Netherlands

THIS EDITION WRITTEN AND RESEARCHED BY

Catherine Le Nevez, Daniel C Schechter

Contents

PLAN YOUR TRIP

ON THE ROAD

CUBE HOUSES, ROTTERDAM
P148

DUTCH TULIPS P255

BRIDGE OVER SINGEL
CANAL, AMSTERDAM P73

Contents

Welcome to the Netherlands

Tradition and innovation intertwine here: artistic masterpieces, windmills, tulips and candlelit cafés coexist with groundbreaking architecture, cutting-edge design and phenomenal nightlife.

Art & Architecture

The legacies of Dutch Masters such as Rembrandt, Vermeer, Van Gogh, Frans Hals, Hieronymus Bosch, Piet Mondrian and MC Escher hang on the walls of the Netherlands' world-renowned museums, along with contemporary Dutch works.

The Dutch influence on construction spans more than a millennia, from Romanesque and Gothic medieval magnum opuses to Dutch Renaissance creations, revolutionary Golden Age gabled houses and engineering endeavours including canals, neoclassicism, Berlage and the Amsterdam School, functionalism, modernism, structuralism, neorationalism, postmodernism and neomodernism, with trailblazing structures making their mark on the cityscapes.

Landscapes

Geography plays a key role in the Netherlands' iconic landscapes. More than half the pancake-flat country is below sea level, and 20% has been reclaimed from the sea, making rows of *polders* (areas of drained land) omnipresent. Uninterrupted North Sea winds have powered windmills since the 13th century, pumping water over the dykes, and milling flour and more. Some two-thirds of the surface is devoted to agriculture, including fields of tulips.

Cycling

The flat, fabulously scenic landscapes make cycling in the Netherlands a pleasure (headwinds notwithstanding). Cycling is an integral part of life and locals live on their *fiets* (bicycle): more than a quarter of all journeys countrywide are by bike, rising to more than a third in big cities.

Experiencing the wind-in-your-hair freedom of cycling is a breeze. Bike-rental outlets are ubiquitous, and the country is criss-crossed with some 32,000km of cycling paths, including the Dutch 'motorways' of cycling, the long-distance LF routes. Grab some wheels and start exploring.

Café Culture

When the Dutch say *café* they mean a pub, and there are thousands of them. In a country that values socialising and conversation more than drinking, *cafés* are places for contemplation and camaraderie. Many *cafés* have outdoor terraces, which are glorious in summer and sometimes covered and heated in winter. Most serve food, from bar snacks to fabulous meals. The most atmospheric is a *bruin café* (brown *café*), named for the nicotine stains of centuries past – the ultimate place to experience the Dutch state of *gezelligheid* (conviviality, cosiness).

Why I Love the Netherlands

By Catherine Le Nevez, Writer

Visionary architecture, vintage-meets-contemporary fashion and interiors, street markets selling rainbows of fresh flowers, *haring* (raw herring), caramel-filled *stroopwafels* (waffles) and cheese, and *borrel* (drinks) at canal-side *cafés* are all reasons I love the Netherlands. But what I love about the country above all is its spirit. If something doesn't exist, the Dutch will design it, build it, manufacture it, recycle it, craft it, launch it (the Netherlands is one of the world's hottest start-up hubs) and make it a reality. There's a sense that anything's possible here (and it invariably is).

For more about our writers, see page 320

Above: Canal, Amsterdam (p38)

The Netherlands

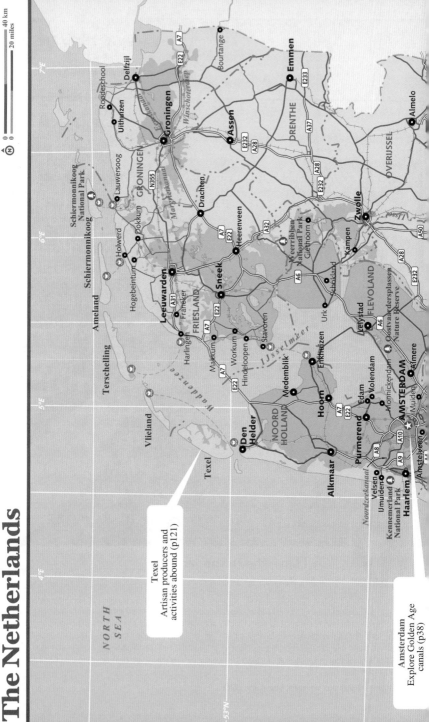

Texel
Artisan producers and activities abound (p121)

Amsterdam
Explore Golden Age canals (p38)

NORTH SEA

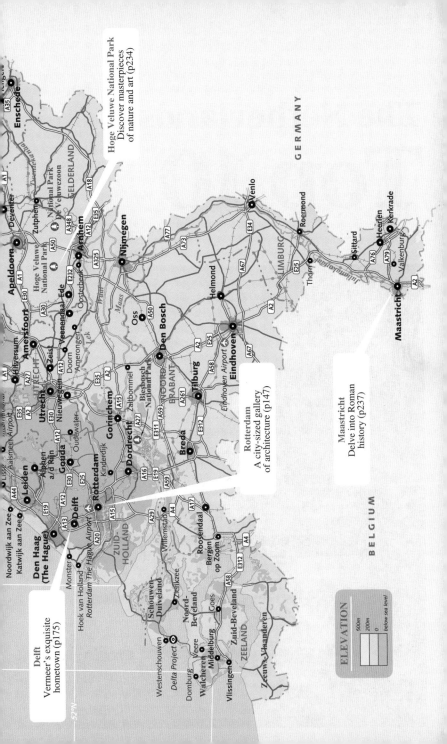

Delft
Vermeer's exquisite
hometown (p175)

Hoge Veluwe National Park
Discover masterpieces
of nature and art (p234)

Rotterdam
A city-sized gallery
of architecture (p147)

Maastricht
Delve into Roman
history (p237)

GERMANY

BELGIUM

52°N

ELEVATION

500m
200m
0
below sea level

Enschede

Deventer

Zutphen National Park
De Veluwezoom

Apeldoorn

GELDERLAND

Hoge Veluwe
National Park Arnhem
Oosterbeek Ede Nijmegen

Veenendaal Venlo

Amersfoort

Hilversum Zeist

UTRECHT Doorn Amerongen Roermond

Utrecht Nieuwegein Oss Helmond

Nieuwegein Den Bosch Heerlen Kerkrade

Leiden Gouda Zaltbommel NOORD- Sittard

Noordwijk aan Zee Alphen Oudewater BRABANT Thorn Valkenburg

Katwijk aan Zee a/d Rijn Gorinchem Tilburg LIMBURG

Den Haag Rotterdam Biesbosch Eindhoven Maastricht
(The Hague) National Park

Kinderdijk Dordrecht Breda Eindhoven Airport

Monster Delft Rotterdam The Hague Airport

Hoek van Holland Willemstad Roosendaal

ZUID- Zierikzee Bergen
HOLLAND op Zoom

Schouwen- Noord-
Duiveland Beveland Goes

Westenschouwen Delta Project Veere Zuid-Beveland

Domburg Walcheren Middelburg

Vlissingen ZEELAND

Zeeuws-Vlaanderen

The Netherlands'
Top 10

Canal Ring, Amsterdam

1 The Dutch capital is a watery wonderland. Amsterdam (p38) made its fortune in maritime trade, and its Canal Ring was constructed during the city's Golden Age. Stroll alongside the canals and check out the narrow, gabled houses and thousands of houseboats; relax on a canal-side *café* (pub) terrace; or, better still, go for a ride. Cruises and boat rentals abound. From boat level you'll see a whole new set of architectural details, such as the ornamentation bedecking the bridges and, come nightfall, glowing lights reflecting in the ripples.

Architecture, Rotterdam

2 Unlike many European cities that emerged from the ashes of WWII with hastily reconstructed city centres, Rotterdam (p148) pursued a different path from the start. Its architecture is striking rather than simply functional and contributes to its glittering, skyscraper-defined skyline. The world's best architects compete here for commissions that result in eye-popping, one-of-a-kind designs, such as a 'vertical city' (the country's largest building), a forest of cube houses, a pencil-shaped residential tower, a swooping white cable-stayed bridge, a fantastical horseshoe-shaped covered market, and an ethereal 'cloud-like' building housing the city's history museum. Markthal Rotterdam (p159)

Artistic Masterpieces

3 The Netherlands has produced a wealth of famous artists. In Amsterdam, Rembrandt's *The Night Watch,* Vermeer's *Kitchen Maid* and other Golden Age treasures fill the mighty Rijksmuseum (p59), the Van Gogh Museum hangs the world's largest collection by tortured native son Vincent, while the Stedelijk Museum shows Mondrian, de Kooning and other Dutch visionaries. Outside the capital, Haarlem's Frans Hals Museum collects the painter's works, Rotterdam's Museum Boijmans van Beuningen spans all eras, and Den Haag's Mauritshuis unfurls a who's who of Dutch Masters.

Rembrandt's *The Night Watch* at the Rijksmuseum

Cycling

4 Grab a bike and go. You can rent them anywhere, and no nation on earth is better suited for cycling (p26). Not only is it as flat as a classic Dutch pancake but there are thousands of kilometres of bike lanes and paths linking virtually every part of the country. You can see *polders* (areas surrounded by dykes where water can be artificially controlled) and creaking traditional windmills (as well as tulips blooming in springtime), and hear cows lowing in expansive green fields before arriving at the next enchanting village.

Brown Cafés

5 *Gezelligheid* has no English translation but is better experienced than defined. It refers to the uniquely Dutch state of conviviality, cosiness, warmth, good humour and sense of togetherness that is a hallmark of the country's famous brown *cafés* (p289). Named for their aged, tobacco-stained walls from centuries past, these small, snug, history-steeped pubs are filled with good cheer. There are around a thousand in Amsterdam alone, and countless others throughout the country. It takes little time, on even your first visit, to be drawn into their welcoming atmosphere.

Maastricht

6 The city where Europe's common currency began has been a meeting place for centuries. The Romans built underground forts here that you can still explore, and every generation since has left its mark. But 2000 years of history, magnificent monuments, mighty ruins, soaring churches and sublime museums aside, where Maastricht (p237) really shines is in how it embraces the moment. Few places in the Netherlands have such a dense concentration of *cafés* and restaurants, filled with people coming together to enjoy every minute of life. Statue of Johannes Petrus Minckelers (p238)

Dutch Cheese

7 Names like Gouda and Edam inspire notions of Dutch cheese (p287) more immediately than the municipalities that spawned them. In both these towns, as well as in Alkmaar, you can visit traditional cheese markets in season that have taken place on the main squares for centuries. The Netherlands' renowned cheese comes in a vast range of styles and flavours, such as aged cheeses that are crystallised like a fine Parmesan, as well as varieties such as caraway-seed-infused and mustard cheese. Shops stocking huge wheels of cheese span the country. Noordermarkt cheese stall (p94)

Texel

8 The vast Waddenzee is recognised by Unesco as a World Heritage site. Its hypnotic tidal mudflats are punctuated by a string of offshore islands, including the largest, Texel (p121). An easy ferry ride from the mainland, Texel offers glorious walks along broad, sandy beaches, near-limitless activities and a stark beauty you can appreciate on land or on a wildlife-spotting boat trip. It has superb places to sleep, eat and drink including a slew of island producers of fruit, cheese, chocolate, ice cream, beer and (rare for the Netherlands) wine.

SARAH COGHILL / LONELY PLANET ©

SARA WINTER / GETTY IMAGES ©

Hoge Veluwe National Park

9 A vast swath of beautiful land that was once private hunting grounds, Hoge Veluwe National Park (p234) combines forests, sand dunes, marshes and ponds. It's a bucolic escape from the densely packed cities and you can easily spend a day here just soaking up the natural environment. But the real treat lies at the park's centre. The Kröller-Müller Museum (p235) is one of the nation's best, with a Van Gogh collection that rivals the namesake museum in Amsterdam. Outside there is a stunning sculpture garden.

Delft

10 The Netherlands has no shortage of evocative old towns that bring the beauty of the Golden Age into the present day. Haarlem, Leiden and Utrecht are some of the more well-known; other historic gems include Enkhuizen and Hoorn. One of the most exquisite (and accessible) of them all is Vermeer's home town, Delft (p175). It's essential to spend an afternoon enjoying the canals, churches and museums, and sitting in a *café* soaking it all in. But Delft is at its most romantic in the evening after the day trippers have left.

Need to Know

For more information, see Survival Guide (p291)

Currency
Euro (€)

Language
Dutch; English widely spoken

Visas
Generally not required for stays of up to three months. Some nationalities require a Schengen visa.

Money
ATMs widely available. Credit cards accepted in most hotels but not all restaurants. Non-European credit cards are sometimes rejected.

Mobile Phones
Local SIM cards can be used in European and Australian phones. Most American smartphones will work.

Time
Central European Time (GMT/UTC plus one hour).

When to Go

Texel
GO Apr–Oct

Amsterdam
GO Year-round

Deventer
GO Apr–Oct

Rotterdam
GO Year-round

Warm to hot summers, mild winters
Warm to hot summers, cold winters

Maastricht
GO Year-round

High Season (Jun–Aug)

➡ Everything is open.

➡ Your best odds of balmy weather to enjoy a *café* (pub) terrace or a countryside bike ride.

➡ Crowds fill the famous museums.

➡ Prices peak, book ahead.

Shoulder (Apr & May, Sep & Oct)

➡ Most sights open.

➡ Few crowds.

➡ Prices are moderate; you'll only need to book popular places in Amsterdam.

➡ Weather can be wet and cold. Bring warm clothes for outdoor *cafés*.

Low Season (Nov–Mar)

➡ Many sights outside major cities close.

➡ It may just be you and a masterpiece at a famous museum.

➡ Weather can be chilly and/or snowy, biking is only for the hardy.

➡ Deals abound.

Useful Websites

Lonely Planet (www.lonely planet.com/netherlands) Destination information, hotel bookings, traveller forum and more.

Netherlands Tourism Board (www.holland.com) Attractions, cultural events and practical info.

Expatica (www.expatica.com/nl) Entertaining guide to life in the Netherlands, with daily news and listings.

Nederland Fietsland (www.nederlandfietsland.nl) Comprehensive cycling information, including maps, route descriptions, rental and repair outlets.

Windmill Database (www.molendatabase.org) Lists every traditional spinner Netherlands-wide.

Weer Online (www.weeronline.nl) The best weather-forecast resource, including a live-update three-hour rain radar.

Important Numbers

Drop the 0 when dialling an area code from abroad.

Emergency	☏112
Netherlands country code	☏31
International access code	☏00

Exchange Rates

Australia	A$1	€0.65
Canada	C$1	€0.66
Japan	¥100	€0.75
New Zealand	NZ$1	€0.61
UK	£1	€1.36
US	US$1	€0.91

For current exchange rates see www.xe.com.

Daily Costs

**Budget:
Less than €100**

➡ Dorm bed €22–€35, private room less than €60

➡ Supermarkets and lunchtime meal specials €15

➡ Free outdoor exploration

Midrange: €100–€200

➡ Double room from €100

➡ Good evening meal in a casual restaurant €30

➡ Museums and trains €20

**Top End:
More than €200**

➡ Luxurious hotel double room from €180

➡ Dinner in top restaurant with drinks from €60

➡ First-class trains, guided tours €40

Opening Hours

Note that hours can vary by season and often decrease during the low season.

Banks 9am–4pm Monday to Friday, some Saturday morning.

Cafés and bars Open noon (exact hours vary); most close 1am Sunday to Thursday, 3am Friday and Saturday.

General office hours 8.30am–5pm Monday to Friday.

Museums 10am–5pm daily, some close Monday.

Restaurants Lunch 11am–2.30pm, dinner 6–10pm.

Shops 10am or noon to 6pm Tuesday to Friday, 10am to 5pm Saturday and Sunday, noon or 1pm to 5pm or 6pm Monday (if at all).

Supermarkets 8am–8pm.

Arriving in the Netherlands

Schiphol International Airport (AMS; www.schiphol.nl)

Train Trains from the airport serve many destinations around the country, often directly, including Amsterdam Centraal Station (€4.10; every 10 minutes or so from 6am to 12.30am, hourly from 1am to 5am).

Shuttle bus A shuttle van (every 30 minutes from 6am to 9pm) runs from the airport to several hotels (€17). Look for the Connexxion desk by Arrivals 4.

Bus Bus 197 (€5 one way, 25 minutes) departs outside the arrivals hall door. Buy a ticket from the driver.

Taxi A taxi to central Amsterdam costs approximately €47.

Getting Around the Netherlands

The Netherlands' compact size makes it a breeze to get around.

Bicycle Short- and long-distance bike routes lace the country and you are often pedalling through beautiful areas. All but the smallest train stations have bike-rental shops, as do most towns and all cities.

Train Service is fast, distances are short and trains are frequent.

Car Good for visiting regions with minimal public transport. Drive on the right.

Bus Cheaper and slower than trains but useful for remote villages that aren't serviced by rail.

For much more on **getting around**, see p299

What's New

Rotterdam Redux

The country's second-largest city has a groundswell of new openings: a state-of-the-art skylit Centraal Station; the country's biggest building, the gleaming, glass De Rotterdam, an eye-popping indoor market hall; a converted former train station with experimental drinking, dining and entertainment venues; a crowd-funded 'air canal' footbridge; the opaque Timmerhuis building housing the Museum Rotterdam; and urban surfing on a wave barrelling through an inner-city canal. (p145)

Eurostar Direct Route

No more switching trains in Belgium. From late 2016, a direct London–Amsterdam route, with stops in Rotterdam and Schiphol International Airport, will cut travel time to four hours. (p301)

A'DAM Tower, Amsterdam

The abandoned Royal Dutch Shell offices have morphed into a hub for electronic-dance-music businesses. Meanwhile, cool-cat spots continue to open in the surrounding district of Amsterdam-Noord. (p49)

Museum Quarter, Den Bosch

With 5000 sq metres of exhibit space wrapped around a stunning swath of greenery, Den Bosch's new Museum Quarter is undoubtedly the cultural highlight of the southern Netherlands. (p244)

'Poshtels'

The Netherlands' burgeoning 'poshtels' (aka posh hostels) include design-savvy Generator in Amsterdam, artist-created King Kong Hostel in Rotterdam, and Eindhoven's Blue Collar Hostel in Strijp-S, the former Philips factory. (p68)

Miffy Museum, Utrecht

Dick Bruna's beloved cartoon bunny now takes centre stage at the artist's former studio. The new museum is designed especially for toddlers with all kinds of imaginative interactive exhibits. (p137)

Craft Breweries

Craft breweries are booming across the country. For a superb introduction, drop by one of the forerunners, Amsterdam's Brouwerij Troost. (p90)

TivoliVredenburg, Utrecht

Utrecht's legendary Tivoli pop-music hall has merged with the city's classical auditorium, expanding into a five-venue music centre with a wildly diverse program. (p141)

Museum De Fundatie, Zwolle

The UFO has landed...on top of the neoclassical building that holds Zwolle's contemporary art museum. The new rooftop's thousands of blue tiles cut a surreal profile on the skyline. (p224)

Kantine de Brandweer, Maastricht

Sparking a renaissance in resplendent Maastricht's northern quarter, the old fire station has been made over as a multipurpose cultural centre and restaurant with fine organic fare. (p242)

Hanzelijn

This new national rail line forges a direct link between Amsterdam and the medieval trade centres of Zwolle and Kampen, where there's a new train station, Kampen Zuid. (p228)

For more recommendations and reviews, see lonelyplanet.com/the-netherlands

If You Like...

Unique Architecture

The Dutch have always excelled at unique architecture, from Golden Age canal houses to attention-grabbing visual statements continuing to be built across the country.

Amsterdam's Canal Ring Each narrow, gabled canal house has its own distinct personality. (p38)

Rotterdam The entire city is a showcase of boundary-pushing modern and contemporary architecture. (p148)

Rietveld-Schröderhuis Utrecht home designed by a leading exponent of the De Stijl movement. (p137)

Groninger Museum Groningen's art and archaeology treasures fill a trio of architect Alessandro Mendini's phantasmagoric buildings. (p209)

Rijksmuseum The facade of Pierre Cuypers' magnificent design from 1875 has Renaissance ornaments carved in stone. (p59)

NEMO Renzo Piano's green-copper, ship-shaped science museum in Amsterdam is a modern classic. (p65)

ARCAM Amsterdam's Centre for Architecture is a one-stop shop for architectural exhibits, guidebooks and maps. (p65)

Art

Powerhouse museums packed with masterpieces proliferate throughout the Netherlands.

Rijksmuseum The Netherlands' top treasure chest overflows with Rembrandts, Vermeers, Delftware and more. (p59)

Van Gogh Museum Hangs the world's largest collection of the tortured artist's vivid swirls. (p59)

Stedelijk Museum Renowned modern art from Picasso to Mondrian to Warhol. (p59)

Hermitage Amsterdam This satellite of Russia's Hermitage Museum features one-off, blockbuster exhibits showing everything from Matisse cut-outs to Byzantine treasures. (p53)

Mauritshuis The magnificent royal collection in Den Haag encapsulates all that's great about Dutch art. (p168)

Museum Boijmans van Beuningen Rotterdam's greatest museum has works from Bosch onwards. (p147)

Kröller-Müller Museum A beautiful national park shelters a supreme collection of Van Goghs and other masterpieces. (p235)

Frans Hals Museum Reason enough for any art lover to visit Haarlem. (p103)

Museum Catharijneconvent Contains Utrecht's cache of religious art tracing the history of Christianity in the Netherlands. (p137)

Markets

Every city and town in the Netherlands has open-air markets at least one day a week. Some specialise in organic foods or antiques; most are held on beautiful central squares.

Albert Cuypmarkt Amsterdam's largest and busiest market sells flowers, clothing, household goods and food of every description. (p60)

Blaak Markt Antiques and ethnic-food stalls unfurl twice-weekly outside the stunning Markthal Rotterdam. (p160)

De Hallen Themed weekend markets (organic produce, Dutch design...) take place inside 1902-built former tram sheds in the capital. (p83)

Waterlooplein Flea Market Amsterdam flea market piling up New Age gifts, cheap bicycle parts, clothing and more. (p94)

Oudemanhuis Book Market Secondhand booksellers' stalls fill a moody, Amsterdam covered alleyway. (p95)

Den Haag Organic Farmers' Market Among the wealth of

local produce, don't miss the superb crêpe stall. (p172)

De Bazaar Beverwijk One of Europe's largest open-air markets, with a truly global flavour. (p106)

Westergasfabriek Sunday Market A quality craft and gourmet food market sets up monthly at these converted gasworks in Amsterdam. (p89)

Haarlem Grote Markt Mondays and Saturdays see stalls fill Haarlem's great square. (p106)

Cycling

While the entire country is a cyclist's dream, there are some good day-trip choices that won't leave you too pooped for a night out. It's easy to rent bikes for the following.

Waterland Near Amsterdam, combining classic Dutch scenery: cows, dykes, canals and lots of expansive green fields. (p29)

Bulb Fields In spring, cycle west from Leiden past fields of tulips exploding in colour. (p30)

Weerribben-Wieden National Park Bike routes circle through this old land of peat farming that is rich with birds. (p228)

Hoge Veluwe National Park Nature and beauty plus the country's best ice cream can be enjoyed while using the park's free bikes. (p234)

Ooijpolder Route Skirt the protected banks of the Waal River from Nijmegen to the German border. (p231)

Nationaal Fietsmuseum Velorama Visit Nijmegen's fascinating collection of vintage bicycles from the golden age of human-powered transport. (p231)

Breda Border Loop Ride to a shrine/brewery on Belgian soil, returning via the bucolic Mark River valley. (p250)

Top: Windmills at Kinderdijk (p161)
Bottom: NEMO museum (p65), Amsterdam

Scheveningen Ride north or south along the invigorating dunes and beaches to leave the crowds behind. (p170)

History

With a history as rich as the Netherlands', you'll find historic sites at every turn.

Anne Frank Huis The secret annex, Anne's melancholy bedroom and her actual diary are chilling reminders of WWII. (p52)

Museum het Valkhof Nijmegen's claim to be 'Netherlands' oldest town' is borne out by the wealth of Roman artefacts here. (p231)

Amsterdam Museum Intriguing multimedia exhibits take you through the twists and turns of Amsterdam's convoluted history. (p39)

Delfshaven Rotterdam's old neighbourhood still has many of the features that greeted the America-bound Pilgrims. (p158)

Kamp Westerbork Disturbing museum/memorial at the site of a Nazi 'transit camp' for deportation of Holland's Jews during WWII. (p218)

Hindeloopen A tiny former fishing village that feels like a time warp to the days when people eked out a living here. (p201)

Deventer The entire old part of the city still has a Hanseatic League echo 800 years on. (p221)

Hunebedden Centrum In Drenthe province, mysterious funerary constructions of giant boulders mark the Netherlands' earliest settlements. (p218)

Airborne Museum Hartenstein Learn about the botched WWII battle Operation Market Garden. (p234)

Bourtange Meticulously restored pentagonal fortress in the remote southeast corner of Groningen province. (p216)

Islands

With so much water around, at times much of the country feels like an island. But there are some proper ones and they are well worth a visit.

Texel The largest Wadden Island has sublime produce including cheese, chocolate, ice cream, beer and wine. (p121)

Vlieland The least visited of the Frisian Islands is almost entirely natural and an ideal escape. (p202)

Schiermonnikoog Home to beautiful beaches, the smallest Frisian Island is also a good *wadlopen* (mudflat-walking) destination. (p205)

Marken Once an island fishing port, this tiny, traditional village is now linked by a causeway. (p109)

Cafés

The Netherlands' *cafés* (pubs) are ideal places to drink, eat, meet and make friends, and experience the country's unique *gezelligheid* (conviviality, cosiness).

't Smalle Amsterdam's most intimate canal-side drinking, with a gorgeous historic interior. (p88)

De Sluyswacht Swig in the lock-keeper's tilted quarters across the street from Rembrandt's house-turned-museum. (p87)

't Oude Pothuys Generations of music students have performed at this ancient Utrecht pub. (p140)

Cafe Derat Unassuming Utrecht spot pouring a changing array of craft brews and sought-after Lambics. (p141)

Take One A Maastricht institution that's everything a Dutch *café* should be: engaging, offbeat, eccentric and with a fab selection of brews. (p242)

De Oude Jan Teensy Delft *café* opening to a sprawling terrace with a live music stage. (p179)

Bierencafé De Heks An amiable Deventer crowd gathers at this *café*, which has an excellent beer selection. (p223)

Cafe Wolthoorn Contender for the country's most authentically vintage *café* is in Groningen, billiard table and all. (p214)

Café De Beyerd Breda's shrine to beer culture brews its own. (p250)

Windmills

Perhaps nothing is more emblematic of the Netherlands than its windmills. Travelling the country you'll see many of the 1200 surviving originals.

Zaanse Schans Tour these still-operating windmills and discover how they did far more than just pump water. (p107)

Kinderdijk The 19 windmills arrayed along a dyke here are recognised by Unesco. (p161)

De Valk A beloved mascot of Leiden, this restored mill has a fine little museum explaining how they work. (p181)

Rotterdam Delfshaven's historic architecture includes a classic Dutch spinner. (p158)

Keukenhof Gardens The Netherlands' most famous flower gardens have a working traditional windmill. (p187)

Ontstaan Uit Iepen van de Molenlaan Climb up inside Texel's beautiful reimagined windmill sculpture for far-reaching views. (p122)

PLAN YOUR TRIP IF YOU LIKE...

Month by Month

January

The first month of the year is unavoidably cold and dark, but on the bright side, museum queues in major cities are nonexistent and you can thaw out in a cosy *café* by a fireplace.

✨ Amsterdam International Fashion Week

Amsterdam's fashion scene takes flight biannually during Fashion Week (www.fashionweek.com), with catwalks, parties, lectures and films around the city. Many events – both free and ticketed – are open to the public. There's a July festival, too.

✨ National Tulip Day

The start of the annual tulip season is celebrated in mid-January. Amsterdam's Dam square fills with around 200,000 tulips, which you can pick and take home at the end of the day.

February

It's still cold and the nights are long but if you head south, you'll find the Catholic provinces getting ready for the year's biggest party.

✨ Carnaval

On the weekend before Shrove Tuesday there are celebrations that would do Rio de Janeiro or New Orleans proud, mostly in the Catholic provinces of Noord Brabant, Gelderland and Limburg. Maastricht's party means days of uninhibited drinking, dancing and street music (p240). On occasion it occurs in early March.

March

If the weather complies, you can get a jump-start on bulb-field viewing in March, and since the season is still off-peak, you won't have to fight the crowds to enjoy them.

✨ European Fine Art Foundation Show (TEFAF)

Europe's largest art show takes place across 10 days in the first half of March in Maastricht. It's your chance to pick up a Monet, or at least do some serious browsing.

◉ Keukenhof Gardens

The world's largest flowering-bulb show (www.keukenhof.nl) runs from mid-March to mid-May at Lisse in the heart of the Netherlands' bulb fields. Buy tickets in advance. (p187)

April

April is all about King's Day in the Netherlands. It's the show-stopping highlight of Amsterdam's jam-packed calendar, but you'll find celebrations taking place all over the country.

✨ King's Day (Koningsdag)

The biggest – and possibly the best – street party in Europe celebrates the monarch on 27 April (26 April if the 27th is a Sunday). In Amsterdam, expect plenty of uproarious boozing, live music and merriment, plus a giant free market where everything under the sun is for sale. (p67)

◉ World Press Photo

An annual show (www.worldpressphoto.org) of stunning and often moving images shot by the best photojournalists on the planet. It's on display at

Amsterdam's Oude Kerk from late April to late June. (p67)

May

Alternating rainy and gorgeous weather and plenty of historic events make post–King's Day a perfect time to explore the country. Hope for a balmy weekend to get out and visit the windmills.

Herdenkingsdag & Bevrijdingsdag

(Remembrance Day and Liberation Day) On 4 and 5 May the fallen from WWII are honoured in an Amsterdam ceremony, followed by live music, debate and a market the following day. (p67)

National Windmill Day

On the second Saturday (and Sunday) in May, 600 windmills throughout the country unfurl their sails and welcome the public inside (www.molens.nl). Look for windmills flying a blue pennant.

June

Visitors start flocking in for the summer peak season. The promise of great weather and very long days draws people outside and keeps them there. It's typically sunny and warm, prime for bicycle rides and drinks on canal-side patios.

Holland Festival

Big-name theatre, dance and opera meet offbeat digital films and experimental music as part of the Netherlands' biggest performing-arts extravaganza (www.holland festival.nl). The month-long, high-art/low-art mash-up happens at venues across Amsterdam.

Ronde om Texel

The largest catamaran race in the world (www.round texel.com) is held off Texel; spectators line the beaches for hours on end watching boats jibe back and forth on the sea. (p124)

Oerol

In the latter half of June, this outdoor performance festival on Terschelling (www.oerol.nl) is revered nationwide as a perfect excuse for going to sea. (p204)

Fashion Festival Arnhem

The modes of the moment take the spotlight with a month of events, exhibits and workshops at locations throughout the nation's fashion capital (www. fashionfestivalarnhem.nl).

July

The days are long, the sun is shining, beaches get busy and outdoor *cafés* are mobbed with locals and tourists alike.

North Sea Jazz Festival

In mid-July, Rotterdam hosts the world's largest jazz festival (www. northseajazz.nl). It attracts around a thousand musicians from around the planet, and even bigger crowds. (p153)

Vierdaagse

In late July, thousands of walkers, both locals and visitors, undertake a four-day, 120km- to 200km-long trek (www.4daagse.nl) around Nijmegen. (p231)

August

August is a surprisingly pleasant time to visit, with temperatures that are much milder than in many other European hotspots. Many Dutch decamp for holidays elsewhere.

Noorderzon

This hugely engaging 11-day arts festival (www. noorderzon.nl), held in mid-August in Groningen, features everything from theatre and music to children's entertainers and electronic installations.

Amsterdam Pride Festival

The rainbow flag blankets Amsterdam on the first weekend of the month, with oodles of parties and special events (www. amsterdampride.nl). The highlight, the Gay Pride Parade, is the world's only waterborne spectacle of its kind.

Lowlands

Held in mid-August in Biddinghuizen, Flevoland, this alternative music and cultural megabash has campgrounds for the masses (http://lowlands.nl) to make a three-day party of it.

Grachtenfestival (Canal Festival)

Classical musicians pop up in Amsterdam's canal-side

parks and hidden gardens during mid-August's 10-day Grachtenfestival (www.grachtenfestival.nl). The highlight of the 'Canal Festival' is the free concert on a floating stage in the Prinsengracht.

September

Summer may be technically over but September is one of the best months to visit the Netherlands. There are some superb festivals along with fair weather and fewer crowds.

Wereldhaven-dagen

In early September Rotterdam celebrates the role of its port, Europe's largest. There are boatloads of ship tours and fireworks. Festival-goers don retro get-ups for the spin-off De Nacht van de Kaap (Night of the Cape), held in Rotterdam's former red-light quarter, Katendrecht. (p153)

Nederlands Film Festival

The Dutch film industry may be tiny, but its output is generally top-notch. Find out for yourself at Utrecht city's NFF in late September, (www.filmfestival.nl) culminating in the awarding of the coveted Golden Calf.

October

A kaleidoscope of autumnal hues colours the country's parks and gardens, and while the weather may remain mild,

low-season prices kick in and queues thin out.

Leidens Ontzet

Leiden grinds to a halt 3 October for Leidens Ontzet, commemorating the day the Spanish-caused starvation ended in 1574. Celebrations ramp up the night before. (p183)

Amsterdam Dance Event

An electronic-music pow-wow on a massive scale, ADE (www.amsterdam-dance-event.nl) sees 2200 DJs and artists and more than 300,000 clubbers attending 450 events across the city over five long, sweaty days and nights late in October.

Dutch Design Week

The southern city of Eindhoven's key event is this design expo, a knowledge exchange and showcase for young designers (www.ddw.nl). It's held at the Dutch Design Academy in late October.

November

Cultural events and reduced low-season rates make up for the shorter days and chillier nights, while the arrival of Sinterklaas heralds the start of the festive season.

Glow

During the second week of November, the home town of Philips, the design hub of Eindhoven, switches on spectacular light installations all over the city.

Sinterklaas Intocht

St Nicholas arrives in Amsterdam by boat from Spain for the Sinterklaas Intocht (www.sintinamsterdam.nl) in mid- to late November and parades on his white horse to the Dam and Leidseplein, to the delight of the city's children.

International Documentary Film Festival

Ten days in late November are dedicated to screening fascinating true stories (www.idfa.nl) from all over the world in Amsterdam.

December

Winter magic blankets the Netherlands (as, some years, does snow), ice-skating rinks set up in open spaces, and the country is a vision of twinkling lights.

Sinterklaas

This long-standing Dutch tradition sees Sinterklaas (St Nicholas) bring presents to children, and families exchange small gifts on 5 December ahead of religious celebrations for Christmas.

New Year's Eve

In Amsterdam: fireworks displays over the Amstel and elsewhere around town (try Nieuwmarkt). Big stages on the Museumplein host live bands and plentiful beer tents for a giant party. Other cities have impromptu raucous celebrations on main squares.

Itineraries

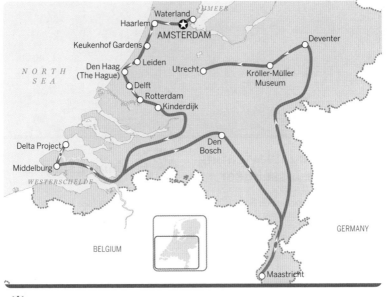

Southern Sojourn

3 WEEKS

Catch the Netherlands most iconic sights on a leisurely spin around the country's south.

Spend three days in lively **Amsterdam**. Visit the big museums, relax in Vondelpark, discover the foodie De Pijp neighbourhood and hang out with the locals at earthy brown *café* Hoppe on the Spui. Plunge into the city's celebrated nightlife in the Southern Canal Ring and escape the city by bicycle to enjoy the classic beauty of the **Waterland** region.

During your second week, visit Golden Age **Haarlem**, **Keukenhof Gardens** (in season), museum-filled **Leiden**, the Dutch seat of government **Den Haag (The Hague)**, and Vermeer's charming home town **Delft**.

Kick off week three in cutting-edge **Rotterdam**. Take the ferry to see the windmills at **Kinderdijk**, then head for Zeeland's restored capital **Middelburg** and the nearby **Delta Project**. Travel through the Netherlands' southern provinces, stopping for the hidden canals of lovely **Den Bosch**. Continue to **Maastricht** to sample some great cuisine and meander through its medieval centre. Head north to Hanseatic **Deventer** and then west to the extraordinary **Kröller-Müller Museum** in the Hoge Veluwe National Park. Polish off your trip in historic, cosmopolitan university-city **Utrecht**.

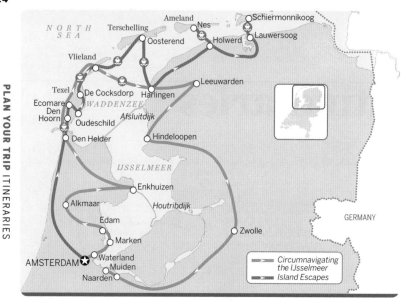

GERMANY

> Circumnavigating the IJsselmeer
> Island Escapes

 ## **Circumnavigating the IJsselmeer**

2 WEEKS

This itinerary focuses on beautiful IJsselmeer – Central Netherlands' vast, shallow 1100-sq-km artificial lake.

Spend three days in **Amsterdam** for museums, parks, canal tours and nightlife. Head north along the IJsselmeer coast through the **Waterland** region to the tiny, traditional fishing village of **Marken**. Cycle the dykes to cute-as-a-button **Edam**. Stay overnight, then reach **Alkmaar** early to experience its centuries-old cheese market (in season), then explore the enthralling Zuiderzeemuseum in **Enkhuizen**.

Travel to **Den Helder**, and take a ferry to **Texel**. Spend two days on the island, enjoying the beach and bike exploration, then catch a ferry to **Vlieland** to appreciate the wilder side of the Frisian Islands. From Vlieland, get a ferry to charming **Harlingen**, from where Friesland's lively capital, **Leeuwarden**, is only a short journey away – as are the nearby chain of coastal towns including boat-filled **Hindeloopen**.

Head to Hanseatic **Zwolle** and also visit the historic fortress towns of **Naarden** and **Muiden**.

 ## **Island Escapes**

1–2 WEEKS

The low-lying Wadden Islands are strung out like pearls in the Unesco-listed Waddenzee and are perfect for island hopping. Some ferry links require advance planning.

From **Amsterdam**, head to **Texel**. Bike along the island's western coast from sleepy **Den Hoorn** through dark copses to the **Ecomare** seal and bird refuge. Comb the eastern side, visiting the superb Maritime & Beachcombers Museum in **Oudeschild**.

From **De Cocksdorp** at the northern end of Texel, board the morning ferry to car-free **Vlieland** to explore its nature and hiking trails before catching the boat to **Terschelling**, Friesland's main tourist island. Hole up in peaceful **Oosterend** and cycle the untouched dunes, then hightail it by ferry to **Harlingen**, a pretty little port on the Frisian coast, and on to **Holwerd**, to ferry across to languid **Ameland**. Stay in the whaling port of **Nes**. Return to the mainland and continue east to the port of **Lauwersoog**. From here catch the ferry to the smallest of the Frisian Islands, **Schiermonnikoog**, home to an evocative, windswept national park, before returning to the mainland.

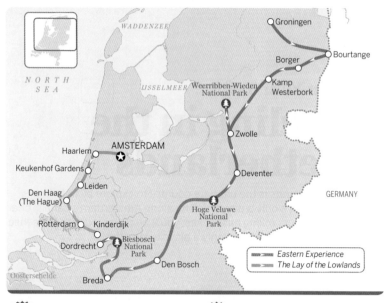

Legend:
- Eastern Experience
- The Lay of the Lowlands

Eastern Experience
2 WEEKS

The Lay of the Lowlands
1 WEEK

The Netherlands' eastern expanse is largely ignored by tourists, but there are myriad highlights to be discovered.

Begin in **Groningen**, a vibrant city with students, bars, cafes and fine museums. Travel southeast to **Bourtange**, a perfectly preserved 17th-century fortified town, then move on to **Borger** and its prehistoric *hunebedden*, stone arrangements once used as burial chambers. Make your way through the woods to **Kamp Westerbork** to encounter its moving, horrible heritage. Head to **Zwolle**, an unhurried Hanseatic town ideal for backstreet meanders, and then to **Weerribben-Wieden National Park** for canoe-paddling.

From Zwolle it's a short hop to **Deventer**, one of the most appealing small towns in the Netherlands. Next, explore **Hoge Veluwe National Park**, a natural oasis that's home to a renowned art museum. Head to **Den Bosch**, which has a dynamite museum dedicated to its namesake artist. Stop at **Breda** to enjoy the city's *cafés*. Go back to nature at **Biesbosch National Park** before finishing in the lovely old streets and canals of **Dordrecht**.

Hit the country's most unmissable highlights. Begin with two days in **Amsterdam**. Visit the big-hitting museums and rent a bicycle to explore the charming Jordaan neighbourhood. On your second day board a canal boat tour and stroll through the Red Light District before getting cosy in a brown *café*.

Travel west to beautiful **Haarlem** – stroll the compact historic core, and view masterpieces at the Frans Hals Museum and the stained glass of the Grote Kerk van St Bavo. In tulip season witness the kaleidoscopic colours of the **Keukenhof Gardens**. Spend a day among old-world splendour in **Leiden**. Next, take a day in **Den Haag (The Hague)** and catch the Mauritshuis' exceptional art collection.

Head south to happening **Rotterdam** to tour the harbour and visit the Museum Boijmans van Beuningen, the Maritiem Museum and the architecturally striking food hall, Markthal Rotterdam. The next morning, take a walking tour of the city's incredible contemporary architecture, then travel to **Kinderdijk** to explore Unesco-recognised windmills.

Plan Your Trip

Cycling in the Netherlands

The Netherlands is the ultimate country to explore by *fiets* (bicycle). Even if it's only a day pedalling along Amsterdam's canals, or a couple of hours rolling past dykes, you'll be rewarded with the sense of freedom (and fun) that only a bicycle can offer.

Good Day Trips by Bike

Just a few of the many possibilities...

Amsterdam to Waterland Loop (37km)

One of the country's most picturesque rides.

Amsterdam to Haarlem (50km to 70km return)

A return trip to a great day-trip town that can include a side jaunt to the beach.

Den Haag to Gouda (70km to 80km return)

A classic day trip through lush Dutch countryside to a cute little cheese-famed town.

Rotterdam to Kinderdijk (25km/50km one way/return)

Cycle out to heritage-listed windmills and take a fast ferry back.

Dordrecht to Biesbosch National Park (25km to 50km return)

A trip to a surprisingly natural park that is best appreciated by bike. Explore vast marshlands and see if you can spot a beaver.

LF Routes

While the Netherlands is webbed with bike routes great and small, one series stands out as the motorway of cycling: the LF routes. Standing for *landelijke fietsroutes* (long-distance routes, also called 'national bike routes') but usually just called LF, this growing network of routes criss-crosses the country and – like motorways – are designed to get you from one locale to another. There are 25 LF routes comprising close to 4500km. All are well marked by distinctive green-and-white signs.

LF routes mostly use existing bicycle lanes and rural roads, which often run beside dykes.

Important LF Routes

➡ LF1 North Sea – Following the Dutch coast from the Belgian border 330km north to Den Helder; it jogs inland briefly near Den Haag and Haarlem.

➡ LF2 Cities Route – From the Belgian border (it starts in Brussels), this 200km route runs via Dordrecht and Rotterdam to Amsterdam.

➡ LF3 – A 555km marathon route that runs north from Maastricht through Nijmegen to Arnhem, then to Zwolle via Deventer and finally to Leeuwarden and the north coast.

⇒ LF4 Central Netherlands Route – Starts at the coast at Den Haag and runs 300km east through Utrecht and Arnhem to the German border.

⇒ LF7 Overland Route – Runs 385km northwest from Maastricht through Den Bosch, Utrecht and Amsterdam to Alkmaar.

Information

Cycling information is copious and widely available. Your biggest challenge will be limiting yourself.

Maps & Books

The best overall maps are the widely available Falk/VVV *Fietskaart met Knooppunten-netwerk* maps (cycling network; www.falk.nl), a series of 22 that blanket the country in 1:50,000 scale, and cost €9 each. The keys are in English and they are highly detailed and very easy to use. Every bike lane, path and other route is shown, along with distances.

Beyond these maps, there is a bewildering array of regional and specialist bike maps, some as detailed as 1:30,000. Many are only available at the local tourist offices of the region covered.

Useful Websites

⇒ Cycling in the Netherlands (http://holland.cyclingaroundtheworld.nl) – Superb English-language site with a vast amount of useful and inspiring information.

⇒ Nederland Fietsland (www.nederlandfietsland.nl) – Dutch site that lists all the LF routes and gives basic details and an outline of each, as well as bike-rental and repair shops.

⇒ Startpagina (http://fiets.startpagina.nl) – Dutch site that lists every conceivable website associated with cycling in the Netherlands.

Clothing & Equipment

Wind and rain are all-too-familiar features of Dutch weather. A lightweight nylon jacket will provide protection, and a breathable variety (Gore-Tex or the like) helps you stay cool and dry. The same thing applies to cycling trousers or shorts.

A standard touring bike is ideal for the Netherlands' flat arena, and for toting a tent and provisions. Gears are useful for riding against the wind, or for tackling a hilly route in Overijssel or Limburg. Other popular items include a frame bag (for a windcheater and lunch pack), water bottles and a handlebar map-holder so you'll always know where you're going. Very few locals wear a helmet, although they're sensible protection, especially for children.

Make sure your set of wheels has a bell: paths can get terribly crowded (at times with blasé pedestrians who don't move) and it becomes a pain if you have to ask to pass every time. Another necessity is a repair kit. Most rental shops will provide one on request. Bike theft is common; you'll want two good locks.

Getting a Bike

Your choices are hiring a bike, buying a bike or using your own. Each has pros and cons.

Hire

Rental shops are available in abundance. Many day trippers avail themselves of the train-station bicycle shops, called Rijwielshops (www.ov-fiets.nl), which are found in more than 100 train stations.

Operating long hours (6am to midnight is common), the shops hire out bikes from €6 to €12 per day with discounts by the week. Many have a selection of models, including increasingly popular e-bikes (electric bikes). You'll have to show a passport or national ID card, and leave a cash or credit-card deposit (usually €25 to €100).

The shops usually offer repairs, sell new bikes and have cheap secured bike parking.

Private shops charge similar rates but may be more flexible on the form of deposit. In summer it's advisable to reserve ahead, as shops regularly hire out their entire stock, especially in places such as the nearly car-free Frisian Islands where everybody arriving wants a bike.

You normally have to return your bike to the place you rented it. Given that distances are short, you can easily just hop a train back to your starting point. Some Rijwielshops do offer a one-way scheme to other shops for €15, so it is worth asking about.

Purchase

Your basic used bicycle (no gears, with coaster brakes, maybe a bit rickety) can be bought for around €100 from bicycle shops or the classified ads. Count on paying €150 or more for a reliable two-wheeler with gears. Good new models start at around €250 on sale. Bike shops are everywhere.

Your Own Bike

Flying policies vary by airline, there are no formalities when crossing the border from Belgium and Germany, and ferries (p300) usually only have a small bicycle surcharge.

Remember the odds of your bike being stolen are high.

On the Train

You may bring your bicycle onto any train as long as there is room; a day pass for bikes (*dagkaart fiets;* €6) is valid in the entire country regardless of the distance involved, but only outside peak periods, from 9am to 4.30pm and 6pm to 6.30am. There are no fees for collapsible bikes so long as they can be considered hand luggage. There are no restrictions on holidays, at weekends or during July and August.

Dutch trains often have special carriages for loading two-wheelers – look for the bicycle logos on the side of the carriage.

Security

➡ Be sure you have two good locks. Hardened chain-link or T-hoop varieties are best for attaching the frame and front wheel to a fixed structure (preferably a bike rack).

➡ Many train-station bike-hire shops also run *fietsenstallingen,* secure storage areas where you can leave your bike cheaply (less than €2 per day).

➡ Some cities have bicycle 'lockers' that can be accessed electronically but these are rare.

➡ Don't ever leave your bike unlocked, even for an instant. Secondhand bikes are a lucrative trade, and hundreds of thousands are stolen in the Netherlands each year. Even if you report the theft to the police, chances of recovery are virtually nil.

Tours

In most cities you'll find companies offering bike tours of the city. There are multi-day trips around the country and many bike-tour operators.

Accommodation

Apart from the recommended campgrounds, there are plenty of nature campsites along bike paths, often adjoined to a local farm. They tend to be smaller, simpler and cheaper than the regular campgrounds, and many don't allow cars or caravans. The Stichting Natuurkampeerterreinen (Nature Campsites Foundation; www.natuurkampeerterreinen.nl) has 141 locations throughout the Netherlands.

You may also wish to try *Trekkershutten* (www.trekkershutten.nl), basic hikers' huts available at many campgrounds.

Many hostels, B&Bs and hotels throughout the country are well geared to cyclists' needs such as bike storage and e-bike charge point. Tourist offices can help you track them down.

BICYCLE ROAD RULES

Heavy road and bike traffic can be intimidating, but observe a few basics and soon you'll be freewheeling like a native:

➡ Watch for cars. Cyclists have the right of way, except when vehicles are entering from the right, although not all motorists respect this.

➡ Watch for pedestrians. Tourists wander in and out of bike paths with no idea they're in a dangerous spot.

➡ Use the bicycle lane on the road's right-hand side; white lines and bike symbols mark the spot.

➡ Cycle in the same direction as traffic, and adhere to all traffic lights and signs.

➡ Make sure you signal when turning by putting out your hand.

➡ By law, after dusk you need to use the lights on your bike (front and rear) and have reflectors on both wheels. If your bike does not have lights, you need to use clip-on lights, both front and rear.

➡ It's polite to give a quick ring of your bell as a warning. If someone's about to hit you, a good sharp yell is effective.

➡ Helmets are not required. Most Dutch don't use them, and they don't come standard with a rental.

Amsterdam to Waterland Loop

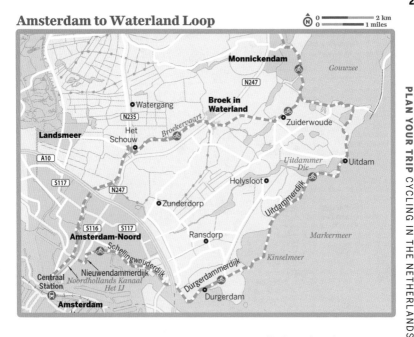

Routes

Amsterdam to Waterland Loop

37km, 3½ to five hours

This is an excellent start to your Dutch cycling experience: pretty scenery, cute towns and easy riding on good bike lanes and roads.

The eastern half of Waterland is culture-shock material: 20 minutes from central Amsterdam you step centuries back in time. This is an area of isolated farming communities and flocks of birds amid ditches, dykes and lakes.

It takes a few minutes to get out of town.

➡ First, take your bike onto the free Buiksloterweg ferry behind Amsterdam's Centraal Station across the IJ River.

➡ Continue 1km along the west bank of the Noordhollands Kanaal. Cross the second bridge, continue along the east bank for a few hundred metres and turn right, under the freeway and along Nieuwendammerdijk.

➡ At the end of Nieuwendammerdijk, turn sharply and then continue along Schellingwouderdijk. Follow this under the two major road bridges, when it becomes Durgerdammerdijk, and you're on your way.

➡ The pretty town of **Durgerdam** looks out across the water to **IJburg**, a major land-reclamation project that will eventually house 45,000 people.

➡ Further north, the dyke road passes several lakes and former sea inlets – low-lying, drained peatlands that were flooded during storms and now form important bird-breeding areas. Colonies include plovers, godwits, bitterns, golden-eyes, snipes, herons and spoonbills. Climb the dyke at one of the viewing points for uninterrupted views to both sides.

➡ The road – now called Uitdammerdijk – passes the town of **Uitdam**, after which you turn left (west) towards **Monnickendam**.

➡ From Monnickendam, return the way you came, but about 1.5km south of town turn right (southwest) towards **Zuiderwoude**. From there, continue to **Broek in Waterland**, a pretty town with old wooden houses.

➡ Cycle along the south bank of the Broekervaart canal towards **Het Schouw** on the Noordhollands Kanaal. Cross the Noordhollands Kanaal (the bridge is slightly to the north); bird-watchers may want to head up the west bank towards Watergang and its bird-breeding areas.

Leiden to the Bulb Fields Loop

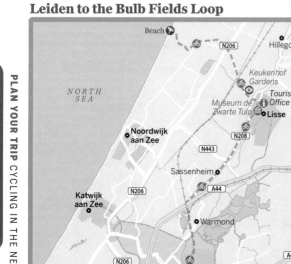

→ Follow the west bank back down to Amsterdam-Noord. From here it's straight cycling all the way to the ferry to Centraal Station.

Leiden to the Bulb Fields Loop
50km to 60km, four to seven hours

The best time to take this route is mid-March to mid-May, when the tulips and daffodils are at their peak and the ribbons of bold colours are astounding. But it's a lovely ride at any time and especially good in summer when you can stop at the beach for a break on the sand and a refreshing dip in the sea.

→ Start in **Leiden**, where you can rent a bike at the train station or from one of the vendors in town.

→ Head north from the station following bike lanes and paths along the east side of the train tracks. Stay with the tracks as they curve north. After crossing several bridges (about 3km), you'll see a fair bit of water and the village of **Warmond** to your right.

→ Stay with the rail path *(spoorpad)* and cross under the A44. You'll be at the Rijksstraatweg. Turn right (northeast) and follow the road for 4km as it changes names to Hoofdstraat and reaches the pretty little village **Sassenheim**.

You'll start to see tulips and the bulb fields. Stay on the little road as it passes the churches and you come to the busy N443.

→ Cross the N443. Stay on the good bike paths along Heereweg for almost 4km to the middle of the village of **Lisse**. Here you can visit the Museum de Zwarte Tulp, which has lots of interesting bulb stories.

→ From Lisse, **Keukenhof Gardens** is just 1.25km west.

→ After you've visited the gardens, cross the road to visit stately castle **Kasteel Keukenhof**. Head west for 7.5km to the beach. Start on Delftweg amid bulb fields and stay on the bike lanes as the road crosses N206 (Oosterduinen). The bike route now separates from the road. Stay with the bike route through the sandy landscape.

→ The route curves south; at Langevelderslag, take the parallel path through the dunes. When you cross national bike route LF1, you're at the **beach**.

→ Try some DIY routing to return. Once past the dunes, take little lanes through the bulb fields that take you due south towards Leiden. You'll be dazzled by the colours in spring. Eventually you'll run into a section of your initial route. Then simply retrace your course back to the train station.

Plan Your Trip
Travel with Children

The Netherlands is one of Europe's most kid-friendly countries. The famous Dutch tolerance extends to children and locals are exceptionally welcoming towards them (and their parents). Many attractions are tailored to or specifically designed for younger visitors, and there are enduring icons such as castles and windmills that captivate all ages.

The Netherlands for Kids

Children's needs have been thought of at every turn in the Netherlands.

Accommodation

Very few hotels have a 'no kids' rule; those that do are mostly in areas of Amsterdam that you wouldn't take kids anyway. Family rooms sleeping four are common. Upscale hotels often offer child-minding services.

Eating Out

Children are welcome in all but the most formal restaurants. In fact, the trend towards stylish bistro-style eateries with high ceilings and a slightly raucous atmosphere are all the better for little ones. Everyone is pretty tolerant of any antics children may get up to when dining out. You'll see Dutch families enjoying meals inside and out at cafes, pubs and restaurants, as well as sitting on benches sharing a quick repast from a fish stall, *frites* (French fries) stand or sandwich shop.

Kids' menus are common and often include deep-fried treats that always go down well. You can also ask for high chairs and even crayons in many restaurants.

Best Regions for Kids

Amsterdam
One of Europe's most kid-friendly cities, with an atmosphere that's cheerfully accommodating to children. In fact, most areas – except the Red Light District, of course – are fair game.

Haarlem & North Holland
Cute old towns, lots of cows, some fun museums and the island of Texel, a huge sandy playground.

Utrecht
Cool canals to explore and castles to bike to.

Rotterdam & South Holland
The neatest old Dutch cities, a fun amusement park in Den Haag, cool things to do in Rotterdam, windmills and beaches in Zeeland.

Friesland
More cows and sandy islands.

Northeast Netherlands
Ancient stones and parks.

Central Netherlands
Fun little towns and parks.

Maastricht & Southeastern Netherlands
The country's best amusement park.

Child-Friendly Facilities

Facilities for changing nappies (diapers) are limited to the big department stores, major museums and train stations, and you'll pay to use them. Breastfeeding is generally OK in public when done discreetly.

On the Road

Most bike-rental shops have bicycle child seats and kid-sized bikes for rent but few offer helmets (for any age); bike helmet use among the Dutch is very limited. You might want to consider bringing your own.

Trains have 'silent' cars where people can escape noise and everyone (youngsters included) is expected to be quiet.

Bargain-Hunting

Family tickets for attractions are common and can yield huge savings. Most museums have half-price entry for children and many major museums offer free admission to kids.

Children's Highlights

Outdoor Fun

Green spaces, parks, windmills and canals galore add up to plenty of fresh-air fun with the little (and not so little) ones. During winter kids will love the skating rinks and outdoor merriment at the carnivals that spring up in many Dutch cities and towns.

➜ **Vondelpark, Amsterdam** This vast play space, with leafy picnic spots and duck ponds, has cool space-age slides at its western end and a great playground in the centre.

➜ **Westerpark, Amsterdam** Kids can splash about in the summer paddling pool.

➜ **Amsterdamse Bos** Tykes can feed goats and climb trees in the woods.

➜ **Apenheul, Apeldoorn** A habitat for apes and monkeys, where children get a chance to observe and even play with the primates.

➜ **Keukenhof Gardens, Lisse** The millions of flowers might delight kids for a while but they'll really love the huge playground.

➜ **Canal Bike, Amsterdam** Take a unique pedal-powered ride through Amsterdam's beautiful canals.

➜ **Canals, Den Bosch** Most canal towns have canal boat tours which last a not-too-long hour

and offer lots of interesting views. The canal tours in Den Bosch travel through underground waterways.

➜ **Artis Royal Zoo, Amsterdam** The big cats, shimmying fish and planetarium will keep young eyes shining for hours; teenagers and adults will love the beautifully landscaped historical grounds. Don't miss the fascinating new microbe museum, Micropia.

➜ **Ecomare, Texel** A nature centre with all sorts of animals from the islands, including injured seals recuperating, and lots of exhibits designed for kids.

➜ **Kinderdijk** Nineteen windmills in a pretty setting near Rotterdam.

➜ **Zaanse Schans** At these windmills north of Haarlem you can go inside to see all the wild gears, pulleys and more.

Sand & Surf

➜ **Beaches** Texel and the Frisian Islands have excellent beaches for kids. Much of the west coast is one long beach; Scheveningen near Den Haag is well-suited for families.

➜ **Surfing** Learn to surf on Texel, which has many other activities – such as horse rides – aimed at kids.

➜ **Windsurfing** Amsterdam's newest neighbourhood, IJburg, offers great windsurfing, with rentals available from **Surfcenter IJburg** (www.surfcenterijburg. nl; Berthaanstrakade; windsurfer/wetsuit rental per hr €17/5; ☺3-9pm Wed & Fri, 11am-6.30pm Sat & Sun Apr-Oct; 🚊26 IJburg).

➜ **Mudflats** North of Groningen, you can spend a day playing out on the mud. *Wadlopen* (mudflat-walking) lets you head out to sea when the vast tidal areas are clear of water at low tide. It's hours of muddy enjoyment and you're expected to get dirty.

Kid Cuisine

Pancakes, *frites,* cheese, ice cream – even adults love fun Dutch food. Every city and town has at least one weekly outdoor market where there are often stalls selling all sorts of tasty items; don't miss the unique holiday treats such as *poffertjes* (tiny Dutch pancakes), that are served up in winter.

➜ **Albert Cuypmarkt, Amsterdam** For *stroopwafels* (caramel-syrup-filled waffles), fruit smoothies, chocolate, sweets and fresh fruit.

A GREAT TRAIN FARE

It may be the best deal in the Netherlands: children aged four to 11 can travel with an adult on Dutch trains anywhere in the country for €2.50. Just buy a **Railrunner** ticket for each child (maximum three kids per adult). Children three years and younger get an even better deal: they travel free.

➡ **Oudt Leyden, Leiden** Some of the biggest, best traditional Dutch pancakes around.

➡ **Villa Augustus Restaurant, Dordrecht** Delicious, healthy dishes made from ingredients growing in the organic garden out front.

➡ **Vleminckx, Amsterdam** This hole in the wall is an old *frites* standby; part of the fun is deciding between dozens of sauces.

➡ **Reitz, Maastricht** A favourite for *frites*.

➡ **De Haerlemsche Vlaamse, Haarlem** Local *frites* institution.

➡ **IJsboerderij Labora, Texel** Working dairy farm where you can see the cows that help make your ice cream.

➡ **IJs van Co, Hoge Veluwe National Park** Sure, the parents want to see the Van Goghs at the Kröller-Müller Museum, but there is also a huge lure near the Hoenderloo entrance to the national park – some of the best soft ice cream in the country.

Kid- & Teen-Friendly Museums

While dragging museum-resistant kids through an exhibition of sombre Dutch Masters' paintings might give parents nightmares, there are plenty of museums that are accessible, educational and fun.

➡ **NEMO, Amsterdam** Tailor-made, kid-focused, hands-on science labs inside; a splashy water feature and amazing views on the roof outside.

➡ **Het Scheepvaartmuseum, Amsterdam** Climb aboard the full-scale, 17th-century replica ship and check out the cannons.

➡ **Rijksmuseum, Amsterdam** Lest the kids be left out of the masterpieces, children get their own audio tour to explore the museum's treasures.

➡ **Maastricht Underground** Explore 2000-year-old tunnels and caves underground. It's spooky and very cool – literally.

➡ **Maritiem Museum, Rotterdam** Ship models any youngster would love to take into the bathtub.

➡ **Miffy Museum, Utrecht** Miffy is one of the most beloved cartoon characters in the Netherlands and you can see a lot of her and other characters at this museum aimed at toddlers.

➡ **Ameland Nature Centre, Nes** The seaquarium here has more than 200 North Sea species, including barracudas and manta rays, plus a viewing theatre.

➡ **Model Train Museum, Sneek** Woo-hoo! Trains roll over bridges and through mountain tunnels in a series of incredibly elaborate dioramas.

➡ **Nederlands Stripmuseum, Groningen** Besides the comic strips by leading Benelux artists, there are films, figurines and more.

➡ **Natuurmuseum Fryslân, Leeuwarden** A fish-eye stroll through a Friesland canal and a simulated bird flight are among the highlights at this kid-friendly nature museum.

➡ **Nederlands Openluchtmuseum, Arnhem** Like a set from a period film, the village re-creates the Netherlands' past with plenty of hands-on activities.

Amusement Parks

➡ **Efteling, Kaatsheuvel** This is the most popular amusement park in the Netherlands and it seems every Dutch person of any age has memories of the fun they've had here. Thrill rides, cartoon characters and more. It's in the south near Tilburg.

➡ **Madurodam, Den Haag** See the Netherlands in miniature outdoors at Madurodam; it's what a kid would build with unlimited time and cash.

➡ **Miniworld Rotterdam** See the Netherlands in miniature indoors at Miniworld; a huge model train layout duplicates much of the country.

➡ **Waterland Neeltje Jans, Zeeland** Amid the amazing and vast Delta Project, kid-friendly exhibits here tell the story of how the Dutch have battled the sea; there are also seals, a water park and rides.

Junior Entertainment

➡ **Amsterdams Marionetten Theater** Puts on captivating shows such as Mozart's *The Magic Flute*.

➡ **Openluchttheater, Amsterdam** A free theatre in Vondelpark hosting performances most Saturday afternoons in summer.

Regions at a Glance

Amsterdam

Museums
Canals
Entertainment

Magnificent Museums

Amsterdam's world-class museums draw millions of visitors each year. The art collections take pride of place – you can't walk a kilometre without bumping into a Van Gogh, Rembrandt or Mondrian masterpiece.

Golden Age Canals

The gabled houses along Amsterdam's remarkably preserved canals look much as they did during the 17th century, and boats travel the same waterways as they did 400 years ago.

Great Entertainment

Amsterdam's nightlife is legendary. Jazz venues abound and you could easily see a live act every night of the week. The dance-music scene thrives, with big-name DJs spinning at clubs around town. Amsterdam's classical venues put on a full slate of shows. Famously hedonistic diversions include the Red Light District's carnival of vice.

p38

Haarlem & North Holland

Historic Towns
Nature
Activities

Picturesque Towns & Villages

Haarlem evokes the Middle Ages and the Golden Age as you stroll its compact centre, and you half expect to see an old merchant's ship sail into Hoorn's harbour. Smaller and cuter still are places such as Edam and Marken, whose traditions let you observe living history.

Birds & Seals

The largest of the Wadden Islands, Texel is ringed by wide beaches and national-park-protected dunes. Birdlife abounds here; out on the water you'll find colonies of seals.

Adventurous Pursuits

You can surf, hike, bike, sail a boat and more in the region's waters. On land, cycling across the dykes and virescent countryside makes for great days exploring.

p100

Utrecht

Canals
Landmarks
Day Trips

Split-Level Canals

As Utrecht's ultramodern new train station draws to completion, the city is looking better than ever. You can stroll along its unique two-level canals – up above at street level or down at the water's edge.

Historic Icons

Utrecht city's soaring surviving church tower, the Domtoren, has sweeping views from the top. The city's fascinating museum includes a side trip to the Unesco-listed Rietveld-Schröder House. Learn about the adorable Dutch cartoon rabbit at the revamped Miffy Museum, in the artist's former studio.

Beyond the Namesake City

Amersfoort was home to Piet Mondrian, the famous 20th-century artist. You can visit his home, along with side trips to country castles and the bewitching town of Oudewater.

p134

Rotterdam & South Holland

Renaissance
Tulips
Cycling

Rotterdam's Renaissance

Rotterdam's urban renaissance not only includes striking new additions to its skyline but a surge of street art, red-hot restaurant and bar openings, and inspired initiatives like inner-city canal surfing.

Blooming Bulbs

Bulb fields fan out around the beautiful city of Leiden and burst into a spectacular display of colour in spring. Keukenhof Gardens puts on dazzling annual displays; the little town of Lisse is home to a tulip museum.

Two-Wheeling

Cycling is as good here as anywhere in the country, whether you're pedalling by Kinderdijk's Unesco-listed windmills, Den Haag's stately palaces and nearby beach Scheveningen, Zeeland's sandy seashore or the medieval buildings gracing Delft's canals.

p145

Friesland (Fryslân)

Islands
History
Adventure

Frisian Islands

Off the north coast of the Netherlands, the Waddenzee's rich environment has been recognised as a Unesco World Heritage site since 2009. The Frisian Islands here are popular for holidays but even on days when the ferries from the mainland all arrive full, there are still endless expanses of empty beach.

History-Steeped Towns

Harlingen is a fascinating historic port town. Leeuwarden has superb museums covering the province's history and natural history, while Hindeloopen is a gem of an old fishing village.

Boats & Bikes

The Frisian Islands offer endless opportunities for outdoor fun. You can island-hop by boat while exploring by bike, or rent a boat yourself to explore the waters.

p193

Northeast Netherlands

······································

History
Parks
Nightlife

······································

Understanding the Past

Some of the oldest finds in the Netherlands are in its far northeast corner: *Hunebedden* (old burial sites) date back 5000 years. The preserved fortress town of Bourtange is a 16th-century time capsule while Groningen still has echoes of the Golden Age. Much more recent and far more terrible, Kamp Westerbork was used by the Nazis for deporting Jews and others.

Green Lands

Protected zones preserve ancient landscapes that are left to evolve naturally. Explore old farms, forests and heaths on a welter of biking and hiking trails.

Party Time

The ancient university town of Groningen has 20,000 students who ensure there's never a dull moment on its streets or in its *cafés* (pubs), bars and pulsating live music venues.

p207

Central Netherlands

······································

Alluring Towns
Canals
History

······································

Backstreet Explorations

One of the greatest pleasures of the Central Netherlands is wandering the backstreets of its towns and making your own discoveries. Old brick buildings unchanged since Deventer was a Hanseatic trading city delight with carved stone details. Nearby Zwolle offers similar rewards, as does compact little Kampen.

Land & Water

Water courses throughout the centre of the Netherlands. Near the canal-laced rural idyll of Giethoorn, you can follow canals and channels dug over the centuries by peat harvesters and farmers in fascinating Weerribben-Wieden National Park.

WWII Reminders

In and around Nijmegen and Arnhem, monuments and museums recall the fierce battles of WWII and their horrific aftermath.

p219

Maastricht & Southeastern Netherlands

······································

History
Art
Cafés

······································

Roman Relics

The land beneath Maastricht is a honeycomb of tunnels and underground forts dating back through centuries of wars and occupiers to Roman times. Above ground, almost every era since is represented by a landmark or building in the city's compact and beautiful centre.

Art, Observed

Hieronymus Bosch was a sharp observer of human frailties and his intricate paintings, which are re-created in his namesake city Den Bosch, still ring true today. Maastricht is home to the world's largest annual sales fair of historic art, and artistic treasures fill its museums.

Café Culture

Café culture is alive and thriving in Maastricht, Den Bosch and Breda. Pull up a chair and soak up the Dutch sense of *gezelligheid* (conviviality, cosiness).

p236

On the Road

Amsterdam

♪ 020 / POP 805,155

Best Places to Eat

➡ Ron Gastrobar (p82)

➡ Dikke Graaf (p82)

➡ Foodhallen (p83)

➡ De Kas (p86)

➡ Ciel Bleu (p84)

Best Places to Stay

➡ Hoxton Amsterdam (p72)

➡ Hotel Not Hotel (p75)

➡ B&B Le Maroxidien (p76)

➡ Sir Albert Hotel (p75)

➡ Cocomama (p73)

Why Go?

Amsterdam works its fairy-tale magic in many ways: via the gabled Golden Age buildings, the glinting boat-filled canals, and especially the cosy, centuries-old brown *cafés*, where candles burn low and beers froth high. Art admirers will be hard-pressed to ogle a more masterpiece-packed city, thanks to rich collections at the Rijks, Van Gogh, Stedelijk and Hermitage museums. Music fans can tune into concert halls booked solid with entertainment from all over the globe. And hedonists? Amsterdam's risqué side beckons, from the women in the Red Light District windows to cannabis-selling *coffeeshops*.

The city is remarkably intimate and accessible, its compact core ripe for rambling. You never know what you'll find among the atmospheric lanes: a hidden garden, an antique-book market, a 17th-century distillery – always worlds-within-worlds, where nothing ever seems the same twice.

When to Go

➡ Summer is the peak time, when *café* terraces boom and festivals rock almost every weekend. Locals go on holiday in late July and August, so you might find your favourite restaurant closed.

➡ Visitor numbers start to taper in October, and by November off-peak rates begin in earnest. Ice skating, fireplace-warmed *cafés* and queue-free museums ease chilly days from December through February.

➡ Crowds start coming back around Easter, and amass in full force around King's Day (27 April), Remembrance Day (4 May) and Liberation Day (5 May).

History

Around 1200, a fishing community known as Aemstelredamme – 'the dam across the Amstel River' – emerged at what is now called the Dam. The town soon grew into a centre for sea trade. Unfettered by high taxes and medieval feudal structures, a society of individualism and capitalism took root. The modern idea of Amsterdam – free, open, progressive – was born.

The city flourished during the 17th-century Golden Age. Merchants and artisans flocked in, Rembrandt painted, and city planners built the canals. By the next century though, international wars and trade competition stagnated the local economy.

In 1806 Napoleon's brother Louis became king of Holland. He eventually moved into the city hall on the Dam and transformed it into the Royal Palace. Infrastructure projects such as Centraal Station, the Rijksmuseum and harbour expansion followed later in the 19th century.

WWI and the Great Depression took their toll in the form of food shortages and increasing poverty. WWII brought hardship, hunger and devastation to the local Jewish community during the Nazi occupation. Only one in every 16 of Amsterdam's 90,000 Jews survived the war.

During the 1960s, Amsterdam became Europe's 'Magic Centre': hippies smoked dope on the Dam and camped in Vondelpark. In 1972 the first *coffeeshop* opened, and in 1976 marijuana was decriminalised to free up police resources for combating hard drugs.

By the 1990s the city's economy had shifted to white-collar jobs and a thriving service industry, while gentrification increased. The ethnic make-up had changed too, with non-Dutch nationalities (particularly Moroccans, Surinamese and Turks) comprising more than 45% of the population.

Two high-profile murders and protests over immigration marked the first years of the 21st century. Recently Amsterdammers have turned their attention to a new metro line, massive artificial suburban islands and other grand urban projects. There are around 200 start-up companies within a 6.5km radius of the centre, working on projects such as building a canal house and canal bridge by 3D printer, honing bitcoin technology, and offering networks where residents can trade surplus green energy with each other.

◉ Sights

Amsterdam is compact and easy to roam on foot. Hop on the occasional tram if you need a rest. The major sights are clustered in the city centre or within a few kilometres, such as the Old South's art museums (3km from Centraal Station).

For more in-depth explorations, pick up Lonely Planet's *Amsterdam* city guide or *Pocket Amsterdam* guide.

◉ Medieval Centre

Amsterdam's heart beats in its tourist-packed medieval core. The Royal Palace rises up here, but the main thing to do is wander the twisting lanes past 17th-century pubs, hidden gardens and eye-popping speciality shops. Centraal Station is the main landmark. Damrak, the main thoroughfare, slices south from the station to the Dam (Amsterdam's central square). The road then becomes Rokin (in the final stages of metro construction) as it continues south.

★**Royal Palace** PALACE
(Koninklijk Paleis; Map p44; ☑620 40 60; www.paleisamsterdam.nl; Dam; adult/child €10/free; ⊗10am-5pm; 🚊4/9/16/24 Dam) Opened as a town hall in 1655, this building became a palace in the 19th century. The interiors gleam, especially the marble work – at its best in a floor inlaid with maps of the world in the great *burgerzaal* (citizens' hall), which occupies the heart of the building. Pick up a free audio tour at the desk after you enter; it will explain everything you see in vivid detail. King Willem-Alexander uses the palace only for ceremonies; check the website for periodic closures.

★**Amsterdam Museum** MUSEUM
(Map p44; ☑523 18 22; www.amsterdammuseum.nl; Kalverstraat 92; adult/child €12/6; ⊗10am-5pm; 🚊1/2/5 Spui) Amsterdam's history museum is a spiffy place to learn about what makes the city tick. Start with the multimedia DNA exhibit, which breaks down Amsterdam's 1000-year history into seven whiz-bang time periods. Afterward, plunge into the maze-like lower floors to see troves of religious artefacts, porcelains and paintings. Bonus points for finding Rembrandt's macabre *Anatomy Lesson of Dr Deijman*. The museum is a good choice during soggy weather, as there's rarely a queue.

Amsterdam Highlights

1 Plunging into the **Rijksmuseum** (p59), housing a trove of Vermeers, Rembrandts and other national riches.

2 Experiencing a young girl's hidden life at **Anne Frank Huis** (p52).

3 Admiring the vivid swirls of a tortured genius at the **Van Gogh Museum** (p59).

4 Visiting the Golden Age painter's inner sanctum at **Museum het Rembrandthuis** (p48).

5 Feeling *gezelligheid* (a cosy sense of wellbeing) in the lanes and *cafés* of the **Jordaan** (p88).

6 Trawling the exotic goods at **Albert Cuypmarkt** (p60), Amsterdam's largest street market.

7 Wandering the **Red Light District** (p43), a contradiction of charming *cafés* and near-naked women in windows.

8 Kicking back amid the ponds, lawns, thickets and paths of **Vondelpark** (p60).

9 Sipping sensational microbrews under an 18th-century windmill at **Brouwerij 't IJ** (p91).

AMSTERDAM IN...

Two Days

On day one, ogle at the masterpieces in the **Van Gogh Museum** and **Rijksmuseum**, side by side in the Old South. Spend the afternoon in the city centre getting a dose of Dutch history at the **Dam**, **Amsterdam Museum**, **Begijnhof** or **Royal Palace**. At night venture into the eye-popping **Red Light District**, then sip in a brown *café* such as **In 't Aepjen**.

Start the next day browsing the **Albert Cuypmarkt**, Amsterdam's largest street bazaar. Head to the Southern Canal Ring and peek in opulent canal houses such as the **Museum Van Loon** and the **Museum Willet-Holthuysen** before taking a **canal boat tour**. At night party at hyperactive, neon-lit **Leidseplein**. **Paradiso** and **Melkweg** host the coolest agendas.

Four Days

On day three head to the Western Canal Ring's **Negen Straatjes** (Nine Streets), a tic-tac-toe board of oddball speciality shops. The haunting **Anne Frank Huis** is nearby, and is a must. Spend the evening in the **Jordaan** for a *gezellig* (cosy) dinner and canal-side drinks.

Begin the following day at **Museum het Rembrandthuis**, then mosey over to the Plantage for the **Hortus Botanicus**, **Royal Artis Zoo** and organic brewery **Brouwerij 't IJ**, at the foot of a windmill.

Civic Guard Gallery
GALLERY

(Map p44; Kalverstraat 92; ⊙10am-5pm; 🚋1/2/5 Spui) **FREE** This cool gallery is part of the Amsterdam Museum – consider it the free 'teaser' – and fills an alleyway next to the museum's entrance. It displays grand posed-group portraits, from medieval guards painted during the Dutch Golden Age (à la Rembrandt's *The Night Watch*) to *Modern Civic Guards,* a rendering of Anne Frank, Alfred Heineken and a joint-smoking personification of Amsterdam.

★ Begijnhof
SQUARE

(Map p44; 🗹622 19 18; www.begijnhofamsterdam.nl; off Gedempte Begijnensloot; ⊙9am-5pm; 🚋1/2/5 Spui) **FREE** This enclosed former convent dates from the early 14th century. It's a surreal oasis of peace, with tiny houses and postage-stamp gardens around a well-kept courtyard. The Beguines were a Catholic order of unmarried or widowed women who cared for the elderly and lived a religious life without taking monastic vows. The last true Beguine died in 1971.

Dam
SQUARE

(Map p44; 🚋4/9/16/24 Dam) This square is the very spot where Amsterdam was founded around 1270. Today pigeons, tourists, buskers and the occasional Ferris-wheel-boasting fair take over the grounds. It's still a national gathering spot, and if there's a major speech or demonstration it's held here.

Nationaal Monument
MONUMENT

(Map p44; Dam; 🚋4/9/16/24 Dam) The obelisk on the Dam's east side was built in 1956 to commemorate WWII's fallen. Fronted by two lions, its pedestal has a number of symbolic statues: four males (war), a woman with child (peace) and men with dogs (resistance). The 12 urns at the rear hold earth from war cemeteries of the 11 provinces and the Dutch East Indies. The war dead are still honoured here at a ceremony every 4 May.

★ Nieuwe Kerk
CHURCH

(New Church; Map p44; 🗹638 69 09; www.nieuwekerk.nl; Dam; admission €8-16; ⊙10am-5pm; 🚋1/2/4/5/9/16/24 Dam) This 15th-century, late-Gothic basilica – a historic stage for Dutch coronations – is only 'new' in relation to the Oude (Old) Kerk. A few monumental items dominate the otherwise spartan interior – a magnificent carved oak chancel, a bronze choir screen, a massive organ and enormous stained-glass windows. The building is now used for exhibitions and organ concerts. Opening times and admission fees can vary, depending on what's going on.

Spui
SQUARE

(Map p44; 🚋1/2/5 Spui) Inviting *cafés* and brainy bookstores ring the Spui, a favoured haunt of academics, students and journalists. On Fridays a book market takes over the square; on Sundays it's an art market. And just so you know, it's pronounced 'spow' (rhymes with 'now').

Sexmuseum Amsterdam MUSEUM
(Map p44; www.sexmuseumamsterdam.nl; Damrak 18; admission €4; ◎9.30am-11.30pm; 🚊1/2/5/13/17 Centraal Station) The Sexmuseum is good for a giggle. You'll find replicas of pornographic Pompeian plates, erotic 14th-century Viennese bronzes, some of the world's earliest nude photographs, an automated farting flasher in a trench coat, and a music box that plays 'Edelweiss' and purports to show a couple *in flagrante delicto*. It's sillier and more fun than other erotic museums in the Red Light District. Minimum age for entry is 16.

Madame Tussauds Amsterdam MUSEUM
(Map p44; www.madametussauds.nl; Dam 20; adult/child €22.50/18.50; ◎9am-9pm Jul & Aug, 10am-7pm Sep-Jun; 🚼; 🚊4/9/16/24 Dam) Sure, Madame Tussauds wax museum is overpriced and cheesy, but its focus on local culture makes it fun: 'meet' the Dutch royals, politicians, painters and pop stars, along with global celebs (Bieber!). Kids love it. Buying tickets online will save you a few euros and get you into the fast-track queue. Going after 3pm also nets discounts.

Centraal Station LANDMARK
(Map p44; Stationsplein; 🚊4/9/16/24 Centraal Station) Beyond being a transport hub, Centraal Station is a sight in itself. The turreted marvel dates from 1889. One of the architects, PJ Cuypers, also designed the Rijksmuseum, and you can see the similarities in the faux-Gothic towers, the fine red brick and the abundant reliefs (for sailing, trade and industry).

Schreierstoren HISTORIC BUILDING
(Map p44; www.schreierstoren.nl; Prins Hendrikkade 94-95; 🚊4/9/16/24 Centraal Station) Built around 1480 as part of the city's defences, this tower is where Henry Hudson set sail for the New World in 1609; a plaque outside marks the spot. It's called the 'wailing tower' in lore – where women waved farewell to sailors' ships – but the name actually comes from the word 'sharp' (for how the corner jutted into the bay).

Beurs van Berlage HISTORIC BUILDING
(Map p44; ☑530 41 41; www.beursvanberlage. nl; Damrak 243; 🚊1/2/5/13/17 Centraal Station) Master architect and ardent socialist HP Berlage (1856–1934) built Amsterdam's financial exchange in 1903. He filled the temple of capitalism with decorations that venerate labour – look inside the *café* to see tile murals of the well-muscled proletariat of the past, present and future. Within two decades trading had outgrown the building and moved elsewhere. The building now hosts conferences and art exhibitions.

◉ Red Light District

The city's famous Red Light District retains the power to make your jaw go limp, even if near-naked prostitutes beckoning passersby from backlit windows is the oldest Amsterdam cliché. But far from being a no-go area, De Wallen (as the district is known locally) has some beautiful historic *cafés* and buildings. Zeedijk and Warmoesstraat are the main commercial thoroughfares chocka-block with restaurants and shops (many with a hedonistic bent). For a seamier scene, walk along neon-lit Oudezijds Achterburgwal, past its fetish shops, sex shows and pot museums. The district is tightly regulated and safe for strolling on the main streets.

★Oude Kerk CHURCH
(Old Church; Map p44; ☑625 82 84; www.oudekerk. nl; Oudekerksplein; adult/child €7.50/free; ◎10am-6pm Mon-Sat, 1-5:30pm Sun; 🚊4/9/16/24 Dam) This is Amsterdam's oldest surviving

---

RED LIGHT DISTRICT FAQ

➡ What year was prostitution legalised in the Netherlands? 1810

➡ When were brothels legalised? 2000

➡ What percentage of working prostitutes were born in the Netherlands? 5%

➡ What is the average rent per window? €75 to €150 per eight-hour shift (paid by prostitute), depending on location.

➡ How much money is generated by the industry? About €650 million annually, according to the Central Bureau of Statistics.

➡ Do prostitutes pay taxes? Yes.

➡ What happens if a patron gets violent? Prostitutes' quarters are equipped with a button that, when pressed, activates a light outside. The police or other protectors show up in a hurry.

➡ Why red light? Because it's flattering. Especially when used in combination with black light, it makes teeth sparkle. Even as early as the 1300s, women carrying red lanterns met sailors near the port.

Amsterdam Centre

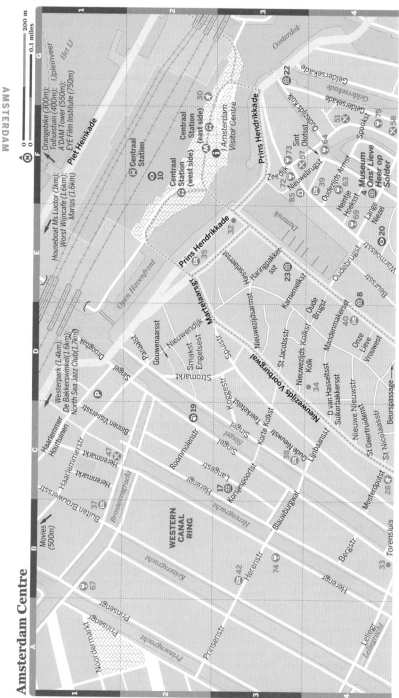

0   0.1 miles
0   200 m

G

Orangebike (300m); IJpleinveer
Tolhuistuin (400m);
A'DAM Tower (550m);
EYE Film Institute (750m)

Piet Heinkade

Het IJ

Oosterdok

Centraal
Station

Centraal
Station
(east side)

I Amsterdam
Visitor Centre

30

22

Gelderskade

Gelderskade

Gelderskade

F

Houseboat Ms Luctor (1km);
Worst Wijncafe (1.6km);
Marius (1.6km)

Centraal
Station

Centraal
Station
(west side)

10

Prins Hendrikkade

Sint
Olofsst

73

57

Oudezijds Kolk

51

75

58

Spooisst

Zee dijk

72

85

Nieuwebrugst

64

39

63

Oudezijds Armst

4 Museum
Ons' Lieve
Heer op
Solder

Heintje

Hoeksst

69

Lange
Niezel

20

E

Open Havenfront

Prins Hendrikkade

32

35

Damrak

Oudebrugst

Warmoesst

Beursst

D

Droogbak

Westerpark (1.4km);
De Bakkerswinkel(1.6km);
North Sea Jazz Club(1.7km)

Singel

Panasst

Gouwenaarsst

Nieuwendijk

Smaksst
Engelsest

Stromarkt

Nieuwezijdsarmst

Haringpakker
sst

Hasselsersst

23

Karnemelkst

Oude
Brugst

St-Jacobsst

Nieuwezijds Kolksst

Kolk

Mandenmakersst

8

40

Onze
Lieve
Vrouwest

C

Haarlemmer
Houttunen

Haarlemmerst

Herenmarkt

47

Binnen Vissersstr

19

Roomolenstr

Korte Kolkst

Teerketelst

Koggestr

Singel
Singel

Oude Nieuwst

38

Nieuwezijds Voorburgwal

34

Lijnbaansst

D-van Hasseltsst
Suikerbakkersst

Nieuwe Nieuwstr

St-Geertruidenst

St-Nicolaasstr

Beurspassage

B

Buiten Brouwersstr

Brouwersgracht

Herengracht

Heren gr

Langestr

17

Korsjespoortst

Herengracht

Blauwburgwal

Herenstr

42

74

Herenstr

Bergstr

Heren gr

Bergstr

33

Torensluis

Mesterdpotst

28

Leliegr
Leliegracht

A

Noordermarkt

Prinsengr

Prinsengr

Prinsengracht

Keizersgracht

67

WESTERN
CANAL
RING

Movies
(500m)

Herenmarkt

45

AMSTERDAM

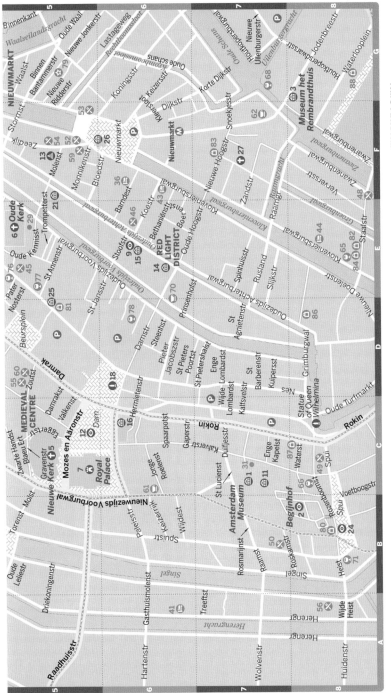

Binnenkant
Waalseilandsgracht
Binnen
Waalst
NIEUWMARKT
Stormst
Zeedijk
Bantammerstr
Nieuwe
Ridderstr
79
Oude Waal
Nieuwe Jonkerstr
Lastageweg
Recht boomssloot
Krom boomssloot
Oude schans
Koningsstr
Keizersstr
Dijkstr
Meijerstr
Korte Dijkstr
Houtkopersburgwal
Nieuwe
Uilenburgerstr
Uilenburgergracht
Jodenbreestr
Houtkopersdwarsstr
Waterlooplein
88
68
Museum het
Rembrandthuis
3
Zwanenburgwal
Zwanenburgwal
Verversstr
Groenburgwal
Staalstr
48
Nieuwe Doelenstr
Nieuwe Hoogstr
Zandstr
Raamgracht
Kloveniersburgwal
44
65
82
84
86
Rusland
Dijkstr
St
Agnietenstr
Spinhuisst
Oudezijds Achterburgwal
Grimburgwal
Oude Hoogstr
Boer
Raavenst
Snoekjesstr
62
27
Nieuwmarkt
13
Molenst
59
Monnikenstr
Bloedstr
Nieuwmarkt
26
36
Barndest
43
Koestr
Bethaniënstr
46
21
Trompetterst
Kennisst
Oude Kerk
6
29
Oude
St Amenstr
Oudezijds Achterburgwal
Oudezijds Voorburgwal
Oudezijds Voorburgwal
9
15
Stoofst
14
RED
LIGHT
DISTRICT
Prinsenhofst
70
78
Pater
Nosterst
76
45
77
25
81
St Jansstr
Beursplein
Damstr
Steenhst
Pieter
Jacobszstr
St Pieters
Poortst
St Pietershalst
Enge
Lombardst
Wijde
Lombardst
St
Barberenstr
Kuipersst
Nes
Statue
of Queen
Wilhelmina
Oude Turfmarkt
Rokin
Damrak
Beurs
Damrakst
Zoutst
55
60
MEDIEVAL
CENTRE
Zwarte Handst
Blaeu Ert
Eggertstr
Valkenst
Damrak
18
Hermerstr
16
Spaarpotst
Gaperstr
Rokin
Kalverstr
Kalverst
Enge
Kapelst
Waterst
87
49
Spui
Voetboogstr
Rosmarijnst
7
Royal
Palace
12
5
Mozes en Aäronstr
Gravenstr
Nieuwe Kerk
Dam
61
Jonge
Roelenst
St Luciensst
Duifjessst
Amsterdam
Museum
1
31
11
65
Begijnhof
2
80
24
71
Heist
Nieuwe Voorburgwal
Nieuwezijds Voorburgwal
Raadhuisstr
Torenst
Molst
Oude
Leliestr
Driekoningenstr
Keizerstr
Paleisstr
Spuistr
Wijdest
Spuistr
Singel
Rosmarijnst
Raamst
Roskamst
Roskamst
50
Singel
Heist
56
Gasthuismolenst
Hartenstr
Herengracht
Treeftst
41
Wolvenstr
Herengracht
Herengracht
Wijde
Heist
Huidenstr

Amsterdam Centre

building (from 1306). It's also an intriguing moral contradiction: a church surrounded by active Red Light District windows. Inside, check out the stunning Müller organ, the naughty 15th-century carvings on the choir stalls, and famous Amsterdammers' tombstones in the floor (including Rembrandt's wife, Saskia van Uylenburgh). The church often holds art exhibitions. You can also climb the tower on a guided tour.

> **ⓘ RED LIGHT PHOTO ETIQUETTE**
>
> Your first instinct might be to take a photo of the barely clad women winking from the crimson-lit windows, but don't do it – out of simple respect, and to avoid having your camera tossed in a canal by the ladies' enforcers.

★**Museum Ons'**
Lieve Heer op Solder　　　　MUSEUM
(Map p44; ☑ 624 66 04; www.opsolder.nl; Oudezijds Voorburgwal 40; adult/child €9/4.50; ⊙10am-5pm Mon-Sat, 1-5pm Sun; ⓖ4/9/16/24 Centraal Station) What looks like an ordinary canal house turns out to have an entire Catholic church stashed inside. Ons' Lieve Heer op Solder (Our Dear Lord in the Attic) was built in the mid-1600s in defiance of the Calvinists. Inside you'll see labyrinthine staircases, rich artworks, period decor and the soaring, two-storey church itself. The museum completed a multi-year restoration project in late 2015, so the interior now sparkles.

Prostitution Information Centre　　LIBRARY
(PIC; Map p44; ☑ 420 73 28; www.pic-amsterdam. com; Enge Kerksteeg 3; ⊙10am-5pm Wed-Fri, to 7pm Sat; ⓖ4/9/16/24 Dam) Established by a former prostitute, the PIC provides frank information about the industry to sex workers, their customers and curious tourists. The small on-site shop sells enlightening reading material and souvenirs, and the centre runs an excellent hour-long walking tour (5pm Saturday, €15 per person, no reservations needed), which takes you around the neighbourhood and into a prostitute's working room.

Cannabis College　　CULTURAL CENTRE
(Map p44; ☑ 423 44 20; www.cannabiscollege. com; Oudezijds Achterburgwal 124; ⊙11am-7pm; ⓖ4/9/16/24 Dam) This nonprofit centre offers visitors tips and tricks for having a positive smoking experience, as well as provides the low-down on local cannabis laws. Browse displays, try out a vaporiser (€3; bring your own smoking material) or view marijuana plants growing sky-high in the basement garden (€3; photos permitted).

Guan Yin Shrine　　BUDDHIST TEMPLE
(Fo Guang Shan He Hua Temple; Map p44; www.ibps. nl; Zeedijk 106-118; ⊙noon-5pm Tue-Sat, 10am-5pm Sun; ⓖ4/9/16/24 Dam) Europe's first Chinese Imperial–style Buddhist temple (2000) is dedicated to Guan Yin, the Buddhist goddess of mercy. Make a donation, light an incense stick and ponder the thousand eyes and hands of the Bodhisattva statue.

Hash, Marijuana & Hemp Museum　　MUSEUM
(Map p44; ☑ 624 89 26; www.hashmuseum.com; Oudezijds Achterburgwal 148; admission €9; ⊙10am-10pm; ⓖ4/9/16/24 Dam) Simple exhibits cover dope botany and the relationship between cannabis and religion. Highlights include an impressive pipe collection, an interactive vaporiser exhibit and a kiosk where you can create an e-postcard of yourself in a marijuana field. Admission also includes the Hemp Gallery (Map p44; Oudezijds Achterburgwal 130), filled with hemp art and historical items, in a separate building a few doors north.

Red Light Secrets Museum of Prostitution　　MUSEUM
(Map p44; ☑ 662 53 00; www.redlightsecrets. com; Oudezijds Achterburgwal 60h; admission €10; ⊙11am-midnight; ⓖ4/9/16/24 Dam) The new prostitution museum is a bit hokey, the kind of place where a tout stands outside and offers discounts if you visit *right now*. But the museum also fills a gap by showing visitors what a Red Light room looks like and answering basic questions about the industry. There are photo opportunities aplenty (ahem, dominatrix room). The venue takes less than an hour to tour.

W139　　GALLERY
(Map p44; www.w139.nl; Warmoesstraat 139; ⊙noon-6pm; ⓖ4/9/16/24 Dam) **FREE** Duck into this contemporary arts centre and ponder the multimedia exhibits, which often have an edgy political angle. Check the website for frequent artists talks.

> **PUT OUT THE RED LIGHT?**
>
> Amsterdam is famously open-minded when it comes to cannabis use and prostitution. But since 2008 a bit of a tussle has ensued as the city embarks on a plan to reduce the number of *coffeeshops* and Red Light District windows. The city says organised crime has entered the scene and must be stopped; opponents say the city simply doesn't like its reputation for sin. The upshot: many spaces in the Red Light area are being converted to galleries, cafes and other more wholesome businesses. The industry certainly won't disappear anytime soon, but it is shrinking (by roughly 20%).

◉ Nieuwmarkt

Nieuwmarkt (New Market) is a district as historic as anything you'll find in Amsterdam. Rembrandt painted canalscapes here, and Jewish merchants generated a fair share of the city's wealth with diamonds and other ventures. The area's focal point is Nieuwmarkt, just east of the Red Light District. This bright, relaxed place – ringed with cafes, shops and restaurants – is arguably the grandest spot in town after the Dam.

★ Museum het Rembrandthuis   MUSEUM
(Rembrandt House Museum; Map p44; ☑ 520 04 00; www.rembrandthuis.nl; Jodenbreestraat 4; adult/child €12.50/4; ☺ 10am-6pm; ☒ 9/14 Waterlooplein) You almost expect to find the master himself at the Museum het Rembrandthuis, where Rembrandt van Rijn ran the Netherlands' largest painting studio, only to lose the lot when profligacy set in, enemies swooped and bankruptcy came a-knocking. The museum has scores of etchings and sketches. Ask for the free audio guide at the entrance. You can buy advance tickets online, though it's not as vital here as at some of the other big museums.

★ Joods Historisch Museum   MUSEUM
(Jewish Historical Museum; Map p62; ☑ 531 03 80; www.jhm.nl; Nieuwe Amstelstraat 1; adult/child €15/7.50; ☺ 11am-5pm; ☒ 9/14 Mr Visserplein) The Joods Historisch Museum is a beautifully restored complex of four Ashkenazic synagogues from the 17th and 18th centuries. Displays show the rise of Jewish enterprise and its role in the Dutch economy, and the history of Jews in the Netherlands. The English-language audio tour is excellent (no extra charge).

Tickets also include admission to the Portuguese-Israelite Synagogue.

Portuguese-Israelite
Synagogue   SYNAGOGUE
(Map p62; www.portugesesynagoge.nl; Mr Visserplein 3; adult/child €15/7.50; ☺ 10am-5pm Sun-Thu, to 4pm Fri, closed Sat Mar-Oct, reduced hours Nov-Feb; ☒ 9/14 Mr Visserplein) This was the largest synagogue in Europe when it was completed in 1675, and it's still in use today. The interior features massive pillars and some two-dozen brass candelabra. The large library belonging to the Ets Haim seminary is one of the oldest and most important Jewish book collections in Europe. Outside (near the entrance) take the stairs underground to the treasure chambers to see 16th-century manuscripts and gold-threaded tapestries.

Admission tickets also provide entry to the Joods Historisch Museum.

Waag   HISTORIC BUILDING
(Map p44; www.indewaag.nl; Nieuwmarkt 4; ⓜ Nieuwmarkt) The multi-turreted Waag dates from 1488, when it was part of the city's fortifications. From the 17th century onward it was Amsterdam's main weigh house, and later a spot for public executions. A bar-restaurant (open 9am-1am) occupies it today. Out the front, Nieuwmarkt square hosts a variety of events, including a Saturday farmers market and a Sunday antiques market.

Gassan Diamonds   FACTORY
(Map p62; www.gassan.com; Nieuwe Uilenburgerstraat 173-175; ☺ 9am-5pm; ☒ 9/14 Waterlooplein) **FREE** At this vast workshop, you'll get a quick primer in assessing the gems for quality, and see diamond cutters and polishers in action. The one-hour tour is the best of its kind in town.

The factory sits on Uilenburg, one of the rectangular islands reclaimed in the 1580s during a sudden influx of Sephardic Jews from Spain and Portugal. In the 1880s Gassan became the first diamond factory to use steam power.

Zuiderkerk   CHURCH
(Map p44; zuiderkerkamsterdam.nl; Zuiderkerkhof 72; ⓜ Nieuwmarkt) Famed Dutch Renaissance architect Hendrick de Keyser built the 'Southern Church' in 1611. This was the first custom-built Protestant church in Amsterdam – still Catholic in design but with no choir. The final church service was held here in 1929. During the 'Hunger Winter' of WWII it served as a morgue.

The interior is now used for private events, but you can tour the tower once it reopens after renovations in 2017 for a sky-high city view.

Scheepvaarthuis   ARCHITECTURE
(Shipping House; Map p62; Prins Hendrikkade 108; ☒ 4/9/16/24 Centraal Station) Now the luxury Grand Hotel Amrath, the grand 1916-built Scheepvaarthuis was the first true example of Amsterdam School architecture. The exterior resembles a ship's bow and is encrusted in elaborate nautical detailing; look for figures of Neptune, his wife and four females that represent the compass points. Step inside to admire stained glass, gorgeous light fixtures and the art-deco-ish central stairwell.

AMSTERDAM-NOORD

The avant-garde thrives in Noord, the vast community across the IJ River from downtown Amsterdam. This northern part of the city has shot up recently to become one of Amsterdam's hippest areas. Free ferries depart from behind Centraal Station and glide to the hotspots.

EYE Film Institute & Around

Some of the most impressive places are a mere five-minute boat ride from Centraal Station. Take the 'Buiksloterweg' ferry – which runs 24 hours a day – to reach the following:

EYE Film Institute (☎589 14 00; www.eyefilm.nl; IJpromenade 1; ⊗10am-7pm Sat-Thu, to 9pm Fri) Inside the mod building, movies from the 40,000-title archive screen in four theatres, sometimes with live music. Exhibits (admission €9 to €15) of costumes, digital art and other cinephile amusements run in conjunction with what's playing. A view-tastic bar-restaurant adds to the hepcat feel. Head to the basement for groovy free displays, including pods where you can sit and watch classic Dutch- and English-language films, and a green screen that injects you into a cartoon.

Tolhuistuin (www.tolhuistuin.nl; IJpromenade 2) This nifty cultural centre hosts African dance troupes, grime DJs and much more on its garden stage under twinkling lights. On sunny days locals pitch up to the brightly coloured picnic tables and beanbag pillows at the venue's cafe (open 10am until late daily) to while away the day. It's steps away from the ferry dock.

A'DAM Tower (www.adamtoren.nl; Overhoeksplein 1) The 22-storey building next to the EYE Film Institute used to be Royal Dutch Shell oil-company offices. As of spring 2016, it's a hip hub for electronic-dance-music businesses. An observatory (with a giant swing for daredevils) crowns the building. There are also two dance clubs (one up high, and one in the basement) and a revolving restaurant on the 19th floor.

Cycling trips This part of Amsterdam-Noord is also great for cycling. After you depart the ferry, pedal north along the Noordhollands Kanaal. Within a few kilometres you're in the countryside, with windmills, cows and small farming communities dotting the landscape. You can buy cycling maps at the visitor centre by Centraal Station. Many bike-rental companies sell maps, and also offer guided tours that cover this very area.

NDSM-werf

NDSM-werf is a derelict shipyard turned edgy arts community 15 minutes upriver. It wafts a post-apocalyptic vibe: an old submarine slumps in the harbour, abandoned trams rust by the water's edge and graffiti splashes across almost every surface. To get here, take the NDSM-werf ferry. It runs between 7am (9am on weekends) and midnight, departing Centraal Station at 15 minutes and 45 minutes past the hour. The ride takes about 15 minutes. There are some top spots to check out here.

Pllek (www.pllek.nl; TT Neveritaweg 59; ⊗9.30am-1am Sun-Thu, to 3am Fri & Sat; ⬛NDSM-werf) Made out of old shipping containers and sporting an artificial sandy beach in front, this cafe is a terrific spot for a waterfront beer or glass of wine. Locals flock here for events, too: al fresco film screenings on Tuesday nights in summer, weekend yoga classes and dance parties under the giant disco ball.

Café Noorderlicht (www.noorderlichtcafe.nl; NDSM-plein 102; mains €17-19; ⊗11am-10pm, closed Mon in winter; ⬛NDSM-werf) Set in a flag-draped greenhouse, Noorderlicht provides food, drinks and a hippy ambience.

Faralda Crane Hotel (☎760 61 61; www.faralda.com; NDSM-plein 78; r €435-535; ✴⚡; ⬛NDSM-werf) This wild hotel has three rooms set at dizzying heights in a repurposed industrial crane. If you can't get a room, you can always bungee jump off the top (€85).

IJ Hallen (www.ij-hallen.nl; Tt Neveritaweg 15; admission €5; ⊗9am-4.30pm Sat & Sun monthly; ⬛NDSM-werf) This whopping flea market – supposedly the largest of its kind in Europe – sprawls through two warehouses. It happens monthly; check the website for the schedule.

Jordaan & the Western Canal Ring

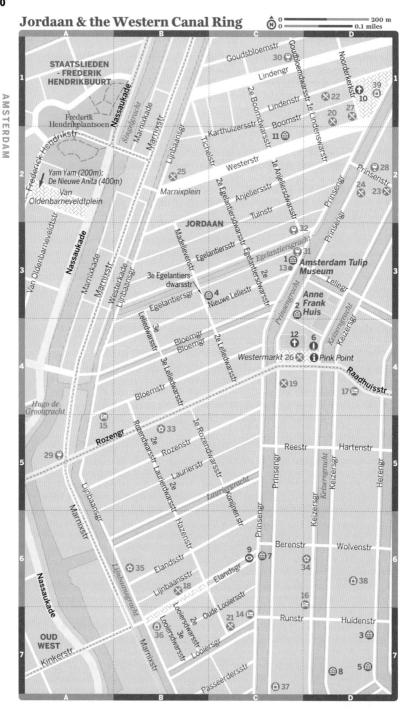

Jordaan & the Western Canal Ring

De Appel ARTS CENTRE
(Map p62; ☑ 625 56 51; www.deappel.nl; Prins Hendrikkade 142; adult/child €7/4.50; ⊙ 11am-6pm Tue-Sun; ⛴ 4/9/16/24 Centraal Station) See what's on at this spiffy contemporary arts centre. The curators have a knack for tapping young international talent and supplementing exhibitions with lectures, film screenings and performances. Admission includes a 45-minute tour departing hourly. **Moes** (Map p62; ☑ 623 54 77; www.totmoes.nl; Prins Hendrikkade 142; mains €11.50-19.50; ⊙ 5-11pm Tue-Fri, 11am-11pm Sat, 11am-6pm Sun; ☑; ⛴ 4/9/16/24 Centraal Station) ✎, the bar-restaurant in the centre's basement, rocks a local crowd of young hipsters.

◉ Jordaan

A former workers' quarter, the Jordaan teems with cosy pubs, galleries and markets squashed into a grid of tiny lanes. It's short on conventional sights, but there's no better place to lose yourself for an afternoon stroll. It abuts the West, industrial badland that has transformed into an avant-garde cultural hub.

Noorderkerk CHURCH
(Northern Church; Map p50; www.noorderkerk.org; Noordermarkt 48; ⊙ 10.30am-12.30pm Mon, 11am-

1pm Sat; ⛴ 3/10 Marnixplein) Near the Prinsengracht's northern end, this imposing Calvinist church was completed in 1623 for the 'common' people in the Jordaan. (The upper classes attended the Westerkerk further south.) It was built in the shape of a broad Greek cross (four arms of equal length) around a central pulpit, giving the entire congregation unimpeded access to the word of God.

Houseboat Museum MUSEUM
(Map p50; ☑ 427 07 50; www.houseboatmuseum.nl; Prinsengracht 296k; adult/child €4.50/3.50; ⊙ 10am-5pm Jul & Aug, Tue-Sun only Mar-Oct, Fri-Sun only Nov-Feb, closed Jan; ⛴ 13/14/17 Westermarkt) This quirky museum, a 23m-long sailing barge from 1914, offers a good sense of how *gezellig* (cosy) life can be on the water. The actual displays are minimal, but you can watch a presentation on houseboats (some pretty and some ghastly) and inspect the sleeping, living, cooking and dining quarters with all the mod cons.

Johnny Jordaanplein SQUARE
(Map p50; cnr Prinsengracht & Elandsgracht; ⛴ 13/14/17 Westermarkt) This shady little square is named for Johnny Jordaan (the pseudonym of Johannes Hendricus van

Musscher), a popular musician in the mid-1900s who sang the romantic music known as *levenslied* (tears-in-your-beer-style ballads). The colourfully painted hut – a municipal transformer station – proudly displays one of his song lyrics '*Amsterdam, wat bent je mooi*' (Amsterdam, how beautiful you are).

Pianola Museum
MUSEUM

(Map p50; ☎627 96 24; www.pianola.nl; Westerstraat 106; adult/child €5/3; ☺2-5pm Thu-Sun Jul & Aug, Sun only Sep-Jun; ☐3/10 Marnixplein) This is a very special place, crammed with pianolas from the early 1900s. The museum has around 50 of the instruments, although only a dozen are on display at any given time, as well as some 30,000 music rolls and a player pipe organ. The curator gives an hour-long (or so) guided tour and music demonstrations with great zest.

Electric Ladyland
MUSEUM

(Map p50; www.electric-lady-land.com; 2e Leliedwarsstraat 5; adult/child €5/free; ☺1-6pm Tue-Sat; ☐13/14/17 Westermarkt) The world's first museum of fluorescent art features owner Nick Padalino's psychedelic sculpture work on one side and cases of naturally luminescent rocks and manufactured glowing objects (money, government ID cards etc) on the other (his art gallery–shop is upstairs). Jimi Hendrix, the Beatles and other trippy artists play on the stereo while Nick lovingly describes each item in the collection.

★Amsterdam Tulip Museum
MUSEUM

(Map p50; ☎421 00 95; www.amsterdamtulipmuseum.com; Prinsengracht 112; adult/child €5/3; ☺10am-6pm; ☐13/14/17 Westermarkt) Don't be dissuaded – or distracted – by the gift shop overflowing with floral souvenirs at the front of this small museum. And yes, it is small, but the Amsterdam Tulip Museum offers a nifty overview of the history of the country's favourite bloom, and is a fascinating way to spend half an hour or so, especially before taking a day trip to the Keukenhof Flower Gardens or Bloemenveiling Aalsmeer flower auction, or strolling the Southern Canal Ring's Bloemenmarkt (p56).

☺ Western Canal Ring

The Western Canal Ring is one of Amsterdam's most gorgeous areas. Grand old buildings and oddball little speciality shops line the glinting waterways. Roaming around them can cause days to vanish.

---

❶ VISITING THE ANNE FRANK HUIS

➡ Come after 6pm to avoid the biggest crowds. Queues can easily be an hour-plus wait otherwise.

➡ Buying tickets in advance allows you to skip the queue entirely and enter via a separate door (left of the main entrance).

➡ Pre-book two ways: via the website (€0.50 surcharge), though you must buy the tickets several days ahead of time and be able to print them or show them on your smartphone; or via the tourist office at Centraal Station (€1 surcharge), which you can do on shorter notice. Both methods give you a set time for entry.

★Anne Frank Huis
MUSEUM

(Map p50; ☎556 71 00; www.annefrank.org; Prinsengracht 267; adult/child €9/4.50; ☺9am-9pm, hours vary seasonally; ☐13/14/17 Westermarkt) The Anne Frank Huis draws almost one million visitors annually (prepurchase tickets online to minimise the queues). With its reconstruction of Anne's melancholy bedroom and her actual diary – sitting alone in its glass case, filled with sunnily optimistic writing tempered by quiet despair – it's a powerful experience.

Westerkerk
CHURCH

(Western Church; Map p50; ☎624 77 66; www.westerkerk.nl; Prinsengracht 281; ☺10am-3pm Mon-Sat; ☐13/14/17 Westermarkt) The main gathering place for Amsterdam's Dutch Reformed community, this church was built for rich Protestants to a 1620 design by Hendrick de Keyser. The nave is the largest in the Netherlands and is covered by a wooden barrel vault. The huge main organ dates from 1686, with panels decorated with instruments and biblical scenes. Rembrandt (1606–69), who died bankrupt at nearby Rozengracht, was buried in a pauper's grave somewhere in the church.

Homomonument
MONUMENT

(Map p50; cnr Keizersgracht & Raadhuisstraat; ☐13/14/17 Westermarkt) Behind the Westerkerk, this 1987 cluster of three 10m by 10m by 10m granite triangles recalls persecution by the Nazis, who forced gay men to wear a pink triangle patch. One of the triangles steps down into the Keizersgracht and is said to represent a jetty from which gay men were sent to the concentration camps.

Het Grachtenhuis
MUSEUM

(Canal House; Map p50; ☑ 421 16 56; www.het grachtenhuis.nl; Herengracht 386; adult/child €12/6; ⊙ 10am-5pm Tue-Sun; ⌂ 1/2/5 Koningsplein) If you're the kind of person who walks through the Canal Ring and marvels over what a feat of engineering it is, you won't want to miss the Canal House, which explains how the canals and houses that line them were built. The museum uses holograms, videos, models, cartoons and other innovative ways to tell the story.

Huis Marseille
MUSEUM

(Map p50; ☑ 531 89 89; www.huismarseille.nl; Keizersgracht 401; adult/child €8/free; ⊙ 11am-6pm Tue-Sun; ⌂ 1/2/5 Keizersgracht) This well-curated photography museum stages large-scale, temporary exhibitions, drawing from its own collection as well as hosting travelling shows. Themes might include portraiture, nature or regional photography, spread out over several floors and in a 'summer house' behind the main house.

Bijbels Museum
MUSEUM

(Bible Museum; Map p50; www.bijbelsmuseum.nl; Herengracht 366-368; adult/child €8/4; ⊙ 11am-5pm Tue-Sun; ⌂ 1/2/5 Spui) This place first gained notoriety thanks to a dedicated minister, Leendert Schouten, who built a scale model of the Jewish Tabernacle described in Exodus. Now on the museum's 3rd floor, the model is said to have attracted thousands of visitors even before it was completed in 1851.

Poezenboot
CAT SANCTUARY

(Cat Boat; Map p44; ☑ 625 87 94; www.depoezen boot.nl; Singel 38; admission by donation; ⊙ 1-3pm Mon, Tue & Thu-Sat; ⌂ 1/2/5/13/17 Nieuwezijds Kolk) This boat on the Singel is a must for cat lovers. It was founded in 1966 by an eccentric woman who became legendary for looking after several hundred stray cats at a time. The boat has since been taken over by a foundation and holds some 50 kitties in proper pens. Fifteen are permanent residents, and the rest are ready to be adopted (after being neutered and implanted with an identifying computer chip, as per Dutch law).

Multatuli Museum
MUSEUM

(Map p44; www.multatuli-museum.nl; Korsjespoortsteeg 20; ⊙ 10am-5pm Tue, 2-5pm Thu & Fri, noon-5pm Sat & Sun Jul & Aug, 10am-5pm Tue, noon-5pm Sat & Sun Sep-Jun; ⌂ 1/2/5/13/17 Nieuwezijds Kolk) **FREE** Better known by the pen name Multatuli – Latin for 'I have suffered greatly' – novelist Eduard Douwes Dekker was best known for *Max Havelaar* (1860), a novel about corrupt colonialists in the Dutch East Indies. This small but fascinating museum-home chronicles his life and works, and shows furniture and artefacts from his period in Indonesia.

◉ Southern Canal Ring

Two clubby nightlife districts anchor the Southern Canal Ring: Leidseplein and Rembrandtplein. Both are neon-lit, one-stop shops for partygoers. In and around them, you'll find intriguing museums, restaurants, *cafés* and shops galore.

★ Hermitage Amsterdam
MUSEUM

(Map p62; ☑ 530 74 88; www.hermitage.nl; Amstel 51; adult/child €15/free; ⊙ 10am-5pm; Ⓜ Waterlooplein, ⌂ 9/14 Waterlooplein) The long-standing ties of Russia and the Netherlands – Tsar Peter the Great learned shipbuilding here in 1697 – led to this local branch of St Petersburg's State Hermitage Museum. Blockbuster temporary exhibitions, such as treasures from the Russian palace or masterworks by Matisse and Picasso, change about twice per year, and they're as stately (and popular) as you'd expect. Come before 11am to avoid the lengthiest queues. Audio guides are available in the entrance hall for €4. Photography isn't permitted.

CHEESE TASTING

Reypenaer Cheese Tasting (Map p44; ☑ 320 63 33; www.reypenaercheese.com; Singel 182; tastings from €15; ⊙ tastings by reservation; ⌂ 1/2/5/13/14/17 Dam/Raadhuisstraat) Here's your chance to become a *kaas* (cheese) connoisseur. The 100-plus-year-old Dutch cheesemaker Reypenaer offers tastings in a rustic classroom under its shop. The hour-long session includes six cheeses – two goat's milk, four cow's milk – from young to old, with wine and port pairings. Staff will guide you through them, helping you appreciate the cheeses' look, smell and taste.

Southern Canal Ring

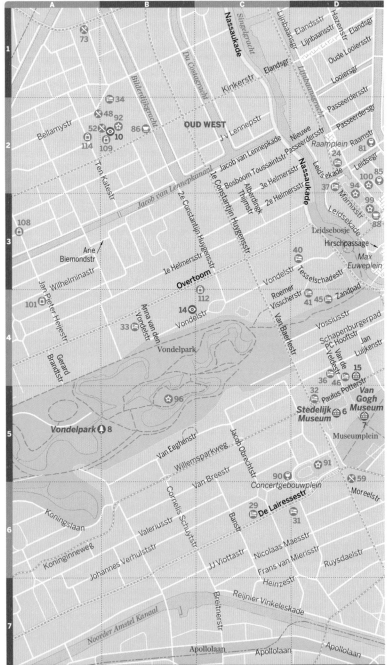

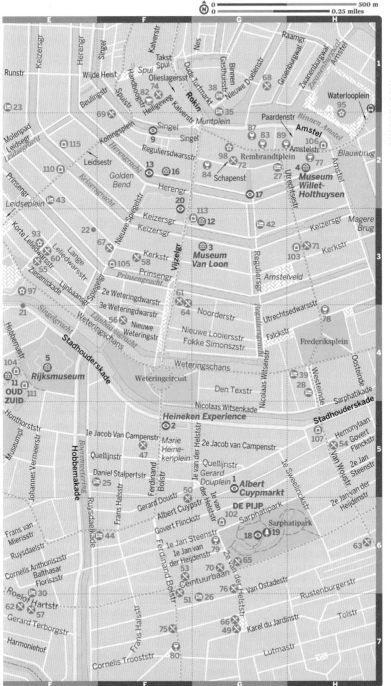

Southern Canal Ring

Bloemenmarkt   MARKET

(Flower Market; Map p54; Singel, btwn Muntplein & Koningsplein; ☺8.30am-7pm Mon-Sat, to 7.30pm Sun Apr-Oct, 9am-5.30pm Mon-Sat, 11am-5.30pm Sun Mar-Nov; ⊞1/2/5 Koningsplein) Since 1860 this famous flower market has been located at the spot where nurserymen and women, having sailed up the Amstel from their small-holdings, would moor their barges to sell their wares directly to customers. No longer floating (it's now perched on piles), the market here offers tulips in season and bulbs year-round, as well as clogs, fridge magnets and other kitsch souvenirs.

Hotels almost always have vases available if you want to brighten your room with colourful blooms.

FOAM   GALLERY

(Fotografiemuseum Amsterdam; Map p54; www.foam.org; Keizersgracht 609; adult/child €10/free; ☺10am-6pm Sat-Wed, to 9pm Thu & Fri; ⊞16/24 Keizersgracht) Simple but spacious galleries, some with skylights or grand windows for natural light, create a superb space for changing exhibitions spanning all genres of photography from world-renowned photographers such as Sir Cecil Beaton, Annie Leibovitz and Henri Cartier-Bresson.

★**Museum Van Loon**   MUSEUM

(Map p54; ☎624 52 55; www.museumvanloon.nl; Keizersgracht 672; adult/child €9/5; ☺10am-5pm; ⊞16/24 Keizersgracht) Museum Van Loon is an opulent 1672 residence that was first home to painter Ferdinand Bol and later to the wealthy Van Loon family. The house recalls canal-side living in Amsterdam when money was no object. Inside there are important paintings such as *Wedding Portrait* by Jan Miense Molenaer and a collection of some 150 portraits of the Van Loons.

Stadsarchief   HISTORIC ARCHIVE

(Municipal Archives; Map p54; ☎251 15 11, tour reservations 251 15 10; www.stadsarchief.amsterdam.nl; Vijzelstraat 32; ☺10am-5pm Tue-Fri, from noon Sat & Sun; ⊞16/24 Keizersgracht) **FREE** The Amsterdam archives occupy a monumental bank building that dates from 1923. When you step inside, head to the left to the enormous tiled basement vault and to displays of archive gems such as the 1942 police report on the theft of Anne Frank's bike. A small cinema at the back shows vintage films about the city. Tours (adult/child €6/free) run at 2pm on Saturday and Sunday and must be reserved in advance.

Kattenkabinet   MUSEUM

(Cats Cabinet; Map p54; 626 90 40; www.kattenkabinet.nl; Herengracht 497; adult/child €7/free; 10am-5pm Mon-Fri, from noon Sat & Sun; 1/2/5 Koningsplein) One Golden Bend house that's open to the public is this offbeat museum, devoted to, of all things, the feline presence in art. It was founded by wealthy financier Bob Meijer in memory of his red tomcat John Pierpont Morgan III. Among the artists, Swiss-born Theopile-Alexandre Steinlen (1859–1923) figures prominently. There's also a small Rembrandt etching (a Madonna and child with a cat and snake) and Picasso's *Le Chat*.

Museum Willet-Holthuysen   MUSEUM

(Map p54; 523 18 22; www.willetholthuysen.nl; Herengracht 605; adult/child €8.50/4.25; 10am-5pm Mon-Fri, from 11am Sat & Sun; Waterlooplein, 4/9/14 Rembrandtplein) Built around 1685 for Amsterdam mayor Jacob Hop and redesigned in 1739, this sumptuous residence, now managed by the Amsterdam Museum, is named after the widow who bequeathed the property to the city in 1895. Highlights include paintings by Jacob de Wit, the *place de milieu* (centrepiece) that was part of the family's 275-piece Meissen table service, and the intimate French-style garden with sundial – you can also peek at the garden through the iron fence at the Amstelstraat end.

Golden Bend   ARCHITECTURE

(Gouden Bocht; Map p54; Herengracht, btwn Leidsestraat & Vijzelstraat; 1/2/5 Koningsplein) One of the ultimate places to mutter 'if only my family had bought that property way back then', the Golden Bend is about the most prestigious stretch of real estate in Amsterdam,

Rijksmuseum

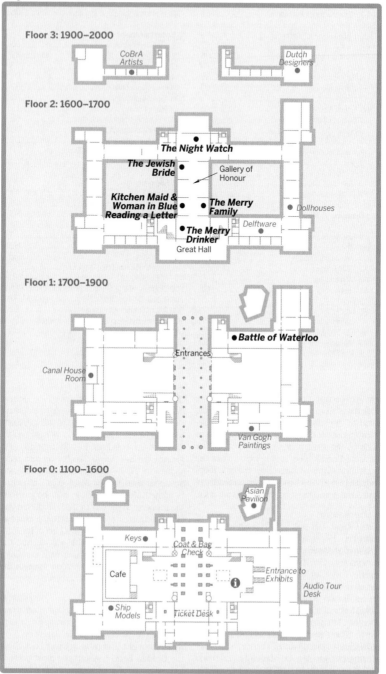

Floor 3: 1900–2000

CoBrA Artists

Dutch Designers

Floor 2: 1600–1700

The Night Watch

The Jewish Bride

Gallery of Honour

Kitchen Maid & Woman in Blue Reading a Letter

The Merry Family

Dollhouses

Delftware

The Merry Drinker

Great Hall

Floor 1: 1700–1900

Entrances

• Battle of Waterloo

Canal House Room

Van Gogh Paintings

Floor 0: 1100–1600

Asian Pavilion

Keys

Coat & Bag Check

Cafe

Entrance to Exhibits

Audio Tour Desk

Ship Models

Ticket Desk

a monument to the Golden Age, when precious goods swelled in cellars of homes already stuffed with valuables. The richest Amsterdammers lived and ruled their affairs from here.

Apart from the Kattenkabinet (p57) museum, the homes are only open on Open Monument Day (Open Monumentendag; second weekend in September).

Reguliersgracht   CANAL
(Map p54; ⊠4/9/14 Rembrandtplein) Amsterdam's prettiest canal was dug in 1658 to link the Herengracht with the canals further south. It was named after an order of monks whose monastery was located nearby. From here you can peer through the arches of at least seven bridges. Many canal boats pass by.

A number of houses along here have intriguing gables, tablets and fancy decorations.

Magere Brug   BRIDGE
(Skinny Bridge; Map p62; btwn Kerkstraat & Nieuwe Kerkstraat; ⊠4 Prinsengracht) Dating from the 1670s, the iconic nine-arched 'Skinny Bridge' has been rebuilt several times in both concrete and timber. It's still operated by hand and remains photogenic even at night, when 1200 tiny lights make the bridge look like a Christmas decoration. You can spot it in many films, including the 1971 James Bond thriller *Diamonds are Forever*. Stand in the middle and feel it sway under the passing traffic.

○ Old South

Often called the Museum Quarter, the Old South (Oud Zuid) holds the top-draw Van Gogh, Stedelijk and Rijksmuseum collections. They cluster around the Museumplein, a grassy, people-filled square that entertains with its skateboard ramp, ice-skating pond (in winter) and *I Amsterdam* sculpture (everyone's favourite climbing structure/photo op). The surrounding genteel neighbourhood is more residential than food- and drink-focused.

★ Rijksmuseum   MUSEUM
(National Museum; Map p54; ☑674 70 00; www.rijksmuseum.nl; Museumstraat 1; adult/child €17.50/free; ⊙9am-5pm; ⊠2/5 Rijksmuseum) The Rijksmuseum is the Netherlands' premier art trove, splashing Rembrandts, Vermeers and 7500 other masterpieces over 1.5km of galleries. To avoid the biggest crowds, come after 3pm. Or pre-book tickets online, which provides fast-track entry.

The Golden Age works are the highlight. Feast your eyes on still lifes, gentlemen in ruffled collars and landscapes bathed in pale yellow light. Rembrandt's *The Night Watch* (1642) takes pride of place. Initially named *Company of Frans Banning Cocq* (the militia's leader), the Night Watch title was bestowed years later due to a layer of grime that gave the impression it was evening.

Other must-sees are the Delftware (blue-and-white pottery), intricately detailed dollhouses and the brand-new Asian Pavilion. The sculpture-studded gardens around the exterior are free to visit.

★ Van Gogh Museum   MUSEUM
(Map p54; ☑570 52 00; www.vangoghmuseum.nl; Paulus Potterstraat 7; adult/child €17/free, audio guide €5; ⊙9am-6pm Sun-Thu, to 10pm Fri & Sat Jul-Oct, 9am-5pm Sat-Thu, to 10pm Fri Nov-Jun; ⊠2/3/5/12 Van Baerlestraat) Framed by a gleaming new glass entrance hall, the world's largest Van Gogh collection offers a superb line-up of masterworks. Trace the artist's life from his tentative start through his giddy-coloured sunflower phase, and on to the black cloud that descended over him and his work. There are also paintings by contemporaries Gauguin, Toulouse-Lautrec, Monet and Bernard.

Queues can be huge; pre-booked e-tickets and discount cards expedite the process with fast-track entry.

★ Stedelijk Museum   MUSEUM
(Map p54; ☑573 29 11; www.stedelijk.nl; Museumplein 10; adult/child €15/free, audio guide €5; ⊙10am-6pm Fri-Wed, to 10pm Thu; ⊠2/3/5/12 Van Baerlestraat) Built in 1895 to a neo-Renaissance design by AM Weissman, the Stedelijk Museum is the permanent home of the National Museum of Modern Art. Amassed by postwar curator Willem Sandberg, the modern classics here are among the world's most admired. The permanent collection includes all the blue chips of 19th- and 20th-century painting – Monet, Picasso and Chagall among them – as well as sculptures by Rodin, abstracts by Mondrian and Kandinsky, and much, much more.

House of Bols   MUSEUM
(Map p54; www.houseofbols.com; Paulus Potterstraat 14; admission incl 1 cocktail €14.50; ⊙noon-5.30pm Sun-Thu, to 9pm Fri, to 7pm Sat; ⊠2/5 Hobbemastraat) An hour's self-guided tour through this *jenever* (Dutch gin) museum includes a confusing sniff test, a distilled history of the Bols company and a cocktail made by one of its formidable bartenders,

who train at the academy upstairs. It's kind of cheesy (especially the 'flair booth' where you try out bottle-flipping skills), but fun. On Friday after 5pm admission is €9.50.

Diamond Museum   MUSEUM
(Map p54; www.diamantmuseumamsterdam.nl; Paulus Potterstraat 8; adult/child €8.50/6; ⊙ 9am-5pm; 🚊 2/5 Hobbemastraat) Almost all of the exhibits at the small, low-tech Diamond Museum are clever recreations. Those on a budget can save money by going next door to **Coster Diamonds** (Map p54; ☑ 305 55 55; www.coster diamonds.com; Paulus Potterstraat 2; ⊙ 9am-5pm; 🚊 2/5 Hobbemastraat) – the company owns the museum and is attached to it – and taking a free workshop tour, where you can see gem cutters and polishers doing their thing.

◎ Vondelpark

The city's bucolic playground unfurls next door to the busy Museum Quarter.

★Vondelpark   PARK
(Map p54; www.vondelpark.nl; 🚊 2/5 Hobbemastraat) The lush urban idyll of the Vondelpark is one of Amsterdam's most magical places – sprawling, English-style gardens, with ponds, lawns, footbridges and winding footpaths. On a sunny day, an open-air party atmosphere ensues when tourists, lovers, cyclists, in-line skaters, pram-pushing parents, cartwheeling children, football-kicking teenagers, spliff-sharing friends and champagne-swilling picnickers all come out to play.

Hollandsche Manege   RIDING SCHOOL
(Map p54; ☑ 618 09 42; www.dehollandschemanege. nl; Vondelstraat 140; adult/child €8/4, private riding lessons per 30min/1hr €37/61; ⊙ 10am-5pm; 🚊 1 1e Constantijn Huygensstraat) Just outside Vondelpark is the neoclassical Hollandsche Manege, an indoor riding school inspired by the famous Spanish Riding School in Vienna. Designed by AL van Gendt and built in 1882, it retains its charming horse-head facade. Take a riding lesson and/or watch the instructors put the horses through their paces during high tea (€24.50) at the elevated cafe.

◎ De Pijp

De Pijp's village-like character is due in part to the fact that it's an island, connected to the rest of the city by 16 bridges. Its name, 'the Pipe', is thought to reflect its straight, narrow streets that resemble the stems of old clay pipes. But it's more attributable to its history. The area's 1860s tenement blocks provided cheap housing for newly arrived industrial-revolution workers. In the 1960s and '70s many working-class residents left for greener pastures and the government refurbished the tenement blocks for immigrants. Inhabited today by all walks of life, with gentrification continuing apace, this arty, foodie neighbourhood retains a community-oriented bohemian spirit.

★Albert Cuypmarkt   MARKET
(Map p54; www.albertcuypmarkt.nl; Albert Cuypstraat, btwn Ferdinand Bolstraat & Van Woustraat; ⊙ 9am-5pm Mon-Sat; 🚊 16/24 Albert Cuypstraat) The best place to marvel at De Pijp's colourful scene is the Albert Cuypmarkt, Amsterdam's largest and busiest market. Vendors loudly tout their odd gadgets and their arrays of fruit, vegetables, herbs and spices. They sell clothes and other general goods too, often cheaper than anywhere else. Snack vendors tempt passers-by with herring sandwiches, egg rolls, doughnuts and caramel-syrup-filled *stroopwafels*. If you have room after all that, the surrounding area teems with cosy cafes and eateries.

★Heineken Experience   BREWERY
(Map p54; ☑ 523 92 22; www.heinekenexperience. com; Stadhouderskade 78; adult/child €18/12.50; ⊙ 10.30am-9pm Jul & Aug, to 7.30pm Mon-Thu, to 9pm Fri-Sun Sep-Jun; 🚊 16/24 Stadhouderskade) On the site of the company's old brewery, the crowning glory of this self-guided 'Experience' (samples aside) is a multimedia exhibit where you 'become' a beer by getting shaken up, sprayed with water and subjected to heat. True beer connoisseurs will shudder, but it's a lot of fun. Admission includes a 15-minute shuttle-boat ride to the **Heineken Brand Store** (Map p54; www.heinekenthecity. nl; Amstelstraat 31; ⊙ noon-6pm Mon, from 10am Tue-Sun; 🚊 4/9/14 Rembrandtplein) near Rembrandtplein. Pre-booking tickets online saves you €2 on the entry fee and allows you to skip the ticket queues.

Sarphatipark   PARK
(Map p54; Ceintuurbaan; 🚊 16/24 Albert Cuypstraat) While the Vondelpark is bigger in size and reputation, this tranquil English-style park delivers an equally potent shot of pastoral summertime relaxation, with far fewer crowds. Named after Samuel Sarphati (1813–66), a Jewish doctor, businessman and urban innovator, the grounds are a mix of ponds, gently rolling meadows and wooded fringes.

ℹ MUSEUM TIPS

Amsterdam's world-class museums draw millions of visitors each year, and queues at the Van Gogh Museum, Rijksmuseum, Anne Frank Huis and others can be an hour or more, particularly in summer. Want to avoid the mobs and save money? Here are some strategies.

How to Beat the Crowds

Take advantage of e-tickets Most sights sell them and there's little to no surcharge. They typically allow you to enter via a separate, faster queue. Note you need to be able to print the tickets in many cases.

Go late Queues are shortest during late afternoon and evening. Visit after 3pm for the Rijksmuseum and the Van Gogh Museum (the latter is also open Friday nights) and after 6pm for the Anne Frank Huis (open late nightly in summer).

Try tourist offices You can also buy advance tickets at tourist offices, but often the queues are as lengthy as those at the sights.

Buy a discount card In addition to saving on entrance fees, discount cards commonly provide fast-track entry.

How to Save Money

Discount cards can save you lots of cash, as long as you choose wisely.

I Amsterdam Card (p99) Good for quick visits to the city. Provides admission to more than 30 museums (many of the same venues as the Museumkaart, though not the Rijksmuseum), plus a GVB transit pass, a canal cruise, and restaurant and shop discounts. You'll need to visit three or so museums per day to make it pay for itself.

Museumkaart (p293) This card works well if you plan to be in the Netherlands a while. It provides free entry to some 400 museums nationwide for a year. Great for queue-jumping; no transit pass or other perks though.

Holland Pass (p293) It's similar to the I Amsterdam Card, but without the rush for usage; you can visit sights over a month. It's tricky to figure out how much money you're saving because you pick from tiers of attractions (the most popular/expensive sights are gold tier, others are silver tier). It also includes a train ticket from the airport.

Priopass (www.priopass.com) A new ticketing platform many hotels offer customers. The pass – either a hard-copy or a smartphone version – provides fast-track entry to most attractions. It's not a discount card: you pay normal rates for museums and tours. But you skip queues, there's no deadline for use, and you only pay for what you use (ie it's not bundled with transit passes, canal cruises etc). The pass itself is free; you link it to your credit card and get charged as you go.

In the centre you'll see the Sarphati memorial (Map p54; 🚊 16/24 Albert Cuypstraat) from 1886, a bombastic temple with a fountain, gargoyles and a bust of the great man himself.

◉ Plantage

Located next door to Nieuwmarkt, the Plantage was laid out as a garden district originally, and it still has a graceful, leafy air.

Hortus Botanicus   GARDENS
(Botanical Garden; Map p62; www.dehortus.nl; Plantage Middenlaan 2a; adult/child €8.50/4.50; ⊙10am-5pm daily, to 7pm Sun Jul & Aug; 🚊9/14 Mr Visserplein) Established in 1638, this venerable garden became a repository for tropical seeds and plants brought in (read: smuggled out of other countries) by Dutch trading ships. From here, coffee, pineapple, cinnamon and palmoil plants were distributed throughout the world. The 4000-plus species are kept in wonderful structures, including the colonial-era seed house and a three-climate glasshouse.

★ Verzetsmuseum   MUSEUM
(Dutch Resistance Museum; Map p62; 🚊620 25 35; www.verzetsmuseum.org; Plantage Kerklaan 61; adult/child €10/5; ⊙10am-5pm Tue-Fri, from 11am Sat-Mon; 🚊9/14 Plantage Kerklaan) This museum shows, in no uncertain terms, how much courage it takes to actively resist an adversary so ruthless that you can't trust neighbours, friends, even family. Exhibits give an insight

Eastern Islands & Plantage

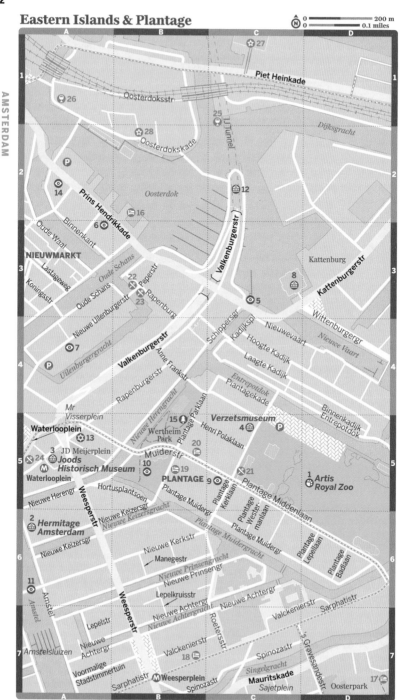

0 200 m
0 0.1 miles

⭐ 27

🚇 26 Oosterdoksstr

Piet Heinkade

25

IJ Tunnel Dijksgracht

⭐ 28 Oosterdokskade

🅿

👁 14 Prins Hendrikkade Oosterdok 🏛 12

Binnenkant 🏛 16

Oude Waal 🏛 6

NIEUWMARKT Kattenburg

Lastageweg Oude Schans 22 Peperstr 8 🏛

Koningsstr Oude Schans Nieuwe Uilenburgerstr 23 Rapenburg Kattenburgerstr

👁 7 Schippersgr Kadijkspl ● 5 Wittenburgergr Nieuwe Vaart

🅿 Uilenburgergracht Valkenburgerstr Anne Frankstr Nieuwevaart Hoogte Kadijk

Rapenburgerstr Laagte Kadijk Nieuwe Vaart

Mr Nieuwe Herengracht Entrepotdok Plantagekade Binnenkadijk Entrepotdok

Visserplein 15 ⚕ Plantage Parklaan Verzetsmuseum

Waterlooplein 🏛 13 Wertheim Henri Polaklaan 4 🏛 🅿

3 JD Meijerplein Park 20 🍴

24 🍴 Joods Muiderstr 🍴 21 Artis

Ⓜ Historisch Museum 10 🍴 19 1 Royal Zoo

Waterlooplein PLANTAGE 9 ● Plantage Middenlaan

Nieuwe Herengr Hortusplantsoen Plantage Muidergr Plantage Kerkstr Plantage Wester- Plantage Lepellaan

Weesperstr Nieuwe Keizersgr manlaan

2 🏛 Hermitage Nieuwe Keizersgracht Plantage Muidergr Plantage Badlaan

Amsterdam Nieuwe Kerkstr Plantage Muidergracht

Nieuwe Keizersgr Manegestr

👁 11 Nieuwe Prinsengracht Nieuwe Prinsengr

Amstel Lepelkruisstr

Lepelstr Nieuwe Achtergr Nieuwe Achtergr Valckenierstr Sarphatistr

Nieuwe Nieuwe Achtergracht Roetersstr

Amstelsluizen Achtergr 18 🍴 Singelgracht

Voormalige Valckenierstr Spinozastr 's Gravesandest 17 🏛

Stadstimmertuin Sarphatistr Ⓜ Weesperplein Mauritskade Oosterpark

Weesperstr Spinozastr Sajetplein

Eastern Islands & Plantage

AMSTERDAM SIGHTS

into the difficulties faced by those who fought the German occupation during WWII from within – as well as the minority who went along with the Nazis. Labels are in Dutch and English.

Its **Verzetsmuseum Junior** relates the stories of four Dutch children, putting the resistance into context for kids.

Hollandsche Schouwburg   MEMORIAL
(Holland Theatre; Map p62; ☑ 531 03 10; www.hollandscheschouwburg.nl; Plantage Middenlaan 24; suggested donation €3; ⊙ 11am-5pm; ⎚ 9/14 Plantage Kerklaan) This historic theatre – first known as the Artis Theatre after its inception in 1892 – quickly became a hub of cultural life in Amsterdam, staging major dramas and operettas. In WWII the occupying Germans turned it into a Jewish theatre, then, tragically, a detention centre for Jews held for deportation.

Wertheimpark   PARK
(Map p62; Plantage Parklaan; ⊙ 7am-9pm; ⎚ 9/14 Mr Visserplein) Opposite the Hortus Botanicus, this park is a brilliant, willow-shaded spot for lazing by the Nieuwe Herengracht. Its most significant feature is the **Auschwitz Memorial**, designed by Dutch writer Jan Wolkers: a panel of broken mirrors installed in the ground reflects the sky.

★ Artis Royal Zoo   ZOO
(Map p62; ☑ 523 34 00; www.artis.nl; Plantage Kerklaan 38-40; adult/child €19.95/16.50, incl Micropia €27/23; ⊙ 9am-6pm Mar-Oct, to 5pm Nov-

Feb; ⎚ 9/14 Plantage Kerklaan) Laid out with delightful ponds, statues, and leafy, winding pathways, mainland Europe's oldest zoo has an alphabet soup of wildlife: alligators, birds, chimps and so on up to zebras. Highlights include convincing themed habitats like African savannah and tropical rainforest, and the aquarium complex featuring coral reefs, shark tanks and an Amsterdam canal displayed from a fish's point of view, plus a planetarium and kids' petting zoo.

⊙ Eastern Islands

In the past 15 years, the crumbling shipyard and warehouse district that used to be the city's fringe has morphed into a hub for cutting-edge Dutch architecture. Because the neighbourhood is more spread out than others, it's a good one to explore by bicycle, gawping at innovative structures along the way.

Het Scheepvaartmuseum   MUSEUM
(Maritime Museum; Map p62; ☑ 523 22 22; www.scheepvaartmuseum.nl; Kattenburgerplein 1; adult/child €15/7.50; ⊙ 9am-5pm; ⎚ 22/48 Kattenburgerplein) An immense, 17th-century admiralty building houses one of the world's most extensive collections of maritime memorabilia. Early shipping routes, naval combat, fishing and whaling are all detailed, and there are some 500 models of boats and ships. A full-scale replica of the Dutch East India Company's 700-tonne *Amsterdam*, one of the largest ships of the fleet, is moored outside.

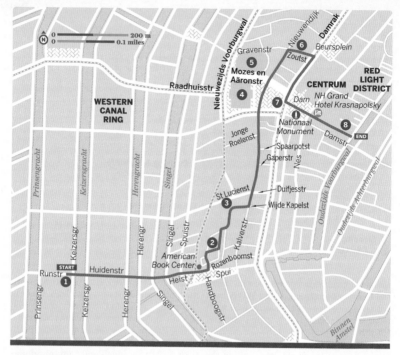

Walking Tour
Cheese, Gin & Monuments

START DE KAASKAMER
FINISH WYNAND FOCKINK
LENGTH 2KM; 1½ HOURS WITH STOPS

This tour is a hit parade of Amsterdam's favourite food, drinks and historic sights.

The Dutch eat more than 14kg of cheese per person annually, and much of it is sold in ❶ **De Kaaskamer** (p94). Wheels of Gouda, Edam and other locally made types are stacked to the rafters. Get a wedge to go.

As you make your way through the Spui, keep an eye out just past the American Book Center for a humble wooden door. Push it open and behold the hidden community known as the ❷ **Begijnhof** (p42), surrounding two historic churches and gardens. Cross the courtyard to the other entrance.

From the Begijnhof turn north and walk a short way to the ❸ **Civic Guard Gallery** (p42). Paintings of stern folks in ruffled collars stare down from the walls. Cross the gallery and depart through the Amsterdam Museum's courtyard restaurant onto Kalverstraat.

Follow Kalverstraat to the ❹ **Royal Palace** (p39), home to King Willem-Alexander and Queen Máxima. The sumptuous interior deserves a look. The palace's neighbour is the ❺ **Nieuwe Kerk** (p42), the stage for Dutch investitures. Afterwards, get onto crowded Nieuwendijk, and walk to Zoutsteeg. Swallow any misgivings about eating raw fish and order the famed Dutch herring at ❻ **Rob Wigboldus Vishandel** (p77), a wee, three-table shop. Then depart Zoutsteeg onto Damrak.

Cross Damrak to the Nationaal Monument side of the ❼ **Dam** (p42) – Amsterdam's birthplace. Wade through the sea of bikes – the urns behind the monument hold earth from East Indies war cemeteries. Follow the street leading behind the NH Grand Hotel Krasnapolsky to ❽ **Wynand Fockink** (p87). The Dutch gin maker's tasting room dates from 1679. The barkeep will pour your drink to the brim, so do like the locals to prevent spillage: lean over it and sip without lifting.

ARCAM
ARCHITECTURE

(Stichting Architectuurcentrum Amsterdam; Map p62; ☑620 48 78; www.arcam.nl; Prins Hendrik-kade 600; ⊙1-5pm Tue-Sat; 🚊22/48 Kadijksplein) **FREE** This showpiece building of the Amsterdam Architecture Foundation is a one-stop shop for all your architectural needs. Expert staff are on hand to interpret the fascinating changing exhibits, and you can find books, guide maps and suggestions for tours on foot, by bike and by public transport.

NEMO
MUSEUM

(Map p62; ☑531 32 33; www.e-nemo.nl; Oosterdok 2; admission €15, roof terrace free; ⊙10am-5.30pm, closed Mon Sep-Mar; 🚊22/48 IJ-Tunnel) Perched atop the entrance to the IJ Tunnel is the science and technology museum, NEMO. The dramatic, green-copper building rises from the waterfront like a ship setting sail. Its hands-on exhibits (with English explanations) are winners with kids and adults: drawing with a laser, 'antigravity' trick mirrors, and a 'lab' for answering such questions as 'How black is black?' and 'How do you make cheese?'.

NEMO's stepped, decklike roof is the city's largest summer terrace with panoramic views.

⊙ Oosterpark

Oosterpark is one of Amsterdam's most culturally diverse neighbourhoods, with Moroccan and Turkish enclaves, and sights that are off the everyday tourist path.

Tropenmuseum
MUSEUM

(Tropics Museum; ☑0880 042 800; www.tropenmuseum.nl; Linnaeusstraat 2; adult/child €12.50/8; ⊙10am-5pm Tue-Sun; ♿; 🚊9/10/14 Alexanderplein) The Tropenmuseum houses a three-storey collection of colonial artefacts, presented with insight, imagination and a fair amount of multimedia. You can stroll through an African market or sit in a Central Asian yurt (traditional felt hut), see ritual masks and spiky spears and listen to recordings of exotic musical instruments. There's a children's section, a great gift shop and a cafe serving global foods.

Oosterpark
PARK

(⊙dawn-dusk; ♿; 🚊9 1e Van Swindenstraat) Oosterpark was laid out in 1891 to accommodate the diamond traders who found their fortunes in the South African mines, and it still has an elegant, rambling feel, complete with regal grey herons swooping around the ponds and wild parrots chattering in the trees.

🏃 Activities

Cycling

Fiets (bicycles) outnumber cars in Amsterdam. Rental shops are everywhere. Vondelpark and the Eastern Islands are easy destinations for DIY cycling.

Travel 20 minutes north of the city centre, and the landscape morphs to windmills, cows and wee farming communities – all accessible via an afternoon bike ride. Take your wheels onto the free Buiksloterweg ferry behind Centraal Station, and cross the IJ River. The crossing takes about five minutes, and boats depart continuously throughout the day. Then pedal north along the Noordhollands Kanaal. Within a few kilometres you're in the countryside. Cycling maps are available at the visitor centre by Centraal Station. Tour companies also cover the area.

Boating

Boaty
BOATING

(☑06 2714 9493; www.boaty.nl; Jozef Israëlskade; boat rental per 3hr from €79; ⊙9am-30min before sunset Apr–mid-Oct; 🚊12 Scheldestraat) Boaty's location on the peaceful Amstelkanaal makes it an ideal launching pad for exploring the waterways before approaching the crowded city-centre canals. Rental includes a map outlining suggested routes; you don't need a boat licence or prior experience. Book ahead online, or phone for same-day reservations. The season can run longer or shorter depending on weather conditions.

Canal Bike
BOATING

(www.canal.nl; per person per hr €8; ⊙10am-6pm Apr-Oct) These pedal boats allow you to splash around the canals at your own speed. Landing stages are by the Rijksmuseum, Leidseplein and Anne Frank Huis. Deposit of €20 required. Affiliated with Canal Bus/boat tours.

Ice Skating

In winter the pond at the Museumplein becomes a popular ice-skating rink, and the scene looks like the top of a wind-up jewellery box. The rink is free; there's a modest fee for skate rentals.

Occasionally the canals freeze over for skating, but stay away unless you see large groups of people gliding. The ice can be weak, especially at the edges and under bridges.

🧭 Tours

Bicycle Tours

The companies following also rent bikes.

AMSTERDAM ACTIVITIES

AMSTERDAMSE BOS & COBRA MUSEUM

Goats in the forest and wild art reward those who venture southwest of the city to the quiet neighbourhood of Amstelveen, near Schiphol Airport.

The jewel here is **Amsterdamse Bos** (Amsterdam Forest; www.amsterdamsebos.nl; Bosbaanweg 5; ⊙ park 24hr, visitor centre noon-5pm; 🚼; 📖 170, 172), a vast 2km by 5km tract of lakes, woods and meadows criss-crossed by paths, about a 40-minute bus ride from Centraal Station. **Bike rentals** (www.amsterdamsebosfietsverhuur.nl; rental per 2hr/day €6/9.50; ⊙ 10am-6pm, closed Mon & Tue in winter; 📖 170, 172) are available at the main entrance and are vital for park exploration. The **Fun Forest** (www.funforest.nl; Bosbaanweg 3; adult/child €24/20; ⊙ 11am-7pm Jul & Aug, to 6pm Sep & Oct; 🚼; 📖 170, 172) tree-top climbing park is also by the main gate.

From here head west for 2.5km and you'll come to the **open-air theatre** (www.bostheater.nl; Bosbaanweg 5; ⊙ Jun–early Sep; 📖 170, 172). It stages classic plays (in Dutch) throughout summer. Nearby at Grote Speelweide you can rent **canoes** and **kayaks** (per hour €6) and **pedal boats** (per hour €10).

About 750m south is the park's most delightful attraction. **De Ridammerhoeve** (www.geitenboerderij.nl; ⊙ 10am-5pm Wed-Mon; 📖 170, 172) FREE is an organic, working goat farm where kids can feed bottles of milk to, well, kids (€8 for two bottles). The cafeteria sells goat's-milk ice cream and other dairy products.

The fascinating **CoBrA Museum** (www.cobra-museum.nl; Sandbergplein 1; adult/child €9.50/6; ⊙ 11am-5pm Tue-Sun; 📖 170, 172, 📖 5 Binnenhof) lies near the park. Formed by artists from Copenhagen, Brussels and Amsterdam after WWII, the CoBrA movement produced semi-abstract works known for their primitive, childlike qualities. The two-storey building holds a trove of boldly coloured, avant-garde paintings, ceramics and statues, including many by Karel Appel, the style's most famous practitioner.

Mike's Bike Tours   BICYCLE TOUR
(Map p54; ☏ 622 79 70; www.mikesbiketours amsterdam.com; Kerkstraat 134; city tours per adult/ child from €22/19, countryside from €25/18; ⊙ office 9am-6pm Mar-Oct, from 10am Nov-Feb; 📖 16/24 Keizersgracht) Tours depart across the road from the office, at Kerkstraat 123. You can also hire bikes (per four/24 hours from €5/10).

Orangebike   BICYCLE TOUR
(www.orange-bike.nl; Buiksloterweg 5c; tours €22.50-32.50; ⊙ office 9am-5.45pm Mon-Fri, 10am-5pm Sat & Sun; 🚢 Buiksloterweg) Traditional city and countryside tours (including a beach tour), plus themed options like the Snack Tour, sampling *bitterballen* (croquettes) and *jenever* (gin), and architectural tours. The shop is in Amsterdam-Noord, a five-minute ferry ride from Centraal Station.

Yellow Bike   BICYCLE TOUR
(Map p44; ☏ 620 69 40; www.yellowbike. nl; Nieuwezijds Kolk 29; city/countryside tours €27.50/32.50; 📖 1/2/5/13/17 Nieuwezijds Kolk) The original. Choose from city tours or the longer countryside tour through the pretty Waterland district to the north.

Boat Tours

Sure they're touristy, but canal tours are also a delightful way to see the city. Several operators depart from moorings at Centraal Station, Damrak, Rokin and opposite the Rijksmuseum. Costs are similar (around €16 per adult). To avoid the steamed-up glass-window effect, look for a boat with an open seating area. On a night tour, there's the bonus of seeing the bridges lit up (though these tours usually cost a bit more).

Canal Bus   BOAT TOUR
(☏ 217 05 00; www.canal.nl; day pass adult/child €23/11.50; ⊙ 10am-6pm; 🚢; 📖 1/2/5 Leidseplein) Offers a handy hop-on, hop-off service. Its 14 docks around the city are located near the big museums and landmarks.

Those Dam Boat Guys   BOAT TOUR
(Map p50; ☏ 06 1885 5219; www.thosedamboat guys.com; per person €20; ⊙ 1pm, 3pm & 5pm; 📖 13/14/17 Westermarkt) Here's your least-touristy canal-cruise option. The guys offer cheeky small tours (no more than 11 people) on electric boats. Feel free to bring food, beer, smoking material and whatever else you want for the 90-minute jaunt. Departure is from Cafe Wester (Nieuwe Leliestraat 2).

Blue Boat Company BOAT TOUR
(Map p54; ☑ 679 13 70; www.blueboat.nl; Stadhouderskade 30; 75-minute tour adult/child €16/8.50; ☺ half-hourly 10am-6pm Mar-Oct, hourly Nov-Feb; ☐ 1/2/5/7/10 Leidseplein) Blue Boat's 75-minute main tour glides by the top sights. Ninety-minute evening cruises (adult/child €19.50/15.50) are offered at 8pm, 9pm and 10pm from March to October and at 8pm November to February. Other cruises include a children's pirate-themed tour, a dinner cruise and a tour in a smaller, open-top boat. The dock is near the Max Euweplein.

Walking Tours

Prostitution Information
Centre Red Light District Tour WALKING TOUR
(Map p44; www.pic-amsterdam.com; Enge Kerksteeg 3; tours €15; ☺ 5pm Sat year-round, plus 6.30pm Wed Jun-Aug; ☐ 4/9/16/24 Dam) The nonprofit Prostitution Information Centre (p47) offers fascinating one-hour tours of the Red Light District, where guides explain the details of how the business works and take you into a Red Light room. Profits go to the centre; reservations are not necessary.

Sandeman's New Amsterdam Tours WALKING TOUR
(Map p44; www.newamsterdamtours.com; donations encouraged; ☺ 10am, 11.15am & 2.15pm; ☐ 4/9/16/24 Dam) Energetic young guides working on a tip-only basis lead a three-hour jaunt past the top sights of the Medieval Centre and Red Light District (with a dip into the Jordaan). Meet at the Nationaal Monument on the Dam, regardless of the weather. The tour is first-come, first served; to guarantee a spot you can make a reservation.

Hungry Birds Street Food Tours WALKING TOUR
(☑ 06 1898 6268; www.hungrybirds.nl; per person €69; ☺ 11am Mon-Sat) Guides take you 'off the eaten track' to chow on Dutch and ethnic specialities. Tours visit around 10 spots over four hours in De Pijp, Utrechtsestraat, Rembrandtplein and the Spui, from family-run eateries to street vendors. The price includes all food. The Birds offer a tour by bike as well. Book in advance; the meet-up location is given after you make reservations.

Randy Roy's Redlight Tours WALKING TOUR
(Map p44; ☑ 06 4185 3288; www.randyroysredlighttours.com; tours €15; ☺ 8pm Sun-Thu, 8pm & 10pm Fri & Sat, closed Dec-Feb; ☐ 1/2/5/13/17 Centraal Station) Fun guides provide in-the-know anecdotes about the city's sex life and celebrity secrets on Randy Roy's lively 1½-hour tour.

The jaunt ends at a local bar with a free drink. Meet in front of the Victoria Hotel (Damrak 1-5), opposite Centraal Station, rain or shine. Reserving in advance is a good idea.

Drugs Tour WALKING TOUR
(Map p44; www.drugstour.nl; tours by donation; ☺ 6pm Fri; ☐ 4/9/16/24 Dam) The illuminating, 1½-hour itinerary looks at Amsterdam's drug culture, both its myths and reality. It includes smart shops, a 'user room' (the tour doesn't go inside) and a look at fake drugs being sold on the street. Tours depart by the Oude Kerk. Reserve in advance. Private tours also can be arranged (€40 per four people) in multiple languages.

Mee in Mokum WALKING TOUR
(Map p44; www.gildeamsterdam.nl; Kalverstraat 92; tours €7.50; ☺ 11am & 2pm Tue-Sun; ☐ 1/2/5 Spui) Mee in Mokum's low-priced walkabouts are led by senior-citizen volunteers who often have personal recollections to add. The tours can be a bit hit-or-miss, depending on the guide. They depart from the cafe in the Amsterdam Museum. Reserve at least a day in advance.

★ Festivals & Events

5 Days Off MUSIC
(www.5daysoff.nl; ☺ early Mar) Electronic music gets its due at this fest in the major club venues. The programming is edgier and more selective than Amsterdam Dance Event, and the feeling more intimate.

King's Day CULTURAL
(Koningsdag; ☺ 27 Apr) King's Day, 27 April, is a celebration of the House of Orange, with more than 400,000 orange-clad people filling Amsterdam's streets for drinking and dancing. The city also becomes one big flea market, as people sell off all their unwanted junk.

World Press Photo Show CULTURAL
(www.worldpressphoto.org; ☺ late Apr-Jun) This gripping display of the year's best photojournalism debuts in the Nieuwe Kerk in late April, and stays on display through June.

Herdenkingsdag CULTURAL
(Remembrance Day; ☺ 4 May) For the fallen of WWII. King Willem-Alexander lays a wreath on the Dam and the city observes two minutes' silence at 8pm.

Holland Festival CULTURAL
(www.hollandfestival.nl; ☺ Jun) June's big-name theatre, dance and opera meet offbeat digital

films and experimental music in the Netherlands' biggest performing-arts extravaganza. The month-long, high-art/low-art mash-up happens at venues citywide.

Roots Festival   MUSIC

(www.amsterdamroots.nl; ⊘ early Jul) Early July's four-day Roots Festival programs world music in key venues around town, culminating in the vibrant Roots Open Air all-day fest at the Park Frankendael.

Over het IJ Festival   CULTURAL

(www.overhetij.nl; ⊘ early Jul) Big performing-arts events (dance, theatre, music) take place for 10 days at the NDSM shipyards in Amsterdam-Noord.

Amsterdam Gay Pride   CULTURAL

(www.pride.amsterdam; ⊘ late Jul-Aug) Amsterdam flies the rainbow flag from late July to early August. Highlights of over-the-top fest include the Drag Queen Olympics and a raucous, waterborne Pride Parade (the first Saturday of August).

Grachtenfestival   MUSIC

(www.grachtenfestival.nl; ⊘ mid-Aug) Classical musicians pop up in canal-side parks and hidden gardens during the 10-day Grachtenfestival. The highlight of the 'Canal Festival' is the free concert on a floating stage in the Prinsengracht.

Inside Design   DESIGN

(www.elle.nl/specials/elle-festival; ⊘ late Oct) Held over a weekend in late October and open to the public, showcasing emerging Dutch-designed furniture and products.

Amsterdam Dance Event   MUSIC

(www.amsterdam-dance-event.nl; ⊘ late Oct) An electronic music powwow on a massive scale, ADE sees 2200 DJs and artists and more than 300,000 clubbers attending 450 events all over the city over five long, sweaty days and nights late in October.

🛏 Sleeping

In its typically charming way, Amsterdam has loads of hotels in wild and wonderful spaces: inspired architects have breathed new life into old buildings, from converted schools and industrial lofts to entire rows of canal houses joined at the hip. Many lodgings overlook gorgeous waterways or courtyards.

Crowds – and rates – peak in summer and on weekends at any time of the year. Book well in advance. Prices are lowest from October to April (excluding Christmas, New Year and Easter).

Amsterdam's hostel scene – and especially its 'poshtel' scene – is thriving; look out for the 2016-opened, 566-bed Generator Amsterdam (Map p62; www.generatorhostels. com; Mauritskade 57; dm €30-50; ⬚ 9/14 9/10/14 Alexanderplein).

Any hotel with more than 20 rooms is considered large, and most rooms are on the snug side. Free wi-fi is nearly universal, but air-conditioning and lifts are not. Prepare to carry your luggage up steep staircases.

Rates generally include a 5% city-hotel tax; however, this is sometimes added separately to the bill, so ask before booking. If you're paying by credit card, some hotels add a surcharge of up to 5%.

Lodgings in the centre can be noisy and poor value for money. Western Canal Ring places are near the action but more dignified and quiet. Vondelpark and the Old South offer quality digs that are close to the museums and only a short walk from the action at Leidseplein, but they can slide up the price scale. Apartment rentals work well for local-life areas such as the Jordaan and De Pijp: Airbnb (www.airbnb.com) can turn up lots of Amsterdam options.

🛏 Medieval Centre & Red Light District

St Christopher's at the Winston   HOSTEL, HOTEL €

(Map p44; ☑ 623 13 80; www.winston.nl; Warmoesstraat 129; dm €40-45, s €95, d €124-144; ⬚; ⬚ 4/9/16/24 Dam) This place hops 24/7 with rock 'n' roll rooms, and a busy club, bar, beer garden and smoking deck downstairs. Ensuite dorms sleep up to eight. Most private rooms are 'art' rooms: local artists were given free rein, with super-edgy (entirely stainless steel) to questionably raunchy results. Rates include breakfast (and ear plugs!).

Hotel The Exchange   DESIGN HOTEL €€

(Map p44; ☑ 523 00 89; www.hoteltheexchange. com; Damrak 50; d €100-225; @ ⬚; ⬚ 1/2/5/13/17 Centraal Station) The Exchange's 61 rooms have been dressed 'like models' in eye-popping style by students from the Amsterdam Fashion Institute. Anything goes, from oversized button-adorned walls to a Marie Antoinette dress tented over the bed. If you like plain decor, this isn't your place. Rooms range from small and viewless to spacious sanctums, but all have en-suite bathrooms.

FOR FREE

It's possible to spend a fortune in Amsterdam, but many enjoyable sights and activities cost nothing.

Sights

Civic Guard Gallery (p42) Stroll through the monumental collection of portraits, from Golden Age to modern.

Begijnhof (p42) Explore the14th-century hidden courtyard and its clandestine churches.

Stadsarchief (p56) You never know what treasures you'll find in the vaults of the city's archives.

Albert Cuypmarkt (p60) Amsterdam's biggest market bursts with cheeses, bike locks and socks, as do the city's many other bazaars – all free to browse.

Entertainment

Concertgebouw (p91) Sharpen your elbows to get in for Wednesday's lunchtime concert, often a public rehearsal for musicians playing later that evening.

Muziektheater (p92) More classical freebies fill the air during lunch, this time on Tuesdays.

Bimhuis (p92) Jazzy jam sessions hot up the revered venue on Tuesday nights.

Tours

Sandeman's New Amsterdam Tours (p67) Young guides show you the centre's top sights.

Gassan Diamonds (p48) Don't know your princess from marquise, river from top cape? Get the shiny lowdown here.

Yellow Backie (www.yellowbackie.org) This program lets visitors hitch a free ride on the back of a local's bike. When you see someone cycling by with a bright yellow luggage rack on the rear, yell 'Backie!'. The rider will stop, let you hop on, and pedal you onward.

DIY

Canals Walk along the 400-year-old waterways and decide which old gabled house leans the most.

Ferry rides Free ferries depart behind Centraal Station to NDSM-werf, northern Amsterdam's edgy art community 15 minutes up-harbour, and to the EYE Film Institute, five minutes across the river.

Red Light District Keep your eyes on the architecture and you needn't spend a cent.

Hotel Résidence Le Coin APARTMENT €€
(Map p54; ☏524 68 00; www.lecoin.nl; Nieuwe Doelenstraat 5; s/f €125/250, d €145-160; ☏; ☐4/9/14/16/24 Muntplein) This shiny inn, owned by the University of Amsterdam, offers 42 small, high-class apartments spread over seven historical buildings, all equipped with designer furniture, wood floors and kitchenettes – and all reachable by lift. It's in the thick of things, opposite the popular grand Café de Jaren and just a five-minute stroll to pretty Nieuwmarkt. Wi-fi is free, with decent speed.

Hotel Brouwer HOTEL €€
(Map p44; ☏624 63 58; www.hotelbrouwer.nl; Singel 83; s €78-98, d €128-148, tr €160-180; @☏; ☐1/2/5/13/17 Nieuwezijds Kolk) A bargain-priced (for Amsterdam) favourite, Brouwer has just eight rooms in a house dating back to 1652. Each chamber is named for a Dutch painter and furnished with simplicity, but all have canal views. There's a mix of Delft-blue tiles and early-20th-century decor, plus a tiny lift. Staff dispense friendly advice. Reserve well in advance. Rates include a hearty breakfast. Cash only.

GAY & LESBIAN AMSTERDAM

Information

Gay Amsterdam (www.gayamsterdam.com) Lists hotels, shops, restaurants and clubs, and provides maps.

Pink Point (Map p50; ☎428 10 70; www.facebook.com/pinkpointamsterdam; Westermarkt; ⊙10.30am-6pm; ◻13/14/17 Westermarkt) Located behind the Westerkerk, this is part information kiosk, part souvenir shop. It's a good place to pick up gay and lesbian publications, and news about parties, events and social groups.

Entertainment

Amsterdam's gay scene is among the world's largest. Five hubs party hardest.

Warmoesstraat In the Red Light District (between the Dam and Centraal Station); hosts the infamous, kink-filled leather and fetish bars.

Zeedijk Near Warmoesstraat; crowds spill onto laid-back bar terraces.

Rembrandtplein In the Southern Canal Ring; this area has traditional pubs and brown *cafés*, some with a campy bent.

Leidseplein A smattering of trendy venues along Kerkstraat.

Reguliersdwarsstraat Draws the beautiful crowd.

't Mandje (Map p44; www.cafetmandje.nl; Zeedijk 63; ⊙5pm-1am Tue-Thu, 4pm-1am Fri, 3pm-1am Sat & Sun; ◻4/9/16/24 Centraal Station) Amsterdam's oldest gay bar opened in 1927, then shut in 1982, when the Zeedijk grew too seedy. But its trinket-covered interior was lovingly dusted every week until it reopened in 2008. The devoted bartenders can tell you stories about the bar's brassy lesbian founder. It's one of the most *gezellig* (cosy, convivial) places in the centre, gay or straight.

Hotel Luxer HOTEL €€
(Map p44; ☎330 32 05; www.hotelluxer.nl; Warmoesstraat 11; r €100-190; ✳@🛜; ◻4/9/16/24 Centraal Station) A pleasant surprise if ever there was one, this smart little number is probably the best option for your money in the thick of the Red Light District. Rooms are small, but well equipped (air-con!), and at night the breakfast area becomes a chic little bar. Breakfast costs €8.

Hotel de L'Europe HOTEL €€€
(Map p54; ☎531 17 77; www.leurope.nl; Nieuwe Doelenstraat 2-8; r from €340; ✳@🛜✳; ◻4/9/14/16/24 Muntplein) Owned by the Heineken family, luxury L'Europe mixes classical elements (glass chandeliers, doorkeepers in top hats) with whimsical Dutch design. The 111 rooms are grand, with iPads, canal views, heated floors and white marble bathtubs; wi-fi is free. The on-site cigar lounge and Freddy's Bar, with brass-topped tables and leather chairs, attract a professional crowd.

art'otel amsterdam BOUTIQUE HOTEL €€€
(Map p44; ☎719 72 00; www.artotels.com; Prins Hendrikkade 33; r €289-389; ✳🛜✳; ◻1/2/5/13/17 Centraal Station) Located opposite Centraal Station, this stylish hotel offers 107 rooms with mod decor and original artworks on the wall. To add to the creative theme, there's an open-to-the-public gallery in the basement. The lobby is a swank refuge with a fireplace and library. A free, beyond-the-norm hot breakfast is included.

🛏 Nieuwmarkt

Stayokay Amsterdam Stadsdoelen HOSTEL €
(Map p44; ☎624 68 32; www.stayokay.com; Kloveniersburgwal 97; dm €29.50-45, tw/d from €85; @🛜; ◻4/9/14/16/24 Muntplein) Efficient Stadsdoelen is always bustling with backpackers. Staff are friendly and the 11 single-sex and mixed rooms (each with up to 20 beds and free lockers) offer a modicum of privacy. There's a big TV room, a pool table, a laundry, free wi-fi throughout the building and free continental breakfast. Towel rental costs €4.50.

Christian Youth Hostel 'The Shelter City' HOSTEL €
(Map p44; ☎625 32 30; www.shelterhostel amsterdam.com; Barndesteeg 21; dm €19-37.50; @🛜; Ⓜ Nieuwmarkt) The price is right at this rambling hostel just outside the Red

Café de Barderij (Map p44; Zeedijk 14; ⊘4pm-1am; 🚇4/9/16/24 Centraal Station) This super-friendly, candlelit bar draws a mixture of local gay regulars and tourists. It has killer views of the canal out back and Zeedijk in front. The crowd skews a bit older, the soundtrack toward fun pop music.

Montmartre (Map p54; www.cafemontmartre.nl; Halvemaansteeg 17; ⊘5pm-1am Sun-Thu, to 4am Fri & Sat; 🚇4/9/14 Rembrandtplein) Regarded by many as the best gay bar in the Benelux, and a busy weekend will show why. Patrons sing along (or scream along) to recordings of Dutch ballads and old top-40 hits.

Getto (Map p44; www.getto.nl; Warmoesstraat 51; ⊘4.30pm-1am Tue-Thu, to 2am Fri & Sat, to midnight Sun; 🚇4/9/16/24 Centraal Station) This groovy, long restaurant-bar is loved for its open, welcoming attitude, great people-watching from the front and a rear lounge where you can chill. It's a haven for the younger gay and lesbian crowd and anyone who wants a little bohemian subculture in the Red Light District's midst. The food (burgers, vegetarian samosas, deer and mushroom stew etc) is good and cheap, too.

Vivelavie (Map p54; www.vivelavie.net; Amstelstraat 7; ⊘4pm-3am Sun-Thu, 3pm-4am Fri, 1pm-4am Sat; ☎; 🚇4/9/14 Rembrandtplein) Flirty girls, good-natured staff, loud music, large windows and dancing make this one of Amsterdam's most popular lesbian *cafés*. In summer the outdoor terrace buzzes.

Warehouse Amsterdam (Map p44; www.warehouse-amsterdam.com; Warmoesstraat 96; ⊘11pm-4am Thu & Sun, to 5am Fri & Sat; 🚇4/9/16/24 Centraal Station) It's mostly men dancing to the international array of hardcore DJs, but women are equally welcome.

Festivals

The centrepiece of **Amsterdam Gay Pride** (p68) celebrations are its waterborne parade with outlandishly decorated boats plying the canals.

Light District, but only if you can handle a bit of religious zeal and a tough no-drugs-or-alcohol policy. The pros of staying here include large, airy, single-sex dorms, filling free breakfasts, a quiet cafe, and a garden courtyard with a ping-pong table. Towel/padlock rental costs €1/4.

There's a partner hostel in the Jordaan.

Misc EatDrinkSleep   BOUTIQUE HOTEL €€€
(Map p44; ☎330 62 41; www.misceatdrinksleep.com; Kloveniersburgwal 20; s/d from €155/165; ❄☎; Ⓜ Nieuwmarkt) Steps from Nieuwmarkt square, the Misc's six themed rooms range from 'baroque' (quite romantic) to 'the room of wonders' (a modern Moroccan escapade); two rooms contain quirky 'bumblebee' ceiling fans. Canal View rooms cost more, but have air-conditioning; the Garden View rooms are equally charming (if smaller, and with fans only). Breakfast is included in the rate.

Jordaan

**Christian Youth
Hostel 'The Shelter Jordaan'**   HOSTEL €
(Map p50; ☎624 47 17; www.shelter.nl; Bloemstraat 179; dm €25-39; @☎; 🚇10/13/14/17 Marnixstraat)

Putting up with the 'no-everything' (drinking, smoking, partying) policy at this small hostel isn't hard, because it's such a gem. Single-sex dorms are quiet and clean, there's a piano, and breakfasts – especially the fluffy pancakes – are great. The cafe serves cheap meals the rest of the day.

★**Amsterdam Wiechmann Hotel**   HOTEL €€
(Map p50; ☎626 33 21; www.hotelwiechmann.nl; Prinsengracht 328; s/d from €85/155; @☎; 🚇7/10/17 Elandsgracht) Lovingly cared-for rooms at this family-run hotel in three canal houses are furnished like an antique shop, with country quilts and chintz, while the lobby knick-knacks have been here for some 75 years. It's an ace location right on the pretty Prinsengracht. Rates include breakfast.

★**Houseboat Ms Luctor**   B&B €€
(☎06 2268 9506; www.boatbedandbreakfast.nl; Westerdok 103; d from €130; ☎; 🚇48 Barentszplein) 🌿 A brimming organic breakfast basket is delivered to you each morning at this self-contained mahogany-panelled 1913 houseboat, moored in a quiet waterway 10 minutes' walk from Centraal Station (five from the Jordaan). Eco initiatives include solar power, two

bikes to borrow and a canoe for canal explorations. Minimum stay two nights.

BackStage Hotel
HOTEL €€

(Map p54; ☑624 40 44; www.backstagehotel. com; Leidsegracht 114; s without bathroom from €65, d with/without bathroom from €100/85; @☎; ⓓ1/2/5 Leidseplein) Seriously fun, this music-themed hotel is a favourite among musicians jamming at nearby Melkweg and Paradiso, as evidenced by the lobby bar's band-signature-covered piano and pool table. Gig posters (many signed) line the corridors, and rooms are done up in neo-retro black and white, with iPod docking stations, and drum-kit overhead lights.

Late at night, bands (and their fans) hold court in the lively bar.

Western Canal Ring

★Hoxton Amsterdam
DESIGN HOTEL €€

(Map p44; ☑888 55 55; www.thehoxton.com; Herengracht 255; r €120-200; ✳☎; ⓓ13/14/17 Westermarkt) Part of a European-based chain known for high style at affordable prices, the Hoxton opened in 2015 to great hipster fanfare. The 111 rooms splash through five canal houses and come in sizes from 'shoebox' to 'roomy'. The breakfast snack, speedy wi-fi, free international calls and low-priced canteen items are nice touches.

The hotel also organises events with local artists and designers, so you get to meet creative locals.

Frederic Rentabike
APARTMENT €€

(Map p44; ☑624 55 09; www.frederic.nl; Brouwersgracht 78; houseboat from €145; ☎; ⓓ18/21/22 Brouwersstraat) Frederic offers nicely outfit-

---

AIRPORT ACCOMMODATION

Citizen M (☑811 70 80; www.citizenm. com/destinations/amsterdam; Plezierweg 2; r €89-179; ✳@☎) A five-minute walk from the terminals, the Starship Enterprise–like rooms are snug, but maximise space to the utmost, with plush, wall-to-wall beds, and shower and toilet pods. Each room includes a lighting control – command central for the lighting (purple, red or white), blinds, flat-screen TV (free on-demand movies), music, temperature and rain shower.

Sushi, sake and self-service snacks are for sale in the club-like canteen.

---

ted houseboats on the Prinsengracht, Brouwersgracht and Bloemgracht that are bona fide floating holiday homes with all mod cons. On land, the company also has various rooms and apartments in central locations. (And yes, bikes, too.)

Hotel Clemens Amsterdam
HOTEL €€

(Map p50; ☑624 60 89; www.clemenshotel.nl; Raadhuisstraat 39; d €135-185; ✳@☎; ⓓ13/14/17 Westermarkt) Very reasonably priced for its near-everything location, the 14 bright rooms at Clemens have rain showers, speedy free wi-fi and air-conditioning. If you don't score a room with a private balcony (some others have window seats or fireplaces), there's a lovely terrace for breakfast (included in the rate). There is no lift, so be prepared for stairs.

Maes B&B
B&B €€

(Map p44; ☑427 51 65; www.bedandbreakfast amsterdam.com; Herenstraat 26; r €115-155; @☎; ⓓ1/2/5/13/17 Nieuwezijds Kolk) If you were designing a traditional home in the Western Canal Ring, it would probably turn out a lot like this property: oriental carpets, wood floors and exposed brick. It's actually fairly spacious for such an old building, but the kitchen (open all day for guests to use) is definitely *gezellig* (convivial, cosy).

Dylan
BOUTIQUE HOTEL €€€

(Map p50; ☑530 20 10; www.dylanamsterdam. com; Keizersgracht 384; d/ste from €350/500; ✳@☎; ⓓ1/2/5 Spui) Exquisite boutique hotel the Dylan occupies an 18th-century Keizersgracht canal house that is set around a herringbone-paved, topiary-filled inner courtyard. Bespoke furniture such as silver-leaf and mother-of-pearl drinks cabinets adorn its 40 individually decorated rooms and suites (some duplex). Its Michelin-star Restaurant Vinkeles also hosts private chef's tables aboard its boat, the *Muze*, as it cruises the canals.

Andaz Amsterdam
DESIGN HOTEL €€€

(Map p54; ☑523 12 34; www.amsterdam.prinsen gracht.andaz.hyatt.com; Prinsengracht 587; d €375-650; @☎; ⓓ1/2/5 Prinsengracht) Visionary Dutch designer Marcel Wanders has transformed Amsterdam's former public library into a fantasy of giant gold and silver cutlery, fish murals, Delftware-inspired carpets, library-book pages writ large on the walls and other flights of imagination. The 122 guest rooms have Geneva sound systems with iPod docks, king-size beds, and complimentary

CANALS OF AMSTERDAM

In Dutch a canal is a *gracht* (pronounced 'khrakht'), and the main canals form the central *grachtengordel* (canal ring). The beauties came to life in the early 1600s, after Amsterdam's population grew beyond its medieval walls and city planners put together an ambitious design for expansion. Far from being simply decorative or picturesque, or even just waterways for transport, the canals were necessary to drain and reclaim the waterlogged land.

In 2010, Unesco listed the waterways as a World Heritage site. The city's canals outnumber those in Venice, and Amsterdam also has three times as many bridges – more than any other city worldwide.

The core canals are the semicircular Singel, Herengracht, Keizersgracht and Prinsengracht. An easy way to remember them is that, apart from the singular Singel, these canals are in alphabetical order as you move outward.

➡ **Singel** Originally a moat that defended Amsterdam's outer limits.

➡ **Herengracht** This is where Amsterdam's wealthiest residents moved once the canals were completed. They named the waterway after the Heeren XVII (17 Gentlemen) of the Dutch East India Company, and built their mansions alongside it.

➡ **Keizersgracht** Almost as swanky, the Keizersgracht (Emperor's Canal) was a nod to Holy Roman Emperor Maximilian I.

➡ **Prinsengracht** Named after Willem the Silent, Prince of Orange and the first Dutch royal, Prinsengracht was designed as a slightly cheaper canal with smaller residences and warehouses. It also acted as a barrier against the crusty working-class quarter beyond, aka the Jordaan. Today the Prinsengracht is the liveliest of Amsterdam's inner canals, with cafes, shops and houseboats lining the quays.

➡ **Brouwersgracht** The Brouwersgracht (Brewers' Canal) is a radial canal that cuts across the others. It takes its name from the many breweries that used to operate along the banks. It's often cited as the city's most beautiful waterway.

snacks and non-alcoholic drinks. Free bikes to use, too.

🛏 Southern Canal Ring

★ **Cocomama** HOSTEL €
(Map p54; ☑ 627 24 54; www.cocomama.nl; Westeinde 18; dm/d/tr from €38/109/146; @ 🛜; 🚊 4/25 Stadhouderskade) Amsterdam's first self-proclaimed 'boutique hostel' plays up its salacious past (the building was once home to a high-end brothel) in some themed bunk rooms, while others are more demure, with Delftware or windmill themes. Private rooms (check out the monarchy-themed 'Royal' room) have iPod docking stations and flat-screen TVs.

City Hotel HOTEL €
(Map p54; ☑ 627 23 23; www.city-hotel.nl; Utrechtsestraat 2; 1-2 people €69, 3-6 people €99-189, 5-8 people without bathroom €149-239; @ 🛜; 🚊 4/9/14 Rembrandtplein) Above the Old Bell pub, practically on Rembrandtplein, is this unexpectedly fabulous budget hotel, run by a friendly family. Rooms sleeping two to six have private bathrooms; larger rooms, sleep-

ing five to eight people, share bathroom facilities; all come with crisp linen. The attic annex has a wonderful view of town.

Seven Bridges BOUTIQUE HOTEL €€
(Map p54; ☑ 623 13 29; www.sevenbridgeshotel.nl; Reguliersgracht 31; d €115-220; 🛜; 🚊 4 Keizersgracht) Sophisticated and intimate, the Seven Bridges is one of the city's most exquisite little hotels on one of its loveliest canals. It has eight tastefully decorated rooms (all incorporating lush oriental rugs and elegant antiques). The urge to sightsee may fade once breakfast (€10), served on fine china, is delivered to your room.

Hotel V BOUTIQUE HOTEL €€
(Map p54; ☑ 662 32 33; www.hotelv.nl; Weteringschans 136; d €101-260; 🛜; 🚊 4/7/10 Frederiksplein) Facing lush Frederiksplein and footsteps away from Utrechtsestraat, the retro-chic Hotel V offers fantastic value given its style and location. Its 48 artsy rooms are done up in charcoal colours and feature stone-wall bathrooms. Ask for rates for its four-person loft apartment, which has a private entrance and a kitchenette.

Hotel Freeland
HOTEL **€€**

(Map p54; ☑ 622 75 11; www.hotelfreeland.com; Marnixstraat 386; s without bathroom from €60, s/d/tr from €70/110/130; ☎; ☒1/2/5/7/10 Leidseplein) In a prime canal-side location, Freeland has 15 tidy themed rooms (tulips, roses and sunflowers, and a few with Moroccan details). Add in a tasty breakfast and it pretty much kills the Leidseplein competition. It's gay-friendly and all-welcoming.

★ Seven One Seven
LUXURY HOTEL **€€€**

(Map p54; ☑ 427 07 17; www.717hotel.nl; Prinsengracht 717; d €500-650; ☀☎; ☒1/2/5 Prinsengracht) The nine hyperplush, deliciously appointed rooms at this breathtaking hotel come with that all-too-rare luxury: space. Step into the prodigious Picasso suite – with its soaring ceiling, elongated sofa, and contemporary and antique decorations – and you may never, ever want to leave. Rates include breakfast, afternoon tea, house wine, beer and personalised service.

🛏 Old South

Van Gogh Hostel & Hotel
HOSTEL, HOTEL **€**

(Map p54; ☑ 262 92 00; www.hotelvangogh.nl; Van de Veldestraat 5; dm/d/tr/q from €28/119/149/179; ☀@☎; ☒2/3/5/12 Van Baerlestraat) No false advertising here: it sits about 14 steps from the Van Gogh Museum, and every room has a Van Gogh mural. The set-up puts the 200-bed hostel on one side, the hotel on the other, and the common area for breakfast (€5) between them. The hostel dorms have six to eight beds, en-suite bathroom and flat-screen TV.

★ Hotel Fita
HOTEL **€€**

(Map p54; ☑ 679 09 76; www.fita.nl; Jan Luijkenstraat 37; s/d from €115/149; ☎; ☒2/3/5/12 Van Baerlestraat) Family-owned Fita, on a quiet street off the Museumplein and PC Hooftstraat, has 15 handsome rooms with nicely appointed bathrooms; a bountiful free breakfast of eggs, pancakes, cheeses and breads; and a lift. The dynamic young owner keeps the property in mint condition (new furniture, new artwork, fresh paint), and service could not be more attentive.

★ Collector
B&B **€€**

(Map p54; ☑ 673 67 79; www.the-collector.nl; De Lairessestraat 46; s/d/tr from €80/95/115; @☎; ☒5/16/24 Museumplein) This spotless B&B near the Concertgebouw is furnished with museum-style displays of clocks, wooden clogs and ice skates – things the owner, Karel, collects. Each of the three rooms has balcony

access and a TV. Karel stocks the kitchen for guests to prepare breakfast at their leisure (the eggs come from his hens in the garden).

Conscious Hotel Museum Square
BOUTIQUE HOTEL **€€**

(Map p54; ☑ 671 95 96; www.conscioushotels.com; De Lairessestraat 7; d/f from €90/171; @☎; ☒5/16/24 Museumplein) ☏ This is a fantastic place to go green. It starts with the living plant wall in the lobby and the organic breakfast (€10 extra), and continues with the modern rooms – beds made with 100% natural materials, desks constructed from recycled yogurt containers, and energy-saving plasma TVs. There is a second location near Vondelpark (☑ 820 33 33; www.conscioushotels.com; Overtoom 519; d/tr from €90/121.50; ☎; ☒1 Rhijnvis Feithstraat) ☏, and a third in the works.

Xaviera Hollander's Happy House
B&B **€€**

(☑ 673 39 34; www.xavierahollander.com; Stadionweg 17; d from €120; ☎; ☒5/24 Gerrit van der Veenstraat) The former madam and author of *The Happy Hooker* welcomes guests to her home in the ritzy Beethovenstraat neighbourhood (minimum two-night stay). The two rooms (which share a bathroom) are decked out with erotic photos, red-heart pillows, and books such as her recent *Guide to Mind-Blowing Sex*. There's also a garden hut with its own facilities (bathroom, refrigerator, terrace).

College Hotel
BOUTIQUE HOTEL **€€€**

(Map p54; ☑ 571 15 11; www.thecollegehotel.com; Roelof Hartstraat 1; d from €178; ☀☎; ☒3/5/12/24 Roelof Hartplein) Originally a 19th-century school, the College Hotel has fashioned its 40 chambers – with high ceilings, tasteful furnishings and the occasional stained-glass window – from former classrooms. Hospitality-school students now staff the hotel to earn their stripes, while celebs from Brooke Shields to Fatboy Slim enjoy the swanky end product.

Conservatorium Hotel
DESIGN HOTEL **€€€**

(Map p54; ☑ 570 00 00; www.conservatoriumhotel.com; Van Baerlestraat 27; d from €460; ☀☎☒; ☒2/5 Van Baerlestraat) Opposite the Royal Concertgebouw, this palatial neo-Gothic building was originally a bank, then the city's conservatorium of music. Its most recent incarnation sees it stunningly converted into an eight-storey, 129-room hotel with soaring glass and steel connecting the 19th-century brickwork (especially in the light-filled atrium lounge) and a 1000-sq-metre gym and spa – the largest of Amsterdam's hotels.

Nods to the building's musical history include a light fitting incorporating dozens of suspended violins.

Vondelpark

Stayokay Amsterdam Vondelpark   HOSTEL €
(Map p54; ☑ 589 89 96; www.stayokay.com; Zandpad 5; dm €31-48, tw €75-152; ☞; ☐ 1 1e Constantijn Huygensstraat) A frisbee's throw from the Vondelpark, this HI-affiliated 536-bed hostel attracts over 75,000 guests a year – no wonder the lobby feels like a mini-UN. It's the best Stayokay in town, with renovated rooms sporting lockers, private bathrooms and well-spaced bunks. Chill out in the congenial bar-cafe, or shoot some pool.

★ Hotel Not Hotel   DESIGN HOTEL €€
(☑ 820 45 38; www.hotelnothotel.com; Piri Reisplein 34; d €75-200, without bathroom €82-120; ☐ 7 Postjesweg) The name's apt: rooms here are wild, no-holds-barred art installations. You can sleep inside Amsterdam Tram 965 (in a king-size bed), hide behind a secret bookcase, lounge on a private Spanish villa al fresco terrace, escape the daily grind in the Crisis Free Zone framed by Transylvanian-inspired woodcarvings to deter evil spirits, or climb a ladder to a crow's nest.

Students from Eindhoven's Design Academy created the rooms. Kevin Bacon (its bar, named in homage of the actor) mixes rockin' cocktails.

Hotel de Filosoof   BOUTIQUE HOTEL €€
(Map p54; ☑ 683 30 13; www.sandton.eu; Anna van den Vondelstraat 6; s/d/tr from €109/119/179; ☞; ☐ 1 Jan Pieter Heijestraat) It's easy to clear your mind in rooms named after philosophers. Each room has its own theme representing its namesake, from Thoreau (with a mural of Walden Pond) to Nietzsche (lots of red, representing his book *Morgenröte,* meaning 'The Dawn'). There's an elegant bar, and the tranquil English garden is a pastoral pleasure come summer.

The hotel features in the novel *The Fault in Our Stars* by John Green, though it wasn't used as a filming location in the hugely popular 2014 film adaptation (in the movie, the American Hotel on Leidseplein is used as its stand-in).

Owl Hotel   HOTEL €€
(Map p54; ☑ 618 94 84; www.owl-hotel.nl; Roemer Visscherstraat 1; s/d from €91/120; ☞; ☐ 1 1e Constantijn Huygensstraat) Some guests love this 34-room place so much that they send in owl figurines from all over the world to add to the hotel's collection. Staff are warm and welcoming, and rooms are bright and quiet. The buffet breakfast (included in the rate) is served in a serene, light-filled room overlooking a delightful garden.

★ Hotel Vondel   BOUTIQUE HOTEL €€€
(Map p54; ☑ 612 01 20; www.vondelhotels.com; Vondelstraat 26-30; d €150-250; ☞; ☐ 1 1e Constantijn Huygensstraat) Named after the famed Dutch poet Joost van den Vondel (as is the nearby park), this chic hotel has calm, comfortable rooms (lots of plush grey), and a bar opening to decks overlooking the gardens, as well as bike rental and an in-room flower service. Its dramatic, art-lined restaurant, Joost, is excellent; breakfast here costs €19.

De Pijp

Between Art & Kitsch B&B   B&B €€
(Map p54; ☑ 679 04 85; www.between-art-and-kitsch.com; Ruysdaelkade 75; s/d from €85/100; ☞; ☐ 16 Ruysdaelkade) Mondrian once lived here – that's part of the art – while the kitsch includes the crystal chandelier in the baroque room and a smiling brass Buddha. The art-deco room has gorgeous tile work and views of the Rijksmuseum. Husband-and-wife hosts Ebo and Irene couldn't be friendlier. Note that it's on the third floor, with no lift.

Bicycle Hotel Amsterdam   HOTEL €€
(Map p54; ☑ 679 34 52; www.bicyclehotel.com; Van Ostadestraat 123; s/d/tr without bathroom from €30/60/120, d/tr/f from €100/150/170; ☞; ☐ 3 Ferdinand Bolstraat) 🚲 Run by Marjolein and Clemens, this casual, friendly, green-minded hotel has rooms that are comfy and familiar. It also rents bikes (€8 per day) and serves a killer organic breakfast (included in the rate).

★ Sir Albert Hotel   DESIGN HOTEL €€€
(Map p54; ☑ 305 30 20; www.siralberthotel.com; Albert Cuypstraat 2-6; d from €200; ✼ @ ☞; ☐ 16/24 Ruysdaelstraat) A 19th-century diamond factory houses this glitzy design hotel. Its 90 creative rooms and suites have soaring ceilings and large windows, with custom-made linens and Illy espresso machines; iPads are available for guest use in the Persian-rug-floored study. Energetic staff are genuine and professional in equal measure.

It's on the same street as the busy Albert Cuypmarkt, but at the peaceful, leafy western end.

Hotel Okura Amsterdam LUXURY HOTEL €€€
(☑ 678 83 00; www.okura.nl; Ferdinand Bolstraat 333; d/ste from €220/415; ❄ @ 🛜 ☂) Rare-for-Amsterdam amenities that elevate this business-oriented hotel way above the competition include panoramic city views (particularly from higher-priced north-facing rooms), a total of three Michelin stars on the premises (two at top-floor Ciel Bleu; p84; and one at lobby-level Japanese restaurant Yamazato), and an amazing health club with an 18m-long jet-stream swimming pool. Breakfast costs €32.50.

Plantage

Hotel Hortus HOTEL €
(Map p62; ☑ 625 99 96; www.hotelhortus.com; Plantage Parklaan 8; s €63-70, d €72-80, f €144-160; 🅿 🛜; 🚊 9/14 Plantage Kerklaan) Facing the botanical garden, this well-worn, comfortable 20-room hotel is terrific value for this area and contains a large common area with a pool table and several TVs. There are only two doubles with a shower, and two without; all share toilets, but have a safe and a sink.

★**B&B Le Maroxidien** HOUSEBOAT, B&B €€
(Map p62; ☑ 400 40 06; www.lemaroxidien.com; Prins Hendrikkade 534; d without bathroom €110-120; 🛜; 🚊 22/32/34/35/48 Prins Hendrikkade) 🏊 Moored within easy reach of Centraal Station, Kathrin Rduch's wonderful houseboat (a 1920s former freighter) has a guest wing with three exotic cabins – the sky-blue 'Morocco', spacious 'Mexico' and small 'India' – which share two bathrooms and a cosy lounge. Kathrin provides an organic feast each morning for breakfast. There's a minimum two-night stay; children over six are welcome. Cash only.

Hotel Rembrandt HOTEL €€
(Map p62; ☑ 627 27 14; www.hotelrembrandt.nl; Plantage Middenlaan 17; s/d/tr/q from €120/135/195/210; 🛜; 🚊 9/14 Plantage Kerklaan) With its spotless modern rooms, the Rembrandt shines. Most rooms contain pop-art prints of Rembrandt himself, but room 8 is graced with a nearly life-sized mural of *The Night Watch*. Breakfast (€10) is served in a wood-panelled room with chandeliers and 17th-century paintings on linen-covered walls. Take care not to let cute resident cat Bink out of the building.

Hotel Allure HOTEL €€
(Map p62; ☑ 627 27 14; www.hotel-allure.hotels ofamsterdam.net; Sarphatistraat 117; s/d/tr from €89/99/145; 🛜; 🚊 7/10 Weesperplein) Scarlet drapes and carpets and a vivid red dining room add dramatic flair to this gleaming contemporary hotel. It's within walking distance of the Hermitage Amsterdam and the Artis Royal Zoo.

Oosterpark

Stayokay Amsterdam Zeeburg HOSTEL €
(☑ 551 31 90; www.stayokay.com; Timorplein 21; dm €22-42, r from €89; @ 🛜; 🚊 14 Zeeburgerdijk) The sibling of Stayokay Vondelpark and Stayokay Stadsdoelen, Zeeburg might be the best of the bunch. It has 508 beds spread over three floors; most of the spick-and-span rooms are four- or six-bed dorms, all with en-suite bathroom and bright orange decor. Hot breakfast is included. Linens are free, but towels cost €4.50. Wi-fi is in the lobby only.

✗ Eating

Amsterdam's sizzling culinary scene has hundreds of restaurants and *eetcafés* (cafes serving meals).

Note that many restaurants do not accept credit cards – even top-end places. Or if they do, they levy a 5% surcharge. Be sure your wallet is filled before dining out.

Phone ahead and make a reservation for midrange and top-end eateries. Nearly everyone speaks English. Many places also offer online booking options.

Medieval Centre & Red Light District

Zeedijk holds several Thai and Chinese options. Spuistraat is another good hunting ground.

★**Gartine** CAFE €
(Map p44; ☑ 320 41 32; www.gartine.nl; Taksteeg 7; mains €6-12, high tea €16-25; ⊙ 10am-6pm Wed-Sun; 🍴; 🚊 4/9/14/16/24 Spui/Rokin) Gartine is magical, from its covert location in an alley off busy Kalverstraat to its mismatched antique tableware and its sublime breakfast pastries, sandwiches and salads (made from produce grown in its garden plot). The sweet-and-savoury high tea is a scrumptious bonus.

★**Vleminckx** FAST FOOD €
(Map p54; http://vleminckxdesausmeester.nl; Voetboogstraat 31; fries €2.10-4.10, sauces €0.60; ⊙ noon-7pm Sun & Mon, 11am-7pm Tue, Wed, Fri & Sat, to 8pm Thu; 🚊 1/2/5 Koningsplein) Vleminckx has been frying up *frites* (French fries) since 1887, and doing it at this hole-in-the-wall takeaway shack near the Spui for more than

50 years. The standard is smothered in mayonnaise, though you can also ask for ketchup, peanut sauce or a variety of spicy toppings.

Rob Wigboldus Vishandel SANDWICHES **€**
(📞626 33 88; Zoutsteeg 6; sandwiches €2.50-4.50; ☺9am-5pm Tue-Sat; 🚋4/9/16/24 Dam) A wee three-table oasis in the midst of surrounding tourist tat, this fish shop in a tiny alley serves excellent herring sandwiches on a choice of crusty white or brown rolls. Don't like fish? **Van den Berg's Broodjesbar** (Map p44; 📞622 83 56; www.vandenbergsbroodjesbar. nl; Zoutsteeg 4; sandwiches €2-5; ☺9am-6pm Mon-Sat; 🚋4/9/16/24 Dam) is next door for other great sandwich options.

★Thais Snackbar Bird THAI **€€**
(Map p44; 📞420 62 89; www.thai-bird.nl; Zeedijk 77; mains €9-16; ☺2-10pm; 🚋4/9/16/24 Centraal Station) Don't tell the Chinese neighbours, but this is some of the best Asian food on the Zeedijk – the cooks, wedged in a tiny kitchen, don't skimp on lemongrass, fish sauce or chilli. The resulting curries and basil-laden meat and seafood dishes will knock your socks off.

Nam Kee CHINESE **€€**
(Map p44; 📞624 34 70; www.namkee.net; Zeedijk 111-113; mains €11-20; ☺noon-11pm; 🚋4/9/16/24 Dam) It won't win any design awards, but year in, year out, Nam Kee is the most popular Chinese spot in town. The steamed oysters and black bean sauce are legendary. If you want to avoid the fluorescent-light ambience, try Nam Kee's nearby branch (Map p44; 📞638 28 48; www.namkee.net; Geldersekade 117; mains €12-22; ☺4pm-midnight Mon-Fri, 2.30pm-midnight Sat, 2.30-11pm Sun; 📞; Ⓜ Nieuwmarkt) in Nieuwmarkt, which is fancier.

'Skek CAFE **€€**
(Map p44; 📞427 05 51; www.skek.nl; Zeedijk 4-8; sandwiches €4-7, mains €12-14; ☺4-10pm Mon, noon-10pm Tue-Sun; 📶; 🚋4/9/16/24 Centraal Station) Run by students for students (flashing your ID gets you 25% off), this friendly cafe-bar is an excellent place to get fat sandwiches on thick slices of multigrain bread, and healthy main dishes with chicken, fish or pasta. Bands occasionally perform at night (the bar stays open to 1am weekdays, and 3am on weekends).

Haesje Claes DUTCH **€€**
(Map p44; 📞624 99 98; www.haesjeclaes.nl; Spuistraat 273-275; mains €16-26, set menus from €32.50; ☺noon-10pm; 🚋1/2/5 Spui) Haesje Claes' warm surrounds – a tad touristy, but with lots of dark wood and antique knick-knacks – are

just the place to sample comforting pea soup and *stamppot* (mashed pot: potatoes mashed with another vegetable). The fish starter has a great sampling of different Dutch fish.

Hofje van Wijs CAFE **€€**
(Map p44; 📞624 04 36; www.hofjevanwijs.nl; Zeedijk 43; mains €9-16; ☺noon-10pm Tue-Sun; 🚋4/9/16/24 Centraal Station) The 200-year-old coffee and tea vendor Wijs & Zonen (the monarch's purveyor) maintains this pretty courtyard cafe. It serves Dutch stews, fondue and a couple of fish dishes, plus local beers and liqueurs. But what you're really here for are the yummy cakes.

Blauw aan de Wal INTERNATIONAL **€€€**
(Map p44; 📞330 22 57; www.blauwaandewal.com; Oudezijds Achterburgwal 99; 3-/4-course menu €55/67.50; ☺6-11.30pm Tue-Sat; 🚋4/9/16/24 Dam) Definitely a rose among thorns: a long, often graffiti-covered hallway in the middle of the Red Light District leads to this Garden of Eden. Originally a 17th-century herb warehouse, the whitewashed, exposed-brick, multilevel space still features old steel weights and measures, plus friendly, knowledgeable service and refined French- and Italian-inspired cooking. In summer grab a table in the romantic garden.

Anna MODERN DUTCH **€€€**
(Map p44; 📞428 11 11; www.restaurantanna.nl; Warmoesstraat 111; mains €19-26, 4-course menu €47.50; ☺6-10.30pm Mon-Sat; 🚋4/9/16/24 Dam) It's quite a contrast: Anna's sleek line of white-clothed tables topped by plates of curry-sauced monkfish and truffle-and-veal risotto, while steps away the world's oldest profession is in full swing. The restaurant sits right by the Oude Kerk and the active Red Light windows surrounding it. A robust list of organic and global wines complements the brilliantly executed fare.

🍴 Nieuwmarkt

Nieuwmarkt brims with cafes where locals hang out.

★Sterk Staaltje DELI **€**
(Map p54; sterkstaaltje.com; Staalstraat 12; dishes €4-7.60; ☺8am-7pm Mon-Fri, 8am-6pm Sat, 11am-5pm Sun; 🚋4/9/14/16/24 Muntplein) From the fruit stacked up in crates on the pavement, Sterk Staaltje looks like an unassuming greengrocer's, but inside it's a veritable treasure chest of ready-to-eat treats: teriyaki meatballs, feta and sundried tomato quiche,

pumpkin-stuffed wraps, a soup of the day, and fantastic sandwiches (roast beef, horseradish and rocket; marinated chicken with guacamole and sour cream) plus salads and pastas.

★ Tokoman
SURINAMESE €

(Map p62; Waterlooplein 327; sandwiches €3-4.50, dishes €6.50-12.50; ⊙ 11am-8pm Mon-Sat; ⊠ 9/14 Waterlooplein) Queue with the folks getting their Surinamese spice on at Tokoman. It makes a sensational *broodje pom* (a sandwich filled with a tasty mash of chicken and a starchy Surinamese tuber). You'll want the *zuur* (pickled-cabbage relish) and *peper* (chilli) on it, plus a cold can of coconut water to wash it down.

A second, newer **branch** (Map p44; Zeedijk 136; sandwiches €3-4.50, dishes €6.50-12.50; ⊙ 11am-9.30pm Mon-Sat; ⊠ 9/14 Waterlooplein) in the neighbourhood has proved equally popular.

Frenzi
MEDITERRANEAN €€

(Map p44; ☑ 423 51 12; www.frenzi-restaurant.nl; Zwanenburgwal 232; mains lunch €7-14, dinner €14.50-18.50, dinner €4.50-6; ⊙ 11am-10pm; ⊠ 4/9/14/16/24 Muntplein) Stunning tapas at this casual spot will sate your hunger – Manchego cheese and fig compote; marinated sardines; portobello mushrooms with melted Gorgonzola – but save room for mains like pan-fried cod with fennel mash, pumpkin gnocchi with wilted spinach, and leg of lamb with roast asparagus. It stocks 110 types of grappa; live jazz plays on Saturdays at 3pm.

Latei
CAFE €€

(Map p44; www.latei.net; Zeedijk 143; lunch dishes €3.75-6.50, dinner mains €6-16; ⊙ 8am-6pm Mon-Wed, to 10pm Thu & Fri, 9am-10pm Sat, 11am-6pm Sun; ⊘; Ⓜ Nieuwmarkt) Young locals throng groovy Latei, where you can buy the lamps (or any of the vintage decor) right off the wall. The split-level cafe does unusual dinners Thursday through Saturday, often an Ethiopian, Indian or Indonesian dish by the local 'cooking collective'. Otherwise it serves sandwiches, apple pie and *koffie verkeerd* (milky coffee). A cat named Elvis roams the premises.

✕ Jordaan

Convivial little places are the Jordaan's hallmark. At the northern edge, Haarlemmerstraat and Haarlemmerdijk have the latest hotspots. Foodie favourites also fan out into the West.

Boca's
CAFE €

(Map p50; ☑ 820 37 27; www.bar-bocas.nl; Westerstraat 30; bar snacks €5-8, platters from €16; ⊙ 10am-1am Mon-Thu, 10am-3am Fri, 9am-3am Sat, 11am-1am Sun; ⊠ 3/10 Marnixplein) Fronted by a red-and-white-striped awning and white-timber facade, this hip little bar is a perfect place for a drink accompanied by bar snacks. Try the mini lasagnes, burgers, bruschetta and steak tartare, or bigger platters on wooden boards: cheese platters, veggie platters, seafood platters, meat platters, sweet platters. If you can't decide, go for Boca's combination platter.

Festina Lente
CAFE €

(Map p50; ☑ 638 14 12; www.cafefestinalente.nl; Looiersgracht 40b; sandwiches €6-8, small plates €4-8; ⊙ noon-10.30pm Mon & Sun, 10.30am-10.30pm Tue-Sat; ⊘; ⊠ 7/10/17 Elandsgracht) This canal-side neighbourhood hang-out is typical Jordaan *gezelligheid* (cosiness), packed with regulars playing board games, reading poetry and snacking on small-portion Mediterranean dishes and big sandwiches.

Worst Wijncafe
TAPAS €

(☑ 625 61 67; www.deworst.nl; Barentszstraat 171; tapas €8-15, brunch mains €10; ⊙ noon-midnight Tue-Sat, 10am-10pm Sun; ⊠ 48 Barentszplein) Named for its sausage-skewed tapas dishes (veal-tongue white sausage, chorizo, lobster sausage with spinach and asparagus), this chequerboard-tiled wine bar is the more casual sibling of esteemed restaurant Marius next door. Other dishes include pigs' trotters. There's a fantastic range of mostly French wines by the glass. Sunday brunch is a local event.

Winkel
CAFE €

(Map p50; www.winkel43.nl; Noordermarkt 43; mains €4.50-15.50; ⊙ kitchen 7am-10pm Mon & Sat, from 8am Tue-Fri, from 10am Sun; ⊛; ⊠ 3/10 Marnixplein) This sprawling, indoor-outdoor space is great for people-watching, popular for coffees and small meals, and out-of-the-park for its tall, cakey apple pie. On market days (Monday and Saturday) there's almost always a queue out the door.

★ Balthazar's Keuken
MEDITERRANEAN €€

(Map p50; ☑ 420 21 14; www.balthazarskeuken.nl; Elandsgracht 108; 3-course menu €32.50; ⊙ 6-10.30pm Wed-Sat; ⊠ 7/10/17 Elandsgracht) In a former blacksmith's forge, with a modern-rustic look, this is consistently one of Amsterdam's top-rated restaurants. Don't expect a wide-ranging menu: the philosophy is basically 'whatever we have on hand', which might mean wild sea bass with mushroom risotto or confit of rabbit, but it's invariably delectable. Reservations recommended.

★Pont 13   ITALIAN €€

(☑770 27 22; www.pont13.nl; Haparandadam 50; lunch mains €7.50-12.50, dinner mains €16-22.50; ⊗noon-10pm; ☎; ☐48 Oostzaanstraat) With sunny decks at either end and a cavernous interior, this vintage 1927 former car and passenger ferry once plied the IJ and now serves stunning Mediterranean fare such as seafood antipasti platters and mains like lasagne with goat's cheese or mozzarella-topped burgers from its open kitchen.

Amazing views of REM Eiland extend across the pier from Pont 13's decks.

REM Eiland   MODERN DUTCH €€

(☑688 55 01; www.remeiland.com; Haparandadam 45; lunch mains €8-14, dinner mains €18-20, 3-course menu €31; ⊗kitchen noon-4pm & 6-10pm; ☐48 Oostzaanstraat) Towering 22m above the IJ, this vivid red, oil-rig-like structure was built in the 1960s as a pirate radio and TV broadcaster and now houses an extraordinary restaurant, with a 360-degree panorama over the industrial docklands and passing river traffic. Reached by steep metal staircases (or a lift), the dining rooms open onto wraparound platforms; the rooftop ex-helipad has an outdoor bar.

Casual lunches (gourmet sandwiches et al) segue to bar snacks then dinner mains like lamb with marinated artichokes and port wine sauce or polenta with roasted pumpkin. Reservations recommended, especially for window and platform tables.

Restaurant Fraîche   FRENCH €€

(Map p50; ☑627 99 32; www.restaurantfraiche. nl; Westerstraat 264; mains €17-22; ⊗6.30-11.30pm Wed-Sat, noon-3pm Sun; ☐3/10 Marnixplein) Cutting-edge French cuisine at this glass-fronted bistro changes seasonally but might include roast turbot and squid with pickled fennel and smoked carrot purée, or roast duck breast with butterscotch and foie gras sauce. There are various tasting plates too, plus brunch specials.

Koevoet   ITALIAN €€

(Map p50; ☑624 08 46; Lindenstraat 17; mains €14-26; ⊗6-10pm Tue-Sat; ☎; ☐3/10 Marnixplein) The congenial Italian owners of Koevoet took over a former cafe on a quiet side street, left the *gezellig* (cosy) decor untouched and started cooking up their home-country staples such as handmade ravioli. Don't miss the signa-

ture, drinkable dessert, *sgroppino limone*: sorbet, vodka and Prosecco whisked at your table and poured into a champagne flute.

Yam Yam   ITALIAN €€

(☑681 50 97; www.yamyam.nl; Frederik Hendrikstraat 88-90; mains €13-16; ⊗5.30-10pm Tue-Sun; ☐3 Hugo de Grootplein) Ask Amsterdammers to name the city's best pizza and chances are it's this hip, contemporary trattoria. The wood-fired oven turns out thin-crust pizzas such as salami and fennel seed, and the signature Yam Yam (organic smoked ham, mascarpone and truffle sauce). There are mouthwatering pastas and fish- and meat-based mains. Creative desserts include orange-caramel *panna cotta* with balsamic and strawberries. Reservations recommended.

★Marius   INTERNATIONAL €€€

(☑422 78 80; www.deworst.nl; Barentszstraat 173; 4-course menu €47.50; ⊗6.30-10pm Tue-Sat; ☐48 Barentszplein) Foodies swoon over pocket-sized Marius, tucked in amid artists' studios in the Western Islands. Chef Kees Elfring shops at local markets, then creates his daily four-course, no-choice menu from what he finds. The result might be grilled prawns with fava bean purée or beef rib with polenta and ratatouille. Marius also runs the fabulous wine/tapas bar Worst Wijncafe next door.

✗ Western Canal Ring

Ridiculously cute cafes and small restaurants line the Negen Straatjes; Berenstraat is a bountiful lane.

Letting   DUTCH €

(Map p50; www.letting.nl; Prinsenstraat 3; mains €7-13; ⊗8.30am-5pm Mon & Thu-Sat, to 3pm Wed, 9am-5pm Sun; ☎; ☐13/14/17 Westermarkt) Start your day in traditional Dutch style with authentic breakfast dishes such as *wentelteefjes* (sugar bread dipped in egg and cinnamon), *uitsmijter rosbief* (eggs served sunny side up, with cheese and roast beef) and scrambled eggs with smoked halibut. At lunch choose from soups and sandwiches. Or book ahead for royal high tea (€25), accompanied by champagne.

Pancake Bakery   DUTCH €

(Map p50; ☑625 13 33; www.pancake.nl; Prinsengracht 191; mains €9-15; ⊗9am-9.30pm; ☞; ☐13/14/17 Westermarkt) This basement restaurant in a restored warehouse features a dizzying 79 varieties of pancakes, from sweet (chocolate, banana or peach) to savoury (the

'Canadian', topped with bacon, cheese and barbecue sauce, or the 'Norwegian' with smoked salmon, cream cheese and sour cream).

Singel 404   CAFE €

(Map p44; ☑428 01 54; Singel 404; dishes €5-9; ☺10.30am-7pm; ☑; ☐1/2/5 Spui) It's easy to miss this tucked-away spot, despite its location near the bustling Spui (look for the cobalt-blue awning). Sure, the menu is as simple as can be – smoked salmon sandwiches, pumpkin soup, honey mint lemonade – but the prices are rock bottom, portions are generous and the quality is superb.

Wil Graanstra Friteshuis   FAST FOOD €

(Map p50; ☑624 40 71; Westermarkt 11; frites €2.50-4.50; ☺noon-7pm Mon-Sat; ☐13/14/17 Westermarkt) Legions of Amsterdammers swear by the crispy spuds at Wil Graanstra Friteshuis. The family-run business has been frying on the square by the Westerkerk since 1956. Most locals top their cones with mayonnaise, though *oorlog* (a peanut sauce–mayo combo), curry sauce and picalilly (relish) rock the taste buds, too.

★ De Belhamel   FRENCH €€

(Map p44; ☑622 10 95; www.belhamel.nl; Brouwersgracht 60; mains lunch €15-24.50, dinner €22.50-26.50; ☺noon-4pm & 6-11pm; ☐1/2/5/13/17 Central Station) In warm weather the canal-side tables at the head of the Herengracht are an aphrodisiac, and the sumptuous art nouveau interior provides the perfect backdrop for superb French- and Italian-inspired dishes such as truffle-parsley-stuffed guinea fowl with polenta, a rack of lamb with aubergine biscuit and pepper coulis, or honey- and mustard-marinated veal.

Bistro Bij Ons   DUTCH €€

(Map p50; ☑627 90 16; www.bistrobijons.nl; Prinsengracht 287; mains €13.50-19; ☺10am-10pm Tue-Sun; ☑; ☐13/14/17 Westermarkt) If you're not in town visiting your Dutch *oma* (grandma), try the honest-to-goodness cooking at this charming retro bistro instead. Classics include *stamppot* (potatoes mashed with another vegetable) with sausage, *raasdonders* (split peas with bacon, onion and pickles) and *poffertjes* (small pancakes with butter and powdered sugar).

✗ Southern Canal Ring

A few steps south of gaudy Rembrandtplein, Utrechtsestraat is a relaxed artery lined by enticing shops, designer bars and cosy eateries.

Lavinia Good Food   VEGETARIAN €

(Map p54; www.laviniagoodfood.nl; Kerkstraat 176; dishes €4.50-8.50; ☺8.30am-4pm Mon-Fri, 9.30am-5pm Sat & Sun; ☑; ☐16/24 Keizersgracht) Spelt minipizzas, portobello mushroom burgers, salads like pasta or chickpea, and sandwiches with toppings like mango salsa, hummus and guacamole make Lavinia a delicious stop even if you're not vegetarian.

Van Dobben   DUTCH €

(Map p54; ☑624 42 00; www.eetsalonvandobben. nl; Korte Reguliersdwarsstraat 5-9; dishes €2.75-8; ☺10am-9pm Mon-Wed, 10am-1am Thu, 10am-2am Fri & Sat, 10.30am-8pm Sun; ☐4/9/14 Rembrandtplein) Open since the 1940s, Van Dobben has white-tile walls and white-coated staff who specialise in snappy banter. Traditional meaty Dutch fare is its forte: try the *pekelvlees* (something close to corned beef), or make it a *halfom* (if you're keen on that being mixed with liver).

Patisserie Holtkamp   BAKERY, SWEETS €

(Map p54; www.patisserieholtkamp.nl; Vijzelgracht 15; dishes €2.45-6.50; ☺8.30am-6pm Mon-Fri, to 5pm Sat, closed late Jul–mid-Aug; ☐4/7/10/16/24 Weteringcircuit) There's been a bakery on this site since 1886; its gorgeous art-deco interior was added in 1928 by architect Piet Kramer. Look up to spot the gilded royal coat of arms, topped by a crown, attached to the brick facade: it supplies the Dutch royals with sweet and savoury delicacies including *kroketten* (croquettes) with fillings including prawns, lobster and veal. They're also on the menu of some of the city's top restaurants.

Soup en Zo   SOUP BAR €

(Map p54; www.soupenzo.nl; Niewe Spiegelstraat 54; soup €5.40-7; ☺11am-8pm Mon-Fri, noon-7pm Sat & Sun; ☑; ☐7/10 Spiegelgracht) On a chilly day, you can't beat a steaming cup of soup from this little takeaway soup bar. Flavours change every hour but might include potato with Roquefort, lentil and minced beef, prunes and pumpkin or spicy spinach and coconut. It now has two other outlets, in Nieuwmarkt and Museumplein, near Vondelpark. Cash only.

★ La Cacerola   BRAZILIAN €€

(Map p54; ☑627 93 97; www.restaurantlacacerola. nl; Weteringstraat 41; mains €21.50-24.50; ☺6-10.30pm Tue-Sat; ☐7/10 Spiegelgracht) ✔ At this rustic, romantic gem, dishes prepared according to traditional methods and Slow Food principles include wild sea bass marinated in lime juice; spiced rack of milk-fed lamb; and house-speciality *churrasco de picanha* (steak barbecued on a charcoal grill and served with spicy pumpkin purée). If you can't decide, go for the chef's surprise four-course menu (€34.50). Service is superb.

Pantry
DUTCH €€

(Map p54; ☑620 09 22; thepantry.nl; Leidse-kruisstraat 21; mains €13-18, 3-course menus €20-28; ☉11am-10.30pm; ⓘ; ⊟1/2/5 Leidseplein) Wood-panelled walls and sepia lighting make this *gezellig* (cosy, convivial) little restaurant an atmospheric place for classic Dutch cooking: *haring met uitjes en zuur* (salted herring with onions and pickles); *zuurkool stamppot* (sauerkraut and potato mash served with a smoked sausage or meatball); *hutspot* ('hotchpotch', with stewed beef, carrots and onions); and *stroopwafelijs* (caramel-syrup-filled wafer-like waffles with ice cream).

In de Buurt
INTERNATIONAL €€

(Map p54; www.inderbuurt-amsterdam.nl; Lijn-baansgracht 246; mains €14.50-20.50; ☉kitchen 5-10pm Mon-Thu, from 3pm Fri, from 2pm Sat & Sun; ⊟1/2/5 Leidseplein) A canal-side summer terrace and interior of exposed brick walls and stainless-steel downlights provide a relaxed backdrop for fantastic miniburgers with truffle mayo and roasted cherry tomatoes, cannelloni stuffed with Dutch goat's cheese and spinach, and grilled whole sea bream with tarragon oil, but the star of the show is the homemade chocolate and pecan brownie with white-chocolate sauce.

★ Restaurant Fyra
MODERN EUROPEAN €€€

(Map p54; ☑428 36 32; www.restaurantfyra.nl; Noorderstraat 19-23; 3-/4-/5-/6-course menus €36/42.50/47.50/52.50; ☉6-11pm; ⊟16/24 Weteringcircuit) Many of the vegetables and herbs at this local foodies' favourite are grown in the owner-chef's garden and used in stunning creations like pea and mint soup with local prawns; barbecued tenderloin with potato mousseline; and marinated peaches with Dutch yogurt, meringue and pomegranate syrup. There's a wonderful selection of artisan cheeses and well-chosen wines.

The setting, inside a traditional brick building framed by French doors, is contemporary and elegant.

Tempo Doeloe
INDONESIAN €€€

(Map p54; ☑625 67 18; www.tempodoeloerestaurant.nl; Utrechtsestraat 75; mains €23.50-38.50, rijsttafel & set menus €29-49; ☉6-11.30pm Mon-Sat; ☑; ⊟4 Prinsengracht) Consistently ranked among Amsterdam's finest Indonesian restaurants, Tempo Doeloe's setting and service

are elegant without being overdone. The same applies to the rijsttafel (ricetable): a ridiculously overblown affair at many places, here it's a fine sampling of the range of flavours found in the country. Warning: dishes marked 'very hot' are indeed like napalm. The wine list is excellent.

SupperClub
MODERN DUTCH €€€

(Map p54; ☑638 05 13; www.supperclub.com; Singel 460; 5-course menu €69; ☉from 8pm; ⊟1/2/5 Koningsplein) If you're looking for a scene, you've found one. Enter the theatrical room, snuggle on the mattresses (here beds take the place of tables and chairs) and snack on victuals as DJs spin house music. Meals are accompanied by provocative and entertaining performance art. If the five-course menu is too much, you can also order à la carte.

✕ Old South

Around the Old South's big museums are some lovely local options.

l'Entrecôte et les Dames
FRENCH €€

(Map p54; ☑679 88 88; www.entrecote-et-les-dames.nl; Van Baerlestraat 47-49; lunch mains €12.50, 2-course dinner menu €24; ☉noon-3pm & 5.30-10pm; ⊟16/24 Museumplein) With a double-height wall made from wooden drawers and a wrought-iron-balustraded mezzanine seating area, the decor is stunning – but still secondary to the food. The two-course dinner menu offers a meat or fish option, but everyone's here for the entrecôte (premium beef steak). Save room for scrumptious desserts: perhaps chocolate mousse, *tarte au citron* (lemon tart) or *crêpes au Grand Marnier*.

La Falote
DUTCH €€

(Map p54; ☑662 54 54; www.lafalote.nl; Roelof Hartstraat 26; mains €15-23; ☉2-9pm Mon-Sat; ⊟3/5/12/24 Roelof Hartplein) Wee La Falote, with its chequered tableclothes, focuses on daily-changing Dutch home-style dishes such as calf liver, meatballs with endives, or stewed fish with beets and mustard sauce. The prices are a bargain in an otherwise ritzy neighbourhood; and wait till the owner brings out the accordion. Cash only.

Restaurant Elements
INTERNATIONAL €€

(Map p54; ☑579 17 17; www.heerlijkamsterdam.nl; Roelof Hartstraat 6-8; 4-course menu €24.50; ☉seatings 5.30pm & 7pm Mon-Fri; ⊟3/5/12/24 Roelof Hartplein) Students – the same ones who run the nearby College Hotel (p74) – prepare and serve contemporary international dishes at this mod restaurant. The result is white-glove service at an excellent price. Reserve in advance. No credit cards.

⚔ Vondelpark

The streets around Vondelpark teem with global options. They're not far – and are a nice escape – from Leidseplein's madness.

★ Braai BBQ Bar BARBECUE €
(www.braaiamsterdam.nl; Schinkelhavenkade 1; dishes €5-11; ⊙11am-10pm; ⓧ1 Overtoomsesluis) A canal-side *haringhuis* (herring stand) has been brilliantly converted into a street-food-style barbecue bar. Snacks span sandwiches such as hummus and grilled veggies or smoked *ossenworst* (raw-beef sausage originating from Amsterdam), a cheese and bacon burger and Braai's speciality – marinated, barbecued ribs (half or full rack). PIN cards are preferred, but it accepts cash. Tables scatter under the trees.

Breakfast Club CAFE €
(Map p54; www.thebreakfastclub.nl; Bellamystraat 2; dishes €4.50-16; ⊙8am-4pm Mon-Fri, to 5pm Sat & Sun; ⓧ17 Ten Katestraat) All-day breakfasts are the speciality of the laid-back Breakfast Club: ricotta flapjacks with honeycomb butter; a full English breakfast with homemade baked beans, bacon, eggs, mushrooms and sausages; buckwheat pancakes with maple syrup; or home-baked croissants and seasonal jam. It also does super-charged smoothies such as beetroot, apple and strawberry, or banana, coconut milk and cocoa powder.

Alchemist Garden VEGAN €
(☎334 33 35; www.alchemistgarden.nl; Overtoom 409; dishes €4-12.50; ⊙8am-10pm Tue-Sat; ⓧ; ⓧ1 Rhijnvis Feithstraat) 🍃 Proving that gluten-, lactose- and glucose-free food can be delicious, this bright, contemporary space serves a vitamin-filled organic menu (raw vegetable pies, sunflower burgers, avocado dumplings and pesto-stuffed portobello mushrooms), plus smoothies, juices and guilt-free treats like raw chocolate cake. Many ingredients are from the owner's garden. Ask about wild food foraging walks in the Vondelpark.

Tarot readings and hand chakra massages are available.

★ Ron Gastrobar MODERN DUTCH €€
(☎496 19 43; www.rongastrobar.nl; Sophialaan 55; dishes €15, desserts €9; ⊙noon-2.30pm & 5.30-10.30pm Mon-Fri, noon-10.30pm Sat & Sun; ☎; ⓧ2 Amstelveenseweg) Ron Blaauw ran his two-Michelin-star restaurant in these stunning designer premises before trading in the stars to transform the space into an egalitarian 'gastrobar', serving around 25 one-flat-price tapas-style dishes such as steak tartare with crispy veal brains, mushroom ravioli with sweet-potato foam, barbecue-smoked bone marrow, Dutch asparagus with lobster-and-champagne sauce, and Wagyu burgers – with no minimum order restrictions.

The crafting and flavour combinations remain haute-cuisine standard (the new format was recently awarded a Michelin star in its own right), and are affordable, too.

★ Dikke Graaf MEDITERRANEAN €€
(☎223 77 56; www.dikkegraaf.nl; Wilhelminastraat 153; bar snacks €3.50-15, mains €12.50-22.50; ⊙kitchen 3-10pm Wed-Sun; ⓧ1 Rhijnvis Feithstraat) Heavenly cooking aromas tip you off to this local secret adorned with copper lamps and black tiling, and opening to a terrace. It's a truly fabulous spot for *borrel* (drinks), with gin cocktails, by-the-glass wines and bar snacks such as oysters, bruschetta, charcuterie and Manchego sheep's cheese, and/or heartier, nightly changing meat, fish and pasta dishes.

Van 't Spit ROTISSERIE €€
(Map p54; www.vantspit.nl; De Clercqstraat 95; half/whole chicken €10/19.50, sides €3.50-5; ⊙kitchen 5pm-midnight; ⓧ12/13/14 Willem de Zwijgerlaan) Cut timber logs line the walls at hip, stripped-back Van 't Spit, but they're not just for show – they're the fuel for the wood-fired rotisserie that spit-roasts delicious chicken. Decisions here are limited simply to a half or whole chicken (there are no other mains), and whether you want sides (corn on the cob, fries, salad and homemade coleslaw). The bar stays open until 1am.

★ Adam GASTRONOMY €€
(☎233 98 52; www.restaurantadam.nl; Overtoom 515; mains €21-24.50, 3-/4-/5-/6-course menus €35/42.50/50/57.50; ⊙6-10.30pm Sat-Sun; ⓧ1 Overtoomsesluis) Widely tipped around town for a Michelin star, this chic restaurant serves exquisitely presented gastronomic fare, such as steak tartare with quail's egg, crispy pork belly with celeriac, sea bass with white asparagus, and *côte de bœuf* (on-the-bone rib steak) for two. Dessert is either a cheese platter or a chef's surprise. Paired wines are available for €7.50 per glass.

Restaurant Blauw INDONESIAN €€€
(☎675 50 00; www.restaurantblauw.nl; Amstelveenseweg 158; mains €21.50-27.50, rijsttafel

DON'T MISS

DE HALLEN

Disused red-brick 1902 tram sheds were stunningly converted in 2014 to create the vast, skylit **De Hallen** (Map p54; www.dehallen-amsterdam.nl; Bellamyplein 51; 🚊17 Ten Katestraat), a cultural complex incorporating a food hall, steak restaurant, library, design shops, boutiques, a bike seller/repairer, a cinema – **Filmhallen** (Map p54; www.filmhallen.nl; Hannie Dankbaar Passage 12, De Hallen; tickets adult/child from €10/7.50; ⊙10am-midnight; 🚊17 Ten Katestraat) – and a hotel, **Hotel de Hallen** (Map p54; 📞515 04 53; www.hoteldehallen.com; Bellamyplein 47; d from €145; ❄🞲; 🚊17 Ten Katestraat).

Regular events held inside include themed **weekend markets** (such as organic produce or Dutch design); check www.localgoodsmarkets.nl to find out what's happening.

A lively street market, **Ten Katemarkt** (Map p54; www.tenkatemarkt.nl; Ten Katestraat; ⊙9am-5pm Mon-Sat; 🚊17 Ten Katestraat), is right outside.

★**Foodhallen** (Map p54; www.foodhallen.nl; Hannie Dankbaar Passage 3, De Hallen; dishes €5-15; ⊙11am-8pm Sun-Wed, to 9pm Thu-Sat; 🚊17 Ten Katestraat) Inside De Hallen, this glorious international food hall has 21 stands surrounding an airy open-plan eating area. Some are offshoots of popular Amsterdam eateries, such as the **Butcher** (Map p54; 📞470 78 75; www.the-butcher.com; Albert Cuypstraat 129; burgers €6.50-12.50; ⊙11am-late; 🞲; 🚊16/24 Albert Cuypstraat) and **Wild Moa Pies** (Map p54; www.pies.nu; Van Ostadestraat 147; dishes €3-4; ⊙10am-6.30pm Tue-Sat; 🞲📞; 🚊3 2e Van der Helststraat); also look out for Viet View Vietnamese street food, Jabugo Iberico Bar ham, Pink Flamingo pizza, Bulls & Dogs hot dogs, Rough Kitchen ribs and De Ballenbar *bitterballen* (croquettes).

Local Goods Store (Map p54; www.localgoodsstore.nl; Hannie Dankbaar Passage 39, De Hallen; ⊙noon-7pm Tue-Fri & Sun, 11am-7pm Sat; 🚊17 Ten Katestraat) As the name implies, everything at this concept shop inside De Hallen is created by Dutch designers. Look for Woody skateboards, I Made Gin gin production kits, Carhusa purses and handbags, Timbies wooden bow ties, Lucila Kenny hand-dyed scarves and jewellery, and Neef Louis industrial vintage homewares, as well as racks of great Dutch-designed casual men's and women's fashion.

per person €26.50-31.50; ⊙6-10.30pm Mon-Fri, 5-10.30pm Sat & Sun; 🚊2 Amstelveenseweg) The *New York Times* voted Blauw the 'best Indonesian restaurant in the Netherlands' and legions agree, because the large, contemporary dining room is always packed (reserve well ahead). Menu standouts include *ikan pesmol* (fried fish with candlenut sauce) and *ayam singgand* (chicken in semi-spicy coconut sauce with tumeric leaf) and mouthwatering Indonesian desserts.

🍴 De Pijp

De Pijp is one of the city's best foodie 'hoods. The Albert Cuypmarkt (p60) offers good grazing.

★**Fat Dog** HOT DOGS €
(www.thefatdog.nl; Ruysdaelkade 251; dishes €4.50-12; ⊙5pm-midnight Mon & Tue, from noon Wed-Sun; 🚊12 Cornelis Troostplein) Überchef Ron Blaauw, of Ron Gastrobar, elevates the humble hot dog to an art form. Ultra-gourmet options include Naughty Bangkok (pickled vegetables, red curry mayo, and dry crispy rice); Vive La France (fried mushrooms, foie gras

and truffle mayo); Gangs of New York (sauerkraut, bacon, and smoked-onion marmalade) and Vega Gonzalez (vegetarian sausage, corn, guacamole, sour cream and jalapeño mayo).

Sir Hummus MIDDLE EASTERN €
(Map p54; sirhummus.nl; Van der Helstplein 2; dishes €6.8.50; ⊙noon-7pm Tue-Fri, to 5pm Sat & Sun; 📞; 🚊3 2e Van der Helststraat) 🌿 Sir Hummus is the brainchild of three young Israelis whose passion for the chickpea dip led to a London street-market stall and then to this hummus-dedicated cafe. Creamy all-natural, preservative- and additive-free hummus is served with pita bread and salad; SH also does fantastic falafel. You can eat in or take away but arrive early before it sells out.

Geflipt BURGERS €
(Map p54; www.gefliptburgers.nl; Van Woustraat 15; dishes €8-9.50; ⊙11am-9.30pm Sun-Thu, to 10.30pm Fri & Sat; 📞; 🚊4 Stadhouderskade) Competition is fierce in this foodie neighbourhood for the best burgers, but Geflipt is a serious contender. In a stripped-back, industrial-chic interior, it serves luscious creations (like Gasconne beef, bacon, golden

cheddar, red-onion compote and fried egg) on brioche buns with sauces cooked daily on the premises from locally sourced ingredients. Bonus points for its Amsterdam-brewed Brouwerij 't IJ beers.

Brezel & Bratwurst   GERMAN €

(Map p54; www.brezelenbratwurst.nl; Van der Helstplein 10; dishes €1-8.50; ☺4-10pm Wed-Sun; ☷3 2e Van der Helststraat) A brilliant addition to De Pijp's line-up of top-quality cheap eats, Brezel & Bratwurst serves authentic German *Bratwurst* (sausages), either on a bun, as currywurst, or with fries and salad. For something lighter, go for a homemade bio, spelt or natural *Brezel* (pretzel) with traditional dips such as Bavarian *Obatzda*, made with soft cheese, paprika and raw veggies.

★ Restaurant Elmar   MODERN DUTCH €€

(Map p54; ☑664 66 29; www.restaurantelmar.nl; Van Woustraat 110; mains lunch €7.50-12.50, dinner €19.50-24.50; ☺noon-3pm & 6-10pm Tue-Sat; ☷4 Ceintuurbaan) ✐ Seriously good cooking at this charming little locavore restaurant utilises organic Dutch produce (Flevopolder beef, Texel lamb, Noord-Holland pigs, *polder* chickens and locally milled flour, along with seasonal fruit and vegetables). Original flavour combinations include ham-wrapped chicken stuffed with liver and sage in marsala jus, and bitter-chocolate mousse with apple compote and iced-coffee foam. There's a delightful courtyard garden.

★ Volt   MEDITERRANEAN €€

(Map p54; ☑471 55 44; www.restaurantvolt.nl; Ferdinand Bolstraat 178; mains €14-20, tapas €4-14; ☺4-10pm; ☷12 Cornelis Troostplein) Strung with coloured lightbulbs, Volt is a neighbourhood gem for light tapas-style bites (olives and marinated sardines; aioli and tapenade) and more substantial mains (artichoke ravioli with walnuts and rucola; squid stuffed with chorizo and rice; and plaice with mozzarella risotto croquette. Its bar stays open until late, or head across the street to its brown *café* sibling, Gambrinus (Map p54; www.gambrinus.nl; Ferdinand Bolstraat 180; ☺11am-1am Sun-Thu, to 3am Fri & Sat; ☏; ☷12 Cornelis Troostplein).

Surya   INDIAN €€

(Map p54; www.suryarestaurant.nl; Ceintuurbaan 147; mains €12-20; ☺5-11pm Tue-Sun; ☷3 2e Van der Helststraat) Indian restaurants can be surprisingly hit-and-miss in this multicultural city, making Surya an invaluable address for fans of subcontinental cuisine. Menu standouts include a feisty madras, fire-breathing vindaloo,

tandoori tikka dishes and silky tomato-based *paneer makhni* with soft cottage cheese made fresh on the premises each day. Mains come with poppadoms, rice and salad.

Friterie par Hasard   DUTCH €€

(Map p54; www.cafeparhasard.nl; Ceintuurbaan 113; mains €17.50, 3-course menu €27.50; ☺noon-10pm Sun-Thu, to 10.30pm Fri & Sat; ☷3 Ferdinand Bolstraat) Fronted by a red-and-white chequered awning, low-lit Friterie par Hasard is feted for its *frites* (fries), served with dishes like ribs in traditional Limburg stew with apple, elderberry and bay leaf sauce; marinated chicken thighs with satay sauce and pickled cucumber; bavette steak; and beer-battered cod. Its adjacent Frites uit Zuyd (Map p54; www.fritesuitzuyd.nl; Ceintuurbaan; dishes €3-5.50; ☺noon-10pm Sun & Mon, to 11pm Tue-Thu, to midnight Fri & Sat; ☷3 Ferdinand Bolstraat) fries up takeaway *frites*.

★ Ciel Bleu   FRENCH €€€

(☑450 67 87; www.okura.nl; Ferdinand Bolstraat 333, Hotel Okura Amsterdam; mains €60, 7-course menu €110, with paired wines €170; ☺6.30-10.30pm Mon-Sat, closed late Jul–mid-Aug; ☷12 Cornelius Trootsplein) Mindblowing, two-Michelin-star creations at this pinnacle of gastronomy change with the seasons, so springtime might see scallops and oysters with vanilla sea salt and gin-and-tonic foam, king crab with salted lemon, beurre blanc ice cream and caviar, or saddle of lamb with star anise. Just as incomparable is the 23rd-floor setting with aerial views north across the city.

If your budget doesn't stretch to dining here, head to the adjacent Twenty Third Bar (www.okura.nl; Ferdinand Bolstraat 333, Hotel Okura Amsterdam; ☺6pm-1am Sun-Thu, to 2am Fri & Sat; ☷12 Cornelius Trootsplein).

✕ Plantage

IJsmolen   ICE CREAM €

(Zeeburgerstraat 2; 1/2/4 scoops €1.50/2.75/4.75; ☺noon-9pm; ☷10 Hoogte Kadijk) Homemade ice cream at this spot near the De Gooyer windmill comes in Dutch flavours like *stroopwafel* (classic caramel-syrup-filled wafers) and *speculaas* (spicy Christmas biscuits) as well as mango and mint; *stracciatella* (vanilla with shredded chocolate); watermelon; and lemon cheesecake. On hot days it stays open to 10pm.

De Plantage   MODERN EUROPEAN €€

(Map p62; ☑760 68 00; caferestaurantdeplantage.nl; Plantage Kerklaan 36; mains lunch €7.50-21.50, dinner €17.50-21.50; ☺9am-10pm; ☷9/14 Plantage

Kerklaan) A beautiful 1870-built, 1900-expanded former greenhouse with wrought-iron struts and glass-paned windows houses this restaurant by the Artis Royal Zoo's gates. Creative dishes include sea wolf with roasted carrots, lavender and beluga lentils; lamb's tongue stew with turnip and artichokes; and almond cake with raspberry compote and almond ice cream. Tables scatter beneath trees strung with fairy lights in summer.

🍴 Eastern Islands

⭐ **Gebr Hartering** MODERN DUTCH €€
(Map p62; ☑ 421 06 99; www.gebr-hartering.nl; Peperstraat 10; 4-/7-course menu €40/65 Tue, Wed & Sun, 6-/9-course menu €50/75 Thu-Sat; ☺ 6-10.30pm Tue-Sun; ☐ 32/33 Prins Hendrikkade) At this jewel of a restaurant founded by two brothers, the menu changes daily so you never know what you'll be tasting, but dishes are unfailingly delicious and exquisitely presented. The wine list is succinct and the timber dining room and canal-side location impossibly romantic.

⭐ **Greetje** MODERN DUTCH €€€
(Map p62; ☑ 779 74 50; www.restaurantgreetje.nl; Peperstraat 23-25; mains €23-27; ☺ 6-10pm Sun-Fri, to 11pm Sat; ☐ 22/34/35/48 Prins Hendrikkade) 🌿

Using market-fresh organic produce, Greetje resurrects and re-creates traditional Dutch recipes like pickled beef, braised veal with apricots and leek *stamppot* (traditional mashed potatoes and vegetables), and pork belly with Dutch mustard sauce. A good place to start is the two-person Big Beginning (per person €15), with a sampling of hot and cold starters.

🍴 Oosterpark

Strike out east from the park down 1e van Swindenstraat, which eventually turns into Javastraat, and you'll strike a vein of delicious Moroccan and Turkish bakeries.

Wilde Zwijnen MODERN DUTCH €€
(☑ 463 30 43; www.wildezwijnen.com; Javaplein 23; mains €19-22, 3-/4-course menu €30.50/36.50; ☺ 6-10pm Mon-Thu, noon-4pm & 6-10pm Fri-Sun; 🕾; ☐ 14 Javaplein) 🌿 The name means 'wild boar' and if it's the right time of year, you may indeed find it on the menu. The rustic, wood-tabled restaurant serves locally sourced, seasonal fare with bold results. There's usually a vegetarian option and chocolate ganache for dessert. The *eetbar* next door offers small plates for €7 to €12 if you don't want a full-on meal.

BRUNCH IN DE PIJP

Amsterdam's brunch scene is booming, with much of the deliciousness happening in De Pijp.

Bakers & Roasters (Map p54; bakersandroasters.com; 1e Jacob van Campenstraat 54; dishes €7.50-15.50; ☺ 8.30am-4pm; ☐ 16/24 Stadhouderskade) Sumptuous brunch dishes served up at Brazilian/Kiwi-owned Bakers & Roasters include banana nutbread French toast with homemade banana marmalade and crispy bacon; Navajo eggs with pulled pork, avocado, mango salsa and chipotle cream; and a smoked salmon stack with poached eggs, potato cakes and hollandaise. Wash them down with a fiery Bloody Mary. Fantastic pies, cakes and slices, too.

CT Coffee & Coconuts (Map p54; www.ctamsterdam.nl; Ceintuurbaan 282-284; mains €6.50-21.50; ☺ 7am-11pm Mon-Fri, from 8am Sat & Sun; 🕾; ☐ 3 Ceintuurbaan) A 1920s art-deco cinema has been stunningly transformed into this open-plan, triple-level cathedral-like space (with a giant print of John Lennon at the top). Brunch dishes like coconut, almond and buckwheat pancakes; French-toast brioche with apricots; avocado-slathered toast with *dukkah* (North African spice-and-nut blend) and lemon dressing; scrambled eggs on sourdough with crumbled feta are served to 1pm.

Scandinavian Embassy (Map p54; scandinavianembassy.nl; Sarphatipark 34; dishes €4.40-12; ☺ 8am-6pm Mon-Fri, 10am-5pm Sat & Sun; ☐ 3 2e Van der Helststraat) Oatmeal porridge with blueberries, honey and coconut, served with goat's milk yogurt; salt-cured salmon on Danish rye with sheep's milk yogurt; muesli with strawberries; and freshly baked pastries, including cinnamon buns, make this blond-wood-panelled spot a perfect place to start the day. As does its phenomenal coffee sourced from Scandinavian micro-roasteries (including a refreshing cold-brewed coffee with tonic water).

★ **De Kas** INTERNATIONAL €€€
(☏462 45 62; www.restaurantdekas.nl; Kamerlingh Onneslaan 3, Park Frankendael; lunch/dinner menu €39/49.50; ⊙noon-2pm & 6.30-10pm Mon-Fri, 6.30-10pm Sat; ☑; ☐9 Hogeweg) ✿ Admired by gourmets citywide, De Kas has an organic attitude to match its chic glass greenhouse setting – try to visit during a thunderstorm! It grows most of its own herbs and produce right here and the result is incredibly pure flavours with innovative combinations.

There's one set menu each day, based on whatever has been freshly harvested. Reserve in advance.

🍷 Drinking & Nightlife

Atmospheric brown *cafés* are Amsterdam's crowning glory. The time-hewn pubs have candle-topped tables and sandy wooden floors, and they induce a cosy vibe that prompts friends to linger and chat for hours over drinks.

COFFEESHOPS

First things first: a '*café*' means 'pub' throughout the Netherlands; a '*coffeeshop*' is where one procures marijuana.

While cannabis is not technically legal in the Netherlands, the possession and purchase of small amounts (5g) of 'soft drugs' (ie marijuana, hashish, space cakes and mushroom-based truffles) is allowed and users won't be prosecuted for smoking or carrying this amount. This means that *coffeeshops* are actually conducting an illegal business – but this is tolerated to a certain extent.

The government has let individual municipalities decide for themselves whether to enforce the national *wietpas* ('weed pass') law banning tourists from *coffeeshops* and requiring locals to have ID. While this is in a state of flux in parts of the Netherlands, in tourist-busy Amsterdam, the city has decreed it will conduct business as usual.

Keep in mind the following:

➡ Ask staff for the menu of goods on offer, usually packaged in small bags. You can also buy ready-made joints. Most shops offer rolling papers, pipes or even bongs.

➡ Don't light up anywhere besides a *coffeeshop* without checking that it's OK to do so.

➡ Alcohol and tobacco products are not permitted in *coffeeshops*.

➡ Don't ask for hard (illegal) drugs.

➡ Be aware that some local varieties can contain up to 15% tetrahydrocannabinol (THC; the active substance that gets people high), and lead to an intense. long-lasting, unpleasant experience; ask the staff's advice about what and how much to consume and heed it, even if nothing happens after an hour.

Dampkring (Map p54; www.dampkring-coffeeshop-amsterdam.nl; Handboogstraat 29; ⊙10am-1am; ☎; ☐1/2/5 Koningsplein) With an interior that resembles a larger-than-life lava lamp, Dampkring is a consistent Cannabis Cup winner, and known for having the most comprehensive menu in town (including details about smell, taste and effect). Its name references the ring of the earth's atmosphere where smaller items combust.

Abraxas (Map p44; www.abraxas.tv; Jonge Roelensteeg 12; ⊙10am-1am; ☎; ☐1/2/5/14 Dam/Paleisstraat) It's young stoner heaven: mellow music, comfy sofas, thick milkshakes and rooms with different energy levels spread across three floors. The considerate staff make it a great place for *coffeeshop* newbies (though the fairy-tale artwork can get a bit intense).

Greenhouse (Map p44; www.greenhouse.org; Oudezijds Voorburgwal 191; ⊙9am-1am; ☎; ☐4/9/16/24 Dam) This is one of the most popular *coffeeshops* in town. Smokers love the funky music, multicoloured mosaics, psychedelic stained-glass windows and high-quality weed and hash. It also serves breakfast, lunch and dinner to suit all levels of the munchies. It's mostly a young, backpacking crowd partaking of the wares.

Bluebird (Map p44; Sint Antoniesbreestraat 71; ⊙9.30am-1am; Ⓜ Nieuwmarkt) Away from Nieuwmarkt's main cluster of *coffeeshops*, Bluebird has a less touristy, more local vibe. The multiroom space has beautiful murals and local artists' paintings, lounge with leather chairs, non-alcoholic bar and kitchen serving superior snacks such as freshly made pancakes. It's especially well-known for its hash, including varieties not available elsewhere in Amsterdam.

Amsterdam's craft-beer scene has exploded in recent years. Alongside long-standing microbreweries are a wave of new ones along with craft-beer specialist bars and/or shops.

Amsterdam's merchants introduced coffee to Europe and it's still the hot drink of choice. Roasteries and micro-roasteries are springing up around the city, and baristas are increasingly using connoisseur styles of drip coffee.

The city centre holds the mother lode of boozers. To drink with locals try the Jordaan or De Pijp neighbourhoods.

Medieval Centre & Red Light District

★**Wynand Fockink**   TASTING HOUSE
(www.wynand-fockink.nl; Pijlsteeg 31; ⊙3-9pm; ▣4/9/16/24 Dam) This small tasting house (dating from 1679) serves scores of *jenever* (Dutch gin) and liqueurs in an arcade behind Grand Hotel Krasnapolsky. Although there are no seats or stools, it's an intimate place to knock back a shot glass or two. Guides give an English-language tour of the distillery and tastings (six samples) on weekends at 3pm, 4.30pm, 6pm and 7.30pm (€17.50, reservations not required).

★**Hoppe**   BROWN CAFE
(Map p44; www.cafehoppe.com; Spui 18-20; ⊙8am-1am; ▣1/2/5 Spui) Gritty Hoppe has been filling glasses for more than 340 years. Journalists, barflies, socialites and raconteurs toss back brews amid the ancient wood panelling. Most months the energetic crowd spews out from the dark interior and onto the Spui. Note Hoppe has two parts: the brown *café* and a modern pub with a terrace, located next door (to the left).

★**In 't Aepjen**   BROWN CAFE
(Map p44; Zeedijk 1; ⊙noon-1am Mon-Thu, to 3am Fri & Sat; ▣4/9/16/24 Centraal Station) Candles burn even during the day at this bar based in a mid-16th-century house, which is one of two remaining wooden buildings in the city. The name allegedly comes from the bar's role in the 16th and 17th centuries as a crash pad for sailors from the Far East, who often toted *aapjes* (monkeys) with them.

★**Café de Dokter**   BROWN CAFE
(Map p44; ☑626 44 27; www.cafe-de-dokter.nl; Rozenboomsteeg 4; ⊙4am-1am Tue-Sat; ▣1/2/5 Spui) Very atmospheric and slightly spooky, Café de Dokter is said to be Amsterdam's smallest pub. Candles flicker on the tables,

music from old jazz records drifts in the background, and a couple of centuries of dust drapes over the chandeliers and bird-cage hanging from the ceiling. Whiskies and smoked beef sausage are the specialities, but good beers flow, too.

A surgeon opened the bar in 1798, hence the name. His descendents still run it.

★**In de Olofspoort**   TASTING HOUSE
(Map p44; ☑624 39 18; www.olofspoort.com; Nieuwebrugsteeg 13; ⊙4pm-12.30am Tue-Thu, 3pm-1.30am Fri & Sat, 3-10pm Sun; ▣4/9/16/24 Centraal Station) The door of this brown *café*-tasting room was once the city gate. A crew of regulars has *jenever* bottles stocked just for them. Check out the jaw-dropping selection behind the back-room bar. Occasional singalongs add to the atmosphere.

Brouwerij De Prael   BEER CAFE
(Map p44; ☑408 44 69; www.deprael.nl; Oudezijds Armsteeg 26; ⊙noon-midnight Mon-Wed, to 1am Thu-Sat, to 11pm Sun; ▣4/9/16/24 Centraal Station) Sample organic beers (Scotch ale, IPA, barley-wine and many more varieties) at the multi-level tasting room of socially minded De Prael brewery, known for employing people with a history of mental illness. A mostly younger crowd hoists suds and forks into well-priced stews and other Dutch standards at the comfy couches and big wood tables strewn about. There's often live music.

Winston Kingdom   CLUB
(Map p44; www.winston.nl; Warmoesstraat 127, Hotel Winston; ⊙9pm-4am Sun-Thu, to 5am Fri & Sat; ▣4/9/16/24 Centraal Station) This is a club that even nonclubbers will love for its indie-alternative music beats, smiling DJs and solid, stiff drinks. No matter what's on – from 'dubstep mayhem' to Thailand-style full-moon parties – the scene can get pretty wild in this good-time little space.

Nieuwmarkt

★**De Sluyswacht**   BROWN CAFE
(Map p44; www.sluyswacht.nl; Jodenbreestraat 1; ⊙12.30pm-1am Mon-Thu, to 3am Fri & Sat, to 7pm Sun; ▣9/14 Waterlooplein) Built in 1695 and listing like a ship in a high wind, this tiny black building was once a lock-keeper's house on the Oude Schans. Today the canal-side terrace with gorgeous views of the Mon-telbaanstoren is one of the most idyllic spots in town to relax with a Dutch beer (Dommelsch is the house speciality).

TILTED ARCHITECTURE

Yes, Amsterdam's buildings *are* leaning. Some – like **De Sluyswacht** (p87) – have shifted over the centuries, but many canal houses were deliberately constructed to tip forward. Interior staircases were narrow, so owners needed an easy way to move large goods and furniture to the upper floors. The solution: a hoist built into the gable, to lift objects up and in through the windows. The tilt allows loading without bumping into the facade.

Café de Doelen
BROWN CAFE

(Map p44; Kloveniersburgwal 125; ⊙9am-1am Mon-Thu, 9am-3am Fri & Sat, 10am-1am Sun; ⊟4/9/14/16/24 Muntplein) Set on a busy canalside crossroad between the Amstel and the Red Light District, De Doelen dates back to 1895 and looks it: there's a carved wooden goat's head, stained-glass lamps and sand on the floor. In fine weather the tables spill across the street for picture-perfect canal views.

Jordaan

★ 't Smalle
BROWN CAFE

(Map p50; www.t-smalle.nl; Egelantiersgracht 12; ⊙10am-1am Sun-Thu, to 2am Fri & Sat; ⊟13/14/17 Westermarkt) Dating back to 1786 as a *jenever* (Dutch gin) distillery and tasting house, and restored during the 1970s with antique porcelain beer pumps and lead-framed windows, locals' favourite 't Smalle is one of Amsterdam's most charming brown *cafés*. Dock your boat right by the pretty stone terrace, which is wonderfully convivial by day and impossibly romantic at night.

De Kat in de Wijngaert
BROWN CAFE

(Map p50; ✆620 45 54; www.dekatindewijngaert.nl; Lindengracht 160; ⊙10am-1am Sun-Thu, 10am-3am Fri, 9am-3am Sat; ⊟3/10 Marnixplein) Rivalling 't Smalle for overwhelming *gezelligheid*, this gorgeous bar is the kind of place where one beer soon turns to half a dozen – maybe it's the influence of the old-guard arts types who hang out here. At least you can soak it all up with what many people vote as the best *tosti* (toasted sandwich) in town.

Café Pieper
BROWN CAFE

(Map p54; Prinsengracht 424; ⊙noon-1am Mon-Thu, noon-2am Fri & Sat, 2-8pm Sun; ⊟1/2/5 Prinsengracht/Leidsestraat) Small, unassuming and unmistakably old (1665), Café Pieper features stained-glass windows, fresh sand on the floors, antique beer mugs hanging from the bar and a working Belgian beer pump (1875). Sip a Wieckse Witte beer or a terrific cappuccino as you marvel at the claustrophobia of the low-ceilinged bar (after all, people were shorter back in the 17th century – even the Dutch).

Cafe Soundgarden
BAR

(Map p50; www.cafesoundgarden.nl; Marnixstraat 164-166; ⊙1pm-1am Mon-Thu, 1pm-3am Fri, 3pm-3am Sat, 3pm-1am Sun; ⊟13/14/17 Marnixstraat) In this grungy, all-ages dive bar, the 'Old Masters' are the Ramones and Black Sabbath. Somehow a handful of pool tables, 1980s pinball machines, unkempt DJs and lovably surly bartenders add up to an ineffable magic. Bands occasionally make an appearance, and the waterfront terrace scene is more like an impromptu party in someone's backyard.

De Twee Zwaantjes
BROWN CAFE

(Map p50; ✆625 27 29; www.detweezwaantjes.nl; Prinsengracht 114; ⊙3pm-1am Sun-Thu, to 3am Fri & Sat; ⊟13/14/17 Westermarkt) The small, authentic 'Two Swans' is at its hilarious best on weekend nights, when you can join locals and visitors belting out classics and traditional Dutch tunes in a rollicking, unforgettable cabaret-meets-karaoke evening. The fact that singers are often fuelled by liquid courage only adds to the spirited fun. Don't be afraid to join in.

Western Canal Ring

★ 't Arendsnest
BEER CAFE

(Map p44; www.arendsnest.nl; Herengracht 90; ⊙noon-midnight Sun-Thu, to 2am Fri & Sat; ⊟1/2/5/13/17 Nieuwezijds Kolk) This gorgeous, restyled brown *café*, with its glowing copper *jenever* (Dutch gin) boilers behind the bar, only serves Dutch beer – but with nearly 200 varieties (many from small breweries), including 30 on tap, you'll need to move here to try them all.

Café Tabac
BAR

(Map p44; www.cafetabac.eu; Brouwersgracht 101; ⊙4pm-1am Mon-Thu, to 3am Fri, 10am-3am Sat, to 1am Sun; ☎; ⊟18/21/22 Buiten Brouwersstraat) Is Café Tabac a brown *café*, a designer bar or simply an effortlessly cool place to while away a few blissful hours at the intersection of two of Amsterdam's most stunning canals? The regulars don't seem concerned about definitions, but simply enjoy the views and kicking back beneath the beamed ceilings.

Café de Vergulde Gaper   BROWN CAFE
(Map p50; www.deverguldegaper.nl; Prinsenstraat
30; ⊙11am-1am Sun-Thu, to 3am Fri & Sat; 🔊;
🚋13/14/17 Westermarkt) Decorated with old
chemists' bottles and vintage posters, this
former pharmacy has amiable staff and a
terrace with afternoon sun. It's popular with
locals, especially for after-work drinks. The
name translates to the 'Golden Gaper', for
the open-mouthed bust of a Moor traditionally posted at Dutch apothecaries.

🍷 Southern Canal Ring

★Air   CLUB
(Map p54; www.air.nl; Amstelstraat 16; ⊙Thu-Sun;
🚋4/9/14 Rembrandtplein) One of Amsterdam's
'it' clubs, Air has an environmentally friendly design by Dutch designer Marcel Wanders including a unique tiered dance floor.
Bonuses include lockers and refillable cards
that preclude fussing with change at the five
bars. The awesome sound system attracts
cutting-edge DJs spinning everything from
disco to house and techno to hip hop. Hours
vary; dress to impress.

★Eijlders   BROWN CAFE
(Map p54; www.cafeeijlders.nl; Korte Leliedwarsstraat
47; ⊙4.30pm-1am Mon-Wed, noon-1am Thu & Sun,
noon-2am Fri & Sat; 🚋1/2/5/7/10 Leidseplein)
During WWII, this beautiful stained-glass
brown *café* was a meeting place for artists
who refused to toe the cultural line imposed
by the Nazis, and the spirit lingers on. It's
still an artists' cafe, hosting regular poetry
readings (sometimes in English – call to be
sure), jam sessions and exhibitions.

★Bar Moustache   BAR
(Map p54; www.barmoustache.nl; Utrechtsestraat
141; ⊙8am-1am Mon-Thu, 8am-3am Fri, 9am-3am
Sat, 9am-1am Sun; 🚋4 Prinsengracht) With an
exposed-brick, minimalist interior designed
by Stella Willing, this loft-style cafe-bar has

WESTERGASFABRIEK

A stone's throw northwest of the Jordaan, the late-19th-century Dutch Renaissance
Westergasfabriek (☎586 07 10; www.westergasfabriek.nl; Haarlemmerweg 8-10; 🚋3 Haarlemmerplein) complex and the adjacent Westerpark (Spaarndammerstraat & Zeeheldenbuurt; 🚋3
Haarlemmerplein) were the city's western gasworks until gas production ceased in 1967. The
site was heavily polluted and underwent a major clean-up before it re-emerged as a cultural
and recreational park, with lush lawns, a long wading pool, cycleways and sports facilities.

The postindustrial buildings now house creative spaces including advertising agencies
and TV production studios, as well as regular festivals and events – including the Sunday
Market (www.sundaymarket.nl; Westergasfabriek; ⊙noon-6pm 1st Sun of month; 🚋10 Van
Limburg Stirumstraat), a quality craft and gourmet food soiree that sets up here monthly.

Westergasfabriek has a slew of dining, drinking and entertainment options:

De Bakkerswinkel (☎688 06 32; www.debakkerswinkel.nl; Polonceaukade 1, Westergasfabriek; dishes €7-14; ⊙8.30am-6pm Mon-Fri, from 10am Sat & Sun; 🚋10 Van Limburg Stirumstraat) Split-level cafe inside the gasworks' former regulator's house.

Raïnaraï (☎486 71 09; www.rainarai.nl; Polonceaukade 40, Westergasfabriek; mains €16.50-23,
3-course menu €38.50; ⊙6-11pm Tue-Sun, lunch by reservation; 🖋; 🚋21 Van Hallstraat) Algerian
cuisine amid exotic decor.

Westergasterras (www.westergasterras.nl; Klönneplein 4, Westergasfabriek; ⊙11am-1am
Sun-Thu, 11am-3am Fri, 10am-3am Sat, 10am-1am Sun; 🚋10 Van Limburg Stirumstraat) One of
the hottest terraces in Amsterdam.

Brouwerij Troost Westergas (☎737 10 28; www.brouwerijtroostwestergas.nl; Pazzanistraat 27,
Westergasfabriek; ⊙4pm-1am Mon-Thu, 4pm-3am Fri, noon-3am Sat, noon-midnight Sun; 🔊; 🚋10 Van
Limburg Stirumstraat) Brewery for hop heads and cool cats.

North Sea Jazz Club (☎722 09 81; www.northseajazzclub.com; Pazzanistraat 1, Westergasfabriek; 🚋10 Van Limburg Stirumstraat) Swingin' live jazz.

Het Ketelhuis (☎684 00 90; www.ketelhuis.nl; Pazzanistraat 4, Westergasfabriek; 🚋10 Van
Limburg Stirumstraat) Art-house cinema.

Pacific Parc (☎488 77 78; www.pacificparc.nl; Polonceaukade 23, Westergasfabriek; 🚋10 Van
Limburg Stirumstraat) Indie gigs and DJ sets.

a mix of communal and private tables that fill with hip locals, and a couple of coveted windowsill benches to watch the action along Utrechtsestraat. There's a stunning, pared-down Italian menu and a great drink selection including Italian wines by the glass.

Door 74
COCKTAIL BAR

(Map p54; ☑ 06 3404 5122; www.door-74.nl; Reguliersdwarsstraat 74; ⊙ 8pm-3am Sun-Thu, to 4am Fri & Sat; ☐ 9/14 Rembrandtplein) You'll need to leave a voice message or, better yet, send a text for a reservation to gain entry to this cocktail bar behind an unmarked door. Some of Amsterdam's most amazing cocktails are served in a classy, dark-timbered speakeasy atmosphere beneath pressed-tin ceilings. Themed cocktail lists change regularly. Very cool.

De Kroon
GRAND CAFE

(Map p54; www.dekroon.nl; Rembrandtplein 17; ⊙ 4pm-1am Mon-Thu, 4pm-4am Fri, 11am-4am Sat, 11am-1am Sun; ☐ 4/9/14 Rembrandtplein) Restored to its original 1898 splendour, De Kroon has high ceilings, velvet chairs, and a beautiful art-deco-tiled staircase up the two floors above Rembrandtplein (there's also a lift). Sit at the atmospheric English-library-themed bar and be mesmerised by the curious display of 19th-century medical and scientific equipment.

🍸 Old South

Welling
BROWN CAFE

(Map p54; www.cafewelling.nl; Jan Willem Brouwersstraat 32; ⊙ 4pm-1am Mon-Fri, 3pm-1am Sat & Sun; ☐ 3/5/12/16/24 Museumplein) Tucked away behind the Concertgebouw, this is a relaxed spot to sip a frothy, cold *biertje* (glass of beer) and mingle with intellectuals and artists. Don't be surprised if the cafe's friendly cat hops onto your lap. There's often live music such as by jazz musicians after their gigs at the Concertgebouw wrap up.

🍸 Vondelpark

★ Franklin
COCKTAIL BAR

(www.barfranklin.nl; Amstelveenseweg 156; ⊙ 5pm-1am Tue-Thu, to 3am Fri & Sat; ☐ 2 Amstelveenseweg) Creative cocktails at this split-level, stained-glass-windowed bar include Picnic at Vondel (lemon-infused gin, summer fruit syrup and chardonnay), Smoke on the Water (mezcal, lime syrup and dandelion bitters) and a Porn Star Martini (vanilla-infused vodka, passion fruit purée and Prosecco). Warm

evenings see its summer terrace get packed to capacity – arrive early to get a seat.

★ Craft & Draft
BEER CAFE

(www.craftanddraft.nl; Overtoom 417; ⊙ bar 2pm-midnight Sun-Thu, to 2am Fri & Sat, shop 2-10pm daily; ☐ 1 Rhijnvis Feithstraat) Craft-beer fans are spoilt for choice, with no fewer than 40 different beers on tap. A huge blackboard chalks up each day's draught – or draft – offerings, such as Belgian 3 Floyds' Lips of Faith, American Coronado's Stupid Stout and Evil Twin's Yang, British Red Willow's Thoughtless, Swedish Sigtuna's Organic Ale and Danish Mikkeller's Peter, Pale & Mary.

★ Lot Sixty One
COFFEE

(Map p54; www.lotsixtyonecoffee.com; Kinkerstraat 112; ⊙ 8am-5pm Mon-Fri, 9am-5pm Sat, 10am-5pm Sun; ☐ 3/12 Bilderdijkstraat) ∅ Look downstairs to the open cellar to see (and better yet, smell) coffee being roasted at this streetwise spot. Beans are sourced from individual ecofriendly farms; varieties include Ethiopian Tchembe, Tanzanian Aranga, Colombian Gerado, Costa Rican Don Mayo, Guatemalan Maravilla and Rwandan Mahembe. All coffees are double shots (unless you specify otherwise); watch Kinkerstraat's passing parade from benches out front.

Butcher's Tears
BREWERY

(www.butchers-tears.com; Karperweg 45; ⊙ 4-9pm Wed-Sun; ☐ 16 Haarlemmermeerstation) Butcher's Tears' beers have a cult following in Amsterdam. Hop heads like to go straight to the source – the brewery's artsy tap room, tucked down an industrial alley – to get their fix. Six brews flow from the taps, and several more varieties are available in bottles. Look for Far Out (a *saison*) and Misery King (a triple-hopped amber ale).

Check the schedule for bands, films and other entertainment that the brewery hosts.

🍷 De Pijp

★ Brouwerij Troost
BREWERY

(Map p54; ☑ 737 10 28; www.brouwerijtroost.nl; Cornelis Troostplein 21; ⊙ 4pm-1am Mon-Thu, 4pm-3am Fri, 2pm-3am Sat, 2pm-midnight Sun; 🐾; ☐ 12 Cornelis Troostplein) ∅ Watch beer being brewed in copper vats behind a glass wall at this outstanding craft brewery. Its dozen beers include a summery blonde, smoked porter, strong tripel, and deep-red Imperial IPA; it also distils gin from its beer and serves fantastic bar food including humongous burgers.

Troost's popularity (book ahead on weekend evenings) saw its second premises open in Westergasfabriek (p89).

Boca's   BAR
(Map p54; www.bar-bocas.nl; Sarphatipark 4; ⊙10am-1am Mon-Thu, 10am-3am Fri & Sat, 11am-1am Sun; 🛜; 🚃3 2e Van der Helststraat) Boca's (Italian for 'mouth') is the ultimate spot for *borrel* (drinks). Mezzanine seating overlooks the cushion-strewn interior but in summer the best seats are on the terrace facing leafy Sarphatipark. Its pared-down wine list (seven by-the-glass choices) goes perfectly with its lavish sharing platters.

Plantage

★**Brouwerij 't IJ**   BREWERY
(www.brouwerijhetij.nl; Funenkade 7; ⊙brewery 2-8pm, English tour 3.30pm Fri-Sun; 🚃10 Hoogte Kadijk) 🚲 Beneath the creaking sails of the 1725-built De Gooyer windmill, Amsterdam's leading organic microbrewery produces delicious (and often very potent) standard, seasonal and limited-edition brews. Pop in for a beer in the tiled tasting room, lined by an amazing bottle collection, or on the plane-tree-shaded terrace. A beer is included in the 30-minute brewery tour (€4.50).

★**SkyLounge**   COCKTAIL BAR
(Map p62; doubletree3.hilton.com; Oosterdoksstraat 4; ⊙11am-1am Sun-Thu, to 3am Fri & Sat; 🚃1/2/4/5/9/14/16/24 Centraal Station) An unrivalled 360-degree panorama of Amsterdam extends from the glass-walled SkyLounge on the 11th floor of the DoubleTree Amsterdam Centraal Station hotel – and just gets better when you head out to its vast, sofa-strewn SkyTerrace, with an outdoor bar. Deliberate over more than 500 different cocktails; DJs regularly hit the decks.

Eastern Islands

★**Amsterdam Roest**   BEER GARDEN
(www.amsterdamroest.nl; Jacob Bontiusplaats 1; ⊙11am-1am Sun-Thu, to 3pm Fri & Sat; 🚃22 Wittenburgergracht) Derelict shipyards have been transformed into a super-cool artist collective/bar/restaurant, Amsterdam Roest (Dutch for 'Rust'), with a canal-facing terrace, huge backyard beneath towering blue cranes and an industrial warehouse interior. Regular events held here include films, live music, festivals, fashion shows and markets; there's a sandy urban beach in summer and toasty bonfires in winter.

★**Hannekes Boom**   BEER GARDEN
(Map p62; www.hannekesboom.nl; Dijksgracht 4; ⊙10am-1am Sun-Thu, to 3am Fri & Sat; 🚃26 Muziekgebouw) Just across the water from NEMO, yet a local secret, this laidback waterside *café* built from recycled materials has a beer garden that really feels like a garden, with timber benches, picnic tables and summer barbecues. Mellow live music such as jazz or singer-songwriters takes place from 3.30pm on Sundays.

The site dates back to 1662, when it was a guard post monitoring maritime traffic into the city.

☆ Entertainment

I Amsterdam (www.iamsterdam.com) lists all sorts of music and cultural goings-on.

★**Concertgebouw**   CLASSICAL MUSIC
(Map p54; 📞671 83 45; www.concertgebouw.nl; Concertgebouwplein 10; ⊙box office 1-7pm Mon-Fri, 10am-7pm Sat & Sun; 🚃3/5/12/16/24 Museumplein) Bernard Haitink, former conductor of the venerable Royal Concertgebouw Orchestra, once remarked that the world-famous hall – built in 1888 with near-perfect acoustics – was the orchestra's best instrument. Free half-hour concerts take place every Wednesday at 12.30pm from mid-September to late June; arrive early. Try the Last Minute Ticket Shop (p92) for half-price seats to all other performances.

Melkweg   LIVE MUSIC
(Map p54; www.melkweg.nl; Lijnbaansgracht 234a; ⊙6pm-1am; 🚃1/2/5/7/10 Leidseplein) In a former dairy, the nonprofit 'Milky Way' is a dazzling galaxy of diverse music. One night it's electronica, the next reggae or punk, and the next heavy metal. Roots, rock and mellow singer-songwriters all get stage time too.

FOOTBALL FEVER

Amsterdam ArenA (www.amsterdam arena.nl; Arena Blvd 1; 🛜; Ⓜ Bijlmer ArenA) Amsterdam ArenA is a high-tech complex with a retractable roof and seating for 52,000 spectators. Four-times European champion Ajax, the Netherlands' most famous football team, play here. Football games usually take place on Saturday evenings and Sunday afternoons from August to May. The arena is about 7km southeast of the centre; the metro will get you there with ease.

ℹ LAST-MINUTE TICKETS

Uitburo & Last Minute Ticket Shop

(Map p54; ☑ 624 23 11; www.lastminute ticketshop.nl; Leidseplein 26; ☺ shop noon-6pm, online ticket sales from 10am; 🚊 1/2/5/7/10 Leidseplein) Not sure how to spend the evening? The Uitburo sells tickets (with a surcharge), and has a Last Minute Ticket Shop, selling same-day half-price seats. They're located in the Stadsschouwburg, on the terrace side. Comedy, dance, concerts and even club nights are often available at a significant discount, and are handily marked 'LNP' (language no problem) if understanding Dutch isn't vital.

Check out the website for cutting-edge cinema, theatre and multimedia offerings.

Paradiso   LIVE MUSIC

(Map p54; ☑ 622 45 21; www.paradiso.nl; Weteringschans 6; ☺ hours vary; 🚊 1/2/5/7/10 Leidseplein) This historic club in a gorgeous old church opened in 1968 as 'Cosmic Relaxation Center Paradiso'. Midweek club nights have low cover charges; the Small Hall upstairs is an intimate venue for up-and-coming bands. The real attraction, of course, is hearing artists like the White Stripes and Lady Gaga rock the Main Hall, wondering if the stained-glass windows might shatter.

De Nieuwe Anita   LIVE MUSIC

(www.denieuweanita.nl; Frederik Hendrikstraat 111; 🚊 3 Hugo de Grootplein) This living-room venue expanded for noise rockers has a great *café*. Behind the bookcase-concealed door, in the back, the main room has a stage and screens cult movies on Mondays. DJs and vaudeville-type acts are also on the eclectic agenda. Entrance fees range from €3 to €7.

Sugar Factory   LIVE MUSIC

(Map p54; www.sugarfactory.nl; Lijnbaansgracht 238; ☺ 6pm-5am; 🚊 1/2/5/7/10 Leidseplein) The vibe at this self-described 'cutting-edge multidisciplinary night theatre' is always welcoming and creative. It's definitely not your average club – most nights start with music, cinema, dance or a spoken-word performance, followed by late-night DJs and dancing. Sunday's Wicked Jazz Sounds party is a sweet one, bringing DJs, musicians, singers and actors together to improvise.

Bimhuis   JAZZ

(Map p62; ☑ 788 21 88; bimhuis.nl; Piet Heinkade 3; tickets free-€28; ☺ closed Aug; 🚊 26 Muziekgebouw) Bimhuis is the beating jazz heart of the Netherlands, and its stylish digs at the Muziekgebouw aan 't IJ draw international jazz greats.

Jazz Café Alto   JAZZ

(Map p54; www.jazz-cafe-alto.nl; Korte Leidsedwarsstraat 115; ☺ from 9pm; 🚊 1/2/5/7/10 Leidseplein) Serious jazz and blues play at this respected cafe near Leidseplein. Doors open at 9pm but music starts around 10pm – get here early if you want to snag a seat.

Maloe Melo   BLUES

(Map p50; ☑ 420 45 92; www.maloemelo.com; Lijnbaansgracht 163; ☺ 9pm-3am Sun-Thu, to 4am Fri & Sat; 🚊 7/10/17 Elandsgracht) This is the free-wheeling, fun-loving altar of Amsterdam's tiny blues scene. Music ranges from garage and Irish punk to Texas blues and rockabilly. The cover charge is usually around €5.

Muziekgebouw aan 't IJ   CONCERT VENUE

(☑ tickets 788 20 00; www.muziekgebouw.nl; Piet Heinkade 1; tickets free-€37; ☺ box office noon-6pm Mon-Sat & 90min before performance; 🚊 26 Muziekgebouw) Behind this multidisciplinary performing-arts venue's high-tech exterior, the dramatically lit main hall has a flexible stage layout and great acoustics. Its jazz stage, Bimhuis, is more intimate. Under-30s can get €10 tickets at the box office 30 minutes before show time. Everyone else should try the Last Minute Ticket Shop (www.last minuteticketshop.nl) for discounts.

Muziektheater   CLASSICAL MUSIC

(Map p54; ☑ 625 54 55; www.operaballet.nl; Waterlooplein 22; ☺ box office noon-6pm Mon-Fr, to 3pm Sat & Sun or until performance Sep-Jul; 🚊 9/14 Waterlooplein) The Muziektheater is home to the Netherlands Opera and the National Ballet. Big-name performers and international dance troupes also take the stage here. Visitors aged under 30 can get tickets for €10 to €15 by showing up 90 minutes before show time. Free classical concerts (12.30pm to 1pm) are held most Tuesdays from September to May in its Boekmanzaal.

Conservatorium van Amsterdam   CLASSICAL MUSIC

(Map p62; ☑ 527 78 37; www.ahk.nl/conservatorium; Oosterdokskade 151; 🚊 4/9/16/24 Centraal Station) Catch a classical recital by students at the Netherlands' largest conservatory of music.

It's in a snazzy contemporary building with state-of-the-art acoustics, endless glass walls and light-flooded interiors.

Felix Meritis
THEATRE

(Map p50; ☑626 23 21; www.felix.meritis.nl; Keizersgracht 324; ☺box office 9am-7pm; ☎; ☐1/2/5 Spui) Amsterdam's centre for arts, culture and science puts on innovative modern theatre, music and dance, as well as talks on politics, diversity, art, technology and literature. Its adjoining cafe is exceptional for coffee or cocktails by the huge windows or outside overlooking the canal.

Boom Chicago
COMEDY

(Map p50; www.boomchicago.nl; Rozengracht 117; ☎; ☐13/14/17 Marnixstraat) Boom Chicago stages seriously funny improv-style comedy shows in English. They make fun of Dutch culture, American culture and everything that gets in the cross hairs. They take place Wednesday through Sunday in the main theatre. Edgier shows happen in the smaller upstairs theatre. Saturday's late-night show is a low-cost good time.

Amsterdams Marionetten Theater
THEATRE

(Map p44; ☑620 80 27; www.marionettentheater.nl; Nieuwe Jonkerstraat 8; adult/child €15/7.50; ⓜNieuwmarkt) In a former blacksmith's shop, the marionette theatre has a limited repertoire (mainly Mozart operas such as *The Magic Flute*), but kids and adults alike are enthralled by the fairy-tale stage sets, period costumes and beautiful singing voices that bring the diminutive cast to life. From June to August the theatre performs only for groups; check the website for a schedule.

Openluchttheater
THEATRE

(Open-Air Theatre; Map p54; www.openluchttheater.nl; Vondelpark 5a; ☺May–mid-Sep; ⓐ; ☐1 1e Constantijn Huygensstraat) Each summer the Vondelpark hosts free concerts in its intimate open-air theatre. It's a fantastic experience to share with others. Expect world music, dance, theatre and more. You can make a reservation (€5 per seat) on the website up to two hours in advance of showtime.

Stadsschouwburg
THEATRE

(Map p54; ☑624 23 11; www.stadsschouwburg amsterdam.nl; Leidseplein 26; ☺box office noon-6pm Mon-Sat; ☐1/2/5/7/10 Leidseplein) In 1894, when this theatre with the grand balcony arcade was completed, public criticism was so fierce that funds for the exterior decorations never materialised. Architect Jan Springer couldn't handle this and promptly retired. The theatre is used for large-scale plays, operettas and festivals. Don't miss the chandeliered splendour of its Stanislavski (Map p54; Leidseplein 26, Stadsschouwburg; ☺10am-1am Sun-Thu, to 3am Fri & Sat; ☎; ☐1/2/5/7/10 Leidseplein) theatre café, and International Theatre & Film Books (Map p54; www.theatreandfilmbooks.com; Leidseplein 26, Stadsschouwburg; ☺noon-6pm Mon, from 11am Tue-Sat; ☐1/2/5/7/10 Leidseplein) shop.

Pathé Tuschinskitheater
CINEMA

(Map p54; www.pathe.nl; Reguliersbreestraat 26-34; ☺11.30am-12.30am; ☐4/9/14 Rembrandtplein) Amsterdam's most famous cinema is worth visiting for its sumptuous art-deco/Amsterdam School interior alone. The *grote zaal* (main auditorium) is the most stunning and generally screens blockbusters; the smaller theatres play art-house and indie films.

Movies
CINEMA

(☑638 60 16; www.themovies.nl; Haarlemmerdijk 161; ☐3 Haarlemmerplein) This *gezellig* (cosy) art-deco cinema (the oldest in Amsterdam, dating from 1912) screens indie films alongside mainstream flicks. From Sunday to Thursday you can treat yourself to a meal in the restaurant (open 5.30pm to 10pm) or have a pre-movie tipple at its inviting *café*-bar.

🔒 Shopping

The capital's cupboards are still stocked with all kinds of exotica (just look at that Red Light gear), but the real pleasure here is finding some odd, tiny shop selling something you'd find nowhere else. Specialities include Dutch-designed clothing and homewares, known for their cool, practical qualities. Antiques, art and vintage goodies also rank high on the local list. Popular gifts include

---

DON'T MISS

NINE STREETS

Negen Straatjes (Nine Streets; Map p50; www.de9straatjes.nl; ☐1/2/5 Spui) In a city packed with countless shopping opportunities, each seemingly more alluring than the next, the Negen Straatjes represent the very densest concentration of consumer pleasures. These nine little streets are indeed small, each just a block long. The shops are tiny, too, and many are highly specialised. Eyeglasses? Cheese? Toothbrushes? Single-edition art books? Each has its own dedicated boutique.

tulip bulbs, bottles of *jenever* (Dutch gin) and blue-and-white Delftware pottery.

Nieuwmarkt

Several good streets (such as Staalstraat) with typically eccentric local stores wend through the neighbourhood.

★Droog   DESIGN, HOMEWARES
(Map p44; www.droog.com; Staalstraat 7; ⊙11am-6pm Tue-Sun; ⌷4/9/14/16/24 Muntplein) Droog means 'dry' in Dutch, and this slick local design house's products are strong on dry wit. You'll find all kinds of smart items you never knew you needed, like super-powerful suction cups. Also here is a gallery space, whimsical blue-and-white cafe, and fairytale-inspired courtyard garden that Alice in Wonderland would love, as well as a top-floor apartment (double €275).

Juggle   CIRCUS SUPPLIES
(Map p44; www.juggle-store.com; Staalstraat 3; ⊙noon-5.30pm Tue-Sat; ⌷4/9/14/16/24 Muntplein) Wee Juggle puts more than mere balls in the air: it also sells circus supplies, from unicycles to fire hoops to magic tricks.

Joe's Vliegerwinkel   KITES
(Map p44; www.joesvliegerwinkel.nl; Nieuwe Hoogstraat 19; ⊙noon-6pm Tue-Fri, to 5pm Sat; ⌷;

AMSTERDAM'S BEST MARKETS

Albert Cuypmarkt (p60) Soak up local colour and snap up exotic goods at Amsterdam's largest market.

Waterlooplein Flea Market (Map p44; www.waterloopleinmarkt.nl; Waterlooplein; ⊙9am-6pm Mon-Sat; ⌷9/14 Waterlooplein) Piles of curios, used footwear and cheap bicycle parts for bargain hunters.

Bloemenmarkt (p56) Bag beautiful bloomin' bulbs at the canal-side flower market.

Noordermarkt It's morning bliss trawling for organic foods and vintage clothes.

Dappermarkt (www.dappermarkt.nl; Dapperstraat, btwn Mauritskade & Wijttenbachstraat; ⊙9am-5pm Mon-Sat; ⌷3/7 Dapperstraat) The Oost's multicultural bazaar reflects its diverse immigrant population.

M Nieuwmarkt) Whether you're after a kite for the kids, you're looking for something more exotic, or just want to have fun in one of the city's parks, head to this specialised kite shop. You can also buy build-it-yourself kits.

Jordaan

In the north of the Jordaan, Haarlemmerstraat and Haarlemmerdijk are lined with hip boutiques and food shops.

Noordermarkt   MARKET
(Northern Market; Map p50; www.jordaanmarkten.nl; Noordermarkt; ⊙flea market 9am-1pm Mon, farmers market 9am-4pm Sat; ⌷3/10 Marnixplein) A market square since the early 1600s, the plaza in front of the Noorderkerk hosts a couple of lively markets each week. Monday morning's **flea market** has some amazing bargains; Saturday mornings see local shoppers flock to the lush **boerenmarkt** (farmers market) overflowing with organic produce.

Antiekcentrum Amsterdam   ANTIQUES
(Amsterdam Antique Centre; Map p50; www.antiekcentrumamsterdam.nl; Elandsgracht 109; ⊙11am-6pm Mon & Wed-Fri, to 5pm Sat & Sun; ⌷7/10/17 Elandsgracht) Anyone with an affinity for odd antiques and bric-a-brac may enter this knick-knack mini-mall and never come out. Spanning 1750 sq metres, there are 72 stalls, plus a handful of larger shops, displays and a private dealers' table market on Wednesday, Saturday and Sunday. You're just as likely to find 1940s silk dresses as you are 1970s Swedish porn.

Western Canal Ring

The Negen Straatjes (Nine Streets; p93) offer a satisfying browse among offbeat, pint-sized shops.

★Frozen Fountain   HOMEWARES
(Map p50; www.frozenfountain.nl; Prinsengracht 645; ⊙1-6pm Mon, 10am-6pm Tue-Sat, noon-5pm Sun; ⌷1/2/5 Prinsengracht) The city's best-known showcase of furniture and interior design. Prices are not cheap, but the daring designs are offbeat and very memorable (designer pen-knives, kitchen gadgets and that birthday gift for the impossible-to-wow friend). Best of all, it's an unpretentious place where you can browse at length without feeling uncomfortable.

De Kaaskamer   FOOD
(www.kaaskamer.nl; Runstraat 7; ⊙noon-6pm Mon, 9am-6pm Tue-Fri, to 5pm Sat, noon-5pm

MEDIEVAL CENTRE & RED LIGHT DISTRICT

The big department stores cluster around the Dam. Chain stores line the pedestrian Kalverstraat.

Condomerie Het Gulden Vlies (Map p44; www.condomerie.com; Warmoesstraat 141; ⊙11am-6pm Mon-Sat, 1-5pm Sun; ⌂4/9/14/16/24 Dam) Perfectly positioned for the Red Light District, this boutique sells condoms in every imaginable size, colour, flavour and design (horned devils, marijuana leaves, Delftware tiles...), along with lubricants and saucy gifts.

American Book Center (ABC; www.abc.nl; Spui 12; ⊙noon-8pm Mon, 10am-8pm Tue-Sat, 11am-6.30pm Sun; ⌂1/2/5 Spui) This excellent three-storey shop is the biggest source of English-language books in Amsterdam. Its greatest strengths are in the artsy ground-floor department, but on the upper floors there's fiction and oodles of special-interest titles, plus a good travel section. It also stocks foreign periodicals such as the *New York Times*. Top-notch postcards, too!

PGC Hajenius (Map p44; www.hajenius.com; Rokin 96; ⊙noon-6pm Mon, 9.30am-6pm Tue-Sat, noon-5pm Sun; ⌂4/9/14/16/24 Spui/Rokin) Even if you're not a cigar connoisseur, this tobacco emporium is worth a browse. Inside is all art-deco stained glass, gilt trim and soaring ceilings. Regular customers, including members of the Dutch royal family, have private humidors here. You can sample your Cuban stogie and other exotic purchases in the handsome smoking lounge.

Kokopelli (Map p44; www.kokopelli.nl; Warmoesstraat 12; ⊙11am-10pm; ⌂4/9/16/24 Centraal Station) Were it not for its trade in 'magic truffles' (similar to the now-outlawed psilocybin mushrooms, aka 'magic mushrooms') you might swear this large, beautiful space was a fashionable clothing or homewares store. There's a coffee and juice bar and a chill-out lounge area overlooking Damrak.

Oudemanhuis Book Market (Map p44; Oudemanhuispoort; ⊙11am-4pm Mon-Sat; ⌂4/9/14/16/24 Spui/Rokin) Secondhand books weigh down the tables in the atmospheric covered alleyway between Oudezijds Achterburgwal and Kloveniersburgwal, where you'll rub tweed-patched elbows with University of Amsterdam professors thumbing through volumes of Marx, Aristotle and other classics. Old posters, maps and sheet music are for sale, too. Most tomes are in Dutch, though you'll find a few in English mixed in.

Sun; ⌂1/2/5 Spui) The name means 'cheese room' and it is indeed stacked to the rafters with Dutch and organic varieties, as well as olives, tapenades, salads and other picnic ingredients. You can try before you buy, and if it's too much to take home a mondo wheel of Gouda, you can at least procure a cheese and/or meat baguette to take away.

Southern Canal Ring

The Spiegel Quarter, along Spiegelgracht and Nieuwe Spiegelstraat, is ground zero for quality antiques and art.

Young Designers United CLOTHING
(YDU; Map p54; www.ydu.nl; Keizersgracht 447; ⊙1-6pm Mon, 10am-6pm Tue, Wed, Fri & Sat, 10am-8pm Thu; ⌂1/2/5 Keizersgracht) Racks are rotated regularly at this affordable women's clothing boutique showcasing young designers working in the Netherlands. You might spot durable basics by Agna K, handmade leggings by

Leg-Inc; geometric dresses by Fenny Faber; and 'punk rock grunge meets fairytale romance' fashion by Jutka en Riska. Accessorise with YDU's select range of jewellery and bags.

Skateboards Amsterdam SPORTS
(Map p54; skateboardsamsterdam.nl; Vijzelstraat 77; ⊙1-6pm Sun & Mon, 11am-6pm Tue, Wed, Fri & Sat, 11am-8pm Thu; ⌂16/24 Keizersgracht) Local skater dudes and dudettes shop for cruisers, longboards, shoes, laces, clothing including Spitfire and Skate Mental t-shirts, caps, beanies, bags and backpacks, books and music at this independent boutique.

Eduard Kramer ANTIQUES
(Map p54; www.antique-tileshop.nl; Prinsengracht 807; ⊙11am-6pm Mon, 10am-6pm Tue-Sat, 1-6pm Sun; ⌂7/10 Spiegelgracht) Specialising in antique Dutch tiles, this tiny store is also crammed with lots of other interesting stuff – silver candlesticks, crystal decanters, jewellery and pocket watches.

MAGIC TRUFFLES & SMART SHOPS

Smart shops – which deal in organic uppers and natural hallucinogens – have long been known for selling 'magic' mushrooms. But in 2008, the government banned them after a high-profile incident in which a tourist died. Nearly 200 varieties of fungus then went on the forbidden list – though conspicuously missing was the magic truffle.

Truffles come from a different part of the plant, but they contain the same active ingredients as mushrooms. Truffles are now the smart shops' stock-in-trade. Counter staff advise on the nuances of dosages and possible effects, as if at a pharmacy. Listen to them. Every year, emergency-room nurses have to sit with people on bad trips brought on by consuming more than the recommended amount. Also, it seems obvious, but never buy truffles or other drugs on the street.

Concerto   MUSIC
(Map p54; concerto.amsterdam; Utrechtsestraat 52-60; ⊙10am-6pm Mon, Wed & Sat, 10am-7pm Thu & Fri, noon-6pm Sun; 🚊4 Prinsengracht) Spread over several buildings, this rambling shop has Amsterdam's best selection of new and second-hand CDs and vinyl in every imaginable genre, from pop to classical, dance to world music and much more. It's often cheap and always interesting, and has good listening facilities.

Mark Raven Amsterdam Art   ARTS
(Map p54; www.markraven.nl; Leidsestraat 42; ⊙10.30am-6pm; 🚊1/2/5 Keizersgracht) For a souvenir with a difference, visit Dutch artist Mark Raven's gallery where he displays and sells his charming paintings, drawings and sketches of Amsterdam's cityscapes as artworks but also printed on T-shirts, hoodies, posters and coffee mugs.

De Pijp

⭐**Hutspot**   CONCEPT STORE
(Map p54; www.hutspotamsterdam.com; Van Woustraat 4; ⊙shop & cafe 10am-7pm Mon-Sat, noon-6pm Sun, bar 5pm-1am Mon-Thu, 4pm-3am Fri & Sat, 4pm-1am Sun; 🚊4 Stadhouderskade) Named after the Dutch dish of boiled and mashed veggies, 'Hotchpotch' was founded by four young guys with a mission to give young entrepreneurs the chance to sell their work. As a result, this concept store is an inspired mishmash of Dutch-designed furniture, furnishings, art, homewares and clothing plus a cool in-store cafe and bar.

Old South

Ultraluxe shopping avenue PC Hooftstraat teems with brands that need no introduction (Chanel, Gucci et al).

Museum Shop at the Museumplein   SOUVENIRS
(Map p54; Hobbemastraat; ⊙shop 10am-6pm, ticket window for museum entrance 8.30am-6pm; 🚊2/5 Hobbemastraat) The Van Gogh Museum and Rijksmuseum jointly operate the Museum Shop at the Museumplein, so you can pick up posters, cards and other art souvenirs from both institutions in one fell swoop (and avoid the museums' entrance queues). While the selection is not as vast as the in-house stores, the shop has enough iconic wares to satisfy most needs.

Vondelpark

Stylish shops line Cornelis Schuytstraat and Willemsparkweg; check www.cornelis schuytstraat.com for new openings.

⭐**Pied à Terre**   BOOKS
(Map p54; 📞627 44 55; www.piedaterre.nl; Overtoom 135-137; ⊙1-6pm Mon, 10am-6pm Tue, Wed & Fri, to 9pm Thu, to 5pm Sat; 🚊1 1e Constantijn Huygensstraat) The galleried, sky-lit interior of Europe's largest travel bookshop feels like a Renaissance centre of learning. If it's travel or outdoor-related, it's likely here: gorgeous globes, travel guides in multiple languages (especially English) and over 600,000 maps. Order a coffee and dream up your next trip at the cafe tables.

Beer Tree   DRINK
(Map p54; www.thebeertree.nl; Jan Pieter Heijestraat 148; ⊙noon-10pm Mon-Fri, 11am-10pm Sat & Sun; 🚊1 Jan Pieter Heijestraat) This is the original branch of this ingenious shop, where many of its 250-plus craft beers from over 25 different countries are available cold from the fridge, making them perfect to take to the Vondelpark on a hot day, as well as four rotating beers on tap that can be bottled to take away cold, too.

It now has a second branch in De Pijp (Map p54; www.thebeertree.nl; 1e Van der Helststraat 53; ⊙noon-10pm; 🚊16/24 Albert Cuypstraat).

Johnny at the Spot FASHION, HOMEWARES
(Map p54; www.johnnyatthespot.com; Jan Pieter Heijestraat 94; ⊘1-6pm Mon, 11am-6pm Tue, Wed & Sat, to 7pm Thu & Fri, 1-5pm Sun; 🚋7/17 Jan Pieter Heijestraat) On up-and-coming Jan Pieter Heijestraat, multipurpose mega-boutique Johnny at the Spot fills several interconnected buildings with super-stylish men's and women's clothing, shoes and raincoats from all over the globe. Groovy homewares include everything from plants and soaps to bowls, vases, crockery and furniture.

ℹ️ Information

INTERNET ACCESS
Wi-fi is widespread. For free wi-fi hotspots around the city, check www.wifi-amsterdam.nl.

MEDIA
Dutch-language newspapers include Amsterdam's *Het Parool* (www.parool.nl), with the scoop on what's happening around town.

MEDICAL SERVICES
BENU Apotheek Dam (📞624 43 31; www.dam.benuapotheek.nl; Damstraat 2; ⊘8.30am-5.30pm Mon-Fri, 10am-5pm Sat, noon-5pm Sun; 🚋4/9/16/24/25 Dam) Pharmacy just off the Dam.

Onze Lieve Vrouwe Gasthuis (📞599 91 11; www.olvg.nl; Oosterpark 9; ⊘24hr; 🚋3/14 Beukenweg) At Oosterpark, near the Tropenmuseum. It's the closest public hospital to the centre of town.

MONEY
ATMs are easy to find in the centre, though they often have queues. To change money try **GWK Travelex** (📞0900 05 66; www.gwk.nl), which also has branches at **Leidseplein** (Leidseplein 31a; ⊘10.15am-5.15pm Mon-Sat; 🚋1/2/5/7/10 Leidseplein) and **Schiphol International Airport** (⊘6am-10pm).

TOURIST INFORMATION
I Amsterdam Visitor Centre (Map p44; www.iamsterdam.com; Stationsplein 10; ⊘9am-6pm; 🚋4/9/16/24 Centraal Station) Located outside Centraal Station, this office can help with just about anything: it sells the I Amsterdam discount card; theatre and museum tickets; a good city map (€2.50); cycling maps; public transit passes (the GVB transport office is attached); and train tickets to Schiphol Airport. It also books hotel rooms (commission charged).

I Amsterdam Visitor Centre Schiphol (⊘7am-10pm) Provides hotel bookings, maps and discount cards inside Schiphol International Airport at the Arrivals 2 hall.

ℹ️ Getting There & Away

AIR
Schiphol International Airport (AMS; www.schiphol.nl),is 18km southwest of the city centre. It has ATMs, currency exchanges, tourist information, car hire, train-ticket sales counters, luggage storage, food and free wi-fi.

BICYCLE
It's easy to get to and from Amsterdam by bike. National bike routes radiate in all directions:

LF20/LF23 East to Muiden and beyond.

LF7 North via ferry across the IJ; before you know it you're in the rural wilds of Waterland.

LF20 West to Haarlem (25km) and onto the coast.

LF2 South to Rotterdam, Dordrecht and Belgium.

For further route planning in the region, visit www.routecraft.com, which calculates the best bike paths; click on 'Bikeplanner' (there's an English version).

NORTH–SOUTH METRO LINE

It's only 9.7km long, but the new Noord/Zuidlijn (north–south metro line) has stretched into a challenge of far greater size. Begun in 2003 and originally targeted for completion in 2011, the project deadline has now been pushed back to 2017.

It's no wonder, given the massive task at hand. To build the metro's route between Amsterdam-Noord and the World Trade Centre in the south, engineers needed to tunnel under the IJ River and the centuries-old buildings of Amsterdam's city centre. When some of the historic monuments in the centre started to shift off their foundations, engineers halted construction.

Debates flared over what to do. Continue, even though the budget was running sky-high? Quit, and lose the millions of euros already spent? How much longer would residents tolerate the inconvenience of their main streets being torn to bits?

The city ultimately decided to proceed. Engineers added additional support beams beneath the affected buildings. Construction is now wrapping up, with new stations, such as De Pijp, being fitted out.

BUS

Eurolines connects with all major European capitals. Buses arrive at **Duivendrecht station** (Stationsplein 3, Duivendrecht), south of the centre, which has an easy metro link to Centraal Station (about a 20-minute trip via metro number 54). The **Eurolines Ticket Office** (www.eurolines.nl; Rokin 38a; ⊙ 9am-5pm Mon-Sat; 🚌 4/9/14/16/24 Dam) is near the Dam. Bus travel is typically the cheapest way to get to Amsterdam.

CAR

If you're arriving by car, it's best to leave your vehicle in a park-and-ride lot near the edge of town. A nominal parking fee (around €8 per 24 hours) also gets you free public transport tickets. For more info see www.bereikbaar.amsterdam.nl.

TRAIN

Centraal Station is in the city centre, with easy onward transport connections. The station has ATMs, currency exchange, tourist information, restaurants, shops, luggage storage (€10 per day), and train-ticket sales.

Amsterdam is the terminus of the high-speed line south to Rotterdam, Antwerp, Brussels and Paris. From late 2016, direct Eurostar trains will link Amsterdam (and Rotterdam, Antwerp and Brussels) with London, with an Amsterdam–London journey time of four hours.

Destination	Price (€)	Duration (min)	Frequency (per hour)
Den Haag	11.20	60	6
Groningen	25	140	3
Maastricht	25	150	3
Rotterdam	14.80	70	8
Rotterdam (high speed)	17.10	40	2
Schiphol Airport	4.10	15	6
Utrecht	7.40	30	3-6

🛈 Getting Around

TO/FROM THE AIRPORT

Trains

Trains run to Amsterdam's Centraal Station (€4.10 one way, 15 minutes) 24 hours a day. From 6am to 12.30am they go every 10 minutes or so; hourly in the wee hours. The rail platform is inside the terminal, down the escalator.

Shuttle Bus

Connexxion (www.schipholhotelshuttle.nl; one way/return €17/27) runs a shuttle van (every 30 minutes from 6am to 9pm) from the airport to several hotels. Look for the Connexxion desk by Arrivals 4.

🛈 NAVIGATING AMSTERDAM

Amsterdam's concentric canals and similarly named streets make it all too easy to get lost. Some pointers: a *gracht* (canal), such as Egelantiersgracht, is distinct from a *straat* (street) such as Egelantiersstraat. A *dwarsstraat* (cross-street) that intersects a *straat* is often preceded by *eerste*, *tweede*, *derde* and *vierde* (first, second, third and fourth; marked 1e, 2e, 3e and 4e on maps).

For example Eerste Egelantiersdwarsstraat is the first cross-street of Egelantiersstraat (ie the nearest cross-street to the city centre).

Streets preceded by *lange* (long) and *korte* (short) simply mean the longer or shorter street. Be aware too that seemingly continuous streets regularly change name along their length.

Bus

Bus 197 (€5 one way, 25 minutes) is the quickest way to places by the Museumplein, Leidseplein or Vondelpark. It departs outside the arrivals hall door. Buy a ticket from the driver.

Taxi

Taxis take 20 to 30 minutes to the centre (longer in rush hour), costing around €47. The taxi stand is just outside the arrivals hall door.

BICYCLE

Bicycles are more common in Amsterdam than cars (or residents, with an estimated 881,000 bikes) and to roll like a local you'll need a two-wheeler. Rent one from the myriad outlets around town or your accommodation, and the whole city becomes your playground. Cycling is *the* quintessential activity while visiting.

To rent a bike, you'll have to show a passport or European national ID card and leave a credit-card imprint or pay a deposit (usually €50). Prices for basic 'coaster-brake' bikes average €11 per 24-hour period. Bikes with gears and handbrakes cost more. Theft insurance costs around €3 extra per day. Bike locks are typically provided; use them, as theft is rampant. Helmets are generally not available (the Dutch don't wear them). Most **cycling tour companies** (p66) also rent bikes.

Bike City (📞 626 37 21; www.bikecity.nl; Bloemgracht 68-70; bike rental per day from €14; ⊙ 9am-5.30pm; 🚋 13/14/17 Westermarkt) These black bikes have no advertising on them, so you can free-wheel like a local.

Black Bikes (Map p44; 📞 670 85 31; www.blackbikes.com; Nieuwezijds Voorburgwal 146; bike rental per 3/24hr from €6/8.50; ⊙ 8am-8pm Mon-Fri, 9am-7pm Sat & Sun; 🚋 1/2/5/13/14/17

Dam/Raadhuisstraat) Signless company offering city, kids', tandem and cargo bikes at 10 shops, including this one in the centre.

MacBike (Map p44; ☑ 620 09 85; www.macbike.nl; Stationsplein 5; bike rental per 3/24hr from €7.50/9.75; ☺ 9am-5.45pm; ⊞ 4/9/16/24 Centraal Station) It's among the most touristy of the rental companies (the bikes are equipped with big logos), but it has several convenient locations (Centraal Station, Waterlooplein 199, Weteringschans 2, among others) and sells great maps.

BOAT

Canal Bus

The **Canal Bus** (p66) offers a unique hop-on, hop-off service among its 16 docks around the city and near the big museums.

Ferries

Free ferries to Amsterdam-Noord depart from piers behind Centraal Station. The ride to Buiksloterweg is the most direct (five minutes) and runs 24 hours; this is how you reach the EYE Film Institute and Tolhuistuin. Another boat runs to NDSM-werf (15 minutes) between 7am and midnight (from 9am weekends). Another goes to IJplein (6.30am to midnight). Bicycles are permitted on all.

CAR & MOTORCYCLE

Parking is expensive and scarce. Street parking in the centre costs around €5/30 per hour/day. It's better to use a park-and-ride lot at the edge of town.

All the big multinational rental companies are in town. Rates start at around €45 per day. Note most cars do not have an automatic transmission. Request automatic cars well in advance and be prepared for a hefty surcharge.

PUBLIC TRANSPORT

The GVB operates the public transport system, a mix of tram, bus, metro and ferry. Pick up tickets, passes and maps at the **GVB Information Office** (www.gvb.nl; Stationsplein 10; ☺ 7am-9pm Mon-Fri, 8am-9pm Sat & Sun; ⊞ 1/2/4/5/9/14/16/24 Centraal Station) across the tram tracks from Centraal Station.

The excellent Journey Planner (www.9292.nl) calculates routes, costs and travel times, and will get you from door to door, wherever you're going.

Tram

Most public transport within the city is by tram. The vehicles are fast, frequent and ubiquitous, operating between 6am and 12.30am.

On trams with conductors, enter at the rear; you can buy a disposable **OV-chipkaart** (www.ov-chipkaart.nl; 1hr €2.90) or day pass (€7.50) when you board. On trams without conductors (line 5, and some on line 24), buy a ticket from the driver.

When you enter and exit, wave your card at the pink machine to 'check in' and 'check out'.

Bus & Metro

➠ Amsterdam's buses and metro (subway) primarily serve outer districts. Fares are the same as for trams.

➠ *Nachtbussen* (night buses) run after other transport stops (from 1am to 6am, every hour). A ticket costs €4.50.

➠ Note that Connexxion buses (which depart from Centraal Station and are useful to reach sights in South Amsterdam) and the No 197 airport bus are not part of the GVB system. They cost more (around €5).

Travel Passes

➠ Travel passes are extremely handy and provide substantial savings over per-ride ticket purchases.

➠ The GVB offers unlimited-ride passes for one to seven days (€7.50/12/16.50/21/26/29.50/32), valid on trams, some buses and the metro, as well as various wider-ranging passes.

➠ Passes are available at the GVB office, I Amsterdam Visitor Centres and from tram conductors (one- and two-day passes only).

➠ The **I Amsterdam Card** (www.iamsterdam.com; per 24/48/72hr €49/59/69) includes a GVB travel pass in its fee.

TAXI

➠ Taxis are expensive and not very speedy given Amsterdam's maze of streets.

➠ You don't hail taxis on the road. Instead, find them at stands at Centraal Station, Leidseplein and other busy spots around town. You needn't take the first car in the queue.

➠ Another method is to book a taxi by phone. **Taxicentrale Amsterdam** (TCA; ☑ 777 77 77; www.tcataxi.nl) is the most reliable company.

➠ Fares are meter-based. The meter starts at €2.95, then it's €2.17 per kilometre thereafter. A ride from Leidseplein to the Dam runs about €12; from Centraal Station to Jordaan is €10 to €15.

ⓘ SIGHTSEEING BY TRAM

For a bit of passive sightseeing, look no further than the tram: the lines rattle through great cross-sections of the city. One of the best routes is tram 10. It starts near Westerpark, swings around the perimeter of the canal loop and heads out to the Eastern Islands, passing 19th-century housing blocks, the Rijksmuseum and Brouwerij 't IJ windmill along the way.

Another good route is tram 5, starting at Centraal Station and cutting south through the centre of town.

Haarlem & North Holland

Best Places to Eat

➡ Brick (p105)

➡ Marque (p117)

➡ Restaurant Mr & Mrs (p105)

➡ De Hoofdtoren (p117)

➡ Texel's island producers (p128)

Best Places to Stay

➡ Camp Silver Island Hideaway (p127)

➡ Gevangenis Hotel Hoorn (p117)

➡ Boutique Hotel Texel (p126)

➡ De Koepoort (p119)

➡ Hello I'm Local Boutique Hostel (p103)

Why Go?

The quintessentially Dutch province of Noord-Holland (North Holland) wraps around Amsterdam like a crown. Less than 20km west of Amsterdam, but entirely its own city, elegant Haarlem is the region's capital and a charming example of 17th-century grandeur. Canals wend through its centre, while wide, sandy beaches fringe its western edge.

Further afield, smaller centres range from mast-filled Golden Age ports such as Hoorn and Enkhuizen with architecturally resplendent historic centres to canal-laced towns and villages like Alkmaar and Edam, famed for their cheese and centuries-old cheese markets. Across the region, bucolic expanses of windswept countryside span extensive *polders* (areas surrounded by dykes where the water can be artificially controlled) to windmill-dotted farmland grazed by cows and sheep, fields of flowers and magnificent dune-scapes, especially on the idyllic, ends-of-the-earth island of Texel.

When to Go

➡ Easily accessible from Amsterdam whatever the weather, Haarlem's outstanding museums, fabulous bars, *cafés*, restaurants and great shopping make it a year-round destination.

➡ Springtime lambing in March and April, around Easter, is an especially delightful time to island hop over to Texel, even though it's still too cold for swimming.

➡ The warmer months of May to September are the prime time to visit smaller towns and villages, which all but hibernate during winter, particularly from November to March, when many sights, activities and attractions close.

Haarlem & North Holland Highlights

❶ Viewing priceless works of Dutch Masters at the **Frans Hals Museum** (p103) in Golden Age Haarlem.

❷ Taking in the centuries-old spectacle of the **Kaasmarkt** (cheese market; p110) in the quaint town of Edam.

❸ Experiencing hardy seafaring life in the days before the Afsluitdijk (Barrier Dyke) at Enkhuizen's **Zuiderzeemuseum** (p118).

❹ Cycling past high sand dunes, deserted beaches, lush forests and green pastures on the island of **Texel** (p121).

❺ Exploring the mighty medieval fortress of **Muiderslot** (p129) in the lively harbour town of Muiden.

❻ Experiencing a 'floating auction' at Broek op Langedijk's fascinating **Museum Broeker Veiling** (p115).

❼ Strolling the elegant streets inside the vast star-shaped fortress at **Naarden** (p130).

NORTH HOLLAND

Its lively capital, Haarlem, aside, this province has enough historic towns and attractions to fill a week or more of touring.

History

The peninsula now known as Noord-Holland (North Holland) was part of Friesland until the 12th century, when storm floods created the Zuiderzee and isolated West Friesland. By this time the mercantile Counts of Holland ruled the area – or thought they did. One of the early counts, Willem II, became king of the Holy Roman Empire in 1247 but perished in a raid against the West Frisians (his horse fell through the ice). His son, Count Floris V, succeeded in taming his defiant subjects 40 years later.

West Friesland was now owned by the county of Holland, a founding member of the Republic of the Seven United Netherlands (1579). North Holland played a key role in the long struggle against Spanish domination, and the town of Alkmaar was the first to throw off the yoke. The era of prosperity known as the Golden Age ensued, and Noord-Holland has a cache of richly ornamented buildings from this period. The fishing and trading ports of Enkhuizen, Hoorn, Medemblik and Edam were at the centre of this boom.

Napoleon invaded in 1795 and split the country in two to break its economic power. Even after Willem I (Willem Frederik, Prince of Orange-Nassau) proclaimed himself Sovereign Prince of the United Netherlands in 1813, a divide remained and the provinces of Noord-Holland and Zuid-Holland were established in 1840.

Today Noord-Holland's main business is agriculture, most famously cheese production.

ⓘ Getting There & Around

This is day-trip country: with the exception of Texel, the entire region is easily reached from Amsterdam, or you can set your own pace and just go and explore.

Noord-Holland is well served by the national rail service, and when the train ends the bus networks take over.

Bike trails lace the province in almost every direction; you can cover the flat stretch from Amsterdam to Den Helder in two days at a leisurely pace.

Haarlem

🌐 023 / POP 156,660

This classic Dutch city of cobbled streets, historic buildings, grand churches, even grander museums, cosy bars, fine cafes and canals is just a 15-minute train ride from Amsterdam, but with so much on offer in such a compact area, you can easily spend a couple of days here.

History

The name Haarlem derives from Haarloheim, meaning a wooded place on high, sandy soil. Its origins date back to the 10th century when the Counts of Holland set up a toll post on the Spaarne River. Haarlem quickly became the most important inland port after Amsterdam until the Spanish invaded in 1572. The city surrendered after a seven-month siege but worse was yet to come: upon capitulation virtually the entire population was slaughtered. After the Spanish were finally repelled by Willem van Oranje, Haarlem soared into the prosperity of the Golden Age, attracting painters and artists from throughout Europe. The 1658-founded Dutch town of Harlem in what's now New York City is named after it.

⊙ Sights

Flanked by historic buildings, restaurants and cafes, the large **Grote Markt** is Haarlem's beating heart.

★**Grote Kerk van St Bavo**   CHURCH
(www.bavo.nl; Oude Groenmarkt 22; adult/child €2.50/free; ⊗10am-5pm Mon-Sat) Topped by a towering 50m-high steeple, the Gothic Grote Kerk van St Bavo cathedral contains some fine Renaissance artworks, but the star attraction is its stunning Müller organ – one of the most magnificent in the world, standing 30m high with about 5000 pipes. It was played by Handel and a 10-year-old Mozart. Free hour-long **organ recitals** take place at 8.15pm Tuesday and 4pm Thursday in July and August, and 2pm on the last Saturday of the month year-round.

Town Hall   HISTORIC BUILDING
(Grote Markt 2) At the western end of the Grote Markt is the florid, 14th-century town hall, which sprouted many extensions including a balcony where judgements from the high court were pronounced. It only opens to the public on Open Monuments Days during the second weekend of September.

De Hallen GALLERY
(www.dehallen.nl; Grote Markt 16; adult/child €7.50/
free; ⊙11am-5pm Tue-Sat, noon-5pm Sun) Haarlem's modern and contemporary art museum
resides within two historic 'halls': the
17th-century Dutch Renaissance Vleeshal, a
former meat market and the sole place that
meat was allowed to be sold in Haarlem from
the 17th through to the 19th century, and the
neoclassical Verweyhal (fish house). Eclectic
exhibits rotate every three months and range
from Dutch impressionists and CoBrA artists
to innovative video, installation art and photography by cutting-edge international artists.

★ **Frans Hals Museum** GALLERY
(www.franshalsmuseum.nl; Groot Heiligland 62;
adult/child €12.50/free; ⊙11am-5pm Tue-Sat, from
noon Sun) A short stroll south of Grote Markt,
the Frans Hals Museum is a must for anyone
interested in the Dutch Masters. Located in
the poorhouse where Hals spent his final
years, the collection focuses on the 17th-
century Haarlem School; its pride and joy are
eight group portraits of the civic guard that
reveal Hals' exceptional attention to mood
and psychological tone. Look out for works
by other greats such as Pieter Brueghel the
Younger and Jacob van Ruysdael.

Among the museum's other treasures are
the works of Hals' teacher, Flemish artist
Carel van Mander: stunning illustrations of
the human anatomy, all ceiling-high with
biblical and mythological references.

Corrie ten Boom House HISTORIC BUILDING
(www.corrietenboom.com; Barteljorisstraat 19; admission by donation; ⊙10am-3pm Apr-Oct, 11am-
2.30pm Nov-Mar) Also known as 'the hiding
place', the Corrie ten Boom House is named
for the matriarch of a family that lived in the
house during WWII. Using a secret compart-
ment in her bedroom, she hid hundreds of
Jews and Dutch resistors until they could be
spirited to safety. In 1944 the family was be-
trayed and sent to concentration camps where
three died. Later, Corrie ten Boom toured the
world preaching peace. English-language
tours take place every 90 minutes.

Proveniershuis HISTORIC BUILDING
(off Grote Houtstraat; ⊙10am-5pm Mon-Sat)
FREE Off Grote Houtstraat to the southwest
of Grote Markt is one of Haarlem's prettiest
buildings, the Proveniershuis. It started life
as a *hofje* (almshouse) and became the former headquarters of St Joris Doelen (the
Civic Guard of St George).

Teylers Museum MUSEUM
(www.teylersmuseum.nl; Spaarne 16; adult/child
€12/2; ⊙10am-5pm Tue-Sat, 11am-5pm Sun)
Dating from 1778, Teylers is the country's
oldest continuously operating museum. Its
array of whiz-bang inventions include an
18th-century electrostatic machine that con-
jures up visions of mad scientists. The eclectic collection also has paintings from the
Dutch and French schools; a magnificent,
sky-lighted Ovale Zaal (Oval Room) displays
natural-history specimens in elegant glass
cases on two levels. Temporary exhibitions
regularly take place.

Nieuwe Kerk CHURCH
(Nieuwe Kerksplein; ⊙10am-5pm Mon-Sat) FREE
Walk down charming Korte Houtstraat to
find the 17th-century Nieuwe Kerk; the ornate tower by Lieven de Key is supported by
a rather boxy design by Jacob van Campen.

ᏟᎦ Tours

Haarlem Canal Tours CANAL TOUR
(www.haarlemcanaltours.com; opposite Spaarne
17; tour per person €13.50; ⊙tours 10am-7pm Apr-
Sep) Fun 1¼-hour tours in vintage open-top
boats depart every 90 minutes.

Ꮮ═ Sleeping

★ **Hello I'm Local**
Boutique Hostel HOSTEL €
(☎844 69 16; www.helloimlocal.com; Spiegelstraat
4; dm €23-33, s/d/tr/q from €75/79/121.50/139; ☎)
In a charming neighbourhood on the edge of
the centre, this quirkily named hostel inside
a traditional brick Dutch house has 56 beds
across 12 rooms, and homey amenities including a patio and open fireplace. All rooms have
showers but some share toilet facilities. Upper
capsule-like timber bunks are accessed by ladder. Bike rental is available for €12 per day.

Ambassador City Centre Hotel HOTEL €
(☎512 53 00; www.ambassadorcitycentrehotel.nl;
Oude Groenmarkt 20; d/tr/f from €84/126/136;
☎) The Ambassador City Centre Hotel's 65
tasteful, individually designed rooms spread
over an entire block near the Grote Kerk. It
also has one studio apartment with a kitchenette (double from €99; minimum two-
night stay).

Stempels HOTEL €€
(☎512 39 10; www.stempelsinhaarlem.nl; Klokhu-
isplein 9; s/d/ste from €97.50/115/157.50; ☎)
A gorgeous old printing house on the east
side of the Grote Kerk shelters 17 spacious

Haarlem

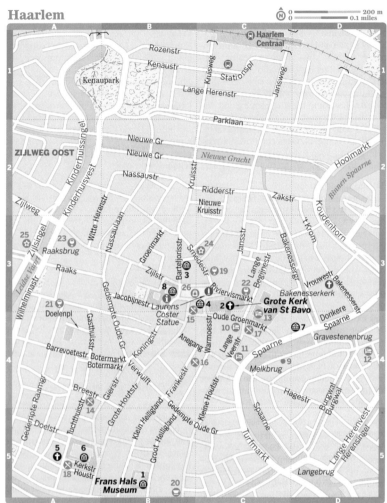

rooms with high ceilings and stark, artistic decor; front rooms face Grote Kerk van St Bavo. Breakfast costs €12.50.

★ **Brasss Hotel Suites** BOUTIQUE HOTEL €€€
(☑ 542 78 04; http://brassshaarlem.nl; Korte Veerstraat 1; ste from €175; ❋ ☎) Each of the 10 luxurious suites at this jewel are named for sea creatures (Octopus, Sardine, Langoustine, Mackerel et al) except for Diamonds of the Sea, which comes with its own sauna. All have heavenly king-size beds, rain showers and velvety bathrobes. Service surpasses expectations.

✖ Eating

Cafes and restaurants abound along Zijlstraat, Spaarne and especially Lange Veerstraat, but you'll find gems scattered all over town.

De Haerlemsche Vlaamse FAST FOOD €
(Spekstraat 3; frites €2.30-4.40; ☉ 9am-6.30pm Mon-Fri, 11am-5.30pm Sat, noon-5.30pm Sun) Line up at this local institution for a cone of crispy, golden fries made from fresh potatoes and one of a dozen sauces, including three kinds of mayonnaise.

Haarlem

★**Brick** MODERN EUROPEAN €€

(☑551 18 70; www.restaurantbrick.nl; Breestraat 24-26; mains lunch €7.50-10.50, dinner €15.50-21.50; ☺noon-10pm Tue-Sun) You can watch Brick's chefs creating inspired dishes such as duck and hazelnut ravioli with black truffle and foie gras sauce, not only from the street-level dining room but also the 1st-floor space, which has a glass floor directly above the open kitchen. There are pavement tables out front but in summer the best seats are on the roof terrace.

★**Restaurant Mr & Mrs** INTERNATIONAL €€

(☑531 59 35; www.restaurantmrandmrs.nl; Lange Veerstraat 4; small plates €9-12, 4-/5-/6-course menu €36/44/52; ☺5-10pm) Unexpectedly gastronomic cooking at this tiny restaurant is artfully conceived and presented. Small hot and cold plates designed for sharing might include steak tartare with black truffles, baby octopus with mango and jalapeño, mackerel with avocado dressing and caviar, hoisin-marinated steak with foie gras and portobello mushrooms, and crème brûlée with whisky meringue. Definitely book ahead.

De Lachende Javaan INDONESIAN €€

(☑532 87 92; www.delachendejavaan.com; Frankestraat 27; mains €11-21.50, rijsttafel per person €23-27.50; ☺5-10pm Tue-Sun) The interior of this old merchant's house glows from stained-glass windows and reflections off the vintage art from Java. The rijsttafel (array of dishes served with rice) is great value.

't Goede Uur BISTRO €€

(☑531 11 74; http://hetgoedeuur.nl; Korte Houtstraat 1; mains €16-18.50; ☺5-11pm Tue-Sun) Six different types of fondue made from organic Gouda and Gruyère, which it has been bubbling up for more than four decades, is the speciality of this rustic little bistro tucked away on one of Haarlem's loveliest, leafiest backstreets.

🍺 Drinking & Nightlife

★**Jopenkerk** BREWERY

(www.jopenkerk.nl; Gedempte Voldersgracht 2; ☺brewery & cafe 10am-1am, restaurant 5.30pm-late Tue-Sat) Haarlem's most atmospheric place to drink is this independent brewery inside a stained-glass-windowed, 1910 church. Enjoy brews such as citrusy Hopen, fruity Lente Bier or chocolatey Koyt along with classic Dutch bar snacks (*bitterballen* or croquettes, cheeses) beneath the gleaming copper vats. Or head to the mezzanine for dishes made from locally sourced, seasonal ingredients and Jopenkerk's beers, with pairings available.

Proeflokaal in den Uiver BROWN CAFE

(www.indenuiver.nl; Riviervischmarkt 13; ☺4pm-1am Mon-Wed, to 2am Thu-Sat, to midnight Sun) One of many atmospheric places overlooking the Grote Markt, this nautical-themed place has shipping knick-knacks and a schooner sailing right over the bar. Live jazz often plays; check the online agenda for dates.

BEVERWIJK

De Bazaar Beverwijk (www.debazaar. nl; Montageweg 35, Beverwijk; ⊙8.30am-6pm Sat & Sun) Every weekend up to 80,000 bargain hunters flock to the town of Beverwijk to visit the covered Bazaar Beverwijk, one of Europe's largest ethnic markets with 2000-plus vendors and 65 eateries. Piled high are Arabian foods and spices, Turkish rugs, garments and handcrafted ornaments. The liveliest of the three biggest halls is the Zwarte Markt, an enormous flea market with a carnival atmosphere.

Parking (per day €5) becomes a problem after 9.30am. Trains run from Amsterdam Centraal (€5.70, 40 minutes, four hourly) and Haarlem €3.10, 15 minutes, up to four hourly) to Beverwijk from where it's a 1km walk.

Utiltje Bar BAR
(http://brouwerijhetuiltje.nl; Zijlstraat 18; ⊙2pm-midnight Tue-Thu & Sun, to 2am Fri & Sat) More than 30 seasonally changing craft beers from around the world are on tap at this passionate beer specialist, with many more by the bottle.

Bar Wigbolt BAR
(www.barwigbolt.nl; Smedestraat 41; ⊙6.30pm-1am Wed & Thu, 4pm-2.30am Fri & Sat, 4pm-1am Sun) Just off the Grote Markt, you can choose from more than 100 different vodkas and cocktails including Haarlem Mule (vodka, ginger beer and lime juice in a copper cup), Thunder Thom (toffee-infused vodka, apple and lemon juice), Monkey Jam Shoulder (whisky, lime juice and strawberry jam) and Bob's Cup of Tea (tequila, Cointreau, OJ and raspberry tea, served in a teapot).

Blender CAFE
(http://blender-haarlem.nl; Klein Houtstraat 138; ⊙8am-9pm Mon-Fri, 9am-9pm Sat & Sun) Amazing fruit juices and smoothies with superfoods such as spirulina, hemp seeds, goji berries and bee pollen are available all day at this groovy spot, as well as health-conscious meals. From noon it also serves organic wines.

☆ Entertainment

Café Stiels LIVE MUSIC
(www.stiels.nl; Smedestraat 21; ⊙8pm-2am Sun-Wed, to 3am Thu, to 4am Fri & Sat) Bands play jazz and rhythm and blues on the back stage almost every night of the week from 10pm onward, to as late as 4am on weekends.

Patronaat LIVE MUSIC
(www.patronaat.nl; Zijlsingel 2; ⊙hours vary) Haarlem's top music and dance club attracts bands with banging tunes. Events in this cavernous venue usually start around 9pm.

🛍 Shopping

★ Grote Markt MARKET
(Grote Markt; ⊙10am-2pm Mon & Sat) Haarlem is at its liveliest during its regular Monday and, especially, Saturday market, when its namesake square fills with stalls selling fresh produce, cheese, preserves, spices, nuts and ready-to-eat Dutch and international snacks, as well as vintage and new clothes, bags, accessories and antiques.

ℹ Information

Tourist office (VVV; ☑531 73 25; www.haarlemmarketing.nl; Grote Markt 2; ⊙9.30am-5.30pm Mon-Fri, 9.30am-5pm Sat, noon-4pm Sun Apr-Sep, 1-5.30pm Mon, 9.30am-5.30pm Tue-Fri, 10am-5pm Sat Oct-Mar) The tourist office sells discount museum tickets.

ℹ Getting There & Away

BICYCLE

Haarlem is linked to Amsterdam by national route **LF20** over a distance of 25km. Given the heavy urbanisation in the area this is not exactly a pastoral ride. Just west you can link up with the much more bucolic **LF1**, which follows the coast north and south.

Rent a Bike Haarlem (☑023-542 11 95; www.rentabikehaarlem.nl; Lange Herenstraat 36; bike rental per day from €10; ⊙9am-5.30pm).

BUS

Bus 300 links Haarlem train station and Schiphol Airport (50 minutes, six daily) between 5.30am and 1am.

TRAIN

Haarlem's 1908 art nouveau station is served by frequent trains linking Amsterdam and Rotterdam.

Destination	Price (€)	Duration (min)	Frequency (per hour)
Alkmaar	6.70	30-50	4
Amsterdam	4.10	15	4-8
Den Haag	8.20	40	4-6
Rotterdam	11.90	60	4-6

Around Haarlem

Zuid-Kennemerland National Park

Some 3800 hectares of classic Dutch coastal dunes are being restored in this vast patch of nature in the midst of the busy Randstad. De Zandwaaier (☑ 023-541 11 23; www.np-zuidkennemerland.nl; Zeeweg 12; ⊘ 10am-5pm Tue-Sun) FREE, the park's visitor centre, has nature displays and is a good source of information, with a range of detailed walking and cycling maps including a great 35km circuit. There are car parks at the Koevlak and Parnassia entrances, from where paths lead into the reserve. Trails snake through hilltop copses of Corsican firs and valleys of low-lying thickets; at the western edge you come to a massive barrier of golden sand that's 1000 years old.

Spring sees the dunes sprout desert orchids, the bright rosettes of the century weed and the white-blooming grass of Parnassus. Red foxes, fallow deer and many species of birds are native to the area. Bats slumber in the park's abandoned bunkers before appearing at dusk.

The Vogelmeer lake has a bird-observation hut above the south shore. The artificial lake 't Wed teems with bathers in summer. Lookout points, with evocative names such as Hazenberg (Hare Mountain), are scattered throughout. At 50m, the Kopje van Bloemendaal is the highest dune in the country, just outside the eastern border of the park, with views of the sea and Amsterdam.

Inside the park, the WWII cemetery Eerebegraafplaats Bloemendaal (☑ 020-660 19 45; www.eerebegraafplaatsbloemendaal.eu; Zeeweg 26; ⊘ 9am-6pm Apr-Sep, to 5pm Oct-Mar) FREE, 5km west of Haarlem, is the resting place of 372 members of the Dutch resistance. Its walled compound in the dunes is isolated from the rest of the park and accessible only via the main road.

Take bus 81 (15 minutes, two hourly) from Haarlem train station or cycle/drive the N200 towards Bloemendaal aan Zee.

Zaanse Schans

Zaanse Schans Windmills   WINDMILLS
(www.dezaanseschans.nl; site free, per windmill adult/child €4/2; ⊘ windmills 10am-5pm Apr-Nov, hours vary Dec-Mar) The working, inhabited village Zaanse Schans functions as an open-air windmill gallery on the Zaan River. Popular with tourists, its mills are completely authentic and operated with enthusiasm and love. You can explore the windmills at will, seeing the vast moving parts first-hand.

The impressive Zaans Museum (☑ 075-616 28 62; www.zaansmuseum.nl; Schansend 7; adult/child €9/5; ⊘ 10am-5pm Apr-Nov, hours vary Dec-Mar) shows how wind and water were harnessed.

Trains (€3.10, 17 minutes, four per hour) run from Amsterdam Centraal Station (direction Alkmaar) to Koog Zaandijk, from where it's a well-signposted 1.5km walk.

The mill with paint pigments for sale will delight artists – you can see the actual materials used in producing Renaissance masterpieces turned into powders. Ask to see the storeroom where ground pigments are for sale.

The other buildings have been brought here from all over the country to re-create a 17th-century community. There's an early Albert Heijn market, a cheesemaker, and a popular clog factory that turns out wooden shoes as if grinding keys (which has a

---

HAARLEM'S BEACHES

Just 5km west of Haarlem's peaceful outskirts lies Zandvoort, a popular seaside resort. It's not pretty as beach towns go, and drab apartment blocks line the main drag, but its proximity to Amsterdam ensures a steady flow of pleasure-seekers.

About 3km north of Zandvoort is Bloemendaal aan Zee, a much less developed spot with a handful of restaurants and cafes and uninterrupted beaches. It's frequented by those looking for a semblance of peace and quiet away from the hustle and bustle of its bigger neighbour to the south.

The closest accommodation to Bloemendaal is De Lakens, but Zandvoort is littered with accommodation.

Trains link Zandvoort to Amsterdam Centraal Station twice hourly (€5.40, 30 minutes) via Haarlem (€2.20, 10 minutes).

surprisingly interesting museum). The engaging pewtersmith will explain the story behind dozens of tiny figures while the soft metal sets in the moulds.

Once you've finished exploring the village, take a **boat** (adult/child €5/3; ⊙ 9am-6pm May-Sep) across the Zaan River. It runs on demand.

Waterland Region

⚑ 075

Time moves slowly in this rural area that starts only 9km north of Amsterdam. Fields of green are watched by herons standing motionless alongside watery furrows amid surrounding farmland. It's glorious cycling country, with plenty to see, including the picturesque towns of Monnickendam, Marken and Edam as well as touristy Volendam.

ℹ Getting There & Around

BICYCLE

The best way to experience the Waterland area is by bike; pick up a rental in Amsterdam and head north on the national bike route **LF7**.

BUS

Regional buses from Amsterdam Centraal are covered with a **Waterland Ticket**.

Monnickendam

⚑ 0299 / POP 9915

Monnickendam gained its name from the Benedictines, who built a dam here, and traces its roots back to 1356. Since the demise of its fishing industry, it has transformed itself into an upmarket port for yachts and sailors.

The beautiful old fishing trawlers mainly operate pleasure cruises. History still pervades the narrow lanes around the shipyards.

◉ Sights

Along the main street, **Noordeinde**, old brick houses tilt at crazy angles as they sink into the soggy ground.

As you stroll the lanes, look for **gable stones** on buildings – many have a story to tell. The one at Kerkstraat 32 dates to 1620, the one at Kerkstraat 12 tells of the five Jews successfully hidden in the building for the duration of WWII.

Speeltoren   HISTORIC BUILDING
(Noordeinde 4) Monnickendam's trademark building is the 15th-century Speeltoren, an

---

ℹ WATERLAND TICKET

If you're planning a day trip by bus north of Amsterdam around the Waterland region, including Monnickendam, Marken and Volendam, as well as Hoorn, save money by purchasing a Waterland Ticket (€10). Available from bus drivers, this great-value pass allows a day's unlimited travel on buses 110, 301, 306, 312, 314, 315, 316 and 319.

---

elegant, Italianate clock tower and former town hall. The tower's 17th-century glockenspiel (carillon) – the world's oldest – performs at 11am and noon on Saturday, when its four mechanical knights prance in the open wooden window twice before retiring.

Inside the clock tower, the newly renovated **Museum De Speeltoren** (www.despeeltoren.nl; Noordeinde 4; adult/child €4.50/3; ⊙ 11am-5pm Tue-Sun Apr-Oct, Sat & Sun Nov-Mar) shows the region through five eras of human occupation and allows you to see the amazing old mechanism that powers the clock.

Grote Kerk   CHURCH
(www.grotekerkmonnickendam.nl; De Zarken; ⊙ 11am-4pm Tue-Sat, 1-4pm Sun May-Oct, hours vary Nov-Feb) FREE The Gothic Grote Kerk, on the southern outskirts of town, is renowned for its triple nave, tower galleries and a dazzling oak choir screen dating from the 16th century. It's impossible to miss the enormous organ in the nave.

Waag   HISTORIC BUILDING
(Middendam 5-7) On the town's central canal, the Waag (weigh house) was the focal point of local economic life. In 1905 it was given grand Tuscan columns, a common trick of the day designed to make it look much older and more impressive. It's now a touristy restaurant.

In de Bonte Os   HISTORIC BUILDING
(Coloured Ox; Noordeinde 26) In de Bonte Os is the only house that's left in its original 17th-century state. In the days before proper glass, the curious vertical shutters at street level were made to let in air and light. If you're interested in staying here, it's listed on Airbnb (www.airbnb.com).

🕴 Activities

As elsewhere on the IJsselmeer, large pleasure boats are popular in Monnickendam.

The harbour is filled with splendid old *tjalken, botters* and *klippers,* historic boats available for hire (as are skippers if need be).

Bootvloot
BOATING

($06 5494 2657; www.bootvloot.nl; Hemmeland 1; half-/full-day rentals from €45/60; 10am-5.30pm Apr-Oct) Small two- to four-person sailboats are available to rent at Bootvloot. It's a 500m walk through the leafy Hemmeland recreation area northeast of Monnickendam marina – follow the sign 'Zeilbootverhuur'.

🍽 Sleeping & Eating

Smoked eel (caught in the IJsselmeer) is a traditional local delicacy. Look for a remaining eel smokehouse on Havenstraat.

★ Posthoorn
BOUTIQUE HOTEL €€€

($0299-654 598; www.posthoorn.eu; Noordeinde 43; d €155-250; 🐾) This beautifully restored building dates to 1697 but the owners suspect it might be older. The six romantic rooms blend traditional comforts with modern style, such as pedestal basins. The long-standing Michelin-star restaurant ($0299-654 598; www.posthoorn.eu; Noordeinde 43; 5-/6-course menu €55/60, paired wines extra €33/40; 6-11pm Tue-Thu, 6pm-midnight Fri & Sat, noon-11pm Sun; 🐾) uses local produce to create stunning multicourse menus that change daily. Book rooms and courtyard dining in advance on weekends.

Theetuin Overleek
CAFE

($0299-652 735; www.theetuinoverleek.nl; Overleek 6a; dishes €4.50-7.50, high tea per person €23.50; 10am-5pm Jul & Aug, Wed-Sun May, Jun & Sep, Sat & Sun Oct-Apr) Right by the water's edge, this wooden teahouse is a charming spot to indulge in high tea, but you can just drop by for light bites such as sandwiches and cakes. It also rents electric boats (per hour €17.50) to explore the waterways and can provide packed picnic lunches (€12.50).

🛍 Shopping

Avontuur in Miniatuur
TOYS, HANDICRAFTS

($0299-652 085; www.avontuurinminiatuur.nl; Noordeinde 76; 10am-5pm Fri & Sat, by appointment Sun-Thu) Doll's houses (and everything you need to furnish, decorate and populate them) are the speciality of this miniature wonderland. When you visit, you may see craftspeople sitting around the shop's large table creating the tiny pieces (many, though not all, are handmade here).

ℹ Information

Tourist office (VVV; $0299-820 046; www.vvv-waterland.nl; Zuideinde 2; 10am-5pm) Waterland's small but excellent regional tourism office can recommend walks, obscure attractions and almost anything fun on the water.

ℹ Getting There & Around

BICYCLE
Like the paths throughout Waterland, good bike routes abound, especially national route **LF21**, which starts in Amsterdam and follows rural dykes along the IJsselmeer. **Ber Koning** ($0299-651 267; www.berkonig.nl; Noordeinde 12; per day €12.50; 9am-8pm Tue-Sat Apr-Sep, to 6pm Tue-Fri, to 4pm Sat Oct-Mar) rents bicycles.

BUS
Bus 315 (25 minutes, up to three per hour), covered on the **Waterland Ticket**, links the centre of Monnickendam to Amsterdam Centraal Station.

Marken

$0299 / POP 1810

Across Gouwzee Bay lies scenic Marken with a small and determined population. It was an isolated island in the Zuiderzee until 1957 when a causeway linked up with the mainland, effectively turning it into a museum-piece village. However, it still manages to exude a fishing-village vibe (well-used wooden shoes sit outside houses), and the car-free centre helps keep at least some of the hordes at bay.

◎ Sights

The colourful **Kerkbuurt** in the village's northeast is the most authentic area, with tarred or painted houses raised on pilings to escape the Zuiderzee floods. The **Havenbuurt** harbourside area is home to most of the souvenir shops and restaurants.

Marker Museum
MUSEUM

(www.markermuseum.nl; Kerkbuurt 44; adult/child €2.50/1.25; 10am-5pm Mon-Sat, noon-4pm Sun Apr-Oct) A row of eel-smoking houses in the Kerkbuurt area have been converted into the Marker Museum, which delves into Marken's history and includes the re-created interior of a fisherman's home, with a wealth of personal odds and ends. It sells a walking-tour brochure (€1), which guides you around the stout wooden structures that line the intricate pattern of lanes.

Marken Kerk CHURCH

(Buurterstraat; ⊘9am-5pm Mon-Sat, noon-4pm Sun Apr-Oct) **FREE** Marken's *kerk* (church) is filled with ship models designed to attract grace to local seamen.

🛏 Sleeping & Eating

★ Hof Van Marken HOTEL €€

(✎ 0299-601 300; www.hofvanmarken.nl; Buurt II 15; s/d from €89/99) Hof Van Marken has big beds, fluffy pillows and heavenly duvets. The seven cosy, pastel-hued rooms reflect this region where land and water blend in the mist. Its **restaurant** serves fresh, stylish takes on local produce and seafood. Book well ahead for both.

ℹ Getting There & Away

If you're driving, you'll need to park in the mandatory open-air car park at the village entrance (per day €5).

BICYCLE

The 8km ride along the dyke from Monnickendam has moody sea views.

BUS

Bus 311 links Marken with Amsterdam (40 minutes, half-hourly) via Monnickendam (12 minutes); it's covered by the **Waterland Ticket** (p108).

FERRY

Marken Express Ferry (www.markenexpress. nl; adult/child return €10/7; ⊘10.30am-6pm Mar-Sep) The Marken Express makes the 45-minute-long crossing from Volendam to Marken every 45 minutes. In Volendam the ferry leaves from the docks at Havendijkje.

Volendam

✎ 0299 / POP 22,000

A former fishing port turned unashamedly tacky tourist trap, Volendam is certainly quaint, with its rows of wooden houses and locals who don traditional dress for church and festive events, but the harbour is awash with kitschy souvenir shops, dress-up-in-Dutch-traditional-costume photo booths, a virtual-reality walk through old Volendam, a huge cheese shop/museum, fish stands, *frites* stands and rapacious seagulls. On weekends it swarms with visitors.

◉ Sights

Volendams Museum MUSEUM

(www.volendamsmuseum.nl; Zeestraat 41; adult/child €3/1.75; ⊘10am-5pm Apr-Oct) Local culture

is covered at Volendam's history museum with traditional costumes, prints, paintings of harbour scenes and even a cramped ship's sleeping quarters, but this place is really devoted to cigar aficionados: some 11 million bands are plastered on its walls.

✖ Eating

Seafood is the undisputed king in Volendam, and the harbour overflows with vendors offering smoked cod, eel, herring and tiny shrimp.

ℹ Information

Tourist office (VVV; ✎ 0299-363 747; www. vvv-volendam.nl; Zeestraat 37; ⊘10am-5pm Mon-Sat, 11am-3pm Sun Apr-Oct, 11am-4pm Mon & Wed-Sat, 11am-3pm Sun Nov-Mar) Regional accommodation info and cycling maps are available at Volendam's busy tourist office.

ℹ Getting There & Around

BICYCLE

National bike route **LF21** passes right along the harbour; Monnickendam is 6km south. Amsterdam lies 22km southwest.

BUS

Buses 110 and 316 link Volendam to Amsterdam (25 minutes) and Edam (eight minutes) every 30 minutes; they're covered on the **Waterland Ticket** (p108).

Edam

✎ 0299 / POP 7380

Once a renowned whaling port – in its 17th-century heyday it had 33 shipyards that built the fleet of legendary admiral Michiel de Ruyter – this scenic little town is another of Noord-Holland's treasures. With its old shipping warehouses, quiet cobblestone streets, hand-operated drawbridges and picture-perfect canals, it's enchanting for a stroll. It's quite astounding that so many tourists flock to Volendam, only 2km away, instead, unless Edam's cheese market is on.

◉ Sights & Activities

Kaasmarkt HISTORIC SITE

(Cheese Market; Kaasmarkt; ⊘10.30am-12.30pm Wed Jul–mid-Aug) In the 16th century Willem van Oranje bestowed on Edam the right to hold a Kaasmarkt, which was the town's economic anchor right through to the 1920s. At its peak, 250,000 rounds of cheese were sold here every year. On the western side of Kaasmarkt stands the 1778 **Kaaswaag** (⊘10am-5pm

Edam

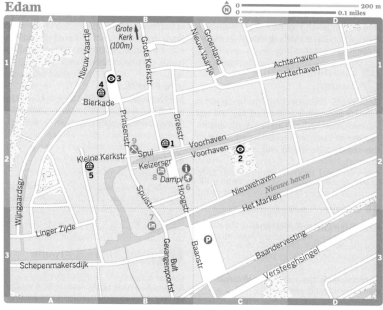

Apr–Sep) **FREE**, the cheese weigh house, which has a display about the town's chief product. Edam's cheese market is smaller than the one in Alkmaar but equally touristy.

Gestam   CHEESE PRODUCER
(www.gestam.com; Voorhaven 127; ⊙10am-4pm Wed & Fri) Sample an astonishing array of cheeses at the wonderful and barely commercial Gestam, a warehouse for regional producers.

Edams Museum   MUSEUM
(www.edamsmuseum.nl; museum Damplein 8, annex Damplein 1; adult/child €5/3; ⊙10am-4.30pm Tue-Sat, 1-4.30pm Sun Apr–late Oct) The Edams Museum's furnishings, porcelain and silverware spread over three cramped floors. Its floating cellar is a remarkable pantry that rises and falls with the river's swell to reduce stress on the structure above. The ornate 1540 brick building is Edam's oldest. Across the canal in an annex in the 1737 town hall, above the tourist office, you'll find more exhibits; among some famous paintings there is an unknown artist's *Tall Girl*, depicting an 8' 4" girl (allegedly the tallest woman ever born).

Grote Kerk   CHURCH
(www.grotekerkedam.nl; Grote Kerkstraat 57; tower €2; ⊙1.30-5pm early Apr–late Oct) **FREE** The 15th-century Grote Kerk bears witness to the

vagaries of Dutch weather. Its 32 dazzling stained-glass windows bearing coats of arms and historical scenes were added after 1602, when the church burnt to a cinder after a lightning strike. Its tower can be climbed for views of the surrounds.

Speeltoren   HISTORIC BUILDING
(Kleine Kerkstraat) Leaning over Kleine Kerkstraat about 100m south of Grote Kerk, the Speeltoren is all that remains of the 15th-century Kleine Kerk.

Fluisterbootjes BOATING
(Whisper Boats; www.fluisterbootverhuur-edam.
nl; VVV, Damplein 1; per hour €23; ⏱9am-5pm
Apr–mid-Oct) Glide through Edam's canals in
a small electric boat you pilot yourself. Pay
and pick up the key from the tourist office.

☞ Tours

Boat Tours BOAT TOUR
(tour €6; ⏱noon & 2pm Wed Jul & Aug) Edam's
tourist office organises 1½-hour tours on
tuindersvelts (small, open-topped boats) in
summer, weather permitting.

Tourist Office Walking Tours WALKING TOUR
(adult/child €4/2; ⏱2pm Sat) One-hour walking tours through the town depart from the
tourist office.

🛏 Sleeping & Eating
The tourist office has a list of private accommodation and farm stays from €25 per
person.

Along with the excellent Gestam (p111)
there are several places to buy cheese and
other picnic supplies.

L'Auberge Dam Hotel BOUTIQUE HOTEL €€
(✆0299-371 766; www.damhotel.nl; Keizersgracht
1; d from €125; 🛜) In the heart of Edam, this
art- and antique-filled hotel makes a romantic retreat. Some of its 11 rooms are on the
small side, but that's counterbalanced by
huge beds and spiffing contemporary bathrooms. Its grand *café* spills onto the main
square; there's also an elegant bistro on-site.

<hr>

WORTH A TRIP

SCENIC DRIVE: DYKES & WINDMILLS

Midway between Edam and Alkmaar,
the village of De Rijp on the N244 is at
the south end of several good drives
and rides along dykes that give an excellent feel for just how low the land is
compared to the waterways coursing
between the earthen walls.

The Oostdijk–Westdijk road travels
north 6km to the hamlet of Schermer-
horn on the N243. Just west, another
dyke road runs parallel and meanders
past several windmills. Both are narrow
and the domain of cyclists and sheep, so
if you're in a car, go slow.

De Fortuna HOTEL €€
(✆0299-371 671; www.fortuna-edam.nl; Spuistraat 3;
s/d/tr/f from €92.50/102.50/157.50/167.50; 🛜) An
Edam gem straight out of an old Dutch painting, De Fortuna's 23 cute rooms have bathrooms best described as snug. Its delightful
restaurant (✆0299-371 671; www.fortuna-edam.
nl; Spuistraat 3; mains lunch €6-20, dinner €22.50
3-/4-/5-course menu €36/43.50/49.50; ⏱kitchen
noon-3pm & 6-9.30pm; 🛜) serves modern European dishes such as beetroot tartare with
smoked-mushroom mayo and red fish with
langoustine bisque amid oil paintings, large
bay windows and buffed leather seats. There
are lush gardens and a waterside terrace.

Edammer Kaaswinkel DELI €
(www.edamcheeseshop.com; Spui 8; ⏱9am-
6pm Mon-Fri, 8.30am-5pm Sat, 9.30am-5pm Sun)
Edammer Kaaswinkel has a wide variety of
cheese as well as a lush adjoining deli.

ℹ Information
Tourist office (VVV; ✆0299-315 125; www.
vvv-edam.nl; Damplein 1; ⏱10am-5pm Mon-
Sat, 11am-4pm Sun Jul & Aug, 10am-5pm
Mon-Sat Apr-Jun, Sep & Oct, noon-4pm Mon,
10am-3pm Tue-Thu, 10am-4pm Fri & Sat Nov-
Mar) Edam's tourist office is located inside
the splendid 18th-century town hall. Pick up
the English-language booklet, *A Stroll Through
Edam* (€2.50), for a 90-minute self-guided tour.

ℹ Getting There & Around

BICYCLE
Edam is on national bike route **LF21**; the many
IJsselmeer dykes make for excellent riding.
Ton Tweewielers (✆0299-371 922; www.
tontweewielers.nl; Schepenmakersdijk 6; bike/
electric bike per day €9/19.50; ⏱8.30am-6pm
Mon-Sat, 9.30am-5pm Sun Apr–mid Sep) Rents
bikes.

BUS
Buses 110 and 316 link Edam with Amsterdam
(35 minutes) via Volendam every 30 minutes;
they're covered on a **Waterland Ticket** (p108).

<hr>

Alkmaar
✆072 / POP 95,076

On Friday mornings from April to early
September, Alkmaar's canal-ringed centre
throngs with tourists eager to catch a glimpse
of the city's famous cheese market. It's a genuine spectacle but even if it's not on, the town
is an engaging place to visit any time of the
year.

Alkmaar

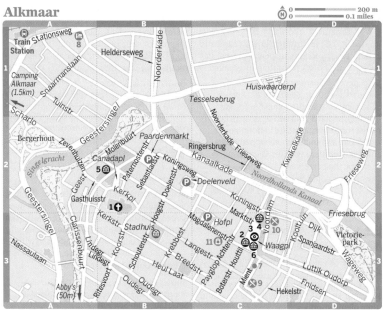

The city holds a special place in Dutch hearts as the first town, in 1573, to repel occupying Spanish troops; locals opened the locks and flooded the area with seawater, forcing the perplexed invaders to retreat. The victory won the town weighing rights, which laid the foundation for its cheese market.

◉ Sights

Before exploring the city, it's worth purchasing a copy of the *Walking Tour of the Town Among the Historic Buildings* booklet (€2.50) from the tourist office. It covers historical buildings such as the Renaissance Stadhuis in extensive detail.

Waaggebouw   HISTORIC BUILDING
(Weigh House; Waagplein 2; ☉ carillon 6.30pm & 7.30pm Thu, 11am & noon Fri, noon & 1pm Sat mid-Apr–mid-Sep) Built as a chapel in the 14th century, the Waaggebouw was pressed into service as a weigh house two centuries later. This handsome building houses the tourist office and the **Hollands Kaasmuseum** (Dutch Cheese Museum; www.kaasmuseum.nl; Waagplein 2; adult/child €3/1.50; ☉ 10am-4pm Mon-Sat Apr-Oct, to 4pm Sat Nov-Mar), with a reverential display of cheesemaking utensils, photos and a curious stock of paintings by 16th-century female artists.

DON'T MISS

ALKMAAR'S CHEESE MARKET

Kaasmarkt (Cheese Market; Waagplein; ⊘10am-noon Fri Apr–early Sep) On Friday mornings, waxed rounds of *kaas* (cheese) are ceremoniously stacked on the main square. Soon, porters appear in colourful hats (denoting the cheese guild), and dealers in white smocks insert a hollow rod to extract a cheese sample, and sniff and crumble to check fat and moisture content. Once deals are struck, the porters whisk the cheeses on wooden sledges to the old cheese scale. It's primarily for show, but as living relics go it's both fascinating and entertaining.

The mechanical tower **carillon** springs to life with jousting knights.

Stedelijk Museum   MUSEUM
(http://stedelijkmuseumalkmaar.nl; Canadaplein 1; adult/child €10/free; ⊘10am-5pm Tue-Sun) The Stedelijk Museum's collection of oil paintings by Dutch Masters, including impressive life-sized portraits of Alkmaar nobles, is alone worth the entry fee. Other works show the city in post–Golden Age decline; sombre scenes of almswomen caring for the poor recall how the church's role grew as trade declined. Modern works on display include Charley Toorop's odd oil painting of the Alkmaar cheese market; her cheese-bearers with grotesque features remain controversial.

Grote Kerk   CHURCH
(www.grotekerkalkmaar.nl; Kerkplein; ⊘11am-5pm Tue-Sun Jun-Aug, Thu-Sat mid-Apr–May) **FREE** Alkmaar's Grote Kerk is renowned for its organs. The most famous is the little 'Swallow Organ' (1511) in the north ambulatory. The 17th-century organ built by Jaco van Campen dominates the nave. Organ recitals – which will thrill any fan of 1930s horror movies – take place on Wednesday evenings and at noon on days when the church is open. The pastel stained-glass windows bathe the interior in spring colour.

Nationaal Biermuseum   MUSEUM
(www.biermuseum.nl; Houttil 1; adult/child €4/2; ⊘10.30am-4.30pm Mon-Sat Jun-Aug, 1-4pm Mon-Sat Sep-May) Housed in the atmospheric old De Boom brewery, the Nationaal Biermuseum has a decent collection of beer-making equipment and wax dummies showing how the suds were made. The video

of Dutch beer commercials since the 1950s will have you in stitches. After your tour, head to the sociable bar, De Boom.

☞ Tours

Grachtenrondvaart Alkmaar   CANAL TOUR
(www.rondvaartalkmaar.nl; Mient; adult/child €6/4.50; ⊘hourly 11am-5pm Apr-Oct) Scenic canal tours with multilingual commentary depart from Mient, near the Waagplein, and last 45 minutes.

🛏 Sleeping

Camping Alkmaar   CAMPGROUND **€**
(☎072-511 69 24; www.campingalkmaar.nl; Bergerweg 201; campsites €23-27, cabins €45; 🛜) This year-round campground lies in a pleasant copse convenient to the ring road, 1km northwest of the train station. Tent sites are sheltered; wooden cabins (without bathrooms) sleep two people. Take bus 6 to Hogeschool (10 minutes).

Hotel Stad en Land   HOTEL **€€**
(☎072-512 39 11; www.stadenlandhotelalkmaar.nl; Stationsweg 92-94; s/d/tr/f from €62.50/85/115/130; 🛜) Close to the train station, with 23 basic yet comfy rooms, Stad en Land is a good choice for a short overnight visit. Rooms at the rear are the quietest and overlook a little pond.

🍴 Eating

Charming restaurants and bars surround the Waag and the Bierkade quay. Away from the cheese-market madness, Koorstraat and Ritesvoort have many excellent bistros and cafes.

De Vlaminck   FRITES **€**
(www.devlaminck.nl; Voordam 2; frites from €2.50; ⊘11am-7pm Fri-Wed, to 9.15pm Thu) The fries are superb at this storefront counter, as are the 17 different sauces, including peanut, *sambal oelek* (Indonesian chilli sauce), garlic, and tomato ketchup. Take your paper cone to the benches in front alongside the canal.

Abby's   INTERNATIONAL **€€**
(☎072-511 11 11; www.restaurantabbys.nl; Ritesvoort 60; mains lunch €6-19.50, dinner €16.50-27.50; ⊘11am-10pm) In the shadow of an old windmill, Abby's has cool jazz inside and cool breezes outside on the terrace. Soups, salads and sandwiches are the mainstays at lunch, but dinner has more adventurous offerings: tournedos (small, round pieces of

tenderloin beef) with caramelised fennel, squid-ink linguine with Norwegian lobster, and shredded daikon (peppery radish) with prawns in vodka tempura.

Cafe Restaurant De Buren   INTERNATIONAL **€€**
(www.restaurant-deburen.nl; Mient 37; mains €15.50-26.50; ⊙10am-10pm Mon-Sat, 11am-9pm Sun) Outside tables at this vintage cafe/restaurant stretch along the canal and wrap around to the old fish market. The menu spans the globe, with dishes such as *coq au vin blanc* (chicken thighs in white wine), steak and *frites* with pepper-cognac sauce, pumpkin ravioli, smoked spare ribs with corn on the cob, and feisty Thai curries.

🍷 Drinking & Nightlife

⭐**De Boom**   BROWN CAFE
(http://proeflokaaldeboom.nl; Houttil 1; ⊙2pm-midnight Sun & Mon, 1pm-midnight Tue & Wed, 1pm-2am Thu-Sat) The pub on the ground floor of the Nationaal Biermuseum lives up to its location. The inside is unchanged since the 1930s – you expect to hear a scratchy 78rpm playing. Outside you can enjoy the fine selection of brews at seats on a moored old canal boat. Live jazz plays on Thursday nights.

☆ Entertainment

Alkmaar has a lively arts scene – pick up a copy of the monthly *Alkmaar Agenda* (free) from the tourist office to see what's on.

Theater De Vest   PERFORMING ARTS
(⌨072-548 98 88; www.theaterdevest.nl; Canada-plein 2; ⊙box office noon-4pm Mon-Sat, 30min before performance Sun) The centre for Alk-maar's highbrow entertainment, De Vest runs the gamut from traditional plays and puppet shows to avant-garde dance. In sum-mer Canadaplein turns into a stage for the performing-arts festival Zomer op het Plein (Summer on the Square).

🛍 Shopping

Langestraat is the pedestrianised shopping street with mainstream stores. Laat has a more interesting and diverse collection.

De Tromp Kaashuis   CHEESE
(www.kaashuistromp.nl; Magdalenenstraat 11; ⊙9am-6pm Mon-Fri, to 5pm Sat) If you're look-ing to pick up some cheese after seeing so much of it, check out this quality-certified shop where samples abound.

ℹ Information

Tourist office (VVV; ⌨072-511 42 84; www.vvvalkmaar.nl; Waagplein 2; ⊙10am-4pm Mon-Thu & Sat, 9am-4pm Fri Apr-Sep, 10am-4pm Mon-Sat Oct, 1-4pm Mon, 10am-4pm Tue-Sat Nov-Mar) In the Waaggebouw, the towering old weigh house.

ℹ Getting There & Away

BICYCLE

National route **LF7** runs west 9km to link with the **LF1** coastal route. It runs east 28km to join the **LF21** which follows the IJsselmeer and links Edam, Hoorn and Amsterdam.

Rent a Scooter Alkmaar (www.ras-alkmaar.nl; Molenbuurt 21; bikes/electric bikes/scooters per 24hr €13.50/35/65; ⊙9am-5pm Mon-Sat) Rents not only scooters but bicycles and electric bikes too.

TRAIN

The train station is 1km northwest of the centre.

Destination	Fare (€)	Duration (min)	Frequency (per hour)
Amsterdam	7.40	35	4
Den Helder	7.80	30	2
Enkhuizen	7.80	50	2
Hoorn	4.90	25	2

Broek op Langedijk

⌨0226

The vast waterlogged area north of Alkmaar was once home to 15,000 tiny, yet produc-tive, farms, each one an island. Rather than tending to their crops by tractor or getting about by road, the farmers used rowboats. Most of the farms have been replaced by developments but in the town of Broek op Langedijk, about 8km northeast of Alkmaar, the fascinating Museum Broeker Veiling (Museum Broeker Auction; www.broekerveiling.nl; Museumweg 2; adult/child €16.50/8.75; ⊙10am-5pm Jul & Aug, Tue-Sun Apr-Jun, Sep & Oct, Wed-Sun Nov-Mar) recalls this way of life.

The centrepiece of this surprisingly fun at-traction is a vast auction house where farmers arrived with boatloads of produce then wait-ed – afloat – inside, until they could paddle through an auction room where wholesale grocery buyers would bid on the produce. Built in 1878, it sits on 1900 piles. You can tour the immense interior and re-created auctions where the winning bid gets a bag of apples. Prices include auction-house and museum entry as well as a boat ride.

On its exterior, the museum shows some of the 15,000 islands. Inside, the exhibits on how the farms worked are a combination of high-tech wizardry and old-fashioned mechanised gadgets. It runs 45-minute tours around some of the 200 surviving island plots nearby. On the grounds you can see some of the traditional crops *in situ*. There's a fine little cafe.

From Alkmaar take bus 10 (30 minutes, hourly) to the museum. A 9km bike route from Alkmaar follows canals and passes through the tiny old village of Sint Pancras.

Hoorn

📞 0229 / POP 71,888

With a magnificent horn-shaped harbour, for which it's named, a string of museums and excellent restaurants, Hoorn attracts both weekenders and skippers alike. It was once the capital of West Friesland and, thanks to the presence of the Dutch merchant fleet, a mighty trading city. As a member of the League of Seven Cities, it helped free the country from the Spanish who occupied the town from 1569 to 1573.

Hoorn's most famous son, explorer Willem Schoutens, named South America's storm-lashed southern tip – Cape Horn – after his home town in 1616.

◉ Sights & Activities

A stroll through Hoorn's streets lined by 16th-century buildings is one of the town's greatest draws. The scenic harbour is lined by stately gabled houses, especially along Veermanskade. Check out the old warehouses on Bierkade, where lager was brought from Germany.

The old quarter begins about 800m southeast of the train station. From the station, walk south along broad Veemarkt to Gedempte Turfhaven, turn right and take the first left into Grote Noord, the pedestrianised shopping street. At the end is the scenic main square, Rode Steen. The main harbour is 300m further southwest, down a road named West.

Rode Steen   SQUARE
Hoorn's heyday as a shipping centre is long gone, but the imposing statue of Jan Peterszoon Coen, founder of the Dutch East India Company, still watches over the

Rode Steen (Red Stone or Fortress), the square named for the blood that once flowed from the gallows. On the northeastern side of the square, the Waag, the 17th-century weigh house, has a carved unicorn, the town symbol.

★ Westfries Museum   MUSEUM
(http://wfm.nl; Rode Steen 1; adult/child €8/free; ⊙ 11am-5pm Mon-Fri, 1-5pm Sat & Sun) Housed in the former seat of the Staten-College (States' Council), the body that once governed seven towns in Noord-Holland, this absorbing museum has a rich collection of historical paintings – so rich that it was the target of art theft in 2005, when paintings worth €10 million were stolen (and are still missing). Fortunately four large group portraits of prominent *schutters* (civic guards) by Jan A Rotius (1624–66) remain.

The building's 1632 wedding-cake facade bears the coat of arms of Oranje-Nassau, the Dutch-German royal dynasty that the Dutch named as rulers when Napoleon left. Its rear courtyard has a number of curious stone tablets from local facades.

Hoofdtoren   HISTORIC BUILDING
(Hoofd 2) Overshadowing surrounding historic buildings, the massive defensive gate Hoofdtoren (1532), topped by a tiny belfry, now houses one of Hoorn's best restaurants.

Museum van de Twintigste Eeuw   MUSEUM
(Museum of the 20th Century; www.museumhoorn.nl; Krententuin 24, Oostereiland; adult/child €8/3.50; ⊙ 10am-5pm Mon-Fri, noon-5pm Sat & Sun) In the vast former prison on Oostereiland, south of the Hoofdtoren, this entertaining museum is devoted to household goods and modern inventions. Among the eye-openers are a 1964 Philips mainframe computer – a clunky bookcase-sized unit with a whole 1KB of memory – and a 30-sq-metre scale *maquette* (model) of Hoorn in 1650.

Affiche Museum   MUSEUM
(Dutch Poster Museum; www.affichemuseum.nl; Grote Oost 2-4; adult/child €3.50/1.75; ⊙ 11am-5pm Tue-Fri, noon-5pm Sat & Sun) The proud graphic-art traditions of the Netherlands are celebrated through the display of scores of posters. Many are beautiful and evocative old prints from the age of steamships and trains.

Museum Stoomtram   STEAM TRAIN
(📞 0229-214 862; www.museumstoomtram.nl; circle ticket adult/child €21/15.80; ⊙ Apr-Oct) Not a museum in the traditional sense, this

historic steam locomotive puffs between Hoorn station and Medemblik (22km; one hour). You can combine train and boat travel on the 'Historic Triangle' (adult/child €26/19.30): from Hoorn to Medemblik by steam train, then by boat to Enkhuizen and finally a regular NS train back to Hoorn. Departure times vary, confirm in advance.

🛏 Sleeping

★**Gevangenis Hotel Hoorn**   DESIGN HOTEL €
(📋0229-820 246; http://gevangenishotelhoorn.nl; Schuijteskade 5; cell s/d €65/73, standard d/f €80/160; 🛜) Oostereiland's enormous former prison – still with bars on its windows – is now partly occupied by this hip hotel. You can sleep in 11 cells (converted to include a private bathroom) behind the original cell doors, or if that's too unnerving, in 14 standard rooms. Also here is a light-filled, harbour-view brasserie. Parking is across the bridge.

The complex also houses a cinema, as well as the Museum van de Twintigste Eeuw.

Hotel de Keizerskroon   HOTEL €
(📋0229-212 717; www.keizerskroonhoorn.nl; Breed 33; s/d/tr from €75/95/105; 🛜) Conveniently situated in the town centre, this 23-room hotel-restaurant has basic dated but perfectly clean, serviceable rooms, though beware that there's no lift and no soundproofing, so it can be noisy until late at night. Walk-in rates are often much cheaper.

Bed & Breakfast Grote Noord   B&B €€
(📋06 2871 9018; www.bedandbreakfastgrotenoord.nl; Grote Noord 3; s/d €84/94; 🛜) The Rode Steen is just metres from this historic B&B. Both of its rooms (medium and large) have exposed 16th-century timbers, as well as toasty open fireplaces and amenities including iPod docks and minibars.

🍴 Eating

Wormsbecher   SEAFOOD €
(📋0229-214 408; http://wormsbechervis.nl; Wijdebrugsteeg 2; dishes €4-13.50; ⊙11am-6pm) Turquoise tiles front this classic fresh-fish takeaway outlet. It's a perfect place to try out the locally loved smoked eel. A fine seafood salad is a bargain at €7.50. There are plenty of picnic spots along the harbour and on Oostereiland.

★**De Hoofdtoren**   MODERN EUROPEAN €€
(📋0229-215 487; www.dehoofdtoren.nl; Hoofd 2; mains lunch €14.50-24.50, dinner €18.50-24.50, 3-/4-/5-course dinner menu €34.50/39.50/44.50;

⊙noon-10pm) A spiralling red-brick staircase leads up to this exquisite restaurant inside Hoorn's historic Hoofdtoren. In a candlelit bare-boards space, it serves high-end fare – truffle risotto; beef steak with polenta, ruccola *staampot* (mash) and red-wine jus; sole with sautéed spinach – at good-value prices; reservations are recommended. On the ground floor, its bar has outdoor pavement seating in summer.

Oude Waegh   GRAND CAFE €€
(www.oudewaegh.nl; Rode Steen 8; mains lunch €5-12.50, dinner €11.50-23.50; ⊙kitchen 8am-9pm Sun-Thu, to 10pm Fri & Sat) On the main square in the splendid Waag building, this local gathering place has a terrace strung with fairy lights and a bustling dining room where you can dine on lunchtime dishes such as steak sandwiches, fish burgers and beef carpaccio with pesto and Parmesan, or evening meals such as steak with pepper sauce, and satay-chicken skewers with cassava chips.

★**Marque**   MODERN EUROPEAN €€€
(📋0229-508 323; www.marquerestaurant.nl; Bierkade 2; mains €29-35, 3-/4-/5-/6-/7-course menu €39.50/45.50/55.50/66.50/72.50; ⊙noon-2pm & 6-10pm Wed-Sun) Marque's kitchen is at the cutting edge, creating dishes like foie gras, beetroot, apple and hibiscus terrine; Gillardeau oysters poached in Champagne; plaice with seaweed and algae; spring lamb with new potatoes and honey jus; and passion fruit soufflé with white chocolate. It's set in a red-shuttered canal-side house, with a mezzanine loft and pavement tables in fine weather. Book ahead.

🛍 Shopping

Hoorn Markt   MARKET
(Breed; ⊙10am-2pm Sat) Hoorn's weekly open-air market unfurls along Breed every Saturday.

ℹ Information

Tourist office (VVV; 📋0229-218 343; www.vvvhartvannoordholland.nl; Rode Steen 1; ⊙11am-5pm Mon-Sat, 1-5pm Sun Jul & Aug, 11am-5pm Mon-Sat Apr-Jun & Sep-Nov, closed Dec-Mar) In the Westfries Museum building.

ℹ Getting There & Around

BICYCLE
National bike route **LF21** runs 20km south to Edam and joins the **LF15** for the 25km coastal run to Enkhuizen.

Fietspoint Ruiter (📞0229-217 096; Station-plein 1; bike rental per day from €9; ⊘4.50am-1am Mon-Thu, 4.50am-2.40am Fri & Sat, 7.30am-1am Sun) Hoorn is a popular Amsterdam commuter town and this bike garage/rental outlet at the station operates virtually around the clock.

BUS

The bus station is outside the train station. Bus 135 serves Den Helder (1¼ hours, hourly). Change buses at Den Oever for trips across the IJsselmeer towards Leeuwarden.

Buses 314 and 317 serve Edam (30 minutes, four times hourly); they're covered on a **Waterland Ticket** (p108).

TRAIN

Destination	Price (€)	Duration (min)	Frequency (per hour)
Alkmaar	4.90	25	2
Amsterdam	8	35	4
Enkhuizen	3.90	25	2

There's a heritage route to Medemblik and Enkhuizen run by the Museum Stoomtram (p116).

Enkhuizen

📞0228 / POP 18,383

Enkhuizen may be a quaint town today but during the Golden Age its strategic harbour sheltered the Dutch merchant fleet. It slipped into relative obscurity in the late 17th century but now possesses one of the largest recreational vessel fleets on the IJsselmeer.

For many travellers, Enkhuizen's biggest drawcard is the Zuiderzeemuseum, one of the country's finest.

⊙ Sights & Activities

★**Zuiderzeemuseum**   MUSEUM
(📞0228-351 111; www.zuiderzeemuseum.nl; Wierdijk 12-22; adult/child €15/10; ⊘ Binnenmuseum 10am-5pm year-round, Buitenmuseum 10am-5pm Apr–late Oct) This captivating museum consists of two sections, 300m apart: open-air **Buitenmuseum**, with more than 130 rebuilt and relocated dwellings and workshops, and indoor **Binnenmuseum**, devoted to farming, fishing and shipping. Visitors are encouraged to leave their vehicles at a car park (€5) off the N302 at the south edge of town. A ferry (included in admission; every 15 minutes April to October) links the car park with the train station and the Buitenmuseum. Plan to spend half a day here.

➡ **Buitenmuseum**

Opened in 1983, the Buitenmuseum was assembled from houses, farms and sheds trucked in from around the region to show Zuiderzee life as it was from 1880 to 1932. Every conceivable detail has been thought through, from the fence-top decorations and choice of shrubbery to the entire layout of villages, and the look and feel is certainly authentic. An illustrated guide (in English), included in the ticket price, is an essential companion on your tour.

Inhabitants wear traditional dress, and there are real shops such as a bakery, chemist and sweets shop. Workshops run demonstrations throughout the day. Though varying in character, the displays join seamlessly: lime kilns from Akersloot stand a few metres from Zuidende and its row of Monnickendam houses, originally built outside the dykes. Don't miss the Urk quarter, raised to simulate the island town before the Noordoostpolder was drained. For a special postmark, drop your postcards at the old post office from Den Oever. The Marker Haven is a copy of the harbour built in 1830 on what was then the island of Marken. There's a fun playground at the entrance.

While the grounds are open all year, there are activities here only from April to October.

➡ **Binnenmuseum**

Occupying a museum complex adjoining the Peperhuis, this indoor museum is in the former home and warehouse of a Dutch shipping merchant. The displays include a fine shipping hall: paintings, prints and other materials tell of the rise and fall of the fishing industry, and the construction of the dykes. Here too are cultural artefacts, such as regional costumes, porcelain, silver and jewellery, that indicate the extent of the country's riches at the time.

Drommedaris   HISTORIC BUILDING
Located between the Buitenhaven and the Oude Haven, the Drommedaris was built as a defence tower as part of the 16th-century town walls. Once a formidable prison, it now serves as a meeting hall. Its clock-tower carillon tinkles on the hour.

Flessenscheepjes Museum   MUSEUM
(Bottleship Museum; www.flessenscheepjesmuseum. nl; Zuiderspui 1; adult/child €4/2.50; ⊘noon-5pm mid-Feb–Oct, Sat-Mon Nov–mid-Feb) Almost as tiny as the boats in its collection, this enchanting museum has a fascinating collection of ships in bottles carved by seamen

through the ages. There are more than 1000 examples, some up to 750 years old. A film shows the secret to their construction.

Waag HISTORIC BUILDING
(Waagstraat 1) At the east end of Westerstraat, the 16th-century Waag (weigh house) overlooks the old cheese market.

Town Hall HISTORIC BUILDING
(Breedstraat 53) Enkhuizen's classical town hall was modelled after the Amsterdam town hall that once stood on the Dam. You can peek through the windows at the lavish Gobelins tapestries.

Westerkerk CHURCH
(www.westerkerkenkhuizen.nl; Westerstraat 138; ⊙10am-5pm Sat Jul–mid-Sep) Along Westerstraat you'll spot the remarkable Westerkerk, a 15th-century Gothic church with a removable wooden belfry. The ornate choir screen and imposing pulpit are worth a look. Opposite the church is the Weeshuis, a 17th-century orphanage with a sugary, curlicued portal.

🛏 Sleeping

Camping Enkhuizer Zand CAMPGROUND €
(☑0228-317 289; www.campingenkhuizerzand.nl; Kooizandweg 4; campsites €16.50-27.50; ⊙Apr-Sep) On the north side of the Zuiderzeemuseum's Buitenmuseum, this popular site is a model of self-sufficiency with beautiful white-sand beaches, tennis courts and a grocery store.

★ De Koepoort BOUTIQUE HOTEL €€
(☑0228-314 966; Westerstraat 294; s/d/tr/f from €80/95/130/150; P❋☎) Adjacent to the historic city gate De Koepoort, the western gateway to the city, its namesake hotel has 25 timber-trimmed designer rooms (some with balconies) with ultracomfortable beds. Amenities include a lobby lounge with leather armchairs, bar, restaurant using seasonal

local produce, a lift and 24-hour reception, as well as a fabulous rooftop terrace overlooking the gate.

Hotel Garni RecuerDos B&B €€
(☑0228-562 469; www.recuerdos.nl; Westerstraat 217; s/d from €63/88; ☎) Owned by a warm and welcoming music-society patron, this stately manor house has three immaculate rooms, each with its own garden terrace. Enjoy breakfast in the glassed-in conservatory where there are often live music performances.

🍴 Eating

De Smederij MODERN DUTCH €€
(☑0228-323 079; www.restaurantdesmederij.nl; Breedstraat 158; mains €21-25.50, 3-/4-course menu €36.50/39.50; ⊙5-9pm Fri-Tue) Cute as a button, this cosy restaurant was once a forge, and is now decorated with beautiful old framed maps. Hearty, highly creative seasonal fare includes pumpkin and duck ravioli, guinea fowl in dark beer sauce, and salmon with truffled hollandaise sauce.

De Drie Haringhe SEAFOOD €€€
(☑0288-318 610; www.diedrieharinghe.nl; Dijk 28; 3-/4-course menu €39.50/45; ⊙lunch by reservation, dinner 5-9pm Wed-Sun) Specialising in seafood, this upmarket locale has been receiving rave reviews for years for its seasonally changing Dutch- and French-inspired dishes such as smoked-eel terrine with saffron mayo, smoked salmon and crab cannelloni, and grilled sea bass with green-asparagus risotto. It's ensconced in an old East India Company warehouse, with a lovely walled summer garden.

🍷 Drinking & Nightlife

★ De Mastenbar BAR
(www.demastenbar.nl; Compagnieshaven 3; ⊙10am-10pm) Hidden away down at the harbour, local

HAARLEM & NORTH HOLLAND ENKHUIZEN

ℹ DYKE ROAD

The N302 between Enkhuizen and Lelystad is one of the country's most extraordinary routes. It runs along a narrow, causeway-like 32km-long dyke, completed in 1976 as the first step of the reclamation of the Markerwaard. A cycling path parallels the road along its length.

Along the way you'll pass below a high-tech causeway that connects Enkhuizen harbour with the IJsselmeer, with ships floating over the motorway. A stone monument at the halfway mark in the form of a chain link symbolises the joining of West Friesland with Flevoland.

Checkpoint Charlie (www.roadhousecheckpointcharlie.nl; N302; dishes €7.50-13.50; ⊙10am-2pm Mar-Sep, Fri-Mon Oct) Despite having no running water and generator-only power, this outpost by the Dyke Road's halfway-point monument at N52° 38' .03" E05° 25' .0" still manages to dish up pancakes, omelettes, sandwiches, toasties, schnitzel and apple tart, which you can wash down with beer or rosé.

favourite De Masten has a cavernous nautical-themed interior with printed maps on the ceiling, old ship's wheels, compasses and copper lanterns, and a panoramic sun-drenched terrace where you can watch cruise boats and working barges float past. Its kitchen specialises in fresh seafood, Flemish onion soup and tasting plates including wild game.

ℹ️ Information

Tourist office (VVV; ☑ 0228-313 164; www.vvvhartvannoordholland.nl; Tussen Twee Havens 1; ⊙ 8am-5pm Jul & Aug, 9am-5pm Apr-Jun & Sep–late Oct) Just east of the train station, Enkhuizen's tourist office sells ferry tickets and a self-guided tour booklet in English (€1.50).

ℹ️ Getting There & Away

You can take a fun and historic trip between Enkhuizen and Hoorn and Medemblik on a steam train (p116) and boat combo.

BICYCLE

From Enkhuizen, Hoorn is 25km west along the coastal national routes **LF15** and **LF21**.

John Brandhoff Tweewielers (☑ 0228-325 771; www.johnbrandhofftweewielers.nl; Westerstraat 25; bike rental per day from €8; ⊙ 9am-6pm Tue-Fri, to 5pm Sat) Rents bikes.

FERRY

Enkhuizen-Stavoren Ferry (☑ 0228-326 006; www.veerboot.info; adult/child one way €11/7; ⊙ mid-Apr–Oct) The Enkhuizen–Stavoren Ferry plies the IJsselmeer connecting Noord-Holland with Friesland. The 90-minute trips depart once or twice daily from near the tourist office, which sells tickets. Boats dock in Stavoren, which is on the train line to Leeuwarden via Sneek.

TRAIN

Destination	Price (€)	Duration (min)	Frequency (per hour)
Alkmaar	7.80	50	2
Amsterdam	10.90	60	2
Den Helder	12.40	90	2
Hoorn	3.90	25	2

For Alkmaar, change at Hoorn. Den Helder requires a change at both Hoorn and Heerhugowaard, which is inconvenient but the fastest public-transport option.

Medemblik

☑ 0227 / POP 43,391

About 12km northwest of Enkhuizen, Medemblik is the oldest port on the IJsselmeer, dating to the 12th century and the Hanseatic League. Parts of the town are especially beautiful, including its busy harbour, old waterfront streets and medieval fortress.

⊙ Sights & Activities

Stroll along Kaasmarkt, Torenstraat, Nieuwstraat and the Achterom canal to see richly decorated building facades.

Kasteel Radboud   CASTLE
(www.kasteelradboud.nl; Oudevaartsgat 8; adult/child €6/4; ⊙ 11am-5pm Mon-Sat, 12.30-5pm Sun May–mid-Sep, 2-5pm Sun mid-Sep–Apr) Pint-sized Kasteel Radboud was built by Count Floris V in the 13th century and served as a prison before a 19th-century remodelling by Pierre Cuypers, the designer of Amsterdam's Rijksmuseum. The original floor plan has been preserved and the imposing **Ridderzaal** (Knights' Hall) still looks much as it did in the Middle Ages. Interpretive signs (in English) detail the castle's long history and the count's undoing. It's signposted from the harbour on the eastern side of town.

Stoommachine Museum   MUSEUM
(Steam Engine Museum; http://stoommachinemuseum.nl; Oosterdijk 4; adult/child €5.50/4.25; ⊙ 10am-5pm Jul & Aug, Tue-Sun mid-Feb–Jun & Sep–mid-Nov) Ever wondered what drove the Industrial Revolution? Part of the answer lies at the Stoommachine Museum, in the old pump station outside Medemblik. Thirty handsome old steam engines from the Netherlands, England and Germany are fired up for demonstrations on various days; check the website for dates.

The Museum Stoomtram (p116) departs from the old train station for Hoorn. You can also catch a boat to Enkhuizen as part of a triangle tour.

🍴 Eating

De Twee Schouwtjes   MODERN DUTCH €€
(☑ 0227-547 077; http://detweeschouwtjes.nl; Oosterhaven 27; mains €19.50, 3-/4-course menu €30/36; ⊙ 2-10pm Tue-Sun; 🐾) Overlooking a boat-filled canal, this rustic restaurant with heavy timber beams and butter-coloured walls serves stunning contemporary fare: salmon and asparagus crème brûlée, mustard soup with smoked eel, lamb with crispy quinoa and mint jus, plaice with parsley sauce, and lemon tiramisu with orange and tarragon crystallina granita. Owner Frank Groot often plays the piano and sings of an evening.

ℹ Information

Tourist office (VVV; ☑ 0227-542 852; www.
vvvhartvannoordholland.nl; ⊙10am-5pm Jul & Aug, 11am-3pm Apr-Jun &
Sep-Oct) At the back of the local stationers,
post office and tobacconist; hours can vary.

ℹ Getting There & Around

BICYCLE
The national bike route **LF21** runs south and east
along dykes 21km to Enkhuizen.

BUS
The nearest train station is in Hoorn; bus 239
makes the 30-minute journey twice hourly.

Den Helder

☑ 0223 / POP 56,506

The workmanlike naval town of Den Helder
has a couple of interesting sights worth checking out before you hop on the ferry to Texel.

◉ Sights

Marine Museum   MUSEUM
(www.marinemuseum.nl; Hoofdgracht 3; adult/child
€6/3; ⊙10am-5pm Mon-Fri, noon-5pm Sat & Sun
Apr-Oct, 10am-5pm Tue-Fri Nov-Mar) In the vast
former armoury of the Dutch Royal Navy,
displays at the Marine Museum cover naval
history mainly after 1815, the year the Netherlands became a kingdom. You can run rampant through several vessels moored on the
docks outside, including an ironclad ram ship
and a submarine left high and dry. Check out
the exhibits on modern-day pirates.

Fort Kijkduin   FORT, AQUARIUM
(www.fortkijkduin.nl; Admiraal Verhuellplein 1, Huis-
duinen; museum & aquarium adult/child €8/6;
⊙10am-5pm Apr-Oct, 11am-5pm Nov-Mar) Built
under Napoleon's orders in 1811 to accommodate 1400 soldiers, this hulking hilltop
fortress (originally called Fort Morland) now
houses a military museum incorporating an
armoury, and a fantastic subterranean aquarium with 14 tanks filled with every species of
marine life from the Waddenzee and North
Sea, one with a walk-through tunnel. Kids
love it. It's located 4km east of Den Helder.

✗ Eating

Kade 60   MODERN EUROPEAN €€
(☑ 0223-682 828; www.kade60.nl; Willemsoord 60;
mains lunch €6-16.50, dinner €16-24.50; ⊙kitchen
11am-10pm Tue-Sun) A former iron found-
ry now houses this cavernous canal-side

restaurant near the Marine Museum and
ferry terminal. Gourmet sandwiches such
as smoked beef, egg and truffle mayo are
served at lunch; dinner mains span beetroot-
marinated lamb with baked potatoes to
oven-roasted sea bass with cherry tomatoes.
You can just stop in for a beer, wine or cider.

ℹ Getting There & Away

BICYCLE
The **LF1** Northsea route links Den Helder with
Sluis by the Belgian border, passing dunes along
the North Sea coast and fields of tulips around
Julianadorp, around 9km south of Den Helder.

TRAIN
Direct train services from Den Helder include
Alkmaar (€7.50, 30 minutes, two hourly) and
Amsterdam (€14.10, 1¼ hours, two hourly).

Texel

☑ 0222 / POP 13,641

Sweeping white-sand beaches, wildlife-rich
nature reserves, sun-dappled forests and
quaint villages are among the highlights of
Texel, the largest and most visited of the
Wadden Islands. About 3km north of the
coast of Noord-Holland, Texel (pronounced
tes-sel) is 25km long and 9km wide. It was
actually two islands until 1835 when a spit
of land to Eyerland island was pumped dry.

Before the Noordzeekanaal opened in the
19th century, Texel was a main stop for ships
en route to Asia, Africa and North America:
the first trade mission to the East Indies began and ended here. It was also the scene of a
colossal maritime disaster: on Christmas Day
1593, hurricane-force winds battered a merchant fleet moored off the coast and 44 vessels
sank, drowning about a thousand seamen.

Sheep are everywhere across the island; the
local wool is highly prized and there are numerous dairies producing cheese. Cyclists will
be enchanted and there are enough diversions
to keep you entertained for days on end.

◉ Sights

★**Texel Dunes National Park**   NATIONAL PARK
(Nationaal Park Duinen van Texel; www.npduinen
vantexel.nl) The patchwork of dune-scape
running along the western coast of the island is a prime reason for visiting Texel. Salt
fens and heath alternate with velvety, grass-
covered dunes; plants endemic to the habitat
include the dainty marsh orchid and orange-
berried sea buckthorn. Much of the area is

HAARLEM & NORTH HOLLAND DEN HELDER

bird sanctuary and accessible only on foot. The visitor centre at Ecomare has schedules and makes reservations for excellent two-hour ranger-led dune walks in English and Dutch (from €7.50).

De Slufter became a brackish wetland after an attempt at land reclamation failed; when a storm breached the dykes in the early 1900s the area was allowed to flood and a unique ecosystem developed. To the south, **De Muy** is renowned for its colony of spoonbills that are monitored with great zeal by local naturalists.

A stone's throw from the windswept beach lies the dark, leafy forest of **De Dennen**, between Den Hoorn and De Koog. Originally planted as a source of lumber, today it has an enchanting network of walking and cycling paths. In spring the forest floor is carpeted with snowdrops that were first planted here in the 1930s.

★**Ecomare**   WILDLIFE RESERVE
(www.ecomare.nl; Ruijslaan 92, De Koog; adult/child €12.25/8.25; ☉9.30am-5pm) Initially created as a refuge for sick seals retrieved from the Waddenzee, Ecomare has expanded into an impressive nature centre devoted to the preservation and understanding of Texel's wildlife. It has displays on Texel's development since the last ice age and the islanders' interaction with the sea, as well as large aquariums filled with fish from the Waddenzee and the North Sea (including sharks); outside there are marked nature trails.

The highlight is the *zeehonden* ('sea dogs', ie seals) themselves. Their playful water ballet will delight even the most jaded visitor. Try to catch feeding time at 11.30am or 3.30pm. Porpoise feeding takes place at 10.30am and 1.30pm; fish feeding is at 2.30pm. Rescued birds are the other main tenants. Look out for the six skeletons of whales stranded in the Waddenzee, including a 15m-long sperm whale carcass complete with 52 fearsome teeth.

★**Kaap Skil Museum Van Jutters & Zeelui**   MUSEUM
(Maritime & Beachcombers Museum; www.kaapskil.nl; Heemskerckstraat 9, Oudeschild; adult/child €8.50/6.50; ☉10am-5pm Tue-Sat, noon-5pm Sun) A stunning new slatted-timber-encased reception building made from recycled materials frames the superb Maritime & Beachcombers Museum. Its extraordinary variety of flotsam and jetsam recovered from sunken ships and the shore is mind-boggling. Demonstrations by rope-makers, fish-smokers and blacksmiths take place in the outdoor section, while the indoor displays cover everything from underwater archaeology to windmill technology.

Reede van Texel, which the museum translates accurately as Texel Roads, has nothing to do with asphalt but rather is a vast and amazingly detailed model of the shipping lanes and ports as they existed in the 17th century.

Lighthouse   LIGHTHOUSE
(www.vuurtorentexel.nl; Vuurtorenweg 184, De Cocksdorp; admission €4; ☉10am-5pm Apr-Oct, Wed, Sat & Sun Nov-Mar) Battered by storms and war, Texel's resilient crimson-coloured lighthouse stands 35m high. Climb its 153 steps for sweeping views across the islands and shallow waters.

Ontstaan Uit Iepen van de Molenlaan   SCULPTURE
(Arise From the Mill; Molenlaan, De Cocksdorp) Opposite De Cocksdorp's supermarket, by the car park, you'll spot *Ontstaan Uit Iepen van de Molenlaan* (Arise From the Mill; 2010) by Meijert Boon, a three-storey-high timber sculpture in the shape of a traditional windmill. A 45-step staircase twists up inside; you can climb it for fabulous views.

Eureka Orchideeën & Vogelbush   GARDENS
(Eureka Orchids & Birds; www.eurekatexel.nl; Schorrenweg 20, Oosterend; adult/child €7.50/5; ☉8.30am-6pm Mon-Fri, 8.30am-5pm Sat, 10am-5pm Sun Jul–mid-Sep, 8.30am-6pm Mon-Fri, to 5pm Sat mid-Sep–Jun) June is the time to see wild orchids on Texel, a rarity in the country. Otherwise, head for the steamy Eureka Orchideeën & Vogelbush to view native orchid species along with a menagerie of tropical birds in a large greenhouse.

🏃 **Activities**

Texel has a total of 170km of well-signposted cycling routes. All the roads are suitable for bikes, and you can circumnavigate the island following the dykes in the east and the trails behind the dunes in the west. The tourist office sells maps and booklets of cycling routes and hiking trails.

De Eilander   BOATING
(✆06 2063 4413; www.deeilander.nl; De Volharding 6, De Cocksdorp; catamaran hire per hour from €45; ☉May-Oct) Catamarans can be hired from near the Vlieland boat dock. Five-hour sailing courses cost €160.

Tessel Air SKYDIVING

(☑ 0222-311 434; www.paracentrumtexel.nl; Texel Airport, Postweg 120; 15min scenic flight €39.50, tandem parachute jump €209; ⊙ daily Apr-Oct, Sat by request Nov-Mar) Tessel Air offers 15-minute pleasure flights over Texel (minimum two people), and for a bit more cash they'll explore the other Wadden Islands. To really feel the wind in your face, try a tandem parachute jump.

Kitesurf School Texel KITESURFING

(☑ 06 1097 1992; www.kitesurftexel.nl; Paal 17, De Koog; kitesurfer/windsurfer rental per hour from €15, 3hr lesson from €95; ⊙ 9am-5pm Apr-Oct) Kitesurf School Texel offers exhilarating kitesurfing and windsurfing lessons as well as rentals.

Ozlines WATER SPORTS

(www.ozlines.com; Paal 17, De Koog; equipment rental from €8, lesson adult/child from €80/25; ⊙ 9am-7pm Jul & Aug, 1-7pm Sat & Sun Apr-Jun & Sep-Oct) Rent kite-surfers, SUPs (stand-up paddleboards) and surfboards at this surf shop that sets up on groovy 17 Kilometre Beach. Lessons are also available.

Manege Elzenhof HORSE RIDING

(☑ 0222-317 469; www.manegeelzenhof.nl; Bosrandweg 252, De Koog; horse & pony ride adult/child per hour €16/8, lesson per 30min €17.50; ⊙ 8.30am-5pm May-Oct) One of several horse-riding stables on the island, Manege Elzenhof offers horse and pony rides and lessons on gentle creatures lined up at the troughs with their names inscribed on plaques. It also organises a two-hour beach ride per adult/child for €32/16. In July and August, you can take a 2½-hour evening ride along the shore (adult/child €45/22.50).

ⵣ Tours

The still-working fishing harbour at Oudeschild is filled with former large prawn trawlers that found new life as tour boats. Competition is fierce and the best way to choose a boat is to wander along the docks checking out itineraries and offers. Trips around Texel sail close to an endangered seal colony on the sandbanks.

Departure times are dependent on tides.

Emmie TX10 BOAT TOUR

(☑ 06 5149 8614; www.garnalenvissen.nl; Oudeschild; 2hr tour adult/child €11/9; ⊙ 10.30am & 2pm Mon-Sat Apr-Oct) Prawns caught on the *Emmie*'s journey are prepared fresh for passengers.

Texel 44 BOAT TOUR

(☑ 06 5110 5775; www.tx44.nl; Oudeschild; 2hr tour adult/child €11/9; ⊙ 2pm Mon, 11am & 2pm Tue-Sat, 12.30pm Sun Apr-Oct) Purpose-built for touring, the *Texel 44* has a big upper deck for seal spotting.

Texelstroom BOAT TOUR

(www.texelstroom.nl; Haven, Oudeschild; 3hr tour adult/child €22.50/18; ⊙ 1.30pm Tue, Thu & Sat Jul & Aug, Thu & Sat May, Jun, Sep & Oct) If you prefer traditional sailing to a powered pleasure craft, take a three-hour tour aboard this beautiful 1906 yacht.

Tuk Tuk Express DRIVING TOUR

(☑ 06 2145 2052; www.tuktukexpresstexel.nl; Haven 12, Oudeschild; per day Mon-Fri/Sat & Sun €119/144; ⊙ 9am-7pm Jul & Aug, 10am-5pm Apr-Jun, Sep & Oct, by reservation Nov-Mar) A fun way to spin around the island is behind the wheel of a

---

ℹ NAVIGATING TEXEL

Ferries from the mainland dock at 't Horntje on the south side of the isle, from where buses head north to Texel's six main villages.

Den Burg The island's modest capital and main shopping destination; 6km north of 't Horntje.

De Koog Texel's beachy tourist heart with a distinctly tacky streak; 5km north again.

Den Hoorn A charming village handy to tulip fields and windswept sand dunes; 5km northwest of 't Horntje.

Oudeschild The best harbour facilities on the island, a fine museum and splendid fish restaurants; 7km northeast of 't Horntje.

Oosterend Quiet hamlet with distinctive architecture; 6km northeast of Den Burg.

De Cocksdorp At the northern end of the island, this tiny village is a launch pad for the island of Vlieland and the rest of the Frisian Islands.

Beaches on the west coast are numbered by the kilometre from south to north.

Texel

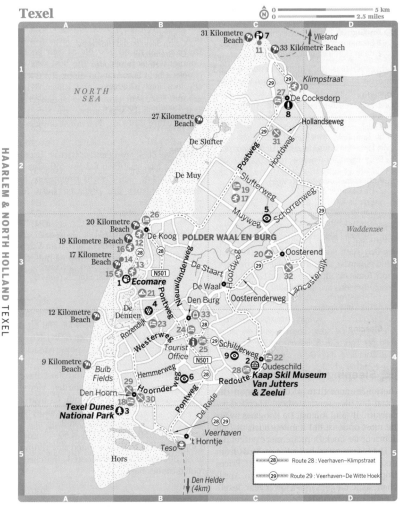

little three-wheeled, four-seater, blue-and-white tuk tuk (Italian Piaggio Calessino convertible, of which only 999 were made).

Jan Plezier   HORSE RIDING
(☎ 0222-316 225; www.janpleziertexel.nl; tour adult/child €16.50/8.50; ⊙10am & 2pm Mon-Sat Apr-Oct) Scenic three-hour horse-drawn wagon rides follow one of two routes: one primarily along the beach, and one through the forest. Tours depart from the lighthouse. It also offers horse riding from €60 for three hours.

★ Festivals & Events

If you're here during lambing season around Easter, you'll see adorable bouncy lambs all over the island; locals enjoy taking a *Lammetjes Wandeltocht* (walk to look at the lambs).

Ronde om Texel   CATAMARAN RACE
(www.roundtexel.com; ⊙early–mid-Jun) The largest catamaran race in the world attracts some 600 participants and thousands of spectators along the beaches.

Texel

🛏 Sleeping & Eating

There are more than 45,000 beds on the island, but it's essential to book ahead, especially in July and August. De Koog has by far the most options, but hamlets such as Den Hoorn or De Cocksdorp are more peaceful.

The tourist office has a list of B&Bs from around €30 per person per night. Prices drop in the low season (October to April) when island life slips into a lower gear. Texel's 11 main campgrounds teem in summer; the tourist office can advise on vacancies. Many farms also offer rooms and campsites.

With more than 27,000 sheep roaming the island, lamb naturally gets top billing on menus, but seafood comes a close second. Asparagus season is celebrated in spring. Look out for local food, beer and wine producers (p128).

🛏 Den Burg

⭐ **Hotel De 14 Sterren** HOTEL **€**
(☑0222-322 679; www.14sterren.nl; Smitsweg 4, Dennenbos, Den Burg; d €70-85; 🐾) On the edge of De Dennen forest, charming Hotel De 14 Sterren's 14 rooms are decorated in warm Mediterranean hues, and most have a terrace or balcony with garden views. Breakfast is served in your room. Its bistro, **De Worsteltent** (☑0222-310 288; www.14sterren.nl; Smitsweg 4, Dennenbos, Den Burg; mains lunch €6.50-13.50, dinner €17.50-24.50; ⊙noon-8.30pm), brings Italian-accented fine dining to a 300-year-old slate-floored thatched-roofed timber barn.

Stayokay Texel HOSTEL **€**
(☑0222-315 441; www.stayokay.com; Haffelderweg 29, Den Burg; dm €22-37, d €50-80; 🐾) Texel's modern HI hostel has 240 beds in clean, colourful rooms, and has a cafe on-site. You can rent bikes to cycle to the beach 6km away.

Peek Lifestyle Lodges BOUTIQUE HOTEL **€€**
(☑0222-313 176; www.peektexel.nl; Gravenstraat 3, Den Burg; d/ste from €95/140; 🐾) In the heart of Den Burg, this boutique gem has three spacious, contemporary rooms in black, white and slate tones. All have balconies; the suite has a kitchenette. All-organic fare at its street-level, blond-timber-panelled restaurant, **Peek** (☑0222-313 176; www.peektexel.nl; Gravenstraat 3, Den Burg; mains €19.50-25, 3-/4-/5-course

DON'T MISS

TEXEL'S BEACHES

The island offers idyllic swimming, cycling, walking, boating, or just relaxation. Its pristine white beaches, lining the western shore in one unbroken ribbon, are numbered by the kilometre and marked with a *paal* (piling) from south to north.

The currents can be treacherous; lifeguards are on duty in July and August from No 9 northeast of Den Hoorn to No 21 near De Koog.

No matter how crowded the island, with a little hiking you can always find a stretch of deserted sand.

Top beaches:

➡ **No 9** Uncrowded, and popular with locals and nudists.

➡ **No 12** Uncrowded, with a sheltered cafe.

➡ **No 17** The party beach (www.paal17.com), where there's always a groovy vibe. Lots of day- and night-time activities, including windsurfing and kitesurfing.

➡ **No 19** The emphasis at this beach (www.paal19.nl) is on lounging with good food and drink, but there's good windsurfing and kitesurfing here, too.

➡ **No 20** Right in front of the tourist enclave of De Koog, and rather built-up.

➡ **No 27** A fairly isolated beach popular with nudists.

➡ **No 31** Near the lighthouse; no swimming due to treacherous rip tides but lots of wind sports.

➡ **No 33** No swimming, but lots of beach sports and occasional seal-spotting.

menu €32.50/39.50/49.50; ◷6-10pm Thu-Mon) 🔪, includes Texel lamb, beef and fish.

★**Freya**   BISTRO €€
(☑0222-321 686; Gravenstraat 4, Den Burg; 3-course menu €26.50; ◷6-9pm Tue-Sat) This petite, welcoming restaurant serves a daily changing set menu (à la carte) of contemporary Dutch cuisine along the lines of smoked duck breast with asparagus, herb-crusted Texel lamb with oven-baked potatoes, and local berries with meringue topped with clouds of whipped Texel cream. Reservations are a must.

Taveerne De Twaalf Balcken   DUTCH €€
(www.12blacken.nl; Weverstraat 20, Den Burg; lunch dishes €3-9, dinner mains €13-22; ◷kitchen 10am-10pm Mon-Sat, 5-9pm Sun; 🔊) The cosy 'Tavern of the 12 Beams' is a locals' haunt that specialises in lamb dishes. Its front section is dark and subdued – perfect for sipping one of the many Trappist beers on offer – while the rear conservatory is light and airy.

De Cocksdorp

At the northern end of the island, little De Cocksdorp has a good-sized supermarket and some appealing cafes along its tidy low-key streets.

★**Boutique Hotel Texel**   BOUTIQUE HOTEL €€
(☑0222-311 237; www.hoteltexel.nl; Postweg 134, De Cocksdorp; d/f/ste from €115/165/175; 🔊💌) Texel's best hotel has 42 stunning rooms (two of which are wheelchair accessible) in natural charcoal tones, fabulous leisure facilities including an indoor swimming pool, sauna and beauty treatments, and an outstanding restaurant, Gusta (☑0222-311 237; www.hotel texel.nl; Postweg 134, De Cocksdorp; mains €20-22, 3-course dinner menu €32.50; ◷noon-9pm), serving seasonal Texel produce such as Waddenzee platters with eels, prawns, cockles, fish and lobster. It's 4.5km south of De Cocksdorp.

't Anker   HOTEL €€
(☑0222-316 274; www.hotelhetankervantexel.nl; Kikkertstraat 24, De Cocksdorp; s/d from €47/93; @🔊) This small, family-run hotel near Roggesloot nature reserve is full of woodsy charm and has basic yet comfy rooms behind a solid brick facade, a lush garden and hearty breakfasts.

Restaurant Topido   BISTRO €€
(☑0222-316 227; www.topido.nl; Kikkertstraat 21-23, De Cocksdorp; mains lunch €7-14.50, dinner €22.50, 3-/4-/5-/6-course dinner menu €36.50/45/50/55; ◷11am-9pm Tue-Sun) In the heart of the village, casual Topido uses island produce in its menus. Lunch is a light affair (soups, burgers, sandwiches), but

dinner dishes are creative: Texel lamb with roast beetroot; sea bass encrusted in locally grown herbs; and local-vegetable strudel.

Den Hoorn

★ Bij Jef BOUTIQUE HOTEL €€€
(📞 0222-319 623; www.bijjef.nl; Herenstraat 34, Den Hoorn; d €195-245; 🛜) The eight simple yet stylish rooms in this former rectory come with a bath, a lavish breakfast, views of the countryside and a sun-drenched balcony. Its sumptuous **restaurant** (📞 0222-319 623; www.bijjef.nl; Herenstraat 34, Den Hoorn; 4-/5-/7-course menu €75/85/100; ⊙ 6-9pm Wed-Fri & Sun, 7-10pm Sat) has a constantly changing menu created from local produce, meat and seafood. Try for a garden table.

Het Kompas MODERN DUTCH €€€
(📞 0222-319 360; www.whiskybarplaza.nl; Herenstraat 7, Den Hoorn; mains €33.50-45; ⊙ noon-10pm Apr-Oct, Wed-Mon Nov-Mar) Behind a dark blueberry-coloured exterior, Het Kompas serves excellent – if pricey – modern Dutch dishes and really comes into its own as a whisky bar. There are more than 3000 different varieties; it also organises rare and closed distillery tastings. There's a flower-filled garden out back.

De Koog

De Koog's main drag, Dorpstraat, Texel's tourist haven, is lined with cheap chipperies, bistros of uncertain provenance and the island's only concentration of boisterous bars.

De Bremakker CAMPGROUND €
(📞 0222-312 863; www.bremakker.nl; Templierweg 40; campsites for 2 people €31.50, chalets per week from €335; ⊙ Apr-Oct; 🌐) This leafy and serene campground is situated between Den Burg and De Koog at the forest's edge, about 1km east of the beach. There's a laundry and snack bar, plus sports facilities including a football field, beach volleyball, a jumping castle and bike hire (per day from €7), plus indoor ping-pong tables for rainy days.

Strandhotel Noordzee HOTEL €€
(📞 0222-317 365; www.strandhotelnoordzeetexel.nl; Badweg 200, De Koog; d from €149) This is one of Texel's few hotels directly on the sand. Its 10 comfy rooms (some with waterbeds) all have North Sea views and some have balconies; you can also unwind on the large beachside terrace.

Oudeschild

If the kids need to work up an appetite, take them to the pirate-themed playground at the north end of the harbour.

Texel Yurts GUESTHOUSE €€
(📞 06 3077 1667; www.texelyurts.nl; Rommelpot 19, Oudeschild; 2-person yurt 3 nights/week from €375/855) Bed down in a luxurious fabric-sided, timber-beamed yurt set in a shady clearing near town, and fitted out with beautiful furniture and a woodstove. Hammocks sway in the grounds. There's a minimum stay of one week in July and August, and three nights the rest of the year.

Design Hotel Texel Suites DESIGN HOTEL €€€
(📞 06 5061 5558; www.texelsuites.com; Haven 8, Oudeschild; ste from €230) Inside a historic harbourside brick warehouse, the three panoramic suites here are bigger than many Dutch apartments: two are 90 sq metres (one is a duplex), and the third is a whopping 140 sq metres with a huge gas-powered fireplace. All have kitchens, baths and rain showers. Seafood caught daily is the speciality of its restaurant, 't Pakhuis (📞 0222-313 581; www.pakhuis.com; Haven 8, Oudeschild; mains €22.50-35.50, 3-/4-/5-/6-course menu €35/45/55/62.50, with paired wines €52.25/68/83.75/97; ⊙ noon-9pm).

Vispaleis Rokerij van der Star SEAFOOD €
(www.vispaleistexel.nl; Heemskerckstraat 15, Oudeschild; dishes €4-9; ⊙ 8.30am-6pm Mon-Sat) Fresh-from-the-ocean seafood is dished up at this cafe, including garlicky seafood soup and sublime smoked fish. Seating is basic – go for a plastic chair on the terrace.

Oosterend

★ Camp Silver
Island Hideaway CARAVAN PARK €€
(📞 0222-318 571; http://campsilver.nl; Eendenkooiweg 2, Oosterend; d €120; ⊙ Apr-Oct; 🅿🛜) ✏ Eight gleaming silver Airstream trailers occupy this glamping paradise 5km northeast of Den Burg, off Oosterenderweg. All are decked out with designer fabrics and shiny stainless-steel bathrooms. Rates include organic breakfast; the camp kitchen has a pantry with ingredients, heat-and-eat homemade meals and drinks on an honesty system; there's a groovy geo-dome-housed lounge. Minimum stay is two nights.

DON'T MISS

ISLAND PRODUCE

Across the island you'll find wonderful local produce, from fruit to cheese, chocolate, ice cream, beer and (rare for the Netherlands) wine.

Texelse Bierbrouwerij (☑ 0222-320 325; www.texels.nl; Schilderweg 214b, Oudeschild; tour adult/child €9.50/4.50; ☺ tour 2pm & 3pm Tue-Fri, 2pm, 3pm & 4pm Sat) See how beer is made at the island's brewery, housed in a former dairy, on an informative 45-minute guided tour (in English and Dutch). Tour prices include four tastings; you can drop in for a drink on the terrace or at the bar. Its flavour-packed beers vary with the seasons and are widely available across Texel.

De Kroon van Texel (www.wijngaarddekroonvantexel.nl; Rozendijk 32, Den Burg; vineyard tour adult/child €9/2.50; ☺ cellar door 10am-5pm May-late Sep, vineyard tour 11am Tue & Sat, 2pm Fri May-late Sep) Wineries across the Netherlands are few, so it's especially worth dropping in to De Kroon, a small but international medal-winning estate. One-hour tours take you through the vines and end with three tastings, or you can just come to sample and buy its Riesling, Johanniter, rosé and Cabernet Sauvignon.

Kaasboerderijk Wezenspyk (☑ 0222-315 090; www.wezenspyk.nl; Hoondernweg 29, Den Hoorn; ☺ 9.30am-5pm Tue-Sat) This small dairy between Den Hoorn and Den Burg is a terrific place to taste and buy rounds produced from the local cows, sheep and goats. A glass viewing window lets you see the cheese being churned. You can just pop by, or book ahead for a one-hour tasting at 2pm Tuesday and Friday (adult/child €5.50/2.75).

IJsboerderij Labora (www.ijsboerderijlabora.nl; Hollandsweg 2, De Cocksdorp; ice cream per scoop €1.25; ☺ noon-8pm Jul & Aug, noon-6pm May & Jun, 1.30-5pm mid-Feb-Apr, Sep & Oct) At this working dairy farm, you can see the cows being milked (by robots) to make Labora's luscious ice cream. Each day there are 18 flavours, such as strawberry, made with strawberries grown on the farm, served in a giant waffle cone and topped with fresh strawberries and handmade strawberry syrup and whipped cream from the cows' milk.

Other varieties range from *strender stropertje* (caramelised Texel raisins) to red-wine and cinnamon sorbet, and apple pie.

De Texelse Chocolaterie (☑ 0222-313 179; www.detexelsechocolaterie.nl; Spinbaan 1a, Den Burg; ☺ 9am-5.30pm Mon-Sat) The heavenly aroma here of melting chocolate made from fresh Texel milk will make you go weak at the knees. Its exquisite pralines and bonbons are laid out like jewels, and come in shapes such as the island's outline, lighthouse, sheep and windmills. You can learn to make bonbons during two-hour workshops (€27; by reservation).

De Kade (Haven 9c, Oudeschild; ☺ 10am-6pm Jul & Aug, 10am-5pm Mon-Sat, noon-5pm Sun Mar-Jun, Sep & Oct) Hundreds of Texel-made products from all over the island are stocked at this one-stop shop at Oudeschild's historic harbour: cheese, wine, jams and preserves, herbs, handicrafts, woollen blankets and clothes.

Rôtisserie Kerckeplein MODERN EUROPEAN €€ (☑ 0222-318 950; www.rotisserie-texel.nl; Oesterstraat 6, Oosterend; mains €11-35.50; ☺ 6-8pm Wed-Sun) This cosy restaurant with loft seating has refined the art of cooking local lamb, with seven varieties of the tender island meat. Wash it down with a dark Texels Speciaalbier.

ⓘ Information

You'll find ATMs in every town. Den Burg has banks, bookshops, pharmacies and other services.

Tourist office (VVV; ☑ 0222-314 741; www.texel.net; Emmalaan 66, Den Burg; ☺ 9am-5.30pm Mon-Fri, to 5pm Sat) Texel's tourist office is signposted from the ferry terminal; on the southern fringe of Den Burg.

ⓘ Getting There & Away

Trains from Amsterdam to Den Helder (€14.10, 75 minutes, twice hourly) are met by **Texel Hopper** (☑ 0222-784 000; www.texelhopper.nl) buses that whisk you onto the ferry, which the bus also boards.

A **ferry** (p203) runs from north of De Cocksdorp to car-free Vlieland in the Frisian Islands.

Teso (☑ 0222-369 600; www.teso.nl; foot passenger/car return €2.50/37, off-peak car return Tue-Thu €25; ☺ to Texel hourly 6.30am-9.30pm, from Texel hourly 6am-9pm) Teso runs crossings from Den Helder to 't Horntje aboard huge ferries; journey time is 20 minutes. On some summer days there's a service every half-hour – check the timetable online. Services start half-hour to an hour later on Sundays. Car queues can be huge in high season; plan to arrive at the docks at least an hour before departure.

Getting Around

BICYCLE

Touring bikes can be rented in every town on Texel and at the ferry terminal for about €6 per day.

BUS

Bus 28 run by **Texel Hopper** (✆ 0222-784 000; www.texelhopper.nl) operates throughout the year; a single trip anywhere on the island has a flat rate of €3. You'll need a paper ticket in advance, available on board Teso ferries and from tourist offices. The route links 't Horntje with Den Burg (seven minutes) and De Koog (another 15 minutes) before returning via the Ecomare wildlife reserve. Buses generally run hourly during daylight (until 10pm in summer).

Texel Hopper also operates minibus services around the rest of the island on demand – reserve at least an hour ahead by phone or online and pay by credit card or give the code of your prepaid bus ticket.

TAXI

Taxi Botax (✆ 0222-315 888; www.taxibotax texel.com) Taxi Botax takes you between the ferry terminal and any destination on the island, including Den Burg (€16), De Koog (€26.50) and De Cocksdorp (€43.50). Book in advance.

Muiden

✆ 0294 / POP 6576

An ideal easy jaunt by bike from Amsterdam, Muiden is an unhurried, historical town renowned for its medieval red-brick castle, the Muiderslot. Life otherwise focuses on the busy central lock that funnels scores of pleasure boats out into the vast IJsselmeer.

Sights

★ Muiderslot   CASTLE
(Muiden Castle; www.muiderslot.nl; Herengracht 1; adult/child €13.50/9; ⊙ 10am-5pm Mon-Fri, from noon Sat & Sun Apr-Oct, noon-5pm Sat & Sun Nov-Mar) Built in 1280 by Count Floris V, son of Willem II, the exceptionally preserved moated fortress Muiderslot is equipped with round towers, a French innovation. The count was a champion of the poor and a French sympathiser, two factors that were bound to spell

trouble; Floris was imprisoned in 1296 and murdered while trying to flee.

Today, Muiderslot is the Netherlands' most visited castle. The interior can be seen only on 30-minute guided tours. The I Amsterdam Card (p99) is valid here.

In the 17th century, historian PC Hooft entertained some of the century's greatest writers, artists and scientists here, a group famously known as the Muiderkring (Muiden Circle). Inside the castle, you'll see precious furnishings, weapons and Gobelin hangings designed to re-create Hooft's era.

Pampus   HISTORIC SITE
(www.pampus.nl; adult/child ferry & tour €20/11; ⊙ 9am-5pm Tue-Sun Apr-Oct) Off the coast of Muiden lies a derelict fort on the island of Pampus. This massive 19th-century bunker was a key member of a ring of 42 fortresses built to defend Amsterdam. Rescued from disrepair by Unesco, it's now a World Heritage site and is great fun to explore. Ferries to Pampus depart from Muiderslot port on a varying schedule in season. Usually there's at least one morning departure which allows a couple of hours to prowl the fort before a mid-afternoon return.

Eating & Drinking

Café Ome Ko   BROWN CAFE
(www.cafeomekomuiden.nl; cnr Herengracht & Naardenstraat; ⊙ 8am-2am Sun-Thu, to 3am Fri & Sat) In warm weather the clientele of little bar Café Ome Ko, with big green-striped awnings, turns the street outside into one big party. When there's no party on, it's a perfect spot to watch the comings and goings through the busy lock right outside. It serves lunchtime sandwiches and classic Dutch bar snacks (croquettes et al).

Getting There & Around

BICYCLE

National bike route **LF20** passes by Amsterdam's Leidseplein. Follow it east for 7km until it passes under the A10 and look for the start of the **LF23** route. Cross the canal and follow the **LF23** for 9km through parklands southeast to Muiden.

BUS

Buses 320, 322 and 327 link Amsterdam's Amstel station with Muiden (20 minutes, two hourly). The castle is then a 1km walk.

FERRY

Ferries operated by **Veerdienst** (www. veerdienstamsterdam.nl; Krijn Taconiskade 124;

DON'T MISS

AALSMEER FLOWER AUCTION
....

Bloemenveiling Aalsmeer (www.floraholland.com; Legmeerdijk 313; adult/child €7/4; ⊙ 7-11am Mon-Wed & Fri, 7-9am Thu) Aalsmeer is home to the world's biggest *bloemenveiling* (flower auction), run by vast flower conglomerate FloraHolland. Get to the viewing gallery before 9am to catch the best action as the flower-laden carts go to Dutch auction, with a huge clock showing the starting price. From the starting bell, the hand drops until a deal is struck.

Take bus 172 from Amsterdam Centraal Station to the Hoofdingang stop (45 minutes, four per hour, from 4.59am). Monday is busiest, Thursday quietest.

The one-million-sq-metre space sees some 90 million flowers and two million plants change hands every day of operation. You can take an aromatic self-guided tour on a 3km-long wheelchair-accessible elevated walkway above the frenetic warehouse floor, overlooking the choreography of flower-laden forklifts and trolleys. Along the route, signboards with push-button audio recordings interpret the action.

The route also passes windows where you can peek into the auction rooms and see blooms being prepped for display as the carts go to auction. More and more transactions are taking place online, so catch it while it's still here.

---

adult/child ferry & tour of either Pampas or Muiderslot €20/15; ⊙ 11am Tue-Fri, 11am & 1.30pm Sat & Sun Apr-Oct) run from the newly built Amsterdam neighbourhood of IJburg (reached from Amsterdam Centraal Station on tram 26 in 20 minutes). The ferry tickets include a tour of either Pampus or Muiderslot. Bicycles travel for free.

Het Gooi

Along the slow-moving Vecht River southeast of Amsterdam lies Het Gooi, a shaded woodland strewn with lakes and heath. In the 17th century this 'Garden of Amsterdam' was a popular retreat for wealthy merchants, and nature-hungry urbanites still flock to its leafy trails to hike and cycle today.

Naarden, on the Gooimeer to the north, has an intriguing fortress. The main town, Hilversum, is really just an Amsterdam suburb with a few interesting early-20th-century buildings, most notably the Raadhuis (town hall; 1931) by Willem Dudok.

Naarden

🚗 035 / POP 17,204

Naarden is a highlight of the Het Gooi area thanks to its remarkable fortress, **Naarden-Vesting**, on its northwest border. This military work of art has the shape of a 12-pointed star, with arrowheads at each tip. This defence system, one of the best preserved in the country, was – like closing a barn door after the horse has bolted – built only after the Spanish massacred the inhabitants in the 16th century. The bastions were staffed by the Dutch army until the 1920s,

long after its strategic importance had become moot.

Today, the walled town of Naarden-Vesting is an upmarket enclave with fine restaurants, galleries and antique shops.

⊙ Sights

Inside the fortress, most of Naarden-Vesting's quaint little houses date from 1572, the year the Spaniards razed the place during their colonisation of Noord-Holland. The bloodbath led by Don Frederick of Toledo is commemorated by a stone tablet on the building at Turfpoortstraat 7.

★**Vestingmuseum**   MUSEUM
(Fortress Museum; www.vestingmuseum.nl; Westwalstraat 6; adult/child €7/5; ⊙ 10.30am-5pm Tue-Fri, noon-5pm Sat & Sun) The Vestingmuseum brings context to the vast star-shaped fortress, which is thought to be the only one in Europe featuring a buffer of two walls and two moats. You can stroll around on the rolling battlements before descending into the cramped casements for insights into a soldier's life here.

Grote Kerk   CHURCH
(www.grotekerknaarden.nl; Markstraat 13; church free, tower adult/child €3/2; ⊙ church 10.30am-4.30pm Tue-Sat, 1.30-4.30pm Sun & Mon mid-Jun–mid-Sep, tower 2-3pm Wed, Sat & Sun) It's easy to spot the tall tower of the fort's central Grote Kerk, a Gothic basilica with stunning 16th-century vault paintings of biblical scenes. You can climb the tower's 235 steps for a view of the leafy Gooi and the Vecht

River. Organ concerts are held throughout the year – check the agenda for times and varying prices.

Comenius Museum MUSEUM
(www.comeniusmuseum.nl; Kloosterstraat 33; adult/child €5/free; ⊙noon-5pm Tue-Sun) The 17th-century Czech educational reformer Jan Amos Komensky (Comenius) is buried in the Waalse Kapel (Walloon Chapel) of the fortress's former monastery. His life and work (he promoted the concepts of universal education for rich and poor) are related next door at the Comenius Museum. Tickets are only available from the tourist office and the Vestingmuseum, not at the Comenius Museum itself.

☞ Tours

Boat Tours BOAT TOUR
(☑035-694 1194; www.vestingvaart.nl; adult/child €6.50/4.50; ⊙1pm & 3pm Mon-Fri, 1pm, 3pm & 5pm Sat & Sun May-Sep, 1pm & 3pm Apr & Oct) Enjoyable one-hour tours on vintage boats explore the moats and some of the reedy natural areas.

✗ Eating

You'll find some excellent dining options inside the walls.

Passionata DELI €
(www.passionata-naarden.nl; Marktstraat 31; dishes €3.50-12; ⊙10am-6pm Tue-Sat, noon-6pm Sun) This stylish Italian deli is a perfect source for picnic supplies you can take to enjoy out on the town walls. Fantastic sandwiches include fillings such as prosciutto, bresaola, ricotta, Gorgonzola, truffle mayo, sundried tomatoes and rocket.

Fine BRASSERIE €€
(☑035-694 48 68; www.restaurantfine.nl; Marktstraat 66; mains €19.50-26.50, 3-course dinner menu €29.50; ⊙noon-10pm Wed-Mon) Aptly named, this cosy bar and restaurant has canal-side wicker chairs and wooden tables, plus regular art exhibitions. You can stop in for a glass of wine and a cheeseboard. The monthly changing menu is superb and highlights local seafood, such as Waddenzee oysters baked with spinach and hollandaise, prawn and crustacean risotto, and mussels with garlic and chilli.

DRAINING THE ZUIDERZEE

The Netherlands' coastline originally extended as far as the sandy beaches of Texel and its Frisian Island companions. The relentless sea, however, never seemed to be in agreement with such borders, and by the end of the 13th century storms had washed seawater over flimsy land barriers and pushed it far inland. The end result was the creation of the Zuiderzee (South Sea).

The ruling Dutch had for centuries dreamed of draining the Zuiderzee to reclaim the huge tracts of valuable farmland. The seafaring folk of the villages lining the sea were of a different opinion, even though the shallow Zuiderzee constantly flooded their homes and businesses, and often took lives with it. A solution needed to be found, and the only way to tame the waves, it seems, was to block them off.

A huge dyke was proposed as early as the mid-17th century, but it wasn't until the late 19th century, when new engineering techniques were developed, that such a dyke could become reality. Engineer Cornelis Lely, who lent his name to Lelystad, was the first to sketch out a retaining barrier. A major flood in 1916 set the plan in motion, and construction began in 1927. Fishermen worried about their livelihood, and fears that the Wadden Islands would vanish in the rising seas were voiced, and while the former concerns were legitimate, the latter proved unfounded.

In 1932 the Zuiderzee was ceremoniously sealed off by the Afsluitdijk (Barrier Dyke), an impressive dam (30km long and 90m wide) that links the provinces of Noord-Holland and Friesland. The water level remained relatively steady, but the fishing industry was effectively killed as the basin gradually filled with fresh water from the river IJssel – this is how the IJsselmeer was born. However, vast tracts of land were created and soon turned into arable *polders* (areas surrounded by dykes where the water can be artificially controlled). A second barrier between Enkhuizen and Lelystad was completed in 1976 – creating the Markermeer – with the idea of ushering in the next phase of land reclamation, but the plan was shelved because of cost and environmental concerns.

For more information on this vast human endeavour, spend some time at Lelystad's Nieuw Land (p133) museum, which details the land reclamation.

WORTH A TRIP

SCHOKLAND

Schokland Museum (www.museumschokland.nl; Middelbuurt 3; adult/child €6/4.50; ⊙10am-5pm Jul & Aug, 11am-5pm Tue-Sun Apr-Jun, Sep & Oct, 11am-5pm Fri-Sun Nov-Mar) Schokland's islanders eked out an existence for hundreds of years on a long, narrow strip of land in the Zuiderzee. By the mid-19th century the clock had run out: fish prices plummeted and vicious storms were eroding the island away. The plucky locals hung on, despite the appalling living conditions, prompting Willem III to order their removal in 1859. Schokland was eventually swallowed up by the Noordoostpolder in the 20th century. The Schokland Museum affords glimpses into this tortured past.

Displays, including a film in English, detail the history of the island, now a Unesco World Heritage site. Views from the lower path hint at just how big the waves were at the prow-shaped barrier, constructed from tall wooden pilings. Ironically, since the area was drained the foundations have begun to dry out. Schokland is sinking but no longer into the sea.

There's no public transport to the museum. By bike, the LF15 from Urk, 14km to the west of Schokland, passes right through. Once here, you can follow a 10km route around the old island.

ℹ Information

Tourist office (VVV; www.vvvgooivecht.nl; Utrecht Gate, Westwalstraat 6; ⊙noon-3pm Wed, Sat & Sun) Set in the old barracks, Naarden's tourist office has a free English-language self-guided walking-tour leaflet of the town.

ℹ Getting There & Around

BICYCLE

National bike route **LF23** passes right through Naarden-Vesting and is an ideal way to explore the extents of the star-shaped moat and nearby waters of the Gooimeer. The castle at Muiden is 11km northwest on the **LF23**.

TRAIN

Direct trains run between Amsterdam Centraal Station and Naarden-Bussum (€4.70, 30 minutes, up to four hourly). From the station, bus 110 (five minutes, twice hourly Monday to Friday, hourly Saturday and Sunday) runs to the fortress, otherwise it's a pleasant 1.8km walk.

FLEVOLAND

Flevoland, the Netherlands' 12th and youngest province, is a masterpiece of Dutch hydro-engineering. From 1927 to 1932 an ambitious scheme went ahead to reclaim more than 1400 sq km of land – an idea mooted as far back as the 17th century. The completion of the Afsluitdijk (Barrier Dyke) paved the way for the creation of Flevoland. Ringed dykes were erected, allowing water to be pumped out at a snail-like pace. Once part of Overijssel province, the Noordoostpolder was inaugurated in 1942, followed by the Southeastern Flevoland (1957) and Southwestern Flevoland

(1968). The first residential rights were granted to workers who'd helped in reclamation and to farmers, especially those from Zeeland, who lost everything in the great flood of 1953.

The cities that sprang up bring to mind anything but the Golden Age. The main hubs – Almere, Lelystad and Emmeloord – are dull places, laid out in unrelieved grid patterns. However, Lelystad has some good attractions and the train line means you can stop off on journeys to the northeast. The top highlights are the old fishing villages Urk and Schokland.

Lelystad

☑0320 / POP 76,285

Unattractive modern architecture dominates the disjointed sprawl of Lelystad, the capital of Flevoland province. Founded in 1967, it is an unfortunate example of urban planning gone awry. This expanse of steel and concrete is, however, home to three superb museums that are winners with kids and adults alike.

◎ Sights

Lelystad's *Batavia* exhibit and Nieuw Land museum are next to Bataviastad, a mock fort containing a huge factory-outlet discount-shopping centre. It's 3km west of the train station and linked by bus 3 (10 minutes, two hourly).

Bataviawerf   HISTORIC SITE

(Batavia Yard; www.bataviawerf.nl; Oostvaardersdijk 1-9; adult/child €11/5.50, combination ticket with Nieuw Land €16/8.50, combination ticket with Luchtvaart Themapark Aviodrome €20/15; ⊙10am-5pm) Bataviawerf is home to a replica of a

17th-century Dutch merchant frigate, the *Batavia,* which took 10 years to reconstruct. The original was a 17th-century *Titanic –* big, expensive and supposedly unsinkable. True to comparison, the *Batavia,* filled to the brim with cannon and goods for the colonies, went down in 1629 on its maiden voyage off the west coast of Australia. The replica, however, redeemed its predecessor in 2000 by sailing around the Pacific.

The huge weathered wooden skeleton alongside belongs to the *Seven Provinces,* a replica of Admiral Michiel de Ruyter's massive 17th-century flagship that's been under construction in fits and starts for years with no completion date in sight. In a separate building, the Netherlands Institute for Maritime Archaeology displays the remains of a 2000-year-old Roman ship found near Utrecht.

Nieuw Land MUSEUM
(www.nieuwlanderfgoed.nl; Oostvaardersdijk 113; adult/child €9/4, combination ticket with Bataviawerf €16/8.50; ⊙10am-5pm Mon-Fri, 11.30am-5pm Sat & Sun Jul & Aug, 10am-5pm Tue-Fri, 11.30am-5pm Sat & Sun Sep-Jun) Nearly half the Netherlands was created by land reclamation. Nieuw Land has exhibits about *polder* reclamation aimed at kids, who can build model bridges or dams, and navigate ships through locks.

Luchtvaart Themapark Aviodrome MUSEUM
(www.aviodrome.nl; Pelikaanweg 50; adult/child €17.50/15, combination ticket with Bataviawerf €20/15; ⊙10am-5pm Tue-Sun) Fronted by a reception area designed like an airport check-in counter, this hugely engaging museum has 70 historic aircraft on display, including a replica of the Wright Brother's 1902 Flyer, Baron von Richthofen's WWI triplane, a Spitfire and a KLM 747. You can also play air-traffic controller in a re-created flight tower or watch aviation films in the mega-cinema. It's at Lelystad Airport, 8km southeast of the train station; take bus 148 (10 minutes, two hourly).

✖ Eating

Chains and fast-food outlets dominate the Lelystad dining scene. The vast plaza by Nieuw Land has a few cafes, but your best option is bringing a picnic.

❶ Getting There & Away

BICYCLE
The national bike route **LF20** starts near Muiden and runs across the reclaimed *polder* for 44km to Lelystad before veering off to the waterfront. From here it continues northeast to Urk.

TRAIN
There are a few regular services to/from Lelystad station.

Destination	Price (€)	Duration (min)	Frequency (per hour)
Amsterdam	9.80	40	2
Groningen	22.10	1½	2
Leeuwarden	21.40	1½	2
Zwolle	10.30	30	2

Urk

☑0527 / POP 19,567

Until 1939, Urk was a proud little island that was home to a sizeable fishing fleet and an important signal post for ships passing into the North Sea. It reluctantly joined the mainland when the surrounding Noordoostpolder was pumped dry. Although now cut off from the North Sea, the town is still a centre of the seafood industry.

Dozens of historic fishing boats are moored around the harbour. At the western end of town, take the coastal walk around the lighthouse. Just 70m off the shore lies the Ommelebommelestien, a slippery rock said to be the birthplace of all native Urkers. Legend also has it that, far from receiving the delivery by stork, dad had to take a rowboat to pick up his newborn.

The supports of the village church, Kerkje aan de Zee (Prinshendrikstraat 1; ⊙10am-5pm Mon-Sat, noon-4pm Sun Apr-Sep), are made entirely out of masts of VOC (Dutch East India Company) ships that brought back exotic goods from the East Indies. Inside are ship models and, at times, haunting recitals by the choir. Across the road by the water's edge you'll spot the Fishermen's Monument, a lonely statue of a woman in a billowing dress gazing seaward where her loved ones were lost. Marble tablets around the perimeter list the Urk seafarers who never returned – name, age and ship's ID number – with new names still being added.

Bus 141 runs between Urk and Kampen (50 minutes, four hourly Monday to Saturday, four daily Sunday) and Zwolle (1½ hours, four hourly Monday to Saturday, four daily Sunday).

Urk is 34km northwest of Lelystad on the national bike route LF20. Zwolle in Overijssel is 50km southeast on the LF15, a scenic ride of dykes, rivers and Schokland.

Utrecht

Best Places to Eat

➡ Blauw (p140)

➡ Lokaal Negen (p140)

➡ Gys (p140)

➡ Corazon Coffee (p144)

Best Places to Drink

➡ Cafe Derat (p141)

➡ Café Ledig Erf (p141)

➡ Kafé België (p141)

➡ Drie Ringen Bierbrouwerij (p144)

Why Go?

Don't underrate the petite province of Utrecht. Its famous namesake city – with its throngs of students, tree-lined canals and medieval quarter – deserves the limelight. No set piece, it has a plethora of hip, fun bars and cafes. Those with calmer tastes can visit more than a dozen museums big and small. Wandering the backstreets, revel in reminders of the 17th century.

And this is no mere city-state. By bike you can explore evocative castles like the splendid Kasteel de Haar on Utrecht's doorstep. To the east stretches the Randstad's largest park, the Utrechtse Heuvelrug, studded with more magnificent estates. Amersfoort radiates medieval character, but also honours native son Piet Mondrian and his minimalist, angular palette.

When to Go

➡ At the heart of the country, Utrecht's weather is perfectly average: cold and wet in the winter, with the potential for damp, chilly conditions the rest of the year as well.

➡ Perfectly clear and sunny days can appear any time, especially from April to October. These are prime times for bike rides round the province.

➡ In Utrecht city, there are tasty bock beer fests in the fall when many *cafés* (pubs) and bars have the seasonal brew on tap.

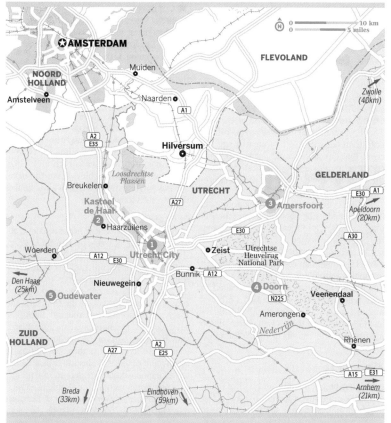

Utrecht Highlights

❶ Seeing clear to Amsterdam from the tippy-top of Utrecht's **Domtoren** (p136) or plunging into the city's vibrant nightlife.

❷ Feeling the weight of history at the **Kasteel de Haar** (p142).

❸ Discovering the narrow canals and medieval confines of **Amersfoort** (p143).

❹ Getting a bike and pedalling out to **Huis Doorn** (p142), a palace in the woods.

❺ Checking your weight in witchiness at **Oudewater** (p144).

UTRECHT CITY

☏ 030 / POP 334,176

Utrecht is one of the Netherlands' oldest cities, with a compact medieval centre set out around canals unique to the Netherlands: there's a lower level where warehouses were located in the 13th century, giving the canals a split-level character and meaning that diners and drinkers can nip off the street and enjoy a snack or a drink down at water level.

While the canals form Utrecht's restful core, elsewhere the city is busy reinventing itself, and part of the excitement is witness-

ing this ongoing transformation. Roads such as Catharijnebaan are being turned back into the canals they once were and the spectacular new train station, nearing completion, adds a vital complement to the old town, adjoined by a greatly expanded concert hall that includes five venues.

Utrecht's student population of 40,000 is the largest in the country, making the city a very vibrant place. From subterranean music cellars to movie-houses-cum-pubs to a slew of special beer *cafés*, the range of social outlets ranks among the nation's broadest.

History

In Roman times the Rhine passed through present-day Utrecht, then called Trajectum. In the following centuries the town had religious ties and formed part of various empires. By the 11th century it was a centre of culture and learning while Amsterdam was still just a grubby fishing town to the west.

In 1579 several regions of today's Netherlands united under the Union of Utrecht. The Protestant religion was made official but, in an early nod to tolerance, it was decreed that Catholics would not be persecuted. Utrecht's university was founded in 1636, the year after René Descartes, a visiting professor, wrote *Discourse on Method*.

In 1702 centuries of simmering animosity between the bishops of Utrecht and the Roman Catholic Church came to a head when the bishop was booted out of his job for failing to recognise the pope's infallibility. This caused a schism that resulted in the creation of the Old Catholics Church in Utrecht. The religion grew in popularity and peaked in 1889 when scores of disgruntled Catholics met in Utrecht. After that the Old Catholics lost following, and there's well under 10,000 members of the church in the Netherlands today.

◉ Sights

A number of key points stand within 500m of the Domtoren (Cathedral Tower); a few hundred metres further south takes you to the museum quarter. Utrecht likes its museums and has over a dozen, some quirkier than a carnival sideshow.

Focus your strolling on the two canals that bisect Utrecht, the Oudegracht and the Nieuwegracht, the old and new canals from the 11th and 14th centuries. A third canal, the Singel, surrounds the old core.

Scene of many a wedding photo, the photogenic bend in the Oudegracht is illuminated by lamplight in the evening; hundreds sit at outside cafes here by day. South of this point is where the canal is at its most evocative, and the streets are quieter, stretching 1km to the southern tip of the old town.

A section of the Singel called the Stadsbuitengracht has its own turn as a lovely canal on the southeastern side of the old quarter, where it follows many parks built on the site of the old fortifications. Stroll down beside this canal and back north through Nieuwegracht, a peaceful stretch of plush canal houses and towering elms.

★ **Domtoren** HISTORIC BUILDING

(Cathedral Tower; ☑236 00 10; www.domtoren.nl; Domplein; tower tour adult/child €9/5; ⊙11am-5pm Tue-Sat, noon-5pm Sun) A remnant of Utrecht's original 14th-century cathedral, this tower is 112m high, with 50 bells. It's worth the 465-step climb to the top for unbeatable city views; on a clear day you can see Amsterdam. Visit is by guided tour only, departing on the hour. Tickets can be purchased online or at the tourist office across the square.

The cathedral and its tower are the city's most striking medieval landmarks. Following almost 300 years' construction, in 1674 hurricane-force winds blew down the nave, leaving only the tower, transept and chancel that we see today.

Domkerk CHURCH

(Cathedral; www.domkerk.nl; Achter de Dom 1; donation requested; ⊙10am-5pm Mon-Sat May-Sep, 11am-4pm Mon-Sat Oct-Apr, 12:30-4pm Sun year-round) Immediately north of the Domtoren, find the row of paving stones that marks the extents of the nave and the position of the columns. Across the way is the Domkerk, the surviving chancel of the cathedral. Back outside, look for the horizontal metallic plates showing the extents of the Roman town.

Behind the church is the most charming component of this ecclesiastical troika: Kloosterhof, a monastic garden and peaceful refuge.

A new component of the Domkerk experience, **DOMunder** (www.domunder.nl; Domplein 4; adult/child €10/7.50; ⊙tours hourly 11am-4pm Tue-Sun), lets you go underground and view the excavated foundations of the Roman fortress that stood here. To purchase tickets and sign up for tours go to the DOMunder outlet next to the tourist office.

Utrecht University HISTORIC BUILDING

On the eastern side of Domplein stand the ceremonial buildings of Utrecht University, surrounding the old church chapterhouse where the Treaty of the Union of Utrecht was signed in 1579. The treaty marked the founding of the Netherlands as a republic.

★ **Centraal Museum** MUSEUM

(☑236 23 62; www.centraalmuseum.nl; Agnietenstraat 1; adult/teen/child €12.50/5/free, incl admission to Rietveld-Schröderhuis plus €3 surcharge; ⊙11am-5pm Tue-Sun) Applied arts are at the heart of a wide-ranging collection that also features paintings by artists of the Utrecht School and a bit of De Stijl to boot. Here too is the world's most extensive Gerrit

FLORA'S HOF

This petite garden, immediately to the right of the Domtoren entrance, makes a peaceful retreat from which to observe the tower.

Rietveld collection, a dream for all minimalists. There's even a Viking longboat that was dug out of the local mud, plus a sumptuous 17th-century dollhouse.

Miffy Museum   MUSEUM
(☑236 23 62; nijntjemuseum.nl; Agnietenstraat 2; child/adult €7.50/2.50; ☺10am-5pm Tue-Sun) One of Utrecht's favourite sons, author and illustrator Dick Bruna is the creator of the beloved cartoon rabbit Miffy (Nijntje as she's known in Dutch) and she naturally takes pride of place at the artist's former studio, across the street from the Centraal Museum. The museum was renovated in 2015 to make it more toddler-friendly (for ages two to six).

Rietveld-Schröderhuis   HISTORIC BUILDING
(☑reservations 236 23 10; www.rietveldschroder huis.nl; Prins Hendriklaan 50; adult/teen/child €15.50/8/3; incl admission to Centraal Museum; ☺11am-5pm Tue-Sun; tours every hour by prior reservation) This Unesco-recognised landmark house is just east of the city centre. Built in 1924 by Utrecht architect Gerrit Rietveld for socialite Truus Schröder-Schräder, it is a stark example of 'form follows function'. Especially notable are the architect's use of primary colours and the transitions between interior and exterior. Visits are by mandatory tour, best booked in advance online.

Nearby, on Erasmuslaan, are a pair of social-housing blocks also designed by Rietveld. It's a 20-minute walk east of the town centre.

★**Museum Catharijneconvent**   MUSEUM
(☑231 38 35; www.catharijneconvent.nl; Lange Nieuwestraat 38; adult/child €12.50/7; ☺10am-5pm Tue-Fri, 11am-5pm Sat & Sun) Museum Catharijneconvent is the pick of Utrecht's museums, with the finest collection of medieval religious art in the Netherlands – virtually the history of Christianity, in fact – housed in a Gothic former convent and an 18th-century canal-side house. Marvel at the many beautiful illuminated manuscripts, look for the odd Rembrandt and hope for one of the often salacious special exhibitions.

Pieterskerk   CHURCH
(Pieterskerkhof 3; ☺11am-5pm Tue-Sat) Walk down Voetiusstraat from behind the Domkerk to Pieterskerk, completed in 1048 and the oldest Romanesque church in the Netherlands.

Universiteitsmuseum   MUSEUM
(☑253 80 08; www.museum.uu.nl; Lange Nieuwstraat 106; adult/child €8/4.50; ☺10am-5pm) On display are the objects of Utrecht University's research through the centuries. There's a recreated late-19th-century classroom, historic dentistry tools and models of medical maladies. Take refuge out back in De Oude Hortus, the old botanical garden, an oasis of calm sheltering trees and plants collected by the Dutch during their world exploits.

Nederlands Spoorwegmuseum   MUSEUM
(Dutch Railway Museum; ☑230 62 06; www.spoor wegmuseum.nl; Maliebaanstation; admission €16; ☺10am-5pm Tue-Sun) The national railway museum features historic trains, including the luxurious cars of the Orient Express and Holland's oldest steam locomotive, a vast collection of model trains and thematic displays in an old station building; a high-speed minitrain takes kids around the grounds. To get there, take bus 3 from Utrecht CS to Maliebaan and walk southeast for five minutes.

Aboriginal Art Museum   MUSEUM
(☑238 01 00; www.aamu.nl; Oudegracht 176; adult/child €9/5; ☺10am-5pm Tue-Fri, 11am-5pm Sat & Sun) Dreamtime in Utrecht: the focus here is on contemporary Australian Aboriginal art, from the paintings of the Central Desert to photography by urban artists.

Sonnenborgh
Museum and Observatory   MUSEUM
(☑820 14 20; www.sonnenborgh.nl; Zonnenburg 2; adult/child €7/4.50; ☺11am-5pm Tue-Fri, 1-5pm Sun) The Sonnenborgh is actually two museums in one: above is an exhibit on the history of astronomy, in a site that was among the foremost astronomical research sites on earth in its heyday. Below are the foundations of the original bastions it's built upon. Though the exhibit could use an overhaul, this site remains special, perched on a hill overlooking the Singel.

On certain days you get a chance to look through the ancient telescopes at the sun (☺1-5pm Sunday) and the moon, stars and planets (☺8-9.30pm Friday April to September; €10). For the latter you'll need to book online. There's also a mini-planetarium (based on the one in Franeker, Friesland) in the library.

Utrecht City

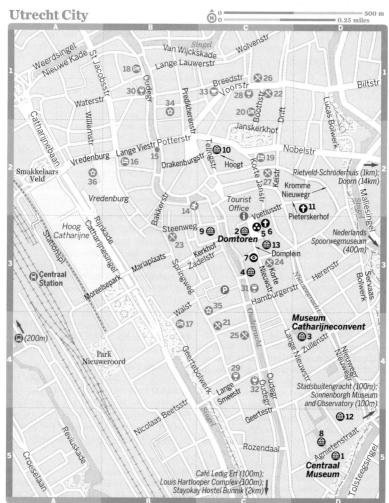

Museum voor het Kruideniersbedrijf MUSEUM
(Grocer's Museum; ☎ 231 66 28; www.kruide niersmuseum.nl; Hoogt 6; ☺ 12.30-4.30pm Tue-Sat) Tucked into a narrow lane is this charming replica of an old grocery store, where lovely ladies in aprons dole out sweets and tea from decorative containers. Pick up a block of white liquorice candy to add to hot milk – an old Dutch tradition.

Museum Speelklok MUSEUM
(☎ 231 27 89; www.museumspeelklok.nl; Steenweg 6; adult/child €11/6; ☺ 10am-5pm Tue-Sun) This museum has a colourful collection of play-er organs from the 18th century onwards. Hourly tours demonstrate them with gusto, and the restoration workshop lets you see how the mechanical marvels work.

🏃 Activities

Canal Tours CANAL TOUR
(☎ 272 01 11; www.schuttevaer.com; Oudegracht a/d Werf 85; adult/child €10/7.50; ☺ 11am-5.30pm) Hour-long canal tours are a fine way to see the old town and the old water-level warehouses. The landing is on Oudegracht just south of Lange Viestraat. Alternatively you can rent **canal bikes** (☎ 030-231 15 27;

Utrecht City

www.canal.nl/canal-bike; 90min per person €9.50; ⊙10am-6pm Jul & Aug, 10am-6pm Wed-Sun Apr-Jun & Sep-Oct) – pedal boats – from in front of the municipal library.

⚘ Festivals & Events

Holland Festival Oude Muziek   MUSIC
(Holland Festival of Ancient Music; www.oudemuziek.nl; ⊙late Aug) This event celebrates music from the Middle Ages to the baroque period.

Nederlands Film Festival   FILM
(NFF; www.filmfestival.nl; ⊙late Sep) The Dutch film industry may be tiny, but its output is generally good. Find out for yourself at the NFF, which culminates with the top prize, the Golden Calf.

Le Guess Who?   CULTURAL
(www.leguesswho.nl ⊙late Nov) Big alternative music and arts fest held at various venues around town for four days.

🛏 Sleeping

Strowis Hostel   HOSTEL €
(📞238 02 80; www.strowis.nl; Boothstraat 8; dm/r from €20/€58; @🛜) This 17th-century building is near the town centre and has been lovingly restored and converted into a hostel (with four- to 14-bed rooms). There's a fine rear garden that is a focus of activity. It's loose and lively and around the corner from its slacker

sister, the ACU (p140). Fruit, muesli and yogurt feature in the vegan breakfast (€6).

Stayokay Hostel Bunnik   HOSTEL €
(📞656 12 77; www.stayokay.com; Rhijnauwenselaan 14; dm/d from €18/49; 🛜) This charming old mansion overlooks a canal on the fringes of a nature reserve, 5km east of the city centre in Bunnik. There are three dining halls, a traditional bar and a lovely terrace. It's on national bike path LF4 or you can take bus 41 from Utrecht CS (direction: Wijk bij Duurstede).

★ Mary K Hotel   HOTEL €€
(📞230 48 88; www.marykhotel.com; Oudegracht 25; d from €120; 🛜) 🌿 A bevy of Utrecht artists decorated the rooms at this ideally situated canal house. Rooms come in three basic sizes ('cosy', medium and large), but no two are alike. All make use of the original 18th-century features and you may find a timber beam running through your bathroom or a stuffed animal snoozing in the rafters.

Grand Hotel Karel V   HOTEL €€
(📞233 75 55; www.karelv.nl; Geertebolwerk 1, off Walsteeg; r from €159; P ❄ @ 🛜) The lushest accommodation in Utrecht can be found in this former knights' gathering hall from the 14th century. The service and decor are understated, and the 117 rooms are split between the old manor and a modern wing. A sunset glass of wine in the walled garden is sublime.

Malie Utrecht
HOTEL €€

(☑231 64 24; www.maliehotel.nl; Maliestraat 2; r from €112; P☀@☎) Tucked away on a beautiful tree-lined avenue, this elegant and comfortable 19th-century house offers 45 large rooms and old-world charm. There's a nice garden out back for a bit of peace and quiet.

NH Centre Utrecht Hotel
HOTEL €€

(☑297 79 77, reservations 020-795 60 88; www.nh-hotels.nl; Janskerkhof 10; r from €115; ☀@☎) Trad style trumps modernity at this atmospheric old hotel (1870). The 47 rooms (minibar, trouser press etc included) are comfortable, with stylish decor and good views of the Janskerk across the way.

Apollo Hotel
Utrecht City Centre
HOTEL €€€

(☑030-233 12 32; www.apollohotelresorts.com; Vredenburg 14; s/d from €119/222; ☎) A low-key business hotel, the Apollo has 90 spacious, comfortable rooms. Those in back are dead quiet, while front units have balconies overlooking the grand boulevard. Though the imposing round yellow facade announces a certain Hotel Smits, that's a throwback from when it was a stock traders' haven.

✖ Eating

The wharfside restaurants on the Oudegracht are an obvious place to explore for dining options. However, it's better known for its views than culinary delights; Utrecht's best restaurants lie elsewhere.

★ Gys
CAFE €

(☑259 17 88; gysutrecht.nl; Voorstraat 77; dishes €10; �lock10am-10pm; ☎☑) ✐ Everything's organic at this bright and airy bistro, from the burgers (tofu or lamb) and sandwiches (smoked mackerel with beet mousse; tempeh with sweet potato, avocado and watercress) to the salads and eggplant schnitzel.

Kimmade
VIETNAMESE €

(☑737 09 93; www.kimmade.nl; Mariastraat 2; dishes €5.50-8; � noon-10pm Mon-Sat, 1-8pm Sun) A hole in the wall on a lane full of restaurants, this one is especially appealing for its authentic street-food-style dishes and low prices. Noodle salads are sublime. It's primarily a takeout but there are a few small tables and a counter in back.

Moksi & Tandoori
SURINAMESE, INDIAN €

(☑231 58 11; www.moksi-tandoori.nl; Oudegracht 235; mains €7-10; � noon-9pm Mon-Sat, 3-9pm Sun) This friendly family joint is as ethnically varied as Suriname: *broodjes* (sandwiches) and *baras* (doughnut-like savoury pastries) all day, and curries and biryanis after 5pm, with plenty of meatless options.

Opium
ASIAN €€

(☑231 55 15; www.restaurant-opium.nl; Voorstraat 80; mains €16-23; � 5-10pm) A high-concept restaurant with a stunning interior, Opium takes flavours from across Asia and mixes them with locally sourced ingredients. Everything is presented with an eye for drama, down to the exotic cocktails.

Polman's
GRAND CAFE €€

(☑231 33 68; www.polmanshuis.nl; cnr Jansdam & Keistraat; mains €18-27; � noon-10pm Mon-Sat) A chic rendezvous in a former gentlemen's club, Polman's has ceiling frescoes, extravagant floral displays and plenty of ambience. French and Italian flavours dominate the menu and extensive wine list.

★ Lokaal Negen
FRENCH €€€

(☑231 13 18; www.lokaalnegen.nl; Trans 7; from €32.50 for 3-course meal; � 5-10pm) Around the corner from the Domtoren, this long-standing option offers intimate dining in the living room of a sturdy old house with an interior garden. Instead of ordering, let yourself be pleasantly surprised by the multi-course set meals, each with an assortment of original starters.

★ Blauw
INDONESIAN €€€

(☑234 24 63; www.restaurantblauw.nl; Springweg 64; set menu from €27; � 6-10pm Mon-Fri, 5-10pm Sat & Sun) Blauw is *the* place for stylish Indonesian food in Utrecht. Young and old alike enjoy superb rijsttafels (an array of spicy dishes served with rice) amid the reddish decor that mixes vintage art with hip minimalism.

🍾 Drinking & Nightlife

't Oude Pothuys
BROWN CAFE

(www.pothuys.nl; Oudegracht 279; � 3pm-2am Mon & Tue, noon-3am Wed-Sun) In a darkened, barrel-vaulted medieval cellar, this cosy pub has nightly music, from jam sessions by emerging bands to funk, blues and electro by established acts. Enjoy drinks on the canal-side pier.

ACU
BAR

(www.acu.nl; Voorstraat 71; � from 6pm Tue-Thu & Sun, from 9pm Fri, from 11pm Sat) Anarcho-slacker reference point in Utrecht, ACU combines bar, music venue, lecture hall and more. Argue about whether Trotsky was too conservative while downing organic vegan food by the inimitable Kitchenpunx (⊘Tuesday to Thursday and Sunday).

Café Ledig Erf   BAR
(www.ledigerf.nl; Tolsteegbrug 3; ⊘10am-2am) Overlooking a confluence of canals at the southern tip of town, the terrace here vies with the beer list; the autumn bock beer fest is a winner.

Kafé België   BAR
(www.kafebelgie.nl; Oudegracht 196; ⊘11am-3am Tue-Sat, 1pm-3am Sun & Mon) This lively bar is an absolute must for beer-lovers. It has 20 Benelux brews on tap and cheap food for absorption. There are a couple of canal-side tables.

The Village   COFFEE
(www.thevillagecoffee.nl; Voorstraat 46; ⊘9am-6pm) This is the place to discuss the difference between a flat white and a latte, ponder the relative merits of French press versus AeroPress or find out the advantages of pour-over brewing. The popular coffee den doubles as a live music venue; ask about upcoming events.

Cafe Derat   PUB
(☑231 95 13; wordpress.cafederat.nl; Lange Smeestraat 37) This cosy corner pub has a lot of soul, with an intriguing selection of craft brews on tap (€3.50 each). Sample *lambieks* and *krieks* – Lambic beers from Belgium and Sweden. Lambic beers are noteworthy as they are spontaneously fermented with the yeast and bacteria that live in the brewing components, resulting in a unique and increasingly sought-after taste.

Cafe Kalff   GAY & LESBIAN
(☑231 09 19; www.cafekallf.nl; Oudegracht 47; ⊘4pm-1am Tue-Fri, 3pm-1am Sat & Sun) This narrow, stylish canal-side pub is a focus of gay and lesbian social life in Utrecht. It's a good place to start the evening before moving on to harder-partying venues such as the one right across the way, Bodytalk.

☆ Entertainment

TivoliVredenburg   CONCERT VENUE
(☑231 45 44; www.tivolivredenburg.nl; Vredenburgkade 11) A fixture on the Oudegracht for decades, the Tivoli pop-music hall merged into this mega concert centre in 2014. Wrapped around the original symphony hall by renowned architect Herman Hertzberger, the new entertainment centre covers a range of musical styles in five different venues.

The Ronda and Pandora halls have taken over the function of the Tivoli while the Hertz, Cloud 9 and 1700-seat Grote Zaal stage classical and jazz events.

Louis Hartlooper Complex   CINEMA
(☑232 04 50; www.hartlooper.nl; Tolsteegbrug 1) Ensconced in a former police station in Amsterdam School style, this is an art-film centre where local cinephiles present each movie (in Dutch) in the tradition of its namesake, who also played piano for silent films. Pre- or post-viewing conversation goes on at the adjacent terrace cafe facing lovely Ledig Erf square.

There's a similar cinema-cafe concept at its sister venue, the **Springhaver Theater** (☑231 37 89; www.springhaver.nl; Springweg 50-52).

RASA   WORLD MUSIC
(☑233 01 23; www.rasa.nl; Pauwstraat 13a) RASA's program spans the globe from klezmer ensembles to Malian bluesmen and salsa combos. The small theatre has comfortable arena seating but more often than not the focus is on the dance floor.

🛍 Shopping

The Hoog Catharijne shopping centre makes a formidable buffer zone between the train station and city centre. Between here and the town hall are pedestrian streets with lots of chains and mainstream shops. For more interesting choices, wander down Voorstraat and especially Twijnstraat, the southern extension of the Oudegracht's east bank.

Huge markets take place on Vredenburg on Wednesday, Friday and Saturday. Most unusual, however, is the Saturday fabric market on Breedstraat.

ℹ Information

Tourist office (VVV; ☑0900 128 87 32; www.visit-utrecht.com; Domplein 9; ⊘noon-5pm Sun & Mon, 10am-5pm Tue-Sat) Sells Domtoren tickets. Another tourist info point is in the corridor between the train station and Hoog Catharijne shopping centre.

ℹ Getting There & Away

Utrecht is a travel hub: bike routes, train lines and motorways converge on the city from all directions.

BICYCLE

National bike route **LF9** runs north through farmlands for 23km to a junction with **LF23**, which covers both Muiden and Flevoland. To the south it runs through rich farmlands towards

Breda. Marathon route **LF7** passes through Utrecht on its 350km route from Alkmaar to Maastricht; Amsterdam is about 50km northwest. **LF4** runs east 80km to Arnhem.

BUS

Regional buses depart from platforms on the west (Jaarbeursplein) side of the train station. For information on bus and tram routes, visit the **U-OV Servicepunt** ([☑] 0900 92 92; u-ov.info; ☺ 6.30am-7pm Mon-Fri, 9am-5.30pm Sat, 10am-5pm Sun) at the Jaarbeursplein side of the station.

Eurolines ([☑] 0880 761 700; www.eurolines. nl; Stationsplein 57; ☺ 9.30am-5.30pm Mon-Sat) has a ticket office opposite the tram station; its buses stop on the west side of the train station on Jaarbeursplein.

TRAIN

As construction of the new station continues, the surroundings are in an ongoing state of transition until at least 2018; expect a fair bit of chaos. Utrecht CS (Centraal Station) is the national hub for Dutch rail services, so you'll probably change trains here at some point. Sample train fares and schedules:

Destination	Price (€)	Duration (min)	Frequency (per hour)
Amsterdam	7.50	30	4
Den Haag	11	40	4
Groningen	24	115	1
Maastricht	23	120	2
Rotterdam	10	40	4

❶ Getting Around

Local buses depart from platforms on the west (Jaarbeursplein) side of the train station; according to current plans, the tram station is to be located on the city-centre side.

AROUND UTRECHT CITY

Kasteel de Haar

Feast your senses on the imposing castle Kasteel de Haar, restored in a fit of nostalgia little more than a century ago, long after its Gothic turrets ceased to have any defensive purpose, by architect PJ Cuypers (of Rijksmuseum fame).

◉ Sights

Kasteel de Haar   CASTLE
([☑] 677 85 15; www.kasteeldehaar.nl; Kasteellaan 1; adult/child tour €14/9, gardens only €4/3; ☺ park 9am-5pm, castle 11am-5pm, tours hourly till 4pm)

The spiffed-up version of the fortress you see now is how it was believed to look around 1500, but equipped with all the creature comforts available in the late 19th century, such as electric lighting and running water. To visit the castle you must join one of the hourly guided tours.

The castle is surrounded by an English landscaped garden with broad paths, canal-like stretches of pond and statues throughout. The French baroque garden near the entrance bears the stamp of Hélène de Rothschild, the baron's wife and heir of the renowned Rothschild banking family – it was her fortune that paid for the 19th-century restoration.

❶ Getting There & Away

To get to the castle from Utrecht, take the train to Vleuten (Sprinter to Den Haag, hourly), and transfer to bus 127. Get off at 'Brink' in Haarzuilens, from where it's a 15-minute walk to the castle. Otherwise, the castle is right on national bike route **LF4**, 13km west of Utrecht.

Utrechtse Heuvelrug National Park

Extending 50km east of Utrecht city between the towns of Zeist and Rhenen, the national park is a 100-sq-km expanse of low meadows and high dunes interspersed with forest. At least seven medieval castles stand in and south of Doorn. Started by noble houses in the 12th century as fortifications, they later lost their defensive function and became vast private estates. Cycling and hiking paths thread across this wealth of formerly private greenery, inhabited by foxes, badgers, pine martens and other wildlife.

Doorn

[☑] 0343 / POP 10,500

Around 20km southeast of Utrecht lies Doorn, a little burg with a claim to an oddment in 20th-century Dutch history: the castle of Huis Doorn.

◉ Sights

Huis Doorn   CASTLE
([☑] 421 020; www.huisdoorn.nl; Langbroekerweg 10; adult/child €9/4.50; ☺ 1-5pm Wed-Fri, noon-5pm Sat & Sun, last tour at 4pm) This 14th-century castle had numerous owners during its time, but none more infamous than Kaiser Wilhelm II of Germany, who inhabited Huis Doorn in exile from 1920 until his death in 1941. Castle visits are by guided tour.

There's a fine collection of German art that it seems the Kaiser brought with him from various German palaces. Afterwards, stroll the grounds and ponder the fate of the Kaiser, who had been allowed into exile by the Dutch as long as he remained under 'house arrest' (some house, hey?).

ℹ Getting There & Away

To get here, catch a local train from Utrecht CS to Driebergen-Zeist, then take bus 50, 56 or 81. It will take about 45 minutes. On national bike route **LF4**, ride 20km southeast from Utrecht.

Kasteel Amerongen

This surreally cubic structure is surrounded by wooded islands that make for an idyllic stroll. You can survey the sumptuous salons by guided tour, then admire it across the great lawn of the terrace cafe. It's 30km southwest from Utrecht on national bike route LF4.

◎ Sights

Kasteel Amerongen　　　　　　CASTLE
(⏺ 454 212; www.kasteelamerongen.nl; Drostestraat 20; adult/child €10/5; ⏱ 11am-5pm Tue-Sun Apr-Oct, 11am-5pm Thu-Sun Nov-Mar) The Kasteel Amerongen, a fortified castle built in the 13th century, is located in the countryside outside the town of Amerongen on the Nederrijn River, a landscape dotted with old wooden tobacco-drying sheds. After being burned by Louis XIV's troops in the late 1600s, it was rebuilt to its present symmetrical appearance by an aristocratic family whose descendants occupied it for the next three centuries.

Amersfoort

⏺ 033 / POP 152,481
Beer, wool and tobacco made Amersfoort an exceedingly rich town from the 16th century onwards. Well-heeled with a touch of the provincial, it has many striking merchants' homes that have been lovingly restored, and the egg-shaped old town offers quiet, wonderfully evocative strolls along canals and narrow alleys that retain their medieval mystery.

Amersfoort makes for a good break on a train journey to/from Friesland or Groningen. You can take an interesting hour-long stroll and then stop for a good meal.

◎ Sights

Much of Amersfoort's appeal comes from wandering the old town, which has at-tractive little canals and more than 300 pre-18th-century buildings.

Zuidsingel is a fine place to start exploring: the inner ring on the north side of town along Muurhuizen is quaint and good for walks. Langestraat is the mainstream shopping strip while Krommestraat has more offbeat choices.

The old town has three surviving gateways, either to the city roads or over the canals: Koppelpoort (north; 15th century), Kamperbinnenpoort (east; 13th century) and picturesque Monnikendam (southeast; 1430).

Kade Museum　　　　　　MUSEUM
(⏺ 422 50 30; www.kunsthalkade.nl; Eemplein 77; adult/child €10/free; ⏱ 11am-5pm Tue-Fri, noon-5pm Sat & Sun) A component of the Eemhuis cultural centre west of the old town, this boldly designed museum hosts large-scale temporary exhibitions devoted to contemporary visual artists or themes. The cafe is excellent.

Mondriaanhuis　　　　　　MUSEUM
(www.mondriaanhuis.nl; Kortegracht 11; adult/child €8/free; ⏱ 11am-5pm Tue-Fri, noon-5pm Sat & Sun) This small but absorbing museum honours the life and work of the famous De Stijl artist Piet Mondrian, with a detailed retrospective that illustrates his development. It's set in the house where the artist was born; Mondrian's primary colours dominate the complex.

Onze Lieve Vrouwe Toren　　HISTORIC BUILDING
(www.olvkerk.nl; Lieve Vrouwekerkhof; adult/child €5/4; ⏱ tours hourly noon-5pm Tue-Sun Jul & Aug, 2pm daily rest of year) The 15th-century Gothic tower is the only surviving component of a church that used to stand on this spot until an unfortunate gunpowder blast in 1787. Tickets to ascend the tower (346 steps, fine views) are sold at the nearby tourist office.

The tower previously marked the exact centre of the Netherlands, as indicated by the subterranean laser light within, and is still used as a reference point in the Dutch geographical coordinate system. The square in front, Lieve Vrouwekerkhof, is Amersfoort's most charming spot.

Sint Joriskerk　　　　　　CHURCH
(www.joriskerk-amersfoort.nl; Hof 1; adult/child €1/free; ⏱ 11am-5pm Wed-Sat May–mid-Oct) If the tower of the Sint Joriskerk appears to be popping out of the roof, that's because it's all that remains of the original 13th-century church; the current structure, dating from 1534, was built around it. Inside, look for the lavishly carved stone chancel screen, a typical medieval feature.

WITCHERY

During the horrific witch-hunts of the 16th century, close to a million women all over Europe were executed – burnt, drowned or otherwise tortured to death – on suspicion of being witches. Weighing was one of the more common methods of determining witchery, as popular belief held that any woman who was too light for the size of her frame was obviously a witch (because hags like that have no soul). A woman who weighed the 'proper' amount was too heavy to ride a broom and thus was not a witch. (Fans of the movie *Monty Python and the Holy Grail* will be familiar with the procedure.) Women who passed the weight test were given a certificate, good for life, proclaiming them to be human.

The town of Oudewater emerges with some honour. No one was ever proved to be a witch here and this is held up as a symbol of the honesty of the locals, as they refused to take bribes to rig the weights. It's also seen as the first stirrings of people power and a turn against the church, which was behind the witch-hunts.

☞ Tours

Fietsboot Eemlijn   CRUISE
(☑ 06 5194 2279; www.eemlijn.nl; Grote Kapel; adult/child €2/free, bike €1; ⊙ excursions 10am mid-Jun–mid-Sep) Embarking from the north bank of the Eem River, about 200m outside the Koppelpoort, the 'bike boat' plies the Gelderse valley to the Eemmeer. You can get off at the villages of Soest or Baarn and cycle back through the woods (or vice-versa, taking the return cruise).

✖ Eating & Drinking

Hof and Lieve Vrouwekerkhof both teem with cafes and pubs.

★ Corazon Coffee   CAFE €
(www.coffeecorazon.nl; Krommestraat 18; snacks from €3; ⊙ 10am-6pm) Excellent choice for a pause: the coffees, teas and fresh juices are superb and the apple cobbler – baked just up the street – is a delight.

Drie Ringen Bierbrouwerij   BREWERY
(www.dedrieringen.nl; Kleine Spui 18; ⊙ 2-7.30pm Tue-Sun) Just below the Koppelpoort is this much-heralded microbrewery, which takes its name from a 17th-century predecessor. Sample the various craft beers on tap, which include the crisp, golden Stadsbier and the velvety Vuurvogel (7.5% alcohol), based on a hallowed Amersfoort recipe.

ℹ Information

Tourist office (VVV; ☑ 0900 112 23 64; www.vvvamersfoort.nl; Breestraat 1; ⊙ 10am-5.30pm Mon-Fri, 10am-4pm Sat & Sun, closed Sun Nov-Mar) Has town walking tours and cycling maps; across from the Onze Lieve Vrouwe Toren.

ℹ Getting There & Around

BICYCLE

A bike-rental outlet, on the left as you exit the train station, rents Batavus three-speed bikes (€7.50 per day). Utrecht is 23km southwest on a beautiful ride through forests and farms on national bike route **LF9**. It also runs north 23km to meet **LF23**, and both continue into Flevoland.

TRAIN

Amersfoort's train station is a 500m walk west of the centre. Frequent trains connect Amersfoort to Utrecht (€4.50, 20 minutes), Amsterdam and Deventer (€10.50, 35 minutes). There are lockers between tracks 4 and 5.

Oudewater

📞 0348 / POP 9,924

There's one real reason to visit Oudewater in the province's southwest: witchcraft. Until the 17th century the **Heksenwaag** (Witches' Weigh House; www.heksenwaag.nl; Leeuweringerstraat 2; adult/child €5/2.50; ⊙ 11am-5pm Tue-Sun Apr-Oct (also Mon Jul-Sep), Fri-Sun Nov-Mar) in the town centre was thought to have the most accurate scales in the land; women who were suspected of being witches came from all over the place to be weighed here.

The house has a modest display of witchcraft history in the loft upstairs; at the end of your visit you'll be invited to step onto the old scale. If you feel light on your feet it's because your *certificaet van weginghe* (weight certificate) makes your weight shrink – an old Dutch pound is 10% heavier than today's unit.

Oudewater is on the route of bus 107 between Gouda (20 minutes) and Utrecht CS (40 minutes), which runs every half-hour. From Woerden (10 minutes west of Utrecht by rail or 18km along national bike route LF4), it's a 10km ride south along the Lange Linschoten River – follow the signs to *knooppunten* 69-94. There's a bike-rental outlet at Woerden station.

Rotterdam & South Holland

Best Places to Eat

➡ FG Food Labs (p155)

➡ Restaurant Allard (p173)

➡ In den Doofpot (p185)

➡ Brasserie 't Crabbetje (p178)

➡ Fenix Food Factory (p156)

Best Places to Stay

➡ Villa Augustus (p164)

➡ King Kong Hostel (p153)

➡ Des Indes (p172)

➡ De Vier Seizoenen (p186)

➡ Hotel The Roosevelt (p188)

Why Go?

In the iconic region southwest of Amsterdam, tulips, windmills, cheese, Dutch Masters and blue-and-white Delftware china abound, but it's the cities here that are the biggest draws.

The country's second-largest, Rotterdam, is riding a wave of urban development, redevelopment and regeneration with striking additions to its dramatic skyline, and electrifying art, food and bar scenes that are fuelling an international buzz. Leiden has a centuries-old university culture, historic canal-laced core and exceptional museums. Den Haag, the seat of government and the Dutch royals, as well as the capital of Zuid-Holland (South Holland), also has a trove of magnificent museums, along with a stately air, luxe shopping and resort beach, while Vermeer's beautiful home town Delft is an exquisite medieval time capsule.

Zeeland (Sea Land), the country's southernmost, dyke-protected province, is anchored by the mast-filled port of Middelburg. Cycling throughout this gentle, mostly sub-sea-level region is unparalleled.

When to Go

➡ Rotterdam's museums, shopping, restaurants, bars and nightlife – as well as its excellent public-transport network – mean you can ignore the weather while indoors, and comfortably visit year-round.

➡ Spring brings an explosion of colour to the glorious tulip-filled gardens at Keukenhof (p187), which open just eight weeks a year and are worth scheduling a trip around.

➡ Between spring and autumn, you'll find many more attractions open throughout the region than in the winter months, and greater odds of enjoying a balmy canal stroll or a beach swim.

Rotterdam & South Holland Highlights

1 Delving into experimental galleries, street art, inspired food and bar scenes, and cutting-edge architecture in 'the city that's never finished', **Rotterdam** (p147).

2 Strolling amid the **Keukenhof Gardens** (p187) in Lisse, filled with thousands of flowering tulips in spring,

and viewing its castle and tulip museum year-round.

3 Touring the splendid **Binnenhof** (p168) palace in regal Den Haag.

4 Climbing the spiralling steps inside the tower of Delft's **Nieuwe Kerk** (p177) for sweeping views over the medieval townscape.

5 Exploring the creaking windmills and windswept dykes at **Kinderdijk** (p161).

6 Boarding the hand-built, full-biblical-scale **Ark van Noach** (p162) in Dordrecht.

7 Unwinding in Leiden's lush 16th-century botanical gardens, the **Hortus Botanicus Leiden** (p181).

SOUTH HOLLAND

Along with the provinces of Noord-Holland (North Holland) and Utrecht, Zuid-Holland (South Holland) is part of the Randstad, the economic and population heart of the Netherlands.

Rotterdam

♫ 010 / POP 616,000

Futuristic architecture, inspired local initiatives such as inner-city canal surfing, a proliferation of art, and a surge of drinking, dining and nightlife venues make Rotterdam one of Europe's most exhilarating cities right now. The Netherlands' second-largest metropolis has a diverse, multiethnic community, an absorbing maritime tradition centred on Europe's busiest port, and a wealth of top-class museums.

Rotterdam is a veritable open-air gallery of modern, postmodern and contemporary construction. It's a remarkable feat for a city largely razed to the ground by WWII bombers. Rebuilding has continued unabated ever since with ingenuity and vision.

Split by the vast Nieuwe Maas shipping channel, Rotterdam is crossed by a series of tunnels and bridges, notably the dramatic Erasmusbrug – the swooping white cable-stayed bridge dubbed de Zwaan (the Swan). On the north side of the water, the city centre is easily strolled.

History

Rotterdam's history as a major port dates to the 16th century. In 1572 Spaniards being pursued by the rebel Sea Beggars were given shelter in the harbour. They rewarded this generosity by pillaging the town. Rotterdam soon joined the revolution.

Astride the major southern rivers, Rotterdam is ideally situated to service trading ships. Large canals first constructed in the 1800s and improved ever since link the port with the Rhine River and other major waterways.

On 14 May 1940 the invading Germans issued an ultimatum to the Dutch government: surrender or cities such as Rotterdam will be destroyed. The government capitulated; however, the bombers were already airborne and the raid was carried out anyway.

Rather than rebuild in historical style, skyscrapers and groundbreaking architectural statements give it an evolving skyline unlike any other in the Netherlands.

Efforts to make the city – 80% of which lies below sea level – fully climate-proof by 2025 include water plazas that double as playgrounds, car-park water-storage tanks and environmentally sustainable floating houses.

◉ Sights

With so many memorable buildings and landmarks, Rotterdam is easy to navigate. The city centre is also a lot smaller than it seems for such a bustling metropolis – you might never need to use the efficient public-transport system of metros, buses and trams. The ultimate way to see the city is by bike.

★ Museum Boijmans van Beuningen   MUSEUM

(www.boijmans.nl; Museumpark 18-20; adult/child €15/free; ⊙ 11am-5pm Tue-Sun) Among Europe's finest museums, the Museum Boijmans van Beuningen has a permanent collection spanning all eras of Dutch and European art, including superb old masters. Among the highlights are *The Marriage Feast at Cana* by Hieronymus Bosch, the *Three Maries at the Open Sepulchre* by Van Eyck, the minutely detailed *Tower of Babel* by Pieter Brueghel the Elder, and *Portrait of Titus* and *Man in a Red Cap* by Rembrandt.

Renaissance Italy is well represented; look for *The Wise and Foolish Virgins* by Tintoretto and *Satyr and Nymph* by Titian.

Paintings and sculpture since the mid-19th century are another strength. There are many Monets and other French Impressionists; Van Gogh and Gauguin are given space; and there are statues by Degas. The museum rightly prides itself on its collection by a group it calls 'the other surrealists', including Marcel Duchamp, René Magritte and Man Ray. Salvador Dalí gained a special room in the recent expansion, and the collection is one of the largest of his work outside Spain and France. All in all, the surrealist wing is utterly absorbing, with ephemera and paraphernalia rubbing against famous works.

Modern modes are not forgotten, and the whole place is nothing if not eclectic: a nude or an old master might be nestled next to a '70s bubble TV, some kind of installation or a vibrating table.

There's also a good cafe and a pleasant sculpture garden (featuring Claes Oldenburg's famous *Bent Screw,* among others).

ARCHITECTURE HIGHLIGHTS

Rotterdam is a vast open-air museum of modern and contemporary design, with architectural wonders such as the new home of the Museum Rotterdam, the Timmerhuis; and the eye-popping Markthal Rotterdam (p159).

Overblaak Development (Overblaak) Designed by Piet Blom and built from 1978 to 1984, this mind-bending development facing the Markthal Rotterdam is marked by its pencil-shaped tower, **De Kolk**, and 'forest' of 45-degree-tilted, cube-shaped apartments on hexagonal pylons. One apartment, the **Kijk-Kubus Museum-House** (www.kubuswoning.nl; Overblaak 70; adult/child €2.50/1.50; ⊙11am-5pm), is open to the public; the Stayokay Rotterdam (p154) youth hostel occupies the supersized cube at the southern end.

Erasmusbrug A symbol of the city, this graceful bridge dubbed 'the Swan' was designed by architect Ben van Berkel in 1996 and spans 802m across the Maas river.

KPN Telecom Headquarters (Wilhelminakade 123) Designed by celebrated architect Renzo Piano and opened in 2000, the KPN Telecom headquarters building leans at a sharp angle, seemingly resting on a long pole.

MaasToren (MaasTower; Wilhelminakade 1) The 2009-built MaasToren is the tallest building in the Netherlands at 165m. Its durable heating and cooling system uses water from the Maas and energy storage in the soil to reduce the building's carbon footprint.

De Rotterdam (Wilhelminakade 177) Completed in 2013, the glitzy 'vertical city' De Rotterdam, designed by Pritzker-winning Rotterdam architect Rem Koolhaas, is the Netherlands' largest building. It incorporates a hotel, superb restaurant HMB (p156), and cocktail bar opening to a panoramic 7th-floor terrace.

Boompjestorens (Boompjes 266-387) Completed in 1989, these three residential towers, Clipper, Schoener and Galjoen (Clipper, Schooner and Galleon), rise to 70m.

Willemswerf (Boompjes 40) Alongside the water is the striking 1988 Willemswerf office building, with a sloping glass trapezium making a diagonal cut-away across the facade.

Willemsbrug Rotterdam's second signature bridge, the 1981-opened Willemsbrug, makes a bold statement with its crimson red pylons.

Van Nelle Fabriek (Van Nelle Factory; Van Nelleweg 1) Unesco World Heritage status is a rarity for an industrial building, but this 'glass palace', a former coffee, tea and tobacco factory built between 1925 and 1931, is a 20th-century icon. It's now filled with design studios and is closed to the public, but Urban Guides (p153) runs 75-minute tours (adult/child €12.50/7.50) at 10.30am Wednesday to Sunday July and August, and 10.30am Saturday and Sunday in May, June, September and October.

Het Nieuwe Instituut (🖉 440 12 00; http://hetnieuweinstituut.nl; Museumpark 25; adult/child €10/free; ⊙10am-5pm Tue-Sat, 11am-5pm Sun) With one side surrounded by a green moat and new garden, and the other comprising a sweeping flow of brick along Rochussenstraat, the Het Nieuwe Instituut is striking. It's a merger of the Netherlands Architecture Institute, the Netherlands Institute for Design and Fashion, and e-culture institute Virtueel Platform, presenting exhibitions on architecture, design, digital culture and fashion.

Included in the admission price is a ticket to **Huis Sonneveld** (Jongkindstraat 25; ⊙10am-5pm Tue-Sat, 11am-5pm Sun), designed by Brinkman and Van der Vlugt and an outstanding example of the Dutch New Building architectural strain (also known as Dutch Functionalism). This 1933 villa has been lovingly restored, with furniture, wallpaper and fixtures present and correct – it is an astonishing experience, almost like virtual reality.

Kunsthal　　　　　　　　GALLERY
(www.kunsthal.nl; Westzeedijk 341; adult/child €12/2; ⊙10am-5pm Tue-Sat, 11am-5pm Sun) At the southern end of Museumpark, the Kunsthal hosts around 20 wildly diverse temporary exhibitions each year, including art and design.

Everything 'from elitist to popular' gets an airing.

It was the victim of a major theft in 2012 when several masterpieces by Monet and Matisse, among others, were stolen (they are still missing).

Witte de With,
Centre for Contemporary Art   MUSEUM
(📞411 01 44; www.wdw.nl; Witte de Withstraat 50; adult/child €6/3; ⊘11am-6pm Tue-Sun) Founded in 1990, the Witte de With, Centre for Contemporary Art has its finger on the pulse of breaking developments in contemporary art worldwide. Its experimental exhibitions, installations and events have a laser-sharp social and political focus, and it has a reputation as a launch pad for up-and-coming talent. It closes between exhibitions while new works are being set up, so check ahead to be sure it's open.

The centre is a linchpin of several contemporary culture institutions on and around Witte de Withstraat that are collectively known as the **Kunstblock Rotterdam** (Arts Block Rotterdam; http://kunstblock.nl). Try to catch **Art Evening**, held on the first Friday of each month, when the venues are free to visit from 6pm to 9pm, and free one-hour introductory tours kick off from 7pm.

Euromast   VIEWPOINT
(www.euromast.nl; Parkhaven 20; adult/child €9.50/6.10; ⊘9.30am-10pm Apr-Sep, 10am-10pm Oct-Mar) A 1960-built landmark, the 185m Euromast offers unparalleled 360-degree views of Rotterdam from its 100m-high observation deck, reached by lift in 30 seconds.

Extra diversions include a brasserie serving lunch, high tea, high wine, dinner and Sunday brunch, as well as summertime abseiling (€52.50). The tower's two suites start from €385, including breakfast.

Het Park   PARK
You can escape the urban jungle surprisingly easily among the lakes of Het Park. In summer locals love to barbecue here on the grassy expanses.

Immediately east is **Tuin Schoonoord** (www.tuinschoonoord.nl; Kievitslaan 8; ⊘8.30am-4.30pm) FREE, a hidden re-creation of an idealised Dutch wilderness that seems to have been taken right from a Renaissance painting.

Maritiem Museum Rotterdam   MUSEUM
(Maritime Museum; www.maritiemmuseum.nl; Leuvehaven 1; adult/child €8.50/4.50; ⊘10am-5pm Tue-Sat, 11am-5pm Sun, plus Mon during school holidays) This comprehensive, kid-friendly museum looks at the Netherlands' rich maritime traditions through an array of models that any youngster would love to take into the tub. There are great explanatory displays such as Mainport Live, giving a 'real time'

view of the port's action in miniature, and a raft of fun temporary exhibitions.

Haven Museum   MUSEUM
(www.maritiemmuseum.nl; Leuvehaven 50) FREE Just south of the Maritime Museum, the Haven Museum comprises all manner of old and historic ships moored in the basin. You can always wander the quays. Signs in English and Dutch let you learn more about what's tied up.

Museum Rotterdam   MUSEUM
(www.museumrotterdam.nl; Meent) Early 2016 sees the Museum Rotterdam reopen inside the 'cloud-like' Rem Koolhaas–designed Timmerhuis building, showcasing Rotterdam's past, present and future.

Wereldmuseum   MUSEUM
(World Museum; www.wereldmuseum.nl; Willemskade 25; adult/child €15/free; ⊘10am-5.30pm Tue-Sun) Inside the 19th-century Royal Yacht Club, the Wereldmuseum celebrates multiculturalism, focusing on rituals, stories and sacred objects, through its permanent collection and major temporary exhibitions. Its magnificent Modern Mediterranean restaurant has a Michelin star.

Miniworld Rotterdam   MODEL TRAINS
(www.miniworldrotterdam.com; Weena 745; adult/child €11/7.50; ⊘weekday hours vary, 10am-5pm Sat & Sun) The Dutch love of the world in miniature is celebrated at the vast Miniworld, a ginormous 535-sq-metre 1:87 scale model railroad re-creating Rotterdam (with landmarks including its new Centraal Station), the Port of Rotterdam and the Randstad, with day and night simulation.

STREET ART

Not only is Rotterdam an architectural gallery, its streets are also filled with art.

Well over 60 sculptures are scattered all over town (with more appearing every year), including many by major artists, such as Paul McCarthy's outsized 2001 **Santa Claus** (Eendrachtsplein), and Picasso's sandblasted 1970 concrete sculpture **Sylvette** (Westersingel), which he designed with Norwegian artist Carl Nesjar.

For a full list of sculptures and an interactive map of their locations, visit Sculpture International Rotterdam (www.sculptureinternationalrotterdam.nl).

ROTTERDAM & SOUTH HOLLAND ROTTERDAM

Rotterdam Central

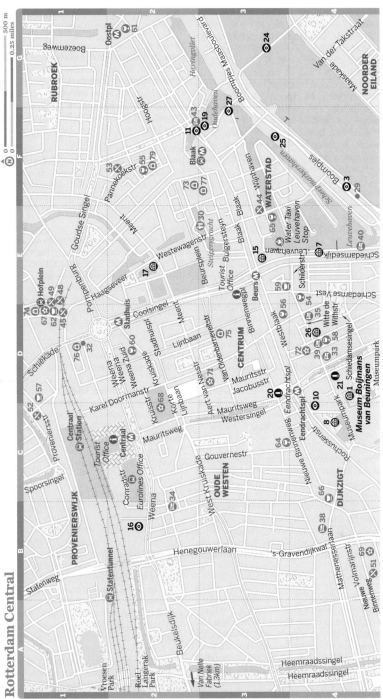

Rotterdam Central

'40-'45 NU   MUSEUM

(War & Resistance Museum; www.40-45nu.nl; Coolhaven 375; adult/child €6/4; ⊙10am-5pm Tue-Fri, noon-5pm Sun) The chilling sounds of Luftwaffe bombers set the scene at this small museum sheltered under a bridge. Displays recount life in Rotterdam during WWII; the fear in the faces of people fleeing the bombing in a 1940 photo is raw.

Nederlands Fotomuseum   MUSEUM

(www.nederlandsfotomuseum.nl; Wilhelminakade 332; adult/child €9/free; ⊙10am-5pm Tue-Fri, 11am-5pm Sat & Sun) On the waterfront across the Maas, the Nederlands Fotomuseum mounts large temporary exhibitions. The highlight is the basement Dark Room, a superb interactive museum with historic photos and films overlaying the history of both the country and photography. Signs and commentary are in English. Allow at least a couple of hours here.

Witte Huis ARCHITECTURE
(White House; Wijnhaven 3) Dating from 1897–98, Europe's first 'skyscraper', the 11-storey, 45m-high Witte Huis, was designed by Willem Molenbroek in art nouveau style using load-bearing brick walls rather than a steel skeleton, and is a rare survivor of the prewar period.

🏃 Activities

RiF010 SURFING
(www.rif010.nl; Steigersgracht) From 2016, surfers, bodyboarders, stand-up paddleboarders and kayakers can take a wild 14-second ride on a naturally purified, barrelling 1.5m-high wave in an inner-city canal. Its water-level beach-house cafe provides up-close views of the action.

👉 Tours

★ Urban Guides TOUR
(☑ 433 22 31; http://urbanguides.nl; Schiekade 205, Hofplein; ⊙ office 10am-7pm Mon-Sat, noon-5pm Sun) Based in the Schieblock (p155), this hip young outfit of passionate Rotterdammers runs a fantastic selection of tours, from 2½-hour 'ByCycle' tours (adult/couple/child €25/45/17.50) to architectural cycling tours (including an option led by architecture students), walking tours, building tours such as the Van Nelle Fabriek (p148), boat tours, exhibition tours and more. It also rents bikes (per day €10).

Spido BOAT TOUR
(www.spido.nl; Willemsplein 85; adult/child €11.75/7.25) Harbour tours lasting 75 minutes depart from the pier at Leuvehoofd near the Erasmusbrug (by the Leuvehaven metro station). There are up to 10 departures daily in July and August, fewer during the rest of the year.

Line 10 TOUR
(☑ 06 5351 3630; www.lijn10.nl; adult/child €7/4.50; ⊙ departures 11am-4.35pm Tue-Sun Jul & Aug, Fri-Sun Sep & Oct) Ride a historical tram through the city on Line 10, which stops at eight key destinations including Markthall Rotterdam, the Euromast and Delfshaven. Tickets are valid all day, so you can hop on and off as you like. Buy tickets on board (cash only). Trams depart near the Spido dock on Willemsplein.

⭐ Festivals & Events

Rotterdam has festivals and events big and small all year long.

International Film Festival Rotterdam FILM
(www.iffr.com; ⊙ late Jan-early Feb) A top-notch selection of independent and experimental films screen over 12 days.

Motel Mozaïque CULTURAL
(http://motelmozaique.nl; ⊙ mid-Apr) Stay in unique locations such as art installations and take artist-guided expeditions during the two-day Motel Mozaïque music, art and performance festival.

Poetry International Festival LITERATURE
(www.poetry.nl; ⊙ early–mid-Jun) Poets from all over the world converge for this five-day festival spanning readings, masterclasses, craft talks and more.

★ North Sea Jazz Festival JAZZ
(www.northseajazz.nl; ⊙ mid-Jul) One of the world's most-respected jazz events sees around a thousand musicians perform. A lot of the acts organise unofficial jams outside the three-day festival, a kind of prefestival festival.

Rotterdam Unlimited Zomercarnaval CULTURAL
(Rotterdam Unlimited Summer Carnival; www.zomercarnaval.nl; ⊙ last weekend in Jul) Rotterdam's multicultural make-up is a vital part of its lifeblood, with some 170 nationalities calling it home. A cacophonous 'battle of drums' and colourful street parade are highlights of this vibrant Caribbean celebration.

★ Wereldhavendagen FAIR
(World Port Days; www.wereldhavendagen.nl; ⊙ 1st weekend in Sep) Tours of normally off-limits industrial areas, nautical displays and sea shanties are part of early September's fascinating World Port Days. Festivalgoers don retro get-ups such as sailor, pirate and prostitute outfits for the spin-off de Nacht van de Kaap (Night of the Cape), held on one crazy Wereldhavendagen night in Katendrecht, Rotterdam's former red-light quarter.

🛏 Sleeping

Rotterdam has a wave of new design hostels and boutique and designer digs, as well as venerable treasures.

★ King Kong Hostel HOSTEL €
(☑ 818 87 78; www.kingkonghostel.com; Witte de Withstraat 74; dm/d/q from €22.50/75/110; @ 🛜)

Outdoor benches made from salvaged timbers and garden hoses by Sander Bokkinga sit outside King Kong, a design haven on Rotterdam's coolest street. Artist-designed rooms and dorms are filled with vintage and industrial furniture; fab features include hammocks, lockers equipped with device-charging points, a gourmet self-catering kitchen, roof garden and barbecue area, and Netflix.

Ani & Haakien
HOSTEL €

(☑236 10 86; www.anihaakien.nl; Coolsestraat 47-49; dm €18.50-25.50, d from €50; ☞) An old-school hostel for the digital generation, Ani and Haakien's homey place has design furniture, lockers with power outlets, and lightning-fast wi-fi, but also a garden with hammocks, a great kitchen, a laundry and an adorable resident cat. It's a 600m walk southwest of Centraal Station.

Stayokay Rotterdam
HOSTEL €

(☑436 57 63; www.stayokay.com; Overblaak 85-87; dm/d from €21/59; ☞) Inside the landmark Overblaak (p148) development, this HI hostel has 245 beds in oddly shaped rooms that sleep two to eight.

★Pincoffs
BOUTIQUE HOTEL €€

(☑297 45 00; www.hotelpincoffs.nl; Stieltjesstraat 34; d/ste from €119/225; P❋☞) A former customs house dating from 1879 encases this exquisite sanctum that blends recycled and vintage art and furniture with 21st-century style. Romantic rooms come with luxuries such as Egyptian cotton robes and towels. A wood-burning fireplace blazes in the bar, and there's a water-taxi stop outside the front door.

SS Rotterdam
DESIGN HOTEL €€

(☑297 30 90; http://ssrotterdam.nl; 3e Katendrechtse Hoofd 25; s/d/f from €98/103/160; P☞☒) Ocean liner SS *Rotterdam* was built in the city in the late 1950s and its 576 original cabins have been converted to 254 '50s-style hotel rooms in three very cool themes: Original, Manhattan and Bahamas. Parking's not a problem (there are 580 spaces); bus 77 drops you at the door. Even if you're not staying here, ship tours are available.

A Small Hotel
BOUTIQUE HOTEL €€

(☑414 03 03; www.asmallhotel.nl; Witte de Withstraat 94; d €99-139; ❋☞) The six rooms at this hotel on where-it's-at Witte de Withstraat are stylishly designed around three themes: Tex, Zen and Coco (for Coco-mat). All rooms have Coco-mat mattresses, along with free stocked minibars, in-room snacks

and tea- and coffee-making facilities. Two caveats: there's no lift and no reception (there's a code-activated key safe).

Hotel Van Walsum
HOTEL €€

(☑436 32 75; www.hotelvanwalsum.nl; Mathenesserlaan 199-201; s/d/tr/q from €90/105/120/135; P❋☞) In a group of grand townhouses dating from 1895, but with mod cons including a lift, this warm, welcoming family-run hotel is just a 10-minute walk from the centre, with great public-transport connections. Comfortable rooms are decorated in autumnal hues; there's a charming back garden and secure parking (per day €15). Rates include breakfast.

Hotel Bazar
HOTEL €€

(☑206 51 51; www.bazarrotterdam.nl; Witte de Withstraat 16; d €80-130) Bazar has 27 over-the-top Middle Eastern, African and South American themed rooms: lush, brocaded curtains, exotically tiled bathrooms and more. Top-floor rooms have balconies and views. It's home to a spectacular restaurant (p157); Turkish bread, international cheeses, yogurt, pancakes and coffee are all on the menu at breakfast.

Hotel Stroom
BOUTIQUE HOTEL €€

(☑221 40 60; www.stroomrotterdam.nl; Lloydstraat 1; d €125-200; ❋☞) Housed in a converted power station, Stroom's designer studios come in a range of configurations, such as the *videstudio* option, a jaw-dropping split-level abode under a glass roof with an open bathroom. It's all sleek, white and metallic. During slow times these luxury rooms are cut-price.

Hotel New York
HISTORIC HOTEL €€€

(☑439 05 00; www.hotelnewyork.nl; Koninginnenhoofd 1; d €99-295; @☞) An art nouveau showpiece, the Holland-America passenger-ship line's former HQ has sweeping vistas, superb dining options including an oyster bar, a barber shop, and a water taxi ferrying guests across the Nieuwe Maas to the city centre. Rooms retain original, painstakingly restored fittings and decor; styles range from standard to timber-panelled suites in the old boardrooms with fireplaces.

Mainport
DESIGN HOTEL €€€

(☑217 57 57; www.mainporthotel.com; Leuvehaven 77; d from €165; P❋☞☒) Locations don't come better than the Mainport, spectacularly set on the harbour a heartbeat from the city's action. Ultraplush rooms are subtly themed to reflect far-flung locations and

STATION HOFPLEIN & AROUND

Among Rotterdam's innovative redevelopments is Station Hofplein (www.station hofplein.nl), the former station of the disused Hofpleinlijn railway, the viaduct arches of which are transforming into cultural and creative spaces, including cutting-edge restaurants, cafes, design and music shops, and a jazz club.

Station Hofplein is connected by the wooden **Luchtsingel** (air canal) footbridge over the train tracks, which was crowd-funded by the sale of inscribed planks. One section skewers the office-building-turned-design-studio-hub Schieblock (www.schieblock. com), topped by the pioneering DakAkker harvestable roof, producing fruit, vegetables and honey. While the Schieblock is closed to the public, there are some great shops, cafes, bars and other initiatives such as tour company Urban Guides (p153) around its base.

Eating & Drinking

FG Noodle Bar (http://fgnoodlebar.nl; Katshoek 33; dishes €10-17.50; ⊘11am-7pm Mon-Sat) Rotterdam's hottest chef, François Geurds, recently opened this noodle bar where you walk through the shop-style space and pick up your ingredients – 15 different types of noodles (including gluten-free seaweed noodles), more than 10 types of tofu, beef, prawns, bok choy, ginger, bean sprouts, eggs – and take them to the chef's station to be whipped up.

De Jong (☑465 79 55; www.restaurantdejong.nl; Rampoortstraat 38; 4-course menu €45; ⊘6-11pm Wed-Sun; ☑) Adventurous chef Jim De Jong wows diners with surprise four-course menus (meat/fish or vegetarian; no à la carte) made from seasonal produce including herbs and flowers from the restaurant's garden.

★FG Food Labs (☑425 05 20; www.fgrestaurant.nl; Katshoek 41; mains €15-32.50; ⊘noon-2pm & 6-10pm) François Geurds' one-Michelin-star molecular-gastronomy lab sits under timber and silvery pressed-tin ceilings within Station Hofplein. You can dine here on his evolving cuisine, pop next door to FG Noodle Bar or even take a culinary electric-bike tour (€95). Tours around Rotterdam start from the lab and include a three-course lunch at his flagship two-Michelin-star premises, FG (p157).

Lokaal (www.lokaal-espresso.nl; Raampoortstraat 34b; ⊘9am-6pm Mon-Fri, 10am-5pm Sat & Sun; ☎) Local Rotterdam products are at the heart of Lokaal (bread, cheese, beer...) but its speciality is brewing Rotterdam-roasted espresso and filter blends from Giraffe Coffee Roasters. The viaduct space is fitted out in warm timbers; there are tables on the pavement out front.

Entertainment

Bird Jazz Club (http://bird-rotterdam.nl; Raampoortstraat 26-28; tickets from €9; ⊘5.30pm-1am Tue-Thu, to 4am Fri & Sat) Jazz but also soul, hip hop, funk and electronica all get a run at Bird, named for American jazz saxophonist Charlie 'Bird' Parker; check the online agenda to see who's playing and prepurchase tickets. Its excellent restaurant serves wood-fired pizzas and small plates; the kitchen closes at 9.30pm.

Shopping

Groos (http://groosrotterdam.nl; Schiekade 203, Hofplein; ⊘10.30am-7pm Wed & Thu, to 9pm Fri, to 6pm Sat, noon-6pm Sun) For made-in-Rotterdam fashion, handmade jewellery, homewares, artworks, books, stationery, music and edibles such as chocolates, coffee and more, browse groovy concept-shop Groos (revived local slang for 'pride'), situated in the Schieblock.

Clone (☑436 95 06; https://clone.nl; Raampoortstraat 12; ⊘10.30am-6pm Mon-Thu & Sat, 10.30am-9pm Fri, noon-5pm Sun) One of the most recent arrivals at Station Hofplein is the relocation of Dutch experimental/underground electronic-dance-music record label and vinyl shop, Clone. It stocks hard-to-find merchandise (especially T-shirts), too.

Rotterdam's role as a port. Many rooms have amenities such as saunas or hot tubs; the heavenly 8th-floor spa has a hammam, Turkish steam bath and gym.

✖ Eating

Rotterdam's foodie scene is booming. Look out for new openings all over the city and especially in hotspots like Station Hofplein (p155). The stunning Markthal Rotterdam (p159) has sit-down and takeaway eating options galore, as does Fenix Food Factory.

★ Tante Nel
FAST FOOD €
(www.tante-nel.com; Pannekoekstraat 53a; dishes €2.25-7.75; ⊙noon-10pm Tue-Sat, to 9pm Sun) New-generation Tante Nel is as tiny as a traditional *frites* (fries) stand but decked out with a stunning Dutch-design painted brick interior and marquee-style canopied terrace for savouring its organic, hand-cut fries (topped by a choice of different sauces), along with house-speciality milkshakes, beer, wine and 13 different gins.

Ter Marsch & Co
BURGERS €
(www.termarschco.nl; Witte de Withstraat 70; burgers €9.50-16.50; ⊙noon-10pm) Butcher-shop-turned-burger-bar Ter Marsch & Co sizzles up monumental burgers (such as Scottish black Angus, pancetta and truffle mayo) that recently saw it awarded the coveted title of Best Burgers in the Netherlands.

La Zia Maria
ITALIAN €
(www.laziamaria.nl; Nieuwe Binnenweg 222a; dishes €5.70-9.50, 3-course lunch menu €27.50; ⊙noon-7pm Mon, 10am-7pm Tue-Fri, 9am-5pm Sat) There are just three tables seating 12 inside this aromatic deli and two more, seating four,

on the pavement outside. If you don't manage to snag one, it's still a fabulous place to pick up Italian specialities such as *formaggi* (cheese), *salumi* (cold cuts), antipasti, fresh ready-to-eat pasta and desserts such as tiramisu and cassata for a canal-side picnic.

Fritez
FAST FOOD €
(Witte de Withstraat 68a; dishes €3.50-7.50; ⊙10am-10pm Tue-Thu, to 2am Fri & Sat, to 8pm Sun) Billed by owner-chef Ruben Kruit as 'haute friture', Fritez serves hand-cut, organic-potato *frites* cooked in premium vegetable oil with six different sauces: mayo, garlic mayo, truffle mayo, pickles and curry, peanut, and tomato ketchup, in pyramid-style recycled cardboard cones. From April to October, it's open to 4am on weekends. Look out for Fritez' food truck at festivals.

HMB
INTERNATIONAL €€
(☑760 06 20; www.hmb-restaurant.nl; Holland Amerika Kade 104; small plates €13-19.50, 3-course lunch menu €35, 4-/5-/6-course dinner menu €49/59/71; ⊙noon-3.30pm & 5.30-10pm Tue-Fri, 5.30-10pm Sat) On the ground floor of the glitzy 'vertical city' De Rotterdam (p148), with dazzling views of the Erasmusbrug, chic HMB serves artistically presented contemporary cuisine (veal meatballs with truffled potatoes; foie gras with eel and apple) at impressively reasonable prices. Afterwards, head to the terrace of the building's 7th-floor cocktail bar.

Alan & Pims
BARBECUE €€
(☑237 32 44; www.alanenpims.nl; Posthoornstraat 524; mains €10-21.50; ⊙11am-11pm) A floor-to-ceiling black-and-white 1930s photo of Rotterdam's main shopping street is a reminder of how much the city's achieved

KATENDRECHT

Known as de Kaap (the Cape), industrial Katendrecht was Rotterdam's one-time red-light district but is now at the forefront of an emerging foodie scene, thanks in large part to market collective **Fenix Food Factory** (www.fenixfoodfactory.nl; Veerlaan 19d; ⊙10am-7pm Wed-Fri, 10am-6pm Sat, noon-5pm Sun). Everything in this vast former warehouse is made locally and sold by separate vendors making their mark on the food scene. They include Booij Kaasmakers (cheese), Cider Cider (cider), Jordy's Bakery (bread and baked goods), Stielman Koffiebranders (coffee roasters), Kaapse Brouwers (craft beer) and Rechtstreex (locally grown fruit and veggies). There's also a bar here that stays open until 11pm.

Every day, the market is also filled with changing food trucks. A large farmers market (outside if it's sunny, inside if it's not) takes place here on the last Saturday of the month.

Opposite the Factory, Deliplein has a string of cafes and bars, and is also where you'll find Katendrecht – and Rotterdam – legend **Tattoo Bob** (☑484 46 94; www.tattoobob.nl; Delistraat 4-10; ⊙1-10pm Mon-Sat), tattooing here on the Cape since 1968.

in postwar rebuilding. Behind the dining room's recycled-timber tables is a full-width white-tiled open kitchen filled with spit-roasting chickens. Chicken marinated in Thai, Provençal or barbecue comes with sides such as jacket-roasted potatoes, fries and corn on the cob.

Le Nord
BISTRO €€

(☑265 44 38; www.lenord.nl; Proveniersstraat 33a; mains €10.50-21.50; ⊗4-10pm Mon-Thu, 3-10pm Fri & Sat, 3-8pm Sun) In the Provenierswijk neighbourhood epicurean hub, Le Nord looks like it might as easily be in a French village for its sage green walls, red-leather bar stools, mezzanine framed by wrought-iron balustrades, and above all its food: steak tartare topped with a quail's egg, Normandy oysters with red-wine vinegar and shallots, and pan-fried turbot meunière in brown-butter sauce, parsley and lemon.

Bazar
MIDDLE EASTERN €€

(www.bazarrotterdam.nl; Witte de Withstraat 16; mains €8.50-16; ⊗8am-11pm Mon-Thu, to midnight Fri, 9am-midnight Sat & Sun) Beneath the exotic Hotel Bazar (p154), this dazzling lantern-lit, souk-style stalwart dishes up dolmades, couscous, hummus, falafel, kebabs, Turkish pizza, baked feta with mint and parsley, Persian lamb and more. Tables spill onto the pavement terrace.

★FG
GASTRONOMY €€€

(☑425 05 20; http://fgrestaurant.nl; Lloydstraat 204; 3-course lunch menu Tue-Fri €45, 4-/5-/7-/9-course menu €91/111/131/151; ⊗noon-2pm & 6.30-9pm Tue-Thu, noon-2pm & 7-9pm Fri & Sat) Quail jelly and langoustine cream; Anjou pigeon with cherry sorbet; truffle macaroni with gold leaf; razor clams with asparagus and pearl barley; lobster with parsnip and caviar; and Masia El Altet extra-virgin olive oil, vanilla and macadamia brittle are among the incomparable dishes on the multicourse menus (no à la carte) at superstar chef François Geurds' flagship, twin-Michelin-starred restaurant.

🍷 Drinking & Nightlife

Witte de Withstraat is easily Rotterdam's coolest street and makes a perfect place to kick off an evening in the city.

★ Bokaal
BAR

(http://bokaalrotterdam.nl; Nieuwemarkt 11; ⊗noon-1pm Sun-Thu, to 2am Fri & Sat) In a *bokaal* (trophy) location at the heart of the enclave around pedestrian Nieuwmarkt

and Pannekoekstraat locally dubbed 'Soho Rotterdam', Bokaal's spectacularly designed bar has butcher-shop tiling, raw concrete floors, and an oak bar and huge all-day-sun terrace. Beer (craft and Trappist) is its speciality, with nine on tap, and more than 80 in bottles, along with charcuterie and cheese.

Vessel 11
PUB

(www.vessel11.nl; Wijnhaven 101; ⊗noon-2am Wed & Thu, noon-4am Fri, 11am-4am Sat, 11am-midnight Sun) This fire-engine-red, 1951-built lighthouse vessel (with a working gas light and foghorn) is now a Brit-influenced pub which brews its own ale, hosts live gigs (mainly rock) and barbecues, and serves full English breakfasts and Sunday roasts. It also rents Rotterdam-designed 'hot-tub boats' (per two hours for two/eight people €139/259) to pilot around the harbour while you soak.

Hopper
COFFEE

(Schiedamse Vest 146; ⊗8.30am-6pm Mon-Fri, 10am-6pm Sat, 11am-6pm Sun; 🛜) Hopper roasts its own coffee using single-source beans and has its own on-site bakery, which makes sourdoughs, pastries and cakes. The huge, airy space with soaring ceilings has rough-polished concrete floors, communal timber tables, and a wraparound mezzanine overlooking the action.

Café LaBru
BAR

(http://cafelabru.nl; Hartmansstraat 18a; ⊗2pm-1am Sun-Thu, to 2am Fri & Sat) Hard-to-find whisky, gin, rum, tequila and craft beers are on the menu at this supercool vintage- and retro-adorned bar.

Blender
CLUB

(http://blenderrotterdam.nl; Schiedamse Vest 9; ⊗4pm-4am Wed-Sat) This scenester's glamorous street-level restaurant and cocktail bar acts as a wraparound balcony looking down into its UV-lit basement club.

Caffè Booon
CAFE

(www.caffebooon.nl; Proveniersstraat 33; ⊗7.30am-6pm Mon-Thu, 7.30am-7pm Fri, 9am-6pm Sat & Sun) Huge glass windows fill Italian-accented Booon with light, and its early opening hours and proximity to Centraal Station make it a perfect spot to jump-start the day with an espresso (it also runs barista workshops), flaky pastries, gourmet sandwiches and bruschetta. It's one of the anchors of the canal-threaded Provenierswijk neighbourhood's local foodie hub of cafes, restaurants and wine bars.

DELFSHAVEN

Just 3km southwest of the Rotterdam centre, Delfshaven, once the official seaport for the city of Delft, survived the war and retains a villagelike atmosphere. In addition to historic sights and a wonderful brewery, there are a string of galleries, artist studios and workshops in its beautiful gabled buildings, as well as charming restaurants and cafes.

Delfshaven is easily reached by foot, bike, trams 4 or 8, or the metro to the Delfshaven station.

Sights

Oude Kerk (www.pilgrimfatherschurch.org; Aelbrechtskolk 20; ⊘noon-4pm Fri & Sat, hours can vary) The Pilgrims prayed for the last time at Delfshaven's 1417-founded Oude Kerk (aka Pilgrim Fathers Church) before leaving the Netherlands for America aboard the *Speedwell* on 22 July 1620. They could barely keep the leaky boat afloat and, in England, eventually transferred to the *Mayflower* – the rest is history. Models of their vaguely seaworthy boats are inside. It closes for events such as weddings and concerts.

Stadsbrouwerij De Pelgrim (www.pelgrimbier.nl; Aelbrechtskolk 12; ⊘noon-midnight Wed-Sun) The heady scent of hops greets you at this vintage brewery abutting the Oude Kerk, with bubbling copper vats by the entrance. Here you can take a voyage through its wonderful seasonal and standard beers such as Rotterdams Stoombier and Mayflower Tripel in the bar, canal-side terrace or courtyard. A tasting flight of five beers costs €5. Ask and they'll usually let you peek at the tanks. There's a restaurant, too.

Windmill (Voorhaven 210) A reconstructed 18th-century windmill overlooks the water at Delfshaven. It still mills grain; the interior is closed to the public.

Eating & Drinking

't Ouwe Bruggetje (www.historisch-delfshaven.nl; Voorhaven 6; mains €17.50-27.50; ⊘6-10pm Wed-Sat, 3-10pm Sun) A Delfshaven jewel, 't Ouwe Bruggetje has a timber-panelled interior with hefty wooden beams, seating by the iron-framed drawbridge out front, and a floating terrace on the canal for dining on dishes such as guinea fowl on sauerkraut with tarragon and mustard, and salmon roulade with cucumber horseradish. It imports more than 100 barrels of wine every year from across Europe.

Restaurant Fritschy (☑477 30 25; www.fritschy.nl; Piet Heynsplein 25; 8-course menu €35; ⊘6-11pm Thu-Sun) Inside a beautiful Delfshaven canal house, with an intimate split-level, dark timber interior, Fritschy serves an astounding-value eight-course surprise menu using ingredients from its own kitchen garden. Although there's no choice on the night (and no à la carte), the chef skilfully adapts to dietary requirements (gluten-free, vegetarian, allergies) so long as you advise when you book (reservations are essential).

De Oude Sluis (Havenstraat 7; ⊘noon-1am Mon-Thu, noon-2am Fri, 2pm-2am Sat, 2pm-1am Sun) The view up the canal from the tables outside goes right out to Delfshaven's windmill at this ideal *bruin café* (brown *café*). The *kriek* (Belgian cherry beer) on tap is a bargain.

Hugh   COCKTAIL BAR
(www.hughrotterdam.nl; Kruiskade 15; ⊘noon-midnight Tue-Sun) A shipping-container bar is the centrepiece bar of Hugh's massive, multilevel space, which has a geometric retro design, DJs on the decks and a lounge vibe. G&T prices are knocked down on Friday's gin night, which showcases a different gin label each week.

Rotown   BAR
(www.rotown.nl; Nieuwe Binnenweg 17-19; ⊘11am-2am Sun-Wed, to 3am Thu-Sat) A smooth bar, a dependable live-rock venue, an agreeable restaurant, a popular meeting place. The musical program features new local talent, established international acts and crossover experiments.

De Witte Aap   BROWN CAFE
(www.dewitteaap.nl; Witte de Withstraat 78; ⊘noon-4am Sun-Thu, to 5am Fri & Sat; ⊗) Anchoring this artist-filled 'hood, the fabulous 'White Monkey' has live music on Wednesdays and DJs on Saturdays and is always crowded with locals. The front opens right up and a huge awning keeps inclement weather at bay.

Delfshaven

⭐ Entertainment

Catch sizzling jazz at Bird (p155), in the Station Hofplein complex.

Schouwburg   THEATRE
(✐411 81 10; www.rotterdamseschouwburg.nl; Schouwburgplein 25) Rotterdam's main cultural centre, the Schouwburg, has a changing calendar of dance, theatre and drama. Check out the intriguing light fixtures with red necks out the front.

Worm   LIVE MUSIC
(www.worm.org; Boomgaardsstraat 71; ⊘hours vary) Music here has a try-anything, do-anything vibe. Media mash-ups, performance art and experimental music are some of the more mundane events. It's part of the Kunstblock (p149) artistic hub.

Dizzy   LIVE MUSIC
(www.dizzy.nl; 's-Gravendijkwal 127; ⊘4pm-midnight Tue-Thu, to 1am Fri & Sat, to 11pm Sun) Live concerts Monday and Tuesday nights and Sunday afternoons. The evening performances are scorching: everything from hot jazz to fast and funky Brazilian and salsa. There are regular jazz jam sessions (and an excellent whisky collection).

De Doelen   CLASSICAL MUSIC
(✐217 17 17; www.dedoelen.nl; Schouwburgplein 50) Home venue of the renowned Rotterdam Philharmonic Orchestra, a sumptuous concert hall that seats 2200, De Deolen is also renowned for its jazz and world-music concerts.

LantarenVenster   CINEMA
(✐010-277 22 77; www.lantarenvenster.nl; Otto Reuchlinweg 996) Great art-house cinema with a good bar and cafe.

🛍 Shopping

Brand-name shops line the bustling, open-air, semisubterranean Beurstraverse, nicknamed de Koopgoot (buying trench).

More alternative options congregate on and around Meent, as well as Nieuwemarkt, Pannekoekstraat, OudeBinnenweg and Nieuwe Binnenweg.

Witte de Withstraat and its offshoots are home to hip boutiques and galleries.

You'll also find one-off shops in the Station Hofplein (p155) complex and its surrounds.

★Markthal Rotterdam   FOOD & DRINK
(http://markthalrotterdam.nl; Nieuwstraat; ⊘10am-8pm Mon-Thu & Sat, to 9pm Fri, noon-6pm Sun) The Netherlands' inaugural indoor food market

Westerpaviljoen   CAFE
(Nieuwe Binnenweg 136; ⊘8am-1am Mon-Fri, 9am-1am Sat & Sun) A huge, buzzy cafe with a very popular terrace, it's the perfect spot for a respite in this prime shopping district but is good at any time of the day when locals of all walks of life drop by. Breakfast is served until 3pm.

Locus Publicus   BROWN CAFE
(www.locus-publicus.com; Oostzeedijk 364; ⊘4pm-1am Sun-Thu, to 2am Fri & Sat) With more than 200 beers on its menu (including 12 always on tap), this is an outstanding specialist beer *café* (pub).

Maassilo   CLUB
(www.maassilo.com; Maashaven Zuidzijde 1-2; ⊘11pm-6am Fri & Sat, hours vary Sun-Thu) Pumpin' club inside a century-old grain silo with a capacity of 6000. Check the agenda to see what party's on when.

hit international headlines when it opened in 2014 due to its extraordinary inverted-U-shaped design, with glass-walled apartments arcing over the food hall's 40m-high fruit- and vegetable-muralled ceiling. There's a tantalising array of produce, prepared food and drinks; shops continue downstairs.

Blaak Markt MARKET
(⊙9am-5pm Tue & Sat) This huge street market sprawls across its namesake square outside the striking new Markthal Rotterdam. Stalls sell all manner of food, gadgets, clothes, antiques, snacks and much more.

Very Cherry FASHION
(www.verycherry.nl; Botersloot 52a; ⊙1-5.30pm Mon, 10am-5.30pm Tue-Sat, noon-5pm Sun) Vintage-inspired shoes, dresses, hats, handbags and swimwear stocked at Very Cherry include pieces by Voodoo Vixen, Pin Up Couture, Heart of Haute, Stop Staring, Lindy Bop, Emily & Finn and King Louis; it also sells its own label of retro '70s-style designs.

Donner BOOKS
(☑413 20 70; www.donner.nl; Coolsingel 119; ⊙11am-6pm Mon, 9.30am-6pm Tue-Thu & Sat, 9.30am-9pm Fri, noon-6pm Sun) This multi-floored place is one of the largest bookshops in the country.

❶ Information

Rotterdam Welcome Card (1/2/3 days per adult €10/13.50/17.50) Great-value savings on museum admission and free public transport. Pick it up at Rotterdam's tourist offices.

Tourist office (☑790 01 85; www.rotterdam. info; Coolsingel 197; ⊙9.30am-6pm; 🛜) Main tourist office.

Tourist office (Centraal Station; ⊙9am-5.30pm) Centraal Station branch of Rotterdam's tourist office.

❶ Getting There & Away

AIR

The Netherlands' huge international airport, Schiphol (AMS; www.schiphol.nl), is roughly equidistant by high-speed train to both Rotterdam and Amsterdam (around 20 to 30 minutes each). **Rotterdam The Hague Airport** (RTM; www.rotterdamthehagueairport.nl) Rotterdam The Hague Airport, serving more than 40 European destinations, is less than 6km northwest of Rotterdam.

BICYCLE

Two important national bike routes converge just east of Het Park. **LF2** runs north through Gouda to Amsterdam and south through Dordrecht to

Belgium. **LF11** runs from Den Haag through Rotterdam and on to Breda. Although the city seems large, 15 minutes of fast pedalling will have you out in the country.

BOAT

The Waterbus (p162) is a fast ferry service linking Rotterdam with Dordrecht via Kinderdijk and is an enjoyable option for day trips, or in place of the train. Boats leave from Willemskade every 30 minutes.

BUS

Rotterdam is a hub for Eurolines bus services to the rest of Europe. The **Eurolines office** (☑0888 076 17 00; Conradstraat 16; ⊙9.30am-5.30pm Mon-Sat) is in the Groothandelsgebouw by Centraal Station. Long-distance buses stop nearby.

TRAIN

Completed in 2014, Rotterdam's skylit, stainless-steel-encased Rotterdam Centraal Station (CS) is an architectural stunner. There are frequent high-speed Thalys trains to/from Brussels (1¼ hours) and Paris (2½ hours). From late 2016, direct Eurostar trains linking Amsterdam with London will stop here, with a Rotterdam–London journey time of 3½ hours.

Major domestic services:

Destination	Price (€)	Duration (min)	Frequency (per hour)
Amsterdam (regular)	14.80	70	8
Amsterdam (high speed)	17.10	40	2
Breda	9.10	30	6
Schiphol	11.90	50	8
Utrecht	10.10	40	4

❶ Getting Around

TO/FROM THE AIRPORT

Bus 33 makes the 20-minute run from the airport to Rotterdam Centraal Station every 15 minutes throughout the day. A taxi takes 10 minutes to get to the centre and costs around €25.

BICYCLE

Rijwielshop (☑412 62 20; www.czwaan.nl; Conradstraat 18; per day €7.50; ⊙4.30am-2am Mon-Thu, 4.30am-1.45am Fri, 5am-1.45am Sat & Sun) Rents bikes almost around the clock.

PUBLIC TRANSPORT

Rotterdam's trams, buses and metro are provided by RET (www.ret.nl). Most converge near Rotterdam Centraal Station. The **RET information booth** (⊙7am-7pm) sells tickets and is down in the Centraal metro station. There are other information booths in the major metro stations.

Day passes are sold for varying durations: 1/2/3 days costs €7.50/12.50/16.50. A single-ride ticket purchased from a bus driver or tram conductor costs €3. Ticket inspections are common.

Trams are the best way to get around the city. They go virtually everywhere and you get to do some sightseeing along the way. The metro (subway) is geared more for trips to the suburbs.

TAXI

Rotterdamse Taxi Centrale (☑ 462 60 60)

WATER TAXI

Fast black-and-yellow **water taxis** (☑ 403 03 03; www.watertaxirotterdam.nl; per 15min around €30) are the Ferraris of the Nieuwe Maas.

Enjoy water-taxi service for a fraction of the cost on two handy fixed routes (two to four times per hour from 11am to 9pm Monday to Thursday and 9am to midnight Friday to Sunday), travelling between the following:

➡ Hotel New York and Veerhaven (€2.90)
➡ Hotel New York and Leuvehaven (€3.60)

Around Rotterdam

Kinderdijk

A Unesco World Heritage site, the **Kinderdijk** (www.kinderdijk.nl; adult/child €7.50/5.50, parking €5; ☺9am-5pm Mon-Sat, 11am-5pm Sun mid-Mar–mid-Oct, 11am-4pm mid-Feb–mid-Mar & Nov-Dec, closed Jan–mid-Feb) has 19 windmills strung out on both sides of canals.

The place has been a focus of Dutch efforts to claim land from the water for centuries. Indeed the name Kinderdijk is said to derive from the horrible St Elizabeth's Day Flood of 1421 when a storm and flood washed a baby in a crib with a cat up onto the dyke. It's a starkly beautiful area, with the windmills rising above the empty marshes and waterways like sentinels.

Several of the most important types of windmill are here, including hollow post mills and rotating cap mills. The latter are

DUTCH WINDMILLS

Long before they became a Dutch icon, the earliest known windmills appeared in the 13th century, simply built around a tree trunk. The next leap in technology came 100 years later, when a series of gears ensured the mill could be used for all manner of activities, the most important of which was pumping water. Hundreds of these windmills were soon built on dykes throughout Holland and the mass drainage of land began.

Technology advanced again in the 16th century with the invention of the rotating cap mill. Rather than having to turn the huge body of the mill to face the wind, the operators could rotate just the tip, which contained the hub of the sails. This made it possible for mills to be operated by just one person.

In addition to pumping water, mills were used for many other industrial purposes, such as sawing wood, making clay for pottery and, most importantly for art lovers, crushing the pigments used by painters.

By the mid-19th century there were more than 10,000 windmills operating in all parts of the Netherlands. But the invention of the steam engine soon made them obsolete. By the end of the 20th century there were only 950 operable windmills left, but this number has stabilised and there is great interest in preserving the survivors. The Dutch government runs a three-year school for prospective windmill operators, who must be licensed.

Running one of the mills on a windy day is as complex as being the skipper of a large sailing ship, and anyone who has been inside a mill and listened to the massive timbers creaking will be aware of the similarities. The greatest hazard is a runaway, when the sails begin turning so fast that they can't be slowed down. This frequently ends in catastrophe as the mill remorselessly tears itself apart.

These days you're more likely to encounter turbine-powered wind farms in the countryside than rows of windmills but there are still plenty of opportunities countrywide.

Kinderdijk , near Rotterdam, has oodles of windmills in a classic *polder* setting (areas surrounded by dykes where water can be artificially controlled). To see mills operating and learn how they work, head to **Zaanse Schans** (www.zaanseschans.nl; Zaans Museum; ☺9am-5pm) near Amsterdam.

Just about every operable windmill in the nation is open to visitors on National Mill Day, usually on the second Saturday of May. Look for windmills flying little blue flags.

among the highest in the country as they were built to better catch the wind. The mills are kept in operating condition and date from the 18th century. In summer tall reeds line the canals, lily pads float on the water and bird calls break the silence. If you venture past the first couple of mills, you leave 90% of the day trippers behind. Admission includes entry to an old pumping station where a film screens about Kinderdijk.

On Saturdays in July and August, from 2pm to 5pm, most of the windmills are in operation, an unforgettable sight.

Boats dock outside the main entrance that can take you along the dykes. The Canal Hopper (adult/child €4.50/2.50) does a short trip to the fifth windmill, from where you can walk back or return by boat. The Canal Cruiser (adult/child €5/3) runs to the furthest windmill, which can't be reached by foot.

ⓘ Getting There & Around

Despite its proximity, there are no viable bus or train services from Rotterdam.

Bicycle Kinderdijk is close to Rotterdam (16km) or Dordrecht (11km) on national bike routes **LF2** and **LF11**.

Ferry The most enjoyable way to visit is by the **Waterbus** (Line 202; www.waterbus.nl; Willemskade, Rotterdam; day-pass adult/child €13/9.50, one-way ticket €4; ⊙ every 30min May-Sep) fast ferry. From either Rotterdam or Dordrecht it takes about an hour. Bikes are carried for free. The ferry dock is 1km from the Kinderdijk entrance.

Rebus (⌨ 010-218 31 31; www.rebus-info.nl; adult/child €15/12; ⊙ noon Tue-Sun Apr-late Oct) runs four-hour boat tours from Rotterdam that allow a fairly quick visit to the mills.

Dordrecht

⌨ 078 / POP 118,782

Centred on its busy port, Dordrecht sits at the confluence of the Oude Maas River and several tributaries and channels. Its strategic trading position (precipitating a boom in the wine trade) and status as the oldest Dutch city (having been granted a town charter in 1220) ensured Dordrecht was one of the most powerful Dutch regions until the mid- to late-16th century. In 1572 town leaders from all over the country met here to declare independence from Spain. Its delightful canal-laced historic centre is easily accessed by train or fast ferry from Rotterdam.

◉ Sights

Most sights are on or near the three old canals: the Nieuwehaven, the Wolwevershaven and the Wijnhaven.

★**Grote Kerk** CHURCH
(www.grotekerk-dordrecht.nl; Langegeldersekade 2; church admission free, tower adult/child €1/0.50; ⊙ church 10.30am-4.30pm Tue-Sat, noon-4pm Sun, tower 10am-4.30pm Tue-Sat, noon-6pm Sun) The massive tower of the 14th- to 15th-century Grote Kerk was originally meant to have been much higher, but it took on a lean during its 150-year-plus construction. You can climb to the top – 275 steps – to enjoy excellent views of the town. Inside the church are finely carved choir stalls and stained-glass windows depicting local historical scenes.

Dordrechts Museum MUSEUM
(www.dordrechtsmuseum.nl; Museumstraat 40; adult/child €12/5; ⊙ 11am-5pm Tue-Sun) Away from the old town, the flashy Dordrechts Museum has works by local artists. Most noteworthy are pieces by Jan van Goyen (1596–1656) and Albert Cuyp (1620–91). Van Goyen was one of the first Dutch painters to capture the interplay of light on landscapes, while Cuyp, who lived in Dordrecht his entire life, is known for his many works painted in and around his home town.

Museum 1940–1945 MUSEUM
(www.dordrechtmuseum19401945.nl; Nieuwehaven 28; adult/child €2/1; ⊙ 10am-5pm Tue, Wed, Fri & Sat, 1-5pm Sun) This small museum shows the privations of the Dordrecht region during WWII.

Museum Simon van Gijn MUSEUM
(www.huisvangijn.nl; Nieuwehaven 29; adult/child €10/3.50; ⊙ 11am-5pm Tue-Sun) The Museum Simon van Gijn depicts the life of an 18th-century patrician, with vintage knick-knacks, furnishings and tapestries.

Het Hof HISTORIC SITE
(Het Hof) It was in this evocative courtyard that the states of Holland and Zeeland met in 1572 to declare independence from Spain.

★**Ark van Noach** MUSEUM
(Noah's Ark; http://arkvannoach.com; Maasstraat 14; adult/child €12.50/7.50, parking per 4hr €2; ⊙ 10am-4pm Mon-Sat) This 20,000-sq-metre ark was hand-built to biblical measurements (30m wide, 23m high, 135m long) by Johan Huibers, following his 1992 dream of the ocean flooding the Netherlands. After trialling a smaller prototype, Huibers completed

Dordrecht

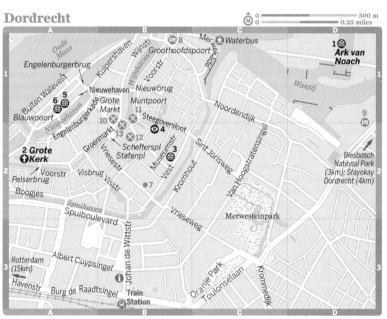

Dordrecht

the football-field-size watercraft in 2012. The towering wooden exterior is adorned with polystyrene elephants and giraffes; on board there's a live petting zoo with rabbits, squirrels and kangaroos, and exhibitions relating the story of Noah. A cafe overlooks the river.

⚒ Courses

Distilleerderij Rutte & Zn   COURSE
(☑ 613 43 67; www.rutte.nl; Vriesestraat 130; tastings €11, jenever-making workshop €34; ⊙ shop 9am-5pm Mon-Fri, 9.30am-5pm Sat) Learn about the local firewater *jenever* (Dutch gin) on a 90-minute tasting at this family-run distillery, in operation since 1872. Better yet, book in for a three-hour workshop to learn

how to make it yourself. The distillery's shop also sells bottles of its prized spirits.

⛵ Tours

De Stroper   TOUR
(☑ 613 00 94; http://destroper.nl; Wijnbrug 1; adult/child €7.50/5; ⊙ hourly 11am-5pm Jun-Aug, 2-5pm Apr, May, Sep & Oct) Seafood restaurant De Stroper (p164) runs boat tours along the town's picturesque waterways.

🛏 Sleeping

De Luthiers   B&B €
(☑ 631 33 90; www.deluthiers.nl; Voorstraat 13; s/d from €85/90) The owners of a violin-, lute- and

guitar-making atelier at street level have two cosy, beautifully furnished rooms tucked up in the attic under the sloped timber eaves. Guests can tour the workshop; four-hour guitar-making courses (€390) are available. Breakfast is served in the music room, where there's a grand piano free to play.

★**Villa Augustus**   DESIGN HOTEL €€
(☑639 31 11; www.villa-augustus.nl; Oranjelaan 7; d/f/ste from €125/145/190; P 🛜) 🅿 An ornate 1882-built art nouveau water tower has been transformed into this ode to Dutch design. Inside the tower, 36 individually designed rooms have stunning art on contrasting feature walls; a suite hides in a secret garden. Views stretch to Rotterdam from the glass-paned rooftop terrace; the organic restaurant in the pumping station is sublime. Private boat rental is available.

🍴 Eating & Drinking

Dordrecht has some superb places to dine. Scheffersplein, a large central square built over a canal, is ringed by cafes and fills with umbrella-shaded terraces in summer.

**Pim's Poffertjes en
Pannenkoekenhuis**   DESSERTS €
(www.pimspofenpan.nl; Nieuwstraat 19; pancakes €6-9.50; ⊙noon-7.30pm Wed & Fri, to 8.30pm Thu, Sat & Sun) Kids (and adults) love this place inside a vintage building with atmospheric, time-worn wooden booths. Thin, cartwheel-size pancakes are filled with dozens of choices of ingredients from savoury to sweet.

★**Villa Augustus
Restaurant**   MODERN EUROPEAN €€
(☑639 31 11; www.villa-augustus.nl; Oranjelaan 7; mains lunch €7.50-13.50, dinner €13.50-24, seafood platters €21-47.50; ⊙7am-10pm Mon-Fri, 8am-10pm Sat & Sun) 🅿 This former pumping station of the historic water tower housing hotel Villa Augustus sits across the complex's rambling market garden and orchard, which supplies ingredients for its menus. The multilevel space with a vast open kitchen is a spectacular setting for freshly squeezed juices to wood-fired pizzas, pork stew, roast duck, and seafood from the surrounding waters.

Behind the restaurant is its bakery and market shop selling fruit, veggies, homemade jams and more, and an emporium with quirky gifts, cookbooks and gardening tools.

Bistro Twee 33   BISTRO €€
(☑740 00 04; www.bistrotwee33.nl; Wijnstraat 233; mains €14.50-26.50; ⊙4-10pm Tue-Fri, 2-10pm Sat &

Sun) French classics such as *escargots bourguignon* (snails in red wine), foie gras and truffle mousse, veal entrecôte with forest-mushroom sauce, and sole meunière (pan-fried and served with brown butter, lemon and parsley sauce) are cooked in a gorgeous space with painted-tile floors, wrought iron and sepia-toned lights. Wine is a passion here; sommelier selections are available by the glass.

Strada del Vino   ITALIAN €€
(☑740 00 01; www.stradadelvino.nl; Wijnstraat 170; pizzas & pastas €7.50-18.50, mains €18.50-27.50; ⊙5-11.30pm Sun-Thu, to midnight Fri & Sat) This inviting bare-brick, bare-boards restaurant is where Dordrecht's chefs dine on their nights off (it's one of the few places in town to open on Mondays). The huge wood-fired oven up the back crisps pizzas to perfection; the pasta is homemade. Fantastic espresso, too.

De Stroper   SEAFOOD €€€
(☑613 00 94; http://destroper.nl; Wijnbrug 1; 2-course lunch menu €25, 4-/6-course dinner menu €42/55; ⊙noon-2pm Mon-Fri, 6-10pm daily) Gaze out on the canal or, in summer, dine on a floating platform at this superb fish restaurant. The menus (no à la carte) change daily; the six-course option at dinner is a culinary tour de force.

🛍 Shopping

Voorstraat is the best street for browsing. To the north it has interesting galleries and boutiques. As it curves to the west, creative shops regularly pop up.

ℹ Information

Tourist office (VVV; ☑0900 46 36 888; www.vvvdordrecht.nl; Spuiboulevard 99; ⊙noon-6pm Mon, 9am-6pm Tue-Fri, 10am-5pm Sat) Dordrecht's vast tourist office is midway between the train station and old town (of which it has a fascinating model).

ℹ Getting There & Away

Buses leave from the area to your right as you exit the train station.

BICYCLE

National bike routes **LF2** and **LF11** run north 27km to Rotterdam along pleasant countryside that includes Kinderdijk. South, **LF11** runs 43km to Breda. Biesbosch National Park is just a 10km ride east by a number of good routes.

Bike Total Zwaan (☑078-635 6830; www.czwaan.nl; Stationplein 10; bike rental per day €9; ⊙4.30am-2am Mon-Thu, 4.30am-1.30am

Fri, 5.30am-1am Sat, 6.30am-1.30am Sun)
Rents bikes at virtually all hours.

BOAT
Waterbus (☑ 0800 023 25 45; www.waterbus.
nl; day-pass adult/child €13/9.50, one way
ticket €6) A fast ferry service linking Dordrecht
with Rotterdam via Kinderdijk and an enjoyable
alternative to the train. The boat leaves from
Merwekade every 30 minutes and takes one
hour to Rotterdam.

TRAIN
From the train station, it's a 700m walk north to
Dordrecht's centre.
  Regular services:

Destination	Price (€)	Duration (min)	Frequency (per hour)
Amsterdam	16	90	4
Breda	5.90	20	4
Rotterdam	4.20	20	8

Biesbosch National Park

Covering 7100 hectares, Biesbosch National
Park encompasses an area on both banks of
the Nieuwe Merwede River, east and south
of Dordrecht. It's so big that it sprawls
across a provincial border; there's a region
known as the Brabantse Biesbosch, further
east, while the part in this province is the
Hollandse Biesbosch.
  In 1970 the Delta Project (p192) shut off
the tides to the area. Reeds, which had been
growing wild, began to die, focusing attention on what is one of the largest expanses of
natural space left in the Netherlands.
  The park is home to beavers (reintroduced to the Brabant area of the park in
1988) and voles, along with scores of birds.
The visitors centre (http://np-debiesbosch.nl;
Biesboschweg 4; 2hr boat tour €11; ⊙10am-5pm
Mar-Oct, 11am-4pm Wed, Sat & Sun Nov-Feb, boat
tour 2pm Apr-Sep) has displays and is where
you can take boat tours of this vast natural
area, and organise kayak and canoe rental. There's an observation point near here
where you can see beavers.
  Right by the park is a Stayokay hostel
(☑ 078-621 21 67; www.stayokay.com; Baanhoek-
weg 25; dm/d from €22.50/49; 🐾).

❶ Getting There & Away

Good bike routes run the 10km east to the park
from Dordrecht.
  The **Waterbus** (☑ 0800 023 25 45; www.
waterbus.nl; day-pass adult/child €13/9.50,

one-way ticket €3) has an hourly boat from
Dordrecht to a dock 500m north of the visitors
centre (€3, 25 minutes).
  Bus service is nonexistent.

Slot Loevestein

Slot Loevestein	CASTLE

(☑ 0183-447 171; www.slotloevestein.nl; Loevestein 1; adult/child €9/6; ⊙ 11am-5pm daily Jul &
Aug, Tue-Sun May, Jun & Sep, Sat & Sun Oct-Apr)
Near the tiny, beautiful little walled town
of Woudrichem you'll find the 14th-century
castle Slot Loevestein. The ancient keep is
wonderfully evocative, perhaps more so for
the difficulty involved in getting here. It
has been a prison, residence and toll castle,
though more recently it has hosted various
cultural events.
  It's best accessed by ferry (www.veer-
dienstgorinchem.nl) from Woudrichem (€3)
or nearby Gorinchem (€5), where there is
a train station. National bike route LF12
passes through between Dordrecht and Den
Bosch.

Gouda

☑ 0182 / POP 70,939

Gouda's association with cheese has made
it famous – the town's namesake export is
among the Netherlands' best known.
  The town enjoyed economic success and
decline from the 16th century onwards. Its
cheese brought more recent wealth, as has
the country's largest candle factory, which
stays busy supplying all those Dutch brown
cafés. The acclaimed 16th-century stained-
glass windows in its church are a highlight.
  Gouda is easily accessible from any city
in Zuid-Holland or from Amsterdam. Its
compact centre, ringed by canals, is just a
five-minute walk from the station.

◉ Sights

The main sights are within a 10-minute walk
of the trapezoidal Markt, one of the largest
such squares in the Netherlands, but wander off down little side streets such as Achter
de Kerk and Lage Gouwe, which pass quiet
canals and seem untouched by the centuries.
Or try the Lange Tiendeweg and Zeugstraat
with its tiny canal and even tinier bridges.

★ Waag	HISTORIC BUILDING

On the north side of the Markt, you can't
miss the Waag, a former cheese-weighing
house built in 1668. Check out the reliefs

Gouda

Gouda

◉ **Top Sights**

◉ **Sights**

◉ **Activities, Courses & Tours**

◉ **Sleeping**

◉ **Eating**

◉ **Shopping**

carved into the side showing the cheese being weighed. Today it houses the **Kaaswaag** (www.goudsewaag.nl; Markt 35; adult/child €4.50/4.25; ⊙noon-5pm Fri-Wed, 10am-5pm Thu Apr-Oct), a museum that follows the history of the cheese trade in the Netherlands, especially its history in Gouda. There is also a scale model of the Markt circa 1990.

Cheese Market   MARKET
(www.goudakaasstad.nl; Markt; ⊙10am-1pm Thu Apr-Aug) Traditional cheese markets on the Markt draw plenty of tourists and stalls selling dairy goods and souvenirs. A few locals dress up in costume and pose for countless photos.

Town Hall   HISTORIC BUILDING
(www.stadhuisgouda.nl; Markt; admission €2; ⊙10am-4pm Tue-Sat, 11am-4pm Sun Apr-Sep, 11am-3pm Tue-Sun Oct-Mar) Right in the middle of the Markt is the mid-15th-century town hall. Constructed from shimmering sand-

stone, this regal Gothic structure bespeaks the wealth Gouda enjoyed from the cloth trade when it was built. The red-and-white shutters provide a fine counterpoint to the carefully maintained stonework. The ceremonial rooms inside are worth a look.

Sint Janskerk   CHURCH
(www.sintjan.com; Achter de Kerk; adult/child €4.50/1; ⊙9am-5pm Mon-Sat Mar-Oct, 10am-4pm Mon-Sat Nov-Feb) Just to the south of the Markt is Sint Janskerk. The church itself had chequered beginnings: it burned down with ungodly regularity every 100 years or so from 1361 until the mid-16th century, when what you see today was completed. At 123m it is the longest church in the country because the ground was so soggy it couldn't support the weight of a tall structure. An audioguide in English costs €2.

Its huge windows set it apart, especially those created by Dirck Crabeth, his brother Wouter, and Lambert van Noort from around 1550 to 1570. Their works, which are numbered, include highlights such as window No 6 (John the Baptist; the folks on either side paid for the window) and No 22 (Jesus purifies the temple; note the look on the face of the money changer).

Museum Gouda   MUSEUM

(www.museumgouda.nl; Achter de Kerk 14; adult/ child €9/2; ☺11am-5pm Tue-Sun) To the imme- diate southwest of the Sint Janskerk church and near a small canal, the city museum is housed in an old hospital, Catherina Gast- huis. It covers Gouda's history and has a few artworks. In the basement a ghoulish section on local torture in the Middle Ages includes devices for the condemned includ- ing an executioner's axe, and a scale model of Gouda as it was in the 1600s. Outside, there's a pretty walled garden.

🏃 Activities

A good circle ride traverses what's billed as the Groene Hart (Green Heart) of the region. It begins just south of the centre and runs 42km through the canal-laced farmlands south of Gouda. Called the Krimpenerwaard Route after the region it covers, it includes stops at dairies where cheese is made. Pick up the free brochure from the tourist office, which also sells detailed maps.

Reederij de IJsel   BOAT TOUR

(☑06 8370 5193; www.reederijdeijsel.nl; Oost- haven 12; adult/child €10/5; ☺1.30pm & 3.30pm Thu & Sat May-Sep) Reederij de IJsel runs 90-minute boat cruises around Gouda's ca- nals and waterways.

Tourist Office Walking Tours   WALKING TOUR

(walking tour €4; ☺11.30am & 2pm daily late Jun-early Aug, 11.30am Thu Apr-late Jun & early-end Aug) Learn about Gouda's architecture, his- tory and its cheese on 40-minute tours run by the tourist office.

🛏 Sleeping

Karmel B&B   B&B €

(☑06 5145 3292; http://bedandbreakfastkarmel. nl; Lange Tiendenweg 54; d €70-75) In a building dating from 1645, this historic B&B has two beautiful pastel-shaded rooms – one art deco and the other, 'Grandma's attic', art nouveau, with timber walls and a counterweight- operated horizontal door. Both have private bathrooms; wonderful breakfasts include Gouda cheese.

Hotel de Utrechtsche Dom   HOTEL €

(☑528 833; www.hotelgouda.nl; Geuzenstraat 6; d with/without bathroom from €67/87, ste from €127; 🖐) On a quiet street, this is a lovely, low-key place to stay, with 14 neat, appealing rooms (the cheapest share bathrooms) and good amenities. It's been an inn for more than 300 years, although the stables get little use from coachmen these days.

🍴 Eating

Kamphuisen   BROWN CAFE €€

(☑0182-514 163; www.kamphuisen.com; Hoge Gou- we 19; mains €16-21.50, 3-course dinner menu €25; ☺5pm-midnight, kitchen to 10pm) This classic *bruin café* (brown *café*; traditional drinking establishment) has a blackboard of drinks overlooking ancient wooden tables and light fixtures. Outside, there are tables under the eaves of the old fish market. The bar menu is ambitious: lamb, steak, fish and more. Book for dinner.

Koeien en Kaas   STEAK €€

(☑656 679; www.koeienenkaas.nl; Achter de Waag 20; mains €15-27; ☺5-10pm) The clue is in the name: the twin specialities at Koeien en Kaas (Cows and Cheese) are steak (10 differ- ent cuts) and fondue (five kinds) made from local cheese. It's set in a rustic space with timber rafters and exposed brick walls.

Brunel   BISTRO €€

(☑518 979; http://restaurantbrunel.nl; Hoge Grouwe 23; mains €17.50-21.50; ☺5-9.30pm Tue-Sat) Re- gional produce is given a creative twist here, such as duck breast on turnip mash with blue- berry sauce, prosciutto-wrapped catfish with asparagus, and lamb with truffle mash and rosemary sauce. In summer dine along the canal in the old colonnaded fish market.

🛍 Shopping

Gouds Kaashuis   FOOD

(www.goudskaashuis.nl; Hoogstraat 1; ☺10am- 6pm Mon, 9.30am-6pm Tue, Wed & Fri, 9.30am-9pm Thu, 9am-6pm Sat) More than 50 types of local cheese are displayed in this knowledgeable cheese shop, with plenty of free samples so you can be sure of what you're buying. It also sells locally milled oils, as well as vinegar.

Slijterij en Bierwinkel
Den Gouwen Aar   DRINK

(www.dengouwenaargouda.nl; Oosthaven 6; ☺10am- 6pm Tue, Wed, Fri & Sat, 10am-9pm Thu, noon-5pm Sun) More than 900 types of beer, spirits and wines are displayed on wooden shelves at this canal-house speciality shop.

ℹ Information

Tourist office (VVV; ☑0182-589 110; www. welkomingouda.com; Waag, Markt 35; ☺10am- 5pm Apr-Oct, to 2pm Nov-Mar) In the historic Waag with the cheese museum and shop; sample cheese while you browse brochures.

❶ Getting There & Around

BICYCLE

National bike route **LF2**, which links Amsterdam and Rotterdam, runs right through the Markt. Follow its twisting route 12km north along dramatic dykes across several large bodies of water to the village of Bodegraven, where you can join the **LF4** for the farm-filled 38km run west to Den Haag.

Fietspoint Gouda (📞 0182-516 111; Stationsplein 10; bike rental per day €7.50) Rents bikes.

BUS

The bus station is immediately to the left as you exit the train station on the Centrum side. Bus 180 runs to Oudewater (30 minutes, twice hourly) and continues to Utrecht.

TRAIN

Gouda's train station is close to the city centre and all you'll need are your feet for local transport.

Regular services:

Destination	Price (€)	Duration (min)	Frequency (per hour)
Amsterdam	11.10	55	6
Den Haag	5.50	20	8
Rotterdam	4.90	20	6
Utrecht	6.20	20	8

Den Haag (The Hague)

📞 070 / POP 515.880

The Netherlands' third-largest city, Den Haag, is a stately, regal place filled with embassies and mansions, green boulevards and parks, a refined culinary scene, a clutch of fine museums and a sybaritic cafe culture. Conversely, its seaside suburb of Scheveningen has a loud and lively kitsch and a long stretch of beach.

Officially known as 's-Gravenhage (the Count's Hedge), Den Haag is the Dutch seat of government and home to the royal family. Prior to 1806, Den Haag was the Dutch capital. However, that year, Louis Bonaparte installed his government in Amsterdam. Eight years later, when the French had been ousted, the government returned to Den Haag, but the title of capital remained with Amsterdam.

In the 20th century Den Haag became the home of several international legal entities, including the UN's International Court of Justice, which regularly holds trials that put Den Haag in the headlines. This is also where foreign embassies in the Netherlands are based, giving the city a significant international community of expats.

◉ Sights & Activities

★ Mauritshuis   MUSEUM

(www.mauritshuis.nl; Plein 29; adult/child €14/free, combined ticket with Galerij Prins Willem V €17.50; ⊙1-6pm Mon, 10am-6pm Tue, Wed & Fri-Sun, 10am-8pm Thu) For a comprehensive introduction to Dutch and Flemish Art, visit the Mauritshuis, a jewel-box of a museum in an old palace and brand-new wing. Almost every work is a masterpiece, among them Vermeer's *Girl with a Pearl Earring*, Rembrandts including a wistful self-portrait from the year of his death, 1669, and *The Anatomy Lesson of Dr Nicolaes Tulp*. A five-minute walk southwest, the recently restored **Galerij Prins Willem V** (www.mauritshuis.nl; Buitenhof 35; adult/child €5/2.50, combined ticket with Mauritshuis €17.50; ⊙noon-5pm Tue-Sun) contains 150 old masters (Steen, Rubens, Potter, et al).

The main building was constructed as a mansion in 1640 in classical style; all its dimensions are roughly the same (25m), and the detailing shows exquisite care. In 1822 it was made the home of the royal collection.

Even if you're just passing through Den Haag on the train, it's well worth hopping off to visit.

★ Binnenhof   PALACE

The Binnenhof's central courtyard (once used for executions) is surrounded by parliamentary buildings. The splendid 17th-century North Wing is still home to the Upper Chamber of the **Dutch Parliament**. The Lower Chamber formerly met in the ballroom, in the 19th-century wing; it now meets in a modern building on the south side. A highlight of the complex is the restored 13th-century **Ridderzaal** (Knights' Hall).

To see the buildings you need to join a tour through visitor organisation **ProDemos** (📞 757 02 00; www.prodemos.nl; Hofweg 1; 45min Ridderzaal tour €5, 90min Ridderzaal & House of Representative tour €8.50, 75min Ridderzaal & Senate tour €8.50, 90min Ridderzaal, House of Representative & Senate tour €10; ⊙office 10am-5pm Mon-Sat, tours by reservation).

Afterwards, stroll around the **Hofvijver**, where the reflections of the Binnenhof and the Mauritshuis have inspired countless snapshots.

Museum de Gevangenpoort   MUSEUM

(Museum of Prison Gate; http://gevangenpoort.nl; Buitenhof 33; adult/child €7.50/5.50, combination ticket Prins Willem V €10/7; ⊙10am-5pm Tue-Fri, noon-5pm Sat & Sun) Across the Hofvijver from the Binnenhof, the Gevangenpoort is a surviving remnant of the 13th-century city fortifications. It has hourly tours showing how justice was dispensed back in the day and new displays bathe the torture tools in radiant light.

Grote Kerk CHURCH
(www.grotekerkdenhaag.nl; Rond de Grote Kerk 12; ⊙11am-5pm Wed-Sun mid-Jul–mid-Aug) The Grote Kerk, dating from 1450, has a fine pulpit that was constructed 100 years later. If you're here outside its limited visitor season, you can take in concerts and organ recitals; check its online agenda for dates.

The neighbouring **Oude Raadhuis** (Old Town Hall; 1565) is a splendid example of Dutch Renaissance architecture.

New Town Hall ARCHITECTURE
(Spui 170) The huge modern town hall is the hotly debated work by US architect Richard Meier. The 'official' nickname of the building is the 'white swan', but locals prefer the 'ice palace'.

Paleis Noordeinde PALACE
The king's and queen's official quarters at Paleis Noordeinde is not open to the public. The Renaissance formality of the structure is fittingly regal.

★**Escher in Het Paleis Museum** MUSEUM
(www.escherinhetpaleis.nl; Lange Voorhout 74; adult/child €9/6.50; ⊙11am-5pm Tue-Sun) The Lange Voorhout Palace was once Queen Emma's winter residence. Now it's home to the work of Dutch graphic artist MC Escher. The permanent exhibition features notes, letters, drafts, photos and fully mature works covering Escher's entire career, from his early realism to the later phantasmagoria. There are some imaginative displays, including a virtual reality reconstruction of Escher's impossible buildings.

Gemeentemuseum MUSEUM
(Municipal Museum; www.gemeentemuseum.nl; Stadhouderslaan 41; adult/child €13.50/free, combination ticket with Foto-Museum Den Haag €18.50/free; ⊙11am-5pm Tue-Sun) Admirers of De Stijl, and in particular of Piet Mondrian, won't want to miss the Berlage-designed Gemeentemuseum. It houses a large collection of works by neo-plasticist artists and others from the late 19th century, as well as extensive exhibits of applied arts, costumes and musical instruments. Take tram 17 from Centraal Station (CS) and Hollands Spoor (HS) to the Statenwartier stop.

Mondrian's unfinished *Victory Boogie Woogie* takes pride of place (as it should –

the museum paid €30 million for it), and there are also a few Picassos and other works by some of the better-known names of the 20th century.

Foto-Museum Den Haag MUSEUM
(www.fotomuseumdenhaag.nl; Stadhouderslaan 43; adult/child €8/free, combination ticket with Gemeentemuseum €18.50/free; ⊙noon-6pm Tue-Sun) Adjoining the Gemeentemuseum, Den Haag's photography museum mounts several major exhibitions a year.

Madurodam AMUSEMENT PARK
(www.madurodam.nl; George Maduroplein 1; admission €15.50; ⊙9am-8pm mid-Mar–Aug, 9am-7pm Sep & Oct, 11am-5pm Nov–mid-Mar) Complete with 1:25 scale versions of Schiphol, Amsterdam, windmills and tulips, Rotterdam harbour and the Delta dykes, Madurodam is a miniaturised Netherlands. It's an enlightening example of the Dutch tendency to put their world under a microscope. Kids love it. Save €2 on entry as well as queuing time by prepurchasing tickets online.

Take tram 9 from CS and HS.

Panorama Mesdag GALLERY
(http://panorama-mesdag.com; Zeestraat 65; adult/child €10/8.50; ⊙10am-5pm Mon-Sat, 11am-5pm Sun) Just past the north end of Noordeinde, the Panorama Mesdag contains the *Panorama* (1881), an immense 120m-long, 14m-high, 360-degree painting of Scheveningen that was painted by Hendrik Willem Mesdag. The panorama is viewed from a constructed dune, with real sand and beach chairs; birdsong and wave sounds are piped through. After admiring the masterful achievement, you can head 4km west of Den Haag to the real thing.

Haagse Toren VIEWPOINT
(✆305 10 00; www.haagsetoren.nl; Rijswijkseplein 786; admission €6; ⊙observation deck noon-10pm) A glass lift whisks you up in just 40 seconds to the observation deck on the 42nd floor (135m) of the city's second-tallest building. (There's a less-dizzying option of riding a windowless lift.) There are indoor viewing areas and an outdoor balcony; on a clear day, panoramas extend for up to 45km, as far as Rotterdam, Leiden and Hoek van Holland. Tickets include a beer, house wine or soft drink at the bar; there's also a restaurant here, the Penthouse.

Vredespaleis HISTORIC SITE
(Peace Palace; ✆302 42 42; www.vredespaleis.nl; Carnegieplein 2; visitor-centre admission free, tours

Den Haag (The Hague) Central

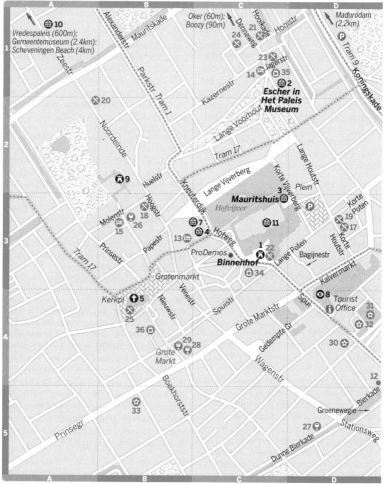

adult/child €9.50/free; ⊙ visitor centre 10am-5pm Tue-Sun) The UN International Court of Justice is housed in the Vredespaleis (Peace Palace). A **visitor centre** details the work of the organisations within. Hour-long guided tours are sometimes offered, but if the courts are in session they are cancelled – check first; you need to book ahead (security is strict). Take tram 1 from HS.

The grand building was donated by American steelmaker Andrew Carnegie for use by the International Court of Arbitration, an early international body whose goal was the prevention of war, which proved elusive as WWI broke out one year after it opened in 1913.

SCHEVENINGEN

The long **beach** at Scheveningen, pronounced – if possible – as s'CHay-fuh-nin-gen, attracts nine million visitors per year. It's horribly developed: architects who lost hospital commissions have designed all manner of modern nightmares overlooking the strand. Scads of cafes elbow each other for space on tiers of promenades by the beach, their themes taken from resorts with more reliable weather worldwide.

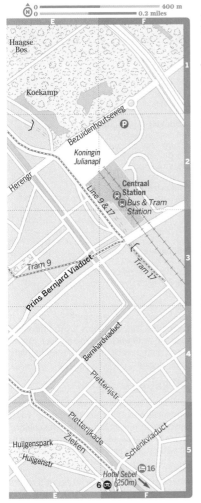

Most Den Haag streets heading west reach Scheveningen, 4km away, or take tram 1, 9 or 11 from HS.

🕝 Tours

The tourist office offers excellent walking- and cycling-route options based around a variety of themes, including 'The Royal Kilometres'.

De Ooievaart   BOAT TOUR
(📞445 18 69; www.ooievaart.nl; Bierkade 18b; adult/child €11/7.50; ⊙daily Jul & Aug, Tue-Sun Apr-Jun & Sep) Offers 90-minute boat tours on routes taking in Den Haag's most interesting sights at canal level. Departure times vary; confirm in advance.

⭐ Festivals & Events

Parkpop   MUSIC
(http://parkpop.nl; ⊙late Jun) Parkpop draws some 200,000 pop-music fans to town for free concerts by big names in Zuiderpark.

🛏 Sleeping

As an expat city, Den Haag has all the major international chains but there are also some interesting smaller hotels. Numerous beach-front possibilities crowd Scheveningen.

Stayokay Den Haag   HOSTEL €
(📞315 78 88; www.stayokay.com; Scheepmaker-straat 27; dm/d from €19/49; 🛜) This Stayokay HI hostel in an Amsterdam School–style building has four- to eight-bed dorms and good facilities including a bar, a restaurant and board games. Towel rental costs €4.50. It's a 500m walk northeast of HS station.

Hotel Sebel   HOTEL €€
(📞345 92 00; www.hotelsebel.nl; Prins Hendrik-plein 20; s/d/tr from €89/99/139, studios from €119; 🛜) This 33-room hotel spreads out across three proud art nouveau corner buildings. The cheapest rooms are minuscule but others have balconies; studios have kitchenettes; and everything has been tastefully updated, including the minimalist lobby. It's on tram line 17 from CS and HS.

Corona   HOTEL €€
(📞363 79 30; www.corona.nl; Buitenhof 39-42; s/d from €90/145; 🅿✳🛜) In a bullseye location by the Binnenhof, 1km southwest of CS, this well-run property occupies three 17th-century, recently renovated townhouses. The 36 rooms span a range of styles that mesh classic details with modernity. On-site parking (€20) is available by reservation.

It's tacky, but you might just find pleasure in the carnival atmosphere, or the waves themselves. Aloha Surf (📞322 71 71; www.alohasurf.nl; Strand Noord 2b, Scheveningen; surfboard/SUP rental per hour €10, 2hr surf lesson €70; ⊙9.30am-6pm) rents surfboards and stand-up paddle boards (SUPs) and also runs lessons. It has hot and cold showers, a cafe, and a surf shop. Rental prices include all-important wetsuits.

Better yet, you can escape to wide-open beaches and nature with just a bit of effort, especially to the south where the hype tapers off as you pass the harbour.

Den Haag (The Hague) Central

Boulevard Hotel   HOTEL €€
(☎354 00 67; www.boulevardhotel.nl; Seinpostduin 1, Scheveningen; s/d/f from €80/85/115; ☎) A classic old beach hotel that's more attractive than its modern neighbours, the Boulevard has simple rooms, but you can enjoy breakfast in the conservatory or in the patio with views down to the surf.

★**Des Indes**   HISTORIC HOTEL
(☎361 23 45; www.hoteldesindesthehague.com; Lange Voorhout 54-56; s/d/ste from €155/175/335; P✳✿♨) Built as a residence in 1858 and a hotel since 1881, this is Den Haag's most resplendent showpiece. In 1899 Tsar Nicholas II held the world's first peace conference here; past guests also include Winston Churchill, Theodore Roosevelt, and ballerina Anna Pavlova, who died here in 1931. Today it's an opulent sanctum with flowing, magnificently decorated rooms and every conceivable luxury.

If money's no object, book into the presidential suite with its own rooftop terrace (from €1450), where many of the most famous patrons have stayed.

Het Paleis Hotel   HOTEL €€€
(☎362 46 21; www.paleis-hotel.nl; Molenstraat 26; d from €149; ✳✿) Near the Noordeinde palace, its location alone is atmospheric, but the antique trimmings in the rooms match

it superbly. The 20 rooms are traditionally luxurious with thick drapes and deep carpet. Fabric patterns are unique to the hotel and richly elegant.

✗ Eating

Den Haag's gastronomic scene is top-notch, with quality matched by the variety you'd expect in an international city. The cobbled streets and canals off Denneweg continue to see adventurous new openings.

Bloem   CAFE €
(www.bloemdenhaag.nl; Korte Houtstraat 6; dishes €3.50-9, high tea per person €21.50; ☺10am-6pm Mon-Sat) Across the Plein from the Binnenhof, this cute little cafe has white tables, chairs and flowers out front. House-made tarts are superb; it also has great sandwiches and smoothies. Stop by for afternoon high tea.

Organic Farmers' Market   MARKET €
(Hofmarkt; ☺10am-6pm Wed) 🌱 Den Haag's organic farmers market offers a dazzling array of local food including a stall selling excellent crêpes.

Brasserie 't Ogenblik   CAFE €
(www.t-ogenblik.nl; Molenstraat 4c; mains €6-15; ☺10am-5pm Mon-Fri, to 6pm Sat & Sun) Staff zip about this hopping cafe at the nexus of several

pedestrianised shopping streets; it has summertime tables along Hoogstraat for people-watching. Coffees and teas offer refreshment, and a creative line-up of salads, sandwiches, soups and more offer sustenance.

★ Restaurant Allard   BISTRO €€

(☑744 79 00; www.restaurantallard.nl; Jagerstraat 6; mains €16-24, 2-/3-/4-course menu €32/39/46; ⊙4-11pm Tue-Sun) Tucked down a charming alleyway with outdoor tables, Allard is a diamond find for flavour-packed creations such as tuna tartare with sundried tomato crème, lamb fillet with honey and fig jus, truffle risotto with wild mushrooms, and grilled sea bass with spinach and potato gratin. It's in a cosy, cellarlike space with exposed brick walls, low-lit chandeliers and black-and-white chessboard-tiled floors.

Oker   TAPAS €€

(☑364 54 53; www.restaurantoker.nl; Denneweg 71; tapas €6.50-13.50; ⊙11.30am-4.30pm & 5.30-10pm Mon-Wed, to 11pm Thu & Fri, noon-4.30pm & 5.30-11pm Sat & Sun) During this hip, sophisticated spot's oyster happy hour (Saturday and Sunday between 3pm and 6pm), you can slurp a dozen Fines de Claire oysters for €15. Any time, you can splurge on Ociëtra caviar (€29.50 per 10g), or share small tapas plates such as goat's cheese, spinach and lemon crème-fraiche ravioli, or plaice with fennel, clams and olive mousseline.

Taveerne de Resident   BISTRO €€

(☑364 87 88; www.deresident.nl; Denneweg 58; mains €16-32; ⊙5.30-10.30pm Mon-Sat, 5-10pm Sun) Facing a romantic square, this cherry-and-cream-painted treasure – here since 1977 – looks like something you might stumble upon in a Parisian backstreet. The elon-gated interior's red-leather booths, stained glass and old French advertising posters do nothing to shatter the illusion, nor does the unfailingly good bistro fare such as calf's liver with apple and bacon.

Marinated spare ribs with potato salad are the house speciality.

De Basiliek   FRENCH, ITALIAN €€

(☑360 61 44; www.debasiliek.nl; Korte Houtstraat 4a; mains €17.50-22.50, 2-/3-course market menu €27.50/30; ⊙noon-4pm & 6-10pm Mon-Fri, 6-10pm Sat) Behind a black-awning-framed facade, classy De Basiliek crafts intricate dishes such as roast hare with red cabbage and figs, or duck cannoli with asparagus and truffle oil. The stellar wine list has full-bottle, half-bottle and by-the-glass options.

Zebedeüs   CAFE €€

(www.zebedeus.nl; Rond de Grote Kerk 8; mains lunch €8-13.50, dinner €10-22.50; ⊙11am-9.30pm) 🍴 Built right into the walls of the Grote Kerk, this organic cafe serves huge, fresh sandwiches (smoked trout, pulled pork) all day, and creative evening dishes such as catfish with pancetta, duck breast with smoked garlic and caramel jus, and mushroom and lentil burgers with celeriac and mash. In fine weather, the best seats are at the chestnut-tree-shaded tables outside.

Mero   SEAFOOD €€

(☑352 36 00; www.merovis.nl; Vissershavenweg 61, Scheveningen; mains €14.50-29.50; ⊙noon-2pm & 5.30-9.30pm Wed & Thu, noon-2pm & 6-9.30pm Fri, noon-9.30pm Sat & Sun) Out at Scheveningen, this industrial-chic harbourside brasserie serves the best fish by the sea. The bold crustacean art on the walls is matched by the intense flavours on the plate. Order a day ahead

ROTTERDAM & SOUTH HOLLAND DEN HAAG (THE HAGUE)

WORTH A TRIP

ESCAPE TO THE DUNES

Open sand, endless beach, hillocks of dunes and the sounds of seagulls and shore are all easily accessible from Den Haag and Scheveningen.

To the south, a mere 1km past the harbour puts you in the heart of nature. From here you can continue along the coast for pretty much as long as you have the fortitude, with only the odd simple beach cafe for relief. Take tram 11 from Hollands Spoor station (HS) to the end of the line right in the heart of the dunes.

Heading north, follow the beach past the end of tram lines 1 and 9. Here the dunes are pristine and the further you walk or cycle, the greater the rewards. You'll also pass a series of WWII bunkers, part of the Nazi Atlantic Wall defence system and an eerie reminder of the Netherlands' place in European history.

National bike route LF1 follows the coast throughout the region. Tellingly, it only diverts inland near Scheveningen when it passes through parks to avoid the chaos.

for its two-person seafood platter (€110), piled high with oysters, prawns, king crab, lobster and other seasonal shellfish. Take tram 11.

Les Ombrelles
SEAFOOD €€€

(✓365 87 89; www.lesombrelles.nl; 3-course lunch menu €32.50, 3-/4-/5-course dinner menu €34.50/42.50/49.50; ⊙noon-2pm & 6-10pm Mon-Fri, 6-10pm Sat) At a confluence of canals in one of the city's most charming districts, this long-running favourite sets up tables across the shady square. The tank with live crabs reaffirms that this is seafood country and the menus (no à la carte) are superb.

It Rains Fishes
SEAFOOD €€€

(✓365 25 98; www.itrainsfishes.nl; Noordeinde 123; mains €24.50-38, 2-/3-course lunch menu €26.50/30, 3-/4-/5-course dinner menu €35/42.50/52.50; ⊙noon-2.30pm & 6-11pm Mon-Fri, 6-11pm Sat) This multi-award-winning seafood place is renowned for its grilled, fried and poached fish, mussels and scallops. The menu reflects what's fresh.

🍷 Drinking

Bouzy
WINE BAR

(http://bouzywineandfood.nl; Denneweg 83; ⊙11am-11pm Tue-Sat) 'Champagne, Wine and Food' is the tag line of this swish new spot in a vintage-industrial space on buzzing Denneweg. Its wine list concentrates on Europe but flirts with the New World; there are dozens of bubbly varieties as well as charcuterie, seafood and cheese platters, *flammkuchen* (Alsatian-style pizza), *bitterballen* (croquettes) and prawn croquettes.

Vavoom
COCKTAIL BAR

(Grote Markt 29; ⊙11am-1am Sun-Wed, to 1.30am Thu-Sat) Jungle Jetsetter (Malibu rum, Maraschino cherry liqueur, lime and pineapple juice), Spiced Pear (spiced rum, Xante pear cognac liqueur, lime juice and pear syrup), Dark Desire (gin, Chambord raspberry, vanilla and cognac liqueur, lime juice and sugar syrup) and La Cucaracha (tequila, passion fruit puree, vanilla syrup and apple juice) are among the knock-out cocktails at this good-time Grote Markt bar.

De Paas
BEER CAFE

(www.depaas.nl; Dunne Bierkade 16a; ⊙3pm-1am Mon-Thu, 3pm-1.30am Fri, 2pm-1am Sat & Sun) A highly atmospheric old bar with a huge selection of Dutch, Belgian and other international beers, De Pass has 10 taps that rotate often and include unusual seasonal

brews. In summer head to its floating terrace aboard a canal boat.

De Zwarte Ruiter
BROWN CAFE

(Grote Markt 27; ⊙11am-1am Sun-Wed, to 1.30am Thu-Sat) De Zwarte Ruiter (The Black Rider) is a perennial Grote Markt favourite for its heated terrace and cavernous light-filled, split-level interior. You can often catch live music here.

Café De Oude Mol
BROWN CAFE

(Oude Molstraat 61; ⊙5pm-1am Sun-Wed, to 2am Thu-Sat) Pass through the ivy-covered door of Café de Oude Mol and you'll find Den Haag without the pretence: an intimate, earthy pub that sums up the Dutch quality of *gezelligheid* (conviviality, cosiness). Live rock music takes to the stage on Mondays.

Strandclub Doen
BAR

(www.strandclubdoen.nl; Strandweg 9, Scheveningen; ⊙9am-midnight mid-Mar–mid-Oct; 🐾) A vision of white, Doen is one of the least tacky of the plethora of beach bars lining the sands. Palm trees shivering in the North Sea breeze add atmosphere to the sprawl of sofas and loungers.

☆ Entertainment

★ Paard van Troje
LIVE MUSIC

(www.paard.nl; Prinsegracht 12; ⊙hours vary) This emporium has an eclectic program of live music – from classical concerts to metal, blues, roots, reggae and soul – as well as Dutch spoken-word poetry, and club nights, such as hip hop and dance. Check the online agenda to find out what's happening.

Nederlands Dans Theater
DANCE

(www.ndt.nl; Schedeldoekshaven 60) This world-famous dance company has two main components: NDT1, the main troupe of 28 dancers, and NDT2, a small group of eight dancers.

Cinematheek Haags Filmhuis
CINEMA

(✓365 60 30; www.filmhuisdenhaag.nl; Spui 191; tickets from €7.50) Screens foreign and indie films.

Dr Anton Philipszaal
CONCERT VENUE

(✓880 03 33; www.zuiderstrandtheater.nl; Spui 150) Home to the Residentie Orkest, Den Haag's classical symphony orchestra.

🛍 Shopping

Den Haag is brilliant for shopping, with several great areas for browsing. Grote Marktstraat is, fittingly enough, where you'll find the major department stores and chains.

Hoogstraat, Noordeinde, Huelstraat and Prinsestraat are all good for eclectic shops and galleries. Denneweg is celebrated not only for its restaurants and bars but also its off-beat boutiques.

De Passage MALL
(www.depassage.nl; cnr Spuistraat & Hofweg; ⊙noon-6pm Mon, 10am-6pm Tue, Wed, Fri & Sat, noon-5pm Sun) De Passage, off Hofweg and Spuistraat, is a beautiful 19th-century covered arcade with high-end brands.

Museumshop Den Haag SOUVENIRS
(www.museumshopdenhaag.nl; Lange Voorhout 58b; ⊙11am-5pm Mon-Sat, noon-5pm Sun) The Netherlands' first-ever independent museum shop is a one-stop-shop for books, prints, postcards, gifts and accessories of artworks and exhibitions from some of the country's most prestigious museums, including Amsterdam's Rijksmuseum and Van Gogh Museum, as well as the Mauritshuis, and Escher in Het Paleis Museum.

Stanley & Livingstone BOOKS
(📞365 73 06; www.stanley-livingstone.eu; School-straat 21; ⊙noon-6pm Mon, 10am-6pm Tue, Wed & Fri, 10am-9pm Thu, 10am-5pm Sat, 1-5pm Sun) Quaint travel bookshop.

ℹ Information

Tourist office (VVV; 📞361 88 60; http://denhaag.com; Spui 68; ⊙noon-8pm Mon, 10am-8pm Tue-Fri, 10am-5pm Sat & Sun; 🐀) On the ground floor of the public library in the landmark New Town Hall (p169).

ℹ Getting There & Away

BICYCLE
The coastal national bike route **LF1** runs just inland of Scheveningen. Leiden can be reached by going 20 miles north and heading inland. **LF11** runs southeast 11km to Delft.
Rijwielshop Centraal (📞070-383 00 39; www.rijwielshopcentraal.nl; Lekstraat 21-25; bike rental per day €10; ⊙8am-6pm Mon-Fri, 10am-5pm Sat) At CS; rents bikes.
Rijwielshop Hollands Spoor (📞070-389 08 30; www.rijwielshop-hollands-spoor.nl; Station-splein 29; bike rental per day €10; ⊙5am-2am Mon-Fri, 6am-2am Sat, 6am-2.30am Sun) At HS station; rents bikes almost around the clock.

BUS
Eurolines long-distance buses and regional buses depart from the bus & tram station above the tracks at CS.

TRAIN
Den Haag has two main train stations.
Centraal Station (CS) A terminus on the eastern edge of the centre. It is a hub for local trams and buses.
Hollands Spoor station (HS) A 1.5km walk south of CS and on the main railway line between Amsterdam and Rotterdam.

Den Haag is also linked to Rotterdam by metro line E (30 minutes).
Regular services:

Destination	Price (€)	Duration (min)	Frequency (per hour)
Amsterdam	11.20	60	6
Leiden	3.40	15	4
Rotterdam	4.70	25	6
Schiphol	8.20	30	6
Utrecht	10.70	40	6

ℹ Getting Around

Most tram routes converge on CS, at the tram and bus station above the tracks and on the western side. A number of routes also serve HS, including the jack-of-all-trades tram 1, which starts in Scheveningen and runs all the way to Delft, passing through the centre of Den Haag along the way. Trams 1, 9 and 11 link Scheveningen with Den Haag. The last tram runs in either direction at about 1.30am.

Tram and bus operator **HTM** (www.htm.net; single ride €3.50, day pass €6.50) sells a highly useful day pass.
TCH Taxis (📞070-390 62 62; www.tch.nl)

Delft

📞015 / POP 98,700
The exquisite medieval centre of Delft is a hugely popular Dutch day-trip destination, with visitors flocking to stroll its narrow, canal-lined streets, gazing at the remarkable architecture and learning about the life and career of Golden Age painter Johannes Vermeer. The artist was born in Delft and lived here; *View of Delft,* one of his best-loved works, is an enigmatic, idealised vision of the town.

Delft is synonymous with its famous Delftware, the distinctive blue-and-white pottery originally duplicated from Chinese porcelain by 17th-century artisans.

Founded around 1100, Delft grew rich from weaving and trade in the 13th and 14th centuries. In the 15th century a canal was dug to the Maas river, and the small port there,

Delft

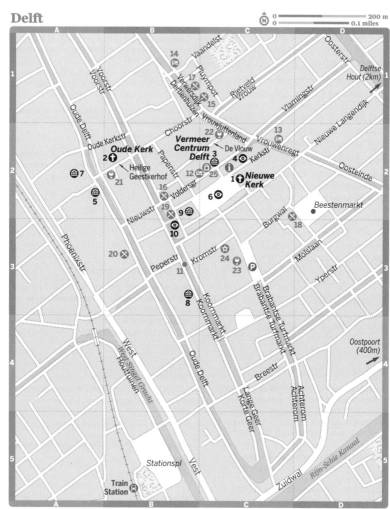

Delfshaven, was eventually absorbed by Rotterdam. Today it has a thriving university which is renowned for its architecture faculty.

In the evenings locals fill the bars and restaurants and the lamplit canals are idyllic for a romantic stroll. It's well worth staying on after the daytime crowds have left.

◉ Sights & Activities

Delft is best seen on foot: almost all the interesting sights lie within a 1km radius of the vast Markt. Much of the town dates from the 17th century and is remarkably well preserved.

★ **Vermeer Centrum Delft** MUSEUM
(www.vermeerdelft.nl; Voldersgracht 21; adult/child €8/4; ⊙10am-5pm) As the place where Vermeer was born, lived, and worked, Delft is 'Vermeer Central' to many art-history and old-masters enthusiasts. Along with viewing life-sized images of Vermeer's oeuvre, you can tour a replica of Vermeer's studio, which reveals the way the artist approached the use of light and colour in his craft. A 'Vermeer's World' exhibit offers insight into his environment and upbringing, while temporary exhibits show how his work continues to inspire other artists.

Delft

At 2pm on Friday and noon on Sunday there's a free one-hour English-language tour.

Markt   SQUARE
The pedestrianised city square is worth a stroll for its pleasant collection of galleries, antiques stores, clothing boutiques and quirky speciality shops.

The **town hall** has an unusual combination of Renaissance construction surrounding a 13th-century tower. Behind it, the **Waag** is a 1536 weigh house; its giant green doors were installed in 1644.

★ **Nieuwe Kerk**   CHURCH
(New Church; http://oudeennieuwekerkdelft.nl; Markt 80; adult/child incl Oude Kerk €3.75/2.25, Nieuwe Kerk tower additional €3.75/2.25; ⊙9am-6pm Mon-Sat Apr-Oct, 11am-4pm Mon-Fri, 10am-5pm Sat Nov-Jan, 10am-5pm Mon-Sat Feb & Mar) Construction on Delft's Nieuwe Kerk began in 1381; it was finally completed in 1655. Amazing views extend from the 108.75m-high tower: after climbing its 376 narrow, spiralling steps you can see as far as Rotterdam and Den Haag on a clear day. It's the resting place of William of Orange (William the Silent), in a mausoleum designed by Hendrick de Keyser.

★ **Oude Kerk**   CHURCH
(Old Church; http://oudeennieuwekerkdelft.nl; Heilige Geestkerkhof 25; adult/child incl Nieuwe Kerk €3.75/2.25; ⊙9am-6pm Apr-Oct, 11am-4pm Nov-Mar, closed Sun) The Gothic Oude Kerk, founded in 1246, is a surreal sight: its 75m-high tower leans nearly 2m from the vertical due to subsidence caused by its canal location, hence its nickname Scheve Jan (Leaning Jan). One of the tombs inside the church is Vermeer's.

Municipal Museum het Prinsenhof   MUSEUM
(http://prinsenhof-delft.nl; St Agathaplein 1; adult/child €10/5; ⊙11am-5pm Tue-Sun) Opposite the Oude Kerk, the former convent where William of Orange (William the Silent) was assassinated in 1584 (the bullet hole in the wall is preserved) is now a museum displaying various objects telling the story of the Eighty Years' War with Spain, as well as 17th-century paintings.

Gemeenlandshuis van Delfland   HISTORIC BUILDING
(Oude Delft 167) Look for the opulent facade of the Gemeenlandshuis van Delfland across the canal from the Oude Kerk. It dates from 1505.

Museum Paul Tetar van Elven   MUSEUM
(www.museumpaultetarvanelven.nl; Koornmarkt 67; adult/child €5/free; ⊙1-5pm Tue-Sun) This off-the-radar museum is the former studio and home of 19th-century Dutch artist Paul Tetar van Elven, who lived and worked here from 1864 until 1894, and bequeathed it to the town. The museum features his works, including reproductions of notable paintings, along with his collection of antique furniture, oriental porcelain and Delftware. The evocative interior retains its original furnishings and lived-in feel.

Oostpoort HISTORIC BUILDING

Oostpoort is the sole surviving piece of the town's walls.

Tours

Canal Boat Tour BOAT TOUR

(www.rondvaartdelft.nl; adult/child €7.50/3; ⊙ hourly 11am-5pm Apr-Oct) Float through Delft's canalscapes on a 45-minute boat tour departing from Koornmarkt 113.

Sleeping

Delft's small size and the proximity of the train station make it a great base for exploring Zuid-Holland. In summer Delft's accommodation is heavily booked and rates at many places shoot up on weekends; reserve well ahead.

Hostel Delft HOSTEL

(✉ 06 1649 6621; www.hosteldelft.nl; Voldersgracht 17a; ⊙ dm from €22; ⑲) In the heart of town a block from the Markt, this 2015-opened independent hostel has roof terraces, a self-catering kitchen and a cosy lounge. Its 43 beds are spread across en suite dorms sleeping between four and 16, with secure lockers.

Delftse Hout CAMPGROUND €

(✉ 213 00 40; www.delftsehout.nl; Korftlaan 5; campsites €24-32, cabins per 3 nights from €295; P ⑲ ≋) This well-equipped, year-round campground is just 1.5km northeast of town. Take bus 80 or 82 from the bus station or use the campground's shuttle. It has 160 sites and is a 15-minute walk from the Markt.

Hotel de Plataan BOUTIQUE HOTEL €€

(✉ 212 60 46; www.hoteldeplataan.nl; Doelenplein 10; s/d from €105/115, themed d from €140; P ⑲) On a pretty canal-side square in the old town, this family-run gem has small but elegant standard rooms and wonderfully opulent theme rooms, including the 'Garden of Eden'; the Eastern-style 'Amber', with a Turkish massage shower; or the desert-island 'Tamarinde'. Modesty alert: many en suites are only partially screened from the room. Rates include breakfast and secure parking.

Hotel de Emauspoort HOTEL €€

(✉ 219 02 19; http://emauspoort.nl; Vrouwenregt 9-11; s/d/tr from €97.50/107.50/142.50, gypsy caravan s/d €89.50/99.50; ⑲) Travellers rave about this well-priced little hotel near the Markt. Spacious rooms balance old-world charm with modern comfort. Extras include a bountiful breakfast and on-site bakery. The lofted Vermeer room is a treat, as are the two gypsy caravans in the courtyard.

Soul Inn B&B €

(✉ 215 72 46; www.soul-inn.nl; Willemstraat 55; s/d/f from €110/135/145, without bathroom s/d from €65/95; ⑲) This quirky B&B is an antidote for those who've experienced an overload of Delft quaintness; rooms play with colour schemes and themes (retro 1970s; Africa). It's 400m west of the centre.

Eating

Stads-Koffyhuis CAFE €

(http://stads-koffyhuis.nl; Oude Delft 133; mains €8-16.50; ⊙ 9am-8pm Mon-Fri, to 6pm Sat) The most coveted seats at this delightful cafe are on the terrace, aboard a barge moored out front. Tuck into award-winning bread rolls, with fillings such as aged artisan Gouda with apple sauce, mustard, fresh figs and walnuts, or house-speciality pancakes, while admiring possibly the best view of the Oude Kerk, just ahead at the end of the canal.

De Visbanken SEAFOOD €

(www.visbanken.nl; Camaretten 2; dishes €3-8.50; ⊙ 10am-6pm Mon, 9am-6pm Tue-Fri, 9am-5pm Sat, 10am-5pm Sun) Fish has been sold on this spot since 1342. Display cases in the old open-air pavilion entice with fresh, marinated, smoked and fried fishy treats.

★ **Brasserie 't Crabbetje** SEAFOOD €€

(✉ 213 8850; www.crabbetjedelft.nl; Verwersdijk 14; mains €11.50-34.50; ⊙ 5.30-10pm Wed-Sun; ⑲) Seafood is given the gourmet treatment at this cool, sophisticated restaurant, from scallops with leek and lobster reduction to skate wing with hazelnut crumb and *beurre noisette* (warm butter sauce), salmon carpaccio with smoked-eel croquette, and grilled lobster with tomato and truffle oil. Lavish seafood platters for two people cost €83. Desserts are exquisite, too.

Spijshuis de Dis MODERN DUTCH €€

(✉ 213 17 82; www.spijshuisdedis.com; Beestenmarkt 36; soups €6-7.50, mains €17-24.50; ⊙ 5-9.30pm Tue-Sun) Fresh fish and amazing soups served in bread bowls take centre stage at this romantic foodie haven, but meat eaters and vegetarians are well catered for too. Creative starters include smoked, marinated mackerel on sliced apple with horseradish. Don't skip the Dutch pudding served in a wooden shoe.

La Fontanella ITALIAN €€

(✉ 212 58 74; www.fontanella.nl; Verwersdijk 30; pizzas & pastas €7-11.50, mains €18-24; ⊙ 5-10pm) The ultimate Italian neighbourhood restaurant, here since 1974, La Fontanella is run by a charming owner-chef who imports his ingredients from his native Italy. Classics such as veal in creamy mushroom and Gorgonzola sauce and salmon in tomato cognac sauce with spaghetti are flawless.

Stadscafé de Waag CAFE
(www.de-waag.nl; Markt 11; mains lunch €7.50-14.50, dinner €14.50-18.50; ☻kitchen 11am-10pm Sun & Mon, 10am-10pm Tue-Sat; 🛜) With a sprawling terrace on the Markt, this is a perfect spot for a postsightseeing beer, but the food is impressive, given the tourist-busy location. Lunch dishes span soups, salads and gourmet sandwiches; dinner mains range from cod with fennel puree to spicy lamb stew, with lush desserts such as apple pie with walnut ice cream to finish.

🍷 Drinking

Locus Publicus BROWN CAFE
(www.locuspublicus.nl; Brabantse Turfmarkt 67; ☻11am-1am Mon-Thu, 11am-2am Fri & Sat, noon-1am Sun) Cosy little Locus Publicus is filled with cheery locals quaffing their way through the 175-strong beer list. There's great people-watching from the front terrace.

De Oude Jan BROWN CAFE
(Heilige Geestkerkhof 4; ☻10am-1am Mon, to 5am Tue, Wed & Sun, to 2am Thu-Sat) Student-friendly

hours and frequent live bands taking to the umbrella-shaded courtyard's outdoor stage (the timber-lined *café* interior's too small) make this one of Delft's most popular hangouts. It's on Delft's oldest square, opposite the Oude Kerk.

Doerak BEER CAFE
(www.cafedoerak.nl; Vrouwjuttenland 17; ☻4pm-1am Mon-Thu, 4pm-2am Fri, noon-2am Sat, 1pm-1am Sun) Canal-side and pavement seating and a vintage-furnished interior with exposed brick walls set the scene for sampling from 160 craft and Trappist bottled beers.

☆ Entertainment

Bebop Jazzcafé LIVE MUSIC
(Kromstraat 33; ☻7pm-1am Mon-Thu, 4pm-2am Fri, 3pm-2am Sat, 3pm-1am Sun) Live jazz plays every Sunday at this dark, intimate venue, which also has jam sessions on Tuesdays, and a great selection of beers.

🛍 Shopping

The most coveted purchase is the iconic Delftware (p180).

Delft Markt MARKET
(Markt; ☻8am-3pm Thu) Delft's general market fills the main square on Thursdays, and is a lively time to visit.

VERMEER'S DELFT

Johannes Vermeer, one of the greatest of the Dutch Masters, lived his entire life in Delft (1632–75), fathering 11 children and leaving behind just 34 (possibly 35) incredible paintings that are attributed to him (although some estimates are as high as 66 works). Vermeer's works have rich and meticulous colouring and he captures light as few other painters have ever managed to. His scenes come from everyday life in Delft, his interiors capturing simple things such as the famous *Girl with a Pearl Earring,* giving a photographic quality to his compositions.

Vermeer's best-known exterior work, *View of Delft,* brilliantly captures the play of light and shadow of a partly cloudy day. Visit the location where he painted it, across the canal at Hooikade, southeast of the train station. Unfortunately, none of Vermeer's works remain in Delft, although the Vermeer Centrum Delft (p176) is a fine resource and the tourist office has a good free walking-tour brochure. Both *Girl with a Pearl Earring* and *View of Delft* can be seen at the Mauritshuis (p168) in Den Haag, while arguably his most famous painting, *The Milkmaid,* resides in Amsterdam's Rijksmuseum (p59).

Vermeer's life is something of an enigma. What little is known about him is not flattering. His fame grows by the year, however. The 2003 film *Girl with a Pearl Earring* (based on Tracy Chevalier's novel) speculated on his relationship with the eponymous girl. The following year, a work long thought to be a forgery was finally confirmed as authentic – *Young Woman Seated at the Virginals* was the first Vermeer to be auctioned in more than 80 years, selling to an anonymous buyer for €24 million.

The excellent website www.essentialvermeer.com has exhaustive details on the painter and his works, including where they are exhibited at any given time.

DELFTWARE

Delft's eponymous blue-and-white china is ubiquitous throughout town. Given that the process was first developed in China, it's ironic that the mass of fake Delftware sold in tourist shops also comes from China.

The real stuff is produced in fairly small quantities at four factories in and around Delft. There are three places where you can actually see the artists at work.

Koninklijke Porceleyne Fles (Royal Delft; www.royaldelft.com; Rotterdamseweg 196; factory tour adult/child €12.50/6.25; ⊙9am-5pm mid-Mar–Oct, 9am-5pm Mon-Sat, noon-5pm Sun Nov–mid-Mar) Pottery fans will love Royal Delft, 1km southeast of the centre. Tour tickets include an audiotour which leads you through a painting demonstration, the company museum and the factory production process. You can also take a workshop (€26.50 to €32) where you get to paint your own piece of Delft blue (tiles, plates and vases). For many, of course, the real thrill begins in the gift shop.

De Candelaer (www.candelaer.nl; Kerkstraat 13; ⊙9.30am-5.30pm Mon-Fri, to 5pm Sat May-Sep, shorter hours Oct-Mar) The most central and modest Delftware outfit is de Candelaer, just off the Markt. It has five artists, a few of whom work most days. When it's quiet they'll give you a detailed tour of the manufacturing process.

De Delftse Pauw (The Delft Peacock; ☎015-212 49 20; www.delftpottery.com; Delftweg 133; ⊙9am-4.30pm mid-Mar–Oct, 9am-4.30pm Mon-Fri, 11am-1pm Sat & Sun Nov–mid-Mar) De Delftse Pauw employs 35 painters who work mainly from home. It has daily tours, but you won't see the painters on weekends. Take tram 1 to Vrijenbanselaan.

Antiques, Bric-a-Brac & Book Market　　　MARKET
(Markt; ⊙8am-3pm early Apr–mid-Oct) Come early for the best bargains.

Plek　　　HOMEWARES, HANDICRAFTS
(www.plek.eu; Voldersgracht 17a; ⊙10am-7pm Tue-Sun; ☎) One-of-a-kind fashion, gifts, homewares, furniture and artworks, most made by local Delft artists, fill this colourful shop, with a cafe also tucked inside. It also has a book swap (and courtyard garden for reading).

❶ Information

Tourist office (VVV; ☎215 40 51; www.delft.nl; Kerkstraat 3; ⊙10am-4pm Sun & Mon, 10am-5pm Tue-Sat Apr-Oct, noon-4pm Mon, 10am-4pm Tue-Sat, 11am-3pm Sun Nov-Mar) Sells excellent walking-tour brochures.

❶ Getting There & Around

BICYCLE

National bike route **LF11** goes right through town: Den Haag is 11km northwest (after about 8km you pass a windmill) and Rotterdam is 28km southeast on a meandering route that enters Rotterdam from the west at pretty Delfshaven.

Delft's train station rents bikes (per day €10).

TRAIN

Delft's gleaming new train station opened in 2015.
Regular services:

Destination	Price (€)	Duration (min)	Frequency (per hour)
Amsterdam	12.70	60	4
Den Haag	2.40	15	6
Rotterdam	3.20	15	8

Den Haag is also linked to Delft by tram 1, which takes 30 minutes.

Leiden

☑071 / POP 121,249

Vibrant Leiden is one of the Netherlands' great cities. Woven with canals lined by beautiful 17th-century buildings, it's renowned for being Rembrandt's birthplace, the home of the Netherlands' oldest and most prestigious university (Einstein was a regular professor), and the place America's pilgrims raised money to lease the leaky *Mayflower* that took them to the New World in 1620.

Leiden's cache of museums, all within walking distance of each other, is a major draw, as is wandering along its picturesque canals and soaking up nightlife fuelled by a 23,000-strong student population.

History

Leiden's university – the Netherlands' oldest – was a gift from Willem the Silent in

1575 for withstanding two Spanish sieges in 1573 and 1574. It was a terrible time, ending when the Sea Beggars arrived and repelled the invaders. According to lore, the retreating Spanish legged it so quickly, they abandoned a kettle of *hutspot* (hotchpotch, stew) – today it's still a staple of Dutch menus in restaurants and in homes.

Decades later, Protestants fleeing persecution elsewhere in the Low Countries, France and England arrived in Leiden to a somewhat warmer welcome. Most notable was the group led by John Robinson, who would sail to America and into history as the pilgrims aboard the *Mayflower*.

Wealth from the linen industry buttressed Leiden's growing prosperity, and during the 17th century the town produced several brilliant artists, most famously Rembrandt van Rijn, better known by his first name alone. Rembrandt was born in Leiden in 1606, and remained here for 26 years before achieving fame in Amsterdam.

Today, the university campus comprises an interesting mix of modern and antique buildings that are scattered around town.

◉ Sights

As you walk five minutes southeast from its striking Centraal Station, the city's traditional character unfolds, especially around the Pieterskerk and south. Leiden's district of historic waterways is worth at least half a day of wandering.

Museum De Lakenhal   MUSEUM
(www.lakenhal.nl; Oude Singel 28-32) Leiden's foremost museum, the Lakenhal, displaying works by native son Rembrandt among others, will close its doors between 2016 and 2018 while it undergoes a major renovation and expansion. Check online or with the tourist office for updates.

★Rijksmuseum van Oudheden   MUSEUM
(National Museum of Antiquities; www.rmo.nl; Rapenburg 28; adult/child €9.50/3; ☺10am-5pm Tue-Sun) This museum has a world-class collection of Greek, Roman and Egyptian artefacts, the pride of which is the extraordinary Temple of Taffeh, a gift from former Egyptian president Anwar Sadat to the Netherlands for helping to save ancient Egyptian monuments from flood.

Note: the Egyptian collection is closed until October 2016.

★Rijksmuseum Volkenkunde   MUSEUM
(National Museum of Ethnology; www.volkenkunde. nl; Steenstraat 1; adult/child €12/6; ☺10am-5pm Tue-Sun) Cultural achievements by civilisations worldwide are on show at the Museum Volkenkunde. More than 200,000 artefacts span China, South America and Africa, much like Amsterdam's Tropenmuseum. There's a rich Indonesian collection; watch for performances by the museum's gamelan troupe.

De Valk   MUSEUM
(The Falcon; ☑071-516 53 53; http://molenmuseum-devalk.nl; 2e Binnenvestgracht 1; adult/child €4/2; ☺10am-5pm Tue-Sat, 1-5pm Sun) Leiden's landmark windmill museum receives loving care, with constant renovation, and many consider it the best example of its kind. Its arms are free to turn 'whenever possible', when wind conditions are right, and can still grind grain.

Museum Boerhaave   MUSEUM
(www.museumboerhaave.nl; Lange St Agnietenstraat 10; adult/child €9.50/4.50; ☺10am-5pm Tue-Sun) Leiden University was an early centre for Dutch medical research. This museum displays the often-grisly results (five centuries of pickled organs and surgical tools and skeletons) plus you can have a gander at the anatomical theatre with skeletons in stiff relief.

★Hortus Botanicus Leiden   GARDENS
(www.hortusleiden.nl; Rapenburg 73; adult/child €7/3; ☺10am-6pm daily Apr-Oct, to 4pm Tue-Sun Nov-Mar) The lush Hortus Botanicus is one of Europe's oldest botanical gardens (1590; the oldest was created in Padua, Italy, in 1545), and is home to the Netherlands' oldest descendants of the Dutch tulips. It's a wonderful place to relax, with explosions of tropical colour and a fascinating (and steamy) greenhouse.

Naturalis Biodiversity Centre   MUSEUM
(www.naturalis.nl; Darwinweg 2; adult/child €12/9; ☺10am-5pm) A stuffed elephant greets you at this large, well-funded collection of all the usual dead critters and, notably, the skullcap of the million-year-old Java Man discovered by Dutch anthropologist Eugène Dubois in 1891. It's 300m west of the town centre.

De Burcht   PARK, MONUMENT
(☺sunrise-sunset) `FREE` De Burcht, an 11th-century citadel on an artificial hill, lost its protective functions as the city grew around it. It's now a park with lovely places to view the steeples and rooftops, with a cafe at its base.

Leiden

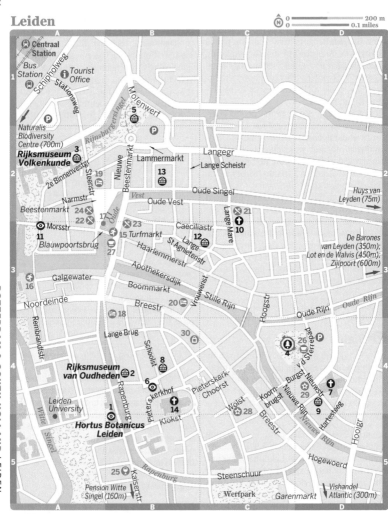

Hooglandse Kerk CHURCH
(www.hooglandsekerk.com; Nieuwstraat 20; ⊙11am-4pm Tue-Sat May-Sep) This huge pile of bricks is the 15th-century Hooglandse Kerk, an agglomeration of styles.

Pieterskerk CHURCH
(www.pieterskerk.com; Pieterskerkhof 1; admission €2; ⊙11am-6pm) Crowned by its huge steeple, Pieterskerk is often under restoration – a good thing as it has been prone to collapse since it was built in the 14th century.

The precinct here includes the gabled old **Latin School** (Lokhorststraat 16), which was graced by a pupil named Rembrandt from

1616 to 1620. Across the plaza, look for the **Gravensteen** (Pieterskerkhof 6), which dates to the 13th century and was once a prison. The gallery facing the plaza was where judges watched executions.

Leiden American Pilgrim Museum MUSEUM
(☑512 24 13; www.leidenamericanpilgrimmuseum. org/index.htm; Beschuitsteeg 9; admission €5; ⊙1-5pm Wed-Sat) The Leiden American Pilgrim Museum is a fascinating restoration of a one-room house occupied around 1610 by the soon-to-be Pilgrims (p184). The house itself dates from 1375 (check out the original 14th-century floor tiles), but the furnishings

Leiden

are from the Pilgrims' period. Curator Jeremy Bangs is an author who has written extensively on the Pilgrims and has a vast knowledge of their Leiden links.

Marekerk   CHURCH
(www.marekerk.com; Lange Mare 48; ☺10am-5pm) The Marekerk dates to 1639 and has a beautiful eight-sided wooden interior. Regular concerts and theatre performances take place here; check the agenda online.

Zijlpoort   GATE
Built in 1667 by Willem van der Helm, this grand stone edifice at Leiden's eastern edge is one of only two surviving city gates (there were originally eight), along with the Morspoort. Today, the Zijlpoort houses a cafe/restaurant and events venue.

Morspoort   GATE
Leiden's mighty western gate is the Morspoort, built in 1669 by Willem van der Helm, who also designed the other surviving gate, the Zijlpoort, and five of the original eight in total.

☆ Activities

Bootjes en Broodjes   BOATING
(🖉514 39 33; www.bootjesenbroodjes.nl; Blauwpoortsbrug 1; 2hr electric-boat rental €75, canal tours adult/child €9.50/5; ☺noon-7pm Mon-Thu, 11am-7pm Fri-Sun mid-Apr–early Oct) As the name (Boats and Bread Rolls) implies, you can buy sandwiches to take on your voyage.

Rent a quiet electric boat (no boat licence required) or join a 50-minute guided tour. Private tours are also available on request.

Botenverhuur 't Galgewater   BOAT RENTAL
(🖉514 97 90; www.botenverhuurleiden.nl; Galgewater 44a; kayak/rowboat/canoe/boat per hour from €6/7/8/50; ☺noon-10pm Mon-Thu, 11am-10pm Fri-Sun mid-May–mid-Aug, noon-7pm Mon-Thu, 11am-7pm Fri-Sun mid-Apr–mid-May & mid-Aug–early Oct) Rent a kayak, rowboat, canoe or *sloepen* (traditional Dutch powered boat) here to explore Leiden's meandering canals. Minimum *sloepen* rental is two hours (no boat licence required).

☞ Tours

Rederij Rembrandt   BOAT TOUR
(🖉513 49 38; www.rederij-rembrandt.nl; Blauwpoortshaven 5; adult/child €10/6.50; ☺11am, 1.30pm & 2.45pm May-Oct) Leisurely one-hour canal boat tours taken in the channel around the old town centre, accompanied by multilingual commentary (including English).

⚑ Festivals & Events

Leidens Ontzet   CULTURAL
(☺3 Oct) Leiden grinds to a halt for Leidens Ontzet, commemorating the day the Spanish-caused starvation ended in 1574. The revelry is undiminished more than four centuries later, and there is much eating of the ceremonial *hutspot*, herring and white bread. Beer-fuelled celebrations kick off the night before.

ROTTERDAM & SOUTH HOLLAND LEIDEN

🛏 Sleeping

You can get good online deals but true budget accommodation is hard to come by in Leiden and there are no hostels.

Huys van Leyden   BOUTIQUE HOTEL €€
(☑ 260 07 00; www.huysvanleyden.nl; Oude Singel 212; d from €134; 🛜) Steeped in history, this 1611 canal house has luxurious rooms and amenities including a sauna, roof terrace, and Nespresso machines in each of the five Golden Age-meets-21st-century rooms richly decorated with shimmering fabrics and canopied beds. Its sister property, De Barones van Leyden, is even more opulent.

Nieuw Minerva   HOTEL €€
(☑ 512 63 58; www.nieuwminerva.nl; Boommarkt 23; s/d from €75/83; @🛜) Located in six canal-side houses dating from the 16th century, this central hotel has a mix of 40 regular (ie nothing special) and very fun themed rooms, including a room with a bed in which King Lodewijk Bonaparte (aka Louis Bonaparte) slept; the 'room of angels' – a luminous vision of white; the 'Delft blue room'; and the Rembrandt room.

Hotel de Doelen   HOTEL €€
(☑ 512 05 27; www.dedoelen.com; Rapenburg 2; s/d from €85/105; @🛜) Built in 1638, this regal former patrician's mansion in a peaceful location just 150m from the Beestenmarkt has an air of slightly faded classical elegance. Some of the canal-side rooms are larger and better appointed than others. There are 128 rooms overall, some on the ground floor.

Hotel Mayflower   HOTEL €€
(☑ 514 26 41; www.hotelmayflower.nl; Beestenmarkt 2; s/d/tr from €75/95/115) The 25 large rooms are bright but are something of a throwback to another era of lodging – say the 1980s. But the hotel is well located on the Beestenmarkt and a short 200m walk from the train station, and it lays out a good buffet breakfast. Apartments are also available on request.

De Barones van Leyden   BOUTIQUE HOTEL €€€
(☑ 260 07 00; www.debaronesvanleyden.nl; Oude Herengracht 22; d from €146; 🛜) While its sister property Huys van Leyden has the ambience of a merchant's house, the 1644 De Barones van Leyden lets you experience Golden Age aristocracy, albeit with all mod cons (including a lift). Sweeping rooms are done up in dazzling shades such as turquoise and plum, with gilt-edged mirrors adorning the breakfast room.

Guests can use Huys van Leyden's wellness facilities.

PILGRIMS' PROGRESS

In 1608 a group of Calvinist Protestants split from the Anglican church and left persecution in Nottinghamshire, England, for a journey that would span decades and thousands of miles. Travelling first to Amsterdam under the leadership of John Robinson, they encountered theological clashes with local Dutch Protestants.

In Leiden they found a more liberal atmosphere, thanks to the university and some like-minded Calvinists who already lived there. They also found company with refugees who had escaped from persecution elsewhere. However, the group's past was to catch up with them. In 1618 James I of England announced he would assume control over the Calvinists living in Leiden. In addition, the local Dutch were becoming less tolerant of religious splinter groups.

The first group of English left Leiden in 1620 for Delfshaven in what is now Rotterdam, where they bought the *Speedwell* with the intention of sailing to the New World. Unfortunately, the leaky *Speedwell* didn't live up to its name; after several attempts to cross the Atlantic, the group gave up and, against their better judgement, sailed into Southampton in England. After repairs to their ship and a thwarted attempt to restart their journey, the group joined the much more seaworthy *Mayflower* in Dartmouth and sailed, as it were, into history as the Pilgrims.

This legendary voyage was actually just one of many involving the Leiden group. It wasn't until 1630 that most had made their way to the American colonies founded in what is today New England. Some 1000 people made the voyages, including a number of Dutch who were considered oddballs for their unusual beliefs.

In Leiden today, traces of the Pilgrims are elusive. The best place to start is the Leiden American Pilgrim Museum (p182).

✖ Eating

Vishandel Atlantic SEAFOOD €
(http://vishandelatlantic.nl; Levendaal 118; dishes €3-12.50; ⊘9am-8pm) Two Turkish brothers opened this fish stand in 1989 and their attention to quality has propelled them to the Netherlands' top ranks of seafood vendors. Their raw herring rates 10 out of 10 in contests where 5.5 is considered a good score. You can also try all types of smoked fish as well as dishes like fish and chips.

David's Burger BURGERS €
(www.davidsburger.nl; Steenstraat 57; mains €10-13.50; ⊘5-11pm) 🍴 Cowhide covers the timber booths, and horseshoes and farm equipment hang on the walls at David's, serving Leiden's best, all-organic burgers such as the gaucho (beef with grilled pepper, courgette and *chimichurri*), spicy veggie (bean and chipotle-pepper patty with guacamole and cheese), lams (lamb with red-onion relish) and classic (beef with lettuce, tomato and pickles), plus corn on the cob.

Oudt Leyden PANCAKES €
(www.oudtleyden.nl; Steenstraat 49; pancakes €6.50-15.50, mains €16-24.50; ⊘11.30am-9.30pm; 🚻🖐) The giant Dutch-style pancakes here make kids and adults alike go wide-eyed. Whether you're after something savoury (marinated salmon, sour cream and capers), sweet (apple, raisins, almond paste, sugar and cinnamon) or simply adventurous (ginger and bacon), this welcoming place hits the spot every time. Pancakes aside, choices include mushroom lasagne, sirloin with red-wine jus and salmon fillets.

Lot en de Walvis INTERNATIONAL €€
(🖂763 03 83; www.lotendewalvis.nl; Haven 1; mains €7-19; ⊘9am-10pm) Lot's sun-drenched terrace sits at the water's edge but the reason it's a Leiden hot spot is the outstanding food, from breakfast (French toast with cinnamon sugar; eggs Benedict on sourdough) to lunch (Thai yellow-curry fish burger; smoked mackerel pasta) and dinner (fiery harissa lamb skewers with yogurt dip; pear and hazelnut cake). Book ahead at all times.

Brasserie de Engelenbak MODERN DUTCH €€
(🖂512 54 40; www.deengelenbak.nl; Lange Mare 38; mains lunch €8-19, dinner €17-19, 3-course dinner menu €29; ⊘11am-10pm) In the shadow of the 17th-century octagonal Marekerk, this elegant bistro serves a seasonally changing menu of fresh fare that takes its cues from across the continent. Local organic produce features in many of the dishes. Tables outside enjoy views of the passing crowds. Its adjoining *café* serves snacks until midnight.

★ In den Doofpot MODERN EUROPEAN €€€
(🖂512 24 34; www.indendoofpot.nl; Turfmarkt 9; 3-/4-course lunch menu €39/45, 4-/5-/6-/8-course dinner menu €55/65/70/80; ⊘noon-3pm & 5-10pm Mon-Fri, 5-10pm Sat) Given the sky-high calibre of chef Patrick Brugman's cooking, In den Doofpot's prices are a veritable steal. Pork belly with smoked eel, grilled lobster with truffle butter and microherb salad, organic Dutch beef fillet with Madeira sauce, potatoes and caramelised orange and other intense flavour combinations are all executed with artistic vision. Wines cost €8 per course.

🍷 Drinking

VLOT CAFE
(www.vlotleiden.nl; Prinsessekade 5; ⊘9am-9pm) Angular, glass-paned VLOT sits out on a platform right in the canal, providing great views year-round, but in warm weather the best seats are on its adjoining open-air terrace. It's an equally relaxing spot for coffee, a beer or a glass of wine.

Café L'Esperance BROWN CAFE
(www.lesperance.nl; Kaiserstraat 1; ⊘3pm-1am Mon-Wed, 11am-1am Thu-Sun) Decked out with wood-panelled walls lined with framed photos, this nostalgic *bruin café* overlooks an evocative bend in the canal, with tables propagating along the pavement outside in summer.

Het Koetshuis CAFE
(www.koetshuisdeburcht.nl; Burgsteeg 13; ⊘noon-9.30pm) On a sunny day, it's hard to beat the terrace tables just outside the grand gate to the Burcht, where all walks of life gather for an afternoon coffee or *borrel* (drinks). It also does fantastic cheese platters and desserts, as well as full meals.

☆ Entertainment

De Twee Spieghels LIVE MUSIC
(www.detweespieghels.nl; Nieuwstraat 11; ⊘4pm-1am Mon-Thu, 4pm-2am Fri, 2pm-2am Sat, 3-11pm Sun) Live jazz takes to the stage at this intimate wine bar at least four nights a week; check the agenda to see what's coming up. Concerts are free.

Café de WW
LIVE MUSIC

(www.deww.nl; Wolsteeg 6; ⊙2pm-2am Sun-Wed, to 3am Thu, to 4am Fri & Sat) On Friday and Saturday, live rock in this glossy scarlet bar can expand to an impromptu stage in the alley with crowds trailing up to the main street. On other nights DJs play. Cash only.

🛍 Shopping

Haarlemmerstraat has all the mainstream chain stores. Big department stores spill across to Breestraat. Look for more interesting shops on side streets such as Vrouwenstraat and in the lanes around Pieterskerk.

Mayflower Bookshop
BOOKS

(www.themayflowerbookshop.nl; Breestraat 65; ⊙1-6pm Mon, 10am-6pm Tue, Wed & Fri, 10am-9pm Thu, 9.30am-6pm Sat, 1-5pm Sun) The Mayflower has a compact selection of new and used classics, fiction and travel guides, including English-language titles.

ℹ Information

Tourist office (☑516 60 00; www.visitleiden. nl; Stationsweg 41; ⊙7am-7pm Mon-Fri, 10am-4pm Sat, 11am-3pm Sun) Across from the train station.

ℹ Getting There & Away

BICYCLE

Head west from the station on bike paths along Geversstraat and then via Rijnsburg for 10km to the beach at Katwijk. There you can pick up national route **LF1**, which connects with the **LF20** for the 34km ride north to Haarlem. Head south on the **LF1**, 20km along the shore to Scheveningen and Den Haag.

Oldenburger (☑071-760 05 66; www.oldenburgerfietsspecialist.nl; Stationsplein; bike rental per day from €9.50; ⊙7am-7pm Mon-Fri, 10am-6pm Sat & Sun Apr-Aug, 7am-7pm Mon-Fri Sep-Mar) Rents bikes.

BUS

Regional and local buses leave from the bus station directly in front of Centraal Station.

TRAIN

Leiden's bold, modern Centraal Station is 400m northwest of the centre. Regular services:

Destination	Price (€)	Duration (min)	Frequency (per hour)
Amsterdam	8.80	35	6
Den Haag	3.40	15	6
Rotterdam	7.20	30	4
Schiphol Airport	5.70	15	6

Around Leiden

This is the very heart of the Netherlands' tulip-growing land. In spring you may be lucky enough to fly over the impossibly brightly coloured fields as you fly into Schiphol. It's definitely worth getting a bike and touring the region from either Leiden, Haarlem or Keukenhof Gardens.

Lisse
☑0252 / POP 22,400

The sweet town of Lisse is just 1km east of Keukenhof Gardens and makes a handy base, but you can also visit its castle and tulip museum year-round.

⊙ Sights & Activities

The Keukenhof Gardens are unmissable in spring.

Kasteel Keukenhof
CASTLE, GARDENS

(☑750 690; www.kasteelkeukenhof.nl; Keukenhof-Noord 1; adult/child €12.50/5.50, gardens only €5/2; ⊙8.30am-5pm Mon-Fri, 10.30am-5pm Sat & Sun) Completely restored in 2012, this grand castle across the road from Keukenhof Gardens was built in 1641 by VOC (Dutch East India Company) commander Adriaan Muertenszoon Block. Tickets include a compulsory 30-minute guided tour of its lavish interior. It sits on more than 80 hectares of woodland, meadows and flowering gardens. There's a delightful petting zoo where kids can crawl into the pens with the guinea pigs and rabbits, and an adjacent teahouse (both open from 10am to 5pm).

Museum de Zwarte Tulp
MUSEUM

(Museum of the Black Tulip; ☑0252-417 900; www. museumdezwartetulp.nl; Heereweg 219; adult/child €6/3; ⊙10am-5pm Tue-Sun Mar-Aug, 1-5pm Tue-Sun Sep-Feb) The small Museum de Zwarte Tulp displays everything you might want to know about bulbs, including why there's no such thing as a black tulip, a mythical bloom that helped drive Tulipmania in 1636.

🛏 Sleeping & Eating

★ De Vier Seizoenen
B&B €€

(☑418 023; http://rdvs.nl; Heereweg 224; d from €80; 🌐) Lisse's best places to sleep and eat are in the same building. Upstairs are four exquisite rooms in chocolate-box tones with sloped ceilings and natural-stone bathrooms. Downstairs, the superb **restaurant** (☑0252-418 023; http://rdvs.nl; Heereweg 224;

DON'T MISS

KEUKENHOF GARDENS

Keukenhof Gardens (www.keukenhof.nl; Lisse; adult/child €16/8, parking €6; ◷8am-7.30pm mid-Mar–mid-May, last entry 6pm) One of the Netherlands' top attractions, Keukenhof, 1km west of Lisse, is the world's largest bulb-flower garden. It attracts nearly 800,000 visitors during its eight-week season, which is almost as short-lived as the blooms on the millions of multicoloured tulips, daffodils and hyacinths.

Special buses (€9, every 15 minutes, 30 minutes) link Keukenhof with Amsterdam's Schiphol Airport and Leiden's Centraal Station; combination tickets covering entry and transport are available (adult/child €23.50/12.50). Prepurchase tickets online to help avoid huge queues.

mains lunch €7.50-19, dinner €19-26, 2-/3-/4-course dinner menu €28/31/38; ◷noon-2.30pm Mon-Sat Apr-Oct, 5.30pm-9.30pm Wed-Mon year-round) serves dishes such as gurnard on sweet-potato mash or veal cheeks and sweetbreads on creamed beetroot.

Den Ouden Heere   INTERNATIONAL €€
(☑418 660; www.denoudenheere.nl; Heereweg 207; mains €14.50-25.50; ◷5-10pm Mon-Sat) Set over two floors with a buzzing pavement terrace facing Lisse's main square, Den Ouden Heere is a popular spot for its globally influenced menu: spinach pancakes stuffed with ricotta and rucola (rocket), Uruguay beef steak with Béarnaise sauce and tarragon potato cake, and rack of New Zealand lamb with sweet potato and honey-thyme jus.

❶ Information

Tourist office (☑417 900; www.vvvlisse.nl; Heereweg 219; ◷10am-5pm Tue-Sun Mar-Aug, 1-5pm Tue-Sun Sep-Feb) Inside the Museum de Zwarte Tulp, Lisse's tourist office can give you many options for bulb-field touring.

❶ Getting There & Away

BICYCLE

The LF1 passes 5km west of Lisse along the coast.

BUS

Bus 361 serves Amsterdam's Schiphol Airport (45 minutes, four hourly). Bus 50 serves Haarlem (55 minutes, four hourly) and Leiden (40 minutes, four hourly).

ZEELAND

The province of Zeeland consists of three slivers of land that nestle in the middle of a vast delta through which many of Europe's rivers drain. As you survey the calm, flat landscape, consider that for centuries the resilient Zeelanders have been battling the North Sea waters, and not always with success. In fact the region has suffered two massive waterborne tragedies.

In 1421 the St Elizabeth's Day flood killed more than 100,000, irrevocably altering the landscape – and some say the disposition – of the Netherlands and its people.

In 1953 yet another flood took 2000 lives and destroyed 800km of dykes, leaving 500,000 homeless and leading to the Delta Project, an enormous, nearly 50-year construction program that is hoped to finally ensure the security of these lands.

Peaceful Middelburg is the historic capital, while the coast along the North Sea is lined with beaches. Many people visit this place of tenuous land and omnipresent water just to see the sheer size of the Delta Project's dykes and barriers.

❶ Getting There & Away

National bike route LF1, which follows the entire North Sea coast of the Netherlands, is a vital link in Zeeland, as is LF13, which runs from Breda in the east to Middelburg and on to the coast (and LF1). However, it is also easy to explore on your own as the vast dyke-webbed farmlands make for easy, mellow riding. Regional bike routes are also numbered and maps are widely available.

Middelburg is easily reached by train, but for most other towns you'll need to rely on the bus network. The most important includes bus 395, which makes a one-hour journey every hour between Rotterdam's Zuidplein metro station and Zierikzee, where you can transfer to buses for the rest of Zeeland.

Middelburg

☑0118 / POP 47,658

Wandering through Middelburg's majestic former VOC harbour and its winding cobbled streets, you'd never guess that during WWII, in 1940, Germany destroyed much of the town's historic centre.

Zeeland's capital was rebuilt in the same style and you can still get a solid feel for what life must have been like hundreds of years ago. The fortifications built by the Sea Beggars in 1595 can still be traced in the pattern of the main canals encircling the old town.

◉ Sights & Activities

This pretty town is eminently suitable for walking, with snaking alleyways leading in and away from the Markt.

The area around the elongated Damplein (east of the Abdij) preserves many 18th-century houses, some of which have been turned into interesting shops and cafes.

★ Abdij   HISTORIC SITE
(☉ churches 10.30am-5pm Mon-Fri, 1.30-5pm Sat & Sun mid-Apr–Oct) **FREE** This huge abbey complex dates from the 12th century and houses the regional government as well as three churches. It features a vast inner courtyard, the **Abdijplein**, unlike anything elsewhere in the Netherlands; it echoes with history. Its three churches are all in a cluster and reached through one tiny entrance via the Wandelkerk. All surround a gem of a cloister with a tiny herb garden.

➡ **Wandelkerk**

(admission free, tower €4; ☉ tower 10am-5pm mid-Apr–Oct) The Wandelkerk dates from the 1600s and holds the tombs of Jan and Cornelis Evertsen, admirals and brothers killed fighting the English in 1666. It encompasses Lange Jan ('Long John'; it has its own locally brewed beer named after it), the 91m **tower** (207 steps).

➡ **Koorkerk**

Just east of Abdij, parts of Koorkerk date from the 1300s.

➡ **Nieuwe Kerk**

West of Abdij, this church has a famous organ and dates from the 16th century.

➡ **Zeeuws Museum**

(www.zeeuwsmuseum.nl; adult/child €8.50/free; ☉ 11am-5pm Tue-Sun) The Zeeuws Museum is housed in the former monks' dormitories of the Abdij abbey complex. Its collection of art and historic items is excellent, especially the traditional dress.

Town Hall   HISTORIC BUILDING
(☑ 0118-675 452; tours adult/child €4.50/4; ☉ tours 3pm Apr-Oct) Dominating the Markt, the town hall grabs the eye. It's ornately beautiful, and a pastiche of styles: the Gothic side facing the Markt is from the 1400s; the more classical portion on Lange Noordstraat dates from the 1600s.

Inside there are several sumptuous ceremonial rooms that boast treasures such as the ubiquitous Belgian tapestries. Visits to the building are by 40-minute guided tours organised by the tourist shop.

Jewish Cemetery   CEMETERY
The large old Jewish cemetery on the Walensingel has a stark memorial to the many Middelburg Jews taken away to their deaths by the Nazis.

☞ Tours

Rondvaart Middelburg   TOUR
(☑ 643 272; http://rondvaartmiddelburg.nl; Achter de Houttuinen 39; adult/child €6.75/3.75; ☉ on demand from 10.30am Apr-Oct) Scenic 40-minute tours run along the southern canal.

★☆ Festivals & Events

Ringrijdendagen   CULTURAL
(Ring Riding Days; ☉ Jul & Aug) The Ringrijdendagen are held on two separate days, the first in July around the Abbey square, the second in August at the Molenwater. 'Ring riders' charge about on horseback in fancy dress carrying big sticks towards a target, with the aim of trying to tilt it.

🛏 Sleeping

Het Princenjagt   HOTEL €
(☑ 613 416; www.hotelhetprincenjagt.nl; Nederstraat 2; s/d €50/85 without bathroom €40/65; 🖥) By the boat-filled marina, this eight-room B&B has simple but clean, comfortable rooms. There's a kitchen for guests to use, and a little toaster on each table at breakfast. Four rooms share bathrooms.

★ Hotel The Roosevelt   BOUTIQUE HOTEL €€
(☑ 43 63 60; www.hoteltheroosevelt.nl; Nieuwe Burg 42; d/ste from €94/109; ❄🖥) Footsteps from the Abdij, a monumental former dyke warden's mansion has been fabulously converted to house 28 period-meets-contemporary boutique rooms. Rooms high up in the building are snug, but others are duplex and/or huge and some open onto balconies. In chilly

Middelburg

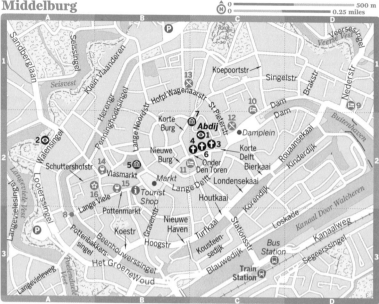

Middelburg

◉ Top Sights

◉ Sights

◉ Activities, Courses & Tours

◉ Sleeping

◉ Eating

◉ Drinking & Nightlife

◉ Entertainment

weather an open fireplace blazes in the bar, which has become a local gathering spot.

Hotel Aan De Dam HOTEL €€
(☎643 773; www.hotelaandedam.nl; Dam 31; s/d from €90/110; 🕸) An opulent 1652 mansion built by Jacob van Campen, who designed the palace on the Dam in Amsterdam, is now an appealing hotel with a great central location. The 13 rooms vary widely in size and view but all have period decor and mod cons. It overlooks a canal and small park.

🍴 Eating & Drinking

Many restaurants shut Sunday night and all day Monday.

De Gouden Bock MODERN DUTCH €€
(www.degoudenbock.nl; Damplein 17; mains lunch €12-22.50, dinner €23-31; ⊙noon-3pm & 6-9pm Tue-Sat) The colours of the coastal dunes add warmth to one of the town's most attractive restaurants. Ingredients are from the region and the menu changes regularly; seafood is a speciality.

Restaurant De Eetkamer
MODERN DUTCH €€€

(☑ 635 676; www.eetkamermiddelburg.nl; Wagenaarstraat 13-15; mains €27-60, 3-/4-/5-/6-course menu €39.50/48/58/67.50; ⊙ noon-2pm & 5.30-9.30pm Tue-Sat) De Eetkamer's produce is sourced locally, meats are house-cured and the menu changes with the seasons but might include the likes of foie gras terrine with rum-marinated raisins, lobster tortellini with bisque, beef and veal sweetbreads braised with chanterelles, and beef Wellington with white mushrooms and fresh herbs.

★ De Mug
BROWN CAFE

(www.demug.nl; Vlasmarkt 54-56) Don't be misled by the Heineken signs; the beer list is long and includes many rare Trappist varieties. Be sure to try the Mug Bitter, heavy on the hops, which is brewed in Middelburg especially for De Mug. There's a great soundtrack of '50s crooners, and hearty food too.

De Zaak
BROWN CAFE

(www.dezaakmiddelburg.nl; Pottenmarkt 24; ⊙ 10am-2am Tue-Sat, noon-2am Sun) De Zaak's rustic interior with hefty beams and wine barrels makes it a cosy spot at any time, but you can't beat it in warm weather when the front terrace spills onto Pottenmarkt and turns into a giant street party.

☆ Entertainment

De Spot
LIVE MUSIC

(http://despotmiddelburg.nl; Beddewijkstraat 15; ⊙ 10pm-4am Thu-Sat, hours vary) Entered through a broad arch, this wide-ranging venue hosts everything from jazz to rock, blues and open-mic nights. Check the online agenda to find out what's coming up.

❶ Information

Tourist shop (☑ 674 300; www.touristshop.nl; Markt 51; ⊙ 9.30am-5.30pm Mon-Sat) There's no official VVV tourist office in Middelburg; there is a tourist shop counter inside the excellent local bookshop, De Drvkkery. It sells various local tours but has little info otherwise.

❶ Getting There & Around

BICYCLE

National bike route **LF1** passes right through town; it crosses the many delta barriers to the north. Head east on **LF13** to Breda (140km) via the fertile countryside and detour to charming villages such as Goes (36km).

Fietsshop (☑ 0118-612 178; Stationplein 2; bike-rental per day €7.50; ⊙ 7.30am-11pm Mon-Sat) Rents bikes.

BUS

Regional buses stop along Kanaalweg close to the train station.

TRAIN

Middelburg's station is 300m southeast of the centre.

Regular services:

Destination	Price (€)	Duration (min)	Frequency (per hour)
Amsterdam	24.60	150	2
Roosendaal	12.20	55	2
Rotterdam	19.40	90	2

Around Middelburg

The Walcheren peninsula is a wonderful place for bicycling: combine journeys to old towns with time at the beach.

Veere

☑ 0118 / POP 1650

Veere is a postcard-perfect former fishing village that turned to tourism when its access to the sea on the Veerse Meer (Veere Lake) was closed as part of the Delta Project. The town now has a busy yacht harbour. Much of Veere dates from the early 16th century and is a lovely place to stroll around.

◉ Sights & Activities

Here, you'll feel like you're in a Vermeer painting: rich Gothic houses abound, a testament to the wealth brought in by the wool trade with the Scots, and at the waterfront, the Campveerse Toren was part of the old fortifications. Look for the indications on the side showing the levels of various floods.

The town hall on the Markt dates from 1474, but was mostly completed in 1599. Its tower is still stuffed with bells – 48 at last count.

At the south end of town is the 16th-century Grote Kerk, another edifice that never matched its designer's intentions – its stump of a steeple (42m) looms ominously.

⨇ Sleeping & Eating

Hotel 't Waepen van Veere
HOTEL €€

(☑ 501 231; http://waepen.nl; Markt 23-27; d €90-145, restaurant mains €16-29.50; ⊙ restaurant noon-10pm Jul & Aug, hours vary Sep-Jun; 🛜) On the central square, this charming hotel has 16 stylish, comfortable rooms and an elegant restaurant with outdoor seating serving adventurous Modern Dutch cuisine with an emphasis on seafood.

ℹ Information

Tourist office (VVV; ☑ 506 110; Markt 5;
🕙10am-5pm Jul & Aug, noon-4pm Tue-Sun
Apr-Jun, Sep & Oct; 🖥) Veere's tourist office
is inside the town hall. Staff can advise on boat
rentals and bike routes.

ℹ Getting There & Away

BICYCLE

Veere is an easy ride from Middelburg on
national bike route **LF1** (8km).

BUS

Bus 54 makes the 10-minute run every hour
(every two hours on Sunday).

Domburg

☑ 0118 / POP 1490

Although Domburg is a low-key seaside town
that's refreshingly untacky, it's still jammed
in summer. To escape the crowds, head south
along the tall dunes. You can keep going past
the golf course for a good 4km.

The tourist office can steer you to one of
many bike-rental shops and provides maps
of the popular 35km Mantelingen bicycle
route, which begins and ends at Domburg.
It takes in beaches, countryside and atmospheric little villages such as Veere.

🛏 Sleeping & Eating

The tourist office has myriad accommodation options, including holiday apartments
and campgrounds.

Stayokay Domburg   HOSTEL €
(☑ 581 254; www.stayokay.com; Duinvlietweg 8;
dm/d from €20/75; 🕙Apr-Oct; 🖥) Domburg's
Stayokay HI hostel is set in a 13th-century
castle, complete with moat, 2km east of the
town and 1km from the beach. It's under-
standably popular; reserve well in advance.
Bus 52 from Middelburg stops along the
N287 near the entrance.

★**Het Badpaviljoen**   SEAFOOD €€
(☑ 582 405; www.hetbadpaviljoen.nl; Badhu-
isweg 21; mains lunch €16-28, dinner €23-35;
🕙11am-midnight Thu-Mon) Perched on the
grassy dunes of Domburg, this legendary
restaurant is housed in a majestic 19th-
century bathhouse with a huge porch and
terrace. Indulge in splendidly prepared seafood dishes in the restaurant or enjoy drinks
and Dutch bar snacks outside while savouring the seashore views.

ℹ Getting There & Away

BICYCLE

The area is laced with ideal bike paths along
dykes and through the green countryside. Get
a map and start exploring. Middelburg is about
13km via various routes.

BUS

Bus 52 links Domburg to Middelburg directly every
hour, while bus 53 goes via the southern beaches.

ℹ Information

Tourist office (VVV; ☑ 583 484; www.vvvzee
land.nl; Schuitvlotstraat 32; 🕙9.30am-5.30pm
Mon-Sat, 11am-3pm Sun Apr-Sep) Domburg's
tourist office is near the entrance to town on
Roosjesweg.

Waterland Neeltje Jans

Travelling the N57, you are on the front lines
of the Dutch war with the sea as you traverse
the massive developments of the Delta Project, a succession of huge dykes and dams
designed to prevent floods. Possibly the most
impressive stretch is between Noord Beveland
and Schouwen-Duiveland, to the north. This
storm-surge barrier, more than 3km long and
spanning three inlets and two artificial islands,
took 10 years to build, beginning in 1976.

Around the midway point between Noord
Beveland and Schouwen-Duiveland on the
N57, the Delta Project's former visitor centre
has morphed into a theme park, **Waterland Neeltje Jans** (www.neeltjejans.nl; adult/
child €22.50/16.50, cage swimming with sharks per
15min €55, 1hr boat trip €3; 🕙10am-7.30pm Jul &
Aug, to 5.30pm Apr-Jun & Sep), complete with a
mermaid mascot. Alongside absorbing exhibits about floods, dams and Dutch courage are seals, a water park and hurricane
simulator. A boat trip takes you out onto the
Oosterschelde for a panoramic view of the
barriers and beyond.

The island has a long beach at the southern end, which is popular with windsurfers.

The entire region has coastal sections that
are part of the **National Park Oosterschelde**
(www.np-oosterschelde.nl; Neeltje Jans; visitor centre
admission free; 🕙10am-9pm Jun-Aug, to 5pm Apr,
May & Sep); there are interesting displays in the
visitors centre across the N57 from Waterland.

Bus 133 follows the N57 and stops at Waterland on its run from Middelburg train station (30 minutes, every 30 minutes to two
hours) or Zierikzee (40 minutes). National
bike route NF1 passes right by.

THE DELTA PROJECT

Begun in 1958, the Delta Project consumed billions of guilders, millions of labour hours and untold volumes of concrete and rock before it was officially completed in 1997 (although works continued until 2010). The goal was to avoid a repeat of the catastrophic floods of 1953, when a huge storm surge rushed up the Delta estuaries of Zeeland and broke through inland dykes. This caused a serial failure of dykes throughout the region, and much of the province was flooded.

The original idea was to block up the estuaries and create one vast freshwater network. But by the 1960s this kind of sweeping transformation was unacceptable to the Dutch public, who had become more environmentally aware. So the Oosterschelde was left open to the sea tides, and 3km of movable barriers were constructed that could be lowered ahead of a possible storm surge. The barriers, between Noord Beveland and Schouwen-Duiveland, are the most dramatic part of the Delta Project and the focus of Waterland Neeltje Jans (p191), which details the enormous efforts to complete the barrier.

The project raised and strengthened the region's dykes and added a movable barrier at Rotterdam harbour, the last part to be completed. Public opinion later shifted, but large areas of water had already been dammed and made into freshwater lakes. At Veerse Meer the fishing industry has vanished and been replaced by tourists and sailing boats.

The impact of the Delta Project is still being felt. At Biesbosch National Park the reduction of tides is killing reeds that have grown for centuries. But those who recall the 1953 floods will trade some reeds for their farms any day.

Work is ongoing to strengthen and heighten portions to deal with rising water levels due to climate change.

Schouwen-Duiveland

The middle 'finger' of the Delta, Schouwen-Duiveland, is a compact island of dunes. Beaches and holiday developments are southwest from the village of Renesse. Buses hub at Zierikzee; from here you can catch bus 133 to Renesse and on for the ride over the Delta Works to Middelburg.

Bikes are the best mode of transit here. Routes abound, including national bike route LF1, which runs north and south along the coast and over the various parts of the Delta Project.

Zierikzee

🖉 0111 / POP 10,483

Zierikzee grew wealthy in the 14th century from trade with the Hanseatic League, but things took a turn for the worse in 1576 when a bunch of Spaniards waded over from the mainland at low tide and captured the town, precipitating a long economic decline. There's good strolling along the long waterfront.

At the east end of town, at Oude Haven (Old Harbour), the Noordhavenpoort and the Zuidhavenpoort are old city gates from the 16th and 14th centuries, respectively. The town hall has a unique 16th-century wooden tower topped with a statue of Neptune. Hang out at a cafe and admire historic boats.

ℹ Information

Tourist office (VVV; 🖉 412 450; www.vvvzee land.nl; Nieuwe Haven 7; ⏱10am-4pm Mon-Sat) The tourist office can supply you with a list of local rooms for overnight stays, plus cycling maps.

ℹ Getting There & Away

National bike route **LF1** runs north–south along the coast.

The bus stop is north of the town centre, a five-minute walk across the canal along Grachtweg. Bus 395 runs to Rotterdam's Zuidplein metro station (one hour, at least every two hours).

Westerschouwen

🖉 0111 / POP 199

Sheltered by tall dunes, this village at the west end of Schouwen-Duiveland adjoins a vast park set among the sands and woods. There are hiking and biking trails for outdoors enthusiasts and, although busy in summer, you can easily find solitude in some of the remoter parts of the park.

The tourist office (VVV; 🖉 450 524; www. vvvzeeland.nl; Noordstraat 45a; ⏱9am-5pm Mon-Sat), in the neighbouring town of Haamstede, can help with accommodation.

Bus 133 from Middelburg links the villages to Zierikzee.

Friesland (Fryslân)

Best Places to Eat

➡ Restaurant By Ús (p197)

➡ De Tjotter (p199)

➡ Café-Restaurant de Hinde (p201)

➡ De Walrus (p200)

Best Places to Stay

➡ Hotel-Paleis Stadhouderlijk Hof (p196)

➡ 't Heerenlogement (p199)

➡ Hotel Pension van der Werff (p206)

Why Go?

At first, Friesland seems typically Dutch: it's flat, it's green and there are plenty of cows (the namesake black-and-white variety). But explore a bit and you'll find its differences. For one, the province has its own language, as you'll see on road signs.

Even by Dutch standards, Frieslanders are a very self-reliant bunch. Here they didn't just have to build dykes to protect their land, they had to build the land as well. North Friesland segues into the Waddenzee in such a subtle way that the transition from watery mud to muddy water is elusive – albeit Unesco recognised. Across this shallow body of water stretches what is arguably the country's supreme summertime destination: the slender Waddenzee Islands, each an appealing combination of forest, dunes and glorious beaches, ripe for exploration and threaded with many miles of cycling paths.

At the province's centre is Leeuwarden, the sort of beguiling old Dutch town where you soon settle in and have a favourite cafe. Elsewhere, craggy old fishing villages like Hindeloopen are finding new life as evocative tourist destinations.

When to Go

➡ Summer is the obvious time to visit Friesland. Water sports such as sailing on the Ijsselmeer are at their peak and offshore islands have the most to offer.

➡ Arrive on Terschelling in late June for the anything-goes Oerol festival or make it to Sneek in August for its major late-summer sailing event.

➡ Off-season old towns like Leeuwarden and Harlingen reward as well with moody canalscapes and riveting museums.

➡ If conditions are just right in winter – deep frozen, that is – the nation pauses for the province-spanning ice-skating race known as the Elfstedentocht.

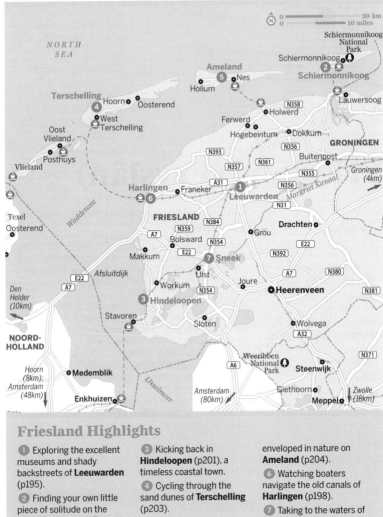

Friesland Highlights

❶ Exploring the excellent museums and shady backstreets of **Leeuwarden** (p195).

❷ Finding your own little piece of solitude on the isle of **Schiermonnikoog** (p205).

❸ Kicking back in **Hindeloopen** (p201), a timeless coastal town.

❹ Cycling through the sand dunes of **Terschelling** (p203).

❺ Spending your days enveloped in nature on **Ameland** (p204).

❻ Watching boaters navigate the old canals of **Harlingen** (p198).

❼ Taking to the waters of the myriad lakes around **Sneek** (p199).

History

Having dredged their home out of the Waddenzee armload by armload, the Frisians are no strangers to struggling with their natural environment.

Farming, fishing and shipbuilding have been the area's principal activities for centuries, and made Friesland one of the wealthiest regions in the Netherlands in the pre-republic era. The Frisians became integrated further into Dutch society – not entirely willingly – in 1932 when the Afsluitdijk (Barrier Dyke) opened, closing the Zuiderzee. This provided better links to Amsterdam and the south but was devastating for small fishing villages, who suddenly found themselves sitting beside a lake.

Language

Frisians speak Frisian, which is actually closer (in some ways) to German and Old English than Dutch; there's an old saying that goes 'As milk is to cheese, are English and Frise'. The majority of Frisians are, however, perfectly conversant in mainstream Dutch.

A ruling in 2002 officially altered the spelling of the province's name from the Dutch 'Friesland' to 'Fryslân', the local version of the name. Likewise, town names are generally presented in two versions, so Leeuwarden is also called 'Ljouwert,' Sneek, the region's second city, 'Snits,' and Hindeloopen is 'Hylpen'. To ingratiate yourself with the locals try uttering the following phrase: *'Fryslân boppe!'* (Friesland rules!)

ⓘ Getting There & Around

The capital, Leeuwarden, is easily reached by train from the south; trains can be caught from there to the coastal towns of the southwest, the port of Harlingen in the west and Groningen in the east. Note that the branch lines are run by Arriva, so if you're using an OV-chipkaart (p302) you must scan it separately from a Nederland Spoorwegen (NS; national railway company) train journey. For example, if you ride an NS train from Amsterdam to Sneek, at Leeuwarden you need to scan off on an NS machine, then scan on again on an Arriva machine for the branch line to Sneek.

The rest of the province requires more patience, but can be reached by bus or, in the case of the islands, by ferry; various day passes are available.

Cycle paths criss-cross Friesland. National bike route **LF3** bisects the province north and south through Leeuwarden; **LF10** cuts across Waddenzee on the Afsluitdijk (30km) from Noord-Holland and takes in the north Frisian coast and all the ferry ports, while **LF22** covers the southern coast before heading inland towards Zwolle.

LEEUWARDEN (LJOUWERT)

📞 058 / POP 107,691

An unexpected combination of style, gritty back alleys, cafe-lined canals and urban renewal, Friesland's capital is well worth a visit, if only to explore its superb trinity of museums. A continuous flow of cyclists ride happily along the broad paths that flank the canals, the tunnels of which are illuminated purple by night. Stick around and sample some of the northern hospitality, something easily found in its many bars and cafes.

Leeuwarden has been selected as the European Capital of Culture for 2018.

⊙ Sights

Most of Leeuwarden's sights are concentrated within a leisurely 10-minute walk of Nieuwestad. Zaailand, the central square otherwise known as Wilhelminaplein, is the cultural centre of town: the Fries Museum occupies a landmark building at one end.

Look for historic ships of all kinds moored along the canals. The pedestrian zone includes the evocative old street Weerd.

★ Fries Museum   MUSEUM
(📞 255 55 00; www.friesmuseum.nl; Wilhelminaplein 92; adult/child €10/5; ⊙ 11am-5pm Tue-Sun) The provincial museum occupies an imposing glass-fronted building sporting a striking wood-and-steel roof that projects out over Wilhelminaplein. The three levels are divided into a series of galleries. A good place to start is the Ferhaal fan Fryslân gallery (1st floor), an overview of the province with representative objects from the collection.

There is also a brilliantly designed section on local efforts to resist the Nazis and a sorrowful examination of the life of Mata Hari (p198), as well as a portrait gallery of the royal Nassaus. An inviting cafe and art cinema round out the complex.

Waag   HISTORIC BUILDING
(Waagplein) The petite weighing house dominates Waagplein; butter and other goods were weighed here from 1598 to 1884.

★ Princessehof Museum   MUSEUM
(📞 294 89 58; www.princessehof.nl; Grote Kerkstraat 11; adult/child/teen €8/free/6.50; ⊙ 11am-5pm Tue-Sun) Pottery lovers will adore the Netherlands ceramics museum. Here you'll find the largest collection of tiles on the planet, an unparalleled selection of Delftware and works from around the globe – the Japanese, Chinese and Vietnamese sections are superbly displayed. It's all atmospherically housed in a 17th-century mansion.

Natuurmuseum Fryslân   MUSEUM
(📞 233 22 44; www.natuurmuseumfryslan.nl; Schoenmakersperk 2; adult/child €7/5; ⊙ 11am-5pm Tue-Sun Sep-Jun, 10am-5pm daily Jul & Aug) Let your angels run rampant in this natural-history museum, covering Friesland's flora and fauna. Highlights include a virtual bird-flight simulation (strap yourself into the hang-glider harness and away you go) and 'Friesland onder Water', an exploration of the bottom of a canal from a fish's perspective.

The museum's skylit cafe makes a cheery refuge on a cold day.

Leeuwarden

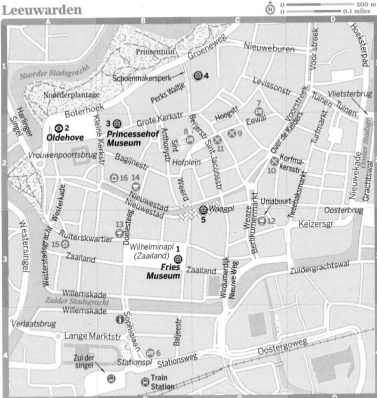

★ **Oldehove** LANDMARK
(www.oldehove.eu; Oldehoofsterkerkhof; adult/teen/ child €3.50/2.50/1.50; ⊙1-5pm mid-Apr–Sep) At the northwest corner of the historic core stands the notoriously off-kilter Oldehove. Things went wrong shortly after the tower was started in 1529 and it never regained its proper posture, nor its intended height. While by no means a Leaning Tower of Pisa, it presents a dramatic sight and may be climbed for the views. Compare the tilt to the very erect neighbouring statue of Pieter Jelles Troelstra, a Dutch socialist who called for revolution after WWI.

🛏 Sleeping

Leeuwarden's accommodation options are limited, but there's enough variety to suit most tastes. For B&Bs from around €30 per person, try the tourist office.

Hotel 't Anker GUESTHOUSE €
(📞212 52 16; www.hotelhetanker.nl; Eewal 73; s/d €31/60 without bathroom, €53/73 with bathroom; 📶) The Anchor is a fine bet for a basic room (ask to see a couple) in an ideally located spot. It's surprisingly quiet, considering the ground floor contains a popular old pub and a string of restaurants and bars line the street. The included breakfast is as simple as the rooms.

Hotel-Paleis Stadhouderlijk Hof HOTEL €€
(📞216 21 80; www.stadhouderlijkhof.nl; Hofplein 29; s/d from €89/104; ✳📶) The austere pink facade of this former royal residence belies its plush interior. Inside, red-carpeted stairwells lead to 28 rooms with wrought-iron details and canopied beds. A regal courtyard garden has terrace seating.

Hampshire Hotel Oranje Leeuwarden HOTEL €€
(📞212 62 41, 035-677 72 17; www.hampshire-hotels. com; Stationsweg 4; r €88-118; ✳@📶) Directly

Leeuwarden

⊙ **Top Sights**
1 Fries Museum......................................B3
2 Oldehove A2
3 Princessehof Museum B2

⊙ **Sights**
4 Natuurmuseum Fryslân......................C1
5 Waag...C3

🛏 **Sleeping**
6 Hampshire Hotel Oranje
    Leeuwarden....................................B4
7 Hotel 't Anker....................................C1
8 Hotel-Paleis Stadhouderlijk Hof B2

🍴 **Eating**
9 Eetcafe Spinoza C2
10 Restaurant By Ús C2
11 Sems..C2

🍷 **Drinking & Nightlife**
12 Café de Ossekop C3
13 De Scamele Ruter B3
14 Grand Cafe De Brass B2

🎭 **Entertainment**
15 De Harmonie A3

🛍 **Shopping**
16 Van der Velde B2

opposite the train station, this business hotel has large rooms with a flash of style (ones at the rear are leafy and quiet). You can park your bike in the garage.

✗ Eating

Leeuwarden has a bevy of restaurants run by creative chefs.

★ Restaurant By Ús   MODERN DUTCH €€
(✆ 215 86 63; www.restaurantby-us.nl; Over de Kelders 24; mains €19-23; ⊙ 5-9pm Wed-Sun; 🚲) Organic local foods are celebrated at this candlelit bistro with a wood-and-leather interior. Frisian-inspired dishes highlight a seasonally changing menu with a range of vegetarian options on offer. There is an excellent wine list and a young and effusive staff.

Eetcafe Spinoza   BISTRO €€
(✆ 212 93 93; www.eetcafespinoza.nl; Eewal 50-52; mains €17-22; ⊙ noon-10pm; 🚲) This often-boisterous locale offers various settings for a hearty meal, from the tree-shaded tables out front to the wood-lined interior to the garden at the rear. The menu features regional specialities and vegetarian options.

Sems   FUSION €€
(✆ 216 22 14; www.semsleeuwarden.nl; Gouverneur-splein 36; dishes €12.50; ⊙ noon-9pm Tue-Sat, 4-9pm Sun) The thing here is *kleine gerechten* (small portions), deftly prepared in an open-air kitchen and beautifully presented at your table. There's a popular terrace and a loungey wine bar, the walls lined with prestige labels.

🍷 Drinking

Bars, cafes and *coffeeshops* line up along Doelesteeg, Kleine Hoogstraat and Grote Hoogstraat while Ruiterskwartier has a few dance clubs.

Grand Cafe De Brass   CAFE
(✆ 843 32 33; www.cafedebrass.nl; Nieuwestad 71) Outdoor tables fan out in all directions from this canal-side cafe. When the weather is even vaguely sympathetic, half of Leeuwarden seems to be here. If it gets too crowded you might take one of the picnic tables atop the nearby canal bridge.

Café de Ossekop   BROWN CAFE
(Uniabuurt 8; ⊙ from 5pm Tue & Thu-Sat) This is the kind of timeless brown *café* (pub) where the installation of a women's toilet in 1970 is still recounted as a recent event. Loyal locals exchange banter with the vintage bartender while sipping lager and tossing back gin.

De Scamele Ruter   PUB
(✆ 215 40 41; Ruiterskwartier 103; ⊙ 11am-1am Mon-Thu, 11am-3am Fri & Sat, 3pm-midnight Sun) In this spot for 27 years running, the 'Weary Horseman' (a former stable) is one of the few pubs in Leeuwarden where Frisian is the tongue of parlance.

☆ Entertainment

De Harmonie   THEATRE
(✆ 233 02 33; www.harmonie.nl; Ruiterskwartier 4) The local home to theatre performances, both mainstream and fringe. Last-minute tickets are half-price.

🔒 Shopping

Look along Kleine Kerkstraat and Tuinen for some of Leeuwarden's more original shops.

Van der Velde   BOOKS
(Nieuwestad NZ 57-59; ⊙ 12.30-6pm Mon, 9.30am-6pm Tue-Fri, 9.30am-5pm Sat) An elegant book-shop with a small but decent selection of English-language and travel books.

MATA HARI

Born Gertrud Margarete Zelle, this daughter of Leeuwarden is best known by her acquired name: Mata Hari (Malaysian for 'sun'). She worked as an exotic dancer in Paris, and her affairs and dalliances were legendary. She favoured rich men-in-uniform, and when WWI broke out she had high-ranking lovers on both sides. Things inevitably became tricky; French officers persuaded her to spy on her German lovers, and German officers managed to do the same. This web of intrigue was not helped by her keen imagination, and mistrust began to rise on both sides.

In 1917, at age 40, she was arrested by the French for spying. There was a dubious trial, during which none of her former 'pals' offered any assistance – probably out of embarrassment – and later that year she was sentenced to death and shot.

Today, Margarete/Mata Hari is still, in a manner of speaking, alive and well in Leeuwarden. Her statue as a sultry dancer can be found on a bridge over the canal close to her birthplace at Over de Kelders 33; the Fries Museum also has an exhibit on her life.

ℹ Information

Tourist office (VVV; ☑ 058-234 75 50; www.vvvleeuwarden.nl; Sophialaan 4; ⊙ noon-5pm Mon, 9.30am-5pm Tue-Fri, 10am-4pm Sat) Stocks a good selection of maps and cycling guides; 150m from train station.

ℹ Getting There & Around

Leeuwarden is at the end of the main train line from the south; it's also the hub for local services in Friesland, with westward branch lines to Harlingen (via Franeker), Stavoren (via Sneek) and Groningen by Arriva. Lockers can be found on platform No 8. Fares and schedules:

Destination	Price (€)	Duration (min)	Frequency (per hour)
Groningen	10	45	3
Utrecht	24	120	2
Zwolle	16	60	3

Buses are to the left as you exit the train station. The **bicycle shop** (☑ 213 98 00; bikes per day €8.50), on the lower level to the right, rents five-speed Batavus bikes. Leeuwarden is about 110km north of Kampen (near Zwolle) on national bike route **LF3**.

WADDENZEE COAST

Between the capital and the picturesque harbour of Harlingen is an intensively farmed area highlighted by one significant town, Franeker, an ancient centre of learning. North of Harlingen, a high dyke parallels the mudflats of the Waddenzee, linking a series of remote villages of stoic farmers whose squat brick houses overlook vast crop fields.

Harlingen (Harns)

☑ 0517 / POP 15,779

Of all the old Frisian ports, only Harlingen has kept its link to the sea. It still plays an important role for shipping in the area, and is the base for ferries to Terschelling and Vlieland.

Harlingen has also managed to retain a semblance of its architectural history; much of the attractive centre is a preserved zone of pretty 16th- and 18th-century buildings that make for a good hour of strolling as you wait for your departure.

◉ Sights & Activities

Harlingen is best enjoyed on foot. Stroll along the canals, many with drawbridges that rise with rhythmic regularity, especially yacht-filled Zuiderhaven and Noorderhaven. The latter has been a place for ocean-going boats to dock since the 16th century. It is lined with houses from the rich era of trading. The deco-style lighthouse has an upper deck for viewing the harbour activity.

Voorstraat has shops, attractions and cafes. It runs into a canal criss-crossed with bridges.

Museum Hannemahuis Harlingen MUSEUM
(www.hannemahuis.nl; Voorstraat 56; adult/child €4.50/2; ⊙ 11am-5pm Tue-Fri, 1.30-5pm Sat & Sun) Housed in the 18th-century mansion of a prominent Harlingen family, the museum deals primarily with the town's maritime heritage, in particular its role in the whaling industry, which brought so much wealth to Friesland in the 1700s. Other exhibits cover

such other noble pursuits as silver crafting and *jenever* (Dutch gin) distilling.

🛏️ Sleeping & Eating

⭐ **'t Heerenlogement**　　　　HOTEL €
(☑ 415 846; www.heerenlogement.nl; Franekereind 23; s/d from €69/90; ⓟ) This 300-year-old relic has been zealously preserved by its owners, down to the period wallpaper in each of the uniquely designed rooms. Overlooking the canal on the east end of town, it's steps away from a lovely English garden that rises along the old ramparts.

⭐ **De Tjotter**　　　　SEAFOOD €€
(☑ 414 691; www.detjotter.nl; St Jacobstraat 1-3; 3-course menu from €28; ⊙ noon-10pm Tue-Sat, 1-10pm Sun & Mon) This seafood specialist gets its fare right off the boats; the catch of the day is deftly prepared with Belgian influences. An adjacent oyster bar has a more casual vibe with a terrace overlooking Noorderhaven, along with fresh and smoked seafood to take away.

Eetcafe Nooitgedagt　　　MODERN DUTCH €€
(☑ 434 211; www.eetcafenooitgedagt.nl; Grote Bredeplaats 35; mains €16.50-18.50; ⊙ 11.30am-10pm) This stylish cafe in an old wine warehouse has a definite seaside vibe with weathered wood tables and a lovely side terrace. The kitchen takes off from Dutch traditional fare and gives it a light, creative spin.

ℹ️ Information

Tourist office (VVV; ☑ 430 207; www.harlingen-friesland.nl; Grote Bredeplaats 12; ⊙ 10am-5pm Mon-Sat)

ℹ️ Getting There & Away

Harlingen is connected to Leeuwarden (€5.40, 25 minutes) by two Arriva trains hourly. There are stations south of the centre and by the harbour (Harlingen Haven), 300m from the ferry terminal. Ferries serve Vlieland and Terschelling.

The ferry port is on national bike route **LF10**, which runs 8km south on the coast to the Afsluitdijk and the crossing to North Holland; going northeast, it passes the ferry ports to Ameland and Schiermonnikoog islands.

SOUTHWESTERN FRIESLAND

The lake-studded region southwest of Leeuwarden is a magnet for sailors, windsurfers and other water recreationists. Since being hemmed in by the Afsluitdijk, the coastal villages of Hindeloopen and Stavoren are sleepier places with echoes of their seagoing past. The latter port is the embarkation point for ferries to Noord-Holland.

Sneek (Snits)

☑ 0515 / POP 33,260
As the saying goes, 'All Frisians know how to sail, and all Frisians know how to fish'. This is certainly true of the residents of Sneek, but then again, they have no choice in the matter: Frisian lakes and rivers are linked to the IJsselmeer (the Central Netherlands' 1100-sq-km artificial lake) and decorate the land not unlike the spots on the local dairy cows. If you've got a hankering to get out under sail, this is the place.

WORTH A TRIP

FRANEKER (FRJENTSJER)

About 6km east of Harlingen, the quaint town of Franeker was once a big player in education, until Napoleon closed its university down in 1810. Today, its well-preserved centre makes for a nice meander, but Franeker's real highlight is its planetarium, which is the world's oldest.

The **Eise Eisinga Planetarium** (☑ 393 070; www.planetarium-friesland.nl; Eise Eisingastraat 3; adult/child €4.75/4; ⊙ 10am-5pm Tue-Sat, 1-5pm Sun year-round, 1-5pm Mon Apr-Oct) is named after its builder, a tradesman with a serious sideline in cosmic mathematics and astrology. Beginning in 1774, he built the planetarium himself to show how the heavens actually worked. It's startling to contemplate how Eisinga could have devised a mechanical timing system built to a viewable working scale that could encompass and illustrate so many different variables of time and motion.

An Arriva train stops in Franeker (from Leeuwarden: €4, 16 minutes, two hourly), 500m from the centre.

SNEEK'S WATER-SPORTS BOUNTY

Sneek is surrounded by water, and any activity associated with it – particularly if it involves wind, of which there is hardly ever a shortage – is big.

Several sailing and windsurfing schools, where you can learn from scratch or top up existing skills, operate in the area. One of the largest is **Zeilschool de Friese Meren** (📞 412 141; www.zeilschoolsneek.nl; Eeltjebaasweg 7; 6-day program €500), which has a range of packages for different age groups.

There are also many boat-rental companies, including the following:

JFT Watersport (📞 443 867; www.jft-watersport.nl; Henry Bulthuisweg 16; rentals per day from €50-200)

Zijda Yachting (📞 432 993; www.zijda.nl; Zoutepoel 2-4; rentals Mon-Fri €500-2000)

Bootverhuur Hospes (📞 412 594; bootverhuurhospes.nl; Burg De Hooppark 3; per weekend €500-1000, depending on type of boat and time of year)

If you'd rather just watch sleek ships skip across the water, then cruise into town in early August to catch **Sneekweek** (www.sneekweek.nl), the largest sailing event on Europe's inland waters. You'll be treated to plenty of racing activity and lots of frivolity.

During the summer months there are **boat cruises** on the local waters. The schedules change according to whim and weather. Most leave from the **Oosterkade**, at the end of Kleinzand, so either wander over or inquire at the tourist office.

⊙ Sights & Activities

A remnant of a time when most traffic plied Sneek's waterways, the **Waterpoort** dates from 1613 and is the former gateway to the old port. Its twin towers are local landmarks. Across from the tourist office, the **town hall** (Marktstraat 15) got its rococo style in the '60s (1760s, that is). Try to guess which of the sculpted allegorical figures represents wisdom, justice or stability.

Fries Scheepvaart Museum   MUSEUM
(📞 414 057; www.friesscheepvaartmuseum.nl; Kleinzand 16; adult/child €6/2; ⊙ 10am-5pm Mon-Sat, noon-5pm Sun) Sneek has been a nexus of Frisian waterways for centuries, and this museum elegantly illustrates many aspects of shipping and seafaring in the province. Pride of place is given to models of the *skûtsjes* and *koffs* that figured so largely in inland and overseas trade.

Model Train Museum   MUSEUM
(📞 430 021; www.modelspoormuseum.nl; Dr Boumaweg 17b; adult/child/senior €5.50/3.50/4.50; ⊙ 1-5pm Sun & Mon, 10am-5pm Tue-Sat) An indispensable attraction for train buffs, the collection here includes some incredibly detailed dioramas. Push the button and watch them run round corners, through tunnels and over bridges.

⊨ Sleeping & Eating

Cafes can be found by the harbour around Oosterkade and on Marktstraat.

De Wijnberg   HOTEL €
(📞 412 421; www.hoteldewijnberg.nl; Marktstraat 23; s/d €68/90; 🛜) An inn of note for over four centuries, the cheerful Wijnberg has 23 simple, bright rooms with either bathtubs or showers. The cafe-pub on the ground floor is often lively.

Stayokay Sneek   HOSTEL €
(📞 412 132; www.stayokay.com/sneek; Oude Oppenhuizerweg 17; dm from €20, d €49; @) This modern, sleekly designed hostel is ideally situated for water recreation: from the canalside dock out back you can sail or row out to the Sneekermeer, and it rents sailboats (€95/day) and canoes (€10). Take breakfast (included) on the waterfront terrace. It's 2km east of the train station.

★ **De Walrus**   MODERN DUTCH €€
(www.dewalrus.nl; Leeuwenburg 11; mains €12-20; ⊙ 11am-midnight) The obvious place for dinner: on summer evenings the terrace tables around the cafe and along the canal-front fill up fast. The menu changes weekly; fish is exceptionally well prepared and comes with enticing sides.

ⓘ Information

Tourist office (VVV; 📞 750 678; www.vvvzuid westfriesland.nl; Kleinzand 16; ⊙ 10am-5pm Mon-Sat, noon-5pm Sat) Located inside the Fries Scheepvaart Museum, the VVV has long lists of boat-rental and charter firms, sailing schools and more. For cycling and walking maps, visit the **ANWB** (☑ 0882 693 580; Marktstraat 18), opposite the Stadhuis.

❶ Getting There & Around

From the train station to the centre of town is a five-minute walk along Stationstraat. Arriva trains on the Leeuwarden–Stavoren line cost €5 (22 minutes, two per hour).

Profile (☑ 413 096; www.profilefietsspecialist.nl; Lemmerweg 13-15), 150m west of the Waterpoort, rents bikes.

Hindeloopen (Hylpen)

☑ 0514 / POP 920

Huddled up against the banks of the IJsselmeer, Hindeloopen has been set apart from Friesland for centuries. As you approach across the flat Frisian countryside, the sudden appearance of a forest of yacht masts marks the town in the distance.

In the 16th and 17th centuries, trade ships from Amsterdam dropped anchor at this Zuiderzee harbour on their way to England and Scandinavia, boosting its prosperity and connecting it with the outside world, though Hindeloopen maintained its own traditions. With its narrow streets, tiny canals, wooden bridges and waterfront, Hindeloopen makes for an atmospheric escape.

❂ Sights & Activities

The dyke that rings the town is a good vantage for admiring the IJsselmeer, and the windblown coast to the south is popular with kitesurfers.

Het Eerste
Friese Schaatsmuseum   MUSEUM
(Frisian Skating Museum; ☑ 521 683; www.schaatsmuseum.nl/home; Kleine Weide 1-3; adult/child €3/2; ☺ 10am-6pm Mon-Sat, 1-5pm Sun) In extraordinarily cold winters Hindeloopen is one of the key towns on the route of the Elfstedentocht race. The icy spectacle and ice skating in general are this museum's focus. Displays covering skating through the centuries are enthralling, as is the history of the competition.

Museum Hindeloopen   MUSEUM
(☑ 521 420; www.museumhindeloopen.nl; Dijkweg 1; adult/child €5/3; ☺ 11am-5pm Mon-Fri, 1.30-5pm Sat & Sun Apr-Oct) Displays here focus on the town's seafaring history and traditional crafts, in particular the fine art of furniture painting, for which Hindeloopen is renowned.

🛏 Sleeping & Eating

There's a sprinkling of restaurants and fish stands overlooking the harbour.

De Stadsboerderij   GUESTHOUSE €
(☑ 521 278; www.destadsboerderij.nl; Nieuwe Weide 7-9; s/d from €51/78; 🕏) An old farmhouse done up vintage-style with four-poster beds and Hindeloopen's signature painted furniture, De Stadsboerderij promises a peaceful night's sleep, while the jointly managed pub next door may come in handy.

De Twee Hondjes   B&B €
(☑ 522 873; www.detweehondjes.nl; Paardepad 2; s/d €55/80; 🅿🕏) Housed in a former shop, this homey option has five simple rooms, two with private bath. The included breakfast, served in the sunny front room, is a typically abundant spread with plenty of smoked fish and cheeses.

★**Café-Restaurant de Hinde**   SEAFOOD €€
(☑ 523 868; www.dehinde.nl; 't Oost 4; mains from €24; ☺ 11am-9pm Thu-Tue) A good place to while away the hours is the terrace at this harbourside spot, which has been in the same family for three generations. The seafood specials are excellent.

❶ Information

Tourist office (VVV; ☑ 522 550; www.vvv hindeloopen.nl; Nieuwstad 26; ☺ 10.30am-3.30pm daily Jul & Aug, 10.30am-3.30pm Fri-Sun Sep & Oct, May & Jun) The staff at Hindeloopen's tourist office can help with accommodation and offer a useful walking map.

❶ Getting There & Away

By bike, it's 27km from Sneek to Hindeloopen via IJlst. From Hindeloopen you can pick up the national bike route **LF22** north to Harlingen or south to Stavoren.

The train station is a 2km walk from town; otherwise, take the half-hourly bus 102 (from Makkum). Arriva has hourly service from Leeuwarden (€8, 45 minutes) via Sneek (€4.20, 17 minutes) and onward to Stavoren, where you can catch a ferry to Enkhuizen (p118) in Noord-Holland.

FRISIAN ISLANDS

The crescent of islands over Friesland – Vlieland, Terschelling, Ameland and Schiermonnikoog – form a unique natural entity and a distinct region of the Netherlands. A natural barrier between the Frisian coast and the open North Sea, they hem in the mud-flats of the Waddenzee, a region that was added to the Unesco World Heritage List in 2009. Accordingly, all of the elongated islands have a dual character: villages, *polders* (areas of drained land) and salt marshes on the Wad-denzee side, broad swaths of beach and dunes on the seaward side, with the two separated by areas of woods and heath.

Populated for at least a thousand years, the remote islands have frequently fallen victim to the whims of nature as the sea washed towns off the map and shifting sands altered the terrain. Challenging as it was to live off the land, inhabitants turned to fishing and whaling for their livelihoods. Since World War II, tourism has been the mainstay, and Dutch and German holidaymakers flock here in the warmer months. Though the proportion of wilderness to tourism development varies from one island to the next, with Schiermonnikoog being the wildest and Ter-schelling the most developed, all have ample space for getting close to nature and beach-combing. Each of the islands is criss-crossed with hiking and cycling trails, and through-out the Waddenzee you'll see opportunities to go *wadlopen* (mudflat walking).

With the huge influx of tourists in the summertime (populations routinely multi-ply tenfold on warm weekends) it can get crowded, so try to make arrangements in advance. Among the myriad accommoda-tion options are hotels, B&Bs and cottages, and there are plenty of campsites.

Getting There & Around

Frequent ferries link the islands with the main-land. There are surcharges for taking cars or bicycles, and only residents may take their cars to Vlieland and Schiermonnikoog. However, all the Frisian Islands have decent bus service as well as bike-rental shops near the ferry docks.

Vlieland

0562 / POP 1113

Historically the most isolated of the islands, and the least visited, Vlieland is a wind-swept and wild place, but this is part of its charm. The ferry arrives at the sole town, Oost Vlieland, at the east end of the island and ringed by forest. It's where you'll find all hotels, restaurants and services. The west end of the island is a sandy wasteland at the mercy of the sea, parts of which are used by the military.

Activities

Nature is the main attraction here. Most of the 72 sq km of island lies waiting to be explored by bike or on foot, including 18km of beaches. Cycling around Vlieland can be exhilarating; there are many unsealed tracks that confident off-roaders can opt to tackle. The tourist office provides English-language self-guided nature walks and bike rides.

Good places to spot birdlife include Kro-on's Polders (spoonbills, kites) and the Noor-doosthoek (terns, ruddy turnstones).

THE GREAT DUTCH RACE: ELFSTEDENTOCHT

Elfstedentocht (Eleven Cities Tour; www.elfstedentocht.nl) Skating and the Dutch culture are interwoven and no event better symbolises this than the Elfstedentocht. Begun officially in 1909, although it had been held for hundreds of years before that, the race is 200km long, starts and finishes in Leeuwarden, and passes through 10 Frisian towns: Sneek, IJlst, Sloten, Stavoren, Hindeloopen, Workum, Bolsward, Harlingen, Franeker and Dokkum.

The record time for completing the race is six hours and 47 minutes, set in 1985 (record-setter Evert van Benthem won again in 1986, making him a living legend).

While it is a marathon, what makes the race a truly special event is that it can only be held in years when it's cold enough for all the canals to freeze totally; this has only hap-pened 15 times since 1909. The last time was in 1997.

In the interim the huge Elfstedentocht committee waits for the mercury to plummet. When it looks as though the canals will be properly frozen, 48 hours' notice is given. All work effectively ends throughout the province as armies of volunteers make prepara-tions for the race, and the thousands of competitors get ready.

On the third day, the race begins at 5.30am. The next few hours are a holiday for the rest of the Netherlands as well, as the population gathers around TVs to watch the live coverage.

Vlieland Outdoor Center KAYAKING
(☑06 5146 0152; www.vlielandoutdoorcenter.nl)
Rents kayaks and kitesurfing equipment;
also offers lessons. Located at Seeduyn
beach.

Vliehors Express DRIVING TOUR
(☑06 2182 0842; www.vliehorsexpres.nl; Dorpstraat 125; adult/child €15.50/10) To experience
the island's desertlike western expanses,
take a ride on the Vliehors Express, a converted army truck.

De Noordwester Information Centre TOUR
(☑451 700; www.denoordwester.nl; Dorpsstraat
150; ⊙11am-5pm Mon-Fri, 2-5pm Sat, 1-4pm Sun
Jun-Sep, hours vary rest of year) Join a hiking or
bird-watching group here. It also offers daily
boat tours around the island that include a
bit of *wadlopen*.

🛏 Sleeping & Eating
Vlieland has several cafes and restaurants,
all with a steak-seafood-bit-of-pasta menu.
Sleeping options are numerous.

Hotelletje de Veerman HOTEL €€
(☑451 378; www.hotelletjedeveerman.nl;
Dorpsstraat 173; r with/without bathroom €118/70;
🖥) The well-run Veerman has 12 neat rooms,
some sharing bathrooms, at the east end of
the main street through town. Nothing is so
fancy you won't want to get sand on it, and
there are also apartments in the village.

ℹ Information
Tourist office (VVV; ☑451 111; www.vlieland.
net; Havenweg 10; ⊙9am-5pm Mon-Fri, 9am-
noon & 1-5pm Sat, 10am-noon & 4-5pm Sun)
Opposite the ferry dock.

ℹ Getting There & Around
Rederij Doeksen (☑0889 000 888; www.
rederij-doeksen.nl) runs regular ferries from
Harlingen to Vlieland (adult/child return
€26/13, bicycle €15) that take approximately
90 minutes. Departures are typically at
8.45am, 2.25pm and 7pm. A fast service
(€39/26) takes 45 minutes direct and 90 minutes via Terschelling. Schedules change often.

In the summer months **De Vriendschap**
(☑022-231 64 51; http://waddenveer.nl; Volharding 2a, De Cocksdorp, Texel; adult/child
€27.50/18.50, bike €10; ⊙May-Sep) connects
Vlieland to nearby Texel island, a 30-minute trip
over the shallow waters. The Vliehors Express
conveys passengers across the sand flats between the harbour on the west end of Vlieland

and Posthuys in the centre. Travel between
Posthuys and Oost Vlieland by bus or bicycle.

Jan van Vlieland (☑451 509; www.janvan
vlieland.nl; Havenweg 7; bikes per day €8) rents
bikes opposite the ferry landing; tandem bikes
and electric bikes are also available. A bus
wanders the few roads of Oost-Vlieland.

Terschelling
☑0562 / POP 4780
Terschelling is the largest of the Frisian
Islands; it's also the most developed and
most visited. A string of villages line up
between *polder* and dunes along its 30km
expanse. West Terschelling, the ferry port at
the island's west end, is the largest. The eastern end of the island is a wild and isolated
place. Overall, there are 250km of walking
and cycling trails.

⊙ Sights & Activities
The iconic 55m **Brandaris lighthouse** in the
centre of West-Terschelling has been a navigational beacon for at least four centuries.

An easy and varied *fietstocht* (bike
ride) can be done cycling northeast from
West-Terschelling through the forest along
the Helmduinweg. About 4km from the
Brandaris you reach the **Bessenschuur**
(☑448 800; http://terschellingercranberry.nl;
Marsakkersweg 5; ⊙10am-5pm), a secluded
cafe offering the bounty from the cranberry
harvests in this part of the island. Continue
north to reach the beach at **West Aan Zee**,
with a pavilion-cafe. Then head west through
dunes to El Dorado, the largest of a string of
salt marshes where you may spot marsh harriers and spoonbills. Return to town through
tranquil woods via the Longway.

De Boschplaat PARK
An extensive natural reserve at the eastern
end of the island, De Boschplaat was a separate island until 1880 when the channel
between the two silted up. Trails criss-cross
a zone of high grassy dunes teeming with
migratory birds.

**Terschelling Museum 't
Behouden Huys** MUSEUM
(☑442 389; www.behouden-huys.nl; Comman-
deurstraat 30-32; adult/child €4/2; ⊙10am-5pm
Mon-Fri, 1-5pm Sat Apr-Oct plus 1-5pm Sun Jul-
Sep, 1-5pm Wed-Sat Nov-Mar) Good for a rainy
day, this small museum covers traditional
Terschelling life and maritime history. It's

named after the cabin on the Novaya Zemblaya archipelago where native son Willem Barentsz and his crew had to hibernate after getting locked in by ice during an exploratory expedition of the Polar Sea in 1596; there's a reconstructed version of their shelter.

Flang in de Pan COOKING COURSE
(☑850 134; http://flangindepan.nl; Dorpsstraat 25; tours per person from €16.50) Island native Flang offers unique culinary tours and workshops, including a *wadlopen* excursion on the Waddenzee to collect oysters, periwinkles and seaweed for a meal he'll then teach you to prepare.

★ Festivals & Events

Oerol PERFORMING ARTS
(www.oerol.nl; ⊗late Jun) The annual Oerol outdoor performance festival is revered nationally as a perfect excuse for going to sea. It started years ago with farmers letting their cows run loose one day each year (hence the name *oerol*, which means 'all over'). It's a wild, arty party, piercing the otherwise unflappable northern facade for 10 days in the latter half of June.

🛏 Sleeping & Eating

Stayokay Terschelling HOSTEL €
(☑442 338; www.stayokay.com/terschelling; 't Land 2; dm/r from €26.50/65; ⊗reception 9am-5pm; 🛜) This branch of the nationwide chain stands on a bluff overlooking the harbour 1.5km east of the lighthouse, with a canteen and terrace to appreciate the view. Bus 121 can drop you off.

Hotel Oepkes HOTEL €€
(☑442 005; www.oepkes.nl; De Ruyterstraat 3; s/d/tr €81/120/149) A couple of blocks up from the ferry port, the Oepkes offers straightforward comfort in the heart of West-Terschelling. Rooms come in a variety of sizes and colours; some pricier units give views of the lighthouse.

Hotel Eetcafé 't Wapen van Terschelling HOTEL €€
(☑448 801; www.twapenvanterschelling.nl; Oosterburen 25; d with/without bathroom €108/80) Located in Midsland, a laid-back village 6km east of the ferry, this long-standing inn is behind a welcoming brown *café* with a good beer selection. Rooms are well-maintained and carpeted; the cheapest share bathrooms while the better ones have balconies. Breakfast is included.

Paviljoen De Walvis SEAFOOD €€
(www.walvis.org; Groene Strand; mains €18-24; ⊗10am-11pm Thu-Tue) At the foot of the western dunes is this casual pavilion with a terrace overlooking the shifting panorama of the Waddenzee, the shipshape interior graced with chandeliers, painted wood and mermaid mascot. Apart from the catch of the day, it does a hearty bouillabaisse and French Limousin beef.

ℹ Information

Tourist office (VVV; ☑443 000; www.vvv-terschelling.nl; Willem Barentszkade 19a; ⊗9.15am-5.30pm Mon-Fri, 10am-3pm Sat) The helpful tourist office has a range of maps, plus cycling and hiking guides (in Dutch). It's just over the road from the ferry landing.

ℹ Getting There & Around

Rederij Doeksen (p203) runs regular ferries from Harlingen to Terschelling (adult/child return €26/13, bicycle €15), a two-hour journey. There are generally three departures daily, with up to five on summer weekends. A fast service (adult/child return €39/26) takes 45 minutes and usually goes three times daily.

In summer there are two fast ferries per day to nearby Vlieland (30 minutes) midweek. Check current schedules online.

Hourly buses (€2) run the length of the main road. **Rijwielverhuur Tijs Knop** (☑442 052; http://www.tijsknop.nl; Torenstraat 10/12; 3-/7-speed bike rentals per day €6.50/8.50), along the main street into West-Terschelling, rents bikes and will transport your luggage to your accommodation.

Ameland
☑0519 / POP 3591
Of the island quartet, Ameland strikes the best balance. Its four peaceful villages – Buren, Nes, Ballum and Hollum – are less developed than those on Terschelling and Texel, but they provide enough social structure for most visitors. Although Mother Nature doesn't rule the roost as on Schiermonnikoog or Vlieland, it still retains generous swaths of untouched natural splendour. All in all, Ameland is an idyll that's just right.

Just 8km from the Frisian mainland, Ameland is a quick ferry ride, and some even choose to hoof it (p216)! Its history may be the strangest of the four isles: it was an independent 'lordship' for almost three centuries until the ruling family died off in

1708. It is actually comprised of three islands that were fused together in the 19th century.

◎ Sights & Activities

Just 25km from end to end, Ameland is easily tackled by pedal power. Bicycle paths cover the entire island and include a 27km packed sand track that runs almost the full length of the northern shore just south of protective sand dunes. The eastern third of the island is given over to a combination of wetlands and dunes, with not a settlement in sight.

Of the villages, the 18th-century former whaling port of Nes is the busiest and cutest, its streets lined with tidy brick houses. Hollum, the most western village, has windswept dunes within an easy walk, and is in sight of a famous red-and-white lighthouse (adult/child €4.50/3.25; ◎10am-5pm Tue-Sun, 1-5pm Mon) with expansive views.

Ameland Nature Centre   MUSEUM
(✐542 737; www.natuurcentrumameland.nl; Strandweg 38; adult/child €6.50/4.50; ◎10am-5pm Mon-Fri, 11am-5pm Sat & Sun Mar-Nov, hours vary rest of year) Just north of Nes village, this centre features an excellent seaquarium in which a number of North Sea species swim around, including manta rays, barracuda and eels. Get shore-to-shore views from the adjacent observation tower and take a 2.2km nature loop walk to Nesserbos forest. The centre offers tours, including *wadlopen*, beach walks and net-fishing excursions.

⊨ Sleeping & Eating

All four villages have accommodation, with Nes being the most convenient to the ferry.

Hotel Restaurant De Jong   HOTEL €
(✐542 016; www.hoteldejong.nl; Reeweg 29, Nes; r with/without bathroom €42/47; 🛜) Standing at the crossroads of Ameland, this friendly inn and cafe buzzes in high season when you can lounge at a terrace table and observe the comings and goings from the ferry pier, 1km south. All 12 rooms have been recently renovated with comfort and style in mind. Seafood stew and herbed eel are among the hits at the cafe.

Stayokay Ameland   HOSTEL €
(✐555 353; www.stayokay.com/ameland; Oranjeweg 59, Hollum; d/q €59/109; 🛜) The atmosphere here is decidedly summer camp. The rooms are basic (two, four or six beds) but in great condition, and sand dunes are literally outside the doorstep. Meals, packed lunches and bicycles are available. It's outside Hol-

lum, 200m past the lighthouse. Bus 130 can drop you there.

Camping Middelpôlle   CAMPGROUND €
(✐06 2386 8480; www.staatsbosbeheer.nl/kamperen/middelpolle; Westerpad 3; campsites €5.50 plus adult/child €5/3.50; ◎Apr-Sep) Shhh... peaceful: no RVs at this nature campground with 40 sites on grassy knolls between trees. It's at the edge of the forest, a 15-minute walk from the beach or easy bike ride from Nes. There are three Quonset tents with kitchens available (maximum three nights).

❶ Information

Tourist office (VVV; ✐546 546; www.vvv ameland.nl; Bureweg 2, Nes; ◎9am-noon & 1.30-5pm Mon-Fri, 10am-3pm Sat) The island's main tourist office is seven minutes' walk, or one bus stop, from the ferry terminal.

❶ Getting There & Around

Wagenborg (✐546 111; www.wpd.nl; adult/child return €14/8, bicycle €9) operates ferries between Nes and the large ferry port at Holwerd on the mainland. The ferries run almost every two hours (€14.70 return, bicycle €9.30, 45 minutes) all year from 7.30am to 7.30pm, and hourly on Friday and Saturday from July to August.

To reach the Holwerd ferry terminal from Leeuwarden, take Arriva bus 66 (€5, 40 minutes, hourly). By bike, it's 26km via the **LF3b**.

Taxis and a small network of public buses that serve the island's four towns meet the ferries. Bus day passes cost €6.50. **Kiewiet Fietsverhuur** (✐542 130; www.fietsenopameland.nl; Oude Steiger 1; bikes per day €8.70; ◎8.30am-6pm Sat-Thu, to 8.30pm Fri), with a branch just up from the ferry dock, rents Gazelle sevenspeed bikes.

Schiermonnikoog

✐0519 / POP 942

The smallest and most serene of the Frisian Islands, Schiermonnikoog is the place to get away from it all; the feeling of sheer isolation as you move through Schiermonnikoog's 40 sq km, with 18km of beaches, can be intoxicating. Its name means 'Grey Monk Island', a reference to the 15th-century clerics who once lived here.

◎ Sights & Activities

Schiermonnikoog is a cyclist's dream: paths of packed white gravel wind through low dune forest with turn-offs to the beach. It

ISLAND HOPPING

In summer daily ferries (p203) connect the islands of Texel, Vlieland and Terschelling without the need to return to the mainland.

But if you've got the time, a more adventurous alternative connects all the islands to Noord-Holland.

The **Eilandhopper** (☑ 06 3829 7449; www.eilandhopper.nl; Van Diemenkade 14, Amsterdam; ☉ Jul & Aug) runs a pair of classic clippers, each over 100 years old. The *Avontuur* sails between Amsterdam and Terschelling (via Enkhuizen and Stavoren), the *Willem Jacob* between Texel and Schiermonnikoog, visiting all the islands en route. A week's journey, say, from Amsterdam to Terschelling, then onward to Schiermonnikoog and Lauwersoog, costs €420/305 adult/child. Meals are served on board.

goes this way round the whole island and one can wander endlessly. The best idea is to grab a map, rent a bike, pack a picnic and head off in any direction that takes your fancy. Even when the ferry is packed on the way over, the endless beach absorbs like a sponge and you'll soon hardly see a soul.

Schiermonnikoog is also a popular destination for *wadlopers* (mud-walkers) from the mainland. By night the island, almost entirely free of light pollution, rewards stargazers with stunning celestial vistas.

Schiermonnikoog National Park   NATIONAL PARK
(☑ 531 641; www.np-schiermonnikoog.nl; Torenstreek 20) The entire island, except for the single town and surrounding *polder*, was designated the Netherlands' first national park in 1989. It's easy to lose yourself exploring its 5400 hectares of beaches, dunes, salt marshes and woods. Those who desire a bit more organisation to their wanderings can join a variety of tours.

Book activities and learn more at the visitors centre, located in an old power station at the foot of the white lighthouse in town.

To survey the surroundings, head for the Wassermann, the remains of a German bunker atop high wooded dunes north of town. For birders, bitterns may be spotted amongst the reeds of the Westerplas, a lake just west of town, while salt marshes are populated by herring gulls, terns and spoonbills.

🛏 Sleeping & Eating

Schiermonnikoog has few hotels or B&Bs, but plenty of bungalows and apartments.

Cafes line the few streets of Schiermonnikoog town. Camping is not allowed in the national park.

★**Hotel Pension van der Werff**   HOTEL €
(☑ 531 306; www.hotelvanderwerff.nl; Reeweg 2; r €58-80) Parts of this grand hotel date back 200 years. Rooms are modern and comfortable and some have balconies. The cafe out front is *the* spot for a long breakfast. Its own vintage bus meets the ferries.

ℹ Information

A grocery store, ATM, pharmacy, bicycle-repair shop and other services are all in a tight little knot in town.

Tourist office (VVV; ☑ 531 233; www.vvv schiermonnikoog.nl; Reeweg 5, Schiermonnikoog; ☉ 9:30am-5pm Mon-Sat) The tourist office is in the middle of town.

ℹ Getting There & Away

Wagenborg (☑ 0900 9238; www.wpd.nl; adult/child return €14/8, bicycles €9) runs large ferries between Schiermonnikoog and the port of Lauwersoog in Groningen province.

Bus 50 makes the one-hour run to Lauwersoog almost hourly from Leeuwarden (€7.70). From Groningen, bus 163 takes about the same time to reach the ferry port.

Ferries make the 45-minute voyage up to five times daily between 6.30 am and 6.30pm. Hotel and public buses (return €3.50) meet all incoming ferries at the port, 3km from the town of Schiermonnikoog. There is a bicycle-rental facility at the port. Nonresidents are not allowed to bring cars onto the island.

Northeast Netherlands

Best Places to Drink

→ Cafe Wolthoorn (p214)

→ De Pintelier (p214)

→ Café de Sleutel (p214)

Best Places to Stay

→ Prinsenhof Groningen (p213)

→ Auberge Corps De Garde (p212)

→ Stee in Stad (p212)

Why Go?

Few travellers venture to this far corner of the Netherlands, but they're missing out on the country's rural heart, a place where traditions are kept alive and prehistoric relics dot the landscape.

The provincial capital of Groningen is a buzzing, youthful city. Museums, restaurants, bars, theatres, canals, festivals – it's the cultural point of reference in the north and makes a fine base for further exploration.

On the nearby coast you can try the strangely intriguing pastime of *wadlopen* (mudflat-walking). Or head to Bourtange, on the eastern border with Germany; its hefty defences are just as forbidding now as they were in the 16th century. To the south, the province of Drenthe is like a great garden with shifting tableaux of sheep pastures, stream-cut peat bogs, marshlands and old forest, much of it accessible only by bike or on foot. As a bonus, *hunebedden* (neolithic burial chambers) are scattered amidst the province's eastern hills.

When to Go

→ Summer is the obvious time to visit. The long days provide a surfeit of light that fades ever so slowly into dusk and the cafe terraces overflow with high spirits well into the night. Groningen punctuates this with Noorderzon, an August festival of arts and frolic.

→ Spring and autumn have their own charms, when you'll see few other visitors.

→ In winter an abundance of cultural venues make indoor alternatives.

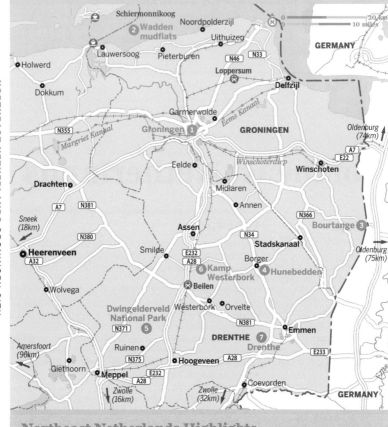

Northeast Netherlands Highlights

1 Experiencing northern culture at its best in vibrant **Groningen** (p208).

2 Stomping out a muddy trail on the **Wadden mudflats** (p216).

3 Walking the fortified ramparts of 16th-century **Bourtange** (p216).

4 Wondering at the **hunebedden** (p218), mighty stone dolmens dotting the landscape.

5 Roaming the beautiful marshlands of **Dwingelderveld National Park** (p218).

6 Pondering the traumatic, not-so-distant past at **Kamp Westerbork** (p218).

7 Cycling the rural byways of **Drenthe** (p217) province.

GRONINGEN CITY

📞 050 / POP 200,336

Looking at a map of the Netherlands, Groningen seems a long way from anywhere – but looks can be deceiving.

This vibrant, youthful city is very much part of the comings and goings of the country, and has all you'd expect of a progressive metropolis. Its student population (which has been around since 1614 when the university opened) of 40,000 ensures a healthy, hedonistic nightlife exists alongside the museums its more mature, established residents (think professors) demand.

Groningen was already an independent city-state and key trading centre by the late Middle Ages; the Martinitoren stands as a reminder of this early boom. The iconic church tower was one of the few remnants of the Golden Age to survive fierce fighting late in World War II before Groningen's liberation on 17 April 1945. Now an ambitious rebuilding scheme looks to transform the zone east of the Grote Markt.

A growing city, Groningen has attempted to combat traffic congestion through zealous pro-cycling initiatives, and it is considered a national leader in this regard. Since the 1970s cycling has been encouraged via severe restrictions on auto movement through the city and investment in cycling infrastructure. Thanks to these policies, the centre remains refreshingly free of traffic.

○ Sights & Activities

The old centre is compact and entirely ringed by canals. Just southwest of the main Grote Markt is Vismarkt, a more intimate and attractive square.

★ Groninger Museum   MUSEUM
(☎366 65 55; www.groningermuseum.nl; Museumeiland 1; adult/child €13/3; ☺10am-5pm Tue-Sun, to 10pm Fri) Those arriving by train can't help but notice the Groninger Museum. Occupying three islands in the ring canal in front of the station, the museum is a striking structure that will draw an opinion from any observer. Within is a scintillating mix of international artworks from through the ages.

The wildly eclectic architecture was the brainchild of Alessandro Mendini, who invited three of his fellow architects to each tackle a section. This explains why, to many, the museum has little consistency and appears thrown together at a whim. Inside, things are quite different; bright, pastel colours add life to the exhibition halls, and natural light seeps in from all angles.

The Mendini Pavilion, a picture of deconstruction, holds temporary exhibitions; like the curatorial direction, they are a wonderfully eccentric mix.

★ Noordelijk Scheepvaartmuseum   MUSEUM
(Northern Shipping Museum; www.noordelijkscheepvaartmuseum.nl; Brugstraat 24-26; adult/child €6/3.50; ☺10am-5pm Tue-Sat, 1-5pm Sun) This engaging tour of the lives of seamen and the ships they sailed unfolds through the set of buildings that once comprised a 16th-century distillery. Going through the labyrinth of 18 rooms is a navigational feat in itself.

Highlights include an intricately carved replica of the church at Paramaribo – the capital of former Dutch colony Surinam – in a bottle (Room 3) and detailed models demonstrating just how the many local shipyards operated throughout the centuries (Room 8).

Grote Markt   SQUARE
The main square holds some gems, of which the Town Hall (Stadhuis), dating from 1810, is the most dazzling. The string of cafes along the south side are perpetually buzzing. A 1950s melange that sprang up on the east side following wartime devastation is in the process of being updated; the socialist-style brick facade in fact belongs to the new university student union.

Martinikerk   CHURCH
(www.martinikerk.nl; Grote Markt; ☺11am-5pm Mon-Sat May-Sep, 2-5pm Sun Jul & Aug) FREE This huge 16th-century church commands the northeast corner of the Grote Markt. By any standard, the 96m-tall Martinitoren (admission €3; ☺11am-5pm Mon-Sat Apr-Oct, also 11am-4pm Sun Jul & Aug, noon-4pm Mon-Sat Nov-Mar) strikes a finely balanced profile. A climb to the summit (251 steps!) yields grand views and worrisome proximity to the giant bells. Purchase admission tokens at the tourist office (p214).

To the northeast the Martinikerkhof, a large square surrounded by historic houses, was used until 1837 as a graveyard. Particularly worthy of admiration is No 25 with an ornately carved gable, the former parsonage of the Sint Walburg church that once stood on the north side.

Prinsenhof   HISTORIC BUILDING
This mansion dates from the 15th century when it was a residence for the Brethren of the Common Life. After a thorough reconstruction in the late 16th century, stadhouders (chief magistrates) resided here for two centuries. In 2013 it became an exclusive hotel (p213). Look for the amazing sundial within the adjacent gardens (Turfsingel; ☺10am-6pm Apr-Oct, to 4.30pm Nov-Mar) FREE.

Nederlands Stripmuseum   MUSEUM
(☎317 84 70; www.stripmuseum.nl; Westerhaven 71; adult/child €8.95/7.50; ☺12.30-5pm Tue-Fri, 10am-5pm Sat & Sun) This museum covers the work of the Netherlands' and Belgium's most renowned comic artists and their creations, including Tintin (here known as Kuifje), Suske & Wiske and, oddly, Donald Duck.

Synagogue   SYNAGOGUE
(☎06 2819 2619; www.synagogegroningen.nl; Folkingestraat 60; adult/child €5/free; ☺1-5pm Wed-Sun Jul & Aug, hours vary rest of year) Groningen's synagogue is one of the few

Groningen City

Simplon Jongerenhotel (250m)
Stee in Stad (1,4km)

Ebbingebrug
Maagdenbrug
Spilsluizen NZ
Kattenhage
Spilsluizen ZZ
Hofstr
Lopendediep NZ
Boteringebrug
Oude Ebbingestr
Kijk in 't Jatbrug
Lopendediep ZZ
Hardewikerstr
16
Muurstr
Oude Boteringestr
Kleine Butjesstr
Butjesstr
Jacobijner-
Noorderhaven NZ
str
Oude Kijk in 't Jatstr
St-Walburgstr
Noorderhaven ZZ
9
Hoekstr
4
Weeshuisstr
Kreupelstr
Visserstr
Broerstr
7 6
26
Kleine
Stalstr
Rechten en
Kromme
Letteren
Elleboog
Poststr
5
Visserbrug
Uurwerkersgang
Grote
Zwanestr
Grote Markt
De Laan
28
23
Kromme
Guldenstr
12
Elleboog
Westerbinnensingel
Hoge Der A
Turftorenstr
Stoeldraaierstr
Tussen Beide
30
Lage Der A
27
Markten
Herestr
Gelkingestr
Lutkenieuwstr
A-Kerkstr
Vismarkt
Citycamp
Stadspark
A-Brug
Brugstr
A-Kerkhof NZ
Korenbeurs
(2,2km)
Noordelijk
A-Str
Scheepvaartmuseum
3
22
Pelsterstr
Haddingestr
8
2
A-Kerkhof ZZ
Folkingestr
Schuitemakersstr
21
Schoolholm
Klein
Bakkers Rijge
13
Pelsterstr
Reitemakersrijge
Munnekeholm
Torenstr
Nieuwstad
Herestr
Museumbrug
Gedempte Zuiderdiep
11
Ganzevoortsingel
Praediniussingel
Sluiskade
Stationsstr
Coehoorn
Singel
Ubbo Emmiusstr
Ruiter-Str
Emmapl
Zuiderhaven
Ubbo Emmiussingel
Ubbo Emmiussingel
Emmabrug
Emmasingel
1
Groninger
Museum
Stationsweg
14
Train Station

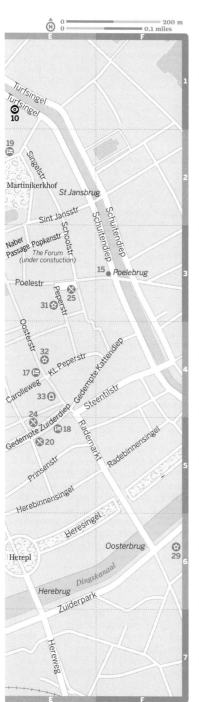

working synagogues left in the country. Sporting Moorish adornments, the century-old structure now houses a school and a temporary exhibition space; its beautifully restored wooden ceiling is one of the interior's highlights.

Aa-kerk   CHURCH
(A-Kerkhof) Located in the old harbour area, Aa-kerk was once a seaman's church; it partially dates back to the 15th century.

Academiegebouw   HISTORIC BUILDING
(Broerstraat) The Academiegebouw is the main building of the university; its richly decorated exterior was completed in 1909. Around the corner on Oude Boteringestraat are a number of appealing buildings dating from the 17th and 18th centuries.

Urinoir   PUBLIC ART
This urinoir was designed by no less than Rem Koolhaas, with an arresting photo collage. For once it also includes a female facility. It's two blocks west of the Aa-kerk, picturesquely standing by the canal.

Tours

Groningen Bike Tours   BICYCLE TOUR
(☑301 18 81; www.fietsstadgroningen.nl; Poelestraat 56; tours €17.50; ☉10.30am Sat) Take a 2½-hour tour of the city, starting from the Fietsverda bike shop. Prices include bikes.

Canal Tours   TOUR
(☑312 83 79; www.rondvaartbedrijfkool.nl; adult/child €12/6.50) Tours of the city's largest canals take approximately one hour and leave from out front of the train station anywhere between one and six times daily, depending on the season.

Festivals & Events

Eurosonic Noorderslag   MUSIC
(www.eurosonic-noorderslag.nl; ☉mid-Jan) A series of concerts by up-and-coming bands.

Noorderzon   PERFORMING ARTS
(www.noorderzon.nl; ☉mid-Aug) Eleven-day arts festival featuring everything from theatre and music to children's entertainment and electronic installations. Huge fun.

Bommen Berend   FIREWORKS
(☉28 Aug) Celebration of the day the city repelled the invading troops of the bishop of Munster. Fireworks and drinking.

Groningen City

Zomer Jazz Fiets Tour JAZZ
(www.zjft.nl; ⊙late Aug) This late-summer event combines two Dutch passions: cycling and jazz.

🛏 Sleeping

The tourist office will book accommodation and carries a list of B&Bs and *pensions* starting at €25 per person.

⭐**Stee in Stad** HOTEL €
(☏577 98 96; http://steeinstad.nl; Floresstrat 75; s/d €52/62; ⊙reception 8am-9pm Mon-Sat, to 3pm Sun; 🛜) 'Stay different' might be its slogan. In the Korreweg neighbourhood, a seven-minute bike ride north of the Martinitoren, these city-owned flats have been creatively renovated for short-term stays. It's a city initiative staffed by workers being trained to re-enter the labour force.

Simplon Jongerenhotel HOSTEL €
(☏313 52 21; www.simplonjongerenhotel.nl; Boterdiep 73-2; 🛜) Housed in an early-20th-century brick structure that served as a cannery, and more famously the Simplon raincoat factory, this is a creatively designed hostel that is affably operated by staff being trained to re-enter the labour force. It also features a fine cafe, the 73-2, with several toothsome, reasonably priced vegetarian options.

Citycamp Stadspark CAMPGROUND €
(☏525 16 24; http://campingstadspark.nl; Campinglaan 6; campsites €6.40 plus per person €3; ⊙mid-Mar–mid-Oct; P🛜) This spacious, green campground takes up the western fringe of the city forest and feels quite remote, yet it's within easy shot of the centre. Facilities include a shop, restaurant and bike rentals. From the train station, take bus 4 (direction: Hoogkerk, stop Kranenburg) about 3km west.

⭐**Auberge Corps De Garde** HOTEL €€
(☏314 54 37; www.corpsdegarde.nl; Oude Boteringestraat 74; r €100-150; ❄🛜) Originally the town guard's quarters, the 17th-century building sports carved animal heads above the door (woodchucks?). The 19 rooms are a mix of vintage and contemporary styles. 'Historic rooms' feature ancient wooden beams that may delight or imperil depending on your height.

Martini Hotel HOTEL €€
(☏312 99 19; www.martinihotel.nl; Gedempte Zuiderdiep 8; r €75-105; ❄@🛜) Parts of the Martini date to 1871 – check out the glass-walled lift. Vintage wallpaper and plush beds highlight a cheery decor; you'll sleep soundly here. There's a lavish spread for breakfast (€12.50) in the old-fashioned dining hall. It's a block from the train station.

Hotel Schimmelpenninck Huys   HOTEL €€
(☑318 95 02; www.schimmelpenninckhuys.nl; Oosterstraat 53; r €99-139; 🛜) The Schimmelpenninck is Groningen's grande dame, and like a dowager of a certain age, it sprawls in several directions. Antique-laden common areas lead to a serene courtyard and bistro, while the seven-building complex features 60 rooms ranging from stylish standard doubles to suites with period pieces and chandeliers.

★Prinsenhof Groningen   HISTORIC HOTEL €€€
(☑317 65 50; www.prinsenhof-groningen.nl; Martinikerkhof 23; P 🛜) The recently inaugurated Prinsenhof is a fabulous rebirth of the 16th-century *stadhouders'* residence (p209) as a modern hotel. Each of the 28 rooms is uniquely designed to accommodate the vagaries of the palace's layout, as is the ground-level cafe, which retains the original walls of the palace chapel.

✖ Eating

Eetcafés (pubs where you can get a meal) dominate the culinary landscape in Groningen, a reflection perhaps of its budget-minded student body.

Eeterie de Globe   DUTCH €
(☑318 22 26; http://eeteriedeglobe.nl; A-kerkhof ZZ 22; 2-course meal €7.50-8.50; ☺noon-3pm & 5-8pm Mon-Fri, 5-8pm Sat; 🍴) Such a deal: soup or appetizer plus a hearty plate of veggies, fish or meat with sides for under €10. No wonder the large, bright dining hall is much patronised by students and other europinchers. The menu changes daily; check its site for the week's offerings.

Amsterdams Broodjeshuis   SANDWICHES €
(☑313 49 21; Gedempte Zuiderdiep 16-18; sandwiches €2-4) An unpretentious purveyor of classic Dutch comfort food, this fluorescent-lit diner has just three formica tables and counter seating. The many *broodjes* (sandwiches) include eel, croquette and salmon salad, but the crown jewel is the tartar special. After hours, use the automat.

Huis De Beurs   CAFE €€
(☑312 03 33; www.huisdebeurs.nl; A-Kerkhof ZZ 4; mains €13-17) From its busy corner of the Vismarkt, pavement tables give a prime vantage for the inevitable speeding cyclist–dawdling shopper catastrophe. The casual menu of salads, sandwiches and hot specials is also served inside, which has an attractive and vaguely Victorian feel. On some nights there's live jazz.

Stadtlander   DUTCH €€
(☑312 71 91; www.eetcafestadtlander.nl; Poelestraat 35; mains €15-18; ☺11am-1am Mon-Thu, 11am-2am Fri & Sat, noon-1am Sun) Last of a line of boisterous terrace cafes, this one is especially *gezellig* (cosy), with a well-demarcated dining area. Go for the weekly and monthly specials – cheap and served up quick. The kitchen's open till 10pm.

Roezemoes   DUTCH €€
(www.eetcafe-roezemoes.nl; Gedempte Zuiderdiep 15; mains €12.50; ☺noon-11pm Sun & Mon, 11am-late Tue-Sat) Come evening, trad Dutch fare is served on the upper level of this brown *café* (pub), featuring three stews nightly. Don't miss the 'Groninger Rijsttafel' – no rice, but plenty of bacon and onions.

★Muller   FUSION €€€
(☑318 32 08; www.restaurantmuller.nl; Grote Kromme Elleboog 13; 5-course menu €58; ☺7-10pm Tue-Sat) You could watch the artistry of chef Jean-Michel Hengge from the street. But why just be a voyeur? Menus change regularly, with lobster, scallops and lamb taking prominent roles. Hengge picks the vegetables from his own garden.

🍷 Drinking

Groningen's student nightlife centres on Poelestraat and its adjoining streets. If there's a hint of good weather, these places are packed.

THE FORUM

Bombed to smithereens during WWII, the entire zone east of the Grote Markt is now being redeveloped. The centrepiece is the Forum, a massive trapezoidal structure with a zigzag hollow section in the middle. Built of the same dolomite stone that makes up the nearby Martinitoren, the 10-storey, 17,000 sq metre Forum will become Groningen's premier cultural centre and contain the main library, tourist office, auditoriums, exhibit spaces, an amazing rooftop terrace and parking for 1250 bicycles. Originally slated for completion in 2017, the project has been held up to implement earthquake-proof measures, a real concern due to intensive drilling for natural gas in the province.

MUSEUM DE BUITENPLAATS

Museum De Buitenplaats (☎ 309 58 18; www.museumdebuitenplaats.nl; Hoofdweg 76; adult/child €9/free; ☺11am-5pm Tue-Sun) In Eelde, 5km south of Groningen, this space is devoted to figurative art from around Europe. The main structure, which blends into its natural surroundings, features paintings from some of the Netherlands' more progressive 20th-century artists, such as Wout Muller, Henk Helmantel, Herman Gordijn and Matthijs Röling.

The gardens are peppered with sculptures and there's also a sun-bathed cafe. In summer an open-air stage is the venue for poetry readings, storytelling and concerts.

From Groningen, take bus 52 (28 minutes, every half-hour); otherwise there's a cycle route along the west side of Paterswolder Meer.

★ **De Pintelier**   BAR
(www.depintelier.nl; Kleine Kromme Elleboog 9; ☺3pm-2am Sun-Wed, to 3am Thu-Sat) Step back to the 1920s at this cosy bar where the selection of beer and *jenever* (Dutch gin) reads like an encyclopedia. Its long wooden bar and atmospheric candlelit tables are timeless. Catch a breeze in the courtyard.

★ **Café de Sleutel**   BROWN CAFE
(☎ 318 14 54; www.cafedesleutel.nl; Noorderhaven 72; ☺from 4pm) In a 17th-century brewery (note the keg hanging outside bearing its namesake key), this vintage bar has a local following for its €10 meals and cosy canal-side vibe.

★ **Cafe Wolthoorn**   BROWN CAFE
(☎ 312 02 82; http://cafewolthoorn.nl; Turftorenstraat 6; ☺4pm-1am Sun-Thu, 3pm-2am Fri & Sat) A highly atmospheric brown *café* with stained glass, red leather upholstery, brass taps and rather perverse art. It's been going since 1923 and the bow-tied tenders can tell you lots of stories about it. In 2008 it was voted 'best *café*' in the Netherlands.

☆ **Entertainment**

To find out what's going on around town, check out the posters that appear everywhere or the website http://uit.groningen.nl.

Jazz Café De Spieghel   LIVE MUSIC
(www.jazzcafedespieghel.nl; Peperstraat 11; ☺music from 10.30pm) A perennial favourite, this lively brown *café* features live music two or three nights per week (though only occasionally jazz) and a smooth sultry atmosphere. There's another bar on the upper level but the most popular spot is the smokers' terrace out back.

Vera   LIVE MUSIC
(☎ 313 46 81; www.vera-groningen.nl; Oosterstraat 44; ☺from 8pm) To see the next big rock act, head to this club. U2 played to 30-odd people in the early 1980s, and Nirvana later gave a performance to a crowd of about 60 people before going supernova. Maybe less is more?

De Oosterpoort   LIVE MUSIC
(☎ 368 03 68; www.de-oosterpoort.nl; Trompsingel 27) De Oosterpoort is *the* place to catch big-name musical acts passing through town. Jazz and classical concerts are the mainstay of its monthly program.

Grand Theatre   PERFORMING ARTS
(☎ 314 46 44; www.grandtheatregroningen.nl; Grote Markt 35) Restored to its original grandeur, this circa 1929 art deco–style venue stages a varied program of classical music, dance and children's theatre.

🛍 **Shopping**

Markets are held on Grote Markt and Vismarkt Tuesday, Friday and Saturday. Chain stores line up along Herestraat; explore Folkingestraat for quirkier options. Galleries abound on the west side, especially on Visserstraat and Oude Kijk in 't Jatstraat.

Kaashandel van der Ley   FOOD
(Oosterstraat 61-63; ☺9am-6pm Tue-Fri, to 5pm Sat) The best cheese from the Netherlands and around the world is sold here. Look for local organic varieties and some of the rare aged numbers that the Dutch never export. There are also deli items and a large array of olives so you can create a dreamy picnic.

ℹ **Information**

Tourist office (VVV; ☎ 313 97 41; www.toerisme.groningen.nl; Grote Markt 29; ☺noon-6pm Mon, 9.30am-6pm Tue-Fri, 10am-5pm Sat year-round, plus 11am-4pm Sun Jul & Aug) Offers advice and sells tickets, tours and excellent walking-tour maps in English. An exhibit illustrates the ongoing construction of the Forum cultural centre, where the VVV is due to move upon completion. Meanwhile, its top terrace remains a popular hangout.

ℹ Getting There & Away

BICYCLE
National bike route **LF9** runs south all the way to Utrecht (about 200km) and beyond. It's been designed to follow what would be the Dutch coastline if there were no dykes. **LF14** heads 48km northwest to Lauwersoog, where you can get the ferry to Schiermonnikoog.

BUS
The regional bus station is to the right as you exit the train station.

TRAIN
The grand 1896 train station, restored to its original glory, is worth seeing even if you're not catching a train. Lockers can be found on platform 2b and there is a good range of services. Two branch lines by Arriva cover the north of the province.

Sample train fares and schedules:

Destination	Fare (€)	Duration (min)	Frequency (per hour)
Leeuwarden	10	40	3
Utrecht	24	120	1
Zwolle	17	60	4

AROUND GRONINGEN

Meandering through the verdant countryside around Groningen by bike is rewarding by itself, but there are also various destinations to pedal for.

Northwest Groningen

The Netherlands' best-known walking trail begins in this corner of the province: the Pieterspad stretches 490 km from Pieterburen to Maastricht.

⊙ Sights

Zeehondencreche Pieterburen   NATURE CENTRE
(Seal Creche; ☑ 0595-526 526; www.zeehonden-creche.nl; Hoofdstraat 94a, Pieterburen; adult/child €7.50/5; ☺ 10am-5pm) Back in the 1970s, seeing how pollution and tourism were taking their toll on the local seal colonies, Lenie 't Hart, a resident of the small coastal town of Pieterburen, began caring for the creatures in her backyard. From this small start arose this centre, which has released hundreds of seals back into the wild since then.

Devoted to the rescue and rehabilitation of sick and injured seals, this centre houses 20 to 30 of the sea mammals, which can be seen lounging and swimming in various pools. Tours of the centre are offered.

The centre also leads seal-watching cruises on the Waddenzee, departing from Lauwersoog. Check schedules and make reservations on the website.

To get to Pieterburen, take the train from Groningen to Winsum (€4, 15 minutes), then bus 68 (20 minutes).

Hoogeland

Stoic churches centuries old dot the flat countryside northeast from Groningen to the coast. They are a lasting testament to the pious people who eked out lives in the muddy, sandy soil. The village of **Zeerijp** (3km northeast from the Loppersum train station) has a large church with a high bell tower and an unusual fake brick motif inside.

⊙ Sights

Menkemaborg   HISTORIC BUILDING
(☑ 0595-431 970; www.menkemaborg.nl; Menkemaweg 2, Uithuizen; adult/child €6/2; ☺ 10am-5pm Tue-Sun Mar-Sep, to 4pm Oct-Dec) Some 25km northeast of Groningen, in the town of Uithuizen, is one of the Netherlands' most authentic manor houses, Menkemaborg. Originally a fortified castle dating from the 14th century, Menkemaborg received its present gentrified appearance – a moated estate of three houses surrounded by lavishly landscaped gardens – early in the 18th century, and it has barely been altered since.

Inside, the rooms retain all the pomp and ceremony of 18th-century aristocratic life, complete with carved-oak mantelpieces, stately beds and fine china.

The gardens surrounding the mansion have been painstakingly restored to their symmetrical design of 1705 and replanted

---

FRACKING OUT

After a farmer discovered natural gas deposits near the town of Slochteren in 1959, Groningen province began major drilling, which fuelled the country's growth. But the rapid extraction of the mineral has resulted in a series of earthquakes centred on the village of Loppersum. Pressure from local residents, bitter about the damage inflicted to their homes and churches, has sparked an antifracking movement and the government has mandated a cessation of the practice.

DON'T MISS

POUNDING MUD: WADLOPEN

When the tide retreats across the Waddenzee, locals and visitors alike attack the mud-flats with abandon, marching, and inevitably sinking, into the sloppy mess. Known as *wadlopen* (mudflat-walking), it's an exercise in minimalism, forcing you to concentrate on the little things as you march towards the featureless horizon.

The mud stretches all the way to the Frisian Islands offshore, and treks over to Schier-monnikoog and Ameland are popular. Because of the treacherous tides, and the fact that some walkers can become muddled and lose their way, *wadlopen* can only be undertaken on a guided tour. Proponents say that it is strenuous but enlivening; the unchanging vista of mud and sky has an almost meditative quality. The centre for *wadlopen* is the coast north of Groningen, where several groups of trained guides are based, including the following:

Stichting Wadloopcentrum (☑ 0595-528 300; www.wadlopen.com; Haven 20, Lauwersoog)

Dijkstra's Wadlooptochten (☑ 0595-528 345; www.wadloop-dijkstra.nl; Hoofdstraat 118)

Wadlopers.nl (☑ 0595-528 689; www.wadlopers.nl; Wierhuisterweg 63, Pieterburen) Guided walks have set rates and take place between May and October. Options range from a short 6km jaunt across the mudflats (€12, three hours) to a gruelling yet exhilarating 25km pound to Schiermonnikoog (€30, five hours); the latter, with its national park, is the most popular destination. The ferry ride back from the islands is included in the price.

It's essential to book around a month in advance. You'll be told what clothes to bring depending on the time of year. You need rubber boots or hi-top sneakers for the trek.

with herbs and flowers from the original plans. The garden in the northeast corner holds a unique sundial and there's a maze to the northwest – enter with some caution as it might take a while to find your way out.

There's a good-value cafe in the old estate farmhouse with tasty soups and sandwiches.

There are hourly Arriva trains that run between Uithuizen and Groningen (€6, 35 minutes). The train station is a 1km walk west of Menkemaborg. National bike route LF10 passes right through.

Noordpolderzijl   HARBOUR
The tiniest harbour in the Netherlands is 29km north of Groningen City and has a desolate beauty. Used until recently by shrimpers from the nearby village of Usquert (the nearest train station), the harbour now serves mainly as a take off point for *wadlopers* (mudflat hikers). To reach it, cycle across flat fields with huge clouds on the horizon.

The old inn that once served the sluice gate, 't Zielhoes, is fortunately still in operation, and its *wadtart*, a rum-infused fruit pie, is worth the trip alone.

Bourtange

☑ 0599 / POP 430
The reconstructed fortress of Bourtange holds an isolated spot in the extreme southeast of the province, 7km east of the sleepy community of Vlagtwedde. Remote as it is,

the surrounding countryside and wetlands – in the process of being restored – are worth exploring and ideal for tackling by bike.

◉ Sights

Bourtange Fortress   FORTRESS
(☑ 354 600; www.bourtange.nl; Willem Lodewijk-straat 33; museums combination ticket adult/child €7.50/4; ⊙ 10am-5pm Apr-Oct, 10am-5pm Mon-Fri, 11am-4pm Sat & Sun Nov-Dec & Feb-Mar) One of the best-preserved fortifications in the country stands at this tiny town near the German border. With its flooded moats, solid defences and quaint houses protected from all sides, it is a sight to behold.

Built in the late 1500s, Bourtange represents the pinnacle of the fortifications of the era. It could withstand months of siege by an invading army, and famously checked the bishop of Münster's advance on Groningen in the 17th century.

In 1964 the regional government restored the battlements and the town itself to its 1742 appearance, when the fortifications around the citadel had reached their maximum size. It took three decades, during which time roads were moved and buildings demolished or reconstructed. The results are impressive. The star-shaped rings of walls and canals have been completely rebuilt and the village returned to a glossier version of its 18th-century self.

From the parking area and information centre, you pass through two gates and across three drawbridges over the moats before you reach the old town proper. From the town's central square, the Marktplein, cobblestone streets lead off in all directions; the pentagram-shaped inner fortification can be crossed in a matter of minutes by foot. The tourist office sells a handy English-language booklet, and docents in period outfits can guide you around.

Inside the walls (which you may walk upon) at the core of the fortification, brick houses make good use of what little space the five bastions afford.

Of the old buildings, four have been turned into museums. Terra Mora houses the main exhibit, with a section on the area's natural history and the chance to engage in simulated cannon volleys. The Captain's Lodge covers the life and times of the militia stationed at Bourtange in the 17th and 18th centuries, while De Baracquen displays artefacts and curios uncovered during the fort's reconstruction. The town's synagogue, built in 1842, explains the life and times of its Jewish population, and includes a plaque listing the 42 locals taken away to their deaths by the Nazis.

🛏 Sleeping & Eating

It's possible to stay in the original soldiers' or captains' quarters (€79). Bookings are taken at the fortress' Information Centre. Rooms are tidy, with polished wooden floors, and breakfast is included.

Two cafes on Marktplein are the only places to eat within the old town.

❶ Getting There & Away

If touring by bike, you can combine Bourtange with visits to the *hunebedden* in Drenthe, some 30km to the west, for a multiday ride.

From Groningen, the trip by train and bus takes about two hours and costs €11. Catch a train east to Winschoten, then bus 14 south to Vlagtwedde; transfer there to bus 11 for Bourtange. Check schedules beforehand on the transport info website www.9292.nl.

DRENTHE

If ever there was a forgotten corner of the Netherlands, this is it. With no sea access or major city to call its own (postwar project Emmen is the largest), Drenthe is as Vincent van Gogh described in 1883: 'Here is peace.' His paintings of the peat collectors in the province's southeast bear him out. But peace is exactly why this mostly rural region de-

serves some of your time. There's a growing collection of national parks, plus you get to explore the mysterious *hunebedden*, dotted liberally along the Hondsrug, an elevated fringe along the province's eastern portion.

Assen

📱 0592 / POP 67,165

Though not as dynamic a spot as nearby Groningen, Assen makes a pleasant enough base for touring the nearby national parks, *hunebedden* and Kamp Westerbork. The tourist office is a good source for bike maps of the region and info on the national parks.

◉ Sights

Drents Museum MUSEUM
(📞 377 773; www.drentsmuseum.nl; Brink 1; adult/child €12/free; ⊙ 11am-5pm Tue-Sun) The galleries of the Drents Museum, near the centre of town, focus on the painting and applied art of the late 19th century, early 20th century and contemporary realism, with a terrific prehistory exhibit on the lower level. The museum's new wing is devoted to temporary exhibitions.

Drentsche Aa
National Landscape NATIONAL PARK
(📞 365 864; www.drentscheaa.nl) Drentsche Aa National Landscape takes in a varied 10-sq-km landscape of ancient farms, deep woods and scraggly heath that bursts into purple bloom come late summer. Cycling through this bell-shaped area just northeast of Assen is sublime, and there are maps posted at each *knooppunt* (numbered marker) to guide you around. National bike route LF14 goes right down the middle.

Several *hunebedden* can be spotted just north of Gasteren, in the centre of the park, and beside a medieval church at Rolde to the south.

★ Festivals & Events

TT SPORTS
(www.tt-assen.com) A frantic motorcycle circuit and Assen's major event, the TT erupts into a festive, week-long blur of activity in late June.

🛏 Sleeping

Hotel De Jonge HOTEL €
(📞 312 023; www.hoteldejonge.nl; Brinkstraat 85; r from €82; 🅿) This hotel stands right in the centre of town over a popular cafe. It has two room types: standard and comfort, the latter with bathtubs.

ⓘ Getting There & Around

Trains connect Assen with both Groningen (€5.50, 20 minutes) and Zwolle (€13.50, 50 minutes). A shop to the left of the station rents three-speed Sparta Railstar bikes at €7.50 per day. National bike route **LF14** runs south 34km from Groningen and on to Emmen (about 40km southeast).

Kamp Westerbork

Of the 107,000 Jews living in the Netherlands before WWII, all but 5000 were deported by the Nazis. Almost all died in the concentration and death camps of Central and Eastern Europe and almost all began their fateful journey here, a rural forest about 10km south of Assen, near the village of Hooghalen.

Kamp Westerbork (☎0593-59 26 00; www.kampwesterbork.nl; Oosthalen 8; adult/child €8.50/4; ⊙10am-5pm Mon-Fri year-round, hours vary Sat & Sun), ironically, was built by the Dutch government in 1939 to house German Jews fleeing the Nazis. When the Germans invaded in May 1940, they found it ideal for their own ends. Beginning in 1942 it became a transit point for those being sent to the death camps, including Anne Frank.

A visit to the camp starts with the excellent museum at the car park, with displays tracing the holocaust in the Netherlands.

The camp itself is a 2km walk through a forest from the museum (or a €2 bus ride). There is little to see here today: after the war the Dutch government rather incredibly used the barracks for South Mollucan refugees, then had them demolished. However, photo blow-ups mark the locations of Nazi-era features such as the punishment building and the workshops where internees worked as virtual slaves; alongside stand rusty posts from which voices of the captives emanate with accounts taken from recovered diaries. But it's more of a place to meditate and reflect than study history.

Of several monuments standing here, perhaps the most moving is at the roll-call site in the centre of the camp, with 102,000 stones set upon a map of the Netherlands.

ⓘ Getting There & Away

The camp is 7km north of Westerbork town (and 7km south of Assen). There is no direct public transport to the site.

By bike, one pretty rural route to follow south from Assen is via *knooppunten* 9-8-33-31-58. By train, use the station at Beilen on the Zwolle–Assen train line (at least two trains per hour), then take bus 22 to Hooghalen, from where it's a 25-minute walk east.

Dwingelderveld National Park

Dwingelderveld National Park NATIONAL PARK (☎0522-472 951; www.nationaalpark-dwingelderveld. nl; Benderse 22, Ruinen; ⊙10am-5pm daily Apr-Sep, 10am-5pm Wed-Sun Oct-Mar) Dwingerveld National Park preserves 37 sq km of the largest wet heathland in Europe. More than 60km of hiking paths and 40km of cycling paths wander amid the bogs, meadows and forest. It's a starkly beautiful place and very popular on summer weekends.

The visitor centre is at the southwest corner of the park outside Ruinen, 7km west of the A28 on the N375. Get maps here.

HUNEBEDDEN

People have been enjoying the quiet in Drenthe since as early as 3000 BC, when prehistoric tribes lived here amid the bogs and peat. These early residents began cultivating the land and created what is arguably the most interesting aspect of Drenthe today, the *hunebedden*.

Hunebedden, which predate Stonehenge, are prehistoric burial chambers constructed with boulders, some of which weigh up to 25,000kg. It is thought the stones arrived in the Netherlands via glaciers from Sweden some 200,000 years ago. Little is known about the builders of the *hunebedden*, who buried their dead along with their personal items and tools, under the monolithic stones. Fifty-two of these impressive groupings of sombre grey stones can be seen in Drenthe and two in Groningen.

The impressive **Hunebedden Centrum** (☎0599-23 63 74; www.hunebedcentrum.nl; Bronnegerstraat 12, Borger; adult/child €7.50/3.50; ⊙10am-5pm Mon-Fri, 11am-5pm Sat & Sun) is the logical place to start a tour. It's in Borger, a little town 17km northwest of Emmen.

The centre has many displays relating to the stones as well as excavated artefacts, and the largest *hunebed* is located just outside its doors. Most are clumped around the villages of Klijndijk, Odoorn, Annen and Midlaren, which are strung out along the N34, a picturesque road linking Emmen and Groningen.

Central Netherlands

Best Places to Eat

➡ Bouwkunde (p222)

➡ Poppe (p225)

➡ Restaurant de
Bottermarck (p227)

➡ Café de Plak (p232)

➡ Sugar Hill (p234)

Best Places to Stay

➡ Hotel de Leeuw (p222)

➡ De Librije (p224)

➡ Hotel Courage (p231)

➡ Hotel Modez (p234)

Why Go?

The 'forgotten' provinces of the Central Netherlands, Over-ijssel and Gelderland, combine historic trade centres of abundant cultural wealth with natural beauty. Hoge Veluwe National Park, containing the Kröller-Müller Museum (with the world's finest Van Gogh collection), should star in any Dutch itinerary.

Deventer, Zwolle and Kampen are centuries-old towns, filled with atmospheric buildings that recall their heritage as members of the Hanseatic League. Nijmegen has a water-front vibe, masses of students and an annual march that now takes the form of a week-long party. On the other side of history, there are many WWII memorials and locations to contemplate around Arnhem.

Cut through by the Rhine and IJssel rivers and their tributaries, this region also offers splendid cycling routes, particularly along the marshy banks of the Waal east of Nijmegen and the IJssel delta north of Kampen, a remote protected area filigreed with silvery channels.

When to Go

➡ Rural Netherlands is at its best in summer when the fields are verdant, the waters are swimmable and the nights are long. Meandering the myriad bike lanes and hiking trails this time of year is a joy – you'll wish it was an endless summer. Activities are at their peak and you can canoe and kayak for hours on end.

➡ The towns and cities, however, have longer seasons. Wandering the narrow streets of Deventer is an atmospheric pleasure almost any time of year.

Central Netherlands Highlights

① Grabbing a free bike and cycling the verdant surrounds of **Hoge Veluwe National Park** (p234).

② Finding your masterpiece at the **Kröller-Müller Museum** (p235).

③ Prowling the backstreets of Hanseatic **Deventer** (p221) for hidden gems.

④ Exploring **Weerribben-Wieden National Park** (p228), encompassing Overijssel's mysterious wetlands.

⑤ Unravelling the Netherlands' war-torn past at **Oosterbeek** (p234).

⑥ Experiencing the ancient walled precinct of **Zwolle** (p224).

⑦ Surveying medieval monuments amongst the 500 in **Kampen** (p227).

OVERIJSSEL

From the Randstad perspective, this is the land 'beyond the IJssel', the river forming much of its western border. The province is hilly in the east near Germany and flat and soggy in the west along the former coastline, now landlocked by Flevoland's Noordoostpolder.

You might like to anchor yourself in Deventer to explore Overijssel, though Zwolle also has its charms. Giethoorn in the north is a novelty.

Deventer

☑ 0570 / POP 98,540

Deventer surprises. It's at its best on a beautiful August night, when you can wander among the Hanseatic ghosts along the twisting streets searching out the odd detail in the ancient facades. What looks like a crack in the wall is really a tiny passage to the IJssel.

Deventer was already a bustling mercantile port by AD 800, and it maintained its prosperous trading ties for centuries, evidence of which you'll see everywhere in its sumptuously detailed old buildings. Think of it as the Delft of the east.

◉ Sights

The Brink is the main square and Deventer's commercial heart. Among the splendid reminders of its Hanseatic past is the Penninckshuis (Brink 89), in the enclosure behind the statue of Albert Schweitzer. Home of the 16th-century cloth merchant Herman Penninck, it has a sculpted facade that's considered a highlight of the Renaissance.

East of the Brink, the Bergkwartier has more examples of restored Hansa-era buildings jammed cheek to jowl and is home to a number of actors and artists.

Waag   HISTORIC BUILDING
(☑693 780; Brink 56; museum €2; ⊙museum 10am-5pm Tue-Sun, 1-5pm Mon) The 1528 weighhouse is in the middle of the square. Look for the cauldron on the north side – legend tells of a 16th-century clerk boiled alive inside after he was discovered substituting cheap metals for precious ones in the local money supply.

There's a small museum upstairs displaying objects from the Deventer treasury.

★ Grote of Lebuïnuskerk   CHURCH
(☑612 548; www.pkn-deventer.nl; Grote Kerkhof 38; admission to tower €2.50; ⊙11am-5pm Mon-

Sat, plus Sun Jul & Aug) The city's main church is named after the English cleric who founded it in 738; the present Gothic structure dates from the late 15th century. Its many wall paintings, whitewashed by Protestant mobs in 1580, were later restored and patient observers can discern scenes of the Last Judgment, among others.

Etty Hillesum Centre   CULTURAL CENTRE
(☑641 003; www.ettyhillesumcentrum.nl; Roggestraat 3; adult/child €3/free; ⊙1-4pm Tue-Sun Jun-Aug, 1-4pm Wed, Sat & Sun Sep-May) The centre is devoted to the writer and philosopher Etty Hillesum, a Jewish woman who lived in Deventer prior to WWII. Like Anne Frank she kept a diary, though she made no attempt to hide and in fact voluntarily chose to dwell in Camp Westerbork to share and document the fate of her people. Housed in the former synagogue, the centre has exhibits on the life and writings of Hillesum and the Deventer Jewish community.

Bergkerk   CHURCH
(⊙11am-5pm Tue-Sun) At the top of Bergstraat, Bergkerk has landmark towers that date to the 13th century.

✦ Activities

The banks of the IJssel River are a scenic place for cycling. A 32km round trip follows the river bank north to Olst, where you can take a ferry across and return along the other side to Deventer. You can do the same thing going south to Zutphen, a 47km loop.

✪ Festivals & Events

Op Stelten   PERFORMING ARTS
(⊙Jul) On the first weekend of July, the old streets of Deventer become a massive theatre with performances of all kinds. The festival name means 'on stilts', as are the scores of street performers who are part of the show.

Bookfest   LITERATURE
(⊙Aug) More than 800 dealers of used and rare books set up shop here on the first Sunday in August.

🛏 Sleeping

Camping De Worp   CAMPGROUND $
(☑613 601; www.stadscamping.eu; Worp 12; campsites €4, plus per person €5.50; ⊙Apr-Oct; 🐾) Right across the IJssel from the centre of town, about two minutes north of the passenger ferry.

Hotel Royal   HOTEL $
(☑ 611 880; www.royal-deventer.nl; Brink 94; r €65-
95; ☎) What it lacks in character, the Royal
makes up for in location, right on the Brink.
The downstairs cafe is a popular spot, and a
nice breakfast buffet is included.

★**Hotel de Leeuw**   HOTEL $
(☑ 610 290; www.hoteldeleeuw.nl; Nieuwstraat 25;
s/d from €79/89; @ ☎) A sweet place to stay,
not just because it has a bakery museum and
old candy store. Every comfort you can think
of is provided. The simple rooms are comfy
and many have kitchenettes.

Hotel Gilde   HOTEL $$
(☑ 641 846; www.hotelgilde.nl; Nieuwstraat 41;
s/d from €94/104; ☎) Once a 17th-century
convent, this 36-room hotel celebrates its
former architectural glory with lavish atten-
tion to trimmings and frills, never mind the
austerity of its former tenants. Rear arcades
overlook a nice courtyard.

✕ Eating

★**Bouwkunde**   BISTRO $$
(☑ 614 075; www.theaterbouwkunde.nl; Klooster 4;
menus from €26; ☹ 6-9pm Tue-Sat) Chef Pieter

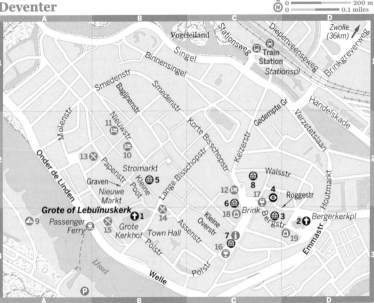

Deventer

Deventer

DON'T MISS

HISTORIC STREETS

Deventer is so well preserved that most streets have something to see. These include the following:

Polstraat Buildings with wall carvings and window decorations created over several centuries.

Walsstr No 20 Shows a woman descending the wall while hanging by a sheet, a reminder of its former use as a women's prison. Nearby are murals from the novels of Charles Dickens, who is celebrated in a December festival.

Bergstraat A street lined with Hanseatic survivors. See Gothic-style **No 29**.

Kleine Poot On a tiny alley just off this street, look for the **oldest stone house** in town, a much-modified AD 1100 vintage building with still-discernible Romanesque details.

adds a French accent to local organic ingredients while sommelier Heleen chooses the right wines at this homey cafe below a small theatre. Service is polished – like the silver. Book ahead.

Cucina Italiana ITALIAN **$$**
(☑615 900; www.cucinadeventer.nl; Grote Poot 1; mains from €20; ☺5.30-10pm Wed-Mon) Authentic southern Italian fare is the draw at this family-run establishment. Chef Raffaele hails from the Apulia region, origin of the local pasta, *orecchiette*. That's his dad on the wall mural crafting the ear-shaped morsels.

Grand Café Dikke van Dale DUTCH **$$**
(☑614 444; www.dikkevandale.nl; Nieuwe Markt 37; mains €14.50; ☺10.30am-midnight Mon-Sat, to 10pm Sun) Unpretentious, stick-to-your-ribs pub fare is served in abundance at this brownish cafe near the big church. With various bookshelf-lined salons, varnished wood tables and friendly, conversant staff, it's conducive to lingering.

🍷 Drinking

Brink is lined with cafes and bars, facilitating the art of hopping from one to another.

Bierencafé De Heks BROWN CAFE
(www.deheks.nl; Brink 63; ☺3pm-2am Sun-Fri, 2pm-3am Sat) At least a dozen brews are on tap at this local favourite where you'll find a jolly mix of regulars, students and even guidebook writers.

De Hip BAR
(☑745 094; www.dehip.nl; Brink 21; ☺noon-late) What is De Hip? An alternative gathering place on the Brink with music events, art exhibits and cheap eats Wednesday to Friday evenings; call to reserve a spot.

🛍 Shopping

The Saturday market on the Brink attracts food, flower and craft vendors from around the region.

Bussink Deventer Koekwinkel FOOD
(www.deventerkoekwinkel.nl; Brink 84; ☺1.30-5.30pm Mon, 9am-5.30pm Tue-Fri, 9am-5pm Sat) Bussink is the long-established purveyor of the local speciality, *Deventer koek*. The mildly spiced gingerbread, made with honey and orange, is so dense that it can sit undisturbed at the bottom of your bag for months.

De Wandelwinkel MAPS
(www.dewandelwinkel.nl; Bergkerkplein 5; ☺noon-6pm Mon, 10am-6pm Tue-Fri, 10am-5pm Sat) This tiny shop opposite the Bergkerk is stuffed to the gills with walking and cycling maps and guidebooks.

ℹ Information

Tourist office (VVV; ☑710 120; www.vvv deventer.nl; Brink 56; ☺10am-5pm Tue-Sat, 1-5pm Sun & Mon) Inside the Waag (p221); has good walking-tour maps.

ℹ Getting There & Around

The bus station is located to the right as you leave the train station.

BICYCLE

National bike route **LF3** runs 36km north through farmlands to Zwolle. Going southwest, it runs 55km to Arnhem and the gateway to Hoge Veluwe National Park, mostly following wide river banks and dykes.

CAR

The best place to park is the free car park on the west bank of the IJssel. A passenger ferry (one way/return €1/1.40; ☺8am-11pm) links it to town. The voyage takes less than five minutes.

TRAIN

Deventer sits at the junction of two train lines. The train station has lockers along track 3.

Destination	Price (€)	Duration (min)	Frequency (per hour)
Amsterdam	17	72	2
Arnhem	8	36	2
Nijmegen	11	60	2
Zwolle	6	24	2

Zwolle

📞 038 / POP 121,861

The capital of Overijssel province is a compact town that can easily occupy a day of exploration – longer in summer, when the weekend market is held and a seemingly endless schedule of small festivals keeps things bubbling.

In the 14th and 15th centuries, Zwolle garnered wealth as the main trading port for the Hanseatic League and became a cultural centre of some repute. While those days are long gone, you can still step back in time, courtesy of the moat and ancient fortifications that surround the town.

○ Sights & Activities

Standing on **Oude Vismarkt**, you have a good view of two key monuments. The **Grote Kerk** is grand but was much grander before lightning knocked down the tower. Much of what's left is from the 15th century. Next door, the **Town Hall** (Stadhuis) has a typically Dutch old part (15th century) and a typically oddball (1976) new part.

★ **Onze Lieve Vrouwe**   CHURCH
(www.peperbus-zwolle.nl; Ossenmarkt 10; tower entry adult/child €2.50/1; ⊙1.30-4.30pm Mon, 11am-4.30pm Tue-Sat) People from Zwolle say they know they're home when they see the Onze Lieve Vrouwetoren (also known as the Peperbus, or Peppermill), the huge former church that dominates the skyline. From atop the **tower** (234 steps!) you can appreciate the Museum De Fundatie's strange new appendage.

Within the church look for a painted case containing the relics of Thomae à Kempis, a German theologian who migrated to Zwolle to become a devotee of the Brethren of the Common Life.

★ **Museum De Fundatie**   MUSEUM
(www.museumdefundatie.nl; Blijmarkt 20; adult/child €9/free; ⊙11am-5pm Tue-Sun) Housed in a neoclassical courthouse, Zwolle's acclaimed art museum stages large-scale temporary exhibits by contemporary figures. The small permanent exhibit traces the trajectory of modern art through representative pieces. The surreal addition to the rooftop is a definite eye-opener.

Stedelijk Museum Zwolle   MUSEUM
(📞421 46 50; www.stedelijkmuseumzwolle.nl; Melkmarkt 41; adult/child €7.50/2.50; ⊙10am-5pm Tue-Sun) The centrepiece of the long-standing city museum is the Drostenhuis, a Golden Age mansion with original furnishings that give a glimpse of how the upper crust lived in the 18th century.

Sassenpoort   HISTORIC BUILDING
The 15th-century Sassenpoort, situated at the corner of Sassenstraat and Wilhelminasingel, is one of the remaining town gates.

🛏 Sleeping

Accommodation is tight here, but thankfully Zwolle is a good day-trip destination.

Hotel Fidder's   HOTEL $$
(📞421 83 95; www.hotelfidder.nl; Koningin Wilhelminastraat 6; r from €100; 🏠) Three late-19th-century homes have been combined into one grand, 21-room, family-run hotel. Inside, antiques abound and many rooms have ornate four-poster beds. It's located 500m southwest of the centre.

Hanze Hotel Zwolle   HOTEL $$
(📞421 81 82; www.hanzehotel.com; Rode Torenplein 10-11; r €94-132; 🏠) Virtually an island of vintage charm, the Hanze has just 11 simple, tidy rooms. Sizes vary and those on the 3rd floor are gut-busters for anyone who overpacked. The hotel's popular tapas bar is on the square out front.

★ **De Librije**   HISTORIC HOTEL $$$
(📞421 20 83; www.librije.com; Spinhuisplein 1; r/ste €295/450; 🅿 ❄ 🏠) The bold creation of Zwolle restaurateurs Jonnie and Thérèse Boer, Zwolle's most luxurious hotel occupies the former prison (1739), retaining such charming reminders as the original window bars and cell doors. The 19 lavishly decorated rooms and suites come with butler service, and Jonnie will lend you one of his sloops.

🍴 Eating

Van Orsouw   BAKERY $
(📞421 68 35; Grote Markt 6; treats from €2; ⊙noon-5pm Mon, 8.30am-6pm Tue-Fri, 8.30am-5pm Sat)

Zwolle

Zwolle

⊙ Top Sights
1 Museum De Fundatie B3
2 Onze Lieve Vrouwe B2

⊙ Sights
3 Grote Kerk B2
4 Sassenpoort C3
5 Stedelijk Museum Zwolle B2
6 Town Hall C3

⛆ Sleeping
7 De Librije D1
8 Hanze Hotel Zwolle B1

⊗ Eating
9 De Vier Jaargetijden B2
10 Het Wijnhuis B3
11 Poppe B3
12 't Pestengasthuys D2
13 Van Orsouw C2

⊛ Entertainment
14 Jack's Music Bar C3
15 Schouwburg Odeon B3

⬢ Shopping
16 Market B2
17 Waanders in de Broeren C1

Get your *blauwvingers* (blue fingers, a local speciality of shortbread dipped in icing) at this locally renowned bakery.

★**Poppe**   MODERN DUTCH $$
(☑ 421 30 50; www.poppezwolle.nl; Luttekestraat 66; menus from €33; ⊙ noon-2.30pm Tue-Fri,

5-10pm Tue-Sun) A former blacksmith's shop has been converted to this simple yet elegant restaurant. The open kitchen issues forth a steady stream of superb seasonal dishes. Spring brings asparagus, summer brings mussels and autumn wild duck and pear compote.

★ 't Pestengasthuys
FUSION $$

(☑ 423 39 86; www.pestengasthuys.nl; Weversgild-eplein 1; 3-course menu €20) Counter-intuitive as it may seem to house an elegant restaurant inside an old hospital for plague victims, the dark past will soon be forgotten by the time you've sampled the appetizers. There's a three- to five-course surprise menu that changes daily; wine pairings are recommended by the staff.

De Vier Jaargetijden
CAFE $$

(☑ 421 99 04; http://devierjaargetijdenzwolle.nl; Melkmarkt 8; dinner mains €15-17.50; ☺ noon-late) Of the many cafes in the centre, this one is always the most crowded and for good reason: fast service, tasty cooking and a long drinks list.

Het Wijnhuis
INTERNATIONAL $$

(☑ 421 74 95; www.wijnhuiszwolle.nl; Grote Kerkplein 7; mains €17.50; ☺ noon-10pm Wed-Sat, 1-10pm Sun) The wine's the thing here: the extensive list includes various organic selections, and the food complements it nicely. The fish is fresh, salads zestily dressed, *frites* (fries) fluffy and the atmosphere, under the chestnut trees beside the Grote Kerk, downright blissful.

☆ Entertainment

Jack's Music Bar
LIVE MUSIC

(Sassenstraat 29) Live music Saturday and sometimes Friday nights spans the genre range from bluegrass to Limp Bizkit cover bands.

Schouwburg Odeon
THEATRE

(☑ 428 82 80; www.odeondespiegel.nl; Blijmarkt 25) This grand building is a multipurpose entertainment venue hosting everything from theatre and dance to live rock and electronica nights.

🛍 Shopping

Diezerstraat is the mainstream strip of chains and big stores.

★ Market
MARKET

(☺ Fri & Sat) The market occupies most of the former Melkmarkt, Oude Vismarkt and the star-shaped centre. Fish, fresh fruit and vegetables, clothes – anything goes. In summer crowds surge and it becomes a party.

Waanders in de Broeren
BOOKS

(Achter de Broeren 1-3; ☺ noon-6pm Mon, 10am-6pm Tue-Sat) A bookshop and cafe magnificently ensconced in the 15th-century Dominican convent.

ℹ Information

Zwolle Tourist Info (☑ 421 53 92; www.zwolletouristinfo.nl; Achter de Broeren 1-3; ☺ noon-6pm Mon, 10am-6pm Tue-Sat) Zwolle's main tourist info centre is inside Waanders in de Broeren bookstore, where you'll find walking-tour brochures and plenty of maps. Other info points are inside the Grote Kerk and Stedelijk Museum.

ℹ Getting There & Around

BUS

Local buses leave from the right as you exit the train station.

BICYCLE

The bicycle shop is to the left as you exit the train station. Historic Urk in Noord-Holland is 50km northwest on national bike route **LF15**, a scenic ride of dykes and rivers. Deventer is 36km south on **LF3** and there are a lot of optional routes along the IJssel.

THE HANSEATIC LEAGUE

The powerful trading community known as the Hanseatic League was organised in the mid-13th century and its member towns quickly grew rich through the import and export of goods that included grain, ore, honey, textiles, timber and flax. The league was not a government as such, but it did defend its ships from attack and it entered into monopolistic trading agreements with other groups, such as the Swedes. That it achieved its powerful trading position through bribery, boycotts and other methods should come as no surprise to anyone who follows the corporate world. The Hanseatic League members did work hard to prevent war among their partners for the simple reason that conflict was bad for business.

Seven Dutch cities along the IJssel River were prosperous members: Hasselt, Zwolle, Kampen, Hattem, Deventer, Zutphen and Doesburg. It's ironic that the Hanseatic League's demise is mostly attributable to the Dutch. The traders of Amsterdam knew a good thing when they saw it and during the 15th century essentially beat the league at its own game, outmuscling it in market after market.

TRAIN

Zwolle is a transfer point with good connections.

Destination	Price (€)	Duration (min)	Frequency (per hour)
Deventer	6	24	2
Groningen	17	60	4
Leeuwarden	16	60	2
Utrecht	15	60	4

Kampen

038 / POP 51,432

Picturesque Kampen, a former Hanseatic city, is 15km west of Zwolle. Its historic centre is one of the country's best preserved, boasting numerous medieval monuments, including houses, gates and towers. The closing of the Zuiderzee ended Kampen's status as an important port and the long economic decline that followed kept modernisation down and old buildings up.

One of the town's most distinctive features is its drawbridge, the latest incarnation graced with golden pulleys; terraces with benches jut off the pedestrian path.

Sights & Activities

Kampen is laid out in a linear fashion, parallel to the IJssel. The main thoroughfare is Oudestraat.

Nieuwe Toren   HISTORIC BUILDING

(Oudestraat) The Nieuwe Toren is immediately obvious: it's the 17th-century tower with the incredible lean. The statue of a cow in front of the tower is linked to a ghastly tale that perhaps only a Kampener could find humour in.

Stedelijk Museum   MUSEUM

(331 73 61; www.stedelijkemuseakampen.nl; Oudestraat 133; adult/child €5/free; 10am-5pm Tue-Sat, 1-5pm Sun) The city museum occupies the old and new town halls, the former a late Gothic masterpiece adorned with sculpted figures. The top-floor exhibit is devoted to water and its crucial role in the town's development; below it hang portraits of all the members of the House of Orange.

Icon Museum   MUSEUM

(www.ikonenmuseumkampen.nl; Buiten Nieuwstraat 2; adult/child €7/free; 1-5pm Tue & Wed, from 10am Thu-Sat) Religious icons are the subject of this museum in a 17th-century monastery. Hundreds from around the world are shown here, spanning the centuries.

City Gates   HISTORIC BUILDING

(Broederweg) Two 15th-century city gates, the Broederpoort and Cellebroederpoort, survive along the bucolic park on Kampen's west side.

Sleeping

Hotel Van Dijk   HOTEL $

(331 49 25; www.hotelvandijk.nl; IJsselkade 30-31; s/d from €60/88;) This solid 18-room riverfront place has decor that dates from the '80s, but it's a real charmer and cyclists are catered for with a locked storage area. Buffet breakfast included.

Eating & Drinking

Banketbakkerij   BAKERY $

(Oudestraat 148; treats from €2; 9am-6pm Mon-Sat) The baked goods on display are as lovely as the fine art nouveau building where they are created. It's beside the Nieuwe Toren.

★ Restaurant de Bottermarck   MODERN DUTCH $$

(331 95 42; www.debottermarck.nl; Broederstraat 23; mains €25-30; noon-9pm Tue-Sat year-round, also open Sun May-Sep) A culinarily innovative couple run this fine bistro in a historic building; the changing menu is fresh and seasonal.

Herberg De Bonte Os   STEAK $$

(230 49 77; www.herbergbonteos.nl; Torenstraat 9; mains €15-18) A simple establishment for those who need their meat and potatoes. The beef, raised on the pastures of Twente, is prepared straight up or Indonesian-style. Enter through the base of the Nieuwe Toren.

De Stomme van Campen   BROWN CAFE

(337 17 21; www.destommevancampen.nl; Oudestraat 218-220) The knowledgeable tenders here will guide you through the ample assortment of special beers flowing from the taps, which include superb seasonal bocks.

Information

Tourist office (VVV; 332 25 22; www.ontdekdeijsseldelta.nl; Oudestraat 41-43; 9am-6pm Mon-Fri, to 5pm Sat) Shares space with a good bookshop, the Read Shop.

Getting There & Around

BICYCLE

LF15 goes northwest to Urk and east to Zwolle (18km); **LF23** follows the old coast below Flevoland and goes 130km west to Amsterdam; **LF22** follows the old coast north and west to Friesland; and **LF3** runs south via Zwolle to Arnhem.

TRAIN

Kampen has two stations: one just across the IJssel for the local run from Zwolle (€3.40, 10 minutes, two per hour), and another 2km south, Kampen-Zuid, on the new direct line to Amsterdam via Lelystad. Bus 74 shuttles passengers between the two stations.

Weerribben-Wieden National Park

A serene and mysterious landscape of watery striations, the Weerribben-Wieden National Park covers 10,000 hectares, the largest freshwater wetland in northwestern Europe. This entire area was once worked by peat and reed harvesters. The elongated ditches across the landscape are the result of peat removal: as one line of peat was dug, it was laid on the adjoining strips of land *(ribben)* to dry. The park consists of two parts: to the north, the Weerribben has the characteristic striated landscape; to the south, the Wieden represents an earlier stage of peat extraction, much of which was swept away by storms and is now covered by lakes. Peat digging later ceded to reed cutting, mainly for roof thatching, which continues today on a small scale.

The Weerribben-Wieden is also an important nesting zone for warblers, bitterns, western marsh harriers and purple herons. A variety of orchids grow in the reed beds.

◉ Sights & Activities

The park is threaded with an extensive network of cycling trails. A wonderfully serene journey can be made from Ossenzijl to Blokzijl along the Kalenburg River, traversing numerous wooden bridges over side canals, by following the LF-22a south. As you pedal along the isolated paths or row the channels, you'll hear the calls, clucks, coos and splashes of birds, fish, frogs, otters, beavers and eels.

Weerribben National
Park Visitor Centre   PARK
(☑0561-477 272; www.np-weerribbenwieden.nl; Hoogeweg 2; ◷10am-5pm Apr-Oct) This visitor centre is at Ossenzijl, a village at the northern end of the park. It has a few small exhibits but it's mostly taken up by a shop. You can sign up for various nature walks and boat tours here.

De Wieden Visitor Centre   NATURE RESERVE
(☑052-724 66 44; www.dewieden.nl; Beulakerpad 1; ◷10am-5pm Thu-Sun Apr-Oct, noon-4pm Wed,

Sat & Sun Nov-Mar) Located at Sint Jansklooster, this centre has informational boards on the landscape and wildlife of the region, plus a tea house with a pleasant terrace. A number of walks and cycle routes take off from here. Immediately behind the centre, a fine 1km boardwalk trail threads through the reeds, a good place to spot black terns.

Eco Waterliner   BOAT TOUR
(www.ecowaterliner.nl; Beulakerpad 1, Sint Jansklooster; day pass €11; ◷10am-5pm May-Sep) The Eco Waterliner gives a relaxed overview of Weerribben-Wieden National Park's unique landscape, running two small craft in opposite directions between Giethoorn and Blokzijl via Sint Jansklooster, a 1½-hour cruise between each point. Between lakes, the boats silently ply lily-pad-strewn canals with abundant bird life, and you may get a glimpse of the reed harvesters at work along the banks.

You can tote along a bike for a combination tour; for example, cruising to Blokzijl, cycling back to Sint Jansklooster and continuing by boat to Giethoorn.

De Gele Lis   BICYCLE/KAYAK RENTAL
(The Yellow Iris; ☑0561-477 442; www.degelelis.nl; Hoogeweg 27a; ◷10am-5pm Apr-Oct) In Ossenzijl, De Gele Lis hires out bikes (€7 per day) and kayaks (from €12 for two hours).

🛏 Sleeping

Recreatiecentrum De Kluft   CAMPGROUND $
(☑0561-477 370; http://dekluft.com; Hoogeweg 26; campsites €7, plus adult/child €4.50/2.50) The full-service campground and RV park is in Ossenzijl at the northern edge of the Weerribben. There are 275 sites and a handful of rooms.

❶ Getting There & Away

From Kampen (21km south), national bike routes **LF3** and **LF22** bisect the park and pass both visitors centres. The former continues north towards Leeuwarden, the latter west to the IJsselmeer coast and Harlingen.

To reach the visitors centre in Ossenzijl, take bus 76 from Steenwijk (35 minutes, hourly Mon-Fri), a stop on the train line from Leeuwarden to Zwolle. Sint Jansklooster is best reached from Zwolle via hourly bus 71 (€5.40, 50 minutes).

Northern Overijssel

Before the Noordoostpolder was created, the region was on the Zuiderzee. Today, the former coastal villages are landlocked, but remain navigable via a spiderweb of canals that criss-cross this marshy area. Buses are infrequent so you'll have to rely on pedal power.

Giethoorn

☑ 0521 / POP 2620

Giethoorn, the region's highlight, is a town with no streets, only canals, walking paths and bike trails. Contrary to most Dutch geography, Giethoorn is built on water crossed by a few bits of land, and farmers even used to move their cows around in row boats filled with hay. Hugely popular in summer, at other times it has an almost mystical charm as you wander its idiosyncratic waterways.

When the tourist hordes get too thick (the site has become a must-visit for Asian tour groups), head to the northern part of the village, which is quieter and quainter.

Near the tourist office, you can rent an electric boat (€15 per hour), canoe (€8 per hour) or bike (€8 per day).

Giethoorn's **tourist office** (VVV; ☑ 360 112; www.giethoorn.com; Eendrachtsplein 1; ◎ 10am-5pm Mon-Sat) is next to the Spar grocery store beside the newish library. It can help navigate the maze of sleeping options: campgrounds, rental cabins, B&Bs and hotel rooms.

Bus 70 serves Giethoorn on its route between Steenwijk (18 minutes) and Zwolle (one hour). Service is hourly.

To get around Giethoorn you'll need a boat, a bike or both. The area is about five scenic cycling kilometres off national bike routes LF3, LF9 and LF22.

Twente

Like a vast garden, Twente forms a distinct region at the southeastern edge of Overijssel, straddling the German border. Walking and cycling paths criss-cross a hilly landscape of old farmsteads and forests. **Ootmarsum** is the medieval showpiece, with a handsome Gothic church and a surfeit of galleries and craft shops.

GELDERLAND

The lush province of Gelderland has some gems amid the green.

Nijmegen honours its distant Roman origins while Arnhem seeks to recreate itself from the ashes of World War II devastation. Hoge Veluwe National Park is the star of the province, with its natural setting and superb museum.

ANOTHER BREACH IN THE WAAL

After a severe storm in 1995, the Waal river nearly overflowed its banks, and the zone from Nijmegen east to the German border had to be evacuated. The storm was a catalyst for preventive action. Water management authorities decided that something had to be done in response to the rising river flows of recent decades. Hence, the project 'Ruimte voor de Waal' (Room for the Waal). The dykes are being moved further north and built higher, and the river itself is being widened by digging a secondary channel to the north. In the process the edge of the northern bank became Lent Island. The whole area will become an ecological park, as new species move into the new eco-niche created in the process. The Waal project is the largest of a nationwide initiative, collectively called 'Space for the River', to widen the Rhine, IJssel, Maas and their tributaries.

Nijmegen

☑ 024 / POP 170,681

Nijmegen is enlivened by the 13,000 students at the Netherlands' only Catholic university. The centre – with its appealing and compact historic quarter – is only 10 minutes from the train station. The Waal River, Europe's busiest waterway, sees a large barge or ferry rolling through every few minutes. Walk or ride a bike along the Waalbrug (the main bridge across the Waal) for breath-stealing sunset views of the old town, with the water and boats below. Atypically, hills mean there are some actual climbs.

History

There's a minor rivalry between Nijmegen and Maastricht to claim the title as the oldest city in the Netherlands. What is known is that the Romans conquered the place in 70 AD and promptly burnt it down. A sad taste of things to come.

Nijmegen built itself up as a trading and manufacturing town. It rolled with the many invasions through the centuries right up until WWII, which was devastating. A marshalling point for German forces, it was bombed heavily by the Americans in February 1944. Later that year, it was pummeled

Nijmegen

Nijmegen

during the Operation Market Garden fiasco (see p233). The postwar years have seen several rebuilding schemes. Nowadays the city bursts with culture, and there are a pack of splendid recreational options in the immediate vicinity.

◉ Sights

Grote Markt   SQUARE
A few important bits of the old town either survived the war or have been reconstructed. The Waag (Weigh House; Grote Markt) was built in 1612 and has a lovely interior. The market on Grote Markt is held Saturday and Monday.

Sint Stevenskerk   CHURCH
(www.stevenskerk.nl; Sint Stevenskerkhof 62; tower adult/child €4/2; ⊗ church open daily Apr-Oct, weekend only Nov-Mar, tower 11am-1pm Mon, 2-4pm Wed & Sat Jul-Oct) Through an arch from Grote Markt, this iconic church dates from the 14th century and has a classic reformist interior: no expense was spared for whitewash. There are 183 steps to the top of the tower.

Stadhuis   HISTORIC BUILDING
(Burchstraat) Just east of Grote Markt, the Stadhuis is a much-restored fairy tale in stone that dates to the 16th century.

★**Museum het Valkhof**   MUSEUM
(⬛360 88 05; www.museumhetvalkhof.nl; Kelfkens-
bos 59; adult/child €8/4; ⊙11am-5pm Tue-Sun)
The museum's rich collections cover regional
history and art, including a first-rate section
of Roman artefacts. In front of the striking
glass building stands a column with a frag-
ment from Nijmegen's Roman foundation.

Valkhof   HISTORIC SITE
Perched in a commanding position over the
Waal, the Valkhof is a lovely park and the
site of a ruined castle (see it in better days
in the Jan Van Goyen painting at the museum across the way). There are plans afoot
to rebuild its tower. At centre stage is the
16-sided **Sint Nicolaaskapel**, which dates
to the time of Charlemagne. It has been re-
modelled and reworked in a multitude of
styles (depending on who held power in Nijmegen) during its 950-year lifespan.

★**Nationaal Fietsmuseum
Velorama**   MUSEUM
(National Cycling Museum; ⬛322 58 51; www.
velorama.nl; Waalkade 107; adult/child €5/3;
⊙10am-5pm Mon-Sat, 11am-5pm Sun) Down
by the riverfront is this museum with more
than 250 bikes: everything from 19th-century
wooden contraptions and hand-propelled
bikes to an entire room devoted to penny
farthings, plus more modern machines. It's
a must-see for anyone who's marvelled at the
Dutch affinity for two-wheelers.

🏃**Activities**

The 16km-long **N70-walk**, starting at the
outskirts of Nijmegen (take the St Maarten-
skliniek bus to its penultimate stop at restaurant Tante Koosje), counts as one of the
best of the Netherlands. The signposted path
takes you across eight hills (up to a *stagger-
ing* 90m) and along beautiful viewpoints over
the Rhine plains and tiny Dutch and German
villages, through wooded valleys with mighty
chestnut trees and enclosed meadows. You
pass the remains of Roman occupation and
a medieval stronghold before reaching the
eastern end of the circuit, where you could
cross the German border, indicated by age-
old posts of natural stone. Bring good walking shoes as the undulating path, especially
after rains, may be a bit slippery.

The **Ooijpolder route** is a classic cycling
excursion east along the protected southern
banks of the Waal, looping back through
bucolic pasturelands. Towards *knooppunt*
(numbered marker) 49 a dyke winds above

the river, which turns swampy with lily
pads, ducks and wooded islands. Big freight
barges ply this section of the river. To the
right are pastures, studded with purple, yellow and white wildflowers.

★**Festivals & Events**

★**Vierdaagse**   SPORTS
(Four Days; www.4daagse.nl; ⊙mid- to late Jul)
Nijmegen's big event is the annual four-
day, 120km- to 200km-long march. It has a
long history, going back to 1909 (the 100th
anniversary in 2016, since it had to be
cancelled during WWII). Thousands walk
a minimum of 30km a day. Routes vary according to gender and age. Completing the
walk is considered a national honour and
comes with a medal. Many suffer debilitat-
ing blisters, while thousands more endure
horrific hangovers, as the Wandelvierdaagse
is the city's excuse for a week-long party.

🛏**Sleeping**

If you're thinking about staying here during
the Vierdaagse, book well in advance.

Credible   HOTEL $
(⬛322 04 98; www.in-credible.nl; Hertogstraat 1;
s/d €55/75) Right in front of the Valkhof is
this old hotel converted into a hipster haven.
Fun is key to the aesthetic in the 18 rooms
on three floors, with naked light fixtures and
inspirational slogans on whitewashed brick
('Why stop dreaming when you wake up?').
The cafe and hang-out is of a piece, with
comfort food reimagined as high cuisine.

Hotel Atlanta   HOTEL $
(⬛360 30 00; www.atlanta-hotel.nl; Grote Markt
38-40; s/d from €65/90; 🐾) Standing on the
Grote Markt is this good-value option with
17 comfy rooms; it's home to a popular cafe.

★**Hotel Courage**   HOTEL $$
(⬛360 49 70; www.hotelcourage.nl; Waalkade 108-
112; r €65-130; ❄🐾) The main draw here is a
superb waterfront location – in the shadow
of the Waalbrug – plus a nice restaurant and
27 cosy rooms; those with river views are
pricier. Includes direct access to the adjoin-
ing cycling museum.

🍴**Eating & Drinking**

Of the dozens of cafes on the Grote Markt,
Cafe Biessels has the distinction of a former
life as an office-supply store, as the neon
fountain pen attests. The Waalkade is an-
other area to explore: though on the touristy

DON'T MISS

LATIN SCHOOL

An oft-overlooked gem, the **Latin School** (St Stevenskerkhof 2) stands beside Sint Stevenskerk. A fine example of Renaissance architecture with sculpted figures of the 12 apostles on the facade, it somehow emerged intact from WWII. The two-headed eagle over the doorway is a symbol of Nijmegen. It is now occupied by an architecture firm.

side, with restaurants coming and going, it's still a romantic spot for dining. The Commanderie van St Jan (a 15th-century hospital for the knights of St John) houses several popular restaurants.

★**Café de Plak**   INTERNATIONAL **$$**
(☑322 27 57; www.cafedeplak.nl; Bloemerstraat 90; mains €11.50-15; ☺noon-10pm; ☑) A perennially popular collective-run eatery with natural, creatively prepared fare and plenty of vegetarian options. The *kaas gehakt* (€10) is its unique variation on the old meatball with two salads and a veggie side. Friendly tattooed servers, and organic bread delivered by bike.

★**Plaats 1**   FUSION **$$**
(☑365 67 08; www.plaats1.com; Franseplaats 1, Commanderie van St Jan; mains €8-20; ☺5.30-10pm Tue-Fri, 10.30am-10pm Sat, noon-10pm Sun) Fresh fare from the lush fields of the province is served much of the year, with tables scattered round the courtyard and a chic, minimalist interior. Order small plates, a sandwich or a lavish menu. Good wine list.

Lux   MODERN DUTCH **$$**
(☑381 68 59; http://lux-nijmegen.nl; Marienburg 38-39; mains €13-17; ☺9am-1am; ☑) The terrace of Lux restaurant – one component of a cinema/cultural centre – faces Marienburg Chapel, a remnant of old Nijmegen miraculously missed by the bombs. Light, healthful fare is the main attraction, with an emphasis on seasonal ingredients and a variety of meal-sized salads. Film-and-dinner packages are offered.

De Hemel   BREWERY **$$**
(Heaven; ☑360 61 67; www.brouwerijdehemel.nl; Franseplaats 1, Commanderie van St Jan; lunch/dinner €19/29, museum visit €11; ☺noon-midnight Tue-Sun, to 6pm Mon) On tap at this local brewery is Luna, a 5% lager and Nieuw Ligt, which is anything but, being heavy in taste, body and colour. Beer-based meals are served in the

courtyard. Tours of the brewery, including tastings, are on weekends from 1pm to 5pm.

Café In De Blauwe Hand   BROWN CAFE
(Blue Hand; ☑360 61 67; www.indeblauwehand.nl; Achter de Hoofdwacht 3; ☺2pm-late Sun-Fri, 1pm-2am Sat) Occupying a corner of the Grote Markt is this inviting spot, as evidenced by its motto: 'A frosty mug of rich beer gives you warmth, joy and sweet pleasure.' An ancient survivor that derives its name from its 17th-century customers: workers at a nearby dye shop.

☆ Entertainment

Doornroosje   LIVE MUSIC
(☑355 42 43; www.doornroosje.nl; Stationsplein 11) In flashy new digs by the station, the long-running concert venue stages an eclectic program, from electronica and house to indie rock and world music.

❶ Information

Tourist office (VVV; ☑0900 112 23 44; www.vvvarnhemnijmegen.nl; Keizer Karelplein 32h; ☺9.30am-5.30pm Tue-Fri, 10am-4pm Sat) Convenient to the train station.

❶ Getting There & Around

BICYCLE

The **bicycle shop** (Stationsplein 7; bike rental per day €8.50; ☺5.30am-late Mon-Fri, 6am-3am Sat, 7am-2am Sun) is underground in front of the train station. Arnhem is 40km along the sinuous riverside course of national bike route **LF3**. Den Bosch is about 70km southwest along the equally curvaceous **LF12**.

BUS

Regional and local buses depart from the north side of the train station.

TRAIN

The train station is large and modern with many services. Lockers are near track 1A and are poorly marked.

Destination	Price (€)	Duration (min)	Frequency (per hour)
Amsterdam	19	85	2
Arnhem	4	15	8
Den Bosch	8	30-40	4

Around Nijmegen

The town of Groesbeek, 10km south of Nijmegen, is home to the **National Liberation Museum 1944–45** (www.bevrijdingsmuseum.nl;

Wylerbaan 4; adult/child €10/5.50). Using interactive displays and historical artefacts, visitors relive the campaign to liberate the Netherlands (which did not go so well).

Though the exhibits are rather low-tech and in sore need of renovation, they still manage to convey the massive carnage that was inflicted during the conflict. The roll-call at the adjacent **Dome of Honor** seems endless.

Bus 5 runs here from Nijmegen every 15 minutes, stopping at the Oude Molen restaurant, 300m from the museum. By bike take the LF3b south to *knooppunt 33* (steep climb), then turn east to point 88, a 13km ride.

Nearby, the **Canadian War Cemetery** is a mausoleum dedicated to the soldiers who fell here during Operation Market Garden.

Arnhem

📋 026 / POP 152,293

With its centre all but levelled during WWII, Arnhem has rebuilt itself as a prosperous township with several fine museums. Thanks to its fashion and design institute, the ArtEZ, the city has become a focus of the industry, and the country's premier fashion expo is held here in June.

🔘 Sights & Activities

A number of young fashion designers' studio-shops can be found in the Modekwartier focusing on Klarendalseweg.

John Frostbrug HISTORIC SITE

The modern and busy replacement for the infamous 'bridge too far' may not look too dramatic, but its symbolic value is immense. Head down to the river bank just west of the bridge where a series of broad granite shelves provide a good vantage point and popular sunset hang-out.

Nederlands Openluchtmuseum MUSEUM
(Netherlands Open Air Museum; 📋 357 61 11; www.openluchtmuseum.nl; Hoeferlaan 4; adult/child €16/12; ⊙ 10am-5pm Apr-Oct) The village-sized open-air museum showcases a nationwide collection of buildings and artefacts with everything from farmhouses and stage-coaches to working windmills. Volunteers in period costumes demonstrate traditional skills. Take bus 3 from the train station in the direction Alteveer.

Museum of Modern Art Arnhem MUSEUM
(Museum voor Moderne Kunst Arnhem; 📋 303 14 00; www.museumarnhem.nl; Utrechtseweg 87; adult/child/teen €10/free/5; ⊙ 11am-5pm Tue-Sun) Arnhem's striking hall of culture is a showcase for realism in modern art and its various movements throughout the past century. The museum also holds a substantial collection of applied art and design. It's 650m west of the station at the top of a riverside park.

🛏 Sleeping & Eating

Cafes and fast-food outlets crowd around the station.

A BRIDGE TOO FAR: OPERATION MARKET GARDEN

The battle they called Operation Market Garden was devised by British General Bernard Montgomery to end WWII in Europe by Christmas 1944. Despite advisers warning that the entire operation was likely to fail, Montgomery pushed on. The plan was for British forces in Belgium to make a huge push along a narrow corridor to Arnhem in the Netherlands, where they would cut off large numbers of German troops from being able to return to Germany, thereby allowing the British to dash east to Berlin and end the war.

Everything went wrong. The British paratroops were only given two days' rations and the forces from the south had to cross 14 bridges, all of which had to remain traversable and lightly defended for the plan to work. The southern forces encountered some of the German army's most hardened troops and the bridges weren't all completely intact. This, in effect, stranded the Arnhem paratroops. They held out there and in neighbouring Oosterbeek for eight days without reinforcements. The survivors, a mere 2163, retreated under darkness. More than 17,000 other British troops were killed.

The results of the debacle were devastating for the Dutch: Arnhem and other towns were destroyed and hundreds of civilians killed. The Dutch resistance, thinking that liberation was at hand, came out of hiding to fight the Germans. But without the anticipated Allied forces supporting them, hundreds were captured and killed.

Finally, Montgomery abandoned the country. The winter of 1944–45 came to be known as the 'Winter of Hunger', as no food could be imported from Allied-held Belgium.

Stayokay Arnhem HOSTEL **$**
(☑️442 01 14; www.stayokay.com/arnhem; Diepen-brocklaan 27; dm/r from €22/49; 🛜) Perched on a wooded hill 2km north of town, Arnhem's hostel is inconvenient to the centre, but that much closer to Hoge Veluwe National Park – and the pub is open till midnight. Take bus 3 (direction: Alteveer) and get off at Ziekenhuis Rijnstate (hospital).

★**Hotel Modez** BOUTIQUE HOTEL **$$**
(☑️442 09 93; www.hotelmodez.com; Elly Lamakerplantsoen 4; s/d €101/114; 🅿️🛜) Beside a delightful square in the heart of Arnhem's fashion district, this unique project has 20 rooms, each individually decorated by a leading fashion designer. The fashionable touch also applies to the food served at the ground-floor bistro, Café Caspar.

★**Sugar Hill** FUSION **$$**
(☑️389 20 10; www.sugarhill.nl; Klarendalseweg 192; mains €18-23; ⊙noon-9.30pm Tue-Sun) Young chef Werry van Leeuwen likes to improvise and experiment in his kitchen – he has a penchant for the stuff that's usually thrown away, for example – and he's cultivated an eager audience for his creations at this 'old-school' corner cafe.

❶ Information

Tourist office (☑️0900 112 23 44; www.vvvarnhemnijmegenregion.com; Stationsplein 13; ⊙9.30am-5.30pm Mon-Sat) Opposite the train station.

❶ Getting There & Around

BICYCLE

The train station has a below-ground bike-rental shop on the left as you exit, with seven-speed Batavuses for rent (€7.50 per day). National bike route **LF3** runs 55km northeast to Deventer; Nijmegen is a twisting 40km south.

BUS

Regional buses leave from in front of the south section of the train station.

TRAIN

Arnhem's monolithic new train station was nearing completion at the time of writing. Services include the following:

Destination	Price (€)	Duration (min)	Frequency (per hour)
Amsterdam	16	65	2
Deventer	8	36	2
Nijmegen	4	15-20	8

Oosterbeek

An old upscale suburb 5km west of Arnhem, Oosterbeek was the scene of heavy combat during Operation Market Garden.

◉ Sights

★**Airborne Museum Hartenstein** MUSEUM
(☑️026-333 77 10; www.airbornemuseum.nl; Utrechtseweg 232; adult/child €8.50/5.50; ⊙10am-5pm Mon-Sat, noon-5pm Sun) Inside a mansion used by both the British and the Germans as HQ during Operation Market Garden, this museum does a good job of laying out the disastrous mission and putting it into context. A subterranean maze simulates a night battle in Arnhem...not for the faint-hearted. The lobby has a useful tourist office, with battlefield and bike maps.

Oosterbeek War Cemetery CEMETERY
More than 1700 Allied (mostly British and Free Polish) troops are buried at this site, 500m east of Oosterbeek train station (follow the signs).

❶ Getting There & Away

By bike, take the **LF4b** west, skirting the railroad tracks much of the way. From Arnhem train station, take bus 52 directly to the museum (nine minutes). Local trains on the line between Arnhem (€2.20, five minutes, every 30 minutes) and Utrecht stop at Oosterbeek station.

Hoge Veluwe National Park

The marshlands, forests, heath and drift sands would be reason enough to visit this 55-sq-km national park, the largest in the Netherlands, but its brilliant museum makes it simply unmissable.

The land was purchased in 1914 by Anton and Helene Kröller-Müller, a wealthy German-Dutch couple. He wanted hunting grounds, she wanted a museum site – they got both. It was given to the state in 1930, and in 1938 a museum opened for Helene's remarkable art collection.

◉ Sights & Activities

Hoge Veluwe National Park PARK
(www.hogeveluwe.nl; adult/child €8.80/4.40; ⊙8am-10pm Jun & Jul, shorter hours rest of year) A visit to Hoge Veluwe can fill an entire day. The ticket booths at each of the three entrances at Schaarsbergen (south), Hoenderloo (east) and Otterlo (west, the busiest of the

three) have basic information and invaluable park maps (€2.50). In the heart of the park, the main visitors centre (⊙9.30am-6pm Apr-Oct, to 5pm Nov-Mar) is an attraction itself, with interactive displays on the flora and fauna and the park's different environments, both above and below the ground. Book guided walks here. There's a restaurant adjacent.

There are myriad bike paths and 42km of hiking trails, with two routes signposted by *paddenstoelen* (mushroom markers). Substantial populations of wild boar, rams and red deer roam wild here and can best be spotted at observation points south of the Kröller-Müller Museum. At the north edge, Jachthuis St Hubert is the baronial hunting lodge that Anton built.

Cyclists in particular will be interested in the campground (⊡055-378 22 32; Houtkampweg; adult/child with tent €8/4.50, park admission not included; ⊙Apr-Oct), which is located at the Hoenderloo entrance. There are 100 sites; you can't reserve but you can call and see what's available.

Kröller-Müller Museum   MUSEUM
(⊡0318-591 241; http://krollermuller.nl; Houtkampweg 6; combination ticket park & museum adult/child €17.60/8.80; ⊙10am-5pm Tue-Sun) The T-shaped museum has works by some of the greatest painters of several centuries, from Bruyn the Elder to Picasso. The Van Gogh collection rivals that of the artist's namesake museum in Amsterdam (Helene was a fan) including *The Potato Eaters* and *Weavers* among many more, all arranged chronologically so you can trace his development as a painter.

Impressionists include Renoir, Sisley, Monet and Manet. A sprawling sculpture garden features works by Rodin, Moore and others.

Art lovers can recharge at a pair of excellent cafes, indoor and out. If you are cycling to the museum from one of the three park entrances, it's 2.5km from Otterlo, 4km from Hoenderloo and 10km from Schaarsbergen.

🚹 Getting There & Around

By bike, the park is easily reached from any direction; national bike route **LF4** through Arnhem is the closest major route. If you don't have your own wheels, you can use the famous free white bicycles, available at the entrances.

From Arnhem train station, take bus 9 (25 minutes, every half-hour) to the Schaarsbergen entrance (stop: Koningsweg) or bus 105 to Otterlo. From Apeldoorn train station in the north, bus 108 travels to Hoenderloo (25 minutes, hourly). Within the park, bus 106 runs between

ICE CREAM DREAM

Ijs van Co (www.ijsvanco.nl; Krimweg 33d, Hoenderloo; treats from €2; ⊙noon-6pm Mon-Thu, to 7.30pm Fri-Sun) After viewing the masterpieces inside Hoge Veluwe, enjoy another kind of artistry at this simple storefront not far from the park entrance in Hoenderloo. Ijs van Co has been making delicious soft-serve ice cream for decades. The creamy treat is firm, yet not too firm, sweet but not too sweet. There are options for toppings like syrupy fruit, but we like ours straight.

To get there by bike from the park entrance, follow signs for *knooppunt* 12.

the Hoenderloo and Otterlo entrances, stopping at the Kröller-Müeller Museum en route.

There is car parking at the visitors centre and museum. It costs €6.25 to take cars into the park, €3 to park them at the entrances.

Apeldoorn

More an agglomeration of towns than a proper city, Apeldoorn may lack cohesion but the compact centre has a cheerful village vibe. Its architectural showpiece, the CODA (⊡055-526 84 00; Vosselmanstraat 299; adult/child €10/free; ⊙10am-5.30pm Tue, Wed & Fri, 10am-8.30pm Thu, 10am-5pm Sat, 1-5pm Sun) museum, holds a terrific collection of costume and fashion jewellery. For the kids, there's the Apenheul (www.apenheul.com; JC Wilslaan 21; adult/child €21/18.50; ⊙10am-5pm Mar-Nov), a unique zoo devoted to monkeys and apes on a jungly hill within the vast forest west of town.

The star attraction, though, is the Paleis Het Loo (⊡055-577 24 00; www.paleishetloo.nl; Amersfoortweg; adult/child €14.50/5; ⊙10am-5pm Tue-Sun), built in 1685 for William III; Queen Wilhelmina lived here until 1962. Now it's a museum celebrating the history of the House of Oranje-Nassau. View the royal bed chambers, regal paintings, the lavish dining room dating from 1686 and the splendid gardens with their symmetrically planted flowerbeds and allusive statuary. Beyond the Colonnades spreads the Palace Park, the immense beautifully landscaped section of the estate where the Oranges took their leisure (entry until 3.30pm).

Apeldoorn is at a junction of train lines to Deventer, Zutphen and Amersfoort. Numerous local buses go near the palace.

Maastricht & Southeastern Netherlands

Best Places to Eat

➡ Cafe Sjiek (p241)

➡ Breton (p246)

➡ Bisschopsmolen (p241)

➡ Eetcafe Ceramique (p242)

Best Places to Stay

➡ Kruisherenhotel (p241)

➡ Stadshotel Jeroen (p246)

➡ Kaboom Hotel (p241)

Why Go?

Things are different below the rivers. Product of their em-battled histories (the Rhine formed the Romans' northern border), the provinces of Noord Brabant and Limburg have a distinctly southern character: more Catholic, more re-laxed and, in the case of Limburg, hillier. Among the obvi-ous southern influences are a preference for good beer and food, as embodied in the concept *bourgondisch:* eating and drinking with a verve worthy of the epicurean inhabitants of France's Burgundy.

Maastricht's medieval ramparts and delicate brick tow-ers, its polyglot inhabitants and its role in brokering the Eu-rozone all suggest a closer kinship with Europe than that of any Dutch town. And the hilly terrain to the east makes for uniquely panoramic (if strenuous) cycling and hiking.

Noord Brabant is an intoxicating combination of histori-cally ambient towns like Den Bosch and Breda, and younger urban centres like Tilburg and Eindhoven which are forging new identities as havens of culture and technology, yet all within cycling distance of supremely tranquil landscapes.

When to Go

➡ Maastricht can be enjoyed in any season, though it'd be a shame to miss the cafe terrace scene from late spring to early autumn. Noord Brabant is striped by rivers which make for curvaceous cycling along their banks during the fair-weather months. It's also prime party time, with major jazz festivals in Breda (early May) and Den Bosch (late May) and Tilburg's boisterous Kermis (mid-July).

➡ The darker months aren't entirely sedate either: the region's most uninhibited party, Carnaval, is in February. It's celebrated with special gusto in Maastricht.

MAASTRICHT

♪ 043 / POP 122,397

Spanish and Roman ruins, sophisticated food and drink, French and Belgian twists in the architecture, a shrugging off of the shackles of Dutch restraint – are we still in the Netherlands?

Maastricht is a lively and energetic place, with appeal and allure out of proportion to its size. The people are irreverent, there are hordes of university students and the streets are steeped in history. No visit to the Netherlands is complete without a visit.

History

Just like that other great afterthought, the appendix, Maastricht hangs down from the rest of the country, hemmed in on all sides by Belgium and Germany. It was this very precarious position that saved the town from war damage in the 20th century; the Dutch government didn't bother mounting a defence.

In previous centuries, however, Maastricht was captured at various times by most of Europe's powers. This legacy has bequeathed the city its pan-European flavour, and makes it all the more fitting that Maastricht was the

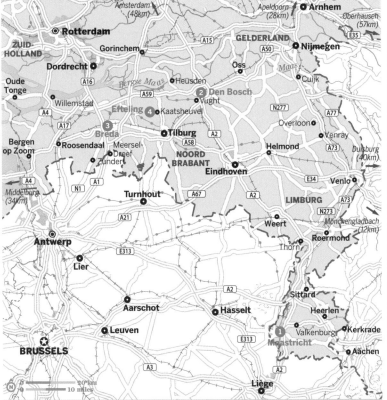

Maastricht & Southeastern Netherlands Highlights

❶ Thrilling in the good life of **Maastricht** (p236), a world apart from the north, and going bonkers at the annual Carnaval.

❷ Exploring the unusual canals of lively Den Bosch and decoding the myriad messages in the artwork at the **Jheronimus Bosch Art Center** (p245).

❸ Hopping off your bike or train to tour **Breda** (p248) and its beautiful Gothic church.

❹ Taking in the attraction the Dutch love most: **Efteling** (p248).

Maastricht

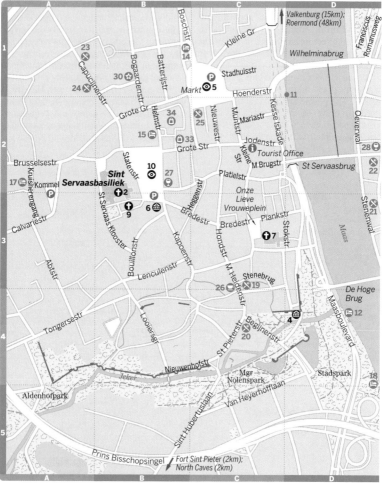

site of two seminal moments in the history of the EU. The first was the signing of the then European Community of the treaty for economic, monetary and political union on 10 December 1991 by the 12 members The following February, the nations gathered again to sign the treaty which created the EU.

◉ Sights & Activities

Maastricht's delights dot a compact area on both sides of the bisecting Maas river. The busy pedestrian Sint Servaasbrug, dating from the 13th century, links the city centre with the Wyck district.

The **Vrijthof**, an expansive square surrounded by grand *cafés*, museums and a pair of magnificent churches, is a focal point. Streets to its south and east form a medieval labyrinth punctuated by interesting shops and any number of places for a drink. The **Markt** is the commercial heart of town. At its north end is a statue of Johannes Petrus Minckelers, holding a flaming rod – he's the chap who invented gaslight.

★**Sint Servaasbasiliek**   CHURCH
(www.sintservaas.nl; Keizer Karelplein 6; basilica free, treasury adult/child €4.50/free; ⊙10am-5pm,

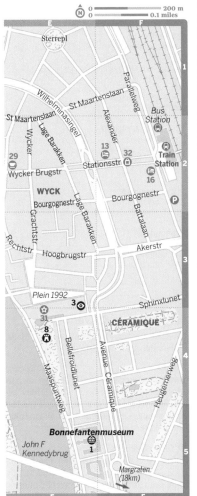

tower got its reddish hue with a coat of ox blood; it was later restored with ordinary paint. Climb to the top for sweeping views.

Museum Aan Het Vrijthof
MUSEUM

(☑ 321 13 27; www.museumaanhetvrijthof.nl; Vrijthof 18; adult/child/teenager €8/2/4; ⊙ 10am-5.30pm Tue-Sun) Housed in Maastricht's oldest civic structure, the museum highlights the city's legacy as a craft guild centre, with fine examples of antique silver, furniture, porcelain, timepieces and weaponry on display. Its most popular feature, though, is the grand cafe, which straddles the original stone loggia to open on a skylit courtyard.

Onze Lieve Vrouwebasiliek
CHURCH

(www.sterre-der-zee.nl; Onze Lieve Vrouweplein 9; treasury adult/child €3/1; ⊙ 7.30am-5pm) Standing on an intimate cafe-filled square, sections of this church date from before 1000. There is a separate treasury area that houses gaudy jewels and riches. The candle-filled shrine to Mary Star of the Sea near the entrance has drawn pilgrims for more than 300 years.

Fortifications
HISTORIC SITE

At the end of Sint Bernardusstraat, the **Helpoort** is the oldest surviving town gate in the Netherlands (1229); this area is laced with old walls. The remains of more 13th-century **ramparts** and fortifications are across the Maas in the Céramique district.

Centre Ceramique
ARCHITECTURE

(☑ 350 56 00; Ave Céramique 50; ⊙ 10.30am-8.30pm Tue & Thu, 10.30am-5pm Wed & Fri, 10am-5pm Sat, 1-5pm Sun) The multifaceted cultural centre, consisting of a library, exhibit space and city archives, is the anchor of the Sphinx Céramique, a residential/office/civic complex standing upon the site of the old ceramics factory. Designed by leading architect Jo Coenen and carried out by over a dozen of his international peers, it's a showcase of Dutch modern architecture.

★ Bonnefantenmuseum
MUSEUM

(☑ 329 01 90; www.bonnefanten.nl; Ave Cèramique 250; adult/child €9/4.50; ⊙ 11am-5pm Tue-Sun) Maastricht's star museum, in the Ceramique district east of the Maas, is easily recognisable by its rocket-shaped tower. Designed by the Italian Aldo Rossi, the E-shaped structure displays early European painting and sculpture on the 1st floor and contemporary works by Limburg artists on the next, linked by a dramatic sweep of stairs. The dome of the tower is reserved for large-scale installations.

to 6pm Jul & Aug) Built around the shrine of St Servatius, the first bishop of Maastricht, the basilica presents an architectural pastiche dating from 1000. Its beautiful curved brick apse and towers dominate the Vrijthof. The Treasury is filled with medieval gold artwork. Be sure to duck around the back to the serene cloister garden.

Sint Janskerk
CHURCH

(Vrijthof 24; church free, tower adult/child €2.50/1.50; ⊙ 11am-4pm Mon-Sat) This small 17th-century Gothic church is among the most beautiful in the Netherlands. Originally the limestone

MAASTRICHT & SOUTHEASTERN NETHERLANDS MAASTRICHT

Maastricht

⊙ Top Sights
1 Bonnefantenmuseum E5
2 Sint Servaasbasiliek B2

⊙ Sights
3 Centre Ceramique E3
4 Helpoort D4
5 Markt C1
6 Museum Aan Het Vrijthof B3
7 Onze Lieve Vrouwebasiliek...................C3
8 Ramparts E4
9 Sint Janskerk..................................... B3
10 Vrijthof.. B2

⊘ Activities, Courses & Tours
11 Stiphout Cruises D1

⊟ Sleeping
12 Botel Maastricht D4
13 Eden Designhotel Maastricht................F2
14 Hotel Beez... B1
15 Hotel DuCasque B2
16 Kaboom Hotel F2
17 Kruisherenhotel A2
18 Stayokay Maastricht D4

⊗ Eating
19 Bisschopsmolen C3
20 Café Sjiek...C4
21 Eetcafé Ceramique D3
22 Gadjah Mas..D2
23 Kantine De Brandweer.......................... A1
24 Marres Kitchen A1
25 Reitz C2

⊖ Drinking & Nightlife
26 Cafe Forum...C3
27 In Den Ouden Vogelstruys B2
28 Take One..D2
29 Zondag...E2

⊗ Entertainment
30 Cinema Lumiere B1
31 Theater De Bordenhal E4

⊙ Shopping
32 aOrganic Market..................................F2
33 Boekhandel Dominicanen B2
34 Entre Deux..B2

Fort Sint Pieter   FORTRESS
(☎325 21 21; www.maastrichtunderground.nl;
Luikerweg 80; fort tour adult/child €6.20/5, combination tour €9.95/6.95; ⊗English tours 12.30pm)
Looming atop a marlstone hill with commanding views of the Maas, the five-sided
Fort Sint Pieter formed the city's southern
defence and is linked to a network of underground tunnels. It's been fully restored to its
original 1701 appearance. Visit is by guided
tour only, which can be combined with a
tunnel tour. Purchase tickets at the visitor
centre below the fort. It's a 2km walk south
of Maastricht, or take bus 4 and get off at
'Mergelweg'.

Three nature walks begin from here, each
marked by colour-coded posts. The fort is
also the southernmost point of the Pieter-
pad, one of the Netherlands' most popular
long-distance hikes, extending 492km to
Pietersburen in Groningen province.

⌨ Tours
The tourist office (p243) can arrange walking tours and cycling expeditions.

Stiphout Cruises   BOAT TOUR
(☎351 53 00; www.stiphout.nl; Maaspromenade
58; adult/child from €9.25/5.10; ⊗daily Apr-Oct,
Sat & Sun Nov-Dec) Runs a variety of boat
cruises on the Maas.

⭒ Festivals & Events
Three events stand out on the busy Maastricht calendar.

Carnaval   CARNIVAL
(www.carnavalinmaastricht.nl) The orgy of partying and carousing begins the Friday before Shrove Tuesday and lasts until the last
person collapses sometime on Wednesday.
Everything stops for Carnaval.

★ European Fine Art Fair   ART
(TEFAF; www.tefaf.com; ⊗mid-Mar) The world's
largest annual art show is in mid-March.
More than 200 exhibitors converge, offering
masterpieces to those with a few million euros to spare. The event is open to the public.

Preuvenemint   FOOD
(www.preuvenemint.nl; ⊗Aug) This foodie festival
takes over the Vrijthof for four days around
the last weekend in August. It's touted as the
'largest open-air restaurant in the world'.

⊟ Sleeping
Maastricht is a popular weekend destination, so reservations are a must. The tourist
office has a list of private rooms.

Botel Maastricht   HOTEL $
(☎321 90 23; www.botelmaastricht.nl; Maasboulevard 95; s/d €63/70) Realize your dream

of staying on a houseboat in one of the 34 compact cabins on this ship moored on the Maas' west bank. Most feature tiny but well-equipped bathrooms. Enjoy breakfast or a sunset drink on deck and admire the barges rolling down the river. Rates drop midweek.

Stayokay Maastricht HOSTEL $
(📞750 17 90; www.stayokay.com/maastricht; Maasboulevard 101; dm €21.50-35, d €59-89; @🛜) A vast terrace right on the Maas highlights this stunner of a hostel with 199 beds in dorms and private rooms. It's 1km south of the centre.

Hotel Beez HOTEL $
(📞321 35 23; http://beezmaastricht.nl; Boschstraat 104-106; s/d €80/95; P🍴@🛜) In an elegant 1855 building just off the Markt, the 24 rooms smartly balance modern styling with rustic touches. Breakfast (included) is a big spread in the ground-floor cafe, which later morphs into a trendy cocktail bar.

★Kaboom Hotel HOTEL $$
(📞321 11 11; www.kaboomhotel.nl; Stationsplein 1; s/d from €58/116; 🍴🛜) This just-unwrapped hotel bills itself as 'a touch rebellious', and its minimal decor strikes an irreverent tone without sacrificing such comforts as flat-screen TVs and hair dryers. It's right across the street from the station.

Eden Designhotel Maastricht HOTEL $$
(📞328 25 25; www.edendesignhotel.com; Stationsstraat 40; r €100-150; P🌸@🛜) On the main drag from the train station to the centre, this regal old hotel has been given a shot of youth and tarted up for a sprightly future. The 105 rooms have stark style with bold colours set against hardwood floors. Breakfast is included.

Hotel DuCasque HOTEL $$
(📞321 43 43; www.amrathhotelducasque.nl; Helmstraat 14; r €80-109; 🛜) There's an air of faded art deco intrigue about this 45-room hotel close to the shopping district. Some rooms on the 4th floor have terraces with views over town.

★Kruisherenhotel BOUTIQUE HOTEL $$$
(📞329 20 20; www.chateauhotels.nl; Kruisherengang 19-23; r from €220; 🌸@🛜) This superb option is housed inside the former Crutched Friar monastery complex, dating from 1483. Modern touches, such as moulded furniture and padded walls, accent the historical surrounds. Each of the 60 sumptuous rooms is unique. Some have murals and artwork,

others are in the rafters of the old church. Breakfast is suitably heavenly.

🍴 Eating

Maastricht has more than its share of excellent places to eat. Clusters worth browsing include the eastern end of Tongersestraat and the little streets around the Vrijthof. Rechtstraat, east of the river, is one of the best streets for dining. Onze Lieve Vrouweplein is easily the best place for a cafe interlude.

★Bisschopsmolen BAKERY, CAFE $
(www.bisschopsmolen.nl; Stenebrug 3; vlaai €2.40, baguette sandwiches €6; ⊘9.30am-5.30pm Tue-Sat, 11am-5pm Sun) A working 7th-century water wheel powers a vintage flour mill that supplies its adjoining bakery. Spelt loaves and *vlaai* (seasonal fruit pies) come direct from the ovens out back. You can dine on-site at the cafe, and, if it's not busy, self-tour the mill and see how flour's been made for aeons.

Reitz FAST FOOD $
(Markt 75; frites €2.50; ⊘11am-6.30pm Tue-Sun) Join the queue at this iconic snack bar, which has been serving scrumptious *frites* (fries) under the classic neon sign for decades.

Marres Kitchen MEDITERRANEAN $
(www.marres.org; Capucijnenstraat 98; mains €14-20) Adjunct to a gallery for contemporary art, the kitchen here is run by a Syrian who previously resided in Tuscany, and dishes span the Mediterranean spectrum. Facing a lush garden, the small dining hall consists of long tables conducive to interaction. Start your noshing from an array of Mideast appetizers.

Gadjah Mas INDONESIAN $$
(📞321 15 68; www.gadjahmas.nl; Rechtstraat 42; rijsttafels €22-32; ⊘5-10pm) This small, lovely Indonesian bistro has rijsttafels (arrays of spicy dishes served with rice) that break with the norm. Flavours are bright and there is no skimping on the spice. Good wine list.

★Café Sjiek DUTCH $$
(www.cafesjiek.nl; St Pieterstraat 13; mains €12.50-24.50; ⊘kitchen 5-11pm Mon-Thu, noon-11pm Fri-Sun; 🛜) Traditional local fare at this cosy spot ranges from *zuurvlees* (sour stew made with horse meat) with apple sauce to hearty venison, fresh fish and Rommedoe cheese with pear syrup and rye bread. It doesn't take reservations and is always busy, but you can eat at the bar. In summer take a terrace table in the park opposite.

MAASTRICHT & SOUTHEASTERN NETHERLANDS MAASTRICHT

DARK AT THE END OF THE TUNNEL

The Romans developed the Sint Pietersberg tunnels by quarrying marlstone at a painstaking rate of just four blocks per day, creating an underground system that provided refuge during the numerous occasions when Maastricht found itself under attack.

The portion known as the Northern Corridor System Tunnels (called the 'North Caves' on the tours) is an amazing feat of pre-industrial engineering: at one stage, there were 20,000 separate passages stretching past the Belgian border, adding up to a length of 230km.

Walking through the tunnels is an eerie experience and you'll feel a deep chill; it's cold (11°C) and wet (95% humidity). People hiding down here during sieges would often die of exposure. **Maastricht Underground** (325 21 21; www.maastrichtunderground.nl; Luikerweg 71; cave tour adult/child €6.20/5, combination tour €9.95/6.95; tours 12.30 & 2pm) runs fascinating tours throughout the year. Among other things, you'll learn that 150 paintings were stored here during WWII, including Rembrandt's *The Night Watch*. You'll also see generations of charcoal drawings on the walls, with everything from ancient Roman stick figures to wartime depictions of movie stars. Hour-long tours of the North Caves start from near the visitor centre at the foot of Fort Sint Pieter.

★**Eetcafé Ceramique**　MODERN DUTCH $$
(325 20 97; www.eetcafeceramique.nl; Rechtstraat 78; mains €17-25; 5.30-10pm;) Their passion is food and they've been indulging it for decades. The dedication shows in such local dishes as Maastricht-style rabbit and *zuurvlees*, with plenty of veggie variations. A fun, relaxed place and the staff know their stuff. Reservations are a must.

Kantine De Brandweer　FUSION $$
(852 22 29; www.debrandweer.com; Capucijnenstraat 21; mains €17-20; 8.30am-6pm Mon, 8.30am-10.30pm Tue-Fri, 10am-10.30pm Sat & Sun) An old firehouse transformed into a hip dining hall/activity centre with amply spaced formica tables and a long book-lined counter. The vibe is friendly and casual. Watch the young chefs work their wizardry on an adventurous melange of cuisines. If it's just a snack you're after, you'll find all the *hapje* (hors d'oeuvre) variations listed on a board.

🍷 Drinking

Maastricht has a thriving cafe scene and most serve food. The east side of the Vrijthof harbours an endless row of options.

★**Take One**　BROWN CAFE
(www.takeonebiercafe.nl; Rechtstraat 28; 4pm-2am Thu-Mon) This narrow, eccentric 1930s tavern has well over 100 beers from the most obscure parts of the Benelux. It's run by a husband-and-wife team who help you select the beer most appropriate to your taste. The Bink Blonde is sweet, tangy and very good.

Zondag　CAFE
(www.cafezondag.nl; Wycker Brugstraat 42; 10am-2am Sun-Thu, to 3am Fri & Sat) On a busy corner of the main drag through Wyck, this old storefront with original tile floors draws a smart, youthful set throughout the day, thanks in part to its well-stuffed bagels (till 4pm) and original tapas (after 5pm). DJs, jazz and art openings boost the buzz considerably.

In Den Ouden Vogelstruys　PUB
(www.vogelstruys.nl; Vrijthof 15; 9.30am-late) On a coveted corner of the Vrijthof, this antique bar is a little bit naughty and a little bit nice. The entrance has heavy red curtains, while inside the bar there are photos of heavy men, heavy light fittings and heavy Trappist beer. But the local cheese is light and creamy...

Cafe Forum　CAFE
(851 94 75; www.cafeforum.eu; Sint Pieterstraat 4; 10am-late) This popular pub has a busy agenda including jazz Mondays, funky Fridays (DJs) and movie Sundays. Craft-beer tastings are another activity. Otherwise just enjoy a *borrel* (alcoholic drink) and brew on the enticing terrace.

☆ Entertainment

Cinema Lumiere　CINEMA
(321 40 80; www.lumiere.nl; Bogaardenstraat 40b) Offbeat and classic films are screened here.

Theater De Bordenhal　PERFORMING ARTS
(350 30 50; www.toneelgroepmaastricht.nl; Plein 1992, 15) A component of the old ceramics factory, the Bordenhal now stages four or five plays per season by the home-grown Toneelgroep.

🛍 Shopping

The Markt is the scene of a produce market Wednesday and a large mass-merchandise market on Friday. An **organic market** fills the median of Stationstraat on Thursday from 2pm to 6.30pm, while a used-everything market occupies the same spot on Saturday.

The streets leading off Grote Straat are lined with mainstream stores, while luxury retailers make up the Entre Deux (Helmstraat 3) shopping arcade. Stokstraat has galleries, boutiques and art stores. In Wyck, Rechtstraat has the most compelling mix of boutiques and shops in the city. Happy browsing!

Boekhandel Dominicanen BOOKS
(☑ 321 08 25; Dominicanenkerkstraat 1; ☺10am-6pm Mon, 9am-6pm Tue-Sat, noon-5pm Sun) A cathedral of books – literally.

❶ Information

Tourist office (VVV; ☑ 325 21 21; www.vvvmaastricht.nl; Kleine Straat 1; ☺10am-6pm Mon-Sat, 11am-5pm Sun) In the 15th-century Dinghuis; cycling tours offered.

❶ Getting There & Away

BICYCLE

National bike route **LF3** heads 156km north to Arnhem (where it continues to the north coast), staying east towards Germany much of the way. **LF7** runs along waterways northwest all the way to Alkmaar (350km) via Den Bosch and Amsterdam.

For an international trip, take **LF6** due east 35km to Vaals on the border with Germany. Attractive Aachen is just 5km further on.

BUS

The bus station is to the right as you exit the train station. Eurolines has buses to/from Brussels. Interliner has hourly buses to/from Aachen.

TRAIN

The classic old train station has full services. Lockers are in an alcove off the main hall. Sample train fares and schedules:

Destination	Price (€)	Duration (min)	Frequency (per hour)
Amsterdam	25	150	2
Den Bosch	20	90	2
Utrecht	23	120	2

There is hourly international service to Liège (30 minutes), from where fast trains depart for Brussels, Paris and Cologne.

❶ Getting Around

It's about 750m from the train station to the Vrijhof.

The **bicycle shop** (☺ 5.15am-1.15am Mon-Fri, 6am-1.15am Sat, 7.15am-1.15am Sun), to the left as you exit the train station, rents city bikes (€10 per day) and 24-speed Gazelle Ultimates (€17).

Around Maastricht

The hills and forests of southern Limburg make for excellent hiking and biking. The Drielandenpunt (the convergence of the Netherlands, Belgium and Germany) is on the highest hill in the country (323m).

Valkenburg

Valkenburg, 12km east of Maastricht, has been a tourist destination for at least a century, mainly for hiking and admiring the natural beauty of the hilly terrain. Among the attractions here is a replica of Roman catacombs, installed in an old limestone mine by architect Pierre Cuypers of Rijksmuseum fame. Above the town loom the ruins of an ancient castle. Valkenburg is an easy rail trip from Maastricht (15 minutes), and the palatial station, the oldest in the Netherlands, is a destination in itself.

Margraten

Netherlands American Cemetery & Memorial CEMETERY, MEMORIAL
(☑ 458 12 08; ☺9am-5pm) In Margraten, 10km southeast of Maastricht, this war memorial is dedicated to US soldiers who died in Operation Market Garden and the general Allied push to liberate the Dutch. It's a sombre memorial with row after row of silent white gravestones – a stark but appropriate testament to the futility of war.

Bus 50 runs from Maastricht's train station (20 minutes, four times per hour).

North Limburg

Clinging to the Maas river, the northern half of Limburg, barely 30km across at its widest point, is a no-nonsense place of industry and agriculture. Venlo, the major town, has a small historic quarter near the train station.

Roermond

The principal town of central Limburg, Roermond stands alongside the Maas, here skirted by a string of excavated gravel ditches turned into lakes and outfitted for recreation and boating. The bustling centre has two ancient churches, the early Gothic **Munsterkerk** and the **Sint Christoffel Kathedral**, each on its own square with plenty of terrace cafes. Sint Christoffel's tower was painstakingly reconstructed after being blown to smithereens by German bombers.

Cuypershuis   MUSEUM
(☑ 047-535 91 02; www.cuypershuisroermond.nl; Pierre Cuypersstraat 1; adult/child €6/4; ⊙ 11am-4.30pm Tue-Sun) Former home and workplace of Pierre Cuypers, the renowned architect, the museum covers his life and voluminous oeuvre. A native of Roermond, the prolific Cuypers not only built Amsterdam's Centraal Station and the Rijksmuseum, but also restored scores of churches and castles, including Roermond's own Munsterkerk. The museum is a 15-minute walk south of the central Munsterplein.

NOORD BRABANT

Wedged between Zeeland and Limburg, the Netherlands' largest province shares a long border with Belgium, and is culturally linked to its southern neighbour, where the adjacent region is simply dubbed Brabant. Cycling the rural backroads you'll encounter Catholic shrines at crossroads, boisterous cafe culture is the norm and every city's calendar is studded with festivals. Richly historic towns like Breda and Den Bosch bear remnants of ancient canals and ramparts while younger siblings Eindhoven and Tilburg revel in contemporary culture. Home to Vincent Van Gogh (who hailed from Zundert south of Breda), Noord Brabant gives its artists pride of place in great museums. And the rural landscapes, river valleys and woods that inspired them are all easily accessed via a superb cycling network.

Den Bosch ('s-Hertogenbosch)

☑ 073 / POP 150,889

The full name of Noord Brabant's capital is 's-Hertogenbosch (Duke's Forest). Den Bosch has two dynamite sights: a remarkable church and a great museum dedicated to its namesake artist. It also has unique tunnel canals to explore.

The significance of the city's full name held true in the 12th century when there was a castle and a large forest here. Both

are long gone. It was hotly contested during the Eighty Years' War and you can still see where the lines of fortifications followed the shape of the canals. It's the birthplace of the 15th-century painter Hieronymous Bosch, who took his surname from the town.

⊙ Sights

You can see the city in one large looping walk.

★ **St Janskathedraal**   CHURCH
(☑ 681 49 33; www.sint-jan.nl; Choorstraat 1; tower adult/child €5/2.50; ⊙ 8.30am-5pm, tower tours 1pm & 3pm Tue-Sun Apr-Oct) One of the finest churches in the Netherlands, the cathedral took from 1336 to 1550 to complete. The interior has late-Gothic stained-glass windows, an organ case from the 17th century and an impressive statue of the Madonna, which in May is the focus of pilgrimages. Take the opportunity to climb the 73m tower, with its carillon and great views.

Take the time to loop around its exterior: notice the contrast between the red-brick tower and the ornate stone buttresses. Look for a score of new angel statues added during a recent massive restoration; one is holding a mobile phone.

Town Hall   HISTORIC BUILDING
(Stadhuis) The town hall was given its classical baroque appearance in 1670. It's the highlight of the vast, trapezoidal Markt.

★ **Noordbrabants Museum**   MUSEUM
(☑ 687 78 77; www.hetnoordbrabantsmuseum.nl; Verwersstraat 41; adult/child €12/free; ⊙ 11am-5pm Tue-Sun) In the 18th-century former governor's residence, this stellar museum features exhibits on Brabant history and southern Dutch art from 1500 to the present, with a separate pavilion housing works by native son Vincent Van Gogh.

Following major renovations to create a Museum Quarter, a corridor connects to the new Stedelijk Museum for modern art. The two museums wrap around a vast inner garden focusing on a giant beech tree.

Stedelijk Museum   MUSEUM
(www.sm-s.nl; De Mortel 4; adult/child €7/free; ⊙ 11am-5pm Tue-Sun) Opened in 2014, this multilevel space focuses on contemporary art and design: tableware, ceramics and jewellery are all coherently arranged and pristinely displayed. The museum brasserie opens on the central lawn from the corridor that connects to the Noordbrabants Museum.

Den Bosch

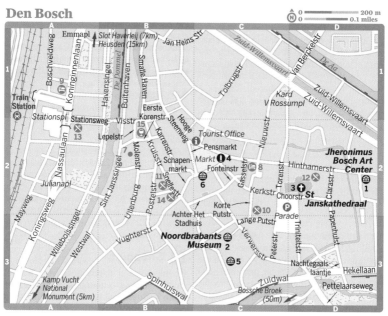

Den Bosch

Jheronimus Bosch Art Center MUSEUM
(☎612 68 90; www.jheronimusbosch-artcenter. nl; Jeroen Boschplein 2; adult/child €6/3; ☺11am-5.30pm Tue-Sun, noon-5.30pm Sat & Sun Apr-Oct, noon-5pm Tue-Sun Nov-Mar) This private museum uses interactive exhibits to explore Hieronymus Bosch's work and life. Housed in an old church, it has reproductions of every Bosch painting and the story to go with it. There's also a sculpture out front modelled on part of *The Garden of Earthly Delights*.

☞ Tours

Canals in Den Bosch are different from the others you've been seeing: many have long stretches that pass under buildings, plazas

and roads. These tunnels add spice to the usual canal tours.

★ Binnendieze TOUR
(www.binnendieze.nl; Molenstraat 15a; adult/child €7/3.50; ☺tours 10am-5.20pm Tue-Sun, 2-5.20pm Mon Apr-Oct) Runs 50-minute tours of the centre's canals. Boats leave three times hourly.

☆☆ Festivals

Jazz in Duketown MUSIC
(http://www.jazzinduketown.nl; ☺May) The many bars and cafes of Duketown (a sly riff on the city's official title) become venues for jazz combos, mostly of the Dixieland variety, during this four-day bash held the last weekend of May.

📛 Sleeping

Hotel Terminus
HOTEL $

(📞 613 06 66; www.hotel-terminus.nl; Boschveldweg 15; s/d €41/76) Close to the train station, as the name suggests, this relaxed hotel holds simple, brightly coloured rooms with nice vintage touches; bathrooms are shared. It's over a cheery pub with a good beer list and regular live folk music, and breakfast (included) is served in the adjacent dining room.

Hotel All-In
GUESTHOUSE $

(📞 613 40 57; www.allin-hotel.nl; Gasselstraat 1; s/d €58/86) Dating from 1905, this friendly pension, close to the Grote Markt, is on the lovably shabby side but comfy and quiet. Showers and sinks are in the rooms, toilets in the hall. Prices are lower from Sunday to Thursday.

★ Stadshotel Jeroen
BOUTIQUE HOTEL $$

(📞 610 35 56; www.stadshoteljeroenbosch.nl; Jeroen Boschplein 6; s/d from €100/130; 📶) Next to the Jheronimus Bosch Art Center, this small hotel is a gem. Each of the seven luxurious rooms has different decor. Guests enjoy the included breakfast in the stylish ground-floor cafe.

🍴 Eating & Drinking

Restaurant-lined Korte Putstraat is usually packed with diners.

Jan de Groot
BAKERY $

(Stationsweg 24; treats from €2; ⊙ 8am-6pm Mon-Fri, to 5pm Sat) Try the local speciality, a calorie-fest known as the *Bossche bol* (Den Bosch ball). It's a chocolate-coated cake the size of a softball, filled with sweetened cream.

Koffiehuis Voltaire
CAFE $

(📞 613 96 72; Stoofstraat 6; mains from €4; ⊙ 10am-6pm Mon-Sat; 🍴) Take a table here for some fab vegetarian fare. The owner cooks up a mean grilled sandwich of organic cheese, pesto, arugula, avocado and more. Great fruit shakes.

Dit
DUTCH $

(www.eetbar-dit.nl; Snellestraat 24; sandwiches €8-13; ⊙ noon-9pm Mon, 10am-9pm Tue-Sun) Fun and funky, 'This' does comfort food with a global twist. The sun-drenched terrace makes a good hangover recovery spot for a beloved *uitsmijter* (three fried eggs) with myriad add-ons.

In de Keulse Kar
CAFE $

(📞 613 61 29; www.dekeulsekar.nl; Hinthamerstraat 101; dinner mains €13-16; ⊙ 11am-2am) Sit outside and enjoy the radiant views of the cathedral at this locally popular corner cafe serving unpretentious pub fare; look out for nightly specials.

★ Breton
BISTRO $$

(📞 513 47 05; https://brasserijbreton.wordpress.com; Korte Putstraat 26; mains €11-18; ⊙ 5-10pm Mon, noon-10pm Tue-Sun) Amid the scads of lively terraces along Korte Putstraat, this cosy bistro stands out for the skills of its chefs, whose performances are on view. Sample-sized portions range from grilled tournedos to an outstanding crab soup; oysters on the half-shell are another popular option.

Café Bar le Duc
PUB

(📞 613 69 15; www.cafebarleduc.nl; Korenbrugstraat 5-7; ⊙ 1.30pm-2am Mon, 11am-2am Tue-Sun) Den Bosch drinks, and Korenbrugstraat is a prime focus for that activity. What makes Le Duc, a narrow haunt cluttered with nautical gear, especially popular is that it brews its own: 't Kolleke blond, amber and *tripel* flow from the tap.

🛍 Shopping

Wednesday and Saturday are the market days on Markt. Uilenburg has antique shops, while Vughterstraat is lined with interesting boutiques. Hinthamerstraat going east is another fine place for upmarket browsing and creative loafing.

ℹ️ Information

Tourist office (📞 612 71 70; www.vvv denbosch.nl; Markt 77; ⊙ 1-5pm Mon, 10am-5pm Tue-Sat)

ℹ️ Getting There & Around

BICYCLE

The bicycle shop is located below the train station. National bike route **LF12** heads due west through lush countryside some 70km to Dordrecht via the north side of Biesbosch National Park. **LF12** goes northeast 70km to Nijmegen along a twisting river route.

TRAIN

The modern train station is 600m east of the Markt. Lockers are on the concourse over the tracks. Buses leave from the area to the right as you exit the station. Sample fares and schedules:

Destination	Price (€)	Duration (min)	Frequency (per hour)
Amsterdam	15	60	2
Breda	8	35	4
Maastricht	20	90	2
Nijmegen	8	30-40	4
Utrecht	9	30	2

Around Den Bosch

Immediately south of Den Bosch, across the Dommel river, the urban landscape gives way to open meadowland, a 202 hectare nature reserve called the **Bossche Broek** that's laced with hiking and cycling trails.

Outside the suburb of Vught, 6km south of Den Bosch is the **Kamp Vught National Monument** (📞656 67 64; www.nmkampvught. nl; Lunettenlaan 600; adult/child €6/3; ⊙noon-5pm Sat & Sun, daily in Jul & Aug), which was the only SS-operated concentration camp outside Germany (Westerbork in the northeast Netherlands was a 'transit camp'). The site has been preserved as a monument to those who suffered and died here, with a reconstructed version of one of the barracks. A museum documents the personal experiences of both prisoners and SS commanders.

Kamp Vught served as both a labour and transit camp for 31,000 captives, including 12,000 Jews, almost all of whom were transported to death camps.

Bus 213 (capacity eight) rides out here from Den Bosch station. Alternatively, a bicycle path skirts the Drongelens Canal, a green corridor for flora and fauna, leading directly to Kamp Vught National Monument via a bridge that spans the canal. It's a serene 5km ride west of town. Heading south along the west bank of the Dommel River, follow *knooppunten* 54-21-22-24-33.

Eindhoven

📞040 / POP 223,209

A mere village in 1900, Eindhoven grew exponentially thanks to electronics giant Philips, founded here in 1891, to become the Netherlands' fifth-largest city. During the 1990s, Philips moved to Amsterdam, but Eindhoven remains a centre of high-tech research and industry with a top technology institute, and is a magnet for 'knowledge workers' from abroad. Due in part to the presence of all the brainiacs, Eindhoven fairly buzzes with cultural activity, much of which revolves around the renovated shell of the former Philips complex. The Dutch Design Academy is ensconced in the ex-Philips lamp factory (locally known as the 'White Lady'), and Dutch Design Week is a major event held here in October. But it is perhaps best known to frugal travellers for the many budget carriers serving its airport, and early departures are reason enough to overnight it here.

◉ Sights

Van Abbemuseum MUSEUM
(📞238 10 00; www.vanabbemuseum.nl; Bilderdijklaan 10; adult/child €12/free; ⊙11am-5pm Tue-Sun; 🚊1) Started in 1936 by the eponymous cigar magnate to boost his town's cultural profile, the Van Abbe holds a first-rate collection of modern art, including works by Picasso, Chagall and Kandinsky. The building itself is impressive, comprising the original brick castle and a 2003 grey-stone addition that incorporates the cascading Dommel river.

Strijp-S CULTURAL CENTRE
(www.strijp-s.nl) The sprawling Philips industrial centre is being redeveloped as a multiuse complex with shops, offices, restaurants, cafes, a concert hall, a hostel and the world's biggest skateboard park, Area 51. It's also the chief venue for Dutch Design Week.

🛏 Sleeping

Blue Collar Hotel HOTEL, HOSTEL $
(📞780 33 34; www.bluecollarhotel.nl; Klokgebouw 10; dm/d from €20/55) This new lodging is in the gleaming white factory building of the former Philips facilities, and its sleek design is a nod to its industrial heritage. The original flooring, fixtures and iron-lattice windows remain part of the 40-bed dorms and private rooms. The downstairs bar brews its own beer and stages events.

❶ Getting There & Around

AIR
Eindhoven Airport (www.eindhovenairport. com) is 6km west of the centre. It's a hub for budget airlines.

Ryanair (www.ryanair.com) London Stansted, Dublin, eastern and Mediterranean Europe.

Transavia (www.transavia.com) Istanbul, Lisbon and other Mediterranean destinations.

Wizzair (www.wizzair.com) Budapest, Warsaw, Belgrade and other destinations.

Bus 401 runs every 10 minutes between the airport and the train station (€3.50, 25 minutes).

BICYCLE
Eindhoven is at the confluence of national bike routes **LF7** and **LF51**, the former a day's ride north to Den Bosch, the latter accessing Belgian Limburg (48km southwest).

TRAIN
There are frequent direct train connections to the rest of the Netherlands, including Schiphol Airport (€20, 1½ hours), Maastricht (€16.30, one hour) and Rotterdam (€17.50, 1¼ hours).

Tilburg

🖉 013 / POP 211,648

A former textile centre, Tilburg lacks the pedigree of places like Breda and Den Bosch, but its industrial heritage has left it a handsome brick motif and an innovative spirit, while a substantial student presence keeps it humming.

◎ Sights

De Pont Museum   MUSEUM

(🖉 543 83 00; www.depont.nl; Wilhelminapark 1; adult/child €10/free; ⊙ 11am-5pm Tue-Sun) The former wool-spinning hangar is now a naturally lit space for large-scale installations by contemporary artists. The museum is 15 minutes north of Tilburg's Central Station, or take bus 6.

Textile Museum   MUSEUM

(Textielmuseum; 🖉 536 74 75; www.textielmuseum. nl; Goirkestraat 96; adult/child/teen €10/free/3.50; ⊙ 10am-5pm Tue-Fri, noon to 5pm Sat & Sun) A monument to Tilburg's leading industry for at least a century, this innovative museum not only traces the development of textile production processes but also exhibits the work of international textile artists. From the station take bus 5 (direction: Noord-Heikant) to the Kasteeldreef stop.

✷ Festivals & Events

Incubate   CULTURAL

(http://incubate.org; ⊙ mid-Sep) A festival of cutting-edge culture, featuring hundreds of envelope-pushing bands at dozens of venues across town.

WORTH A TRIP

EFTELING AMUSEMENT PARK

In the unassuming town of Kaatsheuvel, the 'Dutch Disneyland' (🖉 0416-537 777; www.efteling.nl; Europalaan 1; admission €34; ⊙ 10 or 11am-6pm year-round, to 8pm Jul & Aug) pulls in more than four million visitors annually. All the usual suspects are here: huge rides, walk-through entertainment with robots, scenes from popular stories and fairy tales, live shows performed by 'talent', sticky hands and shrieking kids.

Take bus 300 from Tilburg (30 minutes, half-hourly) train station.

Tilburgse Kermis   FAIR

(Tilburg Fair; www.detilburgsekermis.nl; ⊙ late Jul) A massive street party with rides, beer, bad music, sugary treats and stalls offering stuffed prizes. It's the biggest fair in Benelux, and for that reason alone it's remarkable.

❶ Getting There & Away

Tilburg's train station is midway between Breda (13 minutes) and Den Bosch (15 minutes).

Breda

🖉 076 / POP 180,937

Breda is an unexpected delight. Close as it is to the border, it's usually in a festive mood, the numerous terrace cafes and pubs bubbling away. Its historic core, though perhaps not the most beautiful in the Netherlands, has a real pulse and a vibrant cultural life. This is a place where in midsummer people take to the bucolic Mark River valley to paint landscapes and recite poetry. It also has one of the great parks of the Netherlands, the Valkenburg.

Breda's present peace belies a turbulent past; its strategic proximity to the border meant it was often overrun by invading armies. During the Eighty Years' War it was sacked no less than five times by the Spaniards, who saw it as the gateway to the north.

◎ Sights & Activities

★ Valkenberg   PARK

Between the station and the centre, this idyllic park has a gently rolling landscape with varied trees and a single unadorned jet of water for a fountain. Within the canal that skirts the park's north side stands a fanciful lighthouse designed by the architect Aldo Rossi.

Near the west entrance, the glass-walled pavilion 't Thuis (🖉 515 18 20; www.t-huis breda.nl; JF Kennedylaan 15; ⊙ 10.30am-5pm), with a delightful terrace, makes an ideal spot for morning coffee.

Begijnhof   HISTORIC SITE

(museum €2; ⊙ noon-5pm Tue-Sun) On the south side of Valkenberg Park, this enclave of homes has served as a shelter for unmarried women since 1535. There's a small museum and traditional herb gardens.

Breda Castle   CASTLE

Still an active military base, this remnant from the town's fortified era is off limits but you may wander round the perimeter. The

Breda

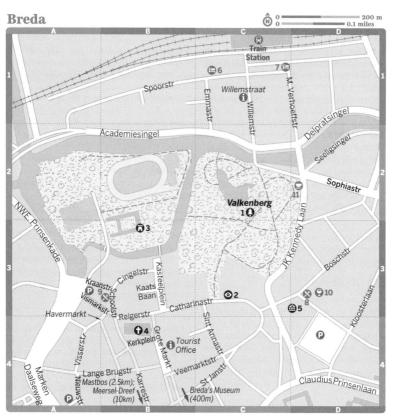

Spanjaardsgat (Spanish gate), a 16th-century survivor, is particularly worthy of admiration.

Grote Kerk CHURCH
(www.grotekerkbreda.nl; Kerkplein 2; tower €5; ⊗10am-5pm Mon-Sat, 1-5pm Sun, tower Thu & Sat) This beautiful Gothic church was built between the 15th and 17th centuries. Its perfect tower is 97m tall and is occasionally open for a climb.

Museum of the Image MUSEUM
(MOTI; ☑529 99 00; www.motimuseum.com; Boschstraat 22; adult/child €7.50/3.75; ⊗10am-5pm Tue-Sun) The Dutch tradition of clear visual communications is explored at this engaging museum, including a historical overview of image making from analog to digital.

Breda's Museum MUSEUM
(☑529 93 00; www.breda-museum.org; Parade 12; adult/child €11/7; ⊗10am-5pm Tue-Sun) Breda's strategic position in the Eighty Years' War

WORTH A TRIP

CYCLING ROUTE: BORDER LOOP

A 22 km circuit south of Breda traverses old woods to reach the Belgian finger of Meersel-Dreef, then returns via the serene Mark River valley. Head south of the centre, following the LF9 to the southern district of Ginneken, then turn right at Ginnekenmarkt. Continue toward *knooppunt* (numbered marker) 5, then turn left at the mushroom marker to Meersel-Dreef. This takes you along a broad sandy path through the Mastbos, a deciduous forest laced with swamps. At the southern tip of the park, cross the A27 to reach the village of Galder, with a shrine that's a station on the Ruta de Santiago. Continuing south to point 43, enter Meersel-Dreef. About a kilometre further, through the village is a Catholic pilgrimage site reminiscent of Lourdes, opposite a Trappist brewery, **Bij de Paters**. Returning, take a right at the *fiets netwerk* sign, then a left to point 43. At the next crossing follow signs to point 41/LF9b. A sliver of a trail skirts the lazy Mark River, flanked by sprays of white and yellow flowers. At the highway take a right, go about 200m, then tunnel under the road and continue along the river. You'll skirt the east bank of the Mark, a delightfully pastoral tableau 6km to Breda. When you see the spire of Ginneken you've returned.

is illustrated by maps, prints, weaponry and filmed re-enactments at the city museum, housed in the former military barracks.

🛏 Sleeping

Breda Hostel HOSTEL $
(☑ 520 57 14; www.bredahostel.nl; Stationsplein 1; dm/s/d €25/40/60) In a handsome brick structure right across from the train station, the hostel is well maintained with imaginative wall paintings. But beware: at weekends it is often occupied by bachelor-party groups.

Apollo Hotel HOTEL $$
(☑ 522 02 00; www.apollohotelsresorts.com; Stationsplein 14; s/d from €99/198; ✺ 🛜) Breda's main post office has been reborn as a stylish business hotel within walking distance of the train station.

🍴 Eating & Drinking

Breda is a great cafe town and on a sunny day it seems the entire population is sitting around having a drink. Make for Grote Markt, Kasteelplein or Haven.

Den Boerenstamppot DUTCH $
(Schoolstraat 3-5; 3-course dinner €8.50; ⊙ 4-7:30pm Mon-Sat) Proprietors Fred and Marloes Weerd take you back to a simpler time before the term 'low-fat' had entered the lexicon. A giant pot of endive *stamppot* (stew) is the basis for most meals here, served in abundance with your choice of *stofvlees* (beef stew), chicken or breaded cutlet. Take a table in the dining hall or belly up to the steel counter.

Dames Pellens FRENCH $$
(☑ 887 69 29; wijnbardamespellens.nl; Boschstraat 24; mains €14-25; ⊙ noon-midnight Tue-Sat, to

10pm Sun) Named after a pair of inseparable sisters who once haunted Breda's cafe society, this cosy bistro is primarily a place to savour fine wines (50 in the rack), and the kitchen does a few wine-based dishes too. Be sure to book ahead.

Café De Beyerd BEER CAFE
(☑ 521 42 65; www.beyerd.nl; Boschstraat 26; ⊙ 10am-late Thu-Tue) The Beyerd is a highly regarded beer *café*, with more than 120 brews, including its own Drie Hoefijzers Klassiek, and a perennially popular terrace. The restaurant, which shares the brewery facility around the corner, prepares fine beer-based meals.

ℹ Information

Tourist office (VVV; ☑ 0900 522 24 44; www.vvvbreda.nl; Grote Markt 38; ⊙ 10am-5.30pm Wed-Fri, to 5pm Sat; 🛜) Has maps and brochures. Another office is near the train station at Willemstraat (Willemstraat 17-19; ⊙ 1-5pm Mon, 10am-5pm Tue-Fri, 10am-2.30pm Sat).

ℹ Getting There & Around

BICYCLE
The bicycle shop is right next to the station. National bike route **LF11** starts here and runs northwest 110km to Den Haag via Dordrecht and Rotterdam. **LF9** runs via Utrecht all the way to the north coast and **LF13** runs via Breda straight east from Middelburg to the German border.

TRAIN
The train station is undergoing a colossal expansion; it has services to Rotterdam (€9, 25–45 minutes) and Den Bosch (€8, 30 minutes) among others.

Understand the
Netherlands

The Netherlands Today

The Netherlands is one of the most upbeat, energetic and socially engaged countries in Europe today. Start-ups proliferate throughout the country, which is one of the world's leading enterprise hubs. Ecominded, tech-enabled initiatives such as solar-panelled bike paths converting energy for the electricity grid are getting off the ground, as are architectural statements that have unparalleled green credentials. And the nation is coming into its own as an epicurean destination, with sizzling-hot drinking and dining scenes.

Best in Print

The Diary of Anne Frank (Anne Frank; 1947) A moving account of a young girl's life hiding from the Nazis.

Amsterdam: A History of the World's Most Liberal City (Russell Shorto; 2013) An American transplant traces the evolution of his adopted city.

In the City of Bikes: The Story of the Amsterdam Cyclist (Pete Jordan; 2013) Amsterdam's evolution into the world's most bike-friendly city.

After the Silence (Jake Woodhouse; 2014) Noir novel in which an Amsterdam detective hunts a murderer in the city's tangled streets.

Best on Film

Oorlogswinter (Winter in Wartime; 2008) A boy's loyalty is tested when he helps the Dutch Resistance shelter a downed British pilot.

Zwartboek (Black Book; 2006) Explores some of the less heroic aspects of the Dutch Resistance in WWII.

The Paradise Suite (2015) A Bulgarian prostitute, a Swedish piano prodigy and a Serbian war criminal cross paths in Amsterdam.

Komt een vrouw bij de dokter (Stricken; 2009) Follows a modern Dutch couple after she discovers she's terminally ill and he goes on philandering.

Holland or the Netherlands?

'Holland' is a popular synonym for the Netherlands, yet it only refers to the combined provinces of Noord-Holland (North Holland) and Zuid-Holland (South Holland). The rest of the country is not Holland, even if the Dutch themselves often make the mistake.

Politics

Among the qualities the Netherlands is best known for is its famous tolerance. However this idea of 'You don't bother me and I won't bother you' seemed under threat recently. Instead of a broad coalition government based near the centre of the political spectrum, the Dutch in 2010 shifted right. The coalition government formed that year included Geert Wilders, leader of the Party for Freedom, a far-right movement with a tough stance on foreigners living in – or immigrating to – the Netherlands.

Prime Minister Mark Rutte made a number of proposals that were a sharp break from previous Dutch policies. They weakened environmental regulations, slashed arts and culture funding, and passed what was thought to be a near-death sentence for the country's marijuana-selling *coffeeshops*. The formerly bedrock Dutch commitment to the EU was openly debated.

But by the time an early election was called for September 2012, it seemed that the Dutch political needle was heading back to the middle. Wilders party went from 24 to 15 seats in the Dutch parliament and Rutte's centre-right Liberal party had to break bread with the left-leaning Labour party (led by a former Greenpeace activist) to form a government.

The next Dutch general election, to elect the members of the House of Representatives, will take place no later than 15 March 2017.

In recent times the Netherlands has assisted refugees from war-torn countries such as Syria. Some 17,000 refugees arrived in the country in the first eight months of 2015, and have been sheltered in tent camps and prisons around the country.

Coffeeshops

A cloud has hung over the future of *coffeeshops* in the current decade. In 2011 the Dutch conservative government passed a law that would have banned foreigners from *coffeeshops* and restricted their customers to locals who signed up for a *wietpas* (weed pass). One of the reasons for its passage was the complaints of southern cities such as Maastricht, which felt inundated by 'drug tourists' from neighbouring Belgium and Germany. However, there was general alarm among civil libertarians and indeed a majority of the Dutch public.

In May 2012 Maastricht was one of the first places where the new law was applied. Most of the city's *coffeeshops* closed due to a lack of customers, and drug dealers returned to the streets, offering not just pot but also hard drugs, which caught the police unprepared. Soon Maastricht's mayor announced he no longer supported the new law.

When Prime Minister Mark Rutte had to open talks with the Labour party to form a government, the odds that the law would be rolled out across the country diminished. Polls showed that the Dutch public (barely 7% of whom use pot) largely disliked the law and that the requirement to register to enter the surviving *coffeeshops* was particularly resisted because of privacy concerns.

Currently, *coffeeshops* are conducting business as usual in Amsterdam – not least due to the tax they generate through tourism. Despite the 2014 commencement of the Dutch law dictating that *coffeeshops* must not operate within 250m of primary schools and 350m of secondary schools in Amsterdam, authorities are also against enforcing this, arguing that minors are already forbidden, *coffeeshops* are monitored and that there are more effective ways to combat youth drug use, such as education.

Elsewhere in the country the '*coffeeshop* issue' remains in a state of flux and is being addressed on a council by council basis. Watch this space.

POPULATION: **16.9 MILLION**

AREA: **41,543 SQ KM**

BULB FIELDS: **225 SQ KM**

PER CAPITA GDP: **€48,317**

UNEMPLOYMENT: **7.9% (2015)**

TRADITIONAL WINDMILLS: **1200**

if the Netherlands were 100 people

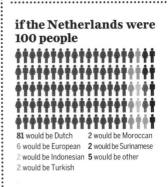

81 would be Dutch **2** would be Moroccan
6 would be European **2** would be Surinamese
2 would be Indonesian **5** would be other
2 would be Turkish

belief systems
(% of population)

47 not religious **26** Catholic
16 Protestant **6** Other **5** Muslim

population per sq km

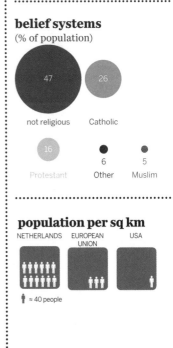

NETHERLANDS EUROPEAN UNION USA

≈ 40 people

History

While the Netherlands seems a peaceful place now, you'd never guess the high drama of its history. Greed, lust and war are prominent in the Dutch story, along with pirates and high-seas adventures. It's the story of land much invaded, whether by armies on land or from the sea. Yet through it all, a society has emerged that has a core belief in human rights, tolerance and, perhaps most surprising given the vicissitudes of its existence, consensus.

Invaders

The first invaders to take note of the locals in today's Netherlands were the Romans, who, under Julius Caesar, conquered a wide region along the Rijn (Rhine) and its tributaries by 59 BC. Celtic and Germanic tribes initially bowed to Caesar's rule and Utrecht became a main outpost of the empire.

As Roman power began to fade, the Franks, a German tribe to the east, began to muscle in. By the end of the 8th century, the Franks had completed their conquest of the Low Countries and began converting the local populace to Christianity, using force whenever necessary. Charlemagne, the first in a long line of Holy Roman emperors, was by far the most successful Frankish king. He built a palace at Nijmegen, but the empire fell apart after his death in 814.

For the next 200 years, Vikings sailed up Dutch rivers to loot and pillage. Local rulers developed their own fortified towns and made up their own government and laws.

Over time, the local lords, who were nominally bound to a German king, began to gain power. When one lord struggled with another for territory, invariably their townsfolk would provide support, but only in return for various freedoms (an equation familiar to any player of sim games today), which were set down in charters. By the beginning of the 12th century, Dutch towns with sea access, such as Deventer and Zwolle, joined the Hanseatic League (a group of powerful trading cities in present-day Germany, including Hamburg and Rostock). Meanwhile, the many little lords met their match in the dukes of Burgundy, who

Early residents of the soggy territory of Friesland built homes on mounds of mud (called *terpen*) to escape the frequent floods.

TIMELINE	3000–2000 BC	59 BC	AD 800
	People living in what is today's Drenthe province bury their dead under monolithic rocks called *hunebedden*. Long before Stonehenge, these people move enormous rocks and create structures.	The Romans extend their empire to what is today the Netherlands. Over the next four centuries, the Romans build advanced towns, farms and the roads that still shape the landscape.	Christianity arrives in the Low Countries by force. It replaces various Celtic belief systems – those who don't convert are killed. Charlemagne builds a church, parts of which survive in Nijmegen.

gradually took over the Low Countries. Duke Philip the Good, who ruled from 1419 to 1467, showed the towns of the Low Countries who was boss by essentially telling them to stuff their charters. Although this limited the towns' freedom, it also brought a degree of stability to the region that had been missing during the era of squabbling lords. The 15th century ushered in great prosperity for the Low Countries, the first of many such periods. The Dutch became adept at shipbuilding in support of the Hanseatic trade, and merchants thrived by selling luxury items such as tapestries, fashionable clothing and paintings, as well as more mundane commodities such as salted herring and beer.

The Dutch National Archive (www.nationaalarchief.nl) has almost a thousand years of historical documents, maps, drawings and photos.

TULIPMANIA

When it comes to investment frenzy, the Dutch tulip craze of 1636 to 1637 ranks alongside the greatest economic booms and busts in history.

Tulips originated as wildflowers in Central Asia and were first cultivated by the Turks, who filled their courts with these beautiful spring blooms ('tulip' derives from the Turkish word for turban). In the mid-1500s, the Habsburg ambassador to Istanbul brought some bulbs back to Vienna, where the imperial botanist, Carolus Clusius, learned how to propagate them. In 1590 Clusius became director of the Hortus Botanicus in Leiden – Europe's oldest botanical garden – and had great success growing and cross-breeding tulips in the cool, damp Dutch climate and fertile delta soil.

The more exotic specimens of tulip featured frilly petals and 'flamed' streaks of colour, which attracted the attention of wealthy merchants, who put them in their living rooms and hallways to impress visitors. Trickle-down wealth and savings stoked the taste for exotica in general, and tulip growers arose to service the demand.

A speculative frenzy ensued, and people paid top florin for the finest bulbs, many of which changed hands time and again before they sprouted. Vast profits were made and speculators fell over themselves to outbid each other.

Of course, this bonanza couldn't last, and when several bulb traders in Haarlem failed to fetch their expected prices in February 1637, the bottom fell out of the market. Within weeks many of the country's wealthiest merchants went bankrupt and many more people of humbler origins lost everything.

However, love of the unusual tulip endured. To this day, the Dutch continue to be the world leaders in tulip cultivation. They also excel in bulbs such as daffodils, hyacinths and crocuses.

So what happened to the flamed, frilly tulips of the past? They're still produced, though have gone out of fashion, and are now known as Rembrandt tulips because of their depiction in so many 17th-century paintings.

For an explosion of modern-day blooms, visit Keukenhof Gardens near Leiden in season. To see wealth in bloom, visit the flower market at Aalsmeer.

1150–1300	1200	1275	1287
Dams are built to retain the IJ River between the Zuiderzee and Haarlem, one of the first efforts in what becomes an ongoing tug of war with the sea.	The age of city states is in full bloom as lords rule in many riverside towns. Trading between the towns is the source of wealth and a powerful inducement against war.	Amsterdam is founded after the Count of Holland grants toll-free status to residents along the Amstel. The city gains its first direct access to the ocean via the Zuiderzee.	The Zuiderzee floods during a storm and upwards of 80,000 die. Except for a few port cities around its periphery, the sea is frequently regarded as a source of trouble.

The Fight for Independence

Philip II of Spain was a staunch Catholic; he'd gained the Low Countries and Spain from his father in 1555 after a period in which control of large swaths of Europe shifted depending on who was marrying who. Conflict with the Low Countries was inevitable; the Protestant reformation had spread throughout the colony, fuelled by the ideas of Erasmus and the actions of Martin Luther. However, before the Spanish arrived, the religious landscape of the Low Countries was quite diverse: Lutherans wielded great influence, but smaller churches had their places too. For instance, the Anabaptists were polygamists and communists, and nudity was promoted as a means of equality among their masses (in the warmer seasons). In the end it was Calvinism that emerged in the Low Countries as the main challenger to the Roman Catholic Church, and to Philip's rule.

In the early 1600s, the Dutch East India Company flooded the local market with cheap porcelain from China. The Dutch responded with what's known today as Delftware. Today, most 'Delftware' is a cheap import from China.

A big believer in the Inquisition, Philip went after the Protestants with a vengeance. Matters came to a head in 1566 when the puritanical Calvinists went on a rampage, destroying art and religious icons of Catholic churches. Evidence of this is still readily apparent in the barren interiors of Dutch churches today.

This sent Philip into action. The duke of Alba was chosen to lead a 10,000-strong army in 1568 to quell the unruly serfs; as the duke wasn't one to take prisoners, his forces slaughtered thousands, and so began the Dutch War of Independence, which lasted 80 years.

The Prince van Oranje, Willem the Silent (thus named for his refusal to argue over religious issues), was one of the few nobles not to side with Philip, and he led the Dutch revolt against Spanish rule. He was hampered by other Dutch nobles content to see which way the political winds blew. In 1572 Willem hired a bunch of English pirates to fight for his cause. Known as the Watergeuzen (Sea Beggars), they sailed up the myriad Dutch rivers and seized towns such as Leiden from the surprised and land-bound Spanish forces.

The *Flying Dutch-man* is a mythical 17th-century ship cursed to sail the seas forever, unable to go home. The story has myriad variations, many embellished by grog-addled seamen.

By 1579, the more Protestant and rebellious provinces in the north formed the Union of Utrecht. This explicitly anti-Spanish alliance became known as the United Provinces, the basis for the Netherlands as we know it today. The southern regions of the Low Countries had always remained Catholic and were much more open to compromise with Spain. They eventually became Belgium.

The battles continued nonetheless until the 1648 Treaty of Westphalia, which included the proviso that Spain recognise the independence of the United Provinces. This ended the Thirty Years' War.

1419	1452	1519	1555–66
The beginning of the end of the powerful city states. The dukes of Burgundy consolidate their power and unify rich trading towns under one geographic empire. Freedom suffers under central rule.	Fire devours wooden Amsterdam. New building laws decree that only brick and tile be used in future. Similar conflagrations in other towns leads to the 'Dutch' look prized today.	Spain's Charles V is crowned Holy Roman Emperor. Treaties and marriages make Amsterdam part of the Catholic Spanish empire. Protestants are tolerated in Holland and the northeast.	In the first major assault on Dutch tolerance, Philip II cracks down on Protestants. Religious wars follow and Calvinists pillage Catholic churches, stripping them of their decor and wealth.

The Golden Age

Throughout the turmoil of the 15th and 16th centuries, merchant cities, particularly Amsterdam, had managed to keep trade alive. Their skill at business and sailing was so great that, even at the peak of the rebellion, the Spanish had no choice but to use Dutch boats for transporting their grain. However, with the arrival of peace the cities began to boom. This era of economic prosperity and cultural fruition came to be known as the Golden Age, which produced artistic and architectural masterpieces still loved today.

The wealth of the merchant class supported numerous artists, including Jan Vermeer, Jan Steen, Frans Hals and Rembrandt. It allowed for excesses such as 'Tulipmania', and the sciences were not forgotten: Dutch physicist and astronomer Christiaan Huygens discovered Saturn's rings and invented the pendulum clock; celebrated philosopher Benedict de Spinoza wrote a brilliant thesis saying that the universe was identical to God; and Frenchman René Descartes, known for his philosophy 'I think, therefore I am', found intellectual freedom in the Netherlands and stayed for two decades.

The Union of Utrecht's promise of religious tolerance led to a surprising amount of religious diversity that was rare in Europe at the time. Calvinism was the official religion of the government, but various other Protestants, Jews and Catholics were allowed to practise their faith. However, in a legacy of the troubles with Spain, Catholics still had to worship in private, leading to the creation of clandestine churches. Many of these unusual buildings have survived to the present day.

Tulipomania: The Story of the World's Most Coveted Flower, by Mike Dash, is an engaging look at the bizarre bulb fever that swept the nation in the 17th century.

Dutch Colonials

Wealth – and the need for more wealth – caused the Dutch to expand their horizons. The merchant fleet known as the Dutch East India Company was formed in 1602 and quickly monopolised key shipping and trade routes east of Africa's Cape of Good Hope and west of the Strait of Magellan, making it the largest trading company of the 17th century. It became almost as powerful as a sovereign state, with the ability to raise its own armed forces and establish colonies.

Its sister, the Dutch West India Company, traded with Africa and the Americas and was at the very centre of the American slave trade. Seamen working for both companies 'discovered' (in a very Western sense of the word) or conquered lands including parts of Australia, New Zealand, Malaysia, Sri Lanka and Mauritius. While employed by the Dutch East India Company, English explorer Henry Hudson landed on the island of Manhattan in 1609 as he searched for the Northwest Passage, and Dutch settlers named it New Amsterdam.

1566–68	1579	1596	1600s
The Low Countries revolt against a lack of religious freedom, launching the Eighty Years' War. In Friesland the rebels win their first battle, immortalised in the Dutch national anthem.	With scores of Dutch towns captured by Calvinist brigands, known as Watergeuzen (Sea Beggars), a Dutch republic made up of seven provinces is declared by Willem the Silent.	A Dutch trade expedition to Indonesia loses half its crew but brings back cargo that's sold for a profit. The Dutch East India Company is formed and the archipelago colonised.	The Golden Age places Amsterdam firmly on the culture map. While Rembrandt paints in his atelier, the grand inner ring of canals is constructed. The city's population surges to 200,000.

CARIBBEAN NETHERLANDS

The Kingdom of the Netherlands shrunk even more with the end of the Netherlands Antilles. Effectively a grab bag of Dutch holdings in the Caribbean, the country came into being in 1954 (as the autonomous successor of the Dutch colony of Curaçao and Dependencies) and islanders always saw themselves as residents of their island first.

Aruba flew the coop first, in 1986, and the Netherlands Antilles was disbanded altogether in 2010. All of the island territories that belonged to the Netherlands Antilles remain part of the Kingdom of the Netherlands today, although the legal status of each island varies. Following the dissolution, Curaçao and Sint Maarten became autonomous countries within the Kingdom, like Aruba, which saves a lot of money on operating embassies, having their own military and the like.

Bonaire, Sint Eustatius and Saba (known as the BES islands) became special municipalities of the Netherlands (nice warm ones popular with Dutch tourists).

Not surprisingly, international conflict was never far away. In 1652 the United Provinces went to war with their old friend England, mainly over the increasing strength of the Dutch merchant fleet. Both countries entered a hotchpotch of alliances with Spain, France and Sweden in an effort to gain the upper hand. During one round of treaties, the Dutch agreed to give New Amsterdam to the English (who promptly renamed it New York) in return for Surinam in South America and full control of the Spice Islands in Indonesia.

This outward perspective coupled with the rich lives being enjoyed by the moneyed class at home caused a certain loss of focus. In 1672 the French army marched into the Netherlands and, as the Dutch had devoted most of their resources to the navy, found little resistance on land. During the decades of conflicts that followed, the Dutch could no longer afford their navy and foreign adventures. The English became the masters of the trade routes and keepers of the resulting wealth.

The Dutch managed to hold onto the Dutch East Indies (today's Indonesia) along with a smattering of spots in the Caribbean. The effectiveness of their rule in the East Indies ebbed and flowed depending on the situation at home. They never approached the intensive colonialism practised by the British. (In Indonesia today it takes real effort to find traces of the Dutch rule or its legacy in most of the country.)

The Dutch East Indies declared itself independent in 1945, and after four years of bitter fighting and negotiations, the independence of Indonesia was recognised at the end of 1949. Surinam also became independent in 1975. In the Caribbean, the Netherlands Antilles disbanded in 2010 but none of the islands severed ties completely.

The official website of the Dutch royal family (www.koninklijkhuis.nl) features minibiographies and virtual tours of the palaces, as well as news.

1602	1620	1650s	1795
Amsterdam becomes the site of the world's first stock exchange when the offices of the Dutch East India Company trade their own shares. Insider trading laws don't yet exist.	The pilgrims arrive in the New World aboard the leaky *Mayflower*, a voyage that began with many fits and starts in the Dutch city of Leiden.	Big mistake: the Dutch infamously trade away the colony of New Amsterdam (now New York) to the British.	French troops install the Batavian Republic, named after the Batavi tribe that rebelled against Roman rule. The fragmented United Provinces become a centralised state, with Amsterdam as its capital.

The Foundation of Today's Netherlands

Wars with France proved the undoing of the Dutch in the 18th century. Shifting allegiances among the Dutch, English, Spanish and various German states did their best to keep the French contained. It was costly and the ties that bound the United Provinces together unravelled, beginning a spiral downwards. The population shrank due to falling fortunes and the dykes fell into a sorry state – there was little money to repair them, and widespread floods swept across the country. The Golden Age was long since over.

Politically, the United Provinces were as unstable as the dykes. A series of struggles between the House of Oranje and its democratic opponents led to a civil war in 1785. The situation reached a nadir when Napoleon renamed it the Kingdom of Holland and installed his brother, Louis Bonaparte, as king in 1806. Fortunately Napoleon's failed Russian invasion allowed the Dutch to establish a monarchy. Prince Willem VI landed at Scheveningen in 1813 and was named prince sovereign of the Netherlands; the following year he was crowned King Willem I, beginning a monarchy that continues to this day.

The Kingdom of the Netherlands – the Netherlands in the north and Belgium in the south – was formed in 1815. However, the marriage was doomed from the start. The partners had little in common, including their dominant religions (Calvinist and Catholic), languages (Dutch and

The Dutch 'bought' (a concept foreign to North American tribes at the time) the island of Manhattan from the Lenape in 1626 for the equivalent of US$24 worth of beads.

THE DUTCH ROYALS

In power now for 200 years, the House of Orange has roots back to the 16th century. Unlike a certain royal family to the west across the Channel, the Dutch royals have proved to be of limited value to tabloid publishers or others hoping to profit from their exploits. The most notable was Queen Wilhelmina, who took a page from Britain's Queen Victoria and approached her job as if she were a general. Although some faulted her for fleeing the Germans in WWII, she ended up winning praise for her stalwart support of her people. During the postwar years, the family were a mostly low-key and benign presence (they have no substantive power within the Dutch government) with the exception of Prince Bernhard, who was caught up in a bribery scandal in the 1970s with the US defence firm Lockheed. Queen Beatrix (born 1938) abdicated in 2013 in favour of her son, ending more than a century of female reign. King Willem-Alexander, father of three daughters, took the throne with his wife, Máxima Zorreguieta, a former banker he met at a party in Spain. Although her father's role in Argentine's Videla government raised a few eyebrows, Máxima has won praise for her work on immigrant issues and support of gay rights. Despite being ranked among Europe's wealthiest royals, the family is considered by many as fairly modest. Beatrix was known for riding her bike in Den Haag. The one day the Dutch think of the House of Orange is on Koningsdag (King's Day).

1813–14	1830	1865–76	1914–20
The French are overthrown, and Willem VI of Orange is crowned as Dutch King Willem I. The Protestant north and Catholic south combine as the United Kingdom of the Netherlands.	With help from the French, the southern provinces secede to form the Kingdom of Belgium. The remaining northern provinces form what continues to be the Netherlands of today.	A period of rapid economic and social change. The North Sea Canal is dug, the Dutch railway system expanded and socialist principles of government are established.	The Netherlands remains neutral in WWI while trading with both sides. Food shortages cripple the country, leading to strikes, unrest and growing support for the Dutch Communist Party.

Jewish Historic Sites

Anne Frank Huis, Amsterdam

Joods Historisch Museum, Amsterdam

Kamp Westerbork, near Groningen

French) and favoured way of making money (trade and manufacturing). Matters weren't helped by Willem, who generally sided with his fellow northerners.

In 1830 the southern states revolted, and nine years later Willem was forced to let the south go. In a nice historical twist, Willem abdicated one year later so that he could marry – surprise! – a Belgian Catholic. It's not known if he ever spoke French at home.

His son, King Willem II, granted a new and more liberal constitution to the people of the Netherlands in 1848. This included a number of democratic ideals and even made the monarchy the servant of the elected government. This document remains the foundation of the Dutch government in the present day. Its role on the world stage long over, the

DUTCH JEWS

The tale of Jews in Europe is often one of repression, persecution and division. In the Netherlands, it is more a tale of acceptance and prosperity, until the coming of the Nazis.

Amsterdam is the focus of Jewish history in the Netherlands, and Jews played a key role in the city's development over the centuries. The first documented evidence of Jewish presence in the city dates back to the 12th century, but numbers began to swell with the expulsion of Sephardic Jews from Spain and Portugal in the 1580s.

As was the case in much of Europe, guilds barred the newcomers from most trades. Some of the Sephardim were diamond cutters, however, for whom there was no guild. The majority eked out a living as labourers and small-time traders on the margins of society. Still, they weren't confined to a ghetto and, with some restrictions, could buy property and exercise their religion – freedoms unheard of elsewhere in Europe.

The 17th century saw another influx of Jewish refugees, this time Ashkenazim fleeing pogroms in Central and Eastern Europe. The two groups didn't always get on well and separate synagogues were established, helping Amsterdam to become one of Europe's major Jewish centres.

The guilds and all restrictions on Jews were abolished during the French occupation, and the Jewish community thrived in the 19th century. Poverty was still considerable, but the economic, social and political emancipation of the Jews helped their middle class move up in society.

All this came to an end with the German occupation of the Netherlands. The Nazis brought about the almost-complete annihilation of the Dutch Jewish community. Before WWII, the Netherlands counted 140,000 Jews, of whom about two-thirds lived in Amsterdam. Fewer than 25,000 survived the war, and Amsterdam's Jewish quarter was left a ghost town. Many homes stood derelict until their demolition in the 1970s, and only a handful of synagogues throughout the country are once again operating as houses of worship.

Estimates put the current Jewish population of the Netherlands at around 50,000, with the largest community living in Amsterdam.

1919	1932	1939	1940
KLM takes to the skies, with a flight from London to Amsterdam. The airline eventually becomes the world's oldest, still flying under its original name.	After centuries of schemes, dyke-building and floods, the Zuiderzee reclamation begins, spurred on by a deadly 1916 storm surge. The completion of the mammoth Afsluitdijk begins the land-reclamation process.	The Dutch government establishes Westerbork as an internment camp to house Jewish refugees. The Nazis later use it as a transit point for 107,000 Jews being sent to death camps.	Germany invades the Netherlands. Rotterdam is destroyed by the Luftwaffe, but Amsterdam suffers only minor damage before capitulating. Queen Wilhemina sets up a Dutch exile government in London.

Netherlands played only a small part in European affairs and concentrated on liberalism at home. It stayed out of WWI, but profited by trading with both sides.

In the 1920s the growing affluence of the middle class fuelled a desire for more liberalism. The Netherlands embarked on innovative social programs that targeted poverty, the rights of women and children, and education. Rotterdam became one of Europe's most important ports and the massive scheme to reclaim the Zuiderzee was launched in 1932.

WWII

The Dutch tried to remain neutral during WWII, but in May 1940 the Germans invaded. The advancing Nazis levelled much of central Rotterdam in a raid designed to force the Dutch to surrender. They obliged.

Queen Wilhelmina issued a proclamation of 'flaming protest' to the nation and escaped with her family to England. The plucky monarch, who had been key in maintaining Dutch neutrality in WWI, now found herself in a much different situation and made encouraging broadcasts to her subjects back home via the BBC and Radio Orange. The Germans put Dutch industry and farms to work for war purposes and there was much deprivation. Dutch resistance was primarily passive and only gained any kind of momentum when thousands of Dutch men were taken to Germany and forced to work in Nazi factories. A far worse fate awaited the country's Jews.

The 'Winter of Hunger' of 1944–45 was a desperate time in the Netherlands. The British-led Operation Market Garden (p233) had been a huge disaster and the Allies abandoned all efforts to liberate the Dutch. The Germans stripped the country of much of its food and resources, and mass starvation ensued. Many people were reduced to eating tulip bulbs for subsistence. Canadian troops finally liberated the country in May 1945.

After the war, the Netherlands was shattered both economically and spiritually. War trials ensued in which 66,000 were convicted of collaborating with the Nazis (with 900 receiving the death penalty). Yet the number of collaborators was much higher and scores – such as the party or parties who ratted out Anne Frank and her family – never saw justice. In contrast, many Dutch people risked everything to help Jews during the war.

Prosperity & Stability

The Dutch set about getting their house in order after the material and mental privations of WWII. During the 1950s a prosperous country began to reemerge. After disastrous flooding in Zeeland and the south in 1953, a four-decades-long campaign began to literally reshape the land and keep the sea forever at bay.

Hans Brinker, who supposedly put his finger in a dyke and saved the Netherlands from a flood, is an American invention and unknown in the Netherlands. He starred in a 19th-century children's book.

WWII Museums

War & Resistance Museum, Rotterdam

Airborne Museum Hartenstein, near Arnhem

National Liberation Museum 1944–45, Groesbeek

1944–45	1946	1958	1960s
The Allies liberate the southern Netherlands, but the north and west are cut off from supplies. The British Operation Market Garden fails and thousands perish in the 'Winter of Hunger'.	The UN-chartered International Court of Justice sets up shop in Den Haag, ensuring that the seat of Dutch government will grace the world's headlines for decades to come.	The Delta Project is launched following the great floods of Zeeland in 1953 which cause widespread destruction and death. Vast construction projects continue for four decades.	Social upheaval leads to the creation of the Provos, a provocative underground countercultural movement. Squatting in empty buildings is widespread. Conservative Dutch culture is challenged.

King Willem-Alexander and his wife Queen Máxima have three daughters: Princess Catharina-Amalia (the Princess of Orange), Princess Alexia and Princess Ariane.

The same social upheavals that swept the world in the 1960s were also felt in the Netherlands. Students, labour groups, hippies and more took to the streets in protest. Among the more colourful were a group that came to be known as the Provos. Amsterdam became the *magisch centrum* (magic centre) of Europe. Hippies flocked to Amsterdam during the 1960s and '70s, a housing shortage saw speculators leaving buildings empty and squatting became widespread. The Dutch authorities turned Vondelpark into a temporary open-air dormitory.

Tolerance towards drug use and gay rights also emerged at the time. The country's drug policy grew out of practical considerations, when Amsterdam's flower-power-era influx made the policing of drug laws impracticable. Official government policy became supportive of same-sex relationships and in 2001, the Netherlands became the first country in the world to introduce marriage equality.

Economically the Netherlands prospered more with each passing decade, allowing a largely drama-free middle-class society to be the norm by the late 1980s.

All governments since 1945 have been coalitions, with parties mainly differing over economic policies. However, coalitions shift constantly based on the political climate, and in recent years there have been winds of change. Tension between different political colours and creeds had never been a problem in the Netherlands, until the murders of Theo van Gogh and Pim Fortuyn stirred emotions and struck fear into the hearts of some.

The leading political parties in the Netherlands responded with a shift to the right. In 2006 the government passed a controversial immigration law requiring newcomers to have competency in Dutch language and culture before they could get a residency permit. However, despite some carping from the sidelines, the Netherlands continued its staunch support of the EU, a role that goes back to the earliest days of the EU-predecessor organisations.

John Lennon and Yoko Ono took to bed at the Amsterdam Hilton for a week in 1969 and invited the world's press to join them. Rather than salacious entertainment, however, they offered bromides about world peace.

The Legacy of Theo & Pim

If the 2004 assassination of Theo van Gogh rocked the Netherlands, it was the assassination of Pim Fortuyn two years earlier that gave the initial push.

The political career of Fortuyn (pronounced fore-town) lasted a mere five months, yet his impact on the Netherlands has proved indelible. His campaign for parliament in 2002 is best remembered for his speeches on immigration: particularly that the Netherlands was 'full' and that immigrants should not be allowed to stay without learning the language or integrating.

1980	1999	2001	2002
The investiture of Queen Beatrix is disrupted by a smoke bomb and riot on the Dam. The term 'proletarian shopping' (ie looting) enters the national lexicon as riotous behaviour becomes widespread.	*Big Brother* premieres on Dutch TV and the concept is soon licensed to television networks worldwide. It starts off the modern-day mania for reality TV shows.	Same-sex marriage is legalised in the Netherlands, the first country in the world to do so. In the next few years Belgium, Spain, Canada and South Africa follow suit.	Leading politician Pim Fortuyn, a hardliner on immigration and integration, is assassinated. The ruling Dutch parties shift to the right after suffering major losses in the national election.

THE PROVOCATIVE PROVOS

The 1960s were a breeding ground for discontent and anti-establishment activity, and in the Netherlands this underground movement led to the formation of the Provos. This small group of anarchic individuals staged street 'happenings' or creative, playful provocations (hence the name) around the Lieverdje (Little Darling) on Amsterdam's Spui.

In 1962 an Amsterdam window cleaner and self-professed sorcerer, Robert Jasper Grootveld, began to deface cigarette billboards with a huge letter 'K' for *kanker* (cancer) to expose the role of advertising in addictive consumerism. Dressed as a medicine man, he held get-togethers in his garage and chanted mantras against cigarette smoking (all under the influence of pot). The movement grew.

The group gained international notoriety in March 1966 with its protests at the marriage of Princess (later Queen) Beatrix to German Claus von Amsberg. Protestors jeered the wedding couple as their procession rolled through Amsterdam.

In the same year the Provos gained enough support to win a seat on Amsterdam's city council. Environmental schemes and social schemes (such as giving everyone a free bike) proved unwieldy and the movement dissolved in the 1970s as some of its liberal policies became entrenched.

Just days before the general election in May 2002, Fortuyn was assassinated by an animal-rights activist in Hilversum, some 20km from Amsterdam. Fortuyn's political party, the Lijst Pim Fortuyn (LPF), had a number of members elected to parliament and was included in the next coalition, but without the figurehead Fortuyn it faded away by 2007.

Enter Theo van Gogh, a film-maker and provocateur who made a short film claiming that Koranic verses could be interpreted as justifying violence against women. The film was a collaboration with Ayaan Hirsi Ali, a Muslim-born woman who had emigrated from Somalia to escape an arranged marriage and eventually became a member of parliament.

The film aired on Dutch TV in 2004, and Van Gogh was killed as he was cycling down an Amsterdam street. A letter threatening the nation, politicians, and Hirsi Ali in particular, was impaled on a knife stuck in Van Gogh's chest. The killing was all the more shocking to locals because the 27-year-old killer, of Moroccan descent, was born and raised in Amsterdam. He proclaimed that he was acting in defence of Islam and would do the same thing again if given the chance (he was sentenced to life imprisonment). Hirsi Ali moved to the US and became a popular figure with American conservatives.

Meanwhile, politicians on the far right such as Geert Wilders have tried to trade on the legacy of Pim and Theo by stoking anti-Islamic feelings.

The largest postwar political party in the Netherlands was the Christian Democratic Union (CDA). Nominally centre-right, it had a historic streak of pragmatism that served it well until 2010, when voters moved to other centrist parties.

2004	2009	2010	2013
Activist film-maker Theo van Gogh, a critic of Islam, is assassinated, sparking debate over the limits of Dutch multiculturalism and the need for immigrants to adopt Dutch values.	Amsterdam courts prosecute Dutch parliamentary leader Geert Wilders for 'incitement to hatred and discrimination'. (He is acquitted of all charges in 2011.)	Members of the Dutch government officially apologise to the Jewish community for failing to protect the Jewish population from genocide.	After a 33-year reign, Queen Beatrix abdicates in favour of her eldest son, Willem-Alexander, who becomes the Netherlands' first king in 123 years.

The Dutch Way of Life

The Netherlands has traditionally been a nation of entrepreneurs: avid seafaring explorers; traders; ambitious engineers working to waterproof the country by building canals, *polders* (areas of drained land) and dykes; artists, architects and designers; and a more recent start-up culture that is an increasingly key part of propelling the economy. But it's not all work, no play – the open-minded, free-spirited Dutch value conversation, camaraderie, socialising and getting out and about, more often than not by bike.

Tolerance

The Dutch flair for engineering extends to social engineering. The nation invented *verzuiling* (pillarisation), a social order in which each religion and political persuasion achieved the right to do its own thing, with its own institutions. This meant not only more churches, but also separate radio stations, newspapers, unions, political parties, sport clubs and so on. The idea got a bit out of hand with pillarised bakeries, but it did promote social harmony by giving everyone a voice.

While the pillars are less distinct today, they left a legacy of tolerance – a pivotal part of the Dutch psyche that's also good for business, including tourism and trade. They also fostered the easy intimacy of *gezelligheid* (cosiness, conviviality). The Dutch are irrepressibly voluble. Sit alone in a pub and you'll soon have a few merry friends. Don't be taken aback if the Dutch seem stunningly blunt – the impulse comes from the desire to be direct and honest.

Perhaps no household item represents Dutch thrift better than the popular *flessenlikker* (bottle-scraper). This miracle tool has a disk on the business end and can scrape the last elusive smears from a mayonnaise jar or salad-dressing bottle.

Dutch Lifestyle

Many Dutch live independent, busy lives, divided into strict schedules. Notice is usually required for everything, including visits to your mother, and it's not done to just 'pop round' anywhere.

Most Dutch families are small, with two or three children. Social housing is prevalent: some 54% of Dutch households live in rented accommodation, but only 13% rent from private landlords. Rent for private rental-market properties is high and demand outstrips supply, so Junior might live with his or her family well into their 20s, or share an apartment.

Dutch citizens earn an average monthly wage of €2158 – more per capita than Germany. Consumer spending is healthy, especially for travel to warm climates.

HEAD & SHOULDERS ABOVE THE REST

The Dutch are the tallest people in the world, averaging 1.81m (5ft, 11in) for men and 1.68m (5ft, 6in) for women, according to Statistics Netherlands. Copious intake of milk proteins, smaller families and superior prenatal care are cited as likely causes, but researchers also suspect there is some magic fertiliser in the Dutch gene pool. Whatever the reason, the Dutch keep growing, as do their doorways. Today, the minimum required height for doors in new homes and businesses is 2.315m (7ft, 6in).

BORREL

Borrel in Dutch means, quite simply, 'drink' – as in a glass of spirits, traditionally *jenever* (Dutch gin). But in social parlance, to be invited to *borrel* means to take part in an informal gathering for drinks, conversation and fun. It usually incorporates food too, especially *borrelhapjes* (bar snacks) such as *borrelnootjes* (peanuts covered in a crisp, spicy outer shell), and *kroketten* (croquettes) including *bitterballen* (small, round meat croquettes) – the name comes from the tradition of serving them with bitters, namely *jenever*.

Any occasion can be a reason for *borrel*: a birthday, a beautiful sunset that invites patio sitting, the end of a work day (*vrijdagmiddagborrel*, usually shortened to *vrijmibo* or just *vrimibo* is specifically Friday afternoon work drinks with colleagues). When you see a group of locals spilling out of a brown *café* (traditional drinking establishment) onto the street with a glass of beer in hand? That's *borrel*. The famously open Dutch rarely mind an addition to the party.

By the Numbers

The Dutch have a great love of detail. Statistics on the most trivial subjects make the news (the number of pigeons on the Dam each year; the incidence of rubbish being put out early), and somewhere down the line this feeds mountains of bureaucracy.

The Dutch are famously thrifty (which is not to say cheap). It's ironic, then, that according to statistics agency Eurostat, Dutch household debt is 250% of disposable income, primarily due to liberal mortgage practices in the lead-up to the 2008 global financial crisis.

An increasing number of Dutch deaths each year result from euthanasia (some 4829 deaths in 2014). The practice is tightly controlled and is administered by doctors at the request of patients.

Sex & Drugs

On sex and drugs, the ever-practical Dutch argue that vice is not going to go away, so you might as well control it. Sex is discussed openly but promiscuity is the last thing on Dutch minds. Only about 5% of customers frequenting the red-light district are Dutch.

By the same token, marijuana and hashish remain tolerated, despite efforts to clamp down, particularly outside Amsterdam. Yet only a fraction of the population partakes: studies show that only 7% of Dutch people had used any form of marijuana in the previous year, less than the average for Europe (7.8%), America (11.5%) and Australia (14%), where enforcement is much stricter. Harder drugs such as heroin, LSD, cocaine and ecstasy are outlawed, and dealers are prosecuted.

Gay & Lesbian Rights

Gay and lesbian locals, expats and visitors enjoy considerable freedom and respect among people of all ages. Discrimination on the basis of sexual orientation is not only illegal, but morally unacceptable. The police advertise in the gay media for applicants and the armed forces have an equal-footing policy. Most significantly, in 2001 the Netherlands became the first country in the world to legalise same-sex marriage, although this is a privilege reserved for local couples.

Population

The need to love thy neighbour is especially strong in the Netherlands, where the population density is the highest in Europe (477 per square kilometre). Nearly half of the country's 16.9 million residents live in the western hoop around Amsterdam, Den Haag and Rotterdam; the provinces of Drenthe, Overijssel and Zeeland in the southwest are sparsely settled, in Dutch terms at least.

More than 80% of the population are of Dutch stock; the rest is mainly made up of people from the former colonies of Indonesia, Surinam and

Traditional Dutch toilets come with a shelf where deposited goods sit until swept away by a flush of water. The reason is tied to health and the supposed benefit of carefully studying what comes out. Not, as some wags say, because the Dutch can't bear to see anything underwater.

the former Netherlands Antilles, plus more recent arrivals from Turkey, Morocco and countries throughout Africa.

Religion

The wonderful Dutch verb *uitwaaien* (out-vwy-ehn) has no direct English translation, but essentially means 'to clear one's head by taking a walk outside in the windy fresh air'.

For centuries, religious preference was split between the two heavyweights of Western society, Catholicism and Protestantism, and if you were Dutch you were one or the other. Today, 51% of the population over the age of 18 claims to have no religious affiliation, and the number of former churches that house offices, art galleries and shops is evidence of today's attitudes.

And faith is falling: 25% of the population follows Catholicism and 15% Protestantism, figures that decrease yearly. Vestiges exist of a religious border between Protestants and Catholics; the area north of a line running roughly from the province of Zeeland in the southwest to the province of Drenthe is home to the majority of Protestants, while anywhere to the south is predominantly Catholic.

The church has little or no influence on societal matters such as same-sex marriage, euthanasia and prescription of cannabis for medical purposes, all of which are legal in the Netherlands.

The latest religion to have any great impact on Dutch society is Islam. Today, nearly 6% of the population classes itself as Muslim and the number is steadily increasing, especially in multicultural Rotterdam.

Multiculturalism

The Netherlands has a long history of tolerance towards immigration and a reputation for welcoming immigrants with open arms. The largest wave of immigration occurred in the 1960s, when the government recruited migrant workers from Turkey and Morocco to bridge a labour gap. In the mid-1970s, the granting of independence to the Dutch colony of Surinam in South America saw an influx of Surinamese.

In the past few years, however, the country's loose immigration policy has been called into question. Politically, there has been a significant swing to the right and consequently a move towards shutting the door on immigration. The assassinations of Pim Fortuyn and Theo van Gogh (p263) caused tensions to rise between the Dutch and Muslim immigrants, which also gave rise to far-right anti-Islam politicians such as Geert Wilders. However, when the former queen, Beatrix, wore a head scarf on a visit to a mosque in Oman and Wilders tried to make an issue out of it, she received overwhelming support from the population.

Golden Age canal houses are typically tall and slender because property used to be taxed on frontage. So the narrower the facade, the less tax was incurred. This also gave rise to the houses' precariously steep, ladderlike *trap* (stairs) that are less than a footstep wide.

Still there is concern about immigrants not becoming 'Dutch'. Strongly urging people to take classes in the Dutch language and culture, where concepts such as tolerance are emphasised, is official government policy. How the paradoxical concept of forcing people to learn to be tolerant will play out remains to be seen.

Sport

The Netherlands is one active country. Some 65% of all Dutch engage in some form of sporty activity, and the average person now spends 20 minutes longer getting sweaty each week than in the 1970s. Sport is organised to a fault: about five million people belong to nearly 30,000 clubs and associations in the Netherlands.

Football (soccer), cycling and skating are the favourites.

Football

Football is the Dutch national game. The country's football team competes in virtually every Euro Cup and World Cup (in 2010, their first trip to the final since 1978, they lost a heartbreaker in overtime to Spain; 2014 saw them beat host country Brazil to place third). 'Local' teams such as Ajax,

Feyenoord and PSV enjoy international renown. The country has produced world-class players, such as Ruud Gullit, Dennis Bergkamp and the legendary Johan Cruyff. The unique Dutch approach to the game – known as Total Football (in which spatial tactics are analysed and carried out with meticulous precision) – fascinated viewers at its peak in the 1970s.

Passion for football runs very high. The national football association counts a million members, and every weekend professional and amateur teams hit pitches across the country. Many pro clubs play in modern, high-tech stadiums, such as Amsterdam ArenA, assisted by a modern, high-tech police force to counteract hooligans.

Cycling

It takes spending all of five minutes in the Netherlands to realise that locals cycle everywhere. Literally everywhere. They bike to the dentist, to work, to the opera and to brunch; they bike in snow, rain, sunshine and fog. Dressing up to bike to dinner and a show, or to drinks and a club, is a typical Dutch activity. Pedal away: no matter what you wear or where you're going, you'll blend in (and have fun).

In sporting terms there's extensive coverage of races in the media, and you'll often see uniformed teams on practice runs. Joop Zoetemelk pedalled to victory in the 1980 Tour de France after finishing second six times.

Leontien van Moorsel is one of the best Dutch athletes ever. She won scores of cycling championships in the 1990s. At the 2000 and 2004 Olympics she won a combined total of four golds, one silver and one bronze. At the 2012 Olympics, Marianne Vos won the gold for the women's road race.

The biggest Dutch cycling race is the Amstel Gold Race around hilly Limburg in mid-April. It's about 260km in length and features dozens of steep hills. It is considered one of the most demanding races on the professional circuit.

Skating

Thousands of Dutch people take to the ice when the country's lakes and ditches freeze over. When the lakes aren't frozen, the Netherlands has dozens of ice rinks with Olympic-sized tracks and areas for hockey and figure skating. The most famous amateur event is Friesland's 200km-long Elfstedentocht.

The Dutch perform exceptionally well in speed skating. At the 2014 Winter Olympics, all of the country's record-breaking 24 medals, made up of eight gold, seven silver and nine bronze, were won on the ice. The Netherlands became the first country to achieve four podium sweeps at a single Winter Olympics.

DOUBLE DUTCH

For better or for worse, the Dutch have maintained close ties with the English for centuries, and this intimate relationship has led to a menagerie of 'Dutch' catchphrases in the English language. Here are some of the more well known.

➡ Double Dutch – nonsense or complete gibberish; a jump-rope game using two skipping ropes. 'Going double Dutch' refers to using two types of contraceptive at the same time.

➡ Dutch courage – strength or confidence gained from drinking alcohol.

➡ Dutch oven – large, thick-walled cooking pot with a tight-fitting lid; the act of breaking wind in bed, then trapping your partner – and the stench – under the covers.

➡ Dutch uncle – a person who sternly gives (often benevolent) advice.

➡ Dutch wife – pillow or frame used for resting the legs on in bed; a prostitute or sex doll.

➡ Going Dutch – splitting the bill at a restaurant. Also known as Dutch date or Dutch treat.

➡ Pass the dutchie – not a phrase as such, but the title of a top-10 hit by Musical Youth in 1982. 'Dutchie' refers to an aluminium cooking pot supposedly manufactured in the Netherlands and used throughout the West Indies.

Swimming

An estimated one-third of all Dutch swim in the pools, lakes or sea, and fancy aquatic complexes have sprung up in many cities to meet demand.

Legendary Dutch swimmer Inge de Bruijn won a total of eight medals (four gold) at the 2000 and 2004 Olympics. In 2008 the Dutch women's water-polo team sunk all competition and took the gold. In 2012 Ranomi Kromowidjojo won two gold medals for the women's 50m and 100m freestyle.

Dutch Design

The Dutch aren't just whizzes at engineering and sport, they also have a keen eye for aesthetics. Contemporary Dutch design has a reputation for minimalist, creative approaches to everyday furniture and homewares products, mixed with vintage twists and tongue-in-cheek humour to keep it fresh. Since the 1990s, what started out as a few innovators has accelerated to become a movement that is putting the Netherlands at the forefront of the industry. Dutch fashion is also reaching far beyond the country's borders, with designs that are vibrant and imaginative, yet practical too.

Providing a key platform to the Dutch design movement was Amsterdam-based Droog, established in 1993. This design collective with signature surreal wit works with a community of designers to help them produce their works and sell them to the world, with the partners to make it happen and the connections to facilitate collaborations with big brands.

Among the contemporary pioneers was Marcel Wanders, who first drew international acclaim for his iconic *Knotted Chair,* produced by Droog in 1996. Made from a knotted aramid and carbon-fibre thread and resin, Wanders' air-drying technique meant it was ultimately shaped by gravity. It's now in the permanent collection of the Museum of Modern Art in New York. In 2001 Wanders founded Moooi (the name is a play on the Dutch word for 'beautiful', with an additional 'o' symbolising extra beauty and uniqueness), now a world-leading design label.

Other revolutionary designers include Jurgen Bey, who has strong architectural links, working with interior and public-space design; Hella Jongerius, whose designs include porcelain plates and tiles using new printing techniques; Piet Hein Eek's works with reclaimed wood; Scholten & Baijings (Stefan Scholten and Carole Baijings), producing colourful textiles and kitchenware; and Ineke Hans, whose celebrated recyclable plastic *Ahrend 380* chair incorporates a table. Furniture-, product- and interior-designer Richard Hutten is famed for his 'no sign of design' humorous, functional furniture; his works have been exhibited worldwide and are held in the permanent collections of museums including Amsterdam's Stedelijk Museum.

Eindhoven is an incubator of Dutch design. The Dutch Design Academy is in the ex-Philips lamp factory and Dutch Design Week is held in October at Strijp-S, the former Philips industrial complex.

Dutch Design Online

Dezeen (www. dezeen.com/tag/ netherlands) Dutch architecture, interiors and design.

Het Nieuwe Instituut (http://het nieuweinstituut.nl) Architecture, Dutch design, fashion and e-culture.

Fashion Council NL (http:// fashioncouncilnl. com) Design and fashion events Netherlands-wide.

ORANGE FEVER

If you've ever attended a sporting event where the Dutch are playing, you'll already be familiar with *oranjegekte* (orange craze), also known as *oranjekoorts* (orange fever). The custom of wearing the traditional colour of the Dutch royal family, the House of Orange-Nassau, was originally limited to celebration days for the monarchy, such as Queen's Day *(Koninginnedag)*, now King's Day *(Koningsdag)*. But particularly since the 1974 football World Cup, when tens of thousands of orange-clad football supporters cheered on every game, the ritual of wearing outlandish orange get-ups – clothes, scarves, wigs, fake-fur top hats, face paint, feather boas, you name it – has become a Dutch phenomenon. To really celebrate like a local, you know what colour to wear.

Dutch Art

They don't call them the Dutch Masters for nothing. Rembrandt, Frans Hals and Jan Vermeer – these iconic artists are some of world's most revered and celebrated painters. And then, of course, there's Vincent van Gogh, the rock star of Impressionism who toiled in ignominy while supported by his loving brother, Theo; and 20th-century artists including De Stijl proponent Piet Mondrian, and graphic genius MC Escher. Understanding these quintessential Dutch painters requires a journey into history.

15th & 16th Century

Flemish School

Prior to the late 16th century, when Belgium was still part of the Low Countries, art focused on the Flemish cities of Ghent, Bruges and Antwerp. Paintings of the Flemish School featured biblical and allegorical subject matter popular with the Church, the court and to a lesser extent the nobility, who, after all, paid the bills and called the shots.

Among the most famous names of the era are Jan van Eyck (1390–1441), the founder of the Flemish School, and the first to perfect the technique of oil painting; Rogier van der Weyden (1400–64), whose religious portraits showed the personalities of his subjects; and Pieter Bruegel the Elder (1525–69), who used Flemish landscapes and peasant life in his allegorical scenes.

Born born Jheronimus van Aken, Hieronymus Bosch (c 1450–1516), a namesake of the city of Den Bosch, created works for the ages with his macabre allegorical paintings full of religious topics. *The Prodigal Son,* which hangs in Rotterdam's Museum Boijmans Van Beuningen, is a study in motion and wit.

Dutch School

In the northern Low Countries, artists began to develop a style of their own. Although the artists of the day never achieved the level of recognition of their Flemish counterparts, the Dutch School, as it came to be called, was known for favouring realism over allegory. Haarlem was the centre of this movement, with artists such as Jan Mostaert (1475–1555), Lucas van Leyden (1494–1533) and Jan van Scorel (1495–1562). Painters in the city of Utrecht were famous for using chiaroscuro (deep contrast of light and shade), a technique associated with the Italian master Caravaggio.

17th Century (Golden Age)

When the Spanish were expelled from the Low Countries, the character of the art market changed. There was no longer the Church to buy artworks – most of its art had been burned by rampaging Calvinists in 1566 during the *Beeldenstorm* (statue storm) – and no court to speak of, so art became a business. Fortunately the wealth pouring into the Dutch economy meant artists could survive in a free market. In place of Church and court emerged a new, bourgeois society of merchants, artisans and shopkeepers who didn't mind spending money to brighten

One-Artist Museums
....
Vermeer Centrum Delft, Delft
....
Jheronimus Bosch Art Center, Den Bosch
....
Museum Het Rembrandthuis, Amsterdam
....
Frans Hals Museum, Haarlem
....
Mondriaanhuis, Amersfoort
....
Escher in het Paleis, Den Haag

If you like Dutch classical music, start with pianist Ronald Brautigam, who has international acclaim. Violinist-violist Isabelle van Keulen has her own Tango Nuevo quartet, the Isabelle van Keulen Ensemble. The country's leading cellist is Pieter Wispelwey, known for his challenging repertoire, while Louis Andriessen is a leading composer.

up their houses and workplaces. The key: they had to produce pictures the buyers could relate to.

Painters became entrepreneurs in their own right, churning out banal works, copies and masterpieces in factory-like studios. Paintings were mass-produced and sold at markets alongside furniture and chickens. Soon the wealthiest households were covered in paintings from top to bottom. Foreign visitors commented that even bakeries and butcher shops seemed to have a painting or two on the wall. Most painters specialised in one of the main genres of the day.

Rembrandt van Rijn

The 17th century's greatest artist, Rembrandt van Rijn (1606–69) grew up a miller's son in Leiden, but had become an accomplished painter by his early 20s.

In 1631 he came to Amsterdam to run the painting studio of wealthy art-dealer Hendrick van Uylenburgh. Portraits were the studio's cash cow, and Rembrandt and his staff (or 'pupils') churned out scores of them, including group portraits such as *The Anatomy Lesson of Dr Nicolaes Tulp*. In 1634 he married Van Uylenburgh's niece Saskia, who had travelled to Amsterdam with the Mennonite painters Govert Flinck and Jacob Backer, and often modelled for him.

Rembrandt fell out with his boss, but his wife's capital helped him buy the sumptuous house next door to Van Uylenburgh's studio (the current Museum Het Rembrandthuis). There Rembrandt set up his own studio, with staff who worked in a warehouse in the Jordaan. These were happy years: his paintings were a success and his studio became the largest in the country, though his gruff manner and open agnosticism didn't win him dinner-party invitations from the elite.

Rembrandt became one of the city's biggest art collectors. He was a master manipulator not only of images; the painter was also known to have his own picture prices inflated at auctions by bidders he planted there. He often sketched and painted for himself, urging his staff to do likewise. Residents of the surrounding Jewish quarter provided perfect material for his dramatic biblical scenes.

TOP 10 GREAT OLD DUTCH PAINTINGS (AND WHERE TO SEE THEM)

Amsterdam

➡ *The Night Watch*, Rembrandt (Rijksmuseum)

➡ *Self Portrait*, Rembrandt (Rijksmuseum)

➡ *The Merry Drinker*, Frans Hals (Rijksmuseum)

➡ *The Merry Family*, Jan Steen (Rijksmuseum)

➡ *Woman in Blue Reading a Letter*, Vermeer (Rijksmuseum)

Den Haag

➡ *Girl with a Pearl Earring*, Vermeer (Mauritshuis)

➡ *The Anatomy Lesson of Dr Nicolaes Tulp*, Rembrandt (Mauritshaus)

Haarlem

➡ *Regents & the Regentesses of the Old Men's Alms House*, Frans Hals (Frans Hals Museum)

Rotterdam

➡ *Tower of Babel*, Bruegel the Elder (Museum Boijmans van Beuningen)

➡ *The Prodigal Son*, Hieronymus Bosch (Museum Boijmans van Beuningen

The Night Watch

After losing three children in their infancy, in 1642 Rembrandt and Saskia's son Titus was born. A year later, Saskia died and business went downhill. Rembrandt's majestic group portrait *The Night Watch* (1642) was hailed by art critics (it's now a prize exhibit at Amsterdam's Rijksmuseum; life-size bronze sculptures re-creating the painting grace the Southern Canal Ring Sq, Rembrandtplein). However, some of the influential people Rembrandt depicted were not pleased. Each subject had paid 100 guilders, and some were unhappy at being shoved in the background. In response, Rembrandt told them where they could shove their complaints. Suddenly he received far fewer orders.

Rembrandt began an affair with his son's governess, Geertje Dircx, but kicked her out a few years later when he fell for the new maid, Hendrickje Stoffels, who bore him a daughter, Cornelia. The public didn't take kindly to the man's lifestyle and his spiralling debts, and in 1656 he applied for *cessio bonorum* (a respectable form of insolvency). His house and rich art collection were sold and he moved to the Rozengracht in the Jordaan.

Etchings

No longer the darling of the wealthy, Rembrandt continued to paint, draw and etch – his etchings on display in the Museum Het Rembrandthuis are some of the finest ever produced. He also received the occasional commission, including the monumental *Conspiracy of Claudius Civilis* (1661) for the city hall (after Govert Flinck, who had originally been commissioned, died before beginning to paint). The authorities disliked Rembrandt's work and had it removed. In 1662 he completed the *Staalmeesters* (the 'Syndics') for the drapers' guild and ensured that everybody remained clearly visible, though it ended up being his last group portrait. It's now in Amsterdam's Rijksmuseum.

Later Works

The works of his later period show that Rembrandt had lost none of his touch. No longer constrained by the wishes of clients, he enjoyed newfound freedom; his works became more unconventional yet showed an ever-stronger empathy with their subject matter, as in *The Jewish Bride* (c 1666), also now in the Rijksmuseum. The many portraits of Titus and Hendrickje, and his ever-gloomier self-portraits, are among the most stirring in the history of art.

A plague epidemic between 1663 and 1666 killed one in seven Amsterdammers, including Hendrickje in 1663. Titus died in 1668, aged 27 and just married, leaving behind a baby daughter, Titia, who was born six months after his death; Rembrandt died a year later, a broken man.

Frans Hals

A great painter of this period, Frans Hals (1583–1666) was born in Antwerp but lived in Haarlem. He devoted most of his career to portraits, dabbling in occasional genre scenes with dramatic chiaroscuro. His ability to capture his subjects' expressions was equal to Rembrandt's, though he didn't explore their characters as much. Both masters used the same expressive, unpolished brush strokes and their styles went from bright exuberance in their early careers to dark and solemn later on. The 19th-century Impressionists also admired Hals' work. In fact, his *The Merry Drinker* (1628) in the Rijksmuseum's collection, with its bold brush strokes, could almost have been painted by an Impressionist.

Great Art Museums

Rijksmuseum, Amsterdam

Van Gogh Museum, Amsterdam

Mauritshuis, Den Haag

Museum Boijmans van Beuningen, Rotterdam

Lakenhal, Leiden

DUTCH ART 17TH CENTURY (GOLDEN AGE)

A new Rembrandt was 'discovered' in 2012 when leading expert Ernst van de Wetering verified its origin and claimed it was one of a pair from 1643. The *Old Man* (or *The Old Rabbi*) is in a private English collection and now thought to be a self-portrait.

Vermeer

The grand trio of 17th-century masters is completed by Johannes (also known as Jan) Vermeer (1632–75) of Delft. There are only 34 (possibly 35) meticulously crafted paintings that are attributed to him (although some estimates are as high as 66 works). Vermeer died poor with 11 children (four more had died in infancy); his baker accepted two paintings from his wife as payment for a debt of more than 600 guilders. Yet Vermeer mastered genre painting like no other artist. His paintings include historical and biblical scenes from his earlier career, his famous *View of Delft* (c 1660–61) in the Mauritshuis in Den Haag, and some tender portraits of unknown women, such as the stunningly beautiful *Girl with a Pearl Earring* (c 1665–67), also hanging in the Mauritshuis.

Girl with a Pearl Earring, a dramatised account of the painting of Vermeer's famous work, is a highly readable 1999 novel by Tracy Chevalier. It was made into a film in 2003, which was nominated for three Academy Awards.

Famous Works

Vermeer's work is known for serene light pouring through tall windows. The calm, spiritual effect is enhanced by dark blues, deep reds, warm yellows and supremely balanced composition. Good examples include the Rijksmuseum's *Kitchen Maid* (also known as *The Milkmaid,* c 1660) and *Woman in Blue Reading a Letter* (c 1663), and, for his use of perspective, *The Love Letter* (c 1669–70).

The Little Street (c 1658), also known as *View of Houses in Delft,* in the Rijksmuseum's collection is Vermeer's only known street scene.

Other Golden Age Painters

Around the middle of the century, the focus on mood and subtle play of light began to make way for the splendour of the baroque. Jacob van Ruysdael (c 1628–82) went for dramatic skies while Albert Cuyp (1620–91) painted Italianate landscapes. Van Ruysdael's pupil Meindert Hobbema (1638–1709) preferred less heroic, more playful scenes full of pretty bucolic detail. Note that Cuyp, Ruysdael and Hobbema all have main streets named after them in Amsterdam's Old South and De Pijp neighbourhoods, and many other streets here are named after other Dutch artists, including Frans Hals, Govert Flinck, Ferdinand Bol, Cornelis Troost and Jan Steen.

The genre paintings of Jan Steen (c 1625–79) show the almost-frivolous aspect of baroque. Steen was also a tavern keeper, and his depictions of domestic chaos led to the Dutch expression 'a Jan Steen household'. A good example is the animated revelry of *The Merry Family* (1668) in the Rijksmuseum; it shows adults having a good time around the dinner table, oblivious to the children in the foreground pouring themselves a drink.

18th Century

The Golden Age of Dutch painting ended almost as suddenly as it began when the French invaded the Low Countries in 1672. The economy

GROUP PORTRAITS BY HALS

Frans Hals specialised in beautiful group portraits in which the participants were depicted in almost natural poses, unlike the rigid line-ups produced by lesser contemporaries – though he wasn't as cavalier as Rembrandt in subordinating faces to the composition. A good example is the pair of paintings known collectively as the *Regents & the Regentesses of the Old Men's Alms House* (1664) in the Frans Hals Museum in Haarlem. The museum occupies a space that Hals knew well; while he never lived in the almshouse (contrary to popular belief), in the 1630s the artist and his family lived in Groot Heiligland, the street where the Old Men's Alms House stood.

collapsed and the market for paintings went south with it. Painters who stayed in business concentrated on 'safe' works that repeated earlier successes. In the 18th century they copied French styles, pandering to the fashion for anything French.

The results were competent but not groundbreaking. Cornelis Troost (1696–1750) was one of the best genre painters, and is sometimes compared to the British artist William Hogarth (1697–1764) for his satirical as well as sensitive portraits of ordinary people; Troost, too, introduced scenes of domestic revelry into his pastels.

Gerard de Lairesse (1641–1711) and Jacob de Wit (1695–1754) specialised in decorating the walls and ceilings of buildings – de Wit's trompe l'œil decorations (painted illusions that look real; French for 'deceive the eye') in the Bijbels Museum in Amsterdam are worth seeing.

19th Century

The late 18th century and most of the 19th century produced little of note, save for the landscapes and seascapes of Johan Barthold Jongkind (1819–91) and the gritty, almost photographic Amsterdam scenes of George Hendrik Breitner (1857–1923). They appear to have inspired French Impressionists, many of whom visited Amsterdam.

Jongkind and Breitner reinvented 17th-century realism and influenced the Hague School of the last decades of the 19th century. Painters such as Hendrik Mesdag (1831–1915), Jozef Israëls (1824–1911) and the three Maris brothers, Jacob (1837–99), Matthijs (1839–1917) and Willem (1844–1910), created landscapes, seascapes and genre works, including Mesdag's impressive 1881 *Panorama Mesdag* (p169), a gigantic 14m-high, 120m-wide, 360-degree cylindrical painting of the seaside town of Scheveningen viewed from a dune.

Vincent van Gogh

Without a doubt, the greatest 19th-century Dutch painter was Vincent van Gogh (1853–90), whose convulsive patterns and furious colours were in a world of their own and still defy comfortable categorisation. (A post-Impressionist? A forerunner of expressionism?)

While the Dutch Masters were known for their dark, brooding paintings, it was Van Gogh who created an identity of suffering as an art form, with a morbid style all his own. Even today, he epitomises the epic struggle of the artist: the wrenching poverty; the lack of public acclaim; the reliance upon a patron – in this case his faithful brother, Theo; the mental instability; the untimely death by suicide. And of course, one of the most iconic images of an artist's self-destruction, the severed ear.

The Artist's Legend: Myths & Facts

Vincent van Gogh may have been poor – he sold only one painting in his lifetime – but he wasn't old. It's easy to forget from his self-portraits, in which he appears much older (partly the effects of his poverty), that he was only 37 when he died. But his short life continues to influence art to this day.

Born in Zundert in 1853, the Dutch painter lived in Paris with his younger brother Theo, an art dealer, who financially supported him from his modest income. In Paris he became acquainted with seminal artists including Edgar Degas, Camille Pissarro, Henri de Toulouse-Lautrec and Paul Gauguin.

Van Gogh moved south to Arles, Provence, in 1888. Revelling in its intense light and bright colours, he painted sunflowers, irises and other vivid subjects with a burning fervour. He sent paintings to Theo in Paris to sell, and dreamed of founding an artists' colony in Provence, but only Gauguin followed up his invitation. Their differing artistic approaches – Gauguin

DUTCH ART 19TH CENTURY

Vincent Van Gogh: The Letters contains all 902 letters between Van Gogh and his brother, friends, lovers, confidantes and fellow artists. It's a moving window into his inner life, plus a testimony to the extraordinary friendship and artistic connection he shared with his brother, Theo.

Van Gogh Films

Lust for Life (1956)
Vincent (1987)
Vincent and Theo (1990)

Van Gogh produced an astonishing output of art during his 10-year artistic career, of which 864 paintings and almost 1200 drawings and prints have survived.

believed in painting from imagination; Van Gogh painting what he saw – and their artistic temperaments, fuelled by absinthe, came to a head with the argument that led to Van Gogh lopping his ear (which he gave to a prostitute acquaintance) and his subsequent committal in Arles.

In May 1889 Van Gogh voluntarily entered an asylum in St-Rémy de Provence, where he painted prolifically during his one-year, one-week and one-day confinement, including masterpieces such as *Irises* and *Starry Night*. While there, Theo sent him a positive French newspaper critique of his work. The following month, Anna Boch, sister of his friend Eugène Boch, bought *The Red Vines* (or *The Red Vineyard;* 1888) for 400 francs (less than €100 today). It now hangs in Moscow's Pushkin Museum.

Legacy of a Tortured Genius

On 16 May 1890 Van Gogh moved to Auverssur-Oise, just outside Paris, to be closer to Theo, but on 27 July that year he shot himself, possibly to avoid further financial burden on his brother, whose wife had just had a baby son, named Vincent, and who was also supporting their ailing mother. Van Gogh died two days later with Theo at his side. Theo subsequently had a breakdown, was also committed, and succumbed to physical illness. He died, aged 33, just six months after Van Gogh.

It would be less than a decade before Van Gogh's talent would start to achieve wide recognition, and by the early 1950s he had become a household name. In 1990 he broke the record for a single painting (*A Portrait of Doctor Gachet*) at Christie's, which fetched US$82.5 million. Accounting for inflation, it's still the highest price paid at a public auction for art to this day.

Van Gogh's Famous Five

....
Sunflowers (Van Gogh Museum, Amsterdam)
....
Wheatfield with Crows (Van Gogh Museum, Amsterdam)
....
Self Portrait with Felt Hat (Van Gogh Museum, Amsterdam)
....
The Potato Eaters (Kröller-Müller Museum, Hoge Veluwe National Park)
....
Weavers (Kröller-Müller Museum, Hoge Veluwe National Park)

20th Century

De Stijl

De Stijl (The Style), also known as neoplasticism, was a Dutch design movement that aimed to harmonise all the arts by bringing artistic expressions back to their essence. Its advocate was the magazine of the same name, first published in 1917 by Theo van Doesburg (1883–1931). Van Doesburg produced similar rectangular patterns to Piet Mondrian's, though he dispensed with the thick, black lines and later tilted his rectangles at 45 degrees, departures serious enough for Mondrian to call off the friendship.

Throughout the 1920s and 1930s, De Stijl attracted sculptors, poets, architects and designers. One of these was Gerrit Rietveld (1888–1964), designer of the Van Gogh Museum and several other buildings, but best known internationally for his furniture, such as the *Red Blue Chair* (1918) and his range of uncomfortable zigzag seats that, viewed side-on, formed a 'z' with a backrest.

Mondrian

A major proponent of De Stijl was Piet Mondrian (originally Mondriaan, 1872–1944), who initially painted in the Hague School tradition. After flirting with Cubism, he began working with bold rectangular patterns, using only the three primary colours (yellow, blue and red) set against the three neutrals (white, grey and black). He named this style neoplasticism and viewed it as an undistorted expression of reality in pure form

VAN GOGH'S LAST WORDS

Even Van Gogh's rumoured last words ring with the kind of excruciating, melancholic beauty that his best paintings express. With Theo at his side, two days after he shot himself in the chest after a manic fit of painting, he is said to have uttered in French *'la tristesse durera toujours'* (the sadness will last forever).

> ## DUTCH GRAPHIC ARTS
>
> It's not all paint on canvas; modern Dutch graphic arts also win acclaim.
>
> ➡ Dick Bruna (1927–) of Utrecht is famous for Miffy (Nijntje in Dutch), an adorable cartoon rabbit. He's written and illustrated 124 children's books and designed thousands of book covers, as well as hundreds of other books, posters, postcards and prints. The Miffy Museum in Utrecht honours him.
>
> ➡ The Dutch tradition of clear visual communications has developed since the start of the 20th century. You'll see examples every day, including on the national railway, which was an early trendsetter in graphic communication. Brilliant examples of Dutch graphic arts are displayed at the Museum of the Image in Breda.

and pure colour. His 1920 Composition in Red, Black, Blue, Yellow and Grey *(Composition No. II)*, in Amsterdam's Stedelijk Museum's collection, is an elaborate example.

Mondrian's later works were more stark (or 'pure') and became dynamic again when he moved to New York in 1940. The world's largest collection of his paintings resides in the Gemeentemuseum (Municipal Museum) in his native Den Haag.

MC Escher

One of the most remarkable graphic artists of the 20th century was Maurits Cornelis Escher (1898-1972). His drawings, lithos and woodcuts of blatantly impossible images continue to fascinate mathematicians: a waterfall feeds itself; people go up and down a staircase that ends where it starts; a pair of hands draw each other. You can see his work at Escher in het Paleis in Den Haag.

CoBrA

After WWII, artists rebelled against artistic conventions and vented their rage in abstract expressionism. In Amsterdam, Karel Appel (1921–2006) and Constant (Constant Nieuwenhuys, 1920-2005) drew on styles pioneered by Paul Klee and Joan Miró, and exploited bright colours and 'uncorrupted' children's art to produce lively works that leaped off the canvas. In Paris in 1945 they met up with the Danish Asger Jorn (1914–73) and the Belgian Corneille (Cornelis van Beverloo, 1922–2010), and together with several other artists and writers formed a group known as CoBrA (Copenhagen, Brussels, Amsterdam). It's been called the last great avant-garde movement.

Their first major exhibition, in the Stedelijk Museum in 1949, aroused a storm of protest (with comments such as 'my child paints like that too'). Still, the CoBrA artists exerted a strong influence in their respective countries, even after they disbanded in 1951. The CoBrA Museum in Amstelveen displays a good range of their works, including colourful ceramics.

Contemporary Artists

Modern Dutch artists are usually well represented at international events and are known for mixing mediums.

Artist duo Liet Heringa (1966–) and Maarten Van Kalsbeek (1962–) are known for their moody, free-form sculptures; Michael Raedecker (1963–) for his dreamy, radiant still lifes; and Roger Braun (1972–) for industrial realism. Harma Heikens (1963–) is also a boundary-pushing sculptor.

Names to watch include Daan Roosegaarde (1979–), who pushes the boundaries between art and technology with interactive landscapes; Levi van Veluw (1985–), famed for using his own body as a canvas; and Anouk Kruithof (1981–), whose main medium is photography.

The Dutch jazz scene has produced some mainstream artists in recent years. Among gifted young chanteuses are Fleurine, Ilse Huizinga and the Surinam-born Denise Jannah, who records for Blue Note and is recognised as the country's best jazz singer. Jannah's repertoire consists of American standards with elements of Surinamese music.

Architecture

The Dutch are masters of architecture and use of space, but this is nothing new. Through the ages, few countries have exerted more influence on the discipline of art and construction than the Netherlands. From the original sober cathedrals to the sleek modern structures, their ideas and designs have spread throughout Europe and beyond. You may not find any bombastic statements such as St Peter's cathedral or the Louvre, but then again, ostentation was never in keeping with the Dutch character.

Romanesque

Romanesque architecture, which took Europe by storm between 900 and 1250, is the earliest architectural style remaining in the country, if you discount the *hunebedden* (chamber tombs). Its main characteristics are an uncomplicated form, thick walls, small windows and round arches.

The oldest church of this style in the Netherlands is the Pieterskerk in Utrecht. Built in 1048, it's one of five churches that form a cross in the city, with the cathedral at its centre. Runner-up is Nijmegen's 16-sided Sint Nicolaaskapel, which is basically a scaled-down copy of Charlemagne's chapel in Aachen, Germany. Another classic example of Romanesque is the Onze Lieve Vrouwebasiliek in Maastricht.

Holland's countryside is also privy to this style of architecture. The windy plains of the north are filled with examples of sturdy brick churches erected in the 12th and 13th centuries, such as the lonely church perched on a human-made hill in Hogebeintum in Friesland.

Gothic

By around 1250 the love affair with Romanesque was over, and the Gothic era was ushered in. Pointed arches, ribbed vaulting and dizzying heights were trademarks of this new architectural style, which was to last until 1600. Although the Dutch buildings didn't match the size of the French Gothic cathedrals, a rich style emerged in Catholic Brabant that could compete with anything abroad. Stone churches with soaring vaults and buttresses, such as Sint Janskathedraal in Den Bosch and Breda's Grote Kerk, were erected. Both are good examples of the Brabant Gothic style, as it was later known.

You'll notice timber vaulting and the widespread use of brick among the stone. Stone is normally a constant fixture of Gothic buildings, but in the marshy lands of the western Netherlands it was too heavy (and too scarce) to use. The basic ingredients of bricks – clay and sand – were in abundance, however. Still, bricks are not exactly light material, and weight limits forced architects to build long or wide to compensate for the lack of height. The Sint Janskerk in Gouda is the longest church in the country, with a nave of 123m, and it has the delicate, stately feel of a variant called Flamboyant Gothic. Stone Gothic structures do exist in the western stretches of Holland, though: Haarlem's Grote Kerk van St Bavo is a wonderful example.

Mannerism

From the middle of the 16th century the Renaissance style that was sweeping through Italy steadily began to filter into the Netherlands. The Dutch naturally put their own spin on this new architectural design, which came to be known as mannerism (c 1550–1650). Also known as Dutch Renaissance, this unique style falls somewhere between Renaissance and baroque; it retained the bold curving forms and rich ornamentation of baroque but merged them with classical Greek and Roman and traditional Dutch styles. Building facades were accentuated with mock columns (pilasters) and the simple spout gables were replaced with step gables that were richly decorated with sculptures, columns and obelisks. The playful interaction of red brick and horizontal bands of white or yellow sandstone was based on mathematical formulas designed to please the eye.

The ultimate in early functionalism, windmills have a variety of distinctive designs and their characteristic look makes them national icons.

Hendrik de Keyser (1565–1621) was the champion of mannerism. His Zuiderkerk, Noorderkerk and Westerkerk in Amsterdam are standout examples; all three show a major break from the sober, stolid lines of brick churches located out in the sticks. Their steeples are ornate and built with a variety of contrasting materials, while the windows are framed in white stone set off by brown brick. Florid details enliven the walls and roof lines.

ARCHITECTURE MANNERISM

Golden Age

After the Netherlands became a world trading power in the 17th century, its rich merchants wanted to splash out on lavish buildings that proclaimed their status.

More than anything, the new architecture had to impress. The leading lights in the architectural field, such as Jacob van Campen (1595–1657) and the brothers Philips and Justus Vingboons, again turned to ancient Greek and Roman designs for ideas. To make buildings look taller, the step gable was replaced by a neck gable, and pilasters were built to look like imperial columns, complete with pedestals. Decorative scrolls were added as finishing flourishes, and the peak wore a triangle or globe to simulate a temple roof.

A wonderful example of this is the Koninklijk Paleis (Royal Palace) in Amsterdam, originally built as the town hall in 1648. Van Campen, the architect, drew on classical designs and dropped many of De Keyser's playful decorations, and the resulting building exuded gravity with its solid lines and shape.

This new form of architecture suited the city's businessmen, who needed to let the world know that they were successful. As red sports cars were still centuries away, canal houses became showpieces. Despite

GABLES

Among the great treasures of the old canals in Amsterdam, Haarlem and elsewhere are the magnificent gables – the roof-level facades that adorn the elegant houses along the canals. The gable hid the roof from public view, and helped to identify the house, until 1795, when the French occupiers introduced house numbers. Gables then became more of a fashion accessory.

There are four main types of gable: the simple spout gable, with diagonal outline and semicircular windows or shutters, that was used mainly for warehouses from the 1580s to the early 1700s; the step gable, a late-Gothic design favoured by Dutch Renaissance architects; the neck gable, also known as the bottle gable, a durable design introduced in the 1640s; and the bell gable, which appeared in the 1660s and became popular in the 18th century.

the narrow plots, each building from this time makes a statement at gable level through sculpture and myriad shapes and forms. Philips and Justus Vingboons were specialists in these swanky residences; their most famous works include the Bijbels Museum (Biblical Museum) and houses scattered throughout Amsterdam's western canal belt.

The capital is not the only city to display such grand architecture. Den Haag has 17th-century showpieces, including the Paleis Noordeinde and the Mauritshuis, and scores of other examples line the picture-perfect canals of Leiden, Delft and Maastricht, to name but a few.

Rotterdam's 12-storey Witte Huis (built 1898) was Europe's first 'skyscraper'. Today it looks almost squat compared to its neighbours; it somehow survived the destruction of Rotterdam in 1940.

French Influence

By the 18th century the wealthy classes had turned their backs on trade for more staid lives in banking or finance, which meant a lot of time at home. Around the same time, Dutch architects began deferring to all things French (which reflected French domination of the country); dainty Louis XV furnishings and florid rococo facades became all the rage. It was then a perfect time for new French building trends to sweep the country. Daniel Marot (1661–1752), together with his assistants Jean and Anthony Coulon, was the first to introduce French interior design with matching exteriors. Good examples of their work can be found along the Lange Voorhout in Den Haag.

Neoclassicism

Architecture took a back seat during the Napoleonic Wars in the late 18th century. Buildings still needed to be built, of course, so designers dug deep into ancient Greek and Roman blueprints once more and eventually came up with neoclassicism (c 1790–1850). Known for its order, symmetry and simplicity, neoclassical design became the mainstay for houses of worship, courtyards and other official buildings. A shining example of neoclassicism is Groningen's town hall; of particular note are the classical pillars, although the use of brick walls is a purely Dutch accent. Many a church was subsidised by the government water ministry and so was named a Waterstaatkerk (state water church), such as the lonely house of worship in Schokland.

Late 19th Century

From the 1850s onwards, many of the country's large architectural projects siphoned as much as they could from the Gothic era, creating neo-Gothic. Soon afterwards, freedom of religion was declared and Catholics were allowed to build new churches in Protestant areas. Neo-Gothic suited the Catholics just fine as it recalled their own glory days, and a boom in church-building took place.

Nationwide, nostalgia for the perceived glory days of the Golden Age inspired neo-Renaissance, which drew heavily on De Keyser's earlier masterpieces. Neo-Renaissance buildings were erected throughout the country, made to look like well-polished veterans from three centuries

---

HOISTS & HOUSES THAT TIP

Many old canal houses deliberately tip forward. Given the narrowness of staircases, owners needed an easy way to move large goods and furniture to the upper floors. The solution: a hoist built into the gable, to lift objects up and in through the windows. The tilt allowed loading without bumping into the house front. Some properties even have huge hoist-wheels in the attic with a rope and hook that run through the hoist beam.

The forward lean also makes the houses seem larger, which makes it easier to admire the facade and gable – a fortunate coincidence for everyone.

earlier. For many observers, these stepped-gable edifices with alternating stone and brick are the epitome of classic Dutch architecture.

One of the leading architects of this period was Pierre Cuypers (1827–1921), who built several neo-Gothic churches but often merged the style with neo-Renaissance, as can be seen in Amsterdam's Centraal Station and Rijksmuseum. These are predominantly Gothic structures but have touches of Dutch Renaissance brickwork.

Berlage & the Amsterdam School

As the 20th century approached, the neo styles and their reliance on the past were strongly criticised by Hendrik Petrus Berlage (1856–1934), the father of modern Dutch architecture. He favoured spartan, practical designs over frivolous ornamentation; Amsterdam's 1902 Beurs van Berlage displays these ideals to the full. Berlage cooperated with sculptors, painters and tilers to ensure that ornamentation was integrated into the overall design in a supportive role, rather than being tacked on as an embellishment to hide the structure. The Gemeentemuseum in Den Haag, Berlage's last major work, was an even more ambitious expression of his principles.

Berlage's residential designs approached a block of buildings as a whole, not as a collection of individual houses. In this he influenced the young architects of what became known as the Amsterdam School, though they rejected his stark rationalism and preferred more creative designs. Leading exponents were Michel de Klerk (1884–1923), Piet Kramer (1881–1961) and Johan van der Mey (1878–1949); the latter ushered in the Amsterdam School (c 1916–30) with his extraordinary Scheepvaarthuis, formerly the headquarters of several shipping firms, now a hotel.

Brick was the material of choice for such architects, and housing blocks were treated as sculptures, with curved corners, oddly placed windows and ornamental, rocket-shaped towers. Their Amsterdam housing estates, such as De Klerk's 'Ship' in the west, have been described as fairytale fortresses rendered in a Dutch version of art deco. Their preference for form over function meant their designs were great to look at but not always fantastic to live in, with small windows and inefficient use of space.

Housing subsidies sparked a frenzy of residential building activity in the 1920s. At the time, many architects of the Amsterdam School worked for the Amsterdam city council and designed the buildings for the Oud Zuid (Old South). This large-scale expansion – mapped out by Berlage – called for good-quality housing, wide boulevards and cosy squares.

Functionalism

While Amsterdam School–type buildings were being erected all over their namesake city, a new generation of architects began to rebel against the school's impractical (not to mention expensive) structures. Influenced by the Bauhaus school in Germany, Frank Lloyd Wright in the USA and Le Corbusier in France, they formed a group called 'the 8'. It was the first stirring of functionalism (1927–70).

Architects such as B Merkelbach (1901–61) and Gerrit Rietveld (1888–1965) believed that form should follow function and sang the praises of steel, glass and concrete. Their spacious designs were practical and allowed for plenty of sunlight; Utrecht's masterpiece Rietveld-Schröderhuis is the only house built completely along functionalist De Stijl (p274) lines.

After the war, functionalism came to the fore and stamped its authority on new suburbs to the west and south of Amsterdam, as well as war-damaged cities such as Rotterdam. High-rise suburbs were built on a large scale yet weren't sufficient to keep up with the population boom

Frank Lloyd Wright acolyte William Dudok's stunning and vast town hall is the one good reason to visit Hilversum, west of Amsterdam.

The *Architectural Guide to the Netherlands,* by Paul Groenendijk and Piet Vollaard, is a comprehensive look at architecture since 1900, arranged by region, with short explanations and photos. It's in two volumes: *1900–2000* and *1980–Present.* The associated website, with a list of the Top 100 structures, is www.architectureguide.nl.

and urbanisation of Dutch life. But functionalism fell from favour as the smart design aspects were watered down in low-cost housing projects for the masses.

Modernism & Beyond

Construction has been booming in the Netherlands since the 1980s, and architects have had ample opportunity to flirt with numerous 'isms' such as structuralism, neorationalism, postmodernism and neomodernism.

Evidence of these styles can be found in Rotterdam, where city planners have encouraged bold designs that range from Piet Blom's startling cube-shaped Boompjestorens to Ben van Berkel's graceful Erasmusbrug. In fact the whole city is a modern architectural showcase where new 'exhibits' are erected all the time. The tallest building in the country, the MaasToren, topped out at 165m, and just a short distance away stands De Rotterdam, a trio of transparent towers that function as a 'vertical city'. The latter is designed by Rotterdam's own Rem Koolhaas, one of the world's most influential architects. His firm, OMA, has been a breeding ground for a new generation of architects.

Other striking examples of bold new architecture can be admired throughout the Netherlands, often combining symbolic references with a sense of play. Near Den Bosch, the Haverleij residential complex reimagines a medieval landscape, with 10 moat-ringed communities, each with its own castle, sharing green pasturelands. In Breda, a surreal copper-plated blob forms an acoustically calibrated dome for the Mezz pop-music hall. In Zwolle, a UFO faced with reflective blue tiles appears to have landed on the rooftop of the stodgy neoclassical Fundatie Museum, shaking up the academy as it were. At the recently unveiled Tivoli/Vredenburg music centre, in Utrecht, four venues (each for a different musical style) hover around and above the original symphony hall like sections in a record store. The new Forum cultural centre of Groningen, still under construction, rises like a great pyramid off the main square. And in Amsterdam, the NEMO Science Centre recalls a resurfacing submarine.

Much of the ground for experimentation is provided by zones or structures whose functions have changed, declined or been abandoned. Throughout the country are numerous fascinating examples of urban transformation and creative building reuse – a sustainable alternative to demolition. As their devotional function goes by the wayside, churches in Zwolle and Maastricht have been reborn as bookshops and a posh hotel. In Eindhoven, the sprawling industrial park of the Philips electronics firm has been retrofitted for creative talent, with an events centre, concert hall, hostel and skateboard park, collectively known as the Strijp-S. On Maastricht's east riverbank, a residential district designed by an all-star team of international architects has sprung up on the site of an old ceramics factory, and is now suitably dubbed Céramique. At the NDSM shipyard in Amsterdam-Noord, the former welding hangar now houses art and film studios; old shipping containers are student housing units; and the crane track (Kranspoor) became the base for an elongated office building.

The shores along Amsterdam's IJ River are a good place to see the vaunted Dutch traditions of urban design in action. Northwest of Centraal Station lies the Westerdokeiland, an imposing clutch of flats, offices and cafes embracing a pleasure harbour; to the northeast is Oosterdokeiland, an A1 office location with housing and home to the Openbare Bibliotheek. Across the river in Amsterdam-Noord there's Overhoeks, a housing estate on the old Shell Oil compound that borders the EYE Film Institute. And so a new city rises where once there was marsh, the story of the Netherlands.

The website of who's who in Holland's architectural scene is www.architecten-web.nl. It also showcases newly commissioned projects and those underway.

The Nederlands Architectuur Instituut (www.nai.nl) in Rotterdam is the top authority on the latest developments in Dutch buildings and design and it has good retrospective shows on the trends that have shaped the nation's architecture.

The Dutch Landscape

There's no arguing with the fact that the Netherlands is a product of human endeavour. Everywhere you look, from the neat rows of *polders* to the omnipresent dykes, everything looks so, well, planned and organised. 'God created the world, but the Dutch created the Netherlands', as the saying goes. Much of this tinkering with nature has been out of necessity – it's hard to live underwater for any length of time. But all of the reorganisation has put a strain on the Dutch environment.

A Land Created

Flanked by Belgium, Germany and the choppy waters of the North Sea, the landmass of the Netherlands is to a great degree artificial, having been reclaimed from the sea over many centuries. Maps from the Middle Ages are a curious sight today, with large chunks of land 'missing' from North Holland and Zeeland. The country now encompasses over 41,500 sq km, making it roughly half the size of Scotland or a touch bigger than the US state of Maryland.

Twelve provinces make up the Netherlands. Almost all of these are as flat as a *pannenkoek;* the only hills to speak of rise from its very southern tip, near Maastricht. The soil in the west and north is relatively young and consists of peat and clay formed less than 10,000 years ago. Much of this area is below sea level, or reclaimed land.

> *Polders* (areas of drained land to facilitate agriculture) form 60% of the Netherlands' landscape – by far the highest percentage of any country in the world.

Dykes

The efforts of the Dutch to create new land are almost superhuman. Over the past century alone three vast *polders* have been created through ingenious engineering: Wieringermeer in North Holland; the province-island of Flevoland; and the adjoining Noordoostpolder. Much of this, just over 1700 sq km, was drained after a barrier dyke closed off the North Sea in 1932. In total, an astounding 20% of the country is reclaimed land.

It's impossible to talk about the Dutch landscape without mentioning water, which covers 20% of the entire country. Most Dutch people shudder at the thought of a leak in the dykes. If the Netherlands were to lose its 2400km of mighty dykes and dunes – some of which are 25m high – the large cities would be inundated. Modern pumping stations (the replacements for windmills) run around the clock to drain off excess water.

The danger of floods is most acute in the southwestern province of Zeeland, a sprawling estuary for the rivers Schelde, Maas, Lek and Waal. The latter two are branches of the Rijn (Rhine), the endpoint of a journey that begins in the Swiss Alps. The Maas rises in France and travels through Belgium before draining into the North Sea in the Delta region.

The floods of 1953 devastated Zeeland and the surrounding region. The resulting Delta Project to prevent future flooding became one of the world's largest public works projects.

Myriad small roads run atop the old dykes and these can make great cycling routes, from which you can appreciate just how far the land lies below the water in the canals, and see the historic windmills once used to keep the water out.

> There's no denying the Netherlands is a low, flat country (Netherlands in Dutch means 'low land'). Its lowest point – the town of Nieuwerkerk aan den IJssel, near Rotterdam – is 6.74m below sea level, while its highest point – the Vaalserberg in Limburg – is a meagre 321m above.

Wildlife

Human encroachment has played a huge role in the wildlife of the Netherlands. Few habitats are left intact in the country, and more than 10% of species are imported. While the Netherlands' flora and fauna will always be in constant change, one fact remains – birds love the place.

In some cases, human activity works in favour of certain species. In Gelderland, the part of the Waal river flowing through the Geldersepoort – an area of lakes, ponds, marshes and willlows – is being widened to accommodate increased flow volumes. As clay is dug from the banks (and made into bricks to finance the project), the river zone opens up, making it attractive to certain birds such as avocets, which settle there. Similar cases of species returning include the great egret, which had inhabited the Austria–Hungary border region until 1988, showing up in Flevoland after establishment of new *polders* there, and the white-tailed eagle appearing in the Biesbosch National Park. In other cases, species are introduced into nature reserves, such as the European bison, highland cattle and Galloway cattle, which behave like extinct species to return the landscape to its original state.

Larger mammals such as the fox, badger and fallow deer have retreated to the national parks and reserves. Some species such as boar, mouflon and red deer have been reintroduced into controlled habitats.

Animals

The Netherlands is a paradise for birds and those who love to follow them around. The wetlands are a major migration stop for European birds, particularly Texel's Duinen van Texel National Park, Flevoland's Oostvaardersplassen Nature Reserve and the Delta. Just take geese: a dozen varieties, from white-fronted to pink-footed, break their V-formations to winter here.

Along urban canals you'll see plenty of mallards, coots and swans as well as the lovely grebe with its regal head plumage. The large and graceful blue heron spears frogs and tiny fish in the ditches of the *polder* lands, but also loiters on canal boats in and out of town. The black cormorant, an accomplished diver with a wingspan of nearly 1m, is another regal bird.

WINDMILLS

Central to the story of the Dutch and their struggles with water are windmills. These national icons were an ingenious development that harnessed the nearly constant winds off the North Sea to keep the waters at bay. First used in the 13th century, windmills pumped water up and over the dykes from land below sea level. Later their uses became myriad, and examples can be spotted among the 1200 windmills still standing.

Standerdmolen – Oldest type of windmill in the Netherlands. The wooden housing can be rotated. Used mostly for milling grain.

Wipmolen – Later variation on the *standerdmolen*; used to pump water out of *polders* (areas of drained land). The smaller mill housing rotates on a fixed pyramidal base.

Stellingmolen – Raised atop a high platform so it can more easily catch the wind in urban areas, with a scaffold around the base, from which operators can rotate the mill and adjust the blades to take best advantage of the wind direction. Used for the production of paper and oil. A good example is De Gooyer beside the Brouwerij 't IJ in east Amsterdam.

Tjasker – Windmill blades placed at top end of an angled shaft that operates as a pump; used by peat diggers to lower the water level to facilitate their work. Examples can be spotted in the Weerribben-Wieden National Park.

Rietmolen – Miniature windmill that looks like a weather vane; used by reed harvesters to keep the reeds wet.

BIRD-WATCHING FOR BEGINNERS

Seen through an amateur birdwatcher's eyes, some of the more interesting sightings might include the following:

Avocet – Common on the Waddenzee and the Delta, with slender upturned bill, and black and white plumage.

Black woodpecker – Drums seldom but loudly. To see it, try woodlands such as Hoge Veluwe National Park.

Bluethroat – Song like a free-wheeling bicycle; seen in Biesbosch National Park, Flevoland and the Delta.

Great white egret – Cranelike species common in marshlands. First bred in Flevoland in the early 1990s.

Marsh harrier – Bird of prey; often hovers over reed beds and arable land.

Spoonbill – Once scarce, this odd-looking fellow has proliferated on coasts in Zeeland and the Wadden Islands.

White stork – Nearly extinct in the 1980s, numbers have since recovered. Enormous nests.

A variety of fish species dart about the canals and estuaries. One of the most interesting is the eel, which thrives in both fresh and salt water. These amazing creatures breed in the Sargasso Sea off Bermuda before making the perilous journey to the North Sea. Herds of seals can be spotted on coastal sandbanks such as those around Texel and off the Groningen coast, where a sanctuary operates to nurse ailing specimens back to health.

Plants

There are thousands of wild varieties on display, such as the marsh orchid (with a pink crown of tiny blooms) and Zeeland masterwort (with bunches of white, compact blooms). Marshy terrain favours purple loosestrife, cattails and water soldiers, a rare white-flowered lily.

Much of the undeveloped land is covered by grass, which is widely used for grazing. Temperate weather means that the grass remains green and grows for much of the year – on coastal dunes and mudflats, and around brackish lakes and river deltas. Marshes, heaths and peatlands are the next most common features. The remnants of oak, beech, ash and pine forests are carefully managed.

Holland's signature flower, the tulip, was imported from elsewhere and then commercially exploited, like much of the country's agriculturally produced flora.

National Parks

With so few corners of the Netherlands left untouched, the Dutch cherish every bit of nature that's left, and that's doubly true for their national parks (www.nationaalpark.nl). But while the first designated natural reserve was born in 1930, it wasn't until 1984 that the first publicly funded park was established.

National parks in the Netherlands tend to be small affairs: for an area to become a park, it must only be bigger than 10 sq km and be important in environmental terms. Most of the 20 national parks in the country average a mere 64 sq km and are as likely to preserve a human-made environment as a wilderness area. A total of 1200 sq km (just over 3%) of the Netherlands is protected in the form of national parks; the most northerly is the island of Schiermonnikoog in Friesland, and the most southerly is the terraced landscape of De Meinweg in central Limburg.

Freshwater species such as white bream, rudd, pike, perch, stickleback and carp enjoy the canal environment. You can admire them up close at Amsterdam's Artis Royal Zoo, in an aquarium that simulates an Amsterdam canal.

NOTABLE NATIONAL PARKS & NATURE RESERVES

NAME	FEATURES	ACTIVITIES	BEST TIME TO VISIT
Biesbosch NP	estuarine reed marsh, woodland	canoeing, hiking, bird-watching, cycling	Mar–Sep
Duinen van Texel NP	dunes, heath, forest	hiking, cycling, bird-watching, swimming	Mar–Sep
Hoge Veluwe NP	marsh, forests, dunes	hiking, cycling, art-viewing	year-round
Oostvaardersplassen NR	wild reed marsh, grassland	hiking, cycling, bird-watching, fishing	year-round
Schiermonnikoog NP	car-free island, dunes, mudflats	hiking, mudflat-walking, bird-watching	Mar–Sep
Weerribben-Wieden NP	peat marsh	kayaking, canoeing, hiking, bird-watching	year-round
Zuid-Kennemerland NP	dunes, heath, forest	hiking, bird-watching, cycling	Mar–Sep

Some national parks are heavily visited, not only because there's plenty of nature to see but also because of their well-developed visitors centres and excellent displays of contemporary flora and fauna. Hoge Veluwe, established in 1935, is a particular favourite with its sandy hills and forests that once were prevalent in this part of the Netherlands. It is the only park that charges admission.

Of the 19 remaining national parks, Weerribben-Wieden in Overijssel is one of the most important as it preserves a landscape once heavily scarred by the peat harvest. Here the modern objective is to allow the land to return to nature, as is the case on Schiermonnikoog, which occupies a good portion of land once used by a sect of monks and which was part of Unesco's 2009 recognition of the broader Waddenzee region.

After the US government granted permission to Shell to start Arctic drilling in August 2015, Dutch Greenpeace called for a boycott on the purchase of fuel from the Anglo-Dutch oil giant.

Environmental Issues

As a society, the Dutch are more aware of environmental issues than most. But then again, with high population density, widespread car ownership, heavy industrialisation, extensive farming and more than a quarter of the country below sea level, they need to be.

As early as the 1980s a succession of Dutch governments began to put in motion plans to tighten the standards for industrial and farm pollution. They also made recycling a part of everyday life, although this has become a subject of some debate. All agree on the need for recycling, but not on how it will be done or by whom. One plan for financing is to charge for waste that goes unsorted.

Drilling for natural gas in Groningen has been linked to increased earthquake activity in the area, prompting the Dutch government to suspend operations in Loppersum at the centre of the province, where the damage has been heaviest.

Conservation Organisations

Dutch Friends of the Earth (www.milieudefensie.nl)

Nature & Environment (www.natuurenmilieu.nl)

Cars

While the Dutch are avid bike riders, they still like having a car at the ready. Despite good, reasonably cheap public transport, private car ownership has risen sharply over the past two decades. Use of vehicles is now about 50% above the levels of the late 1980s. Some critics warn that unless action is taken the country's streets and motorways will become gridlocked (as they already are at rush hour around the Randstad). Stiff parking fees (Amsterdam's, at €55 per day, are the highest in the world), the distinct lack of parking spaces, pedestrian spaces and outlandish fines have helped curb congestion in the inner cities.

Outside of town centres, minor roads are configured to put cyclists first, with drivers sharing single lanes. Such schemes, plus the aggressive building plan for separate cycling routes, have made some headway in slowing the growth in car use.

While elsewhere in the world environmentally concerned drivers are switching to hybrid vehicles, in the Netherlands the trend is towards electric bikes. Netherlanders now own 1.5 million of the battery-operated bicycles, which are ideal for commuting as they make it easier to cover long distances. Perhaps because of this, they're also pedalling nearly 30% more kilometres than five years previous to a total of 1018km per year on average.

Water

The effects of climate change are obvious in the Netherlands. Over the past century the winters have become shorter and milder. The long-distance ice-skating race known as the Elfstedentocht may die out because the waterways in the northern province of Friesland rarely freeze hard enough (the last race was in 1997). The Dutch national weather service KNMI predicts that only four to 10 races will be held this century. Although damp and cold, winter in the Netherlands today is not the ice-covered deep freeze you see in Renaissance paintings.

The lack of ice over winter is simply annoying; a rise in sea levels would constitute a disaster of epic proportions. If the sea level rises as forecast, the country could theoretically sink beneath the waves, like Atlantis, or at least suffer annual flooding. The possibility of a watery onslaught is very real, and not just from the sea. Glaciers in Switzerland are melting and that water finds it way into the Rijn in the Netherlands.

Agriculture

The Dutch chicken population hovers around 100 million, one of the largest concentrations in the industrialised world (six chickens for every citizen; pigs are close to a one-to-one ratio). Such industrialised farming has been the cornerstone of Dutch agriculture since WWII and has brought much wealth to the country. But with concerns about ground-water quality, intensive farming and all the artificial fertilisers, chemicals and animal waste that come with it are under scrutiny. The province of Noord-Brabant in the south was the first to limit farm size and ban antibiotics used in feed.

More attention is being paid to sustainable development. Organic (*biologische*) food is gaining in popularity and the huge agriculture industry is realising that profits can be made from more sustainable practices and by going green. One approach is to make greenhouses more efficient by heating them from warm-air aquifers and having industrial outfits pump in the required CO_2 from the by-products of their own operations.

In the coastal waters there are 12 crustacean species including the invasive Chinese mitten crab. Further out, the stock of North Sea cod, shrimp and sole has suffered from chronic overfishing, and catches are now limited by EU quotas.

A third of the dairy cattle in the world are Holstein Frisian, the black-and-white variety from the north of the Netherlands that are often used as iconic cows in ads worldwide.

THE DUTCH LANDSCAPE ENVIRONMENTAL ISSUES

READYING THE RIVERS

As sea levels rise and the levels of water flowing down rivers increases, more space has to be made to handle the volume. A severe storm in 1995 raised fears that Holland's rivers might overflow and thousands of people had to be evacuated, particularly from the Waal river zone by Nijmegen. This event was a catalyst for a nationwide project to widen the country's rivers and construct higher dykes at greater distances from the rivers, at a cost of €2.3 billion. More than 30 separate cases of flood plain excavation, dyke relocation and removal of obstacles to water flows are under way along the Waal, Lek, Nederrijn and IJssel and all their tributaries. Besides widening the rivers, the project, called 'Room for the River', aims to create more space for nature and seminatural environments. Species return not only due to the new habitat created but because the rivers are cleaner.

Dutch Cuisine

Though it isn't ordinarily included among the world's culinary leaders, the Netherlands is nevertheless increasingly a force to be reckoned with. Hearty, hefty, filling – these are the adjectives with which Dutch cooking is usually tagged. Traditionally, food was given scant attention as there was work to be done. But if the Dutch are anything it's innovative, and that spirit carries over to the kitchen. The new wave of Dutch chefs are busy refining their humble culinary antecedents and giving them a contemporary twist.

On the Menu

Foodie Websites

www.iens.nl – Everyday eaters give their restaurant opinions.

www.lekker.nl – Read reviews and listings for more than 9000 restaurants and cafes.

Dutch

Van Gogh perfectly captured the main ingredient of traditional Dutch cooking in his *Potato Eaters*. Typically boiled to death, these 'earth apples' are accompanied by meat – and more boiled vegetables. Gravy is then added for flavour. It's certainly not fancy, but it is filling.

Few restaurants serve exclusively Dutch cuisine, but many places have several homeland items on the menu, especially in winter. Some time-honoured favourites:

➡ **asperges** (asparagus) – The white version, stout and fleshy, most famously cultivated in Limburg and Noord-Brabant; popular when it's in season (spring); served with ham and butter.

➡ **erwtensoep** (pea soup) – Plenty of peas with onions, carrots, smoked sausage and bacon. And the perfect pea soup? A spoon stuck upright in the pot should remain standing. (Sadly not served in summer.)

➡ **hutspot** (hotchpotch; stew) – Similar to *stamppot,* but with potatoes, carrots, onions, braised meat and more spices. Originated in Leiden, which reputedly inherited (and modified) the recipe from the occupying Spaniards.

➡ **kroketten** (croquettes) – Crumb-coated dough sticks with various fillings that are deep-fried; *bitterballen*, the ball-shaped version, are a popular pub snack served with mustard.

➡ **mosselen** (mussels) – Cooked with white wine, chopped leeks and onions, and served in a bowl or cooking pot with a side dish of *frites* or *patat* (chips); they're best eaten from September to April.

PURELY DUTCH

The sight of a local slowly sliding a raw herring head-first (thankfully headless) down their gullet never fails to get a double-take from newcomers. But the Dutch love this salted delicacy. If an entire fish is too much to stomach, it can be cut into bite-sized pieces and served with onion and pickles. You'll find vendors the length and breadth of the country – look for the words *haring* or *Hollandse niuewe* and dig in. In fact, the arrival of new herring each May is a cause for celebration across the nation.

Another acquired taste in Holland is *drop*. This so-called sweet is a thick, rubbery liquorice root and Arabic gum concoction the Dutch go crazy for – a reputed 30 million kg of the stuff is consumed each year. Its bitter taste is reminiscent of childhood medicine and some foreigners have trouble taking a second bite.

DISTINCTLY CHEESY

Some Dutch say it makes them tall; others complain it causes nightmares. Whatever the case, the Netherlands is justifiably famous for its *kaas* (cheese). The average Dutch person consumes 18.6kg of the stuff every year.

Nearly two-thirds of all cheese sold is Gouda. The tastier varieties have strong, complex flavours and are best enjoyed with a glass of wine. It's classified by how long it's been aged, ranging from *jong* (young) to *belegen* (mature) to *oud*, the last being hard and rich in flavour. Oud Amsterdammer is a delight, deep orange and crumbly with white crystals of ripeness.

Edam is similar to Gouda but slightly drier and less creamy. Leidse or Leiden cheese is another export hit, laced with cumin or caraway seed and light in flavour.

In the shops you'll also find varieties that are virtually unknown outside the country. Frisian *Nagelkaas* might be made with parsley juice, buttermilk, and 'nails' of caraway seed. *Kruidenkaas* has a melange of herbs such as fennel, celery, pepper or onions. *Graskaas* is 'new harvest' Gouda made after cows begin to roam the meadows and munch grass.

➡ **stamppot** (mashed pot) – A simple dish of potatoes mashed with kale, endive or pickled cabbage and served with smoked sausage or strips of pork. Perfect in winter.

Lamb is prominently featured on menus, the most prized variety raised on the isle of Texel. When you're near the coast seafood is on every menu. It is also eaten as a snack. *Haring* (herring) is a national institution, eaten lightly salted or occasionally pickled; *paling* (eel), usually smoked, is another popular delicacy. *Kibbeling*, battered and deep-fried codfish, is a tasty snack commonly sold in street market fish stalls.

For dessert, cafes often serve *appeltaart* (apple pie) with *slagroom* (whipped cream). *Vlaai* is the signature pie of Limburg, filled with fruit or a smooth, subtly sweet cinnamony pudding filling, with a crumbly crust. Ambrosial.

Finally, most towns have at least one place serving *pannenkoeken* (pancakes), like crêpes and often served with fruit and cinnamon, among many other sweet and savoury toppings. *Poffertjes* are the coin-sized version, sprinkled with confectioner's sugar and laced with butter. You can often find these fresh at markets.

The Dutch start the day with a filling breakfast of a few slices of bread accompanied by jam, cheese and a boiled egg. Hotel breakfast buffets may be more lavish but take off from the same concept. A uniquely Dutch breakfast item is *hagelslag* (chocolate sprinkles), which is poured over bread.

Indonesian

Indonesian cooking, a piquant legacy of the colonial era, is a rich and complex blend of many cultures: chilli peppers, peanut sauce and curries from Thailand, lemon grass and fish sauce from Vietnam, intricate Indian spice mixes and Asian cooking methods.

In the Netherlands, Indonesian food is often toned down for sensitive Western palates. If you want it hot (*pedis*, pronounced 'p-dis'), say so, but be prepared for watering eyes and burnt taste buds. You might play it safe by asking for *sambal* (chilli paste) and helping yourself. *Sambal oelek* is red and hot; the dark-brown *sambal badjak* is onion-based, mild and sweet.

The best-known dish is rijsttafel (rice table), an array of spicy savoury dishes such as braised beef, pork satay and ribs served with white rice. *Nasi rames* is a steaming plate of boiled rice covered in several rich condiments, while the same dish with thick noodles is called *bami rames*.

Surinamese

Dishes from this former colony have Caribbean roots, blending African and Indian flavours with Indonesian influences introduced by Javanese labourers. Chicken, lamb and beef curries are common menu items, served either with rice or as sandwich fillings – the ever-popular Surinamese *broodjes*. *Roti*, a chickpea-flour pancake filled with curried potatoes, long beans and meat (vegetarian versions are available), makes a cheap and filling meal.

Drinks

Coffee & Tea

The Dutch drank on average 2.4 cups of coffee per day in 2014, ranking them far and away as the most caffeinated nation in Europe.

The hot drink of choice is coffee – after all, it was Amsterdam's merchants who introduced coffee to Europe – served by the cup (no refills), usually with a cookie on the side.

Ordering a *koffie* will get you a sizeable cup and a separate package or jug of *koffiemelk*, a slightly sour-tasting cream akin to condensed milk. *Koffie verkeerd* is similar to latte, served in a big mug with plenty of real milk. Hard-core aficionados may find the standard cup wanting, but fortunately for them craft espresso vendors are gaining ground: the Coffee Company, a national chain, is Holland's answer to Starbucks.

Tea is usually served Continental-style: a cup or pot of hot water with a tea bag on the side. Varieties might be presented in a humidor-like box for you to pick and choose. If you want milk, say *'met melk, graag'*. Many locals prefer to add a slice of lemon.

Beer

The Dutch love beer. It's seen as the perfect companion for time spent with friends in the sun or out partying till the small hours. And they've had plenty of time to cultivate this unquestioning love – beer has been a popular drink since the 14th century, and at one time the Dutch could lay claim to no fewer than 559 brewers. Most Dutch beer is lager (or Pilsner), a clear, crisp, golden beer with strong hop flavouring.

Beer Bars

't Arendsnest, Amsterdam

Locus Publicus, Delft

De Mug, Middelburg

De Pintelier, Groningen

Take One, Maastricht

Café Derat, Utrecht

De Stomme van Campen, Kampen

Beer is served cool and topped by a head of froth so big it would start a brawl in an Australian bar. Heineken tells us that these are 'flavour bubbles', and requests for no head will earn a steely response. *Een bier* or *een pils* will get you a normal glass; *een kleintje pils* is a small glass and *een fluitje* is a tall but thin glass – perfect for multiple refills.

Heineken is the Netherlands' (and possibly the world's) best-known beer. However, it's often dissed at home – 'the beer your cheap father drinks', to quote one wag. Amstel (owned by Heineken) is also well known, and Grolsch can also claim a certain amount of international fame. Most beers contain around 5% alcohol, and a few of those cute little glasses can pack a strong punch. While the big names are ubiquitous, the Netherlands has scores of small brewers worth trying, including Gulpener (from Gulpen in east Limburg), Jopen (Haarlem), Drie Ringen (Amersfoort), Leeuw (Leeuwarden) and Hettinga (Zwolle). La Trappe is the only Dutch Trappist beer, brewed close to Tilburg. The potent beers made by Amsterdam's Brouwerij 't IJ are sold on tap and in some local pubs – try the Columbus brew (9% alcohol).

Other local breweries worth trying include Texelse Bierbrouwerij on Texel, Rotterdam's Stadsbrouwerij De Pelgrim, Utrecht's Oudaen and Nijmegen's De Hemel. In addition, almost every town has at least one *café* or bar serving a huge range of beers. One of the best is Take One in Maastricht.

If you're around in spring or autumn, don't pass up the chance to sample Grolsch's seasonal bock beers, such as Lentebok (spring bock) and Herfstbok (autumn bock). Sample many at Utrecht's Café Ledig Erf, which has a bock beer fest over an autumn weekend.

THE ART OF BEING GEZELLIG

This particularly Dutch quality, which is most widely found in old brown *cafés* (traditional drinking establishment), is one of the best reasons to visit Amsterdam. It's variously translated as snug, friendly, cosy, informal, companionable and convivial, but *gezelligheid* – the state of being *gezellig* – is something more easily experienced than defined. There's a sense of time stopping, an intimacy of the here and now that leaves all your troubles behind, at least until tomorrow. You can get that warm and fuzzy feeling in many situations, often while nursing a brew with friends.

DUTCH DINING ESSENTIALS

Reservations It never hurts to phone ahead and make a reservation for restaurants in the upper price bracket.

Don't go hungry Dutch kitchens can close early; 'continental' dining times are for elsewhere on the continent. In smaller cities and towns be sure to be dining by 8pm or you might end up at a café (pub) or late-night snack stand (not necessarily a bad thing).

Tipping Diners do tip, but modestly. Round up to the next euro, or around 5%; a 10% tip is considered generous. If your bill comes to €9.50, you might leave €10. If you're paying by credit card, state the amount you want to pay, including tip, as you hand your payment over.

Cash rules Many restaurants don't accept credit cards unless they have an embedded chip. If they do, some levy a 5% surcharge; check first. Lately some places do not accept cash either; just European debit cards.

Saving money *Dagschotel* is the dish of the day; heartier appetites might go for a *dagmenu* (a set menu of three or more courses). Cafe breakfasts tend to be overpriced; consider hitting a bakery instead.

Spirits

It's not all beer here: the Dutch also make the hard stuff. *Jenever* (yanay-ver; Dutch gin; also spelled *genever*) is made from juniper berries and drunk chilled from a tiny glass filled to the brim. Most people prefer *jonge* (young) *jenever*, which is smooth and relatively easy to drink; *oude* (old) *jenever* has a strong juniper flavour and can be an acquired taste. A common combination, known as a *kopstoot* (head butt), is a glass of *jenever* with a beer chaser – few people can handle more than two or three of these. There are plenty of indigenous liqueurs, including *advocaat* (a kind of eggnog) and the herb-based Beerenburg, a Frisian schnapps.

Where to Eat & Drink

Restaurants abound and they cater to a wide variety of tastes and budgets. More casual are *eetcafés,* affordable publike eateries with loyal local followings. You'll also find a growing number of bistros and other types of eatery that draw their style from other cultures.

Cafés

When the Dutch say *'café'* they mean a pub, and there are more than 1000 of them in Amsterdam alone. In a country that values socialising and conversation even more than the art of drinking itself, *cafés* aren't just for drinking: they're places to hang out for literally hours of contemplation or camaraderie. Every town and city has a variety of atmospheric *cafés* that regular customers or a certain type of clientele have considered a 'second home' for years, if not generations.

Many cafes have outside seating on a *terras* (terrace), which are glorious in summer, and sometimes covered and heated in winter. These are fetching places to relax and people-watch, soak up the sun, read a paper or write postcards. Most serve food as well, ranging from snacks like traditional *bitterballen* to surprisingly excellent full meals.

Of course, the Netherlands will go down in cafe history for its historic *bruin cafés* (brown *cafés*). The name comes from the smoke stains from centuries of use. You may find sand on the wooden floor or Persian rugs on the tables to soak up spilled beer.

'Grand *cafés*' are spacious, have comfortable furniture and are, well, just grand. A good tradition in many is an indoor reading table stacked with the day's papers and news magazines, usually with one or two in

Favourite Brown Cafés

De Boom, Alkmaar

Hoppe, Amsterdam

De Heks, Deventer

De Blauwe Hand, Nijmegen

English. They generally have food menus, some quite elaborate. They're perfect for a lazy brunch or pre-theatre supper.

Theatre *cafés* are often similar to grand *cafés*, and are normally attached or adjacent to theatres, serving meals before and drinks after performances. Generally they're good places to catch performers after the show, though they're lovely any time of day.

Quick Eats

Broodjeszaken (sandwich shops) and snack bars proliferate. The latter offer multicoloured treats in a display case, usually based on some sort of meat and spices, and everything is dumped into a deep-fryer when you order. FEBO, the national chain of snack bars, has rows of coin-operated windows à la the Jetsons and are the lifeblood of late-night partiers.

Lebanese and Turkish snack bars specialise in *shoarma*, a pitta bread filled with sliced lamb from a vertical spit – also known as doner kebab – and Turkish pizza, aka *lahmacun*, a baked flat bread that is topped with spiced chopped meat, salad and sauce, then rolled up and served.

Vegetarians

It's surprising how few Dutch consider themselves vegetarians – only about 4% in most polls. Outside the major metropolises you'll be hard-pressed to find a strictly vegetarian-only restaurant in the small town you're visiting; in this case, you'll be relying on the couple of veg options available on most restaurant menus. Check their purity before ordering, though, as often you can't be sure whether they're 100% meat- or fish-free (meat stock is a common culprit). At the ubiquitous Surinamese snack bars, tofu and tempeh are usually available as sandwich fillings.

Top Food Festivals

There are plenty of culinary fests from late spring through early autumn. If you're in the country, don't miss the following:

➡ **Food Truck Festival Trek** (www.festival-trek.nl; multiple Netherlands locations; ◉mid-May–mid-Sep) Dozens of food trucks caravan it to eight different Dutch towns for a truly movable feast, with live music to boot.

➡ **Nijmegen Bierfeesten** (www.nijmeegse Bierfeesten.nl; ◉late May) Some 20 breweries proffer their wares in the heart of the city.

➡ **Taste of Amsterdam** (www.tasteofamsterdam.com; Amsterdam; ◉early Jun) Amsterdam's best restaurants present their signature dishes by the banks of the Amstel.

➡ **Vlaggetjesdag Scheveningen** (www.vlaggetjesdag.com; Scheveningen; ◉mid-Jun) The coastal town ushers in the herring season with a procession of decked-out fishing boats and plenty of *maatjesharing* (soused herring).

➡ **Haarlem Culinair** (www.haarlemculinair.nl; Haarlem; ◉early Aug) Haarlem's master chefs match culinary skills in the shadow of the big church.

➡ **Preuvenemint** (www.preuvenemint.nl; Maastricht; ◉late Aug) Claiming to be the country's biggest food fest, Preuvenemint (Tasting Event) showcases the southern city's myriad restaurants.

Sidebar text:

At any given time the Netherlands has a population of about 12 million pigs against 17 million humans. Despite being small in size, it is Europe's largest exporter of pork and domestic consumption is huge.

FEBO Snacks

Frikandel: skinless sausage of mercifully unspecified ingredients; worrisomely addictive.

Kaas soufflé: lavalike pocket of gooey cheesy goodness.

Bami: Indonesian-style noodles in a deep-fried orange lozenge.

Kroketten: deep-fried crumb-coated sticks with lamb, beef, satay and meatless fillings.

Broodje bal: meatballs on a bun.

FRITES

A national institution, *Vlaamse frites* actually come from Belgium. These fries are made from whole potatoes rather than the potato pulp you will get if the sign only says *frites*. They are supposed to be smothered in mayonnaise, though you can ask for ketchup, curry sauce, garlic sauce or other gloopy toppings. Three favourite vendors: De Haerlemsche Vlaamse (p104) in Haarlem, Vleminckx (p76) in Amsterdam and Reitz (p241) in Maastricht.

Survival Guide

Directory A–Z

Accommodation

The country's wealth of hotels, homestays and hostels provides any traveller – whether backpackers or five-star aficionados – with plenty of choice. Hotels and B&Bs are the mainstay of accommodation in the country and, while most are fairly standard and highly functional, a few gems fly the boutique flag or are simply idiosyncratic.

Note that a good part of the country suffers from the 'Amsterdam effect': because transport is so efficient and the city is so popular, many visitors stay in the capital even if they're travelling further afield. Conversely, some savvy folk use easy-to-access charmers such as Haarlem or Delft as their base, visiting the capital as a day – or night – trip (trains on key lines run all night).

B&Bs

Bed-and-breakfasts are an excellent way to meet the friendly locals face to face, and to see the weird, the wacky and the wonderful interior designs of the Dutch first-hand. While they're not abundant in cities, the countryside is awash with them. Local tourist offices keep a list of B&Bs on file; costs usually start from €30 to €35 per person.

Camping

The Dutch are avid campers, even within their own country. Campgrounds tend to be self-contained communities complete with shops, cafes, playgrounds and swimming pools. Lists of sites with ratings (one to five stars) are available from tourist offices.

A campsite, which costs anything from €10 to €20, covers two people and a small tent; a car is an extra €2 to €6. Caravans are popular and there are oodles of hook-ups.

Simple bungalows or cabins (from €45) with shared bathroom facilities are also an option at many campgrounds.

Hostels

Affiliated with Hostelling International (HI), the Dutch youth-hostel association goes by the banner of Stayokay (www.stayokay.com). Most offer a good variety of rooms. Facilities tend to be impressive, with newly built hostels common. Some, such as Rotterdam's Stayokay, are in landmark buildings.

Almost all Stayokay hostels and most indie hostels have dorm rooms that sleep up to eight people as well as private rooms for one to four people. Nightly rates normally range from €20 to €30 per person for dorm beds and from €60 for private rooms. Book ahead, especially in high season.

Amsterdam has scores of indie hostels (some cutting-edge, some shambolic, some party central filled with high jinks and stoners), with an increasing number appearing around the rest of the country.

Hotels

Any hotel with more than 20 rooms is considered large, and most rooms are on the snug side. You'll see a 'star' plaque on the front of every hotel, indicating its rating according to the Nederlandse Hotel Classificatie (NHC; national hotel classification system). The stars (from one to five) are awarded according to certain facilities, rather than quality. This means that a two-star hotel may be in

---

SLEEPING PRICE RANGES

The following price ranges refer to a double room with bathroom in high season. Unless otherwise stated, breakfast is not included in the price.

€ less than €100

€€ €100–€180

€€€ more than €180

better condition than a hotel of higher rank, albeit with fewer facilities.

Amenities

Wi-fi is nearly universal across the spectrum; air-conditioning and lifts are not. Be prepared for very steep stairs.

➡ **Top End** Expect lifts, minibars and room service. At the top of top end, facilities such as air-conditioning and fitness centres are par for the course. Breakfast is often not included.

➡ **Midrange** Most hotels in this category are big on comfort, low on formality and small enough to offer personal attention. Rooms usually have a toilet and shower, and a TV and phone. Not many hotels in this category over two storeys have lifts, and their narrow stairwells can take some getting used to, especially with luggage. Rates typically include breakfast.

➡ **Budget** Lodgings in the lowest price bracket, other than hostels, are thin on the ground. The better options tend to be spick and span with furnishings that are, at best, cheap and cheerful. Rates often include breakfast.

Rental Accommodation

Renting a property for a few days can be a fun part of a trip. In Amsterdam it gets you a kitchen and other amenities that make coming 'home' after a hard day having fun that much nicer; while out in the countryside it can provide your own retreat. Rentals are often priced competitively with hotels, which offer less in the way of facilities and space.

Climate
Amsterdam

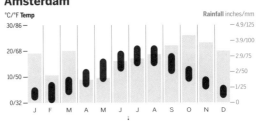

Customs Regulations

For visitors from EU countries, limits only apply for excessive amounts. See www.belastingdienst.nl for details.

Residents of non-EU countries are limited to the following:

Alcohol 1L spirits, wine or beer

Coffee 500g of coffee, or 200g of coffee extracts or coffee essences

Perfume 50g of perfume and 0.25L of eau de toilette

Tea 100g of tea, or 40g of tea extracts or tea essences

Tobacco 200 cigarettes, or 250g of tobacco (shag or pipe tobacco), or 100 cigarillos or 50 cigars

Discount Cards

Visitors of various professions, including artists and teachers, may get discounts at some venues if they show accreditation.

Students regularly get a few euros off museum admission; bring ID.

Seniors over 65, and with partners of 60 or older, benefit from reductions on public transport, museum admission, concerts and more. You may look younger, so bring your passport.

Many cities (eg Amsterdam, Den Haag and Rotterdam) offer discount-card schemes that are good for museums, attractions and local transport. Ask at tourist offices.

Cultureel Jongeren Paspoort (Cultural Youth Passport; www.cjp.nl; card €17.50) Big discounts to museums and cultural events nationwide for people under the age of 30.

Holland Pass (www.holland pass.com; 2/4/6 attractions €42/62/82) Similar to the I Amsterdam Card (p99), but without the rush for usage; you can visit sights over a month. Prices are based on the number of attractions, which you pick from tiers (the most popular/expensive sights are gold tier). Also includes a train ticket from the airport to the city, and a canal cruise. Available from GWK Travelex offices and various hotels.

Museumkaart (Museum Card; www.museumkaart.nl; adult/child €55/27.50, plus for 1st registration €5) Free and discounted entry to some 400 museums all over the country for one year. Purchase at participating museum ticket counters or from ticket shops.

BOOK YOUR STAY ONLINE

For more accommodation reviews by Lonely Planet authors, check out http://lonelyplanet.com/hotels/. You'll find independent reviews, as well as recommendations on the best places to stay. Best of all, you can book online.

Electricity

230V/50Hz

230V/50Hz

Embassies & Consulates

Amsterdam is the country's capital but Den Haag is the seat of government. Many embassies (including those for Australia, Canada, New Zealand and Ireland) are in Den Haag, but Amsterdam has several consulates.

Amsterdam

French Consulate
(☎020-530 69 69; www.consulfrance-amsterdam.org; Vijzelgracht 2; 🚊16/24/25 Keizersgracht)

German Consulate (☎020-574 77 00; www.niederlande.diplo.de; Honthorststraat 36-38; 🚊2/5 Hobbemastraat)

UK Consulate (☎020-676 43 43; www.gov.uk; Konings-laan 44; 🚊2 Valeriusplein)

US Consulate (☎020-575 53 09; http://amsterdam.us-consulate.gov; Museumplein 19; 🚊3/5/12/16/24 Museumplein)

Den Haag

Australian Embassy (☎070-310 82 00; http://netherlands.embassy.gov.au; Carnegielaan 4)

Belgian Embassy (☎070-312 34 56; www.diplomatie.be/thehague; Johan van Olden-barneveltlaan 11)

Canadian Embassy (☎070-311 16 00; www.canadainterna-tional.gc.ca; Sophialaan 7)

French Embassy (☎070-312 58 00; www.ambafrance-nl.org; Smidsplein 1)

Irish Embassy (☎070-363 09 93; www.embassyofireland.nl; Scheveningseweg 112)

New Zealand Embassy
(☎070-346 93 24; www.nzem-bassy.com; Eisenhowerlaan 77)

UK Embassy (☎070-427 04 27; www.gov.uk; Lange Voor-hout 10)

US Embassy (☎070-310 22 09; http://thehague.usem-bassy.gov; Lange Voorhout 102)

Food

Get an in-depth overview of Dutch cuisine on p286.

Gay & Lesbian Travellers

The best national source of information is the government-subsidised COC

(www.coc.nl). It has branches throughout the country that are happy to offer advice.

Amsterdam is one of the gay capitals of Europe. In towns outside Amsterdam, however, the scene is less prominent. Rotterdam is an exception, as are university towns with large gay and lesbian student populations.

Health

It is unlikely that you will encounter unusual health problems in the Netherlands, and if you do, standards of care are world-class. It is still important to have health insurance for your trip.

A few travelling tips:

➡ Bring medications in their original, clearly labelled containers.

➡ Bring a list of your prescriptions (copies of the containers are good) including generic names, so you can get replacements if your bags go on holiday – carry this info separately.

➡ If you have health problems that may need treatment, bring a signed and dated letter from your physician describing your medical conditions and medications.

➡ If carrying syringes or needles, have a physician's letter documenting their medical necessity.

➡ If you need vision correction, carry a spare pair of contact lenses or glasses, and/or take your optical prescription with you.

Recommended Vaccinations

No jabs are necessary for the Netherlands. However, the World Health Organization (WHO) recommends that all travellers should be covered for diphtheria, tetanus, measles, mumps, rubella and polio, regardless of their destination.

Insurance

Travel insurance is a good idea if your policies at home won't cover you in the Netherlands. Although medical or dental costs might already be covered through reciprocal health-care arrangements, you'll still need cover for theft or loss, and for unexpected changes to travel arrangements (ticket cancellation etc). Check what's already covered by your local insurance policies or credit cards.

Worldwide travel insurance is available at www.lonely planet.com/travel_services. You can buy, extend and claim online any time – even if you're already on the road.

Internet Access

Wi-fi is widespread in hotels and cafes (you may need to ask for the code), and can be found for free in many tourist offices and other public places. Open your wireless device and you'll often find paid wi-fi access from KPN (www.kpn.com), the national phone company, and other providers such as T-Mobile (www.t-mobile.nl).

Internet cafes are few and far between, although storefronts selling cheap phonecards with a few terminals can be found near train stations in larger towns. Many libraries, tourist offices, *coffeeshops* and hotels provide internet terminals (sometimes free). Expect to pay anything from €2 to €4 per hour.

If you're surfing on a smartphone that works in the Netherlands, beware of potentially astronomical roaming charges (around €1 per minute depending on your provider).

Legal Matters

The Netherlands *politie* (police) are pretty relaxed and helpful unless you do something clearly wrong, such as

littering or smoking a joint right under their noses.

Police can hold offenders for up to six hours for questioning (plus another six hours if they can't establish your identity, or 24 hours if they consider the matter serious). You won't have the right to a phone call, but they'll notify your consulate. You're presumed innocent until proven guilty.

ID Papers

Anyone over 14 years of age is required by law to carry ID. Foreigners should carry a passport or a photocopy of the relevant data pages; a driver's licence isn't sufficient.

Drugs

➡ Technically, marijuana is illegal. However, possession of soft drugs (eg cannabis) up to 5g is tolerated. Larger amounts are subject to prosecution.

➡ Don't light up in an establishment other than a *coffeeshop* (cafe authorised to sell cannabis) without checking that it's OK to do so.

➡ Hard drugs are treated as a serious crime.

➡ Never buy drugs of any kind on the street; fatalities can and do occur.

Prostitution

Prostitution is legal in the Netherlands. The industry is protected by law and prostitutes pay tax. Much of this open policy stems from a desire to undermine the role of pimps and the underworld in the sex industry.

In Amsterdam's Red Light District you have little to fear as the streets are well-policed, but the back alleys are more dubious.

Maps

The best road maps of the Netherlands are those produced by Michelin and the Dutch automobile association ANWB. The ANWB also puts out provincial maps detailing cycling paths and picturesque road routes. You'll find a wide variety of maps for sale at any tourist office, as well as at bookstores and news-stands.

Tourist offices sell all forms of maps and often have local walking-tour maps in English for sale.

Money

➡ The Netherlands uses the euro (€). Denominations of the currency are €5, €10, €20, €50, €100, €200 and €500 notes, and €0.01, €0.02, €0.05, €0.10, €0.20, €0.50, €1 and €2 coins (amounts under €1 are called cents).

➡ To check the latest exchange rates, visit www.xe.com.

ATMs

Automated teller machines (ATMs, aka cash machines) can be found outside most banks and at airports and most train stations. Credit cards such as Visa and MasterCard/Eurocard are widely accepted, as well as cards from the Plus and Cirrus networks. Using an ATM can be the cheapest way to exchange your money from home but check with your home bank for service charges before you leave.

You can use your ATM card to keep stocked up with euros throughout the Netherlands so there's no need for currency exchange. However, using your ATM card as a debit card, as opposed to a credit card, to pay for purchases won't always work as many businesses only accept Dutch PIN cards.

Cash

Cash is commonly used for everyday purchases throughout the Netherlands.

Credit Cards

All the major international credit cards are recognised, and most hotels and large stores accept them. But a fair number of shops, restaurants and other businesses (including Dutch Railways and supermarket chains) do not accept credit cards, or accept only European cards with security chips.

Some establishments levy a 5% surcharge (or more) on credit cards to offset the commissions charged by card providers. Always check first.

For a backup plan against any security-chip issue, consider getting the Chip and PIN Cash Passport (www.travelex.com/us/products/cash-passport), a preloaded debit MasterCard from Travelex that has a security chip embedded. You won't want to use the card much, as the exchange rates you get when you load it are pretty awful (read the regulations carefully). But it can be helpful to have in emergency situations when/if your home credit card won't work.

PIN Cards

In the Netherlands you'll notice people gleefully using 'PIN' cards everywhere, from shops to supermarkets and vending machines. These direct-debit cards look like credit or bank cards with little circuit chips on them, but they won't be of much use to visitors without a Dutch bank account.

Tipping

The Dutch do tip, but modestly.

Hotel porters €1 to €2

Restaurants Round up, or 5% to 10%

Taxis 5% to 10%

Travellers Cheques

Travellers cheques are rare – you'll be hard-pressed to find a bank that will change them for you.

Opening Hours

As a general rule, opening hours are as follows:

Banks and government offices 9am to 4pm Monday to Friday, some Saturday morning.

Bars and cafes 11am to 1am; some open longer at weekends and others won't open till late afternoon.

Businesses 8.30am to 5pm Monday to Friday.

Clubs Hours vary, but in general 10pm to 4am Friday and Saturday; some also open Wednesday, Thursday and Sunday.

Museums 10am to 5pm daily, some close Monday.

Restaurants 10am or 11am to 10pm, with an afternoon break from 3pm to 6pm.

Shops Noon to 6pm Monday, and 8.30am or 9am to 6pm Tuesday to Saturday. Most towns have *koopavond* (evening shopping), when stores stay open till 9pm on Thursday or Friday. Bigger supermarkets in cities stay open until 8pm. Sunday shopping is becoming more common; large stores are often open noon to 5pm.

Post

The national post office in the Netherlands is privatised and has gone through various name changes.

The current operator is PostNL (www.postnl.nl). It has closed most city post offices and to mail a letter

or package you'll need to go to a postal service shop which may be a supermarket or tobacco shop or something else. Use the website (available in English) to find a location near you. Note that if you're trying to mail a parcel abroad, the staff at the third-party shop may have no idea how to help you.

Public Holidays

Most museums adopt Sunday hours on public holidays (except Christmas and New Year, when they close) even if they fall on a day when the place would otherwise be closed, such as Monday. Many people treat Remembrance Day (4 May) as a day off.

Carnaval is celebrated with vigour in the Catholic south. Huge parties are thrown in the run-up to Shrove Tuesday and little work gets done.

Nieuwjaarsdag (New Year's Day) Parties and fireworks galore

Goede Vrijdag Good Friday

Eerste Paasdag Easter Sunday

Tweede Paasdag Easter Monday

Koningsdag (King's Day) 27 April (26 April if the 27th is a Sunday)

Bevrijdingsdag (Liberation Day) 5 May. Not a universal holiday: government workers have the day off, but almost everyone else has to work

Hemelvaartsdag (Ascension Day) Fortieth day after Easter Sunday

Eerste Pinksterdag (Whit Sunday; Pentecost) Fiftieth day after Easter Sunday

Tweede Pinksterdag (Whit Monday) Fiftieth day after Easter Monday

Eerste Kerstdag (Christmas Day) 25 December

Tweede Kerstdag ('Second Christmas' aka Boxing Day) 26 December

PRACTICALITIES

➡ **Weights & Measures** The Netherlands uses the metric system.

➡ **Media** Dutch-language newspapers include *De Telegraaf*, the Netherlands' biggest seller; and *Het Parool*, Amsterdam's paper, with the scoop on what's happening around town. Keep abreast of news back home via the *International Herald Tribune* or the *Guardian*, or weeklies such as the *Economist* or *Time*, all widely available on news-stands.

➡ **Smoking** The Netherlands bans cigarette smoking inside all bars and restaurants, but you're free to light up outdoors on terraces where they're completely open on one side.

Safe Travel

The Netherlands is one of the safest countries in Europe, but you should still use big-city street sense in larger cities. Bicycle theft is common; always use two locks.

Bicycles can be quite a challenge to pedestrians. Remember when crossing the street to look for speeding bikes as well as cars; straying into a bike lane without looking both ways can cause serious accidents. When cycling yourself, take care with skidding on tram tracks or getting your wheels caught.

Telephone

The Dutch phone network, KPN (www.kpn.com), is efficient, and prices are reasonable by European standards.

Collect Call (Collect Gesprek; ☑domestic 0800 04 10, international ☑0800 01 01) Both numbers are free.

Domestic & International Dialling

To ring abroad, dial ☑00 followed by the country code for your target country, the area code (you usually drop the leading ☑0 if there is one) and the subscriber number.

Netherlands country code ☑31

Free calls ☑0800

Mobile numbers ☑06

Paid information calls ☑0900; cost varies between €0.10 and €1.30 per minute.

Drop the leading ☑0 on city codes if you're calling from outside the Netherlands (eg ☑20 for Amsterdam instead of ☑020). Do not dial the city code if you are in the area covered by it.

Internet Calls

Services such as Skype (www.skype.com), Google Voice (www.google.com/voice) and Viber (www.viber.com) can make calling home cheap. Check the websites for details.

For messaging, a huge percentage of Dutch use WhatsApp (www.whatsapp.com).

Mobile Phones

➡ The Netherlands uses GSM phones compatible with the rest of Europe and Australia but not with some North American GSM phones. Smartphones such as iPhones will work – but beware of enormous roaming costs, especially for data (buy an international plan from your carrier before you leave home).

➡ Prepaid mobile phones are available at mobile-phone shops, starting from around €35 when on special. You can also buy SIM cards (from €5) for your own GSM mobile phone that will give you a Dutch telephone number. Look for Phone House, Orange, T-Mobile and Vodafone shops in major shopping areas.

➡ New prepaid phones generally come with a small amount of call time already stored. To top it up, purchase more minutes at one of the branded stores, newsagents or supermarkets, and follow the instructions.

➡ Incoming calls to Dutch mobile phones are generally free to the recipient.

Phonecards

➡ Public telephones are increasingly scarce.

➡ Phonecards (for €5, €10 and €20) for public telephones are available at train-station counters, tourist offices, GWK offices and tobacco shops.

➡ KPN's card is the most common but there are plenty of competitors (T-Mobile and Vodaphone among them) that usually have better rates.

Time

➡ The Netherlands is in the Central European time zone (same as Berlin and Paris), GMT/UTC plus one hour. Noon in Amsterdam is 11am in London, 6am in New York, 3am in San Francisco and 9pm in Sydney.

➡ For daylight savings time, clocks are put forward one hour at 2am on the last Sunday in March and back again at 3am on the last Sunday in October.

➡ When telling the time, be aware that the Dutch use 'half' to indicate 'half before' the hour. If you say 'half eight' (8.30 in many forms of English), a Dutch person will take this to mean 7.30.

Tourist Information

➡ Outside the Netherlands, www.holland.com is a useful resource.

➡ Within the Netherlands, **VVV** (Vereniging voor Vreemdelingenverkeer, Netherlands Tourism Board; www.vvv.nl) is the official network of tourist offices around the country. Each tourist office is locally run and has local and regional info. Few VVV publications are free but tourist offices are a good place to buy maps and guides.

➡ The Dutch automobile association (ANWB; www. anwb.nl) has maps and guidebooks for sale. It provides a wide range of useful information and assistance if you're travelling with any type of vehicle (car, bicycle, motorcycle, yacht etc). In some cities the VVV and ANWB share offices. You'll have to show proof of membership of your home automobile club to get free maps or discounts.

Travellers with Disabilities

Travellers with restricted mobility will find the Netherlands somewhat accessible despite the limitations of most older buildings.

➡ Most offices and larger museums have lifts and/or ramps, and toilets for people with a disability.

➡ Many budget and midrange hotels have limited accessibility, as they are in old buildings with steep stairs and no lifts.

➡ Cobblestone streets are rough for wheelchairs.

➡ Restaurants tend to be on ground floors, though 'ground' sometimes includes a few steps.

➡ Bathrooms in restaurants may not be wheelchair accessible or fitted with rails.

➡ Train and other public-transport stations sometimes have lifts.

➡ Most train stations and public buildings have toilets for people with a disability.

➡ Trains usually have wheelchair access.

➡ The Dutch national organisation for people with a disability is ANGO (www. ango.nl).

Visas

Tourists from nearly 60 countries – including Australia, Canada, Israel, Japan, New Zealand, Singapore, South Korea, the USA and most of Europe – need only a valid passport to visit the Netherlands for up to three months. EU nationals can enter for up to four months with a passport or national identity card.

Nationals of most other countries need a Schengen visa, valid within the EU member states (except the UK and Ireland), plus Norway and Iceland, for 90 days within a six-month period.

Schengen visas are issued by Dutch embassies or consulates overseas and can take a while to process (up to two months). You'll need a passport valid until at least three months after your visit, and will have to prove you have sufficient funds for your stay and return journey.

➡ **Netherlands Foreign Affairs Ministry** (www. government.nl) Lists consulates and embassies around the world.

➡ **Immigratie en Naturalisatiedienst** (Immigration & Naturalisation Service; ☎0880 430 430; www.ind.nl) Handles visas and extensions. Study visas must be applied for through your college or university in the Netherlands.

Transport

GETTING THERE & AWAY

The Netherlands is an easy place to reach. Amsterdam's Schiphol International Airport has copious air links worldwide, including many on low-cost European airlines. Rotterdam The Hague Airport serves more than 40 European destinations; Eindhoven Airport is a budget-airline hub.

High-speed trains are especially good from France, Belgium and Germany and, from late 2016, London via the Eurostar. Other land options are user friendly and the border crossings are nearly invisible thanks to the EU. There are also ferry links with the UK.

What's more, once you get to the Netherlands the transport remains hassle free. Most journeys by rail, car or bus are so short that you can reach most regional destinations before your next meal. And with its flat terrain, getting around by bicycle is a breeze.

Flights, car rental and tours can be booked online at lonelyplanet.com/bookings

Entering the Country

Passport

In principle, all passengers with passports are allowed entry to the Netherlands. There are relatively few nationalities that need visas.

Air

Airports

Schiphol International Airport (AMS; www.schiphol.nl), conveniently located near both Amsterdam and Rotterdam, is the Netherlands' main international airport and the fourth busiest in Europe. It's the hub of Dutch passenger carrier KLM and is serviced by most of the world's major airlines. The airport is like a small city and is well linked to the rest of the country by train, including the high-speed line south to Rotterdam as well Antwerp and Brussels (Belgium) and Paris (France). It runs efficiently for its size, with a huge shopping mall, Schiphol Plaza, filled with travellers' amenities. You can store luggage for up to a week. There are also airport hotels.

Rotterdam The Hague Airport (RTM; www.rotterdamthe-hagueairport.nl), serving more than 40 European destinations, is less than 6km northwest of Rotterdam. Bus 33 makes the 20-minute run from the airport to Rotterdam Centraal Station every 15 minutes throughout the day. A taxi takes 10 minutes to get to the centre and costs around €25.

Eindhoven Airport (EIN; www.eindhovenairport.com) is a budget-airline hub. It's 6km west of the centre of Eindhoven. Bus 401 runs every 10 minutes between the airport and the train station (€3.50, 25 minutes).

CLIMATE CHANGE & TRAVEL

Every form of transport that relies on carbon-based fuel generates CO_2, the main cause of human-induced climate change. Modern travel is dependent on aeroplanes, which might use less fuel per kilometre per person than most cars but travel much greater distances. The altitude at which aircraft emit gases (including CO_2) and particles also contributes to their climate change impact. Many websites offer 'carbon calculators' that allow people to estimate the carbon emissions generated by their journey and, for those who wish to do so, to offset the impact of the greenhouse gases emitted with contributions to portfolios of climate-friendly initiatives throughout the world. Lonely Planet offsets the carbon footprint of all staff and author travel.

Land

Bicycle

➡ Bringing your own bike into the Netherlands will cause no problems. Ask your carrier to see what you need to do to check it on a plane; by train you usually have to remove the front wheel and put it in a carrier bag.

➡ Long-distance bicycle paths are called *landelijke fietsroutes* (LF) and retain that label in northern Belgium.

BELGIUM

Long-distance cyclists can choose from a variety of safe, easy, specially designated routes to get to the Netherlands from Belgium and Germany. The LF2 route runs 350km from Brussels via Antwerp, Dordrecht and Rotterdam to Amsterdam.

GERMANY

Route LF4 stretches 300km from Enschede near the German border to Den Haag.

The fast German ICE trains from Cologne and Frankfurt are not bike friendly; use regular trains instead.

THE ESSENTIAL TRIP PLANNER

The service 9292.nl (www.9292.nl) is an unrivalled planning resource for getting around the Netherlands. It has comprehensive schedules for every train, tram and bus in the country in English. There is a brilliant free smartphone app.

On the web or app, enter your start and end points (eg an address, train station, museum, hotel); the results include walking details and fares.

UK

Most cross-Channel ferries don't charge foot passengers extra to take a bicycle. You can also bring your two-wheeler on the connecting trains, where it travels for free if it fits into a bike bag as hand luggage.

Bus

Eurolines (www.eurolines.com) A consortium of coach operators that runs cheap international bus services to/from the Netherlands. Coaches have on-board toilets and reclining seats. Some services have on-board wi-fi.

Busabout (www.busabout.com) Operates buses that complete set circuits around Europe, stopping at major cities. The service runs only from May to October and is aimed at younger travellers. Pricing is complex.

Car & Motorcycle

➡ Drivers need vehicle registration papers, third-party insurance and their domestic licence. Get a Green Card from your insurer to show you have coverage.

➡ ANWB (www.anwb.nl) provides information, maps, advice and services if you show a membership card from your own automobile association, such as the AA or AAA.

➡ Hitching is uncommon in the Netherlands. Like most destinations, it poses a small but potentially serious risk and is not recommended.

➡ Ferries take cars and motorcycles to the Netherlands from several ports in the UK including Harwich to Hoek van Holland and Hull to Europoort (both near Rotterdam). There's also a service from Newcastle to IJmuiden near Amsterdam.

Train

International train connections are good. All Eurail and Inter-Rail passes are valid on the Dutch national train service, **NS** (Nederlandse Spoorwegen; www.ns.nl). Many

international services are operated by NS International (www.nsinternational.nl). In addition, Thalys (www.thalys.com) fast trains serve Brussels (where you can connect to the Eurostar) and Paris. From December 2016, direct Eurostar services will link Amsterdam, Schiphol International Airport and Rotterdam with London.

In peak periods it's wise to reserve seats in advance. Buy tickets online at SNCB Europe (www.b-europe.com).

Major Dutch train stations have international ticket offices; you can also buy tickets for local trains to Belgium and Germany at the normal ticket counters.

The excellent website Seat 61 (www.seat61.com) has comprehensive information about train travel.

BELGIUM

Full fares are high (for example Amsterdam to Brussels €80), but advance fares are likely to be cheap (€29).

Thalys operates trains between Paris, Brussels, Rotterdam and Amsterdam (3½ hours from Paris). It also has good advance fares and there is a range of discount schemes.

In the south there is an hourly service between Maastricht and Liège (30 minutes).

GERMANY

German ICE high-speed trains run six times a day between Amsterdam and Cologne (2½ hours) via Utrecht. Many continue on to Frankfurt (four hours) via Frankfurt Airport.

Advance purchase fares bought on the web are as little as €34. Buy tickets in advance at either www.b-europe.com or www.bahn.de, then print them out and present them on the train or show them on a smartphone.

With connections in Cologne or Frankfurt, you can reach any part of Germany easily. Other direct services include several regular trains a day between Amsterdam and Berlin (6½ hours) and a local service from Groningen east across the border to tiny Leer, where you can get trains to Bremen and beyond.

From Maastricht you can reach Cologne via Liège in Belgium and Aachen in Germany (1½ to two hours).

UK

Eurostar (www.eurostar.com) Services take two hours from London St Pancras to Brussels. There you can connect to high-speed trains to the Netherlands and Amsterdam (two hours from Brussels). From late 2016, direct Eurostar services will run from London to Amsterdam, stopping at Brussels, Antwerp, Rotterdam and Schiphol International Airport, with a London–Amsterdam journey time of four hours.

Dutch Flyer (www.stenaline.co.uk) Its services are one of the cheapest ways to reach the Netherlands from the UK. Trains from London (Liverpool St Station), Cambridge and Norwich connect with ferries sailing from Harwich to Hoek van Holland, where a further train travels on to Rotterdam and Amsterdam. The journey takes around nine hours and costs as little as UK£49 one way.

Sea
UK
Several companies operate car/passenger ferries between the Netherlands and the UK. Most travel agents have details of the services but might not always know the finer points. The ferry companies run frequent specials. There are also train–ferry–train services available.

Reservations are essential for cars in high season, although motorcycles can often be squeezed in. Most ferries don't charge for a bike and have no shortage of storage space.

Stena Line (www.stenaline.co.uk) Sails between Harwich

and Hoek van Holland, 31km northwest of Rotterdam, linked to central Rotterdam by train (30 minutes). The fast HSS ferries take 5½ hours and depart in each direction twice a day. Overnight ferries take 8½ hours (one daily), as do normal day ferries (one daily). Foot passengers pay from UK£73 return. Fares for a car and driver range from UK£143 to UK£400 return depending on the season and the day of the week. Options such as reclining chairs and cabins cost extra and are compulsory on night crossings.

P&O Ferries (www.poferries.com) Operates an overnight ferry every evening (11¾ hours) between Hull and Europoort, 39km west of central Rotterdam. Book bus tickets (40 minutes) to/from Rotterdam when you reserve your berth. Return fares start at UK£104 for a foot passenger and UK£120 for a car with driver. Prices include berths in an inside cabin; luxury cabins are available. Prices are much higher in peak season.

DFDS Seaways (www.dfdsseaways.co.uk) Sails between Newcastle and IJmuiden, 30km northwest of Amsterdam, linked to Amsterdam by bus; the 15-hour sailings depart every day. The earlier you book, the lower your fare: return fares start at UK£67 for a foot passenger in an economy berth, plus UK£148 for a car. Prices go up in peak season. The website is relentless in its efforts to upsell.

GETTING AROUND
The Netherlands is very easy to get around. If you are sticking to all but the most remote villages and sights, you won't need a car as the train and bus system blankets the country. Or you can do as the Dutch do and hop on a bike.

Air
With a country as small as the Netherlands (the long-

est train journey, between Groningen and Maastricht, takes 4¼ hours), there are no domestic flights.

Bicycle
The Netherlands is extremely bike friendly and a *fiets* (bicycle) is the way to go. Many people have the trip of a lifetime using nothing but pedal power. Most modes of transport, such as trains and buses, are friendly to cyclists and their bikes. Dedicated bike routes go virtually everywhere.

Boat
Ferry
Ferries connect the mainland with the five Frisian Islands. Passenger ferries span the Westerschelde in the south of Zeeland, providing a link between the southwestern expanse of the country and Belgium. These are popular with people using the Zeebrugge ferry terminal and run frequently year-round.

Regular ferries connect Den Helder with the Waddenzee island of Texel, from where there are also ferries to Vlieland.

The **Waterbus** (☏0800 023 25 45; www.waterbus.nl; day pass adult/child €13/9.50) is an excellent fast ferry service that links Rotterdam and Dordrecht as well as the popular tourist destinations of Kinderdijk and Biesbosch National Park. Boats leave from Willemskade every 30 minutes.

Many more minor services provide links across the myriad Dutch canals and waterways.

Hire
Renting a boat is a popular way to tour rivers, lakes and inland seas. Boats come in all shapes and sizes, from canoes to motor boats, small sailing boats, and large and historic former cargo

sloops. Prices run the gamut and there are hundreds of rental firms throughout the country.

Bus

Buses are used for regional transport rather than for long distances, which are better travelled by train. They provide a vital service, especially in parts of the north and east, where trains are less frequent or nonexistent. The fares are zone-based. You can always buy a temporary paper OV-chipkaart ticket from the driver (€2.70 to €5 for modest distances) but most people pay with a preloaded OV-chipkaart.

There is only one class of travel. Some regions have day passes good for all the buses; ask a driver, they are usually very helpful.

Car & Motorcycle

Dutch freeways are extensive but prone to congestion. Those around Amsterdam, the A4 south to Belgium and the A2 southeast to Maastricht are especially likely to be jammed at rush hour and during busy travel periods; traffic jams with a total length of 350km or more aren't unheard of during the holiday season.

Smaller roads are usually well maintained, but the campaign to discourage car use throws up numerous obstacles: two-lane roads are repainted to be one-lane with wide bike lanes or there are barriers, speed bumps and other 'traffic-calming schemes'.

Parking a car can be both a major headache and expensive. Cities purposely limit parking to discourage car use and rates are high: hotels boast about 'discount' parking rates for overnight guests of €30. Amsterdam has the highest parking rates in the world, averaging €50 per day.

Automobile Associations

ANWB (✆ 070-314 14 14; www. anwb.nl) is the automobile club in the Netherlands;

most big towns and cities have an office. Members of auto associations in their home countries (the AA, AAA, CAA, NRMA etc) can get assistance, free maps, discounts and more.

Driving Licence

Visitors from outside the EU are entitled to drive in the Netherlands on their foreign licences for a period of up to 185 days per calendar year. EU licences are accepted year-round.

You'll need to show a valid driving licence when hiring a car in the Netherlands. An international driving permit (IDP) is not needed.

Fuel

Like much of Western Europe, petrol is very expensive and fluctuates on a regular basis. Prices are generally €1.70 per litre (about US$8.50 per gallon). Gasoline (petrol) is *benzine* in Dutch, while unleaded fuel is *loodvrij*. Leaded fuel is not sold in the Netherlands but diesel (€1.27 per litre) is always available and much cheaper, so it can be worth renting a diesel car. Liquid petroleum gas (€0.73 per litre) can be purchased at petrol stations displaying LPG signs.

To check current fuel prices, visit www.fuel-prices-europe.info.

Hire

➡ The Netherlands is well covered for car hire; all major firms have numerous locations.

➡ Apart from in Amsterdam and at the airports, the car-hire companies can be in inconvenient locations if you're arriving by train.

➡ You must be at least 23 years of age to hire a car in the Netherlands. Some car-hire firms levy a small surcharge for drivers under 25.

➡ A credit card is required to rent.

FARES, TICKETS & OV-CHIPKAARTS

Local transport tickets are smart cards called the OV-chipkaart (www.ov-chipkaart.nl).

➡ Either purchase a reusable OV-chipkaart in advance at a local transport-information office, or purchase a disposable one when you board a bus or tram.

➡ Some trams have conductors responsible for ticketing, while on others the drivers handle tickets.

➡ When you enter *and* exit a bus, tram or metro, hold the card against a reader at the doors or station gates. The system then calculates your fare and deducts it from the card. If you don't check out, the system will deduct the highest fare possible.

➡ Fares for the reusable cards are much lower than the disposable ones (though you do have to pay an initial €7.50 fee; the card is valid for five years).

➡ You can also buy OV-chipkaarts for unlimited use for one or more days, and this often is the most convenient option. Local transport operators sell these.

➡ Stored-value OV-chipkaarts can be used on trains throughout the Netherlands.

ROAD DISTANCES (KM)

	Amsterdam	Apeldoorn	Arnhem	Breda	Den Bosch	Den Haag	Dordrecht	Eindhoven	Enschede	Groningen	Haarlem	Leeuwarden	Leiden	Maastricht	Nijmegen	Rotterdam	Tilburg
Apeldoorn	86																
Arnhem	99	27															
Breda	101	141	111														
Den Bosch	88	91	64	48													
Den Haag	55	133	118	72	102												
Dordrecht	98	133	102	30	65	45											
Eindhoven	121	109	82	57	32	134	92										
Enschede	161	75	98	212	162	224	200	180									
Groningen	203	147	172	260	236	252	248	254	148								
Haarlem	19	117	114	121	103	51	94	136	184	204							
Leeuwarden	139	133	158	248	222	188	234	240	163	62	148						
Leiden	45	125	110	87	99	17	60	132	192	242	42	178					
Maastricht	213	201	167	146	124	223	181	86	274	348	228	334	239				
Nijmegen	122	63	18	101	44	135	98	62	134	208	135	194	131	148			
Rotterdam	73	128	118	51	81	21	24	113	195	251	70	206	36	202	114		
Tilburg	114	115	88	25	25	102	60	34	186	260	129	246	117	123	68	81	
Utrecht	37	72	64	73	55	62	61	88	139	195	54	181	54	180	85	57	81

➡ Less than 4% of European cars have automatic transmission; if you need this, you should reserve well ahead and be prepared to pay a huge surcharge for your rental.

Insurance

Collision damage waiver (CDW), an insurance policy that limits your financial liability for damage, is a costly add-on for rentals but may be necessary. Without insurance you'll be liable for damages up to the full value of the vehicle.

Many credit cards and home auto-insurance policies offer CDW-type coverage; make certain about this before you decline the costly (from €10 per day) CDW.

At most car-rental firms, CDW does not cover the first €500 to €1000 of damages incurred. Yet another add-on, an excess-cover package for around €10 to €20 per day, is normally available to cover this amount. See what your credit card and home auto insurance cover; you may not need anything extra, making that bargain rental an actual bargain.

Road Rules

Rules are similar to the rest of Continental Europe. Full concentration is required because you may need to yield to cars, bikes that appear out of nowhere and pedestrians in quick succession.

➡ Traffic travels on the right.

➡ The minimum driving age is 18 for vehicles and 16 for motorcycles.

➡ Seatbelts are required for everyone in a vehicle, and children under 12 must ride in the back if there's room.

➡ Trams always have right of way.

➡ If you are trying to turn right, bikes have priority.

➡ At roundabouts yield to vehicles already travelling in the circle.

➡ Speed limits are 50km/h in built-up areas, 80km/h in the country, 100km/h on major through-roads and 120km/h on freeways (sometimes 100km/h, clearly marked). Speed cameras are hidden everywhere.

Local Transport

Bicycle

Any Dutch town you visit is liable to be blanketed with bicycle paths. They're either on the streets or in the form of smooth off-road routes.

Bus, Tram & Metro

Buses and trams operate in most cities, and Amsterdam and Rotterdam have the added bonus of metro networks.

Taxi

Taxis are usually booked by phone – officially you're not supposed to wave them down on the street – and also wait outside train stations and hotels. They cost roughly €12 to €15 for 5km. Even short trips in town can get expensive quickly.

Train

Dutch trains are efficient, fast and comfortable. Trains are frequent and serve domestic destinations at regular intervals, sometimes five or six times an hour. It's an excellent system and possibly all you'll need to get around the country, although there are a few caveats.

➡ The national train company **NS** (Nederlandse Spoorwegen; www.ns.nl) operates all the major lines in the Netherlands. Minor lines in the north and east have been hived off to private bus and train operators, although scheduling and fares remain part of the national system.

➡ Bikes are welcome on the train system.

➡ Stations show departure information but the boards don't show trip duration or arrival times, so planning requires the web or a visit to a ticket or information window.

➡ The system shuts down roughly from midnight to 6am except in the Amsterdam–Schiphol–Rotterdam–Den Haag–Leiden circuit where trains run hourly all night.

➡ High-speed NS trains operate between Amsterdam, Schiphol, Rotterdam and Breda.

Train Stations

Medium and large railway stations have a full range of services: currency exchange, ATMs, small groceries, food courts, FEBO-like coin-operated snack-food vending machines, flower shops and much more.

Smaller stations, however, often have no services at all and are merely hollow – often architecturally beautiful – shells of their former selves. At these there may only be ticket vending machines. This is especially true on non-NS lines.

LOCKERS

Many train stations have lockers, much to the delight of day trippers. These are operated using a credit card. The one-day fee is €3.60 to €6 depending on size and location. If you return after more than 24 hours, you have to insert your credit card to pay an extra charge. If it's more than 72 hours, your goods will have been removed and you have to pay a €70 fine.

Note that some stations popular with day trippers (eg Enkhuizen, Delft) do not have lockers.

Train Tickets

Train travel in the Netherlands is reasonably priced. Tickets cost the same during the day as in the evening.

PURCHASING TICKETS

There is one important caveat to buying tickets in the Netherlands for visitors: non-European credit and debit cards are almost impossible to use.

Ticket windows Available at midsize to larger stations. Staff speak English and are often very good at figuring out the lowest fare you need to pay, especially if you have a complex itinerary of day trips in mind. But windows may be closed at night or the lines may be long.

Ticket machines Most only take Dutch bank cards. About 25% do take coins, none take bills. All can be set for English.

If you are at a station with a closed ticket window and don't have the coins for the machines, board the train and find the conductor. Explain your plight (they know where this applies so don't fib) and they will *usually* sell

TIPS FOR BUYING TICKETS

Buying a train ticket is the hardest part of riding Dutch trains.

➡ Only some ticket machines accept cash, and those are coin-only, so you need a pocketful of change.

➡ Ticket machines that accept plastic will not work with most non-European credit and ATM cards. The exceptions are a limited number of machines at Schiphol and Amsterdam Centraal.

➡ Ticket windows do not accept credit or ATM cards, although they will accept paper euros. Lines are often quite long and there is a surcharge for the often-unavoidable need to use a ticket window.

➡ Discounted NS International tickets sold online require a Dutch credit card. The cheap fares can't be bought at ticket windows.

➡ The much-hyped Voordeelurenabonnement (Off-Peak Discount Pass) yields good discounts, but only if you have a Dutch bank account.

➡ To buy domestic and international train tickets online with an international credit card, visit SNCB Europe (www.b-europe.com). You may need to print a copy of the ticket.

you a ticket without levying the fine (€35) for boarding without a ticket on top of the ticket price. If they do fine you, you can apply for a refund at a ticket window.

RESERVATIONS

For national trains, simply turn up at the station: you'll rarely have to wait more than 30 minutes for a train. Reservations are required for international trains.

TICKET TYPES

→ *Enkele reis* (one way) – Single one-way ticket; with a valid ticket you can break your journey along the direct route.

→ *Dagretour* (day return) – Normal day return; costs the same as two one-way tickets.

→ *Dagkaart* (day pass) – €51.40/87.40 for 2nd/1st class and allows unlimited train travel throughout the country. Only good value if you're planning extensive train travel on any one day.

→ *Railrunner* – €2.50; day pass for children aged four to 11 anywhere in the country. Note that for delays in excess of half an hour – irrespective of the cause – you're entitled to a refund. Delays of 30 to 60 minutes warrant a 50% refund and delays of an hour or more a 100% refund.

International trains require passengers to buy tickets in advance and carry surcharges, but also may have cheap fares available in advance.

TRAIN PASSES

There are several train passes for people living both inside and outside the Netherlands. These should be purchased before you arrive in the Netherlands. However, the passes don't offer good value even if you plan on a lot of train travel.

Eurail The Benelux pass is good for five days' travel in a month on all trains within the Netherlands, Belgium and Luxembourg. It costs US$396/255 1st/2nd class.

InterRail A Benelux pass good for six days in one month costs €308/201.

Train Classes

The longest train journey in the Netherlands (Maastricht–Groningen) takes about 4¼ hours, but the majority of trips are far shorter. Trains have 1st-class sections, but these are often little different from the 2nd-class areas and, given the short journeys, not worth the extra cost.

That said, 1st class is worth the extra money during busy periods when seats in 2nd class are oversubscribed.

Train Types

The following are listed in descending order of speed:

Thalys (www.thalys.com) Operates French TGV-style high-speed

HIDDEN TRAFFIC CAMERAS

More than 1600 unmanned and hidden radar cameras (known as *flitspalen*) watch over Dutch motorways. Even if you are in a rental car, the rental company will track you down in your home country and levy a service charge while the traffic authority also bills you for the fine.

trains from Amsterdam, Schiphol and Rotterdam south to Belgium and Paris. Trains are plush and have wi-fi.

ICE (Intercity Express; www.nshispeed.com) German fast trains from Amsterdam to Cologne and onto Frankfurt Airport and Frankfurt. Carries a surcharge for domestic riders.

Intercity The best non-high-speed domestic trains. They run express past small stations on all major lines. Usually air-conditioned double-deck cars.

Sneltrain (Fast Train) Not an Intercity but not as slow as a *stoptrein*. May not be air-conditioned.

Stoptrein (Stop Train) Never misses a stop, never gets up to speed. Some have no toilets.

Language

Dutch has around 20 million speakers worldwide. As a member of the Germanic language family, Dutch has many similarities with English.

The pronunciation of Dutch is fairly straightforward. It distinguishes between long and short vowels, which can affect the meaning of words, for example, *man* (man) and *maan* (moon). Also note that aw is pronounced as in 'law', eu as the 'u' in 'nurse', ew as the 'ee' in 'see' (with rounded lips), oh as the 'o' in 'note', öy as the 'er y' (without the 'r') in 'her year', and uh as in 'ago'.

The consonants are pretty simple to pronounce too. Note that kh is a throaty sound, similar to the 'ch' in the Scottish *loch*, r is trilled and zh is pronounced as the 's' in 'pleasure'. This said, if you read our coloured pronunciation guides as if they were English, you'll be understood just fine. The stressed syllables are indicated with italics.

Where relevant, both polite and informal options in Dutch are included, indicated with 'pol' and 'inf' respectively.

BASICS

Hello.	*Dag./Hallo.*	dakh/ha·*loh*
Goodbye.	*Dag.*	dakh
Yes./No.	*Ja./Nee.*	yaa/ney
Please.	*Alstublieft.* (pol)	al·stew·*bleeft*
	Alsjeblieft. (inf)	a·shuh·*bleeft*
Thank you.	*Dank u/je.* (pol/inf)	dangk ew/yuh

WANT MORE?

For in-depth language information and handy phrases, check out Lonely Planet's *Dutch Phrasebook*. You'll find it at **shop.lonelyplanet.com**, or you can buy Lonely Planet's iPhone phrasebooks at the Apple App Store.

You're welcome.	*Graag gedaan.*	khraakh khuh·*daan*
Excuse me.	*Excuseer mij.*	eks·kew·*zeyr* mey

How are you?
Hoe gaat het met u/jou? (pol/inf)	hoo khaat huht met ew/yaw

Fine. And you?
Goed.	khoot
En met u/jou? (pol/inf)	en met ew/yaw

What's your name?
Hoe heet u/je? (pol/inf)	hoo heyt ew/yuh

My name is ...
Ik heet ...	ik heyt ...

Do you speak English?
Spreekt u Engels?	spreykt ew *eng*·uhls

I don't understand.
Ik begrijp het niet.	ik buh·*khreyp* huht neet

ACCOMMODATION

Do you have a ... room?	*Heeft u een ...?*	heyft ew uhn ...
single	*éénpersoonskamer*	eyn·puhr·sohns·kaa·muhr
double	*tweepersoonskamer met een dubbel bed*	twey·puhr·sohns·kaa·muhr met uhn *du*·buhl bet
twin	*tweepersoonskamer met lits jumeaux*	twey·puhr·sohns·kaa·muhr met lee zhew·*moh*

How much is it per ...?	*Hoeveel kost het per ...?*	hoo·*veyl* kost huht puhr ...
night	*nacht*	nakht
person	*persoon*	puhr·*sohn*

Is breakfast included?
Is het ontbijt inbegrepen?	is huht ont·*beyt* in·buh·khrey·puhn

bathroom	badkamer	bat·kaa·muhr
bed and breakfast	gastenkamer	khas·tuhn· kaa·muhr
campsite	camping	kem·ping
guesthouse	pension	pen·syon
hotel	hotel	hoh·tel
window	raam	raam
youth hostel	jeugdherberg	yeukht·her·berkh

DIRECTIONS

Where's the ...?
Waar is ...? waar is ...

How far is it?
Hoe ver is het? hoo ver is huht

What's the address?
Wat is het adres? wat is huht a·dres

Can you please write it down?
Kunt u dat alstublieft kunt ew dat al·stew·bleeft
opschrijven? op·skhrey·vuhn

Can you show me (on the map)?
Kunt u het mij kunt ew huht mey
tonen (op de kaart)? toh·nuhn (op duh kaart)

at the corner	op de hoek	op duh hook
at the traffic lights	bij de verkeerslichten	bey duh vuhr·keyrs· likh·tuhn
behind	achter	akh·tuhr
in front of	voor	vohr
left	links	lingks
near (to)	dicht bij	dikht bey
next to	naast	naast
opposite	tegenover	tey·khuhn·oh·vuhr
straight ahead	rechtdoor	rekh·dohr
right	rechts	rekhs

EATING & DRINKING

What would you recommend?
Wat kan u wat kan ew
aanbevelen? aan·buh·vey·luhn

What's in that dish?
Wat zit er in dat wat zit uhr in dat
gerecht? khuh·rekht

I'd like the menu, please.
Ik wil graag een menu. ik wil khraakh uhn me·new

Delicious!
Heerlijk/Lekker! heyr·luhk/le·kuhr

Cheers!
Proost! prohst

Please bring the bill.
Mag ik de rekening makh ik duh rey·kuh·ning
alstublieft? al·stew·bleeft

To get by in Dutch, mix and match these simple patterns with words of your choice:

When's (the next bus)?
Hoe laat gaat hoo laat khaat
(de volgende bus)? (duh vol·khun·duh bus)

Where's (the station)?
Waar is (het station)? waar is (huht sta·syon)

I'm looking for (a hotel).
Ik ben op zoek naar ik ben op zook naar
(een hotel). (uhn hoh·tel)

Do you have (a map)?
Heeft u (een kaart)? heyft ew (uhn kaart)

Is there (a toilet)?
Is er (een toilet)? is uhr (uhn twa·let)

I'd like (the menu).
Ik wil graag ik wil khraakh
(een menu). (uhn me·new)

I'd like to (hire a car).
Ik wil graag (een ik wil khraakh (uhn
auto huren). aw·toh hew·ruhn)

Can I (enter)?
Kan ik (binnengaan)? kan ik (bi·nuhn·khaan)

Could you please (help me)?
Kunt u alstublieft kunt ew al·stew·bleeft
(helpen)? (hel·puhn)

Do I have to (get a visa)?
Moet ik (een visum moot ik (uhn vee·zum
hebben)? he·buhn)

I'd like to reserve a table for ...	Ik wil graag een tafel voor ... reserveren.	ik wil khraakh uhn taa·fuhl vohr ... rey·ser·vey·ruhn
(two) people	(twee) personen	(twey) puhr·soh·nuhn
(eight) o'clock	(acht) uur	(akht) ewr

I don't eat ...	Ik eet geen ...	ik eyt kheyn ...
eggs	eieren	ey·yuh·ruhn
fish	vis	vis
(red) meat	(rood) vlees	(roht) vleys
nuts	noten	noh·tuhn

Key Words

bar	bar	bar
bottle	fles	fles
breakfast	ontbijt	ont·beyt
cafe	café	ka·fey
cold	koud	kawt
dinner	avondmaal	aa·vont·maal

drink list	drankkaart	drang·kaart
fork	vork	vork
glass	glas	khlas
grocery store	kruidenier	kröy·duh·neer
hot	heet	heyt
knife	mes	mes
lunch	middagmaal	mi·dakh·maal
market	markt	markt
menu	menu	me·new
plate	bord	bort
pub	kroeg	krookh
restaurant	restaurant	res·toh·rant
spicy	pikant	pee·kant
spoon	lepel	ley·puhl
vegetarian (food)	vegetarisch	vey·khey·taa·ris
with/without	met/zonder	met/zon·duhr

Meat & Fish

beef	rundvlees	runt·vleys
chicken	kip	kip
duck	eend	eynt
fish	vis	vis
herring	haring	haa·ring
lamb	lamsvlees	lams·vleys
lobster	kreeft	kreyft
meat	vlees	vleys
mussels	mosselen	mo·suh·luhn
oysters	oester	oos·tuhr
pork	varkensvlees	var·kuhns·vleys
prawn	steurgarnaal	steur·khar·naal
salmon	zalm	zalm
scallops	kammosselen	ka·mo·suh·luhn
shrimps	garnalen	khar·naa·luhn
squid	inktvis	ingkt·vis
trout	forel	fo·rel
tuna	tonijn	toh·neyn
turkey	kalkoen	kal·koon
veal	kalfsvlees	kalfs·vleys

Question Words

How?	Hoe?	hoo
What?	Wat?	wat
When?	Wanneer?	wa·neyr
Where?	Waar?	waar
Who?	Wie?	wee
Why?	Waarom?	waa·rom

Fruit & Vegetables

apple	appel	a·puhl
banana	banaan	ba·naan
beans	bonen	boh·nuhm
berries	bessen	be·suhn
cabbage	kool	kohl
capsicum	paprika	pa·pree·ka
carrot	wortel	wor·tuhl
cauliflower	bloemkool	bloom·kohl
cucumber	komkommer	kom·ko·muhr
fruit	fruit	fröyt
grapes	druiven	dröy·vuhn
lemon	citroen	see·troon
lentils	linzen	lin·zuhn
mushrooms	paddestoelen	pa·duh·stoo·luhn
nuts	noten	noh·tuhn
onions	uien	öy·yuhn
orange	sinaasappel	see·naas·a·puhl
peach	perzik	per·zik
peas	erwtjes	erw·chus
pineapple	ananas	a·na·nas
plums	pruimen	pröy·muhn
potatoes	aardappels	aart·a·puhls
spinach	spinazie	spee·naa·zee
tomatoes	tomaten	toh·maa·tuhn
vegetables	groenten	khroon·tuhn

Other

bread	brood	broht
butter	boter	boh·tuhr
cheese	kaas	kaas
eggs	eieren	ey·yuh·ruhn
honey	honing	hoh·ning
ice	ijs	eys
jam	jam	zhem
noodles	noedels	noo·duhls
oil	olie	oh·lee
pastry	gebak	khuh·bak
pepper	peper	pey·puhr
rice	rijst	reyst
salt	zout	zawt
soup	soep	soop
soy sauce	sojasaus	soh·ya·saws
sugar	suiker	söy·kuhr
vinegar	azijn	a·zeyn

Drinks

beer	*bier*	beer
coffee	*koffie*	ko·fee
juice	*sap*	sap
milk	*melk*	melk
red wine	*rode wijn*	roh·duh weyn
soft drink	*frisdrank*	fris·drangk
tea	*thee*	tey
water	*water*	waa·tuhr
white wine	*witte wijn*	wi·tuh weyn

EMERGENCIES

Help!
Help! help

Leave me alone!
Laat me met rust! laat muh met rust

Call a doctor!
Bel een dokter! bel uhn *dok*·tuhr

Call the police!
Bel de politie! bel duh poh·*leet*·see

There's been an accident.
Er is een ongeluk uhr is uhn *on*·khuh·luk
gebeurd. khuh·*beurt*

I'm lost.
Ik ben verdwaald. ik ben vuhr·*dwaalt*

I'm sick.
Ik ben ziek. ik ben zeek

It hurts here.
Hier doet het pijn. heer doot huht peyn

Where are the toilets?
Waar zijn de toiletten? waar zeyn duh twa·*le*·tuhn

I'm allergic to (antibiotics).
Ik ben allergisch voor ik ben a·*ler*·khees vohr
(antibiotica). (an·tee·bee·*yoh*·tee·ka)

SHOPPING & SERVICES

I'd like to buy ...
Ik wil graag ... kopen. ik wil khraakh ... *koh*·puhn

I'm just looking.
Ik kijk alleen maar. ik keyk a·*leyn* maar

Can I look at it?
Kan ik het even zien? kan ik huht *ey*·vuhn zeen

Do you have any others?
Heeft u nog andere? heyft ew nokh *an*·duh·ruh

How much is it?
Hoeveel kost het? hoo·*veyl* kost huht

That's too expensive.
Dat is te duur. dat is tuh dewr

Can you lower the price?
Kunt u wat van de kunt ew wat van duh
prijs afdoen? preys *af*·doon

Signs

Ingang	Entrance
Uitgang	Exit
Open	Open
Gesloten	Closed
Inlichtingen	Information
Verboden	Prohibited
Toiletten	Toilets
Heren	Men
Dames	Women

There's a mistake in the bill.
Er zit een fout in de uhr zit uhn fawt in duh
rekening. *rey*·kuh·ning

ATM	*pin-automaat*	pin·aw·toh·maat
foreign exchange	*wisselkantoor*	wi·suhl·kan·tohr
post office	*postkantoor*	post·kan·tohr
shopping centre	*winkel- centrum*	wing·kuhl- sen·trum
tourist office	*VVV*	vey·vey·vey

TIME & DATES

What time is it?
Hoe laat is het? hoo laat is huht

It's (10) o'clock.
Het is (tien) uur. huht is (teen) ewr

Half past (10).
Half (elf). half (elf)
(lit: half eleven)

am (morning)	*'s ochtends*	sokh·tuhns
pm (afternoon)	*'s middags*	smi·dakhs
pm (evening)	*'s avonds*	saa·vonts

yesterday	*gisteren*	khis·tuh·ruhn
today	*vandaag*	van·daakh
tomorrow	*morgen*	mor·khuhn

Monday	*maandag*	maan·dakh
Tuesday	*dinsdag*	dins·dakh
Wednesday	*woensdag*	woons·dakh
Thursday	*donderdag*	don·duhr·dakh
Friday	*vrijdag*	vrey·dakh
Saturday	*zaterdag*	zaa·tuhr·dakh
Sunday	*zondag*	zon·dakh
January	*januari*	ya·new·waa·ree
February	*februari*	fey·brew·waa·ree

March	maart	maart
April	april	a·pril
May	mei	mey
June	juni	yew·nee
July	juli	yew·lee
August	augustus	aw·khus·tus
September	september	sep·tem·buhr
October	oktober	ok·toh·buhr
November	november	noh·vem·buhr
December	december	dey·sem·buhr

TRANSPORT

Public Transport

Is this the ... to (the left bank)?	Is dit de ... naar (de linker- oever)?	is dit duh ... naar (duh ling·kuhr· oo·vuhr)
ferry	veerboot	veyr·boht
metro	metro	mey·troh
tram	tram	trem
platform	perron	pe·ron
timetable	dienst- regeling	deenst· rey·khuh·ling
When's the ... (bus)?	Hoe laat gaat de ... (bus)?	hoo laat khaat duh ... (bus)

Numbers

1	één	eyn
2	twee	twey
3	drie	dree
4	vier	veer
5	vijf	veyf
6	zes	zes
7	zeven	zey·vuhn
8	acht	akht
9	negen	ney·khuhn
10	tien	teen
20	twintig	twin·tikh
30	dertig	der·tikh
40	veertig	feyr·tikh
50	vijftig	feyf·tikh
60	zestig	ses·tikh
70	zeventig	sey·vuhn·tikh
80	tachtig	takh·tikh
90	negentig	ney·khuhn·tikh
100	honderd	hon·duhrt
1000	duizend	döy·zuhnt

first	eerste	eyr·stuh
last	laatste	laat·stuh
next	volgende	vol·khun·duh

A ticket to ..., please.
Een kaartje naar ... graag. — uhn kaar·chuh naar ... khraakh

What time does it leave?
Hoe laat vertrekt het? — hoo laat vuhr·trekt huht

Does it stop at ...?
Stopt het in ...? — stopt huht in ...

What's the next stop?
Welk is de volgende halte? — welk is duh vol·khuhn·duh hal·tuh

I'd like to get off at ...
Ik wil graag in ... uitstappen. — ik wil khraak in ... öyt·sta·puhn

Is this taxi available?
Is deze taxi vrij? — is dey·zuh tak·see vrey

Please take me to ...
Breng me alstublieft naar ... — breng muh al·stew·bleeft naar ...

Cycling

I'd like ...	Ik wil graag ...	ik wil khraakh ...
my bicycle repaired	mijn fiets laten herstellen	meyn feets laa·tuhn her·ste·luhn
to hire a bicycle	een fiets huren	uhn feets hew·ruhn

I'd like to hire a ...	Ik wil graag een ... huren.	ik wil khraakh uhn ... hew·ruhn
basket	mandje	man·chuh
child seat	kinderzitje	kin·duhr·zi·chuh
helmet	helm	helm

Do you have bicycle parking?
Heeft u parking voor fietsen? — heyft ew par·king vohr feet·suhn

Can we get there by bike?
Kunnen we er met de fiets heen? — ku·nuhn wuh uhr met duh feets heyn

I have a puncture.
Ik heb een lekke band. — ik hep uhn le·kuh bant

bicycle path	fietspad	feets·pat
bicycle pump	fietspomp	feets·pomp
bicycle repairman	fietsenmaker	feet·suhn· maa·kuhr
bicycle stand	fietsenrek	feet·suhn·rek

GLOSSARY

abdij – abbey
ANWB – Dutch automobile association
apotheek – chemist/pharmacy

benzine – petrol/gasoline
bevrijding – liberation
bibliotheek – library
bos – woods or forest
botter – type of 19th-century fishing boat
broodje – bread roll (with filling)
bruin café – brown *café*; traditional drinking establishment
buurt – neighbourhood

café – pub, bar; also known as kroeg
coffeeshop – cafe authorised to sell cannabis

eetcafé cafes (pubs) serving meals

fiets – bicycle
fietsenstalling – secure bicycle storage
fietspad – bicycle path

gemeente – municipal, municipality
gezellig – convivial, cosy
GVB – Gemeentevervoerbedrijf; Amsterdam municipal transport authority
GWK – Grenswisselkantoren; official currency-exchange offices

haven – port
hof – courtyard

hofje – almshouse or series of buildings around a small courtyard, also known as begijnhof
hoofd – literally 'head', but in street names it often means 'main'
hunebedden – prehistoric rock masses purportedly used as burial chambers

jenever – Dutch gin; also genever

kaas – cheese
koffiehuis – espresso bar; cafe (as distinct from a coffeeshop)
klooster – cloister, religious house
koningin – queen
koninklijk – royal
kunst – art
kwartier – quarter

LF routes – landelijke fietsroutes; national (long-distance) bike routes
loodvrij – unleaded (petrol/gasoline)

markt – town square; market
meer – lake
molen – windmill; mill

NS – Nederlandse Spoorwegen; national railway company

OV-chipkaart – fare card for Dutch public transit

paleis – palace
polder – strips of farmland separated by canals

postbus – post office box

Randstad – literally 'rim-city'; the urban agglomeration including Amsterdam, Utrecht, Rotterdam and Den Haag
Rijk(s-) – the State

scheepvaart – shipping
schouwburg – theatre
sluis – lock (for boats/ships)
spoor – train platform
stadhuis – town hall
stedelijk – civic, municipal
stichting – foundation, institute
strand – beach

terp – mound of packed mud in Friesland that served as a refuge during floods
treintaxi – taxi for train passengers
tuin – garden
tulp – tulip

verzet – resistance
Vlaams – Flemish
VVV – tourist information office

waag – old weigh-house
wadlopen – mudflat-walking
weeshuis – orphanage
werf – wharf, shipyard
winkel – shop

zaal – room, hall
zee – sea
ziekenhuis – hospital

Behind the Scenes

SEND US YOUR FEEDBACK

We love to hear from travellers – your comments keep us on our toes and help make our books better. Our well-travelled team reads every word on what you loved or loathed about this book. Although we cannot reply individually to postal submissions, we always guarantee that your feedback goes straight to the appropriate authors, in time for the next edition. Each person who sends us information is thanked in the next edition – the most useful submissions are rewarded with a selection of digital PDF chapters.

Visit **lonelyplanet.com/contact** to submit your updates and suggestions or to ask for help. Our award-winning website also features inspirational travel stories, news and discussions.

Note: We may edit, reproduce and incorporate your comments in Lonely Planet products such as guidebooks, websites and digital products, so let us know if you don't want your comments reproduced or your name acknowledged. For a copy of our privacy policy visit lonelyplanet.com/privacy.

OUR READERS

Many thanks to the travellers who used the last edition and wrote to us with helpful hints, useful advice and interesting anecdotes:

A Anne Dirks, Arnout Kors **C** Cornelia Pabijan **D** Douglas Morren **E** Ellen Hermans, Emma Thompson, Erna van Balen **G** Gareth Hartwell, George Moss **H** Hector Del Olmo **J** Jacqueline Mahieu, Jim Koebel, John Baber, John Hodges, Justyna Baber **K** Kevin Geraghty **M** Mac Alphen, Martine Muis **N** Nancy Johnson **R** Ralph Johnson, Rodney Mantle, Ronald Smeltzer **S** Sain Alizada, Sandra Mack, Suzanne Wortel **U** Uta Kreimeier **V** Vincent van der Velde **Y** Yvette van Laar

AUTHOR THANKS

Catherine Le Nevez

Hartelijk bedankt first and foremost to Julian, and to everyone across the Netherlands who provided insights, information and good times. Huge thanks too to my Netherlands co-author Daniel Schechter, Amsterdam city guide co-author Karla Zimmerman, destination editor Kate Morgan and all at LP. As ever, *merci encore* to my parents, brother, *belle-sœur* and *neveu*.

Daniel C Schechter

The following folks gamely pitched in, showing me around, sharing ideas, perusing text and/or providing shelter: in Breda Yvonne Lewin, in Den Bosch Wim & Mieke Verberne and Ria Schouten, Cor van Marion & Ji Tang (Kampen), Frederique Hijink (Deventer), Koen Thuys (Eindhoven), Martin van der Kuil & Briggite Brugger (Nijmegen), Jenne Oosting (Groningen) and Sipke de Jong (Utrecht). Thanks, too, to Amsterdammers Bas Lemmers, Maarten & Jasmijn Hubers, Akke Hoekstra, Alex Hendriksen, Judith Vlug and Mariana Fernández, and, as always, Myra Ingmanson. *Enorm veel dank!*

ACKNOWLEDGMENTS

Climate map data adapted from Peel MC, Finlayson BL & McMahon TA (2007) 'Updated World Map of the Köppen-Geiger Climate Classification', *Hydrology and Earth System Sciences*, 11, 1633–44.

Transit map: Amsterdam Transport Network Map © Map designed by Carto Studio, Amsterdam.

Cover photograph: the Seeker (De Zoeker) oil mill in Zaanse Schans; Alan Copson/AWL.

THIS BOOK

This 6th edition of Lonely Planet's *The Netherlands* guidebook was researched and written by Catherine Le Nevez and Daniel C Schechter. The previous two editions were written by Ryan Ver Berkmoes and Karla Zimmerman, with research by Caroline Sieg and additional content by Simon Sellars. The 3rd edition was written by Neal Bedford and Simon Sellars. This guidebook was produced by the following:

Destination Editor Kate Morgan

Product Editors Grace Dobell, Anne Mason

Regional Senior Cartographer David Kemp

Book Designer Mazzy Prinsep

Assisting Editors Carolyn Bain, Kellie Langdon, Jenna Myers, Charlotte Orr, Christopher Pitts

Cartographer James Leversha

Cover Researcher Naomi Parker

Thanks to Neill Coen, Jo Cooke, Ryan Evans, Andi Jones, Claire Murphy, Wayne Murphy, Karyn Noble, Kirsten Rawlings, Diana Saengkham, Samantha Tyson, Lauren Wellicome, Tony Wheeler

Index

Map Legend

Sights
- Beach
- Bird Sanctuary
- Buddhist
- Castle/Palace
- Christian
- Confucian
- Hindu
- Islamic
- Jain
- Jewish
- Monument
- Museum/Gallery/Historic Building
- Ruin
- Shinto
- Sikh
- Taoist
- Winery/Vineyard
- Zoo/Wildlife Sanctuary
- Other Sight

Activities, Courses & Tours
- Bodysurfing
- Diving
- Canoeing/Kayaking
- Course/Tour
- Sento Hot Baths/Onsen
- Skiing
- Snorkelling
- Surfing
- Swimming/Pool
- Walking
- Windsurfing
- Other Activity

Sleeping
- Sleeping
- Camping

Eating
- Eating

Drinking & Nightlife
- Drinking & Nightlife
- Cafe

Entertainment
- Entertainment

Shopping
- Shopping

Information
- Bank
- Embassy/Consulate
- Hospital/Medical
- @ Internet
- Police
- Post Office
- Telephone
- Toilet
- Tourist Information
- Other Information

Geographic
- Beach
- Gate
- Hut/Shelter
- Lighthouse
- Lookout
- ▲ Mountain/Volcano
- Oasis
- Park
-)(Pass
- Picnic Area
- Waterfall

Population
- Capital (National)
- Capital (State/Province)
- City/Large Town
- Town/Village

Transport
- Airport
- Border crossing
- Bus
- Cable car/Funicular
- Cycling
- Ferry
- Metro station
- Monorail
- Parking
- Petrol station
- S-Bahn/S-train/Subway station
- Taxi
- T-bane/Tunnelbana station
- Train station/Railway
- Tram
- Tube station
- U-Bahn/Underground station
- Other Transport

Note: Not all symbols displayed above appear on the maps in this book

Routes
- Tollway
- Freeway
- Primary
- Secondary
- Tertiary
- Lane
- Unsealed road
- Road under construction
- Plaza/Mall
- Steps
-)==(Tunnel
- Pedestrian overpass
- Walking Tour
- Walking Tour detour
- Path/Walking Trail

Boundaries
- International
- State/Province
- Disputed
- Regional/Suburb
- Marine Park
- Cliff
- Wall

Hydrography
- River, Creek
- Intermittent River
- Canal
- Water
- Dry/Salt/Intermittent Lake
- Reef

Areas

- Airport/Runway
- Beach/Desert
- + Cemetery (Christian)
- × Cemetery (Other)
- Glacier
- Mudflat
- Park/Forest
- Sight (Building)
- Sportsground
- Swamp/Mangrove

5/18 (6) 3/18.

OUR STORY

A beat-up old car, a few dollars in the pocket and a sense of adventure. In 1972 that's all Tony and Maureen Wheeler needed for the trip of a lifetime – across Europe and Asia overland to Australia. It took several months, and at the end – broke but inspired – they sat at their kitchen table writing and stapling together their first travel guide, *Across Asia on the Cheap*. Within a week they'd sold 1500 copies. Lonely Planet was born.

Today, Lonely Planet has offices in Franklin, London, Melbourne, Oakland, Beijing and Delhi, with more than 600 staff and writers. We share Tony's belief that 'a great guidebook should do three things: inform, educate and amuse'.

OUR WRITERS

Catherine Le Nevez

Plan Your Trip, Amsterdam, Haarlem & North Holland, Rotterdam & South Holland, The Netherlands Today, History, The Dutch Way of Life, Dutch Art, Survival Guide

Catherine's wanderlust kicked in when she first roadtripped across Europe, including the Netherlands, aged four, and she's been returning to this spirited, *gezellig* country ever since, completing her Doctorate of Creative Arts in Writing, Masters in Professional Writing, and post-grad qualifications in Editing and Publishing along the way. A freelance writer for many years, Catherine has written scores of Lonely Planet guides and articles over the last decade or so, covering Amsterdam, the Netherlands and destinations all over Europe and beyond.

Read more about Catherine at:
http://auth.lonelyplanet.com/profiles/catherine_le_nevez

Daniel C Schechter

Friesland, Utrecht, Northeast Netherlands, Central Netherlands, Maastricht & Southeastern Netherlands, Architecture, The Dutch Landscape, Dutch Cuisine

Born and raised in Brooklyn, New York, Daniel C Schechter now lives closer to Breukelen, Utrecht. During a 2006 visit to Leiden to see his niece who was studying there, he was so struck by the sight of a steady stream of commuting cyclists that he determined to relocate to the country. In 2010 he moved to Amsterdam, got a second-hand Gazelle and hit the trails. Five years later, he still marvels at the morning commute and has cycled through all 12 of the country's provinces. Follow him around at netherlandsbikeways.blogspot.com

Published by Lonely Planet Publications Pty Ltd
ABN 36 005 607 983
6th edition – May 2016
ISBN 978 1 74321 552 4
© Lonely Planet 2016   Photographs © as indicated 2016
10 9 8 7 6 5 4 3 2 1
Printed in China